PRAISE FOR SARAH HELM'S

# RAVENSBRÜCK



"A profoundly moving c ... ondon)

"*Ravensbrück* helps us un ... thoroughgoing an onslaught on humanity Nazi Germany perpetrated, and how central to its identity was its implacable urge to enslave and kill those it considered undesirable. . . . *Ravensbrück* gives us an agonizing sense of the dark heart of the Nazi ethos." —*The New York Times Book Review*

"Illuminates the attempted escapes, executions, and impossible courage of women history conspired to forget."

—*O, The Oprah Magazine*

"A remarkable and riveting narrative." —*Minneapolis Star Tribune*

"A groundbreaking, detailed biography. . . . There's much to absorb here, from talks of inhumanely cruel punishment to examples of camaraderie, resilience and courage." —*The Jewish Week*

"Compelling. . . . Powerful. . . . Devastating. . . . What one is left with at the end of this momentous book is a sense of the power of human nature, both for good and for evil." —*Irish Independent* (Dublin)

"Using material once locked behind the Iron Curtain, Sarah Helm has performed a tremendous feat of historical rescue. This book at last gives full voice to the women of Ravensbrück, the only Nazi concentration camp for women, for the very first time."

—Anne Applebaum, author of *Gulag*,
winner of the Pulitzer Prize

"An important cautionary tale. . . . A revelation. . . . Helm describes an amazing social structure that, despite all, arose in that encapsulated place, run for and mostly by women. The courage of the prisoners in the face of overwhelming cruelty was extraordinary."

—Lynn H. Nicholas, author of *The Rape of Europa*, winner of the National Book Critics Circle Award

"*Ravensbrück* is a book everyone should read. . . . Beautifully written. . . . Helm has done an amazing job with an enormous and enormously painful topic."

—*PopMatters*

"A beautifully written history of events that offers additional insight into Nazism and those caught in its path. . . . This book deserves significant attention."

—*Publishers Weekly* (starred)

"Chronicles the history of this much-ignored site for women. . . . Helm delivers a gripping story of the women who outlasted them and had the strength to share with the author and us sixty years later."

—*Kirkus Reviews*

## SARAH HELM

# RAVENSBRÜCK

Sarah Helm is the author of *A Life in Secrets: Vera Atkins and the Missing Agents of WWII* and thc play *Loyalty*, about the 2003 Iraq War. She was a staff journalist on *The Sunday Times* (London) and a foreign correspondent on *The Independent*, and now writes for several publications. She lives in London with her husband and two daughters.

Also by Sarah Helm

*A Life in Secrets: Vera Atkins and the Missing Agents of WWII*

# RAVENSBRÜCK

*Life and Death in Hitler's Concentration Camp for Women*

SARAH HELM

ANCHOR BOOKS
A Division of Penguin Random House LLC
New York

FIRST ANCHOR BOOKS EDITION, MARCH 2016

 Published in the United States by Anchor Books, a division of Penguin Random House LLC, New York. Originally published in Great Britain as *If This Is a Woman* by Little, Brown, an imprint of the Little, Brown Book Group, a Hachette UK Company, London, in 2014, and subsequently published in hardcover in the United States by Nan A. Talese/Doubleday, a division of Penguin Random House LLC, New York, in 2015.

Anchor Books and colophon are registered trademarks of Penguin Random House LLC.

The Library of Congress has cataloged the Nan A. Talese/Doubleday edition as follows:
Helm, Sarah.
Ravensbrück : life and death in Hitler's concentration camp for women / Sarah Helm. — First United States edition.
pages cm
Includes index.
1. Ravensbrück (Concentration camp). 2. Women concentration camp inmates—Germany—Ravensbrück. 3. Women prisoners—Germany—Ravensbrück. 4. World War, 1939–1945—Prisoners and prisons, German. I. Title.
D805.5.R38H45 2014 940.53'1853154—dc23 2014014974

**Anchor Books Trade Paperback ISBN: 978-0-307-27871-5**
**eBook ISBN: 978-0-385-53911-1**

*Author photograph © Barney Jones Photography*

www.anchorbooks.com

Printed in the United States of America
10 9 8 7 6 5 4 3 2

*To those who refused*

---

Consider if this is a woman,<br>
Without hair and without name<br>
With no more strength to remember,<br>
Her eyes empty and her womb cold<br>
Like a frog in winter.<br>
Meditate that this came about:<br>
I commend these words to you.

Primo Levi, 'If This Is a Man'

# Contents

DENMARK
SWEDEN
North Sea
Copenhagen
Malmö
Padborg
Lübeck
Barth
Hamburg
Neubrandenburg
Malchow
Neuengamme
Ravensbrück
Fürstenberg
Belsen
ENGLAND
NETHERLANDS
London
Berlin
Sachsenhausen
R. Elbe
Soest
Bernburg
Lichtenburg
Torgau
R. Oder
BELGIUM
Düsseldorf
Buchenwald
Leipzig
GERMANY
LUX.
Frankfurt
Prague
Paris
Verdun
Saarbrücken
Châlons-sur-Marne
Metz
Nuremberg
FRANCE
Ulm
R. Rhine
Dachau
Linz
Mauthausen
Vienna
Bratislava
Munich
Castle Hartheim
Kreuzlingen
SWITZ.
AUSTRIA
ITALY
▲ Barth concentration camps and killing centres
△ Malchow subcamps
Main prisoner routes to the camp
Red Army
French prisoners
Polish prisoners
Hungarian prisoners
Auschwitz death march
Rescue routes from the camp
Swedish Red Cross
ICRC

altic
Sea
LITHUANIA
RUSSIA
Moscow
Königsberg
Stutthof
BELORUSSIA
POLAND
Warsaw
Brest-Litovsk
Lublin
Majdanek
Rovno
Kiev
Slavuta
Kraków
Auschwitz
UKRAINE
LOVAKIA
Budapest
HUNGARY
Odessa
ROMANIA
Simferopol
Sevastopol
Black Sea
LAVIA

A plan of Ravensbrück by the French artist France Audoul, who was one of the '*vingt-sept mille*' – the largest group of French prisoners, who arrived at the camp on 3 February 1944.

The plan shows the main compound on the edge of the lake with the gate, the shower and kitchen building, and the Appellplatz. The gas chamber ('*gaz*') and crematorium are also visible. Against the south wall is the SS garden; just beyond it are the Siemenslager and the warehouses where goods stolen from prisoners ('*marchandises volées*') were sorted and stored. The 'Camp d'Extermination' at Uckermark is also clearly marked, as are the machine-gun posts to the north. On the shore of the lake are the remains of a small fort ('*fortin*') and the '*marais*' – the sandy shore.

From *Ravensbrück: 150,000 femmes en enfer. 32 croquis et portraits faits au camp 1944–1945, 22 compositions et textes manuscrits de France Audoul.*

# Le bagne nazi de Ravensbrück

## Plan subtilisé à la Gestapo

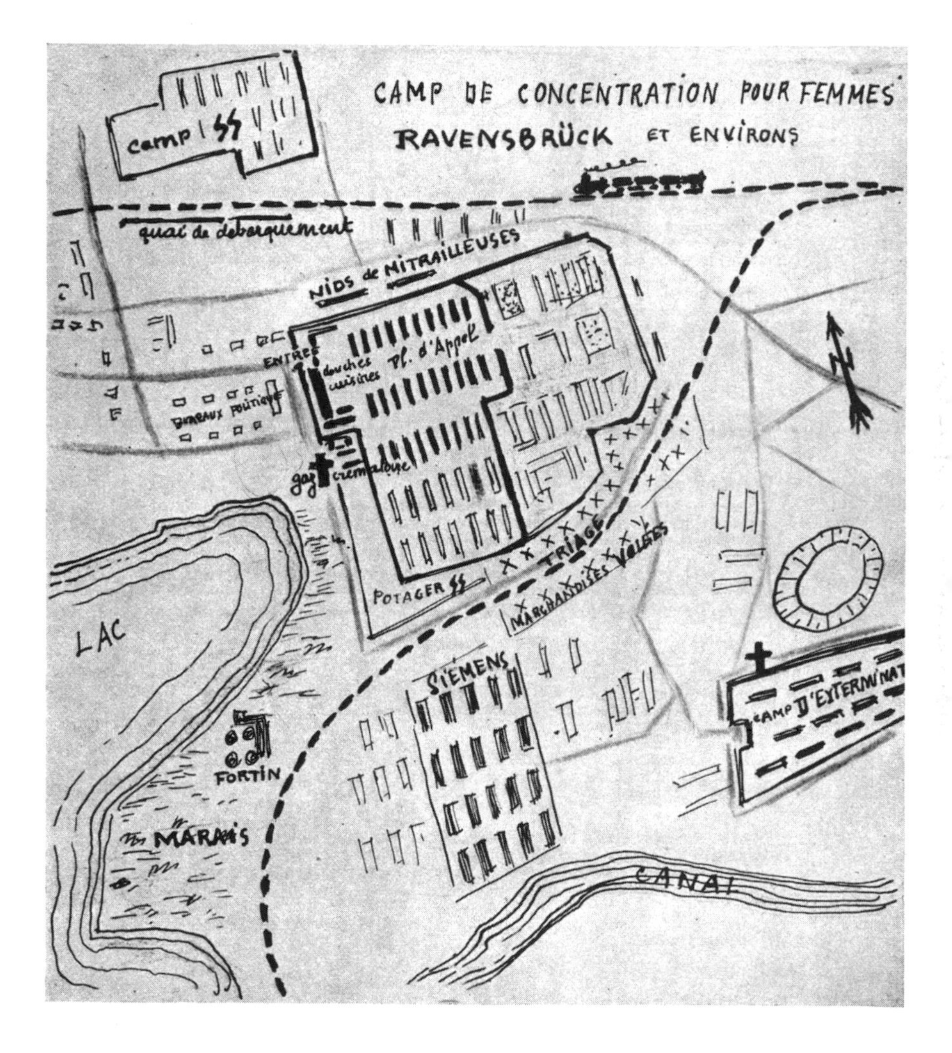

# Prologue

From Berlin's Tegel airport it takes just over an hour to reach Ravensbrück. The first time I drove there, in February 2006, heavy snow was falling and a lorry had jack-knifed on the Berlin ring road, so it would take longer.

Heinrich Himmler often drove out to Ravensbrück, even in atrocious weather like this. The head of the SS had friends in the area and would drop in to inspect the camp as he passed by. He rarely left without issuing new orders. Once he ordered more root vegetables to be put in the prisoners' soup. On another occasion he said the killing wasn't going fast enough.

Ravensbrück was the only Nazi concentration camp built for women. The camp took its name from the small village that adjoins the town of Fürstenberg and lies about fifty miles due north of Berlin, off the road to Rostock on Germany's Baltic coast. Women arriving in the night sometimes thought they were near the coast because they tasted salt on the wind; they also felt sand underfoot. When daylight came they saw that the camp was built on the edge of a lake and surrounded by forest. Himmler liked his camps to be in areas of natural beauty, and preferably hidden from view. Today the camp is still hidden from view; the horrific crimes enacted there and the courage of the victims are largely unknown.

Ravensbrück opened in May 1939, just under four months before the outbreak of war, and was liberated by the Russians six years later – it was one of the very last camps to be reached by the Allies. In the first year there were fewer than 2000 prisoners, almost all of whom were Germans. Many had been arrested because they opposed Hitler – communists, for example, and Jehovah's Witnesses, who called Hitler the Antichrist. Others were rounded up simply because the Nazis considered them inferior beings and wanted them removed from society: prostitutes, criminals, down-and-outs and Gypsies. Later, the camp took in thousands of women captured in countries occupied by the

Nazis, many of whom had been in the resistance. Children were brought there too. A small proportion of the prisoners – about 10 per cent – were Jewish, but the camp was not formally designated a camp for Jews.

At its height, Ravensbrück had a population of about 45,000 women; over the six years of its existence around 130,000 women passed through its gates, to be beaten, starved, worked to death, poisoned, executed and gassed. Estimates of the final death toll have ranged from about 30,000 to 90,000; the real figure probably lies somewhere in between, but so few SS documents on the camp survive nobody will ever know for sure. The wholesale destruction of evidence at Ravensbrück is another reason the camp's story has remained obscured. In the final days, every prisoner's file was burned in the crematorium or on bonfires, along with the bodies. The ashes were thrown in the lake.

I first learned of Ravensbrück when writing an earlier book about Vera Atkins, a wartime officer with the British secret service's Special Operations Executive. Immediately after the war Vera launched a single-handed search for British SOE women who had been parachuted into occupied France to help the resistance, many of whom had gone missing. Vera followed their trails and discovered that several had been captured and taken to concentration camps.

I tried to reconstruct her search, and began with her personal papers, which were filed in brown cardboard boxes and kept by her sister-in-law Phoebe Atkins at her home in Cornwall. The word 'Ravensbrück' was written on one of the boxes. Inside were handwritten notes from interviews with survivors and with SS suspects – some of the earliest evidence gathered about the camp. I flicked through the papers. 'We had to strip naked and were shaved,' one woman told Vera. There was 'a column of choking blue smoke'.

A survivor talked of a camp hospital where 'syphilis germs were injected into the spinal cord'. Another described seeing women arrive at the camp after a 'death march' through the snow from Auschwitz. One of the male SOE agents, imprisoned at Dachau, wrote a note saying he had heard about women from Ravensbrück being forced to work in a Dachau brothel.

Several of the interviewees mentioned a young woman guard called Binz who had 'light, bobbed hair'. Another guard had once been a nanny in Wimbledon. Among the prisoners were 'the cream of Europe's women', according to a British investigator; they included General de Gaulle's niece, a former British women's golf champion and scores of Polish countesses.

I began to look for dates of birth and addresses in case any of the survivors – or even the guards – might still be alive. Someone had given Vera the address of a Mrs Chatenay, 'who knows about the sterilisation of children in Block 11'. A Doctor Louise Le Porz had made a very detailed statement saying the camp was built on an estate belonging to Himmler and his private *Schloss*, or château, was near by. Her address was Mérignac, Gironde, but from her date of birth she was probably dead. A Guernsey woman called Julia Barry lived in Nettlebed in Oxfordshire. Other addresses were impossibly vague. A Russian survivor was thought to be working 'at the mother and baby unit, Leningrad railway station'.

Towards the back of the box I found handwritten lists of prisoners, smuggled out by a Polish woman who had taken notes in the camp as well as sketches and maps. 'The Poles had all the best information,' the note said. The woman who wrote the list turned out to be long dead, but some of the addresses were in London, and the survivors still living.

I took the sketches with me on the first drive out to Ravensbrück, hoping they would help me find my way around when I got there. But as the snow thickened I wondered if I'd reach the camp at all.

Many tried and failed to reach Ravensbrück. Red Cross officials trying to get to the camp in the chaos of the final days of war had to turn back, such was the flow of refugees moving the other way. A few months after the war, when Vera Atkins drove out this way to start her investigation, she was stopped at a Russian checkpoint; the camp was inside the Russian zone of occupation and access by other Allied nationals was restricted. By this time, Vera's hunt for the missing women had become part of a bigger British investigation into the camp, resulting in the first Ravensbrück war crimes trials, which opened in Hamburg in 1946.

In the 1950s, as the Cold War began, Ravensbrück fell behind the Iron Curtain, which split survivors – east from west – and broke the history of the camp in two.

Out of view of the West, the site became a shrine to the camp's communist heroines, and all over East Germany streets and schools were named after them.

Meanwhile, in the West, Ravensbrück literally disappeared from view. Western survivors, historians, journalists couldn't even get near the site. In their own countries the former prisoners struggled to get their stories published. Evidence was hard to access. Transcripts of the Hamburg trials were classified 'secret' and closed for thirty years.

'Where was it?' was one of the most common questions put to me when I began writing about Ravensbrück, along with: 'Why was there a separate women's camp? Were the women Jews? Was it a death camp? Was it a slave labour camp? Is anyone still alive?'

In those countries that lost large numbers in the camp, survivors' groups tried to keep memories alive. An estimated 8000 French, 1000 Dutch, 18,000

Russians and 40,000 Poles were imprisoned. Yet, for different reasons in each country, the story has been obscured.

In Britain, which had no more than twenty women in the camp, the ignorance is startling, as it is in the US. The British may know of Dachau, the first concentration camp, and perhaps of Belsen because British troops liberated it and the horror they found there, captured on film, for ever scarred the British consciousness. Otherwise only Auschwitz, synonymous with the gassing of the Jews, has real resonance.

After reading Vera's files I looked around to see what had been written on the women's camp. Mainstream historians – nearly all of them men – had almost nothing to say. Even books written on the camps since the end of the Cold War seemed to describe an entirely masculine world. Then a friend, working in Berlin, leant me a hefty collection of essays mostly by German women academics. In the 1990s, feminist historians had begun a fightback. This book promised to 'release women from the anonymity that lies behind the word prisoner'. A plethora of further studies had followed as other authors – usually German – carved off sections of Ravensbrück and examined them 'scientifically', which seemed to stifle the story. I noticed mention of a 'Memory Book', which sounded far more interesting, and tried to contact the author.

I had also come across a handful of prisoners' memoirs, mostly from the 1950s and 1960s, hanging around in the back shelves of public libraries, often with sensationalised jackets. The cover for a memoir by a French literature teacher, Micheline Maurel, showed a voluptuous Bond-girl lookalike behind barbed wire. A book about Irma Grese, one of the early Ravensbrück guards, was titled *The Beautiful Beast*. The language of these memoirs seemed dated and, at first, unreal. One writer talked of 'lesbians with brutish faces' and another of the 'bestiality' of German prisoners, which 'gave much food for thought as to the fundamental virtue of the race'. These texts were disorientating; it was as if nobody knew quite how to tell the story. In a preface to one memoir, the French writer François Mauriac wrote that Ravensbrück was 'an abomination that the world has resolved to forget'. Perhaps I should write about something else. I went to see Yvonne Baseden, the only survivor I was then aware was still living, to ask her view.

Yvonne was one of Vera Atkins's SOE women, captured while helping the resistance in France, then sent to Ravensbrück. Yvonne had always willingly talked about her resistance work, but whenever I had broached the subject of Ravensbrück she had said she 'knew nothing' and turned away.

This time I told her I was planning to write a book on the camp, hoping she might say more, but she looked up in horror.

'Oh no,' she said. 'You can't do that.'

I asked why not. 'It is too horrible. Couldn't you write about something else? What are you going to tell your children you are doing?' she asked.

Didn't she think the story should be told? 'Oh yes. Nobody knows about Ravensbrück at all. Nobody ever wanted to know from the moment we came back.' She looked out of the window.

As I left she gave me a small book. It was another memoir, with a particularly monstrous cover, twisted figures in black and white. Yvonne hadn't read it, she said, pushing it on me. It was as if she wanted it out of her sight.

When I got home the sinister jacket fell off the book to reveal a plain blue cover. I read it without putting it down. The author was a young French lawyer called Denise Dufournier who had written a simple and moving account of endurance against all odds. The 'abomination' was not the only part of the Ravensbrück story that was being forgotten; so was the fight for survival.

A few days later a French voice spoke out of my answering machine. It was Dr Louise Le Porz (now Liard), the doctor from Mérignac whom I'd assumed was dead. Instead, she was inviting me to stay with her in Bordeaux, where she now lived. I could stay as long as I liked as there was much to talk about. 'But you'd better hurry. I'm ninety-three years old.'

Soon after this I made contact with Bärbel Shindler-Saefkow, the author of the 'Memory Book'. Bärbel, the daughter of a German communist prisoner, was compiling a database of the prisoners; she had travelled far afield gathering up lists of names hidden in obscure archives. She sent me the address of Valentina Makarova, a Belorussian partisan, who had survived the Auschwitz death march. Valentina wrote back, suggesting I visit her in Minsk.

By the time I reached Berlin's outer suburbs the snow was easing. I passed a sign for Sachsenhausen, the location of the men's concentration camp, which meant I was heading the right way. Sachsenhausen and Ravensbrück had close contacts. The men's camp even baked the women's bread; the loaves were driven out on this road every day. At first each woman got half a loaf each evening. By the end of the war they barely received a slice and the 'useless mouths' – as the Nazis called those they wanted rid of – received none at all.

SS officers, guards and prisoners were frequently moved back and forth between the camps as Himmler's administrators tried to maximise resources. Early in the war a women's section opened at Auschwitz – and later at other male camps – and Ravensbrück provided and trained the women guards. Later in the war several senior SS men from Auschwitz were sent to work at Ravensbrück. Prisoners were also sent back and forth between the two camps. As a result, although Ravensbrück had a distinctive female character it also shared a common culture with the male camps.

Himmler's SS empire was vast: by the middle of the war there were as many as 15,000 Nazi camps, which included temporary labour camps and thousands of subcamps, linked to the main concentration camps, dotted all over Germany and Poland. The biggest and most monstrous were those constructed in 1942, under the terms of the Final Solution. By the end of the war an estimated six million Jews had been exterminated. The facts of the Jewish genocide are today so well known and so overwhelming that many people suppose that Hitler's extermination programme consisted of the Jewish Holocaust alone.

People who ask about Ravensbrück are often surprised that the majority of the women killed there were not Jews.

Today historians differentiate between the camps but labels can mislead. Ravensbrück is often described as a 'slave labour' camp, a term that lessens the horror of what happened and may also have contributed to its marginalisation. It was certainly an important place of slave labour – Siemens, the electrical giant, had a factory there – but slave labour was only a stage on the way to death. Prisoners at the time called Ravensbrück a death camp. The French survivor and ethnologist Germaine Tillion called it a place of 'slow extermination'.

Leaving Berlin, the road north cut across white fields before plunging into trees. From time to time I passed abandoned collective farms, remnants from communist times.

Deep into the forest the snow had drifted and it became hard to find the way. Ravensbrück women were often sent out through the snow to fell trees in the woods. The snow stuck to their wooden clogs so that they walked on snow platforms, their ankles twisting as they went. Alsatian dogs held on leashes by women guards pounced on them if they fell.

The names of forest villages began to seem familiar from testimony I'd read. Altglobsow was the village where the guard with the bobbed hair – Dorothea Binz – came from. Then the spire of Fürstenberg church came into view. From the centre of the town the camp was quite invisible, but I knew it lay just the other side of the lake. Prisoners talked about seeing the spire when they came out of the camp gates. I passed Fürstenberg station, where so many terrible train journeys had ended. Red Army women arrived from the Crimea one February night, packed inside cattle wagons.

On the other side of Fürstenberg a cobbled forest road – built by the prisoners – led to the camp. Houses with pitched roofs appeared on the left; from Vera's map I knew these were the houses where the guards lived. One had been converted into a youth hostel, where I would spend the night. The original guards' decor had long since been stripped away, to be replaced by pristine modern fittings, but the previous occupants still haunted their old rooms.

The lake opened out on to my right, vast and frozen white. Up ahead was the commandant's headquarters and a high wall. A few minutes later I stood at the entrance to the compound. In front lay another vast white expanse, dotted by trees – linden trees, I later learned, planted when the camp was first built. All of the barracks that once sat under the trees had vanished. During the Cold War the Russians used the camp as a base for a tank regiment, and removed most of the buildings. Russian soldiers played football on what had once been the camp Appellplatz, where prisoners stood for roll call. I had heard about the Russian base, but hadn't expected this much destruction.

The Siemens camp, a few hundred yards beyond the south wall, was overgrown and hard to reach, as was the annex, called the Youth Camp, where so much killing had happened. I would have to imagine what they were like, but I didn't have to imagine the cold. The prisoners stood out here on the camp square for hours in their cotton clothes. I sought shelter in the 'bunker', the stone prison building, its cells converted during the Cold War period into memorials to the communist dead. Lists of names were inscribed on shiny black granite.

In one room workmen were taking the memorials down, and redecorating. Now the West had taken over again, camp historians and archivists were working on a new narrative and new memorial exhibition.

Outside the camp walls I found other memorials, more intimate ones. Near the crematorium was a long dark passage with high walls, known as the shooting alley. A small bunch of roses had been placed here; they would have been dead if they weren't frozen. There was a label with a name.

There were three little posies of flowers in the crematorium, lying on the ovens, and a few roses scattered on the edge of the lake. Since the camp had become accessible again, former prisoners were coming to remember their dead friends. I needed to find more survivors while there was still time.

I understood now what this book should be: a biography of Ravensbrück beginning at the beginning and ending at the end, piecing the broken story back together again as best I could. The book would try to throw light on the Nazis' crimes against women, showing, at the same time, how an understanding of what happened at the camp for women can illuminate the wider Nazi story.

So much of the evidence had been destroyed, so much forgotten and distorted. But a great deal had survived, and new evidence was becoming available all the time. The British trial transcripts had been opened long ago and contained a wealth of detail; papers from trials held behind the Iron

Curtain were also becoming available. Since the end of the Cold War the Russians had partially opened up their archives, and testimony never examined before was coming to light in several European capitals. Survivors from East and West were beginning to share memories. Children of prisoners were asking questions, finding hidden letters and hidden diaries.

Most important for this book would be the voices of the prisoners themselves; they would be my guide as to what really happened. A few months later, in the spring, I returned for the anniversary ceremony to mark the liberation and met Valentina Makarova, the survivor of the Auschwitz death march who had written to me from Minsk. She had blue-white hair and a face as sharp as flint. When I asked how she survived she said, 'Because we believed in victory,' as if this was something I should have known.

The sun broke through briefly as I stood near the shooting gallery. Wood pigeons were hooting at the tops of the linden trees, competing with the sound of traffic sweeping past. A coach carrying French schoolchildren had pulled in and they were standing around smoking cigarettes.

I was looking straight across the frozen lake towards the Fürstenberg church spire. In the distance workmen were moving around in a boatyard; summer visitors take the boats out, unaware of the ashes lying at the bottom of the lake. The breeze was blowing a red rose across the ice.

# PART ONE

*Chapter 1*

# Langefeld

'The year is 1957. The doorbell of my flat is ringing,' writes Grete Buber-Neumann, a former Ravensbrück prisoner. 'I open the door. An old woman is standing before me, breathing heavily and missing teeth in the lower jaw. She babbles: "Don't you know me any more? I am Johanna Langefeld, the former head guard at Ravensbrück." The last time I had seen her was fourteen years ago in her office at the camp. I worked as her prisoner secretary ... She would pray to God for strength to stop the evil happening, but if a Jewish woman came into her office her face would fill with hatred ...

'So she sits at the table with me. She tells me she wishes she'd been born a man. She talks of Himmler, whom she somctimes still calls "Reichsführer". She talks for many hours, she gets lost in the different years and tries to explain her behaviour.'

* * *

Early in May 1939 a small convoy of trucks emerged from trees into a clearing near the tiny village of Ravensbrück, deep in the Mecklenburg forest. The trucks drove on past a lake, where their wheels started spinning and axles sank into waterlogged sand. People jumped down to dig out the vehicles while others unloaded boxes.

A woman in uniform – grey jacket and skirt – also jumped down. Her feet sank into the sand, but she pulled herself free, walked a little way up the slope and looked around. Felled trees lay beside the shimmering lake. The air smelt of sawdust. It was hot and there was no shade. To her right, on the far shore, lay the small town of Fürstenberg. Boathouses sprawled by the shore. A church spire was visible.

At the opposite end of the lake, to her left, a vast grey wall about sixteen feet high loomed up. The forest track led towards towering iron-barred gates to the left of the compound. There were signs saying 'Trespassers Keep Out'. The woman – medium height, stocky, brown wavy hair – strode purposefully towards the gates.

Johanna Langefeld had come with a small advance party of guards and prisoners to bring equipment and look around the new women's concentration camp; the camp was due to open in a few days' time and Langefeld was to be the *Oberaufseherin* – chief woman guard. She had seen inside many women's penal institutions in her time, but never a place like this.

For the past year Langefeld had worked as a senior guard at Lichtenburg, a medieval fortress near Torgau, on the River Elbe. Converted into a temporary women's camp while Ravensbrück was built, Lichtenburg's crumbling chambers and wet dungeons were cramped and unhealthy; unsuitable for women prisoners. Ravensbrück was new and purpose-built. The compound comprised about six acres, big enough for the first 1000 or so women expected here, with space to spare.

Langefeld stepped through the iron gates and strode around the sandy Appellplatz, the camp square. The size of a football pitch, it had room enough to drill the entire camp at once. Loudspeakers hung on poles above Langefeld's head, though the only sound for now was the banging of nails. The walls blocked everything outside from view, except the sky.

Unlike male camps, Ravensbrück had no watchtowers along the walls and no gun emplacements. But an electric fence was fixed to the interior of the perimeter wall, and placards along the fence showed a skull and crossbones warning of high voltage. Only beyond the walls to the south, to Langefeld's right, did the ground rise high enough for treetops to be visible on a hill.

Hulking grey barrack blocks dominated the compound. The wooden blocks, arranged in a grid, were single-storey with small windows; they sat squat around the camp square. Two lines of identical blocks – though somewhat larger – were laid out each side of the Lagerstrasse, the main street.

Langefeld inspected the blocks one by one. Immediately inside the gate, the first block on the left was the SS canteen, fitted out with freshly scrubbed chairs and tables. Also to the left of the Appellplatz was the camp *Revier*, a German military term meaning sickbay or infirmary. Across the square, she entered the bathhouse, fitted with dozens of showerheads. Boxes containing striped cotton clothes were stacked at one end and at a table a handful of women were laying out piles of coloured felt triangles.

Next to the bathhouse, under the same roof, was the camp kitchen, which glistened with huge steel pots and kettles. The next building was the prisoners' clothes store, or *Effektenkammer*, where large brown paper bags were piled on a table, and then came the *Wäscherei*, laundry, with its six centrifugal washing machines – Langefeld would have liked more.

Nearby an aviary was being constructed. Heinrich Himmler, head of the SS, which ran the concentration camps and much else in Nazi Germany, wanted his camps to be self-sufficient as far as possible. There was to be a rabbit hutch, chicken coop and vegetable garden, as well as an orchard and flower garden. Gooseberry bushes, dug up from the Lichtenburg gardens and transported in the trucks, were already being replanted here. The contents of the Lichtenburg latrines had been brought to Ravensbrück too, to be spread as fertiliser. Himmler also required his camps to pool resources. As Ravensbrück had no baking ovens of its own, bread was to be brought here daily from Sachsenhausen, the men's camp, fifty miles to the south.

The *Oberaufseherin* strode on down the Lagerstrasse, which started at the far side of the Appellplatz and led towards the back of the camp. The living blocks were laid out, end-on to the Lagerstrasse, in perfect formation so that the windows of one block looked out onto the back wall of the next. They were to be the prisoners' living quarters, eight on each side of the 'street'. Red flowers – salvias – had been planted outside the first block; linden tree saplings stood at regular intervals in between the rest.

As in all concentration camps, the grid layout was used at Ravensbrück mainly to ensure that prisoners could always be seen, which meant fewer guards. A complement of fifty-five women guards were assigned here and a troop of forty SS men, all under overall command of Hauptsturmführer Max Koegel.

Johanna Langefeld believed she could run a women's concentration camp better than any man, and certainly better than Max Koegel, whose methods she despised. Himmler, however, was clear that Ravensbrück should be run, in general, on the same lines as the men's camps, which meant Langefeld and her women guards must be answerable to an SS commandant.

On paper neither she nor any of her guards had any official standing. The women were not merely subordinate to the men, they had no badge or rank and were merely SS 'auxiliaries'. Most of them were unarmed, though some guarding outside work parties carried a pistol and many had dogs. Himmler believed that women were more frightened than men of dogs.

Nevertheless, Koegel's authority here would not be absolute. He was only commandant-designate for now, and he had been refused certain powers. For example there was to be no camp prison or 'bunker' in which to lock up troublemakers, as there was at every male camp. Nor was he to have authority for 'official' beatings. Angered by these omissions, he wrote to his SS superiors requesting greater powers to punish prisoners, but his request was refused.

Langefeld, however, who believed in drill and discipline rather than beating, was content with the arrangements, especially as she had secured significant concessions on day-to-day management. It had been written into the camp's comprehensive rule book, the *Lagerordnung*, that the chief woman guard would advise the Schutzhaftlagerführer (deputy commandant) on 'feminine matters', though what these were was not defined.

Stepping inside one of the accommodation barracks, Langefeld looked around. Like so much else here, the sleeping arrangements were new to her; instead of shared cells, or dormitories, as she was used to, more than 150 women were to sleep in each block. Their interiors were identically set out, with two large sleeping rooms – A and B – on either side of a washing area, with a row of twelve basins and twelve lavatories, as well as a communal day room where the women would eat.

The sleeping areas were filled with scores of three-tiered bunks, made of wooden planks. Every prisoner had a mattress filled with wood shavings and a pillow, as well as a sheet and a blue and white check blanket folded at the foot of the bed.

The value of drill and discipline had been instilled in Langefeld from her earliest years. The daughter of a blacksmith, she was born Johanna May, in the Ruhr town of Kupferdreh, in March 1900. She and her older sister were raised as strict Lutherans; their parents drummed into them the importance of thrift, obedience and daily prayer. Like any good Protestant girl Johanna already knew that her role in life would be that of dutiful wife and mother: '*Kinder, Küche, Kirche*' – children, kitchen, church – was a familiar creed in the May family home. Yet from her childhood Johanna yearned for more. Her parents also talked to her of Germany's past. After church on Sundays they would hark back to the humiliation of the French occupation of their beloved Ruhr under Napoleon and the family would kneel and pray for God's help in making Germany great again. She idolised her namesake, Johanna Prohaska, a heroine of the liberation wars, who had disguised herself as a man to fight the French.

All this Johanna Langefeld told Grete Buber-Neumann, the former prisoner, at whose Frankfurt door she appeared years later, seeking to 'try to explain her behaviour'. Grete, an inmate of Ravensbrück for four years, was startled by the reappearance in 1957 of her chief former guard; she was also gripped by Langefeld's account of her 'odyssey' and wrote it down.

In 1914, as the First World War broke out, Johanna, then fourteen, cheered with the rest as the young men of Kupferdreh marched off to pursue the dream of making Germany great again, only to find that she and all German women had little part to play. Two years later, when it was clear the war would not end soon, German women were suddenly told to get out to work in mines, factories and offices; there on the 'home front', women had a chance to prove themselves doing the jobs of men, only to be expelled from those same jobs again when the men came home.

Two million Germans did not return from the trenches, but several million did, and Johanna now watched as Kupferdreh's soldiers came back, many mutilated and all humiliated. Under the terms of surrender, Germany was to pay reparations, which would cripple the economy, fuelling hyperinflation; in 1924 Langefeld's beloved Ruhr was reoccupied yet again by the French, who 'stole' German coal, in punishment for reparations unpaid. Her parents lost their savings and she was penniless and looking for a job. In 1924 she found a husband, a miner called Wilhelm Langefeld, who died two years later of lung disease.

Johanna's 'odyssey' then faltered; she 'got lost in the years', wrote Grete. The mid-1920s were a dark period that she could not account for other than to say there was a liaison with another man, which left her pregnant, dependent on Protestant aid groups.

While Langefeld and millions like her struggled, other German women found liberation in the 1920s. With American financial support, the socialist-led Weimar Republic stabilised the country and set out on a new liberal path. Women had the vote, and for the first time German women joined political parties, particularly on the left. Inspired by Rosa Luxemburg, leader of the communist Spartacus movement, middle-class girls, Grete Buber-Neumann among them, chopped off their hair, watched plays by Bertolt Brecht and tramped through forests with comrades of the Wandervogel, and other youth movements, talking of revolution. Meanwhile, across the country working-class women raised money for 'Red Help', joined trade unions and stood at factory gates handing out strike leaflets.

In 1922 in Munich, where Adolf Hitler was blaming Germany's strife on the 'bloated Jew', a precocious Jewish girl called Olga Benario ran away from home to join a communist cell, disowning her prosperous middle-class parents. She was fourteen. Within months the dark-eyed schoolgirl was leading comrades on walks through the Bavarian Alps, diving into mountain streams, then reading Marx around the campfire and planning Germany's communist revolution. In 1928 she shot to fame after holding up a Berlin courthouse and snatching a leading German communist to freedom as he faced the guillotine. By 1929 Olga had left Germany for Moscow to train with Stalin's elite, before heading to Brazil to start a revolution.

Back in the stricken Ruhr valley, Johanna Langefeld was by this time a single mother without a future. The 1929 Wall Street Crash triggered world depression, plunging Germany into a new and deeper economic crisis that threw millions out of work and created widespread unrest. Langefeld's deepest fear was that her son, Herbert, would be taken from her if she fell into destitution. Instead of joining the destitute, however, she chose to help them, turning to God. 'It was religious conviction that drew her to work with the poorest of the poor,' so she told Grete all those years later at the Frankfurt kitchen table. She found work with the welfare service, teaching housekeeping skills to unemployed women and 're-educating prostitutes'.

In 1933, Johanna Langefeld found a new saviour in Adolf Hitler. Hitler's programme for women could not have been clearer: German women were to stay at home, rear as many Aryan children as they were able, and obey their husbands. Women were not fit for public life; most jobs would be barred to women and access to university curtailed.

Such attitudes could easily be found in any European country in the 1930s, but Nazi language on women was uniquely toxic; not only did Hitler's entourage openly scorn the 'stupid', 'inferior' female sex, they repeatedly demanded 'separation' of women from men, as if men didn't see the point of women at all except as occasional adornments and, of course, as childbearers.* The Jews were not Hitler's only scapegoats for Germany's ills: women who had been emancipated during the Weimar years were blamed for taking men's jobs and corrupting the country's morals.

Yet Hitler had the power to seduce the millions of German women who yearned for a 'steel-hardened man' to restore pride and order to the Reich. Such female admirers, many deeply religious, and all inflamed by Joseph Goebbels's anti-Semitic propaganda, packed the 1933 Nuremberg victory rally where the American reporter William Shirer mingled with the mob. 'Hitler rode into this medieval town at sundown today past solid phalanxes of wildly cheering Nazis ... Tens of thousands of Swastika flags blot out the Gothic beauties of the place ...' Later that night, outside Hitler's hotel: 'I was a little shocked at the faces, especially those of the women ... They looked up at him as if he were a Messiah ...'

That Langefeld cast her vote for Hitler seems almost certain. She longed to put right her country's humiliation. She also welcomed the new 'respect for family life' proclaimed by Hitler. And Langefeld had personal reasons to be thankful to the new regime: for the first time she had a secure job. For women, and particularly unmarried mothers, most career paths were barred, except the one Langefeld had chosen. From the welfare service she had been promoted into the prison service. In 1935 she was promoted again to the post of *Hausmutter* at Brauweiler, a workhouse for prostitutes near Cologne. The job came with a roof over her head and free care for Herbert.

* Nazis pointed to scientific studies showing that women had smaller brains than men and were therefore obviously inferior.

While at Brauweiler, however, it seems that she didn't take easily to all Nazi methods of helping 'the poorest of the poor'. In July 1933 the Law for the Prevention of Hereditarily Diseased Offspring was passed, legalising mass sterilisation as a means of eliminating the weak, idle, criminal and insane. The Führer believed that all these degenerates were a drain on the public purse, and were to be removed from the chain of heredity in order to strengthen the *Volksgemeinschaft*, the community of pure-bred Germans. The Brauweiler director, Albert Bosse, declared in 1936 that 95 per cent of his women prisoners were 'incapable of improvement and must be sterilised for moral reasons and for the purpose of maintaining the health of the Volk'.

In 1937 Bosse dismissed Langefeld. One reason given in the Brauweiler records is theft, but this was almost certainly a cover for her opposition to his methods. The records also show that Langefeld had so far failed to join the Nazi Party, a duty required of all prison staff.

Hitler's 'respect' for family life had never fooled Lina Haag, wife of a communist state parliament member in Württemberg. As soon as she heard on 30 January 1933 on the wireless that Hitler had been made chancellor, she felt sure that the new security police, the Gestapo, would come and take her husband: 'In our meetings we had warned the country against Hitler. We expected a popular rising, it did not come.'

Then, sure enough, on 31 January Lina and her husband were asleep in bed when at five in the morning the thugs came. The roundup of Reds had begun. 'Chinstraps, revolvers, truncheons. They stamped on the clean linen with repulsive zest. We were not strangers to them – they knew us and we knew them. They were grown-up men, fellow citizens – neighbours, fathers of families. Ordinary common people. And they looked at us now full of hatred with their cocked pistols.'

Lina's husband began to dress. Why did he have his coat on so fast, Lina wondered. Was he just going to go without a word?

'What's up?' she asked him.

'Ah well,' he said, shrugging his shoulders.

'He's a member of the state parliament,' she shouted at the truncheon-wielding police. They laughed.

'Do you hear that? Communist, that's what you are, but now we're clearing all you vermin out.'

Lina pulled the couple's screaming child, Katie, aged ten, away from the window as her father was marched away. 'I thought the people will not long put up with that,' said Lina.

Four weeks later, on 27 February 1933, as Hitler was still struggling to underpin his party's power, the German parliament, the Reichstag, was set on fire. Communists were blamed, although many suspected the blaze was started by Nazi thugs as a pretext to terrorise every political opponent in the country. Hitler at once enforced a catch-all edict called 'preventative detention' which meant that anyone could be arrested for 'treason' and locked up indefinitely. Just ten miles north of Munich a brand-new camp was about to open to hold the 'traitors'.

Opened on 22 March 1933, Dachau was the first Nazi concentration camp. Over the next weeks and months Hitler's police sought out every communist or suspected communist and brought them here to be crushed. Social democrats were rounded up too, along with trade unionists and any other 'enemy of the state'.

Some held here, particularly amongst the communists, were Jews, but in the first years of Nazi rule Jews were not locked up in significant numbers; those held in the early concentration camps were imprisoned, like the rest, for resistance to Hitler, not simply for their race. The sole aim of Hitler's concentration camps in the early days was to crush all internal German opposition; only once this had been done would other objectives be pursued. The crushing was a task assigned to the man most fit for the job: Heinrich Himmler, head of the SS, and soon also to become chief of police, including the Gestapo.

Heinrich Luitpold Himmler was an unlikely police chief, physically slight and podgy, his face chinless and pallid, gold-rimmed spectacles perched on his sharp nose. Born on 7 October 1900, the second of three boys, he was the son of Gebhard Himmler, an assistant head teacher at a school near Munich. Evenings in the family's comfortable Munich apartment were spent helping Himmler senior with his stamp collection or listening to tales of the heroic exploits of their soldier grandfather, while their adored mother, a devout Catholic, sewed in the corner.

The young Heinrich excelled at school, but he was known as a swot and was often bullied; in the gym he could barely reach the parallel bars, so instructors forced him instead to perform torturous knee bends, as peers looked on and jeered. Years later, at male concentration camps, Himmler introduced a torture whereby prisoners were chained together in a circle and forced to jump up and down doing knee bends until they collapsed, only to be kicked to their feet until they fell down for good.

On leaving school Himmler's dream was to be commissioned in the military, but although he served briefly as a cadet, ill health and poor eyesight ruled him out of the officer class. He studied agriculture and bred chickens instead, and became absorbed by another romantic dream, a return to the *Heimat* – the German homeland – passing his spare time walking in his beloved Alps, often with his mother, or studying astrology and genealogy, while making notes in his diary of every trivial detail of his daily life. 'Thoughts and worries chase themselves in my head,' he complained.

By his late teens, Himmler was berating himself for his inadequacies, social and sexual. 'I'm a wretched prattler,' he wrote, and when it came to sex: 'I'm controlling myself with an iron bit.' By the 1920s he had joined Munich's all-male Thule Society, which debated the roots of Aryan supremacy and the threat of the Jews. He was welcomed too into Munich's far-right paramilitary units. 'It is so nice to be in uniform again,' he wrote. In National Socialist (Nazi) Party ranks people began to say of him: 'Heinrich will fix things.' His organisational skills and attention to detail were second to none and he proved adept at anticipating Hitler's wishes. It helped, Himmler discovered, to be 'as crafty as a fox'.

In 1928 he married a nurse called Margarete Boden, seven years his senior. They had a daughter, Gudrun. Himmler's professional fortunes moved on too, and in 1929 he was made head of the SS (*Schutzstaffel*), the paramilitary squad first formed as Hitler's personal bodyguard. By the time Hitler came to power in 1933 Himmler had transformed the SS into an elite force. One of its tasks was to run the new concentration camps.

Hitler proposed the use of concentration camps as places to intern and then crush his opposition, taking as a model the concentration camps used for mass internment by the British during the South African War of 1899–1902. The style of the Nazi camps, however, would be set by Himmler, who personally identified the site for the prototype at Dachau. He also selected the Dachau commandant, Theodor Eicke, who became head of the 'Death's Head' units, as the SS concentration-camp guard squads were called – they wore a skull and crossbones badge on their caps to denote loyalty to death. Himmler charged Eicke with devising a blueprint for terrorising all 'enemies of the state'.

At Dachau Eicke did just that, creating a school for SS men who called him 'Papa Eicke' and whom he 'hardened' before they were sent off to other camps. Hardening meant the men should learn never to show weakness to the enemy and should only 'show their teeth' – in other words, they should hate. Amongst Eicke's early recruits was Max Koegel, the future commandant of Ravensbrück, who came to Dachau looking for work after a short spell in jail for embezzlement.

Born in the south Bavarian mountain town of Füssen, famous for lute making and for Gothic castles, Koegel was the son of a carpenter. Orphaned at the age of twelve, he spent his early years shepherding on the Alps before seeking other work in Munich, where he fell in with far-right '*völkische*' societies and joined the Nazi Party in 1932. 'Papa Eicke' quickly found a use for Koegel, now thirty-eight, his hardness already deeply chiselled.

At Dachau Koegel mixed with other SS men like Rudolf Höss, another early recruit, who went on to become commandant of Auschwitz and who also played a role at Ravensbrück. Höss would later remember his Dachau days with affection, talking of an entire cadre of SS men who learned to 'love' Eicke and never forgot his rules, 'which stayed fast and became part of their flesh and blood'.

Such was Eicke's success that several more camps were soon set up on the Dachau model. But in these early days neither Eicke, Himmler, nor anyone else had contemplated a concentration camp for women; women opponents to Hitler were not taken seriously enough to be viewed as a threat.

In Hitler's purges thousands of women were certainly rounded up. Many had found liberation during the Weimar years – trade unionists, doctors, lecturers, journalists. Often they were communists or wives of communists. On arrest they were ill-treated but these women were not taken to Dachau-style camps, nor was any thought given to opening women's sections in the male camps. Instead, they were put in women's prisons, or converted workhouses where regimes were harsh but not intolerable.

Many of the women political prisoners were taken to Moringen, a converted workhouse near Hanover. The 150 women here in 1935 slept in unlocked dormitories and the guards ran errands for them to buy knitting wool. In the prison hall sewing machines clattered. A table of 'notables' sat apart from the rest, among them the grander members of the Reichstag and the wives of manufacturers.

Nevertheless, as Himmler had calculated, women could be tortured in different ways from men; the simple fact that husbands had been killed and children taken away – usually to Nazi foster homes – was for most women pain enough. Censorship ruled out appealing for help.

Barbara Fürbringer, hearing that her husband, a communist Reichstag member, had been tortured to death at Dachau and her children had been taken to a Nazi foster home, tried to alert her sister in America:

*Dear Sister,*

*Unfortunately we are in a bad way. Theodor, my dear husband, died suddenly in Dachau four months ago. Our three children have been put in the state welfare home in Munich. I am in the women's camp at Moringen. I no longer have a penny to my name.*

The censor rejected the letter so she wrote again:

*Dear Sister,*

*Unfortunately things are not going exactly as we might wish. Theodor, my dear husband, died four months ago. Our three children live in Munich, 27*

*Brenner Strasse, I live in Moringen, near Hanover, 32 Breite Strasse. I would be grateful to you if you could send me a small sum of money.*

Himmler also calculated that as long as the crushing of men was terrible enough, everyone else would soon acquiesce. And this proved largely true, as Lina Haag, arrested just weeks after her husband and locked in another prison, would soon observe. 'Did nobody see where we were heading? Did nobody see through the shameless demagogy of the articles of Goebbels? I could see it even through the thick walls of the prison; yet more and more people outside were toeing the line.'

By 1936 not only was the political opposition entirely eliminated, but humanitarian bodies and the German churches were all toeing the line. The German Red Cross movement had been co-opted to the Nazi cause; at its meetings the Red Cross banner was waved alongside the swastika, while the guardians of the Geneva Conventions, the International Committee of the Red Cross, had inspected Himmler's camps – or, at least, the show blocks – and given their stamp of approval. Western capitals took the view that Nazi concentration camps and prisons were an internal German affair and not a concern of theirs. In the mid-1930s most Western leaders still believed that the greatest threat to world peace was posed by communism, not by Nazi Germany.

Despite the lack of meaningful opposition, at home or abroad, however, the Führer watched public opinion carefully in the early days of his rule. In a speech at an SS training centre in 1937 he said: 'I always know that I must never make a single step that I may have to take back. You have to have a nose to sniff out the situation, to ask: "Now what can I get away with and what can't I get away with?"'

Even the drive against Germany's Jews proceeded more slowly at first than many in the party wanted. In his first years Hitler passed laws to bar Jews from employment and public life, whipping up hatred and persecution, but it would be some time, he judged, before he could get away with more than that. Himmler had a 'nose' to sniff out a situation too.

In November 1936 the Reichsführer SS, who by now was not only head of the SS but also police chief, had to deal with an international storm which erupted over a German woman communist who was brought off a steamer at Hamburg's docks into the waiting hands of the Gestapo. She was eight months pregnant. This was Olga Benario. The leggy girl from Munich who ran away from home to become a communist was now thirty-five, and about to become a cause célèbre for communists around the globe.

After training in Moscow in the early 1930s, Olga had been chosen for the Comintern (the Communist International organisation) and in 1935 was sent by Stalin to help mastermind a coup against President Getulio Vargas of Brazil. The leader of the operation was the legendary Brazilian rebel leader Luis Carlos Prestes. The insurrection was intended to bring about a communist revolution in the biggest country in South America, thereby giving Stalin a foothold in the Americas. As a result of a British intelligence tip-off, however, the plot was foiled, Olga was arrested and along with a co-conspirator, Elise Ewert, sent back to Hitler 'as a gift'.*

From Hamburg docks, Olga was taken to Berlin's Barnimstrasse jail, where she gave birth to a girl, Anita, four weeks later. Communists across the world launched a campaign to free them. The case drew wide attention, largely because the baby's father was the famous Carlos Prestes, the leader of the failed coup; the couple had fallen in love and married in Brazil. Olga's own courage, and her dark, willowy beauty, added to the poignancy of the story.

Such bad publicity abroad was unwelcome, especially as it was the year of the Berlin Olympics and so much had been done to clean up the country's image.† Himmler's Gestapo chiefs first attempted to defuse the row by proposing that the baby be released into the hands of Olga's Jewish mother, Eugenia Benario, who still lived in Munich, but Eugenia didn't want the child: she had long ago disowned her communist daughter and now she disowned the baby too. Himmler then gave permission for Prestes's mother, Leocadia, to take Anita, and in November 1937 the Brazilian grandmother collected the baby from Barnimstrasse jail. Olga, now bereft, remained alone in her cell.

Writing to Leocadia, she explained that she had not had time to prepare for the separation: 'So you have to excuse the state of Anita's things. Did you receive my description of her routine and her weight table? I put the table together as best I could. Are her inner organs all right? What about the bones – her little legs. Perhaps she suffered from the extraordinary circumstances of my pregnancy and her first year in life.'

By 1936 the number of women in Germany's jails was beginning to rise. Despite the terror, German women continued to operate underground, many now inspired by the outbreak of the Spanish civil war. Amongst those taken to the women's 'camp' of Moringen in the mid-1930s were more women communists and former Reichstag members, as well as individuals

* British intelligence also foiled an attempt by communist protesters to get Olga off the steamer when it docked at Southampton en route to Hamburg. Moscow had signalled in advance to the British Communist Party in London, calling for protests to be organised at the port, but the signal was intercepted by MI6 and the steamer went straight to Germany without docking anywhere.

† For example, all Gypsies in Berlin had been rounded up before the Olympics began. In order to remove them from public view they were herded into a vast camp built on a swamp in the Berlin suburb of Marzahn.

operating in tiny groups or alone, like the disabled graphic artist Gerda Lissack, who designed anti-Nazi leaflets. Ilse Gostynski, a young Jewish woman, who helped print articles attacking the Führer on her printing press, was arrested by mistake. The Gestapo wanted her twin sister Else, but Else was in Oslo, arranging escape routes for Jewish children, so they took Ilse instead.

In 1936 500 German housewives carrying bibles and wearing neat white headscarves arrived at Moringen. The women, Jehovah's Witnesses, had protested when their husbands were called up for the army. Hitler was the Antichrist, they said; God was the ruler on earth, not the Führer. Their husbands, and other male Jehovah's Witnesses, were taken to Hitler's newest camp, Buchenwald, where they suffered twenty-five lashes of a leather whip. Himmler knew that even his SS men were not yet hard enough to thrash German housewives, however, so at Moringen the Jehovah's Witness women simply had their bibles taken away by the prison director, a kindly retired soldier with a limp.

In 1937 the passing of a law against '*Rassenschande*' – literally, 'race shame' – which outlawed relationships between Jews and non-Jews, brought a further influx of Jewish women to Moringen. Then in the second half of 1937 the women there noticed a sudden rise in the number of vagrants brought in 'limping, some wearing supports, many others spitting blood'. In 1938 scores of prostitutes arrived.

Else Krug had been at work as usual when a group of Düsseldorf policemen banged on the door at 10 Corneliusstrasse, shouting to her to open up; it was 2 a.m. on 30 July 1938. Police raids were not unusual and Else had no reason to fear, though of late the raids had been on the increase. Prostitution was legal under Nazi law, but the police could use any excuse; perhaps one of the women evaded her syphilis check, or maybe an officer wanted a lead on a new communist cell on the Düsseldorf docks.

Several Düsseldorf officers knew these women personally. Else Krug was always in demand, either for her own particular services – she dealt in sadomasochism – or for her gossip; she kept her ear to the ground. Else was also popular on the street; she'd always take a girl in if she could, especially if the waif was new in town. Else had arrived on the streets of Düsseldorf like this herself ten years ago – out of work, far from home and without a penny to her name.

It soon turned out, however, that the raid of 30 July was different from any that had gone before in Corneliusstrasse. Terrified clients grabbed what they could and ran out half-dressed into the night. The same night similar raids took place at a nearby address where Agnes Petry was at work. Agnes's husband, a local pimp, was rounded up too. After a further sweep through the Bahndamm, the officers had pulled in a total of twenty-four prostitutes, and by six in the morning all were behind bars, with no time given for release.

The treatment of the women at the police station was also different. The desk officer – a Sergeant Peine – knew most of the women as regular overnighters in his cells, and taking out his large black ledger, booked them in painstakingly as usual, noting names, addresses, and personal effects. Under the column headed 'reason for arrest', however, Peine carefully printed '*Asoziale*', 'asocial', against each name – a word he had not used there before. And at the end of the column, likewise for the first time, he wrote in red: 'Transport'.

The raids on Düsseldorf brothels were repeated across Germany throughout 1938, as the Nazi purge against its own unwanted underclasses entered a new stage. A programme called '*Aktion Arbeitsscheu Reich*' (Action Against the Work-shy) had been launched, targeting all those considered social outcasts. Largely unnoticed by the outside world, and unreported within Germany, more than 20,000 so-called 'asocials' – 'vagabonds, prostitutes, work-shy, beggars and thieves' – were rounded up and earmarked for concentration camps.

In mid-1938 war was still a year away, but Germany's war against its own unwanted had been launched. The Führer let it be known that the country must be 'pure and strong' as it prepared for war, so such 'useless mouths' were to be removed. From the moment Hitler came to power, mass sterilisation of the mentally ill and social degenerates had already been carried out. In 1936 Gypsies were locked in reservations near big cities. In 1937 thousands of 'habitual criminals' were sent to concentration camps, with no legal process. Hitler authorised the measures, but the instigator of the crackdown was his police chief and head of the SS, Heinrich Himmler. It was also Himmler who in 1938 called for all 'asocials' to be locked in concentration camps.

The timing was significant. Well before 1937 the camps, established at first to remove political opposition, had begun to empty out. Communists, social democrats and others, rounded up in the first years of Hitler's rule, had been largely crushed, and most were now sent home, broken men. Himmler, who had opposed these mass releases, saw his empire in danger of decline, and looked for new uses for his camps.

To date nobody had seriously suggested using the concentration camps for anything other than the political opposition, but by filling them with criminals and social outcasts, Himmler could start expanding his empire again. He saw himself as far more than a police chief; his interest in science – in all forms of experimentation that might help breed a perfect Aryan race – was always the main objective. By bringing these degenerates inside his camps he had begun to secure a central role for himself in the Führer's most ambitious experiment, which aimed to cleanse the German gene pool. Moreover the new prisoners would provide a ready pool of labour for rebuilding the Reich.

The nature and purpose of the concentration camps would now change. As the number of German political prisoners decreased, social rejects would pour in to replace them. Among those swept up for the first time, there were bound to be as many women – prostitutes, petty criminals, down-and-outs – as men.

A new generation of purpose-built concentration camps was now constructed. And with Moringen and other women's prisons already overflowing, and costly, Himmler proposed a concentration camp for women. Some time in 1938 he called his advisers together to discuss a possible site. A proposal was made, probably by Himmler's friend Gruppenführer Oswald Pohl, a senior SS administrator, that the new camp be built in the Mecklenburg lake district, close to a village called Ravensbrück. Pohl knew the area because he had a country estate there.

Rudolf Höss later claimed that he warned Himmler that the site was too small: the number of women was bound to increase, especially when war broke out. Others pointed out that the ground was a bog and the camp would take too long to build. Himmler brushed aside the objections. Just fifty miles north of Berlin, it was convenient for inspections, and he often drove out that way to visit Pohl or to drop in on his childhood friend, the famous SS surgeon Karl Gebhardt, who ran the Hohenlychen medical clinic just five miles from Ravensbrück.

Himmler therefore ordered male prisoners from the concentration camp of Sachsenhausen, on the edge of Berlin, to start building at Ravensbrück as soon as possible. Meanwhile the male concentration camp at Lichtenburg, near Torgau, which was already half empty, was to be cleared and the rest of the men there taken to the new men's camp of Buchenwald, opened in July 1937. Women earmarked for the new women's camp could be held at Lichtenburg while Ravensbrück was built.

Inside a caged train wagon, Lina Haag had no idea where she was heading. After four years in her prison cell, she and scores of others were told they were going 'on transport'. Every few hours the train would halt at a station, but the names – Frankfurt, Stuttgart, Mannheim – gave little clue. Lina stared at 'ordinary people' on the platforms – a sight she hadn't seen for years – and the ordinary people stared back 'at these ghostly figures with hollow eyes and matted hair'. At night the women were taken off and put up in local prisons. Lina was horrified by the women guards. 'It was inconceivable how in the face of all that misery they could gossip and laugh in the corridors. Most are pious, but with a peculiar sort of piety. They seem to me to be hiding behind God in disgust at their own meanness.'

Women from the Moringen workhouse joined the train and huddled together in shock. A doctor called Doris Maase was brought on at Stuttgart along with a crowd of Düsseldorf prostitutes. Doris, described in her Gestapo file as a 'red student', had half a comb, which she lent to Lina. All around the 'harlots' and 'hags' cackled, although, as Lina admitted to Doris, after four years in a prison, she probably looked like a 'harlot' too.

At Lichtenburg the SS were waiting, wearing buckskin gloves and carrying revolvers. Johanna Langefeld was waiting too. After dismissal from Brauweiler workhouse, Langefeld had been rehired by Himmler's office and offered a promotion as a guard at Lichtenburg. Langefeld would claim later that she only took the job there in the belief that once again she could fulfil her vocation to 're-educate prostitutes', which was obviously a lie: she had been offered a promotion, more money and accommodation for herself and her child. In any case, Brauweiler had already shown Langefeld that prostitutes and other outcasts were to be eliminated from society, not re-educated.

Arriving now at Lichtenburg was Gertrud Kröffges, a woman Langefeld probably even remembered from the workhouse. Kröffges had first been imprisoned at Brauweiler for failing to keep up payments to support her children. Now she had been sent on to Lichtenburg because she was 'incapable of improvement', as her police report noted, and because 'due to her immoral and asocial way of life, the *Volksgemeinschaft* [the racially pure community] must be protected from her'.

Even the prison official who registered the women at Lichtenburg could see no sense in locking up such down-and-outs. Agnes Petry, one of the Düsseldorf crew, arrived 'penniless', he noted on her registration card. All she carried was a photograph of her husband. The word '*Stutze*' was noted on her file, which meant she was a person 'dependent on the state'. 'Could she be sent back?' he asked in a letter to the Düsseldorf police chief. 'Has she anyone in the world who would help her?'

Lina Haag had long ago stopped hoping anyone would help any of them. On 12 March 1938 Austria had been annexed, and soon after that Austrian resisters began arriving at the fortress, including a doctor, an opera singer and a carpenter; all had been beaten and abused. 'If the world was not protesting even against the brutal annexation of foreign territories, was it likely to protest against the whipping of some poor women who had protested against it?' asked Lina.

News that Olga Benario, a name from the glory days of communist resistance, was in the fortress gave some women hope. Olga had been brought alone from Berlin in a Gestapo van, and escorted straight down to the Lichtenburg dungeons. Communist comrades managed to make contact and found her heartbroken at the recent separation from her child. They smuggled messages and tiny gifts to her cell. Recalling Olga's stunning courtroom snatch in 1928, some dreamt of escape, but Lina Haag said there was 'no sense' in attempting anything. 'The Führer always comes out on top and we are just poor devils – absolutely forsaken, miserable devils ...' Then a Gypsy trapeze artist called Katharina Waitz tried to scale the fortress walls. She was captured and beaten. The Lichtenburg commandant, Max Koegel, liked to beat. Lina recalled that on Easter day he beat three naked women 'until he could go on no longer'.

On 1 October 1938, the day Hitler's forces took the Sudetenland, Koegel turned hoses on his prisoners. They had all been ordered to the courtyard to hear the Führer's victory address, but the Jehovah's Witnesses refused to descend the steps, so guards forced them down, dragging old women by their hair. As Prussian tunes struck up someone whispered 'war is coming' and the fortress suddenly erupted. All the Jehovah's Witnesses started shouting hysterically before sinking to their knees and praying. The guards thrashed and the mob hit back. Koegel ordered fire hoses to be turned on the praying women, who were knocked flying, flattened, bitten by dogs. Clinging to one another, they nearly drowned, 'like dripping mice', said Marianne Korn, one of the praying women.

Soon after the riot Himmler visited the fortress to see that order had been restored. The Reichsführer SS inspected Lichtenburg several times, bringing the head of the Nazi women's movement, Gertrud Scholtz-Klink, to show off his prisoners to. On his visits he sometimes authorised releases. One day he released Lina Haag, on condition she didn't speak about her treatment.

Himmler also inspected the women guards. He must have noted that Johanna Langefeld had a certain authority – a knack for quietening prisoners without a fuss – because he marked her down as Ravensbrück's future chief woman guard.

It was the local children who first suspected something was about to be built on the northern shore of the Schwedtsee – or Lake Schwedt – but when they told their parents they were ordered to say nothing. Until 1938 the children played on a piece of scrubland near the lake where the trees were thinner and the bathing was good. One day they were told the area was out of bounds. Over the next few weeks locals in the town of Fürstenberg – of which the village of Ravensbrück is a small suburb – watched as barges delivered building materials up the River Havel. The children told parents they'd seen men in striped uniforms, who chopped down trees.

Ravensbrück, fifty miles north of Berlin, on the southern edge of the Mecklenburg lake district, was, as Himmler identified in 1938, a good location for a concentration camp. Rail and water connections were good. Fürstenberg, cradled by three lakes, the Röblinsee, Baalensee and Schwedtsee, sits astride the River Havel, which divides into several channels as it flows through the town.

Another factor that influenced Himmler's choice was the siting in an area of natural beauty. Himmler believed that the cleansing of German blood should begin close to nature, and the invigorating forces of the German forests played a central role in the mythology of the *Heimat* – German soil. Buchenwald – meaning Beech Forest – was sited in a famous wooded area close to Weimar and several other camps were deliberately located in beauty spots. Just weeks before Ravensbrück was opened a stretch of water here was declared an 'organic source for the Aryan race'. Fürstenberg had always been popular with nature lovers who came to boat on the lakes, or visit the baroque Palace of Fürstenberg.

In the early 1930s the town was briefly a communist stronghold, and as the Nazis first sought a foothold there were several street battles, but before Hitler became chancellor, opposition had been eradicated. A Nazi mayor was appointed and a Nazi priest, Pastor Märker, took over in the town's evangelical church. Hitler's 'German Christians', strong in such rural areas, organised nationalist festivities and parades.

By the late 1930s the Jews of Fürstenberg had largely gone. Eva Hamburger, a Jewish hotelier, resisted expulsion, but after the pogrom of 'Kristallnacht', the 'night of broken glass', of 9–10 November 1938, she too moved out. In Fürstenberg that night the Jewish cemetery was destroyed and Eva Hamburger's hotel was smashed up. Soon after the local paper reported that the last Jewish property at Number 3 Röbinsee was sold.

Like most small German towns, Fürstenberg had suffered badly in the slump, so the arrival of a concentration camp meant jobs and trade. The fact that the prisoners were women was not controversial. Valesca Kaper, the middle-aged wife of a shopkeeper, was an effective leader of the local *Frauenschaft* (Nazi women's group) who often lectured women on the evils of make-up, smoking and alcohol, and explained the burden that 'asocials' placed on the state. Josef Goebbels even made a speech in Fürstenberg telling the townspeople: 'If the family is the nation's source of strength, the woman is its core and centre.'

In the spring of 1939, as the date of the camp opening came nearer, women were urged to 'serve on the home front' – which included working as concentration camp guards, but nothing official was said about recruitment; in fact, nothing official was said about the camp at all. Only a small reference in the *Forest News* to 'an accident near the large construction site' provided a hint that the concentration camp was even being built.

In early May a concert of music by Haydn and Mozart was performed and the local Gestapo hosted a sporting event of shooting and grenade-throwing.

The cinema showed a romantic comedy. The paper reported that, after a hard winter, charitable donations were sought and bankruptcy notices appeared.

All this time, the lock on the river was opening constantly for barges bringing materials and the camp wall became easily visible from the town side of the lake. Several local women put their names down for a job, including Margarete Mewes, a housemaid and young mother. On the first Sunday of May Fürstenberg held its traditional Mother's Day celebrations. Frau Kaper handed out Mother Crosses to those who had borne more than four children, thereby answering Hitler's call to multiply the Aryan gene.

On 15 May, a bright sunny morning, several blue buses drove through the town and turned towards the 'construction site'. Just before dawn that day the same blue buses had pulled up in front of the gates of Lichtenburg Castle, 300 miles to the south. Moments later female figures streamed out over the castle drawbridge, clutching little bags, and climbed into the vehicles. It was a clear night, but inside the buses it was quite dark. No one was sorry to see the black, hulking fortress disappear behind them into the darkness, though none had any idea what awaited them.

Some of the women dared to hope that the journey would lead them somewhere better, and a journey – any journey – was itself a taste of freedom, but the political prisoners warned there was no chance of anything better. Hitler's next advance into Czechoslovakia was only a matter of time. Husbands, brothers, fathers, sons were dying faster than ever in Buchenwald, Sachsenhausen and Dachau. Several women carried official notifications of such deaths in their bags, along with pictures of children and packages of letters.

Jewish women here thought of those rounded up in the Kristallnacht pogrom.* Yet paradoxically, precisely because they were Jewish, these women had more reason to hope at that moment than many others. The horror of Kristallnacht six months previously had traumatised German Jews and shocked the watching world, not into intervention, but into offering more visas to those now desperate to flee. The Nazis were encouraging Jewish flight so that they could snatch the property and assets of the leavers. Six months after the November pogroms more than 100,000 German Jews had emigrated, and many more were still waiting for papers to do the same.

Jews in prisons and camps had learned that they could emigrate too as long as they had proof of a visa and funds for travel. Amongst those hoping to receive their papers soon was Olga Benario. Although her own mother was estranged, Olga's Brazilian mother-in-law, Leocadia, as well as Carlos

* Tens of thousands of German-Jewish men were imprisoned in concentration camps after Kristallnacht, but Jewish women had not been rounded up, probably for fear of creating a backlash and because there was not enough room for them behind bars at this time.

Prestes's sister Ligia, had been working tirelessly on Olga's case ever since securing the release of her baby Anita.

Just before leaving Lichtenburg, Olga had written to Carlos in his Brazilian jail. 'Spring has finally arrived and the light green tips of the trees are looking inquisitively over the tops of our prison yard. More than ever I wish for a little sun, for beauty and luck. Will the day come that brings us together with Anita-Leocadia, the three of us in happiness? Forgive those thoughts, I know I have to be patient.'

As dawn broke over the Mecklenburg countryside, sunlight streamed through the slits in the tarpaulin, and the prisoners' spirits rose. The Austrians sang. When the buses neared Ravensbrück it was midday and stifling hot. The women were gasping for air. The buses turned off the road and stopped. Doors swung open and those in front looked out on a shimmering lake. The scent of the pine forest filled the bus. A German communist, Lisa Ullrich, noticed 'a sparsely populated hamlet situated at a small idyllic sea surrounded by a crown of dark spruce forest'.

The hearts of the women 'leapt for joy', Lisa recalled, but before all the coaches had drawn to a halt came screaming, yelling and a cracking of whips and barking of dogs. 'A stream of orders and insults greeted us as we began to descend. Hordes of women appeared through the trees – guards in skirts, blouses and caps, holding whips, some with yelping dogs rushing at the buses through the trees.'

As the prisoners stepped down several collapsed, and those that stooped to help them were knocked flat themselves by hounds or lashed with a whip. They didn't know it yet, but it was a camp rule that helping another was an offence. 'Bitches, dirty cow, get on your feet. Lazy bitch.' Another rule was that prisoners always lined up in fives. '*Achtung, Achtung*. Ranks of five. Hands by your sides.'

Commands echoed through the trees as stragglers were kicked by jackboots. Stiff with terror, all eyes fixed on the sandy ground, the women did their utmost not to be noticed. They avoided each other's gaze. Some were whimpering. Another crack of a whip and there was total silence.

The well-rehearsed SS routine had served its purpose – causing maximum terror at the moment of arrival. Anyone who had thought of resisting was from now on subdued. The ritual had been performed hundreds of times at male concentration camps, and now it was being enacted for the first time on the banks of the Schwedtsee. It would be worse for those who arrived later, in the dead of night, or in the snow, understanding nothing of the language. But all Ravensbrück survivors would remember the trauma of their arrival; all would recall their own silence.

*

This first group stands silent in the heat for perhaps two hours. As the count begins, Maria Zeh, from Stuttgart, looks up and sees the colza rapeseed is in blossom. She is slapped across the face. '*Die Nase nach vorne!*' shouts a guard – Nose to the front.

The women are counted again and then again – another lesson to learn: if anyone moves out of line, collapses, or if the counting goes wrong, it starts all over. 'And before we march a paper is handed to the head guard with the tally,' recalls Lisa Ullrich. The head guard is Johanna Langefeld. She has been standing apart, and now checks the figures. She signals for the women to march on. The stout figure of Max Koegel is there too.

Heaving forward, the prisoners pass half-built villas to their left, but they are only dimly aware of their surroundings. They come into a vast clearing where every tree and blade of grass has been razed, leaving sand and swamp. In this wasteland stands a massive grey wall. The women pass through a gateway and realise they have entered the new camp.

'*Achtung, Achtung*, ranks of five.' They are standing on a desolate square of sand, marked out as a parade ground. They smell new wood and fresh paint. Stark wooden barracks are positioned all around. Some notice beds of red flowers. The sun beats down. The gate closes behind them.

*Chapter 2*

# Sandgrube

'Hands by your sides. Ranks of five. Eyes ahead.' In groups, the women prisoners are marched forward towards a new building to the right of the gate where the next ritual starts: the bath. The first group enters and sees tables with guards behind them and piles of striped clothes. Everything must come off. Women start to strip. '*Schnell, schnell.*' Some stand there, sanitary straps and towels around their middles, and they look at the guards who shout back: 'Everything off.'

And everything comes off, to be thrown into large brown paper bags, along with all clothes and all possessions. The prisoners give everything up: last letters, photographs of children, embroidered handkerchiefs, knitted hats, little baskets, poems, combs. 'Until there is nothing left.' Wedding rings too.

Stark naked, the women are staring at their feet again, but some look up and shriek to see that male SS officers have been present all along, standing and staring. They laugh and shout insults when they see the women's humiliation.

Then the shavers come, and some of the women are pushed aside. '*Beeilt euch, beeilt euch!*' – Get a move on – and the selected women's hair is shaved off close to the scalp. Then another woman comes through. She makes the same women stand with their legs apart and shaves their pubic hair.

Within hours of their arrival, on 15 May 1939, the first of the 867 prisoners to be transferred from Lichtenburg to Ravensbrück had been stripped, washed, checked for lice, and in many cases shaved, as the *Oberaufseherin* would allow no vermin here. The prisoners were then issued new camp clothes: blue and white striped cotton dresses and jackets, a white headscarf, socks and rough wooden shoes, like clogs.

Each was given a number, printed on a small white piece of cloth. It matched the number they were given on arrival at Lichtenburg – from 1 to 867. The women were also given a coloured triangle made of felt. They were handed a needle and thread and told to sew these on to the left shoulder of their jackets. The triangle indicated which category the prisoner had been placed in: black for 'asocials' – prostitute, beggar, petty criminal, lesbian; green for habitual criminals; red for political prisoners; lilac for Jehovah's Witnesses; yellow for Jews. The Jewish women were subdivided, depending on the reason for arrest. All Jews wore a yellow triangle, but those noted as '*Pol. Jude*' – arrested for political crimes – wore their yellow triangle on a red background. The political Jews included the largest category, those arrested for *Rassenschande*, relations with a non-Jew; of these there were ninety-seven. Those Jews arrested as asocials wore their yellow triangle on a black background.

When numbers and triangles had been sewn on, the tannoy system screamed a siren as the women lined up again in the Appellplatz, before being marched, by category, to separate blocks, led by their *Blockführer*, block guard. The Jews were taken to the '*Judenblock*', except for Olga Benario, who was taken the other way.

Inside the blocks everyone was allocated a bunk bed, a bowl, a plate, an aluminium cup, a knife, fork and spoon, as well as a small cloth for drying and polishing the utensils. Any fuzz on the implements would mean a report to Langefeld, who had given instructions on exactly how the polishing should be done. As agreed under the camp *Lagerordnung*, Langefeld had secured control over 'feminine matters', which included sole authority over the living blocks; Koegel and his men were not allowed inside them unless accompanied by a female guard.

For washing, everyone was given a toothbrush, tooth mug, nugget of soap and small towel. Any item lost would incur 'a report' to the *Oberaufseherin*. Each woman was allocated a tiny shelf to keep her items on; anything misplaced meant 'a report'.

A mass of rules governed making the bed. It had to be done 'Prussian style', as required in all the camps, but on this Langefeld had her own particular instructions too: pillows to be puffed out so that corners pointed at right angles with the bed; the mattress to lie absolutely flat, which was impossible, as it was made of wood chips.

All the women recalled that particular precision was required when folding the blue and white checked blanket on the top. 'The blanket had to be laid just over the pillow and arranged so it ran along the edge of the bed, with its line of checks absolutely straight,' recalled Fritzi Jaroslavsky, an Austrian prisoner, nervously folding the edge of a tablecloth as she spoke. 'Even an inch overlapping the mattress meant the guard would come in shouting "Lazy cow, stupid bitch" and kicking or hitting you and shouting "Report!"'

Worst of all were the rules of the *Appell*, the roll call. At 5 a.m. a siren woke the camp, and prisoners were marched outside their blocks to line up in ranks of five, hands by their sides, standing erect in military fashion while the count took place. Even in these early days it took as long as half an hour to get the numbers right, and at 5 a.m. a cold wind blew off the Schwedtsee, cutting through cotton clothes. '*Achtung! Achtung!* Hands by your sides, ranks of fives.' Langefeld sometimes took *Appell* in person, but usually left the job to her deputy, Emma Zimmer, who had also come from Lichtenburg. Fifty-one-year-old Zimmer, who had a 'loose wrist' – she liked to slap – walked up and down the ranks carrying a large document file, with which she would beat inmates about the head at the slightest movement or sound. Sometimes, usually when drunk, Zimmer – nicknamed 'Aunt Emma' by the prisoners – lashed out with her jackboots too.

Langefeld never hit or kicked, though she would sometimes slap a woman sharply across the face, particularly while hearing 'the report'. The offending prisoner would be brought to Langefeld's office to answer the charge – losing a mug, failing to fold a blanket – to which the prisoner could reply. Langefeld then gave her decision, and if the charge was proven she slapped the prisoner's face and announced the punishment, which might be cleaning lavatories, but Langefeld's preferred punishment was forced standing for several hours without any food. If the standing woman fainted she'd be left lying for a while before being carried away. For serious cases Langefeld was trained in the use of straitjackets and water dousing.

When Zimmer had completed the morning count, the women returned to their blocks, where a black liquid that passed for coffee was doled out with a piece of bread, which was the daily allocation and could either be eaten now or put on the shelf for later. The siren screamed once more and selections for work gangs began. Prisoners were called into line again, then sent to collect tools and marched away to work shovelling sand or building a road, singing German marching songs. On return that evening they were all counted again.

Within a few days most of the Lichtenburg prisoners had been transferred to Ravensbrück. Langefeld's rules had been learned and order established. The brown paper bags containing prisoners' clothes and belongings had been taken for washing in the *Wäscherei* then ironed with a giant steam iron. Each item was then replaced in its numbered brown bag and sent to the *Effektenkammer* next door.

The *Effektenkammer* was divided into four rooms. In one was a long trestle table where all the prisoners' clothes and possessions were tipped out, to be carefully sorted. In an adjoining room was an office with two desks and two typewriters and a big steel cupboard containing hundreds of file index cards, on which was typed every prisoner's name and number, and details of every piece of clothing and every possession, with copies sent to Langefeld's office.*

Valuables were locked in the steel cupboards for safe keeping and carefully noted. The clothes were folded and placed in brand-new brown paper bags, which were attached to hangers; the hangers were taken to be hung on rails in the large roof space above Langefeld's office. When anyone was released she was sent to the *Effektenkammer*, where she gave her number to a worker who then went to the storage loft and retrieved her bag of clothes using a hook on a stick.

When prisoners arrived later from Poland, Russia and France, some brought whole suitcases full of belongings, all of which were put in bags and itemised just the same, said Edith Sparmann, a German-Czech prisoner who worked in the *Effektenkammer*. The bags were enormous strong brown paper sacks, stitched at the sides. One of the rooms held nothing but these brown paper bags, ready for the big transports. 'There was a lot of fancy stuff later,' said Edith, who also recalled how Langefeld would often come to the *Effektenkammer* to check on things. 'She wasn't as bad as some of them. She allowed my mother to keep her wedding ring on.'

During the first days prisoners were also assigned to tasks in the kitchen, and rations carefully calculated for each block, depending on a head count from the night before. In the *Revier*, the sickbay, each prisoner underwent a vaginal examination and if any woman had syphilis, as Agnes Petry did, it was noted on her file. Any woman found to be pregnant was taken away to have her baby at a nearby hospital in Templin. The baby would be sent for adoption, and the woman brought back.

The count after the first seven days – including a few new arrivals in addition to those from Lichtenburg – gave a total figure of 974 prisoners in the camp. Of these, 114 women wore red triangles (political prisoners); 388 Jehovah's Witnesses wore lilac; 119 wore green (habitual criminals); 240 wore black (asocials); 137 wore yellow (Jews) and some of the categories overlapped. From now on each arrival was given a number in sequence, so it would always be clear to guards and other prisoners alike, simply from a prisoner's number, who had been longest in the camp and who had just arrived. The first prisoner to be given a 'pure' Ravensbrück number (i.e. she was not transferred from Lichtenburg) was a thirty-seven-year-old German teacher arrested for communist resistance, called Clara Rupp. She arrived on 25 May and had the number 1415.

* According to prisoner secretaries, by the time the camp was liberated five years later some prisoner files contained enough paperwork to cover three square metres.

By the end of the first week the cards of all the first arrivals had been copied and filed, and their clothes packed in brown paper bags hanging above Langefeld's head. Langefeld's work, however, had only just begun.

Johanna Langefeld's office, inside an ordinary block near the gate, was not as grand as the commandant's extensive stone-built headquarters, but her block was ideally placed. From her desk she had a view out over the Appellplatz, allowing her to observe much of what went on.

Her office was also well staffed. Lines of clerks and secretaries sat at desks, as prisoners queued to give details of their arrest, their medical history and next of kin, all of which was noted on several different files. Langefeld's messenger then took copies of the prisoner information to relevant departments around the camp.

There had been a variety of administrative matters to see to in the first days. Inquiries came from police departments. 'Would the KZ [*Konzentrationslager*: concentration camp] pay the price of a prisoner's train fare?' Hamburg police wanted to know. 'Should Düsseldorf send on a hat?' Letters came from the German Red Cross, passing on inquiries about prisoners received from the International Red Cross in Geneva. A daughter, Tanja Benesch, wanted news of her mother, Susi. And Langefeld was obliged to tell Max Koegel that the camp washing machines were for prisoners' clothes and linen only; he would have to wash his clothes elsewhere.

More prisoner jobs were given out. Hanna Sturm, an Austrian communist and a carpenter, was assigned to put up fences and bang in nails. Many disciplinary problems arose. Another Austrian called Marianne Wachstein arrived in nothing but a nightgown and didn't know who she was.

Hedwig Apfel, who said she was an opera singer and came from Vienna, threw her mattress on the ground on her first day and had barely stopped screaming since. A few days after the camp opened a nationwide hunt was launched for Katharina Waitz, the Gypsy trapeze artist, who escaped again, though nobody knew how.

The Jehovah's Witnesses caused more trouble for Max Koegel, this time by refusing his offer to set them free. In return for their release the women were told they simply had to sign a piece of paper renouncing their faith, but each one refused, repeating that the Führer was the Antichrist. It was largely because of their riot at Lichtenburg that Koegel had first requested the cell block for Ravensbrück. He told his SS superior Theodor Eicke a few weeks before the camp opened: 'It will be impossible to keep order if these hysterical hags can't be broken. Just depriving them of food will not subdue them without a form of rigorous imprisonment.'

Although this first request was refused, Koegel did secure permission to convert an ordinary living block into a 'punishment block' or '*Strafblock*' and several 'hysterical hags' were soon thrown in. The *Strafblock* was set some way apart from the other blocks, behind barbed wire. Prisoners might be sent there for such crimes as repeated lateness for *Appell*, failing to make their bed by the rules, or refusing an order. The *Strafblock* prisoners were forced to work longer hours, on the worst gangs, with no days off. Punishments such as straitjackets and water dousing were used.

Attached to one end of the *Strafblock*, a few makeshift isolation cells were constructed out of wood. The Berlin Gestapo had requested such cells be built for holding prisoners who were still under interrogation, though other women were soon locked in solitary confinement too, among them Marianne Wachstein, the Austrian who had arrived in her nightgown. She was locked up after refusing to sign a document relating to her arrest and protesting that her human rights were being violated.

As Marianne later explained, she refused to sign because she had no idea why she was here; twenty-four hours earlier she had been snatched unconscious from a prison cell in Vienna where she'd been locked up for 'insulting' the Führer. 'Next I remember waking up in a train wagon in my nightclothes. I pinched myself because I thought I was dreaming; it was no dream, it was the truth.'

A guard on the train first told her she was being taken to a mental asylum. 'That made me happy.' Then the train passed Salzburg 'and I realised I had been abducted to Germany. I was very upset, and couldn't stand or walk.' A guard screamed at her and began hitting her over the head. 'I started to vomit. He grabbed me, pulled me up and threw me on a bench and slammed the door.' Before she knew it, Marianne was being marched into Ravensbrück and forced to sign a document that they wouldn't let her read. 'So I said God will avenge me and the communists will have their revenge against what the Nazis have done.'

It was at this point that Marianne was taken to the commandant and given forty-two days of 'aggravated arrest', the maximum term under the *Strafblock* rules, which ran to several pages. For those sentenced to solitary confinement, 'plain arrest' permitted a prisoner to have a mattress and a blanket in her cell, and a small amount of light; coffee and bread were given once a day and a hot meal once every four days. Prisoners sentenced to 'aggravated arrest' received the same rations, but were locked in a dark cell with no mattress and no blanket, just a bucket and nothing more.

Koegel decided on all *Strafblock* cases without consulting Langefeld, though her deputy, Emma Zimmer, who ran the block, kept the *Oberaufseherin* closely informed. According to Ilse Gostynski, some guards were so obviously unhappy about conditions in the early days that they were dismissed. Among those who came from Lichtenburg was one, 'a lesbian, very decent towards the prisoners but often drunk', who was dismissed for being 'too kind'. Three more left 'because they couldn't stand it any more'.

Langefeld herself would claim later that when she first arrived at Ravensbrück she still believed her role was to 're-educate prostitutes'. The truth was that she couldn't refuse such a promotion, especially when it came from the Reichsführer SS himself. She was now the most important woman in Himmler's camp empire. And the living conditions alone were so attractive that it was very hard to walk away.

On viewing their living quarters, Langefeld and all her guards must have been pleasantly surprised. Several of these women were widows or divorcees and, like Langefeld, had transferred here from Lichtenburg, after working for years in prisons and workhouses. A middle-aged woman called Ella Pietsch, trained as a workhouse guard, had nowhere else to go, and nor had Jane Bernigau, who had previously worked in orphanages. Both applied for the job at Ravensbrück because of the salary and security.

Others were factory workers thrown out of work. Ottilie Lotz got the job by chance. After her husband died, Lotz had moved to Lichtenburg to be close to her daughter; she had found work as a clerk in the fortress and was promoted to guard.

These women staff were quartered in smart pitched-roof villas amidst the pine trees looking over the lake. Just a hundred yards or so outside the camp walls, they were convenient for the camp, but far enough away to allow a sense of separation after work. Many of these villas were still being constructed, and prisoners were labouring all around – heaving bricks up from barges moored on the lake – but some of the buildings were complete. The interiors were fitted out in style. Rooms led off a central staircase, and each had pretty curtains and new upholstery. Two women shared a room, and each had her own wardrobe and chest of drawers.

The chief guard's apartment was larger than others, and she was allowed to bring Herbert, now aged eleven, to live with her; he would attend the local school. Mothers were promised free places at the staff kindergarten, which would open soon – several single mothers were bringing their children with them.

Further up the slope, amidst the trees, stood the grander SS officers' villas, surrounded by large gardens. Koegel's villa, where he lived with his wife, Marga, was fitted with parquet floors, and an elegant carved staircase. Around the house hung antlers and other hunting trophies; antlers also hung above the porch outside.

The siting of SS accommodation, away from the camp itself, in a pleasant natural setting, was a common feature of all camps. The intention was to encourage the SS staff to feel content in their home environment. At Ravensbrück the men had their own SS sports field, while the women could go boating on the lake in summer, or picnicking in the woods.

For the younger women it was not only the pay and conditions that drew them: the prospect of meeting a handsome SS officer was another lure; while for those who were lesbians – a significant minority – Ravensbrück offered special opportunities to meet other women, particularly at a time when lesbianism, like all homosexuality, was reviled. The new recruits were also pleased to find a well-stocked staff canteen, and the pretty town of Fürstenberg had a cinema, several bars, and a hair salon, offering the latest permanent wave. Within a short time of arriving the women sent postcards to their families and friends writing about their new jobs with pride. Several former women guards kept photograph albums and diaries of their time at Ravensbrück containing pictures of their 'luxurious' apartment furnishings.

The dog-handlers, who had a special status, took pictures of themselves standing with their dogs. Gertrud Rabenstein, the woman known at Lichtenburg as 'Iron Gustav', took pictures of herself with Britta, her German shepherd, standing just outside the walls. Rabenstein was divorced and had lost custody of her son. She put an album together to show him something of her life at the camp. The dogs had been trained to attack people with prisoner clothes, she said. Next to the pictures of Gertrud with Britta are happy scenes of mother and son on holiday.

At Rabenstein's post-war trial, her son was called to give evidence about his mother and said her motto was: 'Be hard. Be hard. To be hard is good. Do not be sentimental.' He said she used to tell him a story about how she once saw a blacksmith beating metal and watched it grow hard. 'This was good.'

The guards soon settled in and Langefeld assigned their tasks. Several were put in charge of a block while others were to guard outside work parties. Langefeld briefed them all on their behaviour; for example, folding arms or sitting down in front of prisoners was forbidden, and gossiping a sackable offence. Guards could only visit male quarters with Langefeld's permission.

On broader questions regarding treatment of prisoners, however, it was quickly evident that many guards – particularly those on outside work gangs – were following Koegel's lead, not hers. From her office Langefeld could see the women brought in daily from the sandpit with bleeding legs and arms. And even from her apartment she could hear the women's screams.

Edith Fraede let her dog snarl and snap at the women somewhere between the gates of the camp and the sandpit – or *Sandgrube*, as it was known. If a terrified prisoner dropped her shovel, Fraede would kick her on the ground or pick up the shovel and hit her across the back with it. Fraede was about thirty years old, big and blonde. Rabenstein, however, usually waited until the work was underway before she lashed out, but by then Britta would already be straining on his leash.

In the early days the dog-handlers couldn't control their animals. They were new to the job and in the spring and summer it was always hard as the dogs were often on heat. So if a prisoner fell or made a dash for the lake to get a drink, the dogs would pull so hard that the guards simply let them off the leash.

At this time the sandpit lay just outside the camp walls, near the lake, and close to the site where the SS houses were being built.

As soon as the gangs reached the pit they had to line up and start shovelling. By nine, the sun was already beating down and sweat rolled down their backs. They had to fill a shovel from one pile and drop the sand on another, until all the sand had been moved. Then they shovelled it back again, as guards shouted, '*Schnell, schnell*, lazy bitches.' Another gang threw the sand one or two metres up a hill. 'Full shovels, full shovels. Filthy cows. Scum. Bitch. Filthy cows.' The shovels were too short or too long, or bent and broken.

Sometimes a gang had to pile the sand in a wagon and heave the wagon onto makeshift tracks. The wagon often jumped the tracks and the women would try to stop it tipping, but when it fell it spilled the contents and they'd have to fill it again. As the temperature rose the guards yelled and swore even louder; they'd beat the women on the back again and kick those that passed out.

Other gangs unloaded coke and stones from a barge on the lake. The women heaved sacks on their backs, while up the hill another gang pulled stone rollers to flatten land for road building. There was one giant roller and one smaller one. The handles had ropes attached and the women grabbed a rope and pulled. At least the road-rolling had a point. There was no point in shovelling sand.*

Soon the prisoners hated the sand. The Jehovah's Witnesses thought the work was designed especially for them, 'to make them give up their God', but many noticed it was the Jews who suffered most: they seemed weaker, and were less used to hardship, others said. By midday the women in the *Sandgrube* were sunburned on their arms and brows and their mouths were parched. When sand got inside their wooden clogs it burned the soles of their feet and rubbed on blisters. The *Sandgrube* was soon spotted with blood.

Rabenstein and Britta supervised the unloading gang. Standing up the

* In contrast, prisoners at Himmler's new male concentration camps of Mauthausen and Flossenbürg worked in quarries, hacking out granite to rebuild Berlin as Hitler's new fantasy capital Germania.

hill, they watched prisoners heave sacks of coal or stones and pile them into carts at the edge of the lake. The women pushed the carts up the hill to a dump, but to get there they had to cross a makeshift bridge made of planks, and often the older women fell off the planks and into the water. When this happened the guards would yell and kick the fallen woman. One day a woman hit Rabenstein on the head with a hoe to get her own back. She was sent to the *Strafblock* and not seen again.

Sometimes Rabenstein would select a group of women at random, line them up behind a heap of stones, and kick them with her boots. Or she would tell a prisoner to shovel soil from a massive pile by tunnelling from underneath until the pile started caving in. The prisoner had to keep shovelling till eventually the pile collapsed on her and she was buried alive. Rabenstein considered this a game and called it '*Abdecken*' – 'roof falling'. Afterwards, the prisoner, bruised and suffocating, was pulled out by friends.

Standing on a chair inside her wooden cell, Marianne Wachstein saw a similar 'game' enacted outside her window:

> I looked out and saw the following: a weak young woman – I later heard her name was Langer, sick with lupus, and with a piece of flesh sewn on her nose – had refused to shovel sand. They hit her hard but she still refused to pick up the shovel. They dragged her, holding her tight, to a well and sprayed her with a strong stream of water wherever it hit her. They put her like that into a heap of sand with only her head uncovered. They threw sand on her head and face. She constantly tried to break loose. This game went on so long that I got down from the small chair several times and sat down.

Wachstein noticed women guards were watching, and one of the commandant's top men watched too.

Hanna Sturm, the Austrian carpenter, soon began to get the measure of the camp. Not all prisoners were sent on outside work gangs; Hanna's skills – she was a locksmith and a glazier as well as a carpenter – were too valuable to waste on pointless toil, so she was used as a handywoman, which allowed her to snoop inside offices and blocks, and she collected things – an old newspaper, or a knife perhaps – which she smuggled back to her block. Her best early discovery was a dog-eared copy of *War and Peace*. Goebbels had long ago banned all Tolstoy's books, along with other seditious works by authors such as Kipling, Hemingway, Remarque and Gide. They were usually either burned or used as lavatory paper, and Hanna had probably picked the book from a latrine's supply. She hoped to find a chance to read it with her comrades.

Given that every minute of the day was now regimented by blaring sirens and rules, talking to friends was hard. There were no corners, no hidden alleys for prisoners to slip into unseen. Inside the barracks, the women were so tightly packed together, and so carefully watched – always kept constantly on the move – that individual contacts or formation of small groups was virtually impossible, which was precisely the intention of block living.

The doctor Doris Maase loathed the constant company of riffraff, but she phrased her misery carefully in her censored letter home: 'I wish I could be built so that stupidity and dullness wouldn't bother me as much, but I just can't help it. It may sound paradoxical but with time one wishes to be a hermit instead of always being around people.'

Prisoners known as Blockovas had been put in charge of blocks and ordered to enforce discipline. Sometimes, just before the lights went out, if her Blockova was not close by, Hanna Sturm tapped on the bunk below where her communist friend Käthe Rentmeister lay, and Käthe would alert another comrade, Tilde Klose, who lay below her. The women would exchange words about Hanna's latest find, or if the Blockova was in a good mood she might even allow a little conversation from time to time.

One or two of these newly empowered Blockovas – mostly wearing green and black triangles – behaved like tyrants from the start; certain names – Kaiser, Knoll and Ratzeweit – were already known amongst the political prisoners from Lichtenburg as trouble. But most of these first arrivals had been in prisons together many years and had learned to get along, whatever their backgrounds. A different-coloured piece of felt on their striped jackets wasn't going to turn them into enemies overnight.

On Sundays there was some respite. Not everyone had Sundays off work: the Jewish block, Block 11, and the *Strafblock* prisoners had to labour as usual. There was also a Sunday *Appell* at midday and cleaning to be done. But in the late afternoon the prisoners all went for an obligatory 'walk' – a sort of forced recreational stroll along the Lagerstrasse, done to music. The guards in the gatehouse plugged the public address system into German radio and marching songs blared out, which at least meant the women could chat freely, as the minders couldn't hear.

After the marching it was sometimes possible to lie quietly on a bunk, and to wash clothes and be 'normal'. There was a Sunday dollop of jam, a square of margarine and a sausage. Prisoners lucky enough to have received money from home could spend it in the camp shop, which was situated inside the staff canteen, and stocked biscuits, toothpaste, and soap. During this 'free time' Hanna's group tried to get together at the back of the block to read their book; one read out loud while another was lookout. They couldn't believe their luck at finding Tolstoy in a concentration camp.

On Sundays prisoners also read letters from home and wrote back. A letter was allowed once a month, and in these pre-war days as long as no mention was made of politics or the camp the women could still write at length. In her letters home, Doris Maase talked about how she'd been reading books too. Doris was working as a nurse in the *Revier*, where she also spent the night. It was still possible to receive packages from home, including books, and there was even a camp library of sorts – a collection of approved books, including several copies of *Mein Kampf*.

'Today I try to have Sunday,' wrote Doris to her sister in June 1939. 'I'm reading Beyond the Woods by [Trygve] Gulbrannssen.' Doris's husband, Klaus, was in Buchenwald, so the two wrote censored letters back and forth, reading between each other's lines. At least, as an inmate of Buchenwald, Klaus would know something of what Doris was going through; of course she could tell him nothing of the brutality she saw.

We know from her later testimony that Doris used to watch through the *Revier* windows as the work gangs were taken to the gate, led by an SS officer who walked them deliberately through a large pond, so that they'd start work soaking wet.

In June, Olga Benario's comrade Sabo (Elise Saborowski Ewert), her co-conspirator from her Brazilian days, suddenly buckled and collapsed as she worked in the *Sandgrube*. Sabo had been raped and tortured in a Brazilian jail, and had never recovered. Fraede kicked her but Sabo could not get up and was eventually brought into the *Revier*, where Doris was there to help. 'Maase, where is Maase?' was the shout heard every day around the bandaging station. 'There are so many things I can hardly talk about, so much is waiting for you,' she wrote in a letter to Klaus.

On another Sunday Doris's letter to her sister enthused about good news from home – 'At first I could not believe that something this pleasant still exists – I almost feel as if I'd been there' – but her attempt to sound cheerful couldn't hide her fear for her relatives on the outside. Doris's father, also a doctor, was Jewish and she knew that as war approached, his side of the family would be increasingly at risk; new laws were making any form of normal life in Germany impossible and Doris's father had been barred from practising. Though her mother was not Jewish – which explains why Doris received better treatment than other Jews in the camp – the pressure on those in 'mixed marriages' was increasing, with couples forced to consider separating or emigrating.

At one point Doris asks: 'Are the parents relaxing as they should? I imagine roses blooming there and every day something else to harvest in the garden,' but by the next letter she has learned that her mother and father are 'crossing the Channel' and she hoped for news.

'As for me, I'm fine,' wrote Doris to her sister, and it is almost tempting to believe her, because she went on: 'I wear my hair long and neatly knotted and I'm noticeably blossoming inside and out' – though what she meant by 'blossoming' is impossible to say. We know from her later testimony that by late June temperatures in the *Sandgrube* were soaring and the women Doris was treating had burned skin, sores and boils. Worrying the prisoners even more were the terrifying screams now coming from the *Strafblock*. The prisoners had recently discovered that Olga was being held in one of the stifling wooden cells. Doris wrote in a letter home: 'My darlings, it's *so* hot.'

It was Ilse Gostynski who first discovered that Olga was in solitary confinement. Ilse had the job of emptying the cell buckets, and managed to pass a few words with Olga, whom she had got to know at Lichtenburg and whose story had made a deep impression. Ilse remembered Olga as 'a young woman from Munich, very beautiful, very intelligent. In Ravensbrück, she was treated badly, she got almost nothing to eat.'

The cells were made of thin wood, just two metres long by two metres wide, and had no ventilation. Olga had nothing except a straw mattress and a bucket. Ilse made sure that Hanna Sturm knew about Olga's plight and Hanna managed to get together biscuits and bread for Olga, which Ilse smuggled in next time she emptied the buckets. Comrades sent messages. If Zimmer had seen her, Ilse would have been locked up too. 'I left some sweets for her or a slip of paper with comforting words from her fellow prisoners … She was in a very bad way,' Ilse recalled.

Not long after finding Olga, Ilse was told she was to be released, so Olga's go-between was gone.

Perhaps the most startlingly 'normal' aspect of the camp was that even as the brutality increased, prisoners were regularly being freed. Ilse's English contacts had secured her a visa. On being told she could leave, she was sent first to the *Effektenkammer*, where the clothes she arrived in were retrieved, along with her valuables, and then she was free to go. The same day Ilse was on a train to Berlin, and within a week or two she was on another train heading for the Hook of Holland, from where she caught a ferry across the Channel to Harwich on the Essex coast. Here she was met by communist friends, the ones who had secured the papers necessary for release.

Safely in England, Ilse told her friends about Olga Benario and urged them to reach her husband's family in Brazil; Ilse believed her own case would give Olga's family hope that they could secure her release too, but they had to secure a visa before war broke out. A few months after arrival in England, Ilse, as a German, was declared an enemy alien and sent to an internment camp on the Isle of Man.

After the war was over Ilse married and had a daughter, Marlene. She was also reunited with her twin, Else, who had sat out the war in hiding in Norway. Over time the sisters found out that their parents had died in Auschwitz and that many friends had shared the same fate. In 1951 Ilse tried to write down her story, describing briefly her years at Moringen, Lichtenburg and Ravensbrück. Dissatisfied by her inability to describe 'the endless fear and suffering', she wrote a postscript apologising to readers: 'Rereading my report I feel sorry that I don't seem to have been able to depict the real tragedy of the concentration camp.'

According to her daughter, Marlene, after writing her report, Ilse never spoke of the camp again. 'She suffered from the particular pain and guilt of those who had been lucky enough to get out before the worst began.' Sitting in a north London café, Marlene, an artist, held up a picture she had painted showing Ilse and Else as bourgeois German girls with muslin frocks 'before they rebelled and went off camping in the woods to read Marx', says Marlene.

In another picture, called *Bars*, Marlene shows her mother in her last days, lying asleep in bed. 'She has become beautiful again in old age,' says Marlene's inscription. 'She is cared for like a baby and never speaks or smiles. I see the shadow of her imprisonment falling across the end of her life, unfinished business. In another place or time the shadow could have fallen on me or my child. Would I know how to be brave?'

After Ilse left for England, the number of arrivals began to rise. Among the newcomers was a Czech journalist called Jozka Jaburkova, arrested in Prague the day after the Germans invaded, 16 March 1939. As soon as the Czech capital fell, all resistance was rooted out, intellectuals were targeted and newspapers shut down, including *The Soweress*, a communist feminist magazine, which Jozka edited.

On arrival at the camp Jozka was suffering terrible headaches, having been badly beaten about the head under interrogation, but she soon found communist comrades to take care of her. Her arrival boosted morale in the political block, where her name was already known. For her part Jozka was delighted to find Olga Benario was here in the camp; she had worked on Olga's release campaign.

Hanna invited Jozka into the Tolstoy reading group, and Jozka entertained them not only with her predictions of the coming communist revolution but also with her fairy stories; she had once published a collection of fairy tales, called *Eva in Wonderland.*

On 28 June came the biggest convoy of new prisoners since the camp opened two months earlier. In the middle of the night 450 Gypsy women, from Burgenland in Austria, were marched through the gates, many shivering in nightgowns, some chained together, and others pregnant or carrying children. Most had long black plaits and all seemed to be screaming and crying.

With full-scale war now imminent, Hitler opened a new front in the racial war, ordering the roundup of 3000 Austrian Sinti and Roma, most of whom had lived in Burgenland for generations. Women and men were dragged from their beds, and hauled away with no warning, then the sexes were separated. A fifteen-year-old teenager called Bella was still in her nightgown as she was driven away; 'my pregnant mother ran down behind the car, screaming to stop'. Most of the women were herded together, first in a village hall at Pinkafeld, where local thugs, posing as police, were waiting for them as well as German SS. Many were raped 'by the village SS', as they called Hitler's local stooges. Lorries took the women to a prison near Graz. Before they left, a police commander accompanying the convoy offered Bella a sandwich. 'He said, "Here, take it," but I said, "No I won't eat." He said, "Yes you will. I know how hunger hurts," so I took it.'

At Feldbach prison in Graz, there were guards with police dogs. The women gathered here had been snatched from countless Burgenland villages and all talked of the same terror. Gisela Sarkozi was captured with her sister: 'They came in the middle of the night, everywhere, the SS, and the village mayor came too; he was a Hitler "high up". They knocked down the doors and just took people out. They didn't let us dress.' Gisela was taken to the town of Oberwart where her mother brought her clothes; from there she was taken on to Graz.

Theresia Pfeifer and her sister, Anna, were chased from their house, then tied up and put in fetters after some tried to escape. They were put in cattle wagons and sent off on a train for two days and two nights. The men had been sent to Dachau, the women to Ravensbrück. When the train stopped at Fürstenberg it was pitch-black and nobody had any idea where they were. The SS were standing around with dogs.

'We had to line up in pairs and we were led to the bath. First we had to strip naked in front of the SS. Everyone was weeping and crying out. People said you have to be silent or you'll be shot.' Theresia's plaits were cut off, her body hair shaved. She was given a black felt triangle and told to sew it on to her striped prison dress. Several screaming women were taken to the *Strafblock*, where Zimmer dealt with them. Others were put in blocks, and marched out next morning to the *Sandgrube* with the rest.

By July everyone in Germany knew the invasion of Poland was coming. Ethnic Germans living in Poland poured back into Germany and Goebbels's propaganda war against the Poles intensified as camp guards whipped up hatred against 'filthy Slavs'. The women guards also talked of husbands, brothers and sons called up to serve at the front. Even Pastor Märker, the Fürstenberg priest, had volunteered to serve.*

As if the camp itself was on a war footing, military top brass regularly inspected, putting Langefeld on her mettle. After she had kept the entire camp on parade for several hours during a Luftwaffe inspection, an officer was heard to ask: 'Where is the commandant? I hear no commanding voice,' to which Langefeld replied that she had no need to shout.

Ahead of the war, security tightened across the camp in case of 'mutiny'. The *Strafblock* filled up and all around the Appellplatz women stood, hour after hour, barefoot, facing the wall as 'standing punishment' for 'crimes'.

In the political block it was hard for the communist group to talk, as Koegel's spies were all around. Jozka Jaburkova was betrayed by a spy one day after dropping her rag down a lavatory, which caused the sewage system to block up. Hated for her 'arrogant face', Jozka was always given the filthiest jobs. Now she too was made to stand for many hours, face to the wall.

Then on 18 July word got out that Olga Benario's cell was empty; she had been taken from the camp under Gestapo escort. Her comrades in the Tolstoy reading group believed that she must have been taken to Berlin for reinterrogation by Hitler's secret police. The fact that she had been picked out in the run-up to war demonstrated just how much the fascists still feared the communist resistance, they told themselves, and how high a price they still placed on Olga's head. More recent evidence points to a different explanation: she probably left the camp in July 1939 not for further questioning but because the Gestapo had agreed to release her.

The evidence that Olga was about to be released comes in part from a surviving Gestapo report on the circumstances of her leaving Ravensbrück, including a curiously detailed description of what she was wearing: 'A multicoloured dress with red belt, black three-quarter-length coat, beige-coloured sneakers, pale socks and she carried a yellow handbag.' Clearly, before departure she had been taken to the *Effektenkammer* and dressed in civilian clothes; the only prisoners who left Ravensbrück in civilian clothes in 1939 were those about to be set free.

Anita Benario Prestes, Olga's daughter, who lives today in Brazil, a teacher at the University of Rio de Janeiro, has further proof that her mother was about to be freed. Anita was of course too young to understand the

* The pages of the Fürstenberg church record book covering the war years have been torn out, almost certainly by Märker, in order to cover up his activities.

negotiations for Olga's release, but her grandmother, Leocadia, and her aunt, Ligia, told her later what happened. They also gave Anita their correspondence with the Gestapo, as well as every letter written to them, and to Carlos, by her mother.

While Carlos Prestes had remained incarcerated in a Brazilian jail, Leocadia and Ligia had continued their campaign to get Olga out of Ravensbrück. At first they had little hope, said Anita, but they were encouraged by a letter received from Ilse Gostynski in England, persuading them to keep trying. So in June 1939, the Prestes women wrote again to the German authorities, pleading on Olga's behalf. Soon afterwards they received a reply from the German-Jewish emigration office, saying the Gestapo was willing to free Olga 'on the sole condition that she emigrate immediately overseas'. The letter even helpfully suggested that they should apply 'as soon as possible to Mexico' for Olga's visa.

Leocadia travelled to Mexico, and after some delay she secured the visa and other official Mexican documents and posted them on to Germany, sending them via New York, as was necessary at the time. 'She was hopeful that my mother would be released but she knew that time was very short. Once war broke out it would be impossible for Olga to reach us,' said Anita. She stayed on in Mexico to await confirmation that the visa had reached Berlin, but by 25 August no confirmation had come through. 'By now she was in despair,' said Anita. 'And so was my mother.'

Anita knows of her mother's feelings from Olga's numerous letters to Leocadia and to Carlos in which her desperation to be reunited with the child taken from her Berlin cell in 1937 is painfully clear. As if trying to mother Anita from afar, she inquires about every detail of her health and care, issuing instructions to Leocadia that Anita be exposed to the sun, have her hair cut short and wear plain clothes. 'She must not think herself special.' And Olga worried that Anita would not be able to learn her Brazilian family's language. 'In the prison I could at least have spoken French to her. You see I know the children's language only in my mother tongue – and then again I guess my old optimism is to blame that made me hope we would not be separated at all.'*

By mid-August 1939, a month after leaving Ravensbrück, Olga was still waiting in her temporary Berlin prison for confirmation that the documents required for her emigration had arrived. She was allowed to read the Nazi newspaper the *Völkischer Beobachter*, and knew war was imminent. Once hostilities broke out there would be no chance of leaving Germany.

* Today Anita speaks no word of German and has had her mother's letters translated into Portuguese.

'Don't be angry with me but I feel the deepest pessimism,' she wrote to Leocadia on 15 August. In her next letter she seemed to lose the will to write at all: 'Look, I was angry at first about this short sheet of paper but now I find I have nothing else to write. Kiss my beloved child a thousand times for me.'

As Olga waited in Berlin, her comrades back in Ravensbrück were facing new terrors. A short time after Olga had left the camp, Hanna Sturm and her reading group were caught red-handed reciting Tolstoy. Sent to Koegel for punishment, Hanna saw the spy who had betrayed them standing next to him, so she spat at her, at which Koegel hit Hanna across the face, promising to 'teach her some discipline'. The next thing she knew, Hanna was locked in a dark, bare wooden cell, just as Olga had been.

Hanna Sturm was as well equipped as any woman to survive these solitary cells. Born into a poor Burgenland farming family, of minority Czech roots, she had been sent to work in the fields at eight, and was banging nails into fences well before she learned to read. As a young woman she was drawn to 'red Vienna', and during Austria's turmoil of the 1930s she joined a trade union and helped fight anti-fascist battles, frequently ending up behind bars. She'd been imprisoned in Lichtenburg's dungeons too. But Hanna had never seen a cell like this, and when she wrote her story later, her memories of this first cell block were as vivid as anything that happened to her since. Hanna Sturm's account is also invaluable, as only two prisoners left testimony of Ravensbrück's first wooden cell block, which by the end of 1939 had been knocked down, and evidence that it had even existed, destroyed.

Apart from the few cracks in the wall, Hanna's cell was completely dark. It was like 'a small box', she recalled, two metres in length and two wide. As she had been sentenced to 'aggravated arrest', Hanna had no bed, no mattress and nothing but the floor to sit on. A proper meal was provided once a week, on a Thursday. On all other days the only food was 100 grams of bread and a bowl of so-called coffee.

When Hanna was first locked up she closed her eyes to try and get used to the darkness. When she wanted to go to the lavatory she had to feel her way along the wall towards the bucket provided. But although it was impossible to see anything, Hanna could hear a great deal.

It wasn't long before Hanna heard screaming and shouting in the yard outside. Peering through a chink in the wall she saw the screaming was coming from a Gypsy, demented with terror, who was being dragged inside the *Strafblock* opposite. Then came the sounds of beating and Zimmer shouting: 'Wait till I get you into the straitjacket, you'll shut up, you bitch.' Hanna recognised another familiar voice: that of Margot Kaiser, a German prisoner who worked as Zimmer's helper and was much hated throughout the camp. Kaiser went off to get the straitjacket. The screams suddenly stopped and Hanna could hear only whimpering and then nothing. Zimmer seemed to forget about the Gypsy until several hours later, when shouting began again and it became clear that she'd been found dead in another cell.

Hanna heard Zimmer say: 'She's lying here dead like a dog.' Zimmer yelled an order to Kaiser and others to help her. Hanna heard no more, but other prisoners saw the Gypsy's body being dragged out of the *Strafblock* compound by the hair and pulled into the laundry room, her body covered in blood and pine needles.

The prisoners learned later that the Gypsy had been driven wild because her six-week-old baby had been torn out of her arms. The woman was breast-feeding, and her breasts had grown swollen and hard, which added to her pain. Nobody knew the Gypsy's name and there is no official record of her death. She may have been the first prisoner to be murdered in Ravensbrück, although according to the camp records, another Gypsy from the Burgenland transport, Amalie Pfeiffer, fifty years old, was the first prisoner to die in the camp.

Amalie's death was carefully recorded and even certified by a doctor, and the certificate survives. It says that on 24 August 1939 Amalie Pfeiffer, born Karoly, on 5 July 1890 (Gypsy), resident of Neustift an der Lafnitz (Austria), died at 4 p.m. in Ravensbrück women's concentration camp. Cause of death: 'suicide by stab wounds to the left cervical artery'.

After the Gypsy death, the cell block fell quieter. Hanna found ways of improving her cell. Zimmer hadn't searched her thoroughly, and as always she had something useful concealed in her clothes, this time scissors. So thin were the walls that she managed to loosen planks, and soon found she could whisper to the women next door. One neighbour was called Lene who told Hanna she was a Jehovah's Witness. Then Zimmer heard the voices and yelled: 'Quiet, you monkeys.'

After a time Hanna heard peals of mad laughter from the cell on the other side. 'This is what a lunatic asylum must be like,' she thought, but then she noticed the 'mad' woman laughed every time she heard Zimmer's voice. Listening to the gossip of the guards, Hanna discovered that the woman was Hedwig Apfel and she was a musician, perhaps an opera singer. Apfel was Jewish and her family had paid a fortune to the Nazis in an attempt to secure her release. Hanna knew also of an American in the cell block, who 'prayed all the time very loudly, using unintelligible words' – presumably English. The 'American' may have been Olga's fellow conspirator, Sabo, who had lived many years in Canada and was locked in the cell block in the summer. Every time Sabo prayed, she set off Hedwig Apfel's hysterical laughter.

Hedwig was goading Zimmer. When Zimmer opened her door, Hedwig was waiting with a lavatory bucket that she emptied onto her face. Zimmer screamed: '*Judensau!*' (Jewish pig). Hedwig mimicked: '*Judensau, Judensau.*' Sometimes Hedwig ran from her cell out into the open space of the punishment block, at which Margot Kaiser would chase her and catch her.

Hanna had by now used her scissors to make tiny holes in her cell wall, so she could see through into the cells either side. Then one day Zimmer threw Hanna's door open and shoved Hedwig Apfel inside. Hedwig giggled and was obviously scared by the darkness. When she realised Hanna was in the cell she asked Hanna to dance. Hanna suggested singing instead. Hedwig began to sing: 'For you because you are one of us.' And now Hanna thought: 'Perhaps she isn't mad after all.' Hedwig said: 'I'm only acting as if I'm mad. *Die Alte* ['the old woman' – Zimmer] is afraid of me ever since I emptied the bucket into her face. Next time, I'll spit in her face and you'll see how she'll run.'

From this moment on Apfel and Sturm became firm friends, which was not to Zimmer's liking; she took Hedwig away and Hanna was left alone. Hedwig was even moved away from her cell, which was taken by another woman whom Hanna also tried to befriend.

Knocking on the wall she asked: 'Who are you?'

'I'm Susi, and you?'

'I'm Hanna.'

The next day Hanna learned that Susi was the Austrian communist Susi Benesch. Susi was very sick, with boils all over her body. She couldn't lie down or sit, and at night she walked around all the time, so that nobody in the entire cell block could sleep. One morning Zimmer took Susi out of the cell for the day and sent her out to work, apparently thinking if she tired her out carrying stones she'd sleep better at night. When Susi returned in the evening she told Hanna: 'It is hard carrying stones. But at least I have seen the sun and I have been with people.' The next day Susi did not return. Hanna had nobody to talk to again and she started to lose track of time. But she did hear others moving around and sometimes talking and screaming.

One of the prisoners Hanna heard moving around must have been Marianne Wachstein, the woman who had arrived in her nightgown from Vienna. Like Hanna, Marianne left a detailed account of her time in the wooden cell block and much of their experience matched, though the circumstances in which they gave their testimony were very different.

Hanna was not able to tell her story until after the war, but Marianne wrote an uncensored account of what she'd seen just six months after it happened. In February 1940 Marianne was unexpectedly freed, to give evidence in Vienna at the trial of her husband, a Jewish businessman accused of corruption by a Nazi court. She wrote her report in the first weeks after she was freed, while recuperating in a Viennese hospital. Her account is therefore unique, as it is virtually contemporaneous. 'The camp of Ravensbrück near Fürstenberg is a slave labour camp,' she began.

> The work that we have to do there (I myself had bad nerves and could not work for that reason) is pushing rollers by using two ropes and a handle. And this handle the women have to grip and pull. They have to carry sand in wooden boxes, working in the sun, nine hours a day. Three times a day and twice on Saturdays there is so-called roll call. The camp has to line up before the barracks and stand still, soldier-like, with hands on the body until the camp has been counted by the Frau *Oberaufseherin* [Langefeld]. The camp has 17 barracks. One of the barracks is for Jews.

Marianne then talks of her arrival in Ravensbrück and recounts what happened to her in the wooden cell. There was no light at all. The guard, Zimmer, came in and yelled at her: 'Now you will starve and you will not get out of here.' Marianne replied: 'If God wills it, I will die here.' At this Zimmer took her to the hallway and told Marianne to undress, down to her shirt. 'I was put in a straitjacket. My hands were so tightly clasped they swelled up. They took me by the throat and threw me back in the cell, and due to the straitjacket I passed out and had a screaming fit.'

When Marianne woke up a man in uniform was pushing her. It was Koegel's deputy Egon Zill, who thumped her on the nose and on the feet while Zimmer pulled her hair. Helpless to protect herself, as she was still in the straitjacket, she passed out again with the pain and woke to find she was lying in her own excrement, the straitjacket removed. She spent that night in her cell, in a nightshirt, teeth chattering.

The next day she was given a blanket, and the third day a sack of straw and another blanket, but she had no food for three days. Next, Marianne was told she was being sentenced to a further three weeks' arrest 'for screaming in the cell and lying in her own excrement'.

Like Hanna Sturm, Marianne was introduced to Hedwig Apfel. And like Hanna, she was forced to share a cell with Hedwig as a punishment. Unlike Hanna, however, Marianne had no doubt that Hedwig Apfel was insane. When Zimmer came to their door Apfel threw her water at her and spat onto the door and onto the sack of straw. 'She has diarrhoea and does not clean herself at all. She spits into her hands and rubs it into her own face.'

There was a bunk bed in the cell and Apfel slept at the top. At night she came and sat on Marianne's bed, but Marianne had no wish to make friends and told her to go away. So Apfel ripped Marianne's blankets and tore her bed to pieces. 'And she talks all night, swearing at God. Hands and arms and legs as thin as a spider.'

Because of the noise the guards dared not enter the cell. On the third day, the 'mad' Apfel sat on her top bunk, tipped her coffee over Marianne's head and threw things and yelled at her. Zimmer opened the cell door but still didn't dare come in. Eventually Zimmer sent Margot Kaiser into the cell, and Marianne was taken out, and locked up on her own again, before being released and sent back to her block.

In early September, long after Marianne Wachstein had left the cell block, Hanna was still there, locked up alone in the dark, and with no hope of release. She had lost all track of time, but she still peered through the holes into the neighbouring cells to see if anyone was there. One of the cells looked quite comfortable compared with hers; it had a bed with a blanket and a stool, but it was still empty. A little time later – she didn't know how long – Hanna heard someone talking in the cell and recognised the voice. It was Olga Benario.

As both Leocadia and Olga had feared in the last days of August, Olga's Mexican visa had got stuck in the post – in fact it hadn't got past New York. On 1 September German forces marched into Poland and war broke out, removing any chance of Olga leaving Germany. On 8 September the Gestapo took her back to Ravensbrück.

Olga was considered less of a threat now (for reasons not explained), and the conditions of her confinement were not as strict as before; she had regular food and was able to receive mail, which included an envelope from the Mexican consulate in Hamburg, sending on a copy of the visa, which they had by now received. As Olga well knew, however, it was too late – and in any case copies were not good enough.

Writing under new and stricter wartime censorship rules, Olga wrote to Leocadia and Ligia on 13 September:

> *My dears!*
>
> *I am back in Ravensbrück camp. Received entry permit to Mexico from the Mexican consulate, Hamburg, but am afraid that I won't be able to make use of it. However, I know that you will continue to do everything possible for me. Pass the enclosed letter on to Carlos and please write more details about Anita.*
>
> *Lots of love, kiss my little child for me.*
>
> *Yours Olga.*

As soon as she could Hanna made herself known to Olga by whispering through one of the tiny holes she had made in the wall. Olga was amazed to find her friend next door, saying she'd heard about the arrest of the Tolstoy reading group when she first came back to the camp.

Hanna said she was being starved, so Olga offered to share her food, and they managed to enlarge the hole in the wall so that Olga could give Hanna bread – just as Hanna had got food to Olga when she was being starved a few months earlier. 'You need some warm food, but how can we do it?' wondered Olga. 'The best thing would be if you bring your mouth up to the hole and I will feed you. In the morning I'll give you the bread, right after Zimmer has brought the coffee.'

Olga then told Hanna she had news for her, but they had to talk quickly before '*die Alte*' came back. The news was that war had broken out. Sitting in her solitary cell, Hanna had no idea, so Olga passed on all she'd learned in Berlin. Soon everyone in the cell block knew, because Zimmer was 'celebrating and boasting to the prisoners about the "glorious" news of Nazi conquests which are happening every day in the war'.

*Chapter 3*

# Blockovas

Doris Maase saw a great deal from her window in the *Revier*. She watched women guards and SS men enter the staff canteen opposite at lunchtime and then saw them go out 'as courting couples' in the evening. In early September 1939, soon after war began, Doris looked out and saw a prisoner run at the electric fence. She was trying to kill herself, but was stopped by a young blonde guard who dragged her to the *Strafblock*, beating her as she went. Doris learned that the guard's name was Dorothea Binz: 'I saw Binz take the skeletal woman away and beat her with a cane on her naked thighs. Such cruelty in one so young and pretty made a lasting impression on me.'

Binz's appetite for cruelty soon made an impression on everyone in the camp. And yet, until she got the job here, she had been little noticed. The daughter of a forester, Dorothea Binz was one of several local girls who started work over the summer. These recruits were different from the women who arrived with the prisoners five months earlier from Lichtenburg. They had no experience of any other penal institution, and many were so young that they had no meaningful experience of life before Nazi rule. Work at the camp was their first job.

Dorothea had always lived in the woods around Fürstenberg, attending village schools and churches, playing down forest trails, chasing wild pigs, bathing in lakes in the summer, skating on them in winter. The family had moved around the area a great deal, and in the mid-1930s they settled in a village called Altglobsow, a poor hamlet, three miles from Ravensbrück, where villagers scraped a living felling trees or working on the land. As newcomers, the Binz family were viewed as outsiders, especially as Walter Binz's official post as forester meant they were better off and had a bigger house.

At the age of ten Dorothea and her friends joined the Bund Deutscher Mädel (League of German Girls), the female wing of the Hitler Youth. At school she followed the Nazi curriculum, which taught children to despise Jews and revile society's outcasts, although there is some evidence that her parents were not so fond of Hitler's ideas. Walter Binz had not always been in favour with his employers, perhaps due to a reluctance to join the Nazi Party – compulsory for government and state officials. It was also well known that the forester had been before the courts for poaching; he was a drinker too, as was his wife, Rose. The Binz family were not disliked, but people in the village were wary of them, and often heard the shouts and screams that issued from their house. It was not a happy home.

Dorothea had had her own setbacks too: in her early teens she suffered a bout of tuberculosis, not unusual in the damp climate of this low-lying terrain, but Dorothea's infection was severe and had meant many months in a TB clinic, so she missed out on some of her schooling, leaving with few, if any, qualifications.

Stigmatised as a carrier of TB and barred from many jobs due to the danger of contagion, on leaving school Dorothea went to work as a kitchen maid, so when the prospect arose of working as a guard at the new concentration camp she jumped at the chance. Later as she rose up the ladder, she would laughingly relate to other guards how her father had told her not to take the job, but the chance was too good to turn down: to live away from home, in comfortable quarters, with good pay and a smart uniform. Dorothea had already caught the eyes of the young SS officers, stationed at a nearby training depot, who drank in the Altglobsow village bar. Tall, slim and blonde, with rounded cheeks and upturned nose, she was known as a local beauty.

Other local girls were keen to join up too. Margarete Mewes, the mother of three from Fürstenberg, took a job at the same time as Binz, as did Elisabeth Volkenrath, a farmer's daughter.

All SS camp staff were told to toughen up when war broke out. According to Rudolf Höss, by now an officer at Sachsenhausen, on the day the German forces crossed into Poland, Eicke himself had summoned all senior concentration camp officers to tell them they must henceforth 'treat orders as sacrosanct and even those that appear most hard and severe must be implemented without hesitation'. Höss recalled Eicke saying: 'The harsh laws of war now prevailed.' From now on the job of SS camp staff was to 'protect the homeland against all internal enemies' – the fight to suppress those in the camps was as important for the future of the Reich as the fight at the front.

'He, Eicke, therefore demanded the men serving in the camps should show an inflexible harshness towards the prisoners. Only the SS were capable of protecting the National Socialist state from all internal danger. Other organisations lacked the necessary toughness.'

Koegel understood Eicke's orders well. The Ravensbrück enemy within – just 1607 women on 1 September 1939 – was small in number, but Koegel was showing due harshness towards every one of them. More were joining their ranks every day. On 16 September a group of political prisoners were brought in, including Luise Mauer, a courier for the German Communist Party, who had risked her life running secret messages across borders. Luise had little fighting spirit in her after being forced to stand outside the camp gates in the rain for hours, before being stripped, deloused, and shorn in the 'bath', and even less after she was sent to the most back-breaking work, shovelling coal from the bottom of barges. These 'September prisoners' were then assigned to a special block where they could not infect the camp with their dangerous plotting.

While the communists were crushed, however, it was the handful of Poles – the first real foreign 'enemies' to arrive – who were hated most. Within days of crossing into Poland the German forces had set about not only seizing Polish land and property but capturing and killing its ruling classes, including countless women teachers, trade unionists, countesses, community leaders, officers' wives and journalists.

So 'filthy' were these 'Slavs' that when they first passed the Ravensbrück gates they were brutally scrubbed 'clean' before being sent to the *Strafblock* and put on brick-throwing work 'until hands were bloody and raw', in the words of Maria Moldenhawer, a Polish aristocrat and instructor of 'military readiness' in Warsaw girls' schools.

To whip up ever more hatred, stories were spread that the Poles had cut out the tongues of German soldiers or poisoned their tea. Renee Salska had gouged out the eyes of German children, the guards said, though her only crime was to have taught Polish history in a Poznań school.

The first 'internal enemies' to rise up in Ravensbrück, however, were not these Polish newcomers but Koegel's oldest and most hated enemies of all: the Jehovah's Witnesses. The same religious women who rioted at Lichtenburg were now refusing his orders to sew bags for the war effort. A sewing workshop for the military had been established at the camp to make use of their skills, but this was war work, they protested, it was against their pacifist principles. This sent the commandant into another blind rage.

It says a lot about the mindset of Max Koegel that even now the prisoners who riled him most were not the 'communist whores', the 'Slav vermin' or the 'Jewish bitches', but these religious 'hags'. Every threat had been levelled at them and every cruelty inflicted so as to make them renounce their faith by signing on the dotted line. To break their unity, the women had even been split up among different blocks, but they had immediately begun to try converting others to their faith, so they'd been moved back together again. And as punishment they were given the hated Käthe Knoll as their Blockova, a feared green triangle who was said to have murdered her mother. But still the forms lay stacked and unsigned in Langefeld's office.

Langefeld herself seemed unperturbed; in most respects these respectable German housewives were model prisoners who caused her no trouble. Perhaps it was precisely because they were 'model German housewives' that Koegel found them harder to show his teeth to than the communists, the Jews, the Slavs and the whores – and this is what drove him mad.

Nor was the Jehovah's Witnesses' protest insignificant. In the autumn of 1939 they made up more than half of the women in the camp, and Koegel had called for more powers to restrain them, demanding a bigger, more permanent prison building. Now that war had begun, Ravensbrück should be equipped with the same secure cell block as the male camps.

In the autumn of 1939 he finally received permission for the new prison, and male prisoners from Sachsenhausen were brought in to build it, though Koegel saw to it that the Jehovah's Witnesses helped them. Constructed out of stone on two levels, one sunk deep into the ground, it would have seventy-eight cells, replacing the wooden structure where Hanna Sturm was still incarcerated.

After nearly three months in isolation, Hanna had lost track of time, but she knew autumn had come, as it was icy cold in her cell and she still had only a thin summer dress. Olga had left the neighbouring cell long ago, but Hanna could still hear Hedwig Apfel. Each time Mewes, the new *Strafblock* guard, entered Hedwig's cell the opera singer shrieked and laughed and threw her pot back in Mewes's face.

Since war had begun, numbers in the *Strafblock* had swelled, and Mewes was brought in to help Zimmer, handing out the food and patrolling at night. A sullen brute, Mewes had had three children, all by different Fürstenberg men, or so Hanna had picked up by listening to gossiping guards. At least, thought Hanna, she could be thankful that Margot Kaiser had been moved on. Under the commandant's new regime, the twenty-year-old green-triangle prisoner from Chemnitz had been promoted and was now the camp's most powerful inmate.

In any male concentration camp, Margot Kaiser would have been called a Kapo ('trusty', inmate foreman), or Senior Kapo. Here in Ravensbrück the word was less commonly used, but the practice of co-opting prisoners to carry out the day-to-day work of running the camp was to all intents and purposes the same as it was in Buchenwald, Dachau or Sachsenhausen. The female prisoner guards were more likely to be called by their official titles – the Blockova was the block chief, the Stubova the room chief – but they were all put in post to assist the SS, just as the Kapos were in male camps. Such prisoner jobs had existed from the start, but in the autumn of 1939, in line with the new harshness, the Kapo system had been tightened up, with a new hierarchy. The job of *Lagerläuferin* – camp runner – was introduced: prisoners whose job was to carry messages back and forth as required. And a 'head prisoner' was appointed; Margot Kaiser was the first to get the job. Her official title was *Lagerälteste*, camp senior, though the prisoners called her *Lagerschreck* – camp terror.

The Kapo system had always been at the very heart of the concentration camp blueprint. For one thing, it saved on staff and money: without these willing prisoner helpers, the SS would not have been able to control the vast numbers held in their camps. But as Rudolf Höss explained in his memoir, the Kapos were far more than just free labour. 'The more there are rivalries, the more battles between the prisoners, the easier it is to control the camp. Divide and rule – that is the principle not only of high politics but also in a concentration camp.' And the prisoner staff in no way represented the needs or wishes of the prisoners. Their job was to obey SS commands; as soon as they failed to do so they were removed. And this was the trap, as Heinrich Himmler himself explained in a speech to officers of the German army. 'The Kapo must make the men march,' he said, 'and as soon as he doesn't do his job we make him return to his block with fellow prisoners and there they will beat him to death.'

From the beginning, the system worked just as well with women as it had with men; there was no lack of prisoners willing to take bribes of better clothing, more food and their own bed. As in the male camps, the women Kapos also wore green armbands, indicating their privileged jobs and allowing them to move around freely. In the early days, just as in the men's camps, the women chosen were often the green triangles; co-opting the criminal class to rule over political prisoners was the most obvious way to institute 'divide and rule'. The experience of the male camps had proved that the 'greens' were most likely to bring zeal to the work. A 'green' Kapo at Mauthausen called August Adam, a gangland criminal, had the task of assigning work to new arrivals and boasted later about how he used to pick out lawyers, priests and professors and tell them: 'Well, here I am in command. The world has turned upside down.' Then he would beat them with his bat and send them to the *Scheisskompanie* – latrine gang.

The green triangles at Ravensbrück were never in the same criminal league as August Adam; those chosen as Kapos here were more likely to be simply feckless women who'd fallen into a life of petty theft, illegal abortion or dodging work. Even Käthe Knoll – a Kapo of sorts since the earliest days in Lichtenburg – had not, as it later turned out, murdered her mother but was arrested for 'race shame' after relations with a Jewish man; she had also led a life of petty crime. Margot Kaiser, the new *Lagerschreck*, had never murdered anyone before she arrived at Ravensbrück. Throughout her teens she'd tricked and thieved, until she was sent to work in a munitions factory, from which she ran away. By the time she left Ravensbrück, however, she had beaten at least ten women to death, as she admitted at her post-war trial.

Although the green triangles held most power, Ravensbrück also employed a large number of black triangles as Kapos particularly in the blocks, and in this respect the women's camp differed from the men's. Among the black triangles Ravensbrück had a useful resource that the male camp didn't have: *Puffmütter*, brothel madams. Langefeld liked to appoint these women: if a *Puffmutter* could run a brothel, she could run a Ravensbrück block.

Philomena Müssgueller, a forty-one-year-old prostitute who had run a brothel in Munich for many years, was happy to be plucked out of the mayhem of the asocial block to work as a Blockova keeping order over 'politicals', especially as it won her an extra sausage and her own bed. Philomena already had her own gang of black-triangle acolytes, who fawned around her, and together they easily had the muscle to keep down a bunch of red triangles.

Marianne Scharinger, an Austrian, arrested for carrying out illegal abortions, was made Blockova of the Jewish block, while the Düsseldorf prostitute Else Krug had been chosen for the prize job of running the potato cellar. Peeling mountains of root vegetables to a strict deadline was gruelling and repetitive work, but much sought after thanks to the chance of pocketing a potato, cabbage or swede. Since the outbreak of war, prisoners were getting one less ladle of soup a day, and Else had set up a smuggling ring, getting extra vegetables out to the hungry in her block.

As their power spread, nobody despised the Kapos more than the German and Austrian red triangles. The 'September prisoner' Luise Mauer was harassed by a prostitute Blockova called Ratzeweit, a 'despicable' character who lashed out and screeched when the women were late getting up for *Appell*. Ratzeweit liked to pick on older women, and harassed Lisel Plucker, an elderly political prisoner, so Lisel tried to kill herself by walking into the wire.

Maria Wiedmaier, who had organised Red Help committees for the Communist Party, had never had to take orders from such a lowlife as

Müssgueller. 'Zimmer surrounded herself with green triangles,' she said, 'and she made use of their meanness, and their brutish methods.' These Kapos were also used as SS spies; one such spy spotted Minna Rupp, another newly arrived German communist, stealing half a carrot and reported her to Koegel, so Minna was sent to the *Strafblock*. Prisoners were barely able to meet at all any more, as the *Spitzel* (informers) were watching and would report not only to Koegel but to Langefeld as well.

Johanna Langefeld saw the value of the Kapo system too, particularly as Koegel tried to further undermine her authority. In the first six months of the camp the *Oberaufseherin* had lost several battles with the commandant, and now there was to be a new camp prison – or 'bunker' – against her wishes.

Langefeld had been as eager as anyone to fulfil Himmler's edict on 'protecting the homeland from internal enemies'. The mere sight of women standing for hours in the cold and wet demonstrated her iron discipline. Nevertheless, Koegel's methods were not hers, and later she would tell American interrogators that she had always known Koegel was a sadist, though her statement suggests that she was just as angered by Koegel's refusal to inform her of his plans as she was by his brutality.

In particular, he had secured the right – behind her back – to order women to the *Strafblock* and isolation cells without consultation. Worse, women guards – other than those assigned to work there – would be barred from entering the new stone bunker without Koegel's permission. To counter this affront, Langefeld shored up her own power base in the living blocks, kitchen, *Wäscherei* and *Effektenkammer* by making sure that Kapos loyal to her were put in key positions. And she insisted on choosing these prisoner staff herself. She took her time, watching women on the Lagerstrasse and reading their files. She also listened to her informers, often other Kapos.

Doris Maase said later that from the very earliest months, Johanna Langefeld had recruited her 'men of confidence' from amongst the prostitutes. If she heard that a Blockova was losing control, the woman was sacked. Langefeld would then stride out onto the Lagerstrasse at *Appell* and pick another woman who had caught her eye.

In the autumn of 1939 Langefeld was looking for a new Blockova for the Jewish block. The place was in chaos: women always late for *Appell*, the lice count high, food being spilled. A group of orphaned Gypsy children had been put in the block too, which didn't help. Even Doris Maase described the Jewish block as 'a rabble' as she watched the women line up at the *Revier*.

From the start the Jewish prisoners had been deliberately brought lower than any other group. Just 10 per cent of the prisoner strength, the Jews had been isolated in a single block at the end of the Lagerstrasse, subject to constant harassment. Rations were meaner, and they worked longer hours, without a day off. Not surprisingly, many Jewish women soon fell ill, suffering mostly from swollen legs, nervous fits and chest infections. Many were also afflicted by sores and wounds caused by beatings. It was the practice of the night shift guards to sit around in the canteen talking about what they'd read about 'Jewish sluts' and 'rich Jewish bitches', before striding off to lash out at any Jewish 'swine, whore or bitch' they saw.

The outbreak of war brought an escalation in abuse, as Marianne Wachstein observed when she returned to the block after her period in the isolation cells. She saw sick women forced out into the early morning cold by Blockovas, and made to stand at *Appell* having epileptic fits and seizures, while others fainted as they stood to be punished in the rain. 'A Jewish woman called Rosenberg who was at that time in side B of the Jewish barrack, had to undergo a standing punishment inside the block with the door and windows open in the freezing cold – even though she had a bad chest,' said Marianne. 'The Rosenberg woman had been reported for failing to make her bed properly.'

The fear of standing obsessed Marianne because she herself could hardly walk or stand. On arrival in the camp in June a 'humane' SS doctor excused her from *Appell*, but in the autumn a new SS doctor told her she would have to attend. Marianne objected and demanded that he should examine her first to see if she was well enough, but he refused 'and said something rude and disparaging about Jews' and the nurse sitting behind the desk 'followed with a jeering smile'. Marianne said: 'I will tell people abroad how one is treated in a concentration camp,' upon which the doctor grabbed her and threw her out. 'I'll report that too,' Marianne said, clearly believing that the wrongs she was suffering would soon be put right.

After the incident, Marianne returned to her block and told her friends: 'The physician has taken his oath and must examine me, the Jew, just as he examines an Aryan woman when he checks if she is fit or not,' and the others all agreed, including Edith Weiss, Modesta Finkelstein, Leontine Kestenbaum and several more of the Vienna 'rabble'.

Such a rise in anti-Semitic abuse in the camp was hardly surprising given the increasing Jewish persecution across the Reich. The Führer was not yet ready to order wholesale German-Jewish roundups – not least because there were no firm plans about where the Jews would go – but persecution had intensified, and by the time war started in September 1939, 500,000 German Jews had found the means to leave Germany; 250,000 remained, two-thirds of them women – widows, divorcees, single mothers, the destitute and the homeless, none standing any chance of securing a visa and all at high risk of being picked up by the police and accused, like Herta Cohen, of the crime of 'infecting German blood'.

The pickup happened, said Herta, in one of her many statements to the police, in a restaurant called Bremer Hafen in Essen, where she went for a glass of beer.

> It was 5 p.m. And I sat down on the table where there was nobody. On another table were two men in uniform. Grey uniform. The two men came to my table and sat down. They wanted a beer too. One left. And the other stayed. When we were alone I told him I was Jewish but for him this was not important and he wanted to sit here. He gave me a drink. I got dizzy. After two hours I was leaving and the man paid for the drinks. On the way home he asked if I wanted to drink beer near my flat in Adolf Hitler Strasse.

He asked her to go to his flat. 'I say I cannot do this as I am Jewish. And he says be quiet it doesn't matter. I stay with him. He gives me more beer. The next morning I am lying next to him. I don't know what happened to my clothes. The next morning we had sex.'

The interrogator wants to hear more, and now asks exactly what happened, where it happened, and how it happened – 'Was it full sexual intercourse? Was he inside you? ... Was he right inside you?' But that left the man unsatisfied, so the questions resumed next day. To one of them Herta answers: 'I had to clean up the semen,' and the questions go on until finally there is no more to say, so she is sent to Ravensbrück. The 'reason for arrest' given on her file was 'infecting German blood'.

So desperate were some of these abandoned German-Jewish women that several had tried to flee across the Dutch border, but travelling alone made them conspicuous. A Frau Kroch, from Leipzig, had sacrificed her own chance of freedom by letting her husband go on ahead with her children, staying behind to cover their tracks. When the coast was clear she set off to join them but was arrested and brought to Ravensbrück. A German political prisoner who had known her before recognised her in the camp one day. 'They had cut off her hair and she went about in bare feet. I shall never forget the sad look she gave me.'

Mathilde ten Brink never had much hope of getting away, as she had no papers. Mathilde was a fifty-one-year-old homeless woman from Osnabrück. She had lost her job as a cleaner in the family shop when it was destroyed in the Kristallnacht pogrom, which may also explain how she lost her *Reichspass*, identity card. In any event the Dutch police arrested her at Emmerich and handed her back to the Gestapo. A German police report noted that she was 'Not married. 138 cm [4' 6"] tall and weak.' She had Jewish features. 'Nose is very big. Big ears. No teeth. Speaks German and poor Dutch.' Mathilde had 'No children and no home,' said the police report, which included dozens of pages of official correspondence, before Mathilde had even been sent to Ravensbrück, as did the report on Irma Eckler, a Jewish woman accused of *Rassenschande*. Irma and her 'Aryan' husband – who was also jailed – had two little girls who'd been taken away; one was now living with Irma's parents, the other taken to a Nazi orphanage.

Irma received only scraps of news about the girls in censored letters from her parents. In one of her replies it is evident that Irma had been toiling on an outside work gang, because she says she's seen children roller-skating – villagers perhaps, or children of the SS, playing in their villa gardens:

> *Dear Mutti,*
>
> *I was terribly happy about your letter. Yes, that's the way I imagine Ingrid to be. She'll be someone who knows how to stand up for herself in life. Roller-skating seems to be in fashion. Here at work I often see the children roller-skating. Now you'll be getting the garden in order. You don't say anything about emigrating any more?*
>
> *Tender wishes and kisses also to my roller-skater,*
>
> *Your Irma Mutti.*

When Doris Maase described the Jewish block as a rabble, however, she meant not only that these women were the most desperate, but also that they had no discipline, no organisation, no common cause. Though identified as Jews, religion meant little or nothing to them and few shared any political beliefs. In Blocks 2 and 3 the communists and other politicals were planning how to celebrate the anniversary of the Bolshevik Revolution on 7 November, but the tiny group of Jewish communists in Block 11 were reviled by other Jewish women as Reds, and they in turn scorned the 'bourgeois' Viennese women and recoiled from the prostitutes. A minority of the Jewish women could console themselves that they were here for fighting fascism, which was what Maria Wiedmaier and her comrades tried to remember as they were herded every morning into line.

Within weeks of her release from the isolation cell, Marianne Wachstein herself was once again demanding to know why she was in the camp at all, and was brought again before the commandant. Evidently she still thought she could make Koegel see sense, but instead 'The Herr Director took the file that was lying in front of him and hit me several times on the hands and I realised that I was not allowed to defend myself.' Koegel ordered Wachstein back to an isolation cell and told Langefeld to sort out the block of 'Jewish whores'.

Langefeld's response was radical. She dismissed the Blockova of the Jewish block and walked out onto the Lagerstrasse at *Appell* to choose another. But rather than turn to the criminal or asocial blocks, she walked towards the Jewish women, and observed them with silent disgust. Johanna Langefeld hated the Jews as much as anyone, but one of these women stood out. Olga Benario was a striking, handsome figure even in her striped uniform and Langefeld, who had known Olga since Lichtenburg, was well aware of her story. She called her out of line, made her stand to attention, and told her she was the new Blockova of the Jewish block. Till then, no political prisoner – Jew or non-Jew – had been offered the poisoned chalice of ruling over fellow inmates.

The SS burned all documents about the appointment of Kapos and other prisoner staff, so we have no official information on why Olga was given the Blockova job. Accounts from the prisoners in Block 11 are rare, as few of the Jewish prisoners survived.

After the war Olga's communist comrades tried to explain her appointment, but their version of events is not always reliable. By the early 1950s the majority of Ravensbrück's German communist survivors had settled in the East, where they wrote a history of the camp with one main objective in mind: to extol the courageous communist resistance.

In the new German Democratic Republic (GDR) the heroism of camp communists was trumpeted to help bolster the country's image as a bulwark against fascism. Olga Benario, Stalin's own revolutionary, was central to this narrative; streets, schools and buildings across East Germany were named after her. Certain elements of Olga's story, however, did not fit this theme, particularly her appointment as a Blockova – a role that meant she had to implement the orders of the SS.

To sanitise Olga's appointment, these communist historians omitted to mention that such a job came with privileges and made out that her taking it was not collaboration but a sign that the SS had run out of other ways to break her – they made Olga Blockova to 'bring hatred on her head,' they said. And as soon as she was appointed, Olga turned the Blockova role to her advantage, showing these 'bourgeois Jews the evils of fascism', wrote Ruth Werner, Olga's first biographer.

Werner, who was not in Ravensbrück, but trained with Olga in Moscow, and based her biography on interviews with communist survivors, described the other non-communist Jewish prisoners in Ravensbrück as 'feral women' with 'a me-first attitude, stealing clothes and blankets', giving proof – if it were needed – that anti-Semitism was rife amongst many German communist prisoners in the camp too. Olga herself was not really fully Jewish, some comrades suggested. Maria Wiedmaier said that she looked like 'an Aryan' and might have been 'half-Aryan'.

The communists' post-war idolatry of Olga reached its zenith with the inauguration of the Ravensbrück memorial site in 1959, when crowds gathered at the foot of a statue called *Tragende* (Woman Carrying), depicting an emaciated woman, high on a pedestal, carved in bronze, holding the limp figure of another woman in her arms. *Tragende* is meant to be Olga Benario. The Olga who stands there today seems distant, stark and cold, nothing like the tortured Olga – wife and mother – who accepted the role of Blockova in October 1939.

Returning from Berlin in September, there can be no doubt that Olga Benario was at breaking point. Three years spent behind bars, most of them in solitary confinement, had weakened her both physically and spiritually. She came back to Ravensbrück to find the communist group in the camp almost crushed. Hanna Sturm was still in the bunker. Her dear friend and fellow revolutionary, Sabo, was dead, probably from pneumonia, though some reports say beaten to death. Jozka Jaburkova was dangerously ill. And faith in Stalin had been unsettled by news that he had entered into a pact with Hitler.

Olga had her private pain too. She had long ago rejected her Jewishness, but now everything that was happening to her stemmed from it. How she viewed this conflict – did she long to be in the communist block with old comrades, or to join her fellow Jews in Block 11? – we will never know. Nor will we know how deeply she feared for her estranged mother and her brother's safety. An aunt, her mother's sister, had fled to America, but Olga's mother and brother were still in Munich. Her deepest despair, however, clearly lay in the knowledge that during the summer real hopes of seeing Anita and Carlos again had been snatched away.

Olga could have refused the Blockova job – she had shown the courage for such defiance in the past – but that was before she had become a mother. If she refused she risked being shot, or at best put back in the bunker with no mail and no way of hearing news of Anita. If any new chance of emigration came up, she wouldn't know.

Exactly when Olga became Blockova isn't clear, but it must have been by 14 October 1939, as on that day she wrote to Carlos saying she could sometimes read a newspaper, which can only mean that she was receiving a Blockova's privileges, and she was obviously able to move around and see her friends. She adds: 'The few weeks in Berlin reminded me that it is the most difficult thing to be alone. Here I have my comrades who worry about what I eat.' Olga worried about how Carlos was coping, as she knew he was still in solitary confinement. 'Do you walk – do you exercise? It really depresses me to know you are alone.' As always, her letter returned to Anita. 'I'm dreaming of you and the little one again and again, but it's bitter to wake up in the morning.'

'*Achtung! Achtung!*' shouts Olga as soon as the morning siren wails. In October temperatures are already dropping fast, and although there is a stove in the block, nobody can use it. Several women refuse to wake, so Olga marches up and down, shaking them. If they're late, they'll be beaten by guards, she warns. Another scrum forms around the *Kesselkolonne*, the soup wagon. The 'coffee' is quickly drunk. Olga shouts: 'Out, out. *Appell! Appell!*' Those too sick to work stay behind, but everyone else marches out, and by 4.30 a.m. the women of Block 11 are standing under the stars. '*Achtung! Achtung!* Ranks of five,' and the 'crows' appear in their black woollen winter capes, watching the Blockovas for any slipup in the count.

One by one the women with the green armbands – Ratzeweit, Müssgueller, Scharinger, and now Benario – deliver the numbers to Langefeld. Olga's tally is checked and approved. The women are dismissed back to blocks where they just have time to make their beds, before labour roll call. Olga watches them march off, then fills out her record book. As Blockova she takes the sick from her block to the *Revier*, where they line up with others hoping to see a doctor. Olga exchanges a word with Doris Maase, and passes on a message to Maria Wiedmaier in Block 3.

All day Olga has tasks to perform: registering new comers, counting stockings, knickers and vests for the weekly laundry, listing rations, under the block guard's eye. When the women return at midday she serves the lunchtime soup and counts them again, and when they return at the end of the day she counts them again. Evening *Appell* is the worst, as women go missing during the day – hiding in the block, perhaps – so the count starts again, and if the missing person isn't found everyone waits as the food gets cold and temperatures drop. Women slump to the ground and Olga stands and watches as the guard, Fraede, lashes out.

After the evening soup the women trudge to the washroom and fight over the lavatories. They undress and climb onto mattresses. Olga walks up and down. Someone is sleeping in her clothes to keep out the cold. She must take them off and fold them, Olga says, or she'll get a report. Another woman is moaning, complaining of pains in her legs. The woman tells Olga she is blind. Olga sees her ankles are swollen and blue, and she pauses to show the woman how to stretch to ease the pain.

By 9 p.m. the block is locked and the SS guards leave the women alone till morning. Now Olga gathers friends around her to talk. She has her own bed, and locker. Here is Rosa Menzer, from Dresden, whom Olga has known since Lichtenburg, and Lena and Lenza, her other young comrades.

On Sundays, when the SS watch slackens, Olga's comrades come together again to write their letters and talk about their families. Rosa, a seamstress, cannot write, so Olga or another comrade writes her letters for her, and Rosa returns the favour by showing them how to stitch old paper into their shirts to keep out the cold.

Olga brings out letters she has received from Carlos and they all discuss his ideas on philosophy and what Olga might say in reply. And they talk about Anita. They all agree that Anita should be part of a collective as young as possible. Olga writes: 'It is important for her character. I have someone here who says this.'

The days pass. Olga comes to know the women better as she moves around the bunks, and they get to know her and look forward to her rounds; even the 'bourgeois' Viennese stop calling Olga a Red and a Bolshevik cow, because she helps them, telling them to eat slowly to ease the hunger, and to pick off lice from each other's heads. 'Don't give up,' she says. 'Cling close for warmth.'

Olga finds moments to draw and sketch. Saving the scraps of paper she is allowed to have as Blockova, she draws miniature maps so the women can follow the progress of the war. Marking the front in pencil, with tiny arrows, she shows how German forces are advancing across Poland; a dotted line rings off Nazi-occupied lands. Olga's information comes from snippets taken from the Nazi newspaper, the *Völkischer Beobachter*, smuggled to her by Maria Wiedmaier and Doris Maase.

Olga draws beautifully and the women in the block look on in wonder. A new prisoner called Käthe Leichter has arrived from Vienna. She seems to know a lot and tells Olga what is happening in the outside world, saying that before she was arrested the Austrian press were reporting that Churchill would sue for peace by Christmas.

Käthe quickly becomes loved by everyone in the block; she sings to the other women and recites poems. Some say that she seems to know every poem that was ever written. She is older than Olga and seems to want to help her.

And although Käthe is not a 'comrade' as such – she is a social democrat, not a communist – the two women have much in common, as do all the women here; they all have children or family far away. One evening Käthe talks of her last days in Vienna. Her husband and two boys managed to get out to safety across the Czech border and are now in Paris. Käthe despairs that she let them leave ahead of her and berates herself for not following sooner. She knows they reached Paris because she received letters via an aunt in Vienna, but she worries how long it will be before Paris will be taken too, and where they will go next. Käthe recites another poem, this time one she has written to an imaginary 'brother' in a men's concentration camp.

> Brother, have you been with your wife and children during the last night?
> I was with my children.
> I covered them both and said:
> 'Mother will be there soon, be good don't cry.'
> The light of the lamp shines across a book and a couch.
> We were sitting quietly, my husband and I, not to disturb the children.
> I jumped up scared. The pale moonlight reflected on the iron bunks.
> And I lie here among many, so still, so lonely and cold.
> I in Ravensbrück, you in Sachsenhausen, in Dachau or Buchenwald.

Throughout November Olga's letters ceased. Thanks to another Jewish prisoner, Ida Hirschkron, we know why. Ida, arrested in Vienna for resistance activity in July 1939, arrived in Ravensbrück in October. She was sent to the Jewish block, and remained a prisoner there until September 1941, at which point she was suddenly released. 'My release must have been a mistake,' she wrote later, 'because as soon as I returned to Vienna the Gestapo started looking for me again. I was therefore forced to live underground illegally.' But Ida escaped recapture, and after the war she recounted her experience in the camp. Her most vivid memory was the 'lockdown' of the Jewish block that began on 10 November 1939.

On that day all the Jewish women were barricaded inside Block 11. Doors were barred and windows boarded up. Nobody knew why. 'We were not allowed to leave the block to receive mail or write letters, we were completely cut off from the outside world.' Even roll call was taken inside the block, by Emma Zimmer. 'When Zimmer entered the block our hearts beat fast. There was a storm of foul abuse – "Jewish swine", "Jewish rabble", "lazy bunch of Jews". At the same time Zimmer beat us with all her might, haphazardly, and she beat whoever was near her.'

The lockdown went on day after day. Ida does not explain how, or how often, the women received food or water, but they sat in darkness 'terrified of what might happen next' and each day Zimmer came to shout and beat. 'All this time we had no air and were not allowed to open the windows. We nearly went crazy with fear.'

The nightmare continued for three weeks, and it would clearly have gone on much longer if Olga hadn't taken action. 'Then our Blockova Olga

Benario-Prestes dared ask Zimmer to put an end to this almost unbearable state of affairs.' This was unprecedented impudence. To date no prisoner – and certainly no Blockova – had dared confront a guard, and according to Ida, Olga's protest sent Zimmer wild.

'Zimmer screamed like a madwoman and made a report to the camp commandant, Koegel, of the mutiny. She made everyone stand to attention and shouted: "You Jews, you will all be shot now!" This caused tremendous panic and chaos among the prisoners.' But Koegel did not order the women to be shot. The threat was just a 'sadistic little pleasure of Zimmer's', said Ida. 'Instead we had to collect tools and then we went to shovel sand.'

Some time later the women learned the cause of their ordeal. On 8 November 1939, two days before they were incarcerated, a thirty-six-year-old joiner from Württemberg called Georg Elser had tried to kill Hitler and nearly succeeded. He planted a bomb in a beer hall where Hitler was speaking, but by a fluke of timing it went off ten minutes after Hitler left, killing eight bystanders instead. In revenge Jews in all concentration camps were punished.

Ida Hirschkron's testimony, which was not available to the communist historians writing after the war, gives an almost unique view inside the Jewish block at this time of strife. Without it, nothing would be known of Olga's courage in demanding an end to lockdown. As a result of Olga's protest that particular punishment ended, and the doors of the block were opened.

As Hirschkron makes clear, however, being sent to shovel sand instead was no soft option. The guards in the *Sandgrube* made sure the prisoners continued to suffer from morning until night. 'Women were attacked by dogs and there were terrible injuries. I myself often had to help carry women into the camp, who were covered with blood. The women had to be carried to the hospital with frightful frostbite.'

There were many old women amongst them, and one was completely blind, though whether this is the same blind woman comforted earlier by Olga in the block, we don't know. 'The woman's feet were also so badly swollen that she couldn't do the work the rest of us were sent to do. So Zimmer seized the blind woman by the scruff of the neck and beat her down, pulled her up again, and beat her with her hand and again thrust her to the ground so that she was left lying there, moaning.'

It wasn't until 20 December that Olga was able to write to Leocadia and Ligia again, although only very briefly. She thanked them for continuing to 'do all you can for me' and for a telegram she had just received, sent on Anita's third birthday – 27 November – during the lockdown; 'kiss my Anita-child for me'.

Despite the 'mutiny' Olga still held her post of Blockova in December, according to Alice Bernstein, another Jewish survivor. Alice was a Stubova (room chief) in Block 11 at the time, and recalled another incident involving Olga three days before Christmas. That morning she allowed a three-year-old Gypsy girl to sleep in longer than usual. 'The child was ill and the Blockova, Olga Benario-Prestes, had covered her with a woollen blanket.' The girl was discovered by the SS man Johann Kantschuster. 'He grabbed the child by the hair, took her to the lake, and drowned her.'

*Chapter 4*

# Himmler Visits

On 4 January 1940 Heinrich Himmler ordered his driver to head north-west out of Berlin, along the icy roads towards the Mecklenburg forest and on to Ravensbrück. With heavy snowfalls overnight, and temperatures dipping to minus 20°C, the journey was treacherous, with roads often blocked by drifting snow. Given the weather, as well as events in the wider war, particularly in Poland, one might imagine that a visit to the small women's camp at Ravensbrück in January 1940 would have been low on the Reichsführer's list of priorities. But Himmler liked to visit his camps, and this would be his first tour of Ravensbrück since it opened in May.

Adolf Hitler showed little interest in the concentration camps – according to the records, he never visited a single one – but they lay at the centre of Himmler's empire; whatever went on behind their walls was signed off with his pen. Himmler's childhood obsession with detail had grown into an urge to micromanage his entire empire, particularly his camps. As Reichsführer SS he ruled on everything from the prisoners' calorie consumption to SS appointments; he always vetoed a man whose family tree suggested a non-Aryan gene. And during his visits he liked to meet inmates face to face, and might admonish one or two in person, or pick someone out for release.

Himmler would not have been deterred from visiting Ravensbrück by the bad weather; he liked to strike out into the frozen wilderness, indeed he often took the wheel of his Mercedes cabriolet himself. Even now the top would have been down, Himmler warmly wrapped. These woodlands were a far cry from the Bavarian Alps that he had known as a boy, with their tumbling waterfalls and fairy-tale castles, but the forests of the plain were also pure German lands and the woods were a place to seek out the mystical presence of his ancestors.

He also drove out this way to visit his friends. It wasn't only Oswald Pohl, head of the SS economic office, who had an estate near Ravensbrück; several other top Nazis had property out here too, and regularly came out to hunt. Himmler, however, saw blood sports as 'the cold-blooded murder of innocent and defenceless animals'. Criticising the 'bloodhound' Hermann Göring, he once told his masseur and confidant Felix Kersten: 'Imagine, Herr Kersten, some poor deer is grazing peacefully and up comes the hunter with his gun to shoot the poor animal. Could that give you pleasure, Herr Kersten?' Kersten had been hired by Himmler to ease the chronic stomach pains that had afflicted him since boyhood. The Estonian-born masseur – Himmler called him 'my Black Buddha' – was expected both to massage away pain and to listen to his patient's theories on the master race.

None of the Nazi elite believed in the master-race ideology more fanatically than the Reichsführer SS, and none had such an obsession with related theories; for information on Indian mysticism or freemasonry and how they related to ideas of racial hygiene Himmler could recite chapter and verse, so that the British historian Hugh Trevor-Roper, who studied Himmler closely, commented: 'with such a narrow pedantry, such black-letter antiquarianism did Himmler study details of this sad rubbish that many have supposed, but wrongly, that he had been a schoolmaster'. As Trevor-Roper pointed out, however, had Himmler only been a crank, 'we would have heard far less of him'. As a manager, he was also 'very efficient'.

Just weeks after the start of the war, Hitler rewarded Himmler's efficiency on the war front with the rank of Reich Commissar for the Consolidation of Germandom, which required him to remove all unwanted people from newly captured Poland, and transform the land into a perfect living space for a genetically cleansed German super-race. By January the task was well in hand; he had already moved the population of the Warthegau and Gdansk corridor and resettled the areas with ethnic Germans, transported in from the Baltic States. The Polish ruling classes were also being rounded up and two million Polish Jews were being moved to reservations in the so-called 'General Government', a part of annexed eastern Poland. The Führer had not yet ruled on where these Jews would eventually go but many around Hitler assumed they would be pushed further east, or even deported to Africa – an idea to resettle them in the French colony of Madagascar had been floated.

With the largest human experiment ever imagined under way, Himmler had now found the time to head to Ravensbrück to examine more localised experiments. He had also arranged a meeting at Ravensbrück with Oswald Pohl, who had started an experiment of his own. At his nearby estate Pohl was trying out different breeds of poultry, and Himmler, who used to breed chickens too, was eager to pick his brains.

The screech of wheels in icy ruts alerted the camp that Himmler was close. Gangs of prisoners stood knee-deep in snow, shovelling a path. Out on the frozen lake more women were at work, hacking ice for the camp storeroom. The weakest often collapsed on the ice, dragging axes in frostbitten hands. 'Their frozen corpses sometimes had to be hacked free,' recalled Luise Mauer.

Outside the headquarters building the Reichsführer's car pulled to a halt. Koegel, newly promoted to Sturmbannführer (major) and officially confirmed as commandant, stepped out to greet him. Followed by Langefeld, the men strode through the camp gates to inspect a lineup of excited women guards. Himmler then joined Koegel in his office to hear in detail about the ongoing revolt by Jehovah's Witnesses. These women's refusal to sew military mailbags had grown over recent weeks into a full-blown protest, which Koegel had failed to break, and the commandant was raging with anger.

Many prisoners later recalled the protest, marked by the religious women's extraordinary resilience. First they were forced to stand in ice and snow for hours on end, until several collapsed with frostbite. As soon as Koegel's new stone bunker was complete, the women were locked inside, nine to a cell, in total darkness, and given no food. Still not a single woman had broken ranks.

Koegel now appealed to Himmler for even greater powers to break them. The only way, he insisted, was to beat them. Random beating took place every day, but Koegel asked for authorisation to use the *Prügelstrafe*, a method used in male camps. This 'official' beating meant strapping a prisoner, stomach down, over a wooden horse, or *Bock*, and giving them twenty-five lashes on the buttocks with an oxhide whip. Such punishment could only be authorised by Himmler himself, and to date he had refused to permit it. Why he had withheld it at Ravensbrück is not recorded, but we know that Johanna Langefeld believed such thrashing to be unnecessary, and had made clear she was opposed.

Himmler asked first to see the Jehovah's Witnesses in their cells before he made his mind up. Koegel was proud of his new prison. Stone-built, surrounded by pine saplings, it was impenetrable. Dorothea Binz, the forester's daughter, and Maria Mandl, a more experienced Austrian guard, had been chosen to run the new bunker, which made them almost as powerful as Johanna Langefeld – and certainly more feared. No other women guards might enter without Koegel's say-so.

By the time Himmler arrived on 4 January 1940, the Jehovah's Witnesses had been in the bunker for three weeks. A guard unlocked one of the doors. Himmler and Koegel peered into the darkness at a huddle of starving, freezing women crammed inside a wet, stinking cell. The women were praying. Himmler was heard to comment that they were 'in a bad way'.

Amongst the first group were Erna Ludolph and Marianne Korn, their white headscarves barely visible as they prayed in silence in the freezing darkness. Both women had spent at least five years in prisons for refusing to give up their faith; both had been amongst those hosed down like 'drowned mice' during the Lichtenburg riot.

It was day twenty-one of their bunker arrest when Himmler appeared, recalled Erna Ludolph. 'He let the guards open a cell door for him and he got a fright at the sight of us.' Now he spoke. 'Don't you see your God has left you? We can do with you whatever we like.' One of the Jehovah's Witnesses in the cell responded: 'God will save us. And if he does not – we will not serve you.' Himmler stopped outside another cell. Again he asked for the door to be opened and peered inside. He asked a young woman called Ruth Bruch if she was ready to renounce her faith. She said: 'I will only follow God's rules.' Himmler replied, 'Shame on you, girl,' and turned to go.

Himmler and Koegel strode down the Lagerstrasse as the commandant raised other matters of concern, many of which arose due to wider developments in the war. The round-ups in Poland, for example, meant that growing numbers of Polish women were arriving every day; soon more new living blocks would be required.

The Jewish block was already packed to capacity, as was the *Strafblock*, which was filling with new asocials. The *Revier* could not cope with the number of sick, queuing to see a doctor, most of them black or green triangles, covered in sores. To the commandant all such women were 'hags, bitches and whores', but Himmler rarely used such language; to him they were 'useless mouths', 'lives not worth living'.* Although Koegel was not to know – the matter was far too secret – Himmler already had plans for dealing with them; by January 1940 the first extermination of lives not worth living had begun – not in the concentration camps, but in German sanatoria, and in the name of euthanasia.

Hitler's intention to weed out Germany's mentally and physically disabled – including the blind, deaf, mute and epileptic – in order to rejeuvenate the race (and spare the public purse) had long been known inside the party, but as always the Führer trod carefully, wary of public opinion at home and abroad. He knew that such a programme of mass killing could not be authorised by any law, however it was camouflaged, but the cover of war would obscure its criminality. For this reason Hitler waited until war was under way before directing, in October 1939, that the 'euthanasia' begin. Public reaction

* These terms were not invented by the Nazis: other expressions such as 'empty human husks' and 'ballast lives' had been common in the science of eugenics in Germany and many other countries, notably the United States, since the nineteenth century.

could still not be guaranteed, so an elaborate cover story was devised to fool both Germans at home and possible observers abroad.

First, a special office inside Hitler's own Chancellery was set up to run the 'euthanasia' programme, code-named T4 after the address of the office itself, situated at Berlin's Tiergartenstrasse 4. Killing centres were set up inside existing hospitals and sanatoria – five in Germany, one in annexed Austria – and a 'commission' of doctors, all sworn to secrecy, would diagnose the incurably ill and the insane.

Many practical arrangements were made for disguising what was going to happen. A 'Limited company for the transport of invalids in the Public Interest' was established to manage bus transport, while hospital staff in the sanatoria were taught how to send out lying letters to the families of the dead.

The decision on how to kill had been more difficult. In Poland, Himmler had ordered that all mentally ill be shot, but in Germany mass shooting of sanatoria patients was ruled out: it would expose what was happening. After some discussion amongst top doctors, a proposal to use carbon monoxide gas was agreed. One idea was to administer it by releasing the gas into hospital dormitories when patients slept. Others suggested introducing gas into a purpose-built sealed chamber through showerheads. A decision was taken to test the gas-chamber idea at one of the chosen T4 killing centres. The results were satisfactory, and were almost certainly conveyed to Himmler shortly before he arrived for his Ravensbrück tour.

The inspection over, Himmler was eager to return to Koegel's office, where his friend Pohl was waiting to talk about poultry. Johanna Langefeld was also hoping to catch a word with Himmler and entered the room just as his discussions with Pohl began. Her purpose was to lobby against Koegel's request for the *Prügelstrafe*, but when she entered Koegel's office, a curious scene greeted her, as she described to Grete Buber-Neumann after the war:

> In one of the rooms at the commandant's building Himmler sat next to the man who was in charge of the chicken sheds at Pohl's estate nearby. Also present were the upper ranks of the camp administration and several female guards. Himmler was in deep discussion of the business of chicken-rearing both from the point of view of research on racial genetics but also from the point of view of the farmer himself. Pohl had brought his chief chicken farmer with him to join in the talks with Himmler.

Langefeld tried to talk to Himmler about Koegel's request for official beating, and was hopeful that the Reichsführer would agree with her, but he turned a deaf ear. 'Instead he continued his enthusiastic discussion of the business of rearing a racially perfect breed of chickens.'

Langefeld told Grete that she knew Koegel had been trying behind her back to win Himmler over to the *Prügelstrafe* plan. 'This was the time that Langefeld saw Koegel for what he really was, a sadistic criminal,' Grete commented. The commandant had even claimed that the beating was necessary to protect Langefeld herself, telling Himmler that she had been 'attacked by a prisoner with a knife, though this was entirely untrue'.

Commenting further on Langefeld's account, Grete said it was clear to her that Langefeld was already a 'deeply confused woman' at this time in the life of the camp. 'The conflict between morality and immorality was taking place inside Langefeld's head. On the one hand here was a woman who supported the Nazi racist insanity and anti-Semitism, but on the other hand she was ridden with guilt because women were to be sentenced to corporal punishment.'

Langefeld stayed in Koegel's office, and eventually had a chance of speaking to the Reichsführer. 'But when he had heard everything he wanted to hear on the subject of chickens, he ignored what Langefeld had been saying, and issued the order that beating should in future be permitted at Ravensbrück,' said Grete.

However, the imprisoned Jehovah's Witnesses were not the first to be beaten. Instead, Himmler ordered Koegel to release them from the bunker and assign them to hard labour in the snow. He seems to have grasped what Koegel could not: no amount of beating would make the Witnesses renounce their faith. Moreover, apart from their refusal to do war work, or recognise the Führer, they were model prisoners; it was against their faith to lie or escape and they made excellent domestic servants. So not long after his visit to the camp, Himmler ordered that the Jehovah's Witnesses be employed in SS homes as cleaners – he even offered some to Oswald Pohl for use on his nearby estate.

Before he left Ravensbrück Himmler signed the release form for a German communist prisoner who'd tried to escape in July and had been imprisoned in the punishment block ever since. Her release was postdated by three months to 20 April, which was Hitler's fifty-first birthday. It was a tradition to release prisoners on the Führer's birthday.

A month after Himmler's visit the first *Prügelstrafe* lashings took place. The victims were Mariechen Öl and Hilde Schulleit, caught stealing a pot of lard. Himmler had personally approved the beating; under the new orders the Reichsführer had to be consulted each time.

As the orders also required, a doctor attended, and the chief guard, Langefeld, was obliged to look on. The *Bock* was positioned in one of the bunker cells, the women were tied face down, and once their skirts were lifted each was thrashed on the buttocks twenty-five times. On this occasion Koegel himself took the oxhide whip.

By the time that the *Prügelstrafe* lashings began, many new prisoners had been locked inside the bunker cells vacated by the Jehovah's Witnesses. Marianne Wachstein, imprisoned in the wooden cells the previous summer, had continued to protest about her treatment, for which she was locked up in the new bunker in early February 1940. Just as she had described the first prison building, so she was able to give an account of this one, and once again, because she wrote it all down having just been released – she would be set free three weeks later – the details were fresh in her mind. Her writing even switches back and forth from past to present tense, because she knows the events she describes are still going on.

Marianne said she was brought before Langefeld in early February 1940 and told her crime was 'slandering the state', and that the sentence was twenty-eight days in the new bunker. When she protested, Langefeld told her the punishment 'came from Koegel'.

They took her to her cell 'without considering that my feet were bleeding and frozen and that I was so emaciated that every single rib could be counted and in some places my skin was hanging like an empty sack'. She passed out, and Zimmer tried to wake her 'by spilling water on me through the opening where the food is pushed in'. When this didn't wake her, Zimmer ordered an assistant to hit Marianne with a broomstick through the same opening. 'When I woke up from the blows I was wet all over and had to stay in the cold winter in a wet dress and wet socks – in solitary confinement there are no shoes – for several days.'

A guard called Kolb opened Marianne's cell door to insult her.

> Frau Kolb said: 'It stinks in here,' so I replied: 'I beg your pardon, Frau Aufseherin, but I can't possibly stink, I wash my body three times a day.' Upon that she answered: 'All Jews stink,' and I had the feeling that if I said another word she would hit me, so I kept silent. When she opened the door again in order to bring in the food she said again: 'You stink,' and closed the door quickly.

Marianne came across other prisoners in the bunker, including Alma Schulze, 'an Aryan, beaten so badly that she screamed at night: "My eyes, my eyes" because she was afraid she would lose her sight'. The 'mad' opera singer, Hedwig Apfel, had never been released since her days in the wooden cell block; Marianne heard her screaming.

The misery grew worse. Marianne's 'wet pitch-black cell' was one floor below ground level.

> I was in cell 15 and it was so wet that the wall with the window was covered with black mould. In solitary confinement one is not allowed to do anything. Not to read or write, just to sit. Not walk either. It was not heated in any way. The winter was very cold. Even though I am quite tough I was freezing, shivering, teeth chattering in complete darkness. I sat in the prison block with bleeding feet.

After a few days, Marianne was released. As she left her cell she heard Apfel screaming. 'She did not sound human any more, more like an animal. I think that there is another insane woman because another voice could be heard that also had nothing human in it any more.' In her report she wrote that it was precisely five o'clock on 23 February 1940 'when God took me out of there by transporting me here'. 'Here' was the Vienna hospital where she was now recuperating. Her journey back to Vienna had been quite the opposite of her nightmare journey to the camp in her nightgown nine months before.

As Marianne was waiting in a Berlin prison for her place on a train, a doctor put ointment on her frostbitten feet, and at other prisons en route back to Vienna she received more kindness and 'very good food', including on one occasion 'two slices of real rye bread and butter'.

On arrival in Vienna Marianne was admitted to a hospital. The conditions of her return remain unclear, but we know she was released to give evidence at her husband's trial, to be held in Vienna, on trumped-up charges of corruption relating to her Jewish family business. Given her sickness, however, she couldn't testify immediately, so she was allowed to recover, and in hospital she found the strength to write her report on Ravensbrück, addressing it to an official of the court – a Herr Hofrat Dr Wilhelm.

Marianne had no fear of being sent back to the camp, so she made no attempt at self-censorship, even presenting her report as testimony. Just as she had believed in Ravensbrück that she could protest to the SS commandant, as if he hailed from a normal world, so she thought the Viennese courts would listen to her warnings and prosecute the Nazi perpetrators on the basis of her evidence. She even suggested that lawyers check her claims by talking to other witnesses in the camp, and she named some of the Austrian Jewish 'rabble', including Toni Hahn, Ami Smauser, Louise Olhesky and Kate Piscaul. She also mentioned the Austrian prisoner Susi Benesch – the latter 'a communist and Aryan' – who had been in the bunker with her.

'But in order to interview these witnesses it is necessary to get them out of Ravensbrück, as they would not dare to tell the truth in the face of medieval punishments, involving lashes, beating and the straitjacket,' wrote Marianne.

As Marianne wrote her report on Ravensbrück she had no idea where events she had witnessed were leading. At this time the very first gassing centres, commissioned under Hitler's new euthanasia programme, were only just being set up. Her report therefore speaks to us from before the Holocaust, and its innocence is startling. Yet Marianne clearly believed she had witnessed a monstrous crime in the making, and that she had been released by God to tell the world.

Soon after her report was written, however, Marianne Wachstein was sent back to Ravensbrück, and in February 1942 she died in one of those same euthanasia gassing centres. Whoever received her report in Vienna hid it for the duration of the war, and Marianne's warning to the world only came to light in the late 1950s, when it was anonymously handed in to the camp memorial's archives.

*Chapter 5*

# Stalin's Gift

In February 1940 a train from Moscow pulled to a halt on the Soviet side of the Brest-Litovsk Bridge on the Russian–Polish border. Figures climbed down the side of a coach, feet feeling for icy rungs. One by one they jumped the last long gap, thumping down onto snow. Twenty-four passengers in all, including two women, stood staring across the bridge into Poland, wondering what was to happen to them.

The group were Germans, all former communists, released from Stalin's Gulag and now being handed back by Stalin to Hitler. The bridge they stood on had already given its name to many a treacherous pact, as over the years Germany and Russia had fought over Poland. These men and women were a gift to Hitler, this time as part of the Nazi–Soviet pact.

One of the two women was thirty-nine-year-old Margarete Buber-Neumann, widow of Heinz Neumann, once a leading light of German communism, now dead – a victim of Stalin's purges.* During the 1930s Neumann, like others amongst the German communist elite, spent time in Moscow. Grete, his wife, also a true believer, followed her husband there in 1933. After staying in the famous Hotel Lux, where foreign communists – including Olga Benario – gathered to pay homage at Stalin's court, the couple left for Spain to start a communist newspaper but instead became entangled

* Neumann was Grete's second husband. He was Jewish, as was her first husband Rafel Buber, the son of the Jewish religious philosopher Martin Buber. Grete's sister Babette also married a Jew. 'Maybe the fact that they both married Jews was some sort of protest against their father,' says Judith Buber Agassi, Grete's daughter. 'Their narrow-minded father [the director of a Potsdam brewery] did not like the Jews.'

in the lethal internecine power games between the German Communist Party and Moscow. Neumann displeased Stalin in ways that he never understood. Like millions of others he was declared an enemy of the people and on return to Moscow was arrested and shot in 1937 after a show trial. A year later Grete was also arrested and sent to hard labour at Karaganda, a Soviet concentration camp in the Kazak Steppe.

Her husband's execution, and two years in the Gulag, brought Grete low. Before leaving for the border, she and the others spent time in Moscow, where they were restored to a semblance of health in case the Nazis should get the wrong idea about their treatment. But nothing could restore her faith in communism. She returned to her native Germany a bitter woman, disgusted by Stalin and dreading what the return home would bring. The Nazis were certain to punish her for high treason committed during her years as an active communist.

The prisoners were taken off by a German escort and packed into the back of a truck, which headed for the Polish city of Lublin, 170 kilometres southwest, where they were held for a few days in Lublin Castle, in the heart of the old city. Here from the windows Grete could see the marks of the first six months of war. Much of the city had been reduced to rubble, and under the orders of Odilo Globocnik, Himmler's police chief in Lublin, Jews were being herded past the castle towards an area that would become their ghetto.

Inside the castle prison, Grete heard from fellow prisoners – nuns, students, professors, doctors – of the wider Nazi terror, and she met Polish communists, who still hoped to escape east to Moscow in the belief that this offered salvation. She tried to disabuse them of their faith in Stalin, but as she spoke 'their faces turned to stone'.

Grete was moved on west to the Gestapo jail in Alexanderplatz, Berlin. Known as 'the Alex', it functioned as a clearing house for prisoners bound for concentration camps. Each night the women talked about 'the KZ' and when they might be going. On Fridays a list was read out of those being sent the next day. One Friday a Jewish doctor called Jacoby heard her name was on the list. That night she hanged herself from a water cistern, but she was discovered and cut down. The next day she was sent to Ravensbrück.

Here in the Alex Grete met a young German communist called Lotte Henschel, for whom Soviet Russia was still the land of hope. Lotte asked Grete about her experiences there, and when she had heard Grete out, she sat on the mattress beside her and wept. 'What have we got to live for now?' she asked.

On Friday 1 August 1940 Grete heard her name called on the KZ list, and the next day she left for Ravensbrück. Fifty women travelled on Grete's transport, but only two made any impression. One, whom Grete took to be a prostitute, declared she was only going for re-education and would be out in three months. The other was a Jehovah's Witness, who looked like a schoolteacher and who prayed constantly.

They arrived at Fürstenberg station in the mid-morning. Dogs growled as the women were piled into trucks and taken to Ravensbrück. Grete stared with fascination and dread at the Nazi camp, which she instantly compared with what she had known at Karaganda. The high wire, the guards, the shouting – the Russians had yelled '*Davai, Davai*' and the Germans shouted '*Raus, Raus*' – were familiar. But as she came closer differences emerged.

The Nazi camp was tiny by comparison. When Grete arrived it stood at about 4000 women; Karaganda alone held 35,000. Her memory of Siberia would always be of winter, the time of year she left it – a vast, grey, freezing encampment, where armies of prisoners, mostly men, toiled on the Kazak Steppe under a steel grey sky.

When Grete reached Ravensbrück it was early August and the German camp was into its second summer; outside the gates the limpid water of the Schwedtsee was lapping against the reeds in a warm summer breeze. Once inside, she noticed to her astonishment beds of bright red flowers; ahead lay a kind of street lined with sixteen wooden blocks, all of them painted, and beside each block stood a small sapling.

The paths near the gate were covered with sand, which was freshly raked in intricate patterns. To the left, near a watchtower, was an aviary. Peacocks stalked slowly around and a parrot squawked. At Karaganda there were no flowers or green lawns, but this was eerier somehow, and for a few moments all was silent.

Yells and shouts broke out again as a column of prisoners came by and Grete saw German camp inmates for the first time: not the shuffling ramshackle figures – men mixed with women – of the Gulag, but women in orderly ranks, each wearing a clean white kerchief bound round her head, with striped dress and dark blue apron. 'Left, right. Left, right. Heads up. Arms by your side. Line up.' Their faces were impassive. They all appeared identical. A siren howled. Now women came marching in columns of five from all sides. Some carried spades on shoulders, and what most astonished her was that they were singing 'silly marching songs'. It was all very Prussian, and Grete knew about Prussian ways, having been brought up in Potsdam.

Further on, she noticed more and more 'Prussian thoroughness'. The new arrivals' details were registered, files stamped, dossiers checked and double-checked. Some of the women shouting orders were wearing the same striped clothes and were obviously prisoners. In the Gulag too prisoners had been co-opted to do much of the work. Grete had got used to seeing Russians in those roles – they were called the 'brigadiers' and were usually men. To see women, German women, as 'brigadiers', shouting orders at other prisoners, 'some with evident relish', shocked her.

Even the woman now searching Grete's head and pubic hair for lice was a prisoner, a Jehovah's Witness. Meticulously the woman probed, brandishing cutters, but found nothing and Grete was spared the razor. The shower attendants wore white overalls and they too were prisoners.

In the Soviet camp distinctions were made between political and criminal prisoners. Here the inmates were divided into many categories, as Grete discovered when she saw the small coloured triangles. As a political prisoner, she received a red triangle with the number 4208.

After the shower Grete stood before a camp doctor, who slapped his leather-booted calves with a riding whip. Dr Sonntag, a recent arrival, picked Grete out from the line. 'Why are you here?' he demanded. 'Political,' she said. 'Bolshevist shrew,' he snapped. 'Get back in line.' Soon Grete was wearing the clothes she had seen the marchers in: striped dress, blue apron, white headscarf. No shoes were worn in the summer and her group walked barefoot over the sharp gravel to Block 16, the reception block. With the other fifty newcomers, Grete waited outside it, rubbing the soles of her feet to dislodge sharp flints.

Beyond the huts she saw the high camp wall and counted five lines of barbed wire. The midday sun reflected off a blackboard with a skull and crossbones painted in yellow. Earlier that day a Gypsy woman had run into the wire, she heard. 'You'll see where later. When they pulled her body away her fingers were torn off and they're still there.'

A guttural voice yelled names in an accent Grete recognised as Swabian.* The woman was Blockova of Grete's block. She was another political prisoner with a red triangle and a green armband too. Grete found her repulsive; someone said her name was Minna Rupp.

Inside the block rows of women were knitting grey socks. Because of the growing numbers, new arrivals were held separate while their registration was completed, and as they waited they knitted soldiers' socks. The hut 'seemed like a palace' compared with the clay huts in the Gulag. There Grete walked into the steppe when nature called; here there were proper lavatories and basins, as well as furniture – stools, a table and lockers. The new prisoners were each given their mess kit – mug, spoon and bowl – and two woollen blankets, a white sheet and a long, blue and white striped nightdress. They were told the rules about washing, eating and folding.

Later Grete learned from other inmates about the many more rules enforced by Minna Rupp. Rupp treated a scratch on a prisoner's mess tin as

* From Swabia, a region of southwest Germany.

sabotage, and would report the offender, who might get a thrashing or a spell in the bunker. Women must not smile at each other or shake hands, or they'd be sent outside for 'standing punishment'.

The Blockova even checked the way the women put on underclothes, in case they had tried to stuff paper inside for warmth. No one must visit the toilet at night and there must be absolute silence at all times. But nothing mattered more to Minna Rupp than making the bed. A crinkle in the blanket meant the whole of Sunday was spent making beds as punishment. Repeat offenders got the *Strafblock* or the bunker and twenty-five lashes, and Minna Rupp knew the terror of this herself after being sent to the *Strafblock* for stealing half a carrot. She was later thrashed as well.

Grete's friends in the newcomers' block were mostly Poles, resourceful women, many of them teachers. They'd been here some weeks already and had learned a great deal about how to cope. One of them, a music teacher, showed Grete the trick for bed-making. She used a stick to square the mattress off, so that Rupp could not complain. They all loathed Rupp. Until recently only asocials and criminals had held these prisoner posts, but there had recently been a coup, Grete learned, and now communists like Rupp held the jobs too.

As the days passed, Grete watched out for the communists. She probably knew some of them of old and dreaded meeting them. Like the other communists she'd met since leaving Russia, none of them would want to hear what she had to say about Stalin. They wouldn't like the fact that she'd been brought here from Moscow. They'd be suspicious.

After just a week the showdown came. Grete was sitting knitting socks when a group of prisoners wearing red armlets came into the block and called her name out. One was Minna Rupp. The trio took Grete into the sleeping quarters, where normally no prisoner was allowed in the daytime, and their interrogation began.

'You were arrested in Moscow? Why?'

Grete realised this was a political interrogation on behalf of the communists in the camp. She answered frankly, telling the story of Stalin's persecution.

'All right,' said Minna Rupp. 'You're a Trotskyist, that's what you are.' By this, Rupp meant that Grete was a traitor to the true Stalinist cause. From that moment on she was blackballed. Grete had once again been branded an enemy of the people, this time by her former German comrades, now fellow prisoners in a Nazi concentration camp.

The communist coup that ousted the green- and the black-triangle prisoners from their Kapo jobs was a major turning point in the early life of the camp. It took place some time in the spring of 1940. Until then the SS practice of selecting asocials and criminals as Kapos had continued; the appointment in November of Olga Benario as Blockova was an exception. Then early in the New Year the political prisoners took a deliberate decision to try to displace the 'greens' and 'blacks'. They had several reasons.

In January 1940 a skeletal figure came hobbling out of the camp bunker and saw sky above her. Hanna Sturm, the Austrian carpenter, and one of the communist stalwarts, had been released after six months in solitary confinement. She had lived in darkness, on starvation rations, and very nearly died.

Back in her block, Hanna was able to relate to her comrades the horror of the bunker, and how she'd been given up for dead. In the freezing winter months she had fallen sick. She couldn't eat and grew so weak that she just lay on the ground. One day she overheard Zimmer outside the cell door saying, 'She may as well kick the bucket in there,' but Hanna 'didn't want to do Zimmer that favour'. She forced herself to chew on her bread. Spitting out the solid, she managed to swallow enough of the goo that remained to slowly build up strength.

One Sunday a friendly guard called Lena was on duty. Hanna knew that 'Lenchen', as she called her affectionately, was kind because she'd met her once before coming to the bunker. On that occasion the two had gone to repair a window in the commandant's villa, and Lenchen said to Hanna: 'See how well the SS live here, and we work hard and earn a pittance.'

Now Lenchen opened Hanna's cell door and said: 'Oh, so you're in here. You're looking pretty bad, what's up?'

'I'm sick, very sick,' said Hanna.

'How can I help? In here you're going to die, that's for sure.'

Lenchen fetched Hanna food as well as medicine, and the next day she even brought a doctor in to see her – a doctor who was only in the camp a short time. The doctor said Hanna was probably suffering from typhus. Her strength crept back, however, and, suddenly, at the end of January 1940 Koegel came to her cell.

'Do you want to go back to your block again?' he demanded.

'Yes sir,' responded Hanna.

'Well out you go. But I'm warning you – I don't want to hear of you again.' Hanna's release delighted her comrades, but the sight of this once strong Austrian now reduced to skin and bone was further evidence of the plight they were all in.

Since Hanna's confinement many other communist comrades had been brought to breaking point. One had thrown herself on the wire, and the official beatings on the *Bock* had spread a new despair. A woman called Irma von

Strachwich was locked in the bunker for shouting 'Heil Österreich!' When she continued to shout, she was given fifty lashes and died. Soon everyone seemed to know a prisoner who'd been thrashed. Ira Berner, another German communist, said: 'I've seen women whose skin was one big bloody mass so that they couldn't sit down for weeks. Many had damaged kidneys and other injuries.'

It was the 'unofficial' beating of the Austrian communist Susi Benesch that caused the deepest shock of all. Rosemarie von Luenink, another German political prisoner, saw what happened:

> At that time we had to unload bricks from a ship. Benesch was so weak that she couldn't carry the stones any more and she collapsed. Rabenstein hauled her up by force, placed the stone on her shoulder again, and then she collapsed for the last time. Rabenstein thereupon lifted up the stone herself and smashed it down on Benesch's head. Benesch died instantly and we saw how the blood streamed down from her mouth and her tongue hung out.

After Susi's murder the communists' morale plunged, and Käthe Rentmeister, one of the old hands, led a move to restore their pride. She called the faithful to her bunk in Block 1 and they discussed what to do. All had served long terms in prison before the camp. They'd cut their teeth in the 1920s at trade union and communist youth meetings, in the corridors of the Reichstag or at Red Help committees. Most had husbands, brothers, fathers in the camps. Käthe Rentmeister's brother was in Sachsenhausen – he was one of those sent to build Ravensbrück. Maria Wiedmaier was the hardest of all. She'd worked for the secret service of the party and organised strikes in Holland and France. In 1935 the Gestapo told her the man she loved was dead. Maria refused to believe them so they took her to a cemetery and exhumed his corpse for her to see, then locked her up.

The women agreed that Koegel had all but crushed them and there was no defence against the SS, but they could surely defend themselves against the likes of Margot Kaiser, the *Lagerschreck*, and her green- and black-triangle criminal Kapos. Each one of those here had at some point been sold out to the SS by one of Kaiser's 'bandits'. The red-triangle political women couldn't even meet without being betrayed by Kaiser, while the asocial and criminal 'filth' stole from fellow prisoners and enjoyed privileges denied to the rest.

If the communists could somehow procure these Kapo jobs their lives might improve. It was not impossible, especially as there was reason to believe they might have Johanna Langefeld on their side. Langefeld had recently agreed to the women's pleas that the political prisoners should all live together, here in Block 1. The *Oberaufseherin* appeared to approve of the way they kept order, and one or two of their leading figures had won her confidence. Everyone knew that Langefeld was fighting her own war with the SS. She needed new allies, even among the prisoners.

Some argued against doing the work of the fascist SS, but others said that the Jewish block had transformed since Olga Benario had taken the Blockova's job. The Jewish women held their heads higher now, organised poetry readings, and the Jews were even talking of staging a play.

If the communists didn't grab some power, others would beat them to it. The Czechs had jobs and Langefeld was even favouring certain Poles. Maria Wiedmaier was in touch with Olga, who was urging them to go ahead; it was their duty, as communists, to survive. Maria said they should try to get jobs not only in the blocks but in the kitchen and the offices so that they could gather information, work undercover. Like Olga, Maria was Moscow-trained and hadn't forgotten how to infiltrate – she would never forget, as her later Stasi file shows.

Hanna Sturm came up with a plan. Some weeks after her release from the bunker she had been sent to work in the SS supplies cellar, where asocial Kapos were in charge. Prisoners in the cellar were often accused of theft. Hanna proposed framing one of the asocial gang leaders there. She and a group of others set about stealing cigarettes and alcohol from the supplies and planted the loot on a prominent green-triangle block leader. They made sure Langefeld got to hear of it.

The plot worked better than they'd hoped. Furious at the betrayal of trust by her asocial Kapos, Langefeld removed almost all of them from their jobs and threw Margot Kaiser into the *Strafblock*. By late spring it was the political prisoners who held most of the influential camp posts, and a communist called Babette Widmann replaced Kaiser, securing the top prisoner post of *Lagerälteste*. No thought was given to the fate of those ousted; the communists were too busy helping their own.

Barbara Reimann, a young communist from Hamburg, had been arrested in 1940 for writing letters to German soldiers at the front, urging them not to fight. She arrived at the camp just after the communist prisoners seized power and found many comrades ready to help her. Minna Rupp, now Blockova of the newcomers' barracks, signalled to the new *Lagerälteste* that Barbara had arrived, and through Langefeld it was fixed to move her to the political block. Here older German women, some of whom she had once known as mothers of school friends, took her under their wing.

Not surprisingly, the newly empowered communists were determined not to see their influence undermined. When in August word spread that Grete Buber-Neumann had arrived and was telling lies about Stalin, a decision was taken to condemn her as a Trotskyist. The communist women said later that the SS brought Grete out before them one morning like a trophy, saying: 'You want to know how bad a concentration camp can be? Ask her about Stalin's camps.' According to Maria Wiedmaier it was Olga Benario who proposed that Grete be blackballed, and the communist committee agreed.

Grete's daughter, however, doubts that Olga was the one who blackballed her mother. The two women had met briefly in the Hotel Lux in Moscow in the 1930s. 'My mother only ever expressed admiration for Olga,' says Judith Buber Agassi, sitting in a blaze of sunshine in her villa on the Israeli coast. Judith nevertheless makes clear that her mother was always bitter about her treatment by the rest of the communist clique.

> For my mother it was the worst thing. She saw the communists as bigots. Anyone who was not a communist was of less value, even in the camp. If someone was in the camp because she was a prostitute, or a Jehovah's Witness or a Jew it was all the same. The communist women were a narrow-minded bunch. My mother couldn't stomach it. After the war they made out that they had helped the Jews in the camp. But of course that was not possible. They couldn't help.

It was not entirely true that the non-Jewish political prisoners were unable to help the Jews. Through Langefeld and those in her inner circle, the new political Kapos gleaned intelligence that they could pass on to the Jewish women. Maria Wiedmaier continued to smuggle Olga's letters out, so she could write to Carlos and Leocadia more freely than through the camp mail. Furthermore, the Jews themselves clearly believed the new red-triangle Kapos could help them, which was why not only Olga but other Jewish leaders in Block 11 supported the political prisoners' grab for power.

Käthe Leichter had delighted the Jewish block with her poems and storytelling from the moment she arrived in the autumn of 1939, and had since made a name for herself in the camp. A social democrat, Käthe was not privy to the communists' intelligence, but she had her own contacts, and in April she heard that an old friend from Vienna, another social democrat called Rosa Jochmann, was being brought to the camp. Käthe arranged to meet her as soon as she arrived. She told her that she, Rosa, was to be a Blockova.

Rosa recalled later: 'We weren't allowed to talk with Jewish people, but of course we did. On my first day Käthe and I walked all over the camp and she told me what I was going to do and gave me my instructions.' Käthe was sure that Rosa was cut out for a Blockova job, because she knew her strength of character of old.

That Rosa Jochmann should have joined Käthe Leichter in Ravensbrück was in itself extraordinary. The two women knew each other on the Vienna workers council in the late 1920s, battling to improve the conditions of women at work. Their backgrounds were very different. Rosa, born in 1901, the daughter of a washerwoman and a steelworker, started work in a factory at the age of fourteen. By her twenties she was active in Austrian trade union politics, and became head of the Socialist Women of Austria, a social-democratic body.

Four years Rosa's junior, Käthe Leichter, born in Vienna in 1905, came from a prosperous, cultured Jewish family, but rejected her bourgeois roots and went to Heidelberg in Germany to study sociology under the philosopher Max Weber. When the First World War broke out Käthe organised pacifist protests and was sent back to Austria; when the Nazis came to power her doctorate was annulled.

As women's rights rose up the agenda of Austrian liberals, both women were at the forefront of the campaign, though Rosa, who believed in industrial action, did not always see eye to eye with Käthe, who called for negotiation and tried to tell the working classes what to do. Nevertheless, the two became friends and worked together until Austria's new fascist leaders banned their activities. In early 1938, by which time Hitler's annexation of Austria (the *Anschluss*) looked inevitable, both women were active in the anti-fascist resistance and were at risk of arrest; neither took her chance to escape.

Käthe Leichter's husband Otto, editor of an anti-fascist newspaper, and their two boys left for France, expecting her to follow but for reasons her family never quite understood – probably because she found it hard to desert her mother, still living in Vienna, and because she didn't believe she'd be caught – Käthe delayed her departure. Eventually she booked her train out but was arrested the evening before she was due to leave.

When Rosa Jochmann arrived at Ravensbrück about six months after Käthe she was astonished to see her friend there, and even more astonished by what she said. She later recalled Käthe's briefing word for word, giving a rare insight into the desperate rationale behind the prisoners' decisions to cooperate with the SS in the early years of the camp.

As soon as she heard of Rosa's arrival, Käthe negotiated her appointment as a Blockova, and this alone shows the influence that certain prisoners – even Jewish social democrats – had managed to secure. She told Rosa:

> Don't forget that it isn't like being on the trade union works council back home. You will be an extended arm of the SS. And you always have to agree with the SS. And if they beat somebody to death in front of you, you have to ask the person who's being beaten: Why did you do such a thing?

> And so on. At the same time you have to do what you can to try to prevent the guard from giving a report. And as block leader you must stand in the corner and shout at everyone during roll call: 'Attention. Everyone look towards the guard.'

Käthe told Rosa it often happened that a guard would beckon somebody out of line with their stick, perhaps because she hadn't sewn something on right, or for some other irrelevant cause. 'And she beats the woman nearly to death under your eyes,' said Käthe.

> You are standing next to the scene and you are forced to pretend to be outraged by what the prisoner has done as well, and you say: 'Why have you done this, who do you think you are?' And you have to pretend to be outraged as well. But you have to try to take the guard to one side and say to the guard: 'Frau Aufseherin, I cannot understand this, she is normally such a well-behaved person.' And you say, so don't give her a report. I will put her on lavatory duty. Or make her carry the food for two months. You must always agree with the SS. Always.

Käthe's brutal pragmatism about the position of the Jews shocked Rosa most of all. At the end of her speech Käthe turned to her and said: 'Rosa, and if the SS want you to say, "Stinking Jewish women," what are you going to do?'

> I said: 'No I will not say that, Käthe. You can do what you want but I'm not going to say that.'
>
> And Käthe said: 'Then you can't become a leader of the block. You will be unable to do it. You have to say it.'
>
> So Käthe gave me my instructions. She said: 'You cannot contradict the SS. They are all stupid, evil and cruel. But you might just be able to help if you cooperate with them a little by being diplomatic and agreeing with them.' And that was the truth. Käthe Leichter was right.

Käthe's conviction that cooperating with the SS was the only way to survive may have reflected her faith in negotiation, as well as her experience of the 'celebrities' work gang in the camp. The celebrities gang – so called because they had princesses and prima donnas amongst them – were at one point suddenly left to do as they pleased. Clara Rupp (no relation to Minna), the German communist and teacher, was one of the 'celebrities', and recalled in a memoir:

> Prisoners liked nothing more than to fool the guards, break the rules. Some groups were so good at it that they almost didn't care about the SS at all.

> It once happened that a prisoner smuggled a wonderful azalea branch out of the nursery into the political prisoners' block. The theft was discovered because the commandant's fresh flowers were not delivered that day. But the theft was so well organised that the smugglers were not discovered, which gave them great happiness.

Such tricks, she says, were far easier to get away with later on, when the camp numbers grew so vast that the SS reign of terror became more erratic, more diffuse. Like many women imprisoned there from start to finish, Clara looked back on the first years as the most terrifying, simply because the SS control reached into every corner: every individual 'lived in imminent danger'.

And yet, says Clara, back in 1940 one group of women briefly found freedom. They were building a new road to the camp when they were suddenly told to down tools because building materials had run out. As there was no work – and no chance of escape – no guard was assigned to watch them. A friendly green-triangle Kapo was left in charge, recalled Clara.

> So the Jewish prisoner Käthe Leichter starts to talk to the green triangle. And Käthe tells the woman the war will soon be over and that Hitler is finished and the Kapo – a good-natured woman arrested for carrying out abortions – believed her. Soon we were leading the green triangles and not the other way around. This turn of events was mostly due to Käthe from Vienna. She was the most prominent member of the group and developed the most particular abilities in this matter. She was very good at arranging things. Since she was Jewish she wasn't allowed to have newspapers, but as I had friends in high places I got newspapers for her. When Käthe gets her newspaper she forgets the danger and flips it open, studies, and even forgets who and where she is.

Another prisoner, a German called Elisabeth Kunesch, supported Clara's report about the road-building gang. She was there from the start and remembers the gang to this day, in particular a woman called Käthe. 'Käthe was Jewish and very intelligent and very kind. She used to sing to us as we heaved the stones and made us forget the pain.'

According to Clara there was a real princess on the celebrities gang too; she had been denounced by her cook for saying bad things about Hitler and was very musical. 'If you asked her she would hum any part of the orchestra.'

There was another university doctor, Maria, 'a walking encyclopaedia' who taught Clara English history for an hour every evening:

> She herself was an original character: tall, with a lot of brown spots, often with lice, quite a big belly. She used to wrap herself in anything possible as protection against the cold, but usually lost it all again. Many stupid people made fun of her but the clever ones were her friends. I loved the way she longed for open skies, meadows and forests.

There was Anni from Prague, once secretary to Tomáš Masaryk, president of Czechoslovakia between the wars. 'She always knew the best rumours in the camp.' Even when there was work to do the celebrities marched out singing. 'If the Princess is in a particularly good mood she sings the "Rose" aria from *Figaro.*' The friendly green-triangle Kapo gave out the tasks 'with a wink from our side'. Then the women talked philosophy or literature.

> Every day there was discussion in some corner of our road which was under construction indefinitely. Once nearly all of us were in a trench laying stones, and as we had already sung Mozart, Beethoven and Bruckner, Maria began a lecture about Romanticism and we were so absorbed that we hadn't noticed a guard coming from the laundry. I stepped on Maria's foot and she started scolding me till she saw the expression on our faces. The guard chose to take it out on me and yelled 'I will teach you how to work, just you wait,' and I was put to work in the laundry, brushing dirty sheets and coal sacks.

The celebrities talked of returning home soon, or they'd talk of Marx and about the dispute in the Jewish block between the communists and the social democrats. They would hear how Käthe argued with Olga about whether capitalism contained the seeds of its own destruction.

> Some say Hitler's power has been underestimated. Sometimes we move out to work even though it's raining because we're in the middle of a topic that has to be finished. Ours was the best work gang of all; we worked for ourselves and not for the Nazis. Käthe was our real gang leader. She was always lively and gentle. She tells us one day she has a plan to fit a motor on her barrow. We laugh with all our heart. She shows us the letters from her two lovely boys.

Kathy Leichter, Käthe's granddaughter, and daughter of one of the lovely boys, says that even today the family still ask themselves why Käthe didn't leave Austria when she had the chance. 'She could have got out to safety with the others,' says Kathy, a film maker, who lives on New York's Upper East Side. 'Most women didn't think they were in danger. But Käthe knew. So as you trace her story you want to shout at her all the time: Get on that train. Go on, get on it. Why were you not leaving, for God's sake? Leave, Käthe! But she doesn't.'

I asked what she thought Käthe was like. 'She looked a little like me,' said Kathy, who has long black curls tumbling around her shoulders and big dark eyes.

> But she was bigger. She was quite a manly woman. And like me, she was a woman with a job, juggling care of the children. She studied childcare and the rights of home workers and she talked to seamstresses and asked what their problems were. She had been trying to make a better world, especially for women, and in Ravensbrück too she tried to carry on. And she was cultured. She knew every painting in the Louvre. But she is also hard to know. I am searching always for her voice. It was blocked. I just get occasional glimpses. Through others' memories, or her poems. Or the play.

Thanks to Käthe, the celebrities knew all about the play. 'Only the Jewish block could organise something like that,' said Clara. The play was called *Schumm Schumm* and an entire script was written down, but it was fake, so as to seem harmless, in case the play was discovered. Käthe, along with another Austrian Jew, a lawyer called Herta Breuer, devised the real script; the words had to be learned by heart and spoken only on the day. The story was of a Jewish couple and their daughter who were released from a concentration camp. They were sent into exile on an island where Jewish features were seen as divine and Jews were treated as royalty. There were several allusions to the camp: the Jewish mother passed out on arrival and nothing would revive her until '*Appell, Appell*' was whispered in her ear.

Preparations for the play caused excitement, and many non-Jewish women helped the Jewish dramatists, particularly with the costumes, which 'were made with love and care out of nothing,' Clara remembered – from bits and pieces 'organised' – filched – by other prisoners. The women had dresses made of lavender-blue headscarves brought in by Czech prisoners 'and organised for us by friends,' said Clara. Jewels and ornaments were made from silver and gold paper, also organised by friendly prisoners, as was the paper for the men's tailcoats. The island savages wore sand couch-grass skirts; Gypsies in the matting workshop smuggled the grass out.

The play was staged in the Jewish block on a Sunday afternoon. Amongst those in the audience were many Blockovas and Stubovas from other barracks, and because they came, ordinary prisoners came too.

The next day disaster struck. In Block 2, a separate group of prisoners were caught dancing, and when the guards reported them they complained that the Jewish block had staged a play so why shouldn't they dance?

At first it looked as if the entire Jewish block would be punished, along with everyone who attended, but 'negotiations' were carried out, and only those who took part in the production were punished. Clara doesn't tell us who the prisoners were, but they were obviously all from the Jewish block, and must have included the creators, Käthe Leichter and Herta Breuer, as well as Olga Benario, the Jewish Blockova.

There was nothing their non-Jewish comrades could do to help them now, whatever Kapo positions they held. The six were offered a choice of punishment: twenty-five lashes or six weeks in the bunker. They chose the bunker and all six were crammed into one small cell. They had food only every fourth day. The women were 'deeply troubled on release', said Clara. 'One told us: "Being so hungry, I couldn't stand hearing anyone chewing. The one who had something left while the others had already finished their food was hated most. Because they went on chewing." They warned the rest of us to avoid the bunker at any cost. They were in a very bad way.'

*Chapter 6*

# Else Krug

Within weeks of her arrival at the camp, Grete Buber-Neumann found herself standing on the Appellplatz waiting to see if she might be selected for a Blockova's job. Her Polish friends had put her up to it.

By August 1940 the red triangles' takeover had gone further than anyone had predicted: not only were communists being allocated camp jobs once held by the asocials and criminals, but so were other political prisoners of all persuasions. The Poles, fearing they would never secure such posts themselves, hoped nevertheless to benefit from the coup by proposing their own candidates, and they felt sure that Grete had the necessary qualities. They hoped she'd be appointed as their own Blockova instead of the loathed Minna Rupp, but the plan went wrong.

'I was lined up with half a dozen other women in the square, and there we waited, standing to attention. Langefeld came along and subjected us to a detailed inspection, asking each of us where and why we were arrested and how long we had been in the camp. She picked out a number of us, including me, and said I was to go to Block Two.'

When Grete told the Poles her destination they were horrified. Block 2 was full of the dreaded asocials. Sure enough, she found that entering the block was like 'stepping naked into a cage of wild animals'. Her first task was to serve the black triangles their lunchtime soup. As she tried to do so, hungry women seethed around, holding out their bowls, shouting: 'Get on with it! Our table first.' Grete lifted her ladle and froze in panic, with no idea how to control the menacing crowd.

When the politicals ousted the asocials and criminals from power they hadn't reckoned on having to live amongst them as their Blockovas, but for the SS, putting political women in charge of asocials was just another opportunity to 'divide and rule'. The political prisoners appointed to asocial blocks were horrified by what they had to face. When Nanda Herbermann was made Blockova of an asocial block she found characters there 'from Sodom and Gomorrah'. The filth repelled her: 'They took their dishes into the bunks at night and relieved themselves of their greater and smaller needs in them.' The moral 'filth' horrified her more, especially the lesbianism. Nanda had lived a sheltered life, working for the bishop of Münster, editing an anti-Nazi Catholic newspaper. 'Their fate had also made them hard and egotistical,' she said.

> A number of them were true monsters, and I was always afraid of them; morally they were completely ruined, and in addition they were sly and deceitful and therefore dangerous. Others were just children, outcasts from society who, under the terrors of the SS, could only get worse.

Some of the women were driven to such despair that they threw themselves on the wire, 'and in the mornings their charred remains hung from the electric fence'. Bertha Teege, a German communist, saw such a body hanging from the wire the day she arrived in July 1940: 'A young asocial from Vienna had attempted to escape. The body, still hanging, was shown to us as a deterrent.'

Bertha, who already knew other politicals here, soon secured an appointment as Blockova and was sent to Block 9, another asocials block. Here she took over from the ousted Munich *Puffmutter* Philomena Müssgueller, another coup victim, who had been thrown into the *Strafblock*. Teege found asocials on one side of her block and Gypsies on the other. Controlling them was a 'Herculean task', but she soon linked up with her old communist comrade Luise Mauer, now Blockova of the 'notorious criminals block', and together 'we set right what we could – got hold of certain things and never let them catch us'. The two had contacts with the 'camp administration'.

The Gypsies, said Bertha Teege, were more controllable than the prostitutes. 'The Gypsies are like dependent children, squabbling, fighting each other and then friends again.' The asocials however were decrepit and unable to cope. More than 80 per cent had venereal disease as well as TB.

Who these asocial women were, however, Teege doesn't say. Like her fellow politicals, she seems never to have asked a name. Apart from the early notorious Kapos like Müssgueller, Kaiser and Knoll, the camp's common criminals and asocials almost never had names. By the SS and prisoners alike, these women were viewed as an anonymous mob. Prisoners used the SS language to refer to them: they were 'asocials', 'pests', 'hags', or – as Grete said – 'wild animals'.

Even when a black- or green-triangle Kapo is remembered for an act of kindness she is rarely granted a name, though Edith Sparmann did recall Goldhansi, as her Blockova was nicknamed. Goldhansi was kind to Edith, who was very young when she first arrived, and was split up from her mother. 'Goldhansi found my mother for me and arranged for us to meet,' said Edith. Goldhansi probably also lost her job in the coup.

Although we learn a lot about what the political prisoners thought of the asocials, we learn nothing of what the asocials thought of them. Unlike the political women, they left no memoirs. Speaking out after the war would mean revealing the reason for imprisonment in the first place, and incurring more shame. Had compensation been available they might have seen a reason to come forward, but none was offered.

The German associations set up after the war to help camp survivors were dominated by political prisoners. And whether they were based in the communist East or in the West, these bodies saw no reason to help 'asocial' survivors. Such prisoners had not been arrested as 'fighters' against the fascists, so whatever their suffering none of them qualified for financial or any other kind of help. Nor were the Western Allies interested in their fate. Although thousands of asocials died at Ravensbrück, not a single black- or green-triangle survivor was called upon to give evidence for the Hamburg War Crimes trials, or at any later trials.

As a result these women simply disappeared: the red-light districts they came from had been flattened by Allied bombs, so nobody knew where they went. For many decades, Holocaust researchers also considered the asocials' stories irrelevant; they barely rate mention in camp histories. Finding survivors amongst this group was doubly hard because they formed no associations, nor veterans' groups. Today, door-knocking down the Düsseldorf Bahndamm, one of the few pre-war red-light districts not destroyed, brings only angry shouts of 'Get off my patch.'

Only in the 1990s did researchers begin to appeal for asocial survivors to come forward, but of the handful who responded, none gave real names, and none, they said, had been prostitutes themselves. Käthe Datz admitted to having been imprisoned as an asocial for being 'work-shy'; she skipped off from her factory job one day to help her sick mother.

> They said I was a traitor and committed a crime. Then I was put on a mass transport so I cried. Amongst our group were many working girls – prostitutes. I remember them walking in their high heels across the cobbled

> streets of Fürstenberg on the way to the camp. I can tell you how they went for those women: 'You swines. We will teach you a lesson,' and then came the kicking and the beating.

And yet, thanks to Nazi bureaucracy, a few clues have survived as to who these women were. So extensive was the police records system set up by Himmler so as to monitor and then exterminate Germany's underclass that Bomber Command failed to destroy every file. Nowhere was this bureaucracy more extensive than in Cologne, which had one of the biggest red-light districts in Germany. In part because these women served the military, they were extensively monitored and controlled. The city was flattened by Allied bombs in 1942, but during the post-war clear-up a handful of random police files were dug from the rubble and stacked in archives in nearby Düsseldorf, where they have remained unread for nearly seventy years.

Here is Anna Sölzer's file. Just twenty when her police photograph was taken in 1941, Anna was pretty, with a dark felt hat. Found living in a single room, she was arrested on suspicion of spreading venereal disease. She had no papers because they'd been destroyed when a house she was living in was bombed. The arresting officer found her alone in her room, 'but we know men had been there,' he noted. 'At first she refused to get out of bed and go to the police station saying she didn't want to.'

Anna was five months pregnant. She said she didn't know the father. As pregnant women could not be imprisoned, she was put under curfew until the baby was born and then rearrested.

The file contains a statement Anna made as part of a report into the 'genetic history' of the family. She never knew her father. Her mother died when she was six. 'I was in an orphanage until I was eight years old. I went to a house where I learned how to work in a family as a domestic help, but the money was so bad I went to work in a factory.' Even there she only earned twenty marks a week, so she started to work as a prostitute. The police report found that Anna came from a 'genetically worthless' family and showed '*widerspenstiges freches Benehmen*' – wilful, cheeky behaviour.

Anna told police she wanted to continue working as a prostitute until she had the baby. 'I will find work for the sake of the child. I know the police are watching me. If I do something else bad I will go to the KZ.' While she was pregnant she fell ill and went to the baby's father for help. 'But he was married and had a family.' When the baby – Bodo – was born he was taken to a Cologne orphanage. Soon afterwards she was taken to Ravensbrück.

Also on Anna's file is a telegram from the authorities at Ravensbrück to the Cologne Gestapo saying that at 16.00 on 28 December 1944 Anna died of TB. Tuberculosis was certainly prevalent in the camp, but by 1944 it was often given as a cause of death to cover up murder. The Cologne Gestapo received the standard camp letter issued in such cases: 'Please inform her family of the death. They cannot look at the body and it is not possible to have the ashes for reasons of hygiene.' The Cologne Gestapo replied to KZ Ravensbrück saying that Anna's only family was her son Bodo, who was now three. 'The child will inherit. He is now living in an orphanage. Please send her possessions to him via the Cologne Youth Department.'

Ottilie Gorres's life story also emerged from the rubble. Ottilie was in care from the age of two. She was not employed when arrested and 'drinks all day in pubs', said the Gestapo interrogator, who found Ottilie's family to be 'genetically flawed'. Items taken from her when she was admitted to the camp – a brooch and a comb – were awaiting collection, said a note. She had died in Ravensbrück.

More women's faces stare out of more files, all telling similar stories. Elisabeth Fassbender grew up in a Cologne orphanage and was arrested for stealing a coat. She too died in Ravensbrück.

From the start the proportion of asocials in the camp was about one-third of the total population, and throughout the first years prostitutes, homeless and 'work-shy' women continued to pour in through the gates. Overcrowding in the asocial blocks increased fast, order collapsed, and then followed squalor and disease.

Unused to following rules, the asocials were always more likely than most others to be picked on for some small crime such as failing to make a bed correctly, and then they'd be sent for a beating or to the *Strafblock*, returning in a far worse state. From Bertha Teege's testimony it seems that some of the political Blockovas were as ready as the guards themselves to report asocial charges for crimes.

Bertha complains that there was nothing she could do to help these women, as they were always 'fighting, sneaking and lazy' and refused to obey the rules. Women could now be sent to the *Strafblock* just for shortening a dress, shaving eyebrows or cutting their hair, she observed. 'Strangely enough, many asocials liked such vanities, most of all the lesbians.' One young girl was sent to the *Strafblock* for laziness. 'She opens her dress in front of me to show me her breast – eaten away by frost and vermin. Next morning she is dead.'

When a raid on the SS canteen stores took place, the asocials were blamed and all had to stand for hours without food while the block was searched, so they were 'collapsing like flies'. The search was unsuccessful. 'Nothing found apart from pathetic secret messages and love letters by the asocials.'

What struck many of the new political Blockovas was not just the disorder in the asocial blocks but the lesbianism, which spread as the overcrowding crammed bodies close together. Nanda Herberman had no doubt that lesbian sex was most prevalent in the asocial blocks. She watched in astonishment, praying for these 'lost souls'. 'They performed the most depraved acts with each other.'

Her explanation was that the women were so 'morally deprived' that 'sexuality was the only thing left for them'. There were no men around. The SS men reviled the women prisoners, and sexual contact meant dismissal. The only other men seen around the camp in the early days were male prisoners brought in from Sachsenhausen and Dachau to build new blocks. So permanent was this male slave labour force that by the summer of 1942 they had been housed in their own barracks, and a small men's camp had come into being, adjoining the women's camp towards the back. But the men's camp was behind the camp wall and ringed with barbed wire; sexual contact was almost impossible, although not unheard of.*

The prisoner lesbianism took many forms. Some of the women who came here were already openly gay. Although female homosexuality was not a ground for arrest, a handful were listed on the records as *lesbisch* and wore black triangles. Many confirmed lesbians made no attempt to hide their sexuality, some taking on men's names – Max, Charlie or Jules – and sometimes preying on others who were not gay but were easily drawn in. Other women offered sex in return for food. Grete knew of a lesbian 'prostitute' called Gerda; 'prisoners brought their rations of margarine and sausage to her'.

As even Nanda acknowledged, however, many of the women turned to sex because they were lonely. Several of the 'lost souls' – Gisela, Freda and Thea – even sought affection from Nanda herself. Throwing their arms around her, they 'shook with pain over their botched lives'. One woman died in Nanda's arms; she was 'riddled with disease'. Thea was sick and haunted the block at night scaring the sleeping women. 'Thea,' recalled Nanda, 'you no longer knew what you did.'

> One night I lay sleeping on my bunk and you beat me with both fists. You stood there draped with blankets. I wanted to take hold of you, but you began to run and you jumped out of the window and ran, with me and several other inmates behind you until we finally caught you. It was an icy winter night. And the SS came and put Thea in a straitjacket. The SS came with dogs. I had to come with you to the cell building, where a straitjacket was put on you before my eyes. You never made it out of the death house alive.

* According to Maria Bielicka, a Polish prisoner, prostitutes from the asocial blocks sometimes had contacts with men in the small male camp. 'They knew how to do this. One was caught and was put in the bunker and given twenty-five lashes.'

The 'work-shy' Käthe Datz survived the loneliness of the asocial blocks partly because she had a friend, Helga. The two were together when they were shaved. 'When we left the shower I hardly recognised her. She says: "Hey it's me." I said: "Really – is it you?"' Käthe smuggled in a little comb, and when her hair grew back she used it to put her hair up, and to keep down the nits.

> They could have taken anything from me, but not my little comb. I combed my hair every day. You could find red traces, and that finished people off who couldn't bear to scratch all the time. No ointment was given. You couldn't go and see a doctor for lice. So they got eczema. I was fine though. I sorted this lice problem out. Others started to give up. They sat in the corner. In the morning the coffee was given out – water with something in it. Many didn't even get that. When they saw they were almost finished they didn't give them anything any more. They waited till they died, then carried them away.

The asocials who found solace in sex were evidently no good at keeping their lovemaking quiet. Other prisoners often spoke of beds shaking and even collapsing in the night. And as lesbianism was a crime in the camp (though not outside), many were caught and thrown into the *Strafblock*, where, as Bertha Teege put it, 'sexual aberrations got out of hand'.

Erika Buchmann, who became Blockova of the *Strafblock* in 1942, said lovemaking in the block was 'sometimes shameless and unrestrained', but couples tried to seek privacy too. 'If you got up at night to use the toilet, you had to wait because the little couples were in the small compartments with the doors locked.'

Grete Buber-Neumann was also shocked by the lesbian sex, but she was more sanguine than some others, perhaps because her eyes had been opened in the Gulag. As Grete saw it, the prostitutes there had been far better off, precisely because there were men in the Gulag camps too and they could 'continue their work'. Here in Ravensbrück the prostitutes, 'used to long hours and irregular life-styles, were broken and brutalised by the camp discipline'.

More shocking to Grete than the sex was the way the women continually denounced each other. 'Sworn friendships were sealed one day and broken in squabbling and enmity the next. All day the women accused each other, throwing the vilest insults around. The most wounding insults touch on their professional honour, the accusation that they had charged low rates. "Look who's talking," was a typical opening. "Took drunks in a doorway for a mark a time."'

And yet, as with Nanda, Grete's criticisms seem to mask affection for these women too. Perhaps this was due to her friendship with Else Krug.

When in the late summer of 1940 Grete had first entered Block 2 and tried to serve the soup, she panicked as the 'mob' menaced her. But then, to her amazement, one of the mob stepped out and called for order. 'A powerful woman with lively brown eyes, a determined chin and a voice like a sergeant major' was how Grete described her rescuer, who suddenly jumped up on a stool and bellowed: 'If you don't line up properly and stop mobbing the new Blockova the pots will go back to the kitchen and no one will get anything.' It worked like a charm, said Grete. 'After that I had no further trouble – for the moment.'

So thankful was Grete to the woman who helped her that she remembered her in her memoir. She was called Else Krug. And because she helped Grete, and later befriended her, Else Krug became one of the very few prostitutes in Ravensbrück to be given a name.

Unknown to Grete, a newcomer to Ravensbrück, Else was already a well-known figure around the camp; she had arrived with the first transport from Lichtenburg and was one of the first black triangles to be given a Kapo job, running the work gang in the kitchen supplies cellar – a job she had so far held on to, despite the communist coup. As a prisoner of some standing in the block, therefore, Else had a place at the top table in the day room at mealtimes, sitting next to the Blockova. It was here that she and Grete had a chance to chat, and get to know each other.

Else would often hark back to her past, talking of life as a prostitute in Düsseldorf, always with a twinkle in her eye. Her speciality had been sado-masochism, which she described in vivid detail. Some days she would turn to Grete and begin – 'What about a little nature study?' – and she would reminisce. 'Up to then I had considered myself a fairly enlightened person,' Grete recalled, 'and I'd read a certain amount of scientific literature on the subject, but Else's stories of the requests she met with in the course of her profession and how she complied with them made my hair stand on end.'

Yet Grete came to admire Else. 'She told her stories in a dry, matter-of-fact way, and there was a certain professional pride in her attitude. She knew what she was and she insisted she was good at what she did.' Else never 'whined' or claimed as others did that they were going to reform when they got out. Instead she would muse: 'A few more years of camp and I'll find it hard to earn 300 marks in a night. Ah well, I'll have to invent something special to make up for it.'

Grete also learned that Else was very good at managing her kitchen work gang, and took a pride in it. Work on the gang was highly sought after, as the opportunities to smuggle out extra carrots, potatoes and turnips, and sometimes canned food and jam, were considerable – as too were the risks of being caught, or denounced by a political prisoner trying to muscle in. Probably the main reason Else Krug's operation had not yet been damaged, despite Hanna Sturm's smear campaign against asocials, was precisely because she kept her team – all fellow asocials – on a tight rein, making sure that the pickings were fairly shared. Else had become a mother to her kitchen gang, winning their loyalty, observed Grete.

In all their talks, however, Grete never seems to have learned anything about Else's background, or about her own mother, though Grete often heard about others.

Once a month, like all prisoners, the asocials could write a letter, and one of the Blockova's jobs was to pre-censor the mail, so they got to read all the letters. Those to mothers were the most heartrending. One wrote: 'Dear Mother, I know I've been a great shame to you but do write me just a word. I'm so unhappy. When I come out I will make a fresh start; really I will. Send me a mark.' Sometimes on a Saturday, when mail arrived, there would be an unexpected answer for one of them 'as some mother's heart had been touched, and the tears would flow in streams, but by Sunday all remorse had been forgotten and the insults would start flying again.'

In most cases, however, the women never heard back, either because their letters never reached their destinations or because the family had disowned them. Some women never wrote at all, perhaps because they had lost touch with their families long ago and never had the courage to tell them what they'd become, or where they were, which seems to have been the story in Else's case. We know from other sources that Lina Krug, Else's mother, had no idea where her daughter was.

Families of the asocial prisoners are as impossible to trace as the women themselves. Often they had no fixed address, or were themselves behind bars. After the war, if the missing women did not return, such families tended to stay silent. They may have guessed where their loved ones had been sent, but they saw no purpose in trying to make their voices heard; families received no help or compensation either.

Else's mother, however, did make her voice heard. After the war she appealed to the German survivors' body, the communist-run Vereinigung der Verfolgten des Naziregimes (VVN: Organisation for the Victims of Fascism), saying that she sought news of her daughter. Lina Krug seems to have had no idea that her daughter might have been a prostitute, or why she had been arrested. She simply asked the VVN for any information they might have. The letter also set out something of Else's family background, revealing a life story that was quite different to the asocial stereotype as found in the Nazi police files.

The letter states that Elisabeth (Else) was born on 3 March 1900 in Merzig, Saarland, the tiny German state bordering France, and the family lived in the nearby town of Neudorf-Altenkessel. Else's father, Jacob Krug, was a master tailor, a respected figure in his community.

At some time in the 1920s she left home to live in Düsseldorf. Lina doesn't explain when or why Else left, but we know from other records that Jacob Krug died young, so Else may have gone to find work when the family lost its breadwinner. In the 1920s, as unemployment rose, young women flocked to the cities to work for wealthy families as domestics.

Why Else fell into prostitution is unclear, but probably, like so many others, she simply needed money. She was hardly going to tell her mother what she was doing, which was probably why the two lost touch. When she became a prostitute is also hard to pinpoint, but we do know – thanks to further remnants of Nazi documents – that by 1938 she was working at a brothel in Düsseldorf. The address was 10 Corneliusstrasse, then in the heart of the town's red-light district.

As well as the personal files on prostitutes, a number of police logbooks were also pulled from the rubble of German cities, and among them is the daily logbook for 1938 kept by Düsseldorf police. The well-thumbed volume lists every raid on every Düsseldorf brothel carried out that year. The raids happened monthly, and each time about twenty-five regulars were logged in the book and then sent home.

The same addresses and the same names crop up again and again. An address at 10 Corneliusstrasse was often raided. Some of the prostitutes were brought in with a husband, who was often a pimp. Most had a few personal effects – a few Pfennigs and a hat, which they left at the desk and signed for when they were booked in. One of the regulars from 10 Corneliusstrasse also brought a bag, and this was Else Krug.

On the night of 30 July 1938 the brothel at 10 Corneliusstrasse was raided again, but this time the usual suspects were not sent home. They had been arrested under Himmler's new 'asocials' law, one of the very first mass arrests of its kind, which meant they were soon to be sent to Ravensbrück. Before she left the police station, Else Krug signed for her bag in her usual firm, clear hand.

By her second year in Ravensbrück Else must have been out of touch with her mother for at least four years, probably many more. Then she lost any chance to write home even had she wanted to. One by one – thanks to the red triangles' takeover – the remaining asocial Kapos were ousted from their posts, and when eventually Else's smuggling was betrayed, she too lost her job in the kitchen cellar. She was punished with a term in the *Strafblock*, heaving bricks and unpacking coal barges, but it didn't break her, says Grete, who sometimes snatched a word with her friend through the *Strafblock* wire.

'Grete,' said Else once, 'they think they can get me down with work, but they're wrong; I'm tough, I can get through it better than any of them.'

The brutality in the *Strafblock* was worse than it had ever been. A new guard, Gertrud Schreiter, a baker's daughter from Cologne, beat with a leather belt. She 'became savage', said the women, and prisoners said later they could recognise the *Strafblock* prisoners because the brutality 'turned them into beasts' too – 'the last remains of any softness vanished from their faces and their posture'.

Towards the end of 1940 Koegel decided to make use of the beasts by ordering them to carry out the thrashings on the *Bock*. So frequent were the thrashings by now that Dorothea Binz and Maria Mandl were overworked, and they needed help. If they agreed, the *Strafblock* women were given extra food and sent back to their ordinary blocks. There was no shortage of volunteers. Nor was there a shortage of hands ready to beat the trapeze artiste Katharina Waitz after she had escaped for the third time.

Following her two earlier attempts, Katharina had been imprisoned in the *Strafblock* for many months, then some time in 1941 she found a way out again. So breathtaking was her escape this time that many prisoners later recounted how she did it. Under cover of darkness, without alerting guards or dogs, she slipped out of the *Strafblock* and reached the SS canteen. She climbed on top of the building and, using a pillow and blanket to protect herself from the current, she scaled the electric fence and jumped down to the ground on the other side. Using all her high-wire skills she clambered over the five rows of barbed wire and up the four-metre-high wall, also using the pillow and blanket to get over the barbed wire at the top. Katharina then leapt to freedom, but by morning the guards had found the blanket in the barbed wire and the pillow on the roof of the canteen.

The prisoners who remembered how Katharina got away also recalled how she was brought back. While she was being hunted, the whole camp was made to stand in punishment, but it was the *Strafblock* she had escaped from that was punished most severely. These women were forced to keep standing, without food, until Katharina was found.

It took three days and nights. On the fourth morning she was discovered hiding out in Fürstenberg. The female guards with dogs sent to hunt her down reappeared, with Koegel close behind, pushing Katharina in front of him. She was bitten all over and covered in blood and dirt.

Doris Maase, observing from the *Revier* window, watched as Koegel took

Katharina to the *Strafblock*, telling the prisoners, crazed with starvation and anger: 'There she is. You can do what you want.' Another witness heard Koegel say: 'Let's bring her to the beasts – let our beasts have fun with her,' and as soon as he handed Katharina over to the *Strafblock* women 'the worst of them pushed her into the bathroom, swearing at her, and they beat her to death with chair legs'. Her corpse 'must have looked terrible', said Doris Maase, because for the first time in the camp's history a dead body was taken away by the camp doctor, Dr Sonntag, and his medical orderly, and not by prisoners.

Not long after Katharina's death, Koegel organised another mass thrashing, and once again the *Strafblock* was involved. The Jehovah's Witnesses working in the rabbit hutches were refusing to collect angora wool, saying it was being used for soldiers' coats, and therefore amounted to war work. Koegel flew into a rage and ordered scores of the women to be thrashed, but for such multiple flogging he needed extra hands, so he called on volunteers from the *Strafblock*. Once again, inducements were offered and volunteers came forward, but Koegel needed more.

Perhaps because of her powerful appearance, or because he noticed her haughty pride, Koegel specifically selected Else Krug as one of the thrashers. Like the others she was offered the chance of release from the *Strafblock*, but Else said no. Koegel called Else to his office, and Grete got to hear what happened next.

Koegel was not used to prisoners opposing his orders, so he was furious and shouted at Else, ordering her to obey.

'No, Herr Camp Commandant,' said Else. 'I never beat a fellow prisoner.'

'What, you dirty whore? You think you can pick and choose? That's refusal to obey an order.' Else shrugged, but was grimly determined. 'Take the whore away,' snorted Koegel. 'You'll have cause to remember me, I can tell you.'

*Chapter 7*

# Doctor Sonntag

Olga, like all the prisoners, lived in almost constant fear of winter. Only in the earliest weeks of spring was winter absent from her thoughts, but as her letters show, from summer onwards the prospect of the first snows haunted her. 'For me the life in summer is so much easier and I hope not to spend another winter here,' she wrote to Leocadia and Ligia in June 1940.

For now the easier summer prompted pleasant thoughts of Anita. 'Give her lots of sport. In her abilities and character, does she take after me or her father?'

There was even hope of release again, signalled by reference to a money transfer. The recent releases of the Jewish prisoners Ida Hirschkron and Marianne Wachstein may have revived her optimism.

Soon after writing this, however, Olga was shut in the bunker for her part in staging the Block 11 play. The absence of a letter between July and November 1940 suggests that she and the five others were locked up until winter came back, and it was to be a cold one: guards found prisoners' bodies frozen to the bunker floors. Olga's November letter to Carlos – still in his Brazilian jail – hints at her incarceration. 'Here are a few lines as a sign of life for you ... when one has passed so much time it ought to be possible to survive a little more.'

When Olga emerged from the bunker she found many changes. Workshops were being constructed. There were 1000 more prisoners and two new barracks. The Poles were the biggest group, and asserting new authority.

Dismissed as Blockova, Olga was sent to the brick-throwing gang. Barges loaded with bricks for the new buildings moored each day on the Schwedtsee. Women would form a human chain, throwing bricks along the line until the load was cleared. Olga's hands were hardened, but others' softer palms tore to shreds, then froze numb as frostbite set in. Some might get a paper bandage or a dab of iodine at the *Revier*, but not the Jews. The head doctor, Walter Sonntag, refused to treat Jews.

In December Olga heard again from Carlos, and Leocadia enclosed a photograph of Anita. 'The little sweetie is already completely different from the baby I knew,' she wrote back. 'I have been following events through the newspaper as best I can.' She urged him again not to lose hope. 'As for me, I am steeling myself to get to the end of winter.'

That Olga had seen a newspaper meant she was at least back in touch with comrades in other blocks. The events no doubt included Hitler's seizure of France, Belgium and the Netherlands. In the pages of the *Völkischer Beobachter* she would have read the Nazi propaganda claiming that Britain really was about to sue for peace. Hitler had even signed pacts with Japan and Italy.

But how long would Hitler's all-important pact with Stalin last? To Olga and her communist comrades this was the biggest question of all. The women told themselves that Stalin's purpose would soon become clear. Olga now updated her miniature atlas, showing where the fronts had moved, and she began to fashion her own miniature camp newspaper using tiny scraps of paper.

The Reichsführer's desk diary for 14 January 1941 stated: 'Himmler left Berlin at 10.30 hours and spent the day and night in Ravensbrück.' A year after his first visit Himmler was heading out again to the frozen Mecklenburg forest, and this time he was spending the night. Most probably he spent it not at Ravensbrück itself, but five miles down the road at a small forest estate called Brückenthin that he had acquired and where he had installed his mistress, Hedwig Potthast. Aged twenty-seven, she had been his secretary since 1936, and in 1940, as relations with his wife Marga deteriorated, the couple became lovers. He called her 'Häschen' – 'Bunny'.

That Himmler should take a mistress was entirely in keeping with his views on extramarital relationships. It was Himmler who in 1937 had introduced the concept of *Lebensborn* ('Source of Life') homes – institutions where SS officers could procreate outside marriage with selected Aryan women, in order to produce a constant supply of perfect Aryan children. In 1940 he passed a procreation order urging German soldiers to procreate outside marriage in order to produce as many children as possible, to resupply the gene pool. This need not be done secretly, he proclaimed.

His own procreation was a different matter. Perhaps for Häschen's sake – he seems to have had a genuine affection for her – he made sure their encounters were discreet, choosing as a love-nest a simple forester's house on the edge of this tiny village.* Although Brückenthin was secluded, however, it was also convenient. Just five miles from Ravensbrück, Himmler could always combine a visit to Häschen with a visit to the camp, using the latter as cover. Just across the lake lay the village of Comthurey, where Himmler's chicken-breeder friend Oswald Pohl had his estate; Pohl's wife offered to keep an eye on Häschen. Five miles further on lay the village of Hohenlychen, with its famous SS medical clinic. Top officers and Nazi politicians were often to be found there, receiving treatment from Professor Karl Gebhardt, who was only too willing to help out his old friend Himmler by watching out for his lover down the road.

Although Häschen was on Himmler's mind, however, the January visit to Ravensbrück was important to him. He had matters to discuss at the camp, and wished in particular to meet with Walter Sonntag, the senior SS doctor. Snow had even been brushed from the ornamental garden outside Dr Sonntag's office; the *Revier* had been scrubbed from top to bottom and the entire camp smelt of wet wood.

Since his last visit Himmler's priorities had moved on. Poland had been crushed and was being reshaped in order to create the Führer's promised German utopia. A new concentration camp at Oswiecim – in German, Auschwitz – in southern Poland had been opened to hold Polish resisters. And the country's two million Jews were being driven from their homes and forced into ghettos or reservations in parts of annexed Poland – or the Greater Reich – called 'the general government'.

As yet no official solution had been proposed – except perhaps in private – as to what to do next with the Jews. As Hitler was now making plans to invade the Soviet Union – the entire Russian land mass might fall into German hands – one idea was to push the Jews out to the very edge of the continent and leave them there. Such a solution, however, posed its own problems: the Jews would somehow have to be rendered barren, or else they would never be destroyed. Not surprisingly, therefore, one of the subjects on Himmler's mind in early 1941 was mass sterilisation. He had been in discussion with his favoured doctors as to whether such experiments should be conducted here at Ravensbrück.

With the prospect of a new front opening up to the east, Himmler was also thinking about how Ravensbrück and other camps could better use their

* Häschen's parents were unhappy about their daughter's liaison with Himmler, so she insisted that the relationship be conducted in secret.

resources to support the war effort. In the early days hard labour had largely been used as a means of torture and discipline, but the war looked set to last longer than expected, and prisoner labour was being more usefully deployed.

The related question of what to do with those prisoners who could not work was also very much on Himmler's mind. It was now more than a year since Hitler's T4 'euthanasia' programme had been launched, and in that time more than 35,000 German men, women and children seen as a drain on the nation's resources had been killed by carbon monoxide pumped into gas chambers hidden in German sanatoria. In Poland the T4 techniques had also been adapted to kill the country's mentally and physically handicapped, murdered in specially adapted mobile gassing trucks.

The Reichsführer had no authority over the T4 euthanasia programme, but he was always consulted on the operations. Just weeks before his visit to Ravensbrück, Himmler personally intervened when a crisis erupted at Grafeneck Castle, southwest of Stuttgart, one of the T4 gassing centres.

In December 1939 the castle's old coach house was converted into a gas chamber, and over the next twelve months 10,000 mentally and physically ill men and women were bussed to Grafeneck to be murdered. However, later in 1940 buses belonging to the 'Limited Company for the Transport of Invalids in the Public Interest' began to attract attention, and a local judge reported serious unrest. 'For several weeks gossip has been circulating in the villages around Grafeneck that things cannot be right at the castle,' he wrote. 'Patients arrive but they are never seen again, nor can they be visited, and equally suspicious is the frequently visible smoke.'

In November a local aristocrat and ardent Nazi, Else von Löwis, wrote a letter to party chiefs, asking them to tell Hitler that the killings were taxing the loyalty of the local population. She presumed the Führer didn't know of the killings, as no law had been passed authorising them. 'The power over life and death must be legally regulated,' she said. The murders were leaving a 'dreadful impression' on the local population. People were asking: 'Where will this lead us and what will be its limits?'

Else von Löwis's letter reached Himmler, who intervened at once. The letter touched a nerve, because it confirmed the risks of carrying out mass murder of citizens near to where ordinary Germans lived and were bound to take notice.

Himmler instructed that Grafeneck be 'immediately deactivated' in order to quell the unrest. 'The process must be faulty if it has become as public as it appears,' he asserted. Plainly, it was the fact that the killing had become public that was faulty, not the killing itself: soon after Grafeneck was closed two new killing centres opened in Germany, but under better disguise. And not only was the T4 'euthanasia' programme itself to be expanded, Himmler now planned to co-opt its gassing methods. Soon after the Grafeneck episode he wrote to the T4 chief, Philipp Bouhler, also head of Hitler's Chancellery, asking him 'whether and how the personnel and the facilities of T4 can be utilised for the concentration camps'.

Entering Ravensbrück's freshly scrubbed *Revier* for his talks with Dr Sonntag, Himmler would have seen for himself the growing need for a clear-out of useless mouths. The small wards were packed with pallid faces and the corridor lined with enfeebled naked women awaiting treatment. However, the new gassing plans were probably too premature – and too secret – to discuss as yet with a mere camp doctor. Instead, Himmler raised with Dr Sonntag the more urgent matter of gonorrhoea.

A few weeks earlier Himmler had instructed his chief surgeon, Ernst Grawitz, to order Sonntag to start experiments on Ravensbrück prostitutes to find a cure for gonorrhoea, and he was eager to hear the results. Himmler had long been fascinated by medical experimentation, and the outbreak of war had given his interest new purpose – to increase the life expectancy of German forces. Where better to carry out the experiments than on human guinea pigs in the concentration camps? At the male camp of Sachsenhausen mustard-gas tests had been carried out on prisoners to find a way to cure soldiers poisoned at the front, and at Dachau prisoners were being starved of oxygen to find out at what altitude a pilot would die.

The presence in Ravensbrück of scores of infected prostitutes offered a chance to explore curing syphilis and gonorrhoea. On Himmler's instructions, soldiers were being encouraged to use brothels while at the front. Regular sex, he believed, would increase their motivation to fight, especially if they could be protected from VD. But now he was angered to learn from Sonntag that the experiments had not even started yet. Grawitz had apparently failed to pass on the order to Sonntag, either because he had forgotten or perhaps because he didn't trust unqualified camp doctors like Sonntag to do the job properly.

Sonntag's main training was as a dentist and his medical qualifications were limited, but Himmler thought highly of him, as it was he who had carried out the mustard-gas experiments at Sachsenhausen. Sonntag had not hesitated to apply lethal bacteria to the skin of healthy prisoners, inducing monstrous swellings and causing excruciating pain. The Reichsführer SS therefore instructed Sonntag to start the gonorrhoea tests at Ravensbrück without further delay.

A tall man in immaculate black uniform, the skull of the SS Totenkopf (Death's Head) division on his cap, Dr Walter Sonntag struck quite a figure as he strode down the Lagerstrasse to the camp hospital, a bamboo cane tucked into one long leather boot. Prisoners recalled his aquiline nose, angular features and large ears. They also recalled his unusual strength: any woman struck by him invariably collapsed and fell to the ground.

The son of a postmaster, Walter Sonntag was born in 1907 in the town of Metz, in what was then German Lothringen and is now French Lorraine. Coming from such a contested border region – Lorraine had been fought over by Germany and France for centuries – Sonntag's nationalism was fired at an early age. At the outbreak of the First World War the villages he knew were the scene of renewed carnage. Under the terms of the Versailles settlement that followed, the Sonntags, like thousands of other humiliated Germans, were evicted and forced to start new lives. His father found work on the land, and Walter spent his young years playing with animals. By the time he left school he was drawn to the Nazi Party and decided to better himself by training as a dentist.

Though Sonntag first chose dentistry as a career, he later switched to medicine, attracted no doubt by the prominent role doctors were being given in fighting Hitler's new racial war. He quickly joined the Nazi Party, and along with hundreds of fellow medical students enrolled in the SS. The percentage of German doctors applying to join the SS was the largest of any single profession.

National Socialist ethics of racial cleansing were by the mid-1930s at the core of the medical curriculum. Nazi doctors were required to cure the 'whole' of the German race, not simply to focus on the individual. And in order to treat public health, doctors were required to eliminate the racially subhuman or the genetically impure, enabling the German gene pool to cleanse itself and thrive.

Walter Sonntag began a thesis in 1939 on 'social medicine' in which he compared the Führer's ideas to those advocated by the Spartans, or by the scientists of medieval times who would have killed off lepers had religious scruple not intervened. He also set out his views on sterilisation, stating: 'Reproduction by the genetically ill and asocial elements of a people will inevitably lead to the deterioration of the whole nation. Sterilising undesirables and eliminating them as far as possible is therefore a humanitarian project that offers protection to the more worthy parts of society.' His own earlier Catholicism clearly no longer restrained Sonntag, and nor did the fact that his sister Hedwig had developed multiple sclerosis, a chronic genetic disorder that she feared was a punishment from God for marrying a Protestant.

It was one of the many anomalies of the Nazi system that concentration camps should have had such an institution as a hospital at all. Everything about the camps seemed designed to cripple the inmates' health and ultimately to kill one way or another, not to treat or to cure. And yet if fit young prisoners were to be used as slave labourers, it made sense to treat them for day-to-day illnesses. Moreover, the Nazis were terrified of contagious disease spreading from the overcrowded, undernourished prisoners in the camps into the population at large. One of the chief functions of the hospitals, therefore, was to prevent killer plagues breaking out.

When Sonntag started work at Ravensbrück the *Revier* still showed traces of a normal hospital. Housed in an ordinary barracks, the sickbay had a 'ward' with sixty beds, to which the very sick were admitted. Temperatures were monitored and anyone whose fever dropped below 39 was sent back to work. It had a fully equipped operating theatre, as well as a pharmacy, radiography equipment and a pathology lab. Rules on hygiene were enforced, with bed linen changed regularly. There were daily 'surgeries' when in theory any prisoner could line up to see a doctor. The two female doctors, Dr Jansen and Dr Gerda Weyand, had both trained at reputable medical schools. Under them was a qualified nursing sister, Lisbeth Krzok, 'Schwester Lisa', and several other *Schwestern* who wore the brown uniforms of the Reich nursing sisterhood.

There was nothing normal in the daily array of injuries and ailments afflicting the women who lined up every morning, five abreast, outside the hospital entrance, complaining of dog bites, gashes from beatings and frostbite. Nor was there anything normal about the way that Schwester Lisa, known as the hospital *Schreck*, screamed at prisoners to be silent, made them strip, and lashed out at them as they waited in line. Dr Jansen would sit for hours with a mug of coffee, chatting, until her surgery time was over and the patients were sent away untreated. But the other female doctor, Gerda Weyand, showed more patience with the prisoners, more humanity. She asked them about their symptoms, examined them and never hit or abused.

The very presence of the prisoner staff lent a certain air of normality to the *Revier* too. As elsewhere in the camp, prisoners had been co-opted to help, and now they virtually ran the administration of the *Revier*. At a table in the corridor sat prisoner nurses with bandages, ointments and medicines. Surrounded by jostling inmates, they did their best to treat boils, eczema and cuts. The prisoner doctor Doris Maase, who slept at the hospital at night, answered cries long after others had gone.

And in the records office sat a woman with thick red hair and bright eyes. Stuck on the wall beside her was a picture of a sunflower, torn from a magazine left lying around by an SS doctor. Recently arrived from Prague, Milena Jesenska was a journalist, and had once been the lover of Franz Kafka. Now she filed the results of swabs taken from asocial prisoners, as part of Sonntag's test programme. Here too was Erika Buchmann, tall, blonde and blue-eyed.

Once a secretary for a Reichstag communist, Erika was now a *Revier* secretary, typing up long lists of the sick delivered each morning by block leaders.

These women – Maase, Buchmann, Jesenska – had to stay clean to work in the hospital, so they were housed in a privileged block and could change their clothes more often than ordinary prisoners. Like other prisoner staff they wore special armbands – in the case of *Revier* workers, yellow – that allowed them to move freely in the camp. This freedom, and their ability to help some prisoners, allowed them to feel a little normal. With Dr Sonntag's arrival, however, nothing could be normal again.

On his first day they all watched as he passed down the line of waiting women, kicking the weakest with his boots, or lashing out with his stick at any cries of pain. He made one woman undress and kicked her in the stomach. What horrified the women was not only his brutality, it was the smile on his face.

That Sonntag was a sadist none of the prisoners who worked with him at the hospital had any doubt. It was an 'extreme pleasure' for Sonntag to extract otherwise healthy teeth. Women would come with an infected tooth; he would take out instead a perfectly healthy molar. 'These extractions were performed without anaesthetic. The terrible screams could be heard all over the hospital. When he came out of the theatre he was beaming with satisfaction,' recalled Erika Buchmann.

After the war Erika testified about all manner of Ravensbrück atrocities, but none of what she witnessed later was described with the pinpoint clarity with which she recalled Sonntag's treatment of an exhausted woman who came to him with frostbite in the winter of 1940:

> He stood in front of the woman with a bamboo stick in his hands. He hit the woman with the stick in the wounds caused by the frostbite. He tore the bandages away with his stick because at that time bandages were already made of paper. He poked around with his cane in the open, bleeding, matter-filled wounds. It gave him a special pleasure.

Sonntag enjoyed nothing more than the chance to declare a woman fit for flogging. One of the camp doctor's duties was to rule on whether a prisoner sentenced to twenty-five lashes on the *Bock* was physically strong enough to survive. The rules stated that women with high fever or acute disease should not be flogged at all, but Sonntag always sent them to the *Bock*. He would order the flogging stopped only if the woman passed out, and he would feel her pulse and signal that flogging should resume as soon as her pulse revived. He was always in a particularly good mood when he came from the cells where the beating took place.

It was not simply that Sonntag enjoyed the prisoners' suffering; the prisoners evidently disgusted him. He hated them and sometimes even seemed to fear them, making sure patients were kept at a distance from him, which was why, if he examined them at all, he did so with his stick. Yet in among the images of his sadism are other memories of a grotesque and often preposterous figure. He was a lecher and a thief – he stole from prisoners' food parcels – and he liked to strut and show off with his bamboo stick. And he was often seen drunk, marauding around the camp.

'I remember a woman coming for treatment for a broken finger, smashed when she was unloading bricks, and at that moment Sonntag emerged from the hospital kicking the air. He was drunk,' said a prisoner called Maria Apfelkammer. He was also drunk when on another occasion he rode his bicycle around the surgery table. Sonntag's antics infuriated Koegel. As chief doctor, he refused to recognise Koegel's authority. He considered the SS commandant vulgar and uncouth, along with most of his subordinates. He particularly hated Koegel for barring him from the coveted SS living quarters beside the lake. As Sonntag was single, Koegel insisted he live in digs in Fürstenberg.

Just as Walter Sonntag liked to cause pain, so he could not stand to see others show kindness towards the sick or suffering. One day he caught a woman called Vera Mahnke as she tried to stuff a piece of bread through the wire to a Jewish friend in the *Strafblock*. 'Dr Sonntag was passing and without asking what I was doing he shouted: "You old pig. You piece of shit. You give bread to a Jewess, do you?" and he started beating me with his fists. He kicked and beat me until I passed out.'

Sonntag held a particular loathing for Jews. From his office window he watched in disgust as the Jewish brick-throwers trudged back through the gates at the end of the day, blackened by dust, pouring with sweat, and dragging wooden clogs. The summer was no kinder to the brick-throwing gang than the winter. All were sunburnt and those who had not long been in the camp were a pitiful sight.

'Their faces and bare arms and legs were an angry red and their hands which hung down at their sides were raw and bleeding,' recalled Doris Maase.

Sometimes the brick-throwers' gang leader would stop at the *Revier* to ask for bandages, but they knew not to ask if Sonntag was there. And even if bandages were issued, they were never changed, so within days wounds suppurated and crawled with maggots. One day Erika Buchmann saw an old woman crawl into the hospital from such a gang on hands and knees. 'She was a terrible sight. The bandages hung from her in rags. But Sonntag forbade anyone to help her.'

On another occasion, Olga Benario was passing. Her hands were torn and bleeding, but instead of cursing or kicking her, to everyone's astonishment Sonntag appeared to feel sorry for her, and offered to help. After two years in the camp, Olga had made an impression on many of the staff, as well as on other prisoners. Perhaps Sonntag had seen her tall dark figure on the Lagerstrasse, talking to Doris Maase. She had clearly caught his eye at some point. 'Sonntag, the greatest scoundrel, allowed her to wear gloves,' recalled Maria Wiedmaier.

Sonntag would also show an interest, and even a grudging respect, for certain prisoners who worked in the *Revier*. Although Doris Maase was half Jewish, he relied on her for medical expertise. 'Maase, Maase, where is Maase?' he would call, as others had called before him. He made Erika Buchmann his personal secretary and would rarely let her out of his sight, so dependent was he on her skills. Nor could he conceal his adoration for the Czech journalist Milena Jesenska, always seeking her attention. One day he offered her what was left of his breakfast, which she declined without thanks. Another day he stopped her in the corridor and tickled her under the chin with his bamboo cane, at which, to his astonishment, Milena grabbed it and flung it down. She related later how Sonntag had stared into her face and seen her anger and loathing. After that he abandoned his overtures, but continued to turn a blind eye when Milena helped prisoners.

The prisoners who worked for Sonntag certainly acquired a modicum of influence and even power. Maase would smuggle out medicines. Jesenska sometimes switched cards of VD patients to save them from Sonntag's knife. Buchmann found chances to sign sick patients off the labour gangs. And yet the price they paid for this power to help other prisoners was high: for most of the time they were obliged to help Sonntag. They had to stand holding his syringe, passing surgical instruments, filing notes for Berlin and drawing up his lists.

After Himmler's visit in January 1941, Sonntag began to keep new lists. At first he listed women with gonorrhoea and syphilis, seeking to find a cure. No records exist of how he performed his experiments, but everyone knew they were happening. It was Milena Jesenska's job to keep the card index of those suffering from venereal disease. Each time a new prisoner arrived with a suspected infection a blood sample was taken and sent off to labs in Berlin. The results came back to Milena for filing, and knowing of Sonntag's 'barbarous cures', as she called them, she tried whenever possible to forge the results or lose them in the system.

Sonntag had also begun to try his hand at sterilisation. By this time several new ideas for mass sterilisation were being put forward to Himmler. One scientist claimed that the sap from a plant called *Caladium seguinum* (elephant ear) caused sterilisation, and Himmler was so interested in the idea that he set about cultivating the plant in a hothouse, in order to try it on prisoners. Another option explored was to sterilise men and women by exposing them to high doses of X-rays. Himmler placed most faith in the work of Professor Carl Clauberg, who was trying to sterilise women by injecting an irritant into the womb. Himmler had asked Clauberg how long it would take to sterilise 1000 women, and would later suggest he try it out at Ravensbrück.

In the meantime Sonntag used his own methods – what, once again, we don't know – but his guinea pigs appear to have been chosen at random. Doris Maase observed that Sonntag could not stand the idea of Polish or Czech prisoners being unable to speak German, so when one of them claimed not to speak German he said 'She is mad' and chose her for sterilisation. Hanna Sturm recalled taking two Gypsy children to Sonntag aged between nine and eleven, whom he tried to sterilise. After the operation she took them back to their block. 'They staggered across the camp road. About one or two days later they were found dead in their bed.'

More and more pregnant women were arriving at Ravensbrück. From the first days Himmler had insisted that no births must take place there, and all pregnant women were taken to an outside hospital to give birth, but the rising intake meant pre-screening was not always effective. As a result it had become necessary to carry out abortions in the *Revier*. With no trained staff available, Schwester Lisa performed the operations, and often cruelly botched them. Schwester Lisa had 'come under Sonntag's spell', as the prisoners said: she seemed to enjoy the cruellest work, and would show off the result to others, as Erika Buchmann recalled:

> I remember one day a particularly beautiful young Gypsy came to theatre for a delivery and we heard that she had died. Sister Lisa demanded that I come and look at what had happened. I refused but Schwester Lisa got hold of my arm and threw me in front of the bed, tore the sheet off the body and I was forced to see what I did not want to see. I believe that a woman cannot do worse towards living or dead than what Schwester Lisa had done. It was sheer sadism. I can see Sister Lisa's sardonic grin over the horrors I felt.

Schwester Lisa, however, was not alone in falling under Dr Sonntag's spell. Some months after he arrived, the prisoners noticed that the woman doctor Gerda Weyand started behaving differently. At first Weyand was viewed as decent in her attitude towards the prisoners, and even friendly to some, but after Sonntag's arrival she grew indifferent to her medical duties and seemed oblivious to the patients' pain.

Soon it became clear that Sonntag and Weyand had begun a passionate relationship. In the run-up to the Hamburg trial, Weyand wrote to Erika asking her to speak out on her behalf. Erika refused, and reminded Weyand of the atrocities she'd been a party to. 'Neither could I forget the times in the hospital, in Dr Sonntag's room, when you were having fun for hours very noisily and regardless that on the other side of the wall were several ill people with fevers, pining for rest.'

In the summer of 1941 Gerda Weyand and Walter Sonntag were married. This gained Sonntag a higher status within the SS, and the couple moved into a well-appointed centrally heated villa, on the grassy slope above the lake. By now the SS enclave, attractively landscaped, was an idyllic spot to raise a family. The married couples were able to leave their offspring at a kindergarten on the lake shore, cared for by Jehovah's Witnesses, while they went off to work at the camp, just a few minutes' stroll away. Older children were educated at the local school in Fürstenberg.

The Sonntags, like other SS families, had their own domestic servants, selected from amongst reliable prisoners. They chose Hanna Sturm as their home help. Gerda wrote to Walter some time later, 'I have never been happier than I was at Ravensbrück', but Hanna Sturm said later that she often saw Sonntag beat Gerda. Sometimes he would drink so heavily that he would forget that Hanna was standing by, while he lashed out at his new wife.

An insight into the Sonntags' life at Ravensbrück is provided by Walter Sonntag himself, in letters he wrote to Gerda after leaving the camp in December 1941. By this time Max Koegel, who loathed Sonntag, had managed to have him removed; he was sent to the front at Leningrad. However the Sonntags had refused to give up their SS villa, despite Koegel's efforts to evict them. Gerda Weyand, pregnant with their first child, had stayed on at Ravensbrück to give birth.

In his letters sent from Leningrad, Walter Sonntag often dwelled on his life at Ravensbrück. He addressed his wife as 'Podgy' and asked about the villa, the furniture, his car and the chickens: 'My dear good Podgy ... make sure everything is in order. Is the car in the garage? Are the windows boarded up? How will you organise the dog, the chickens and the dovecote?' He asks if she has had a receipt for 200 marks' worth of wine he bought from the local wine merchant.

The letters show Sonntag bitter and angry at the treatment he received before leaving, particularly over the appointment of a new woman doctor, Herta Oberheuser, which he took as a deliberate snub to him. 'Dear Gerda, you won't believe how often I think of you, and it worries me when I imagine you being there without me, completely at the mercy of the furious

Oberheuser and her entourage.' He urges Gerda not to work too hard because 'nobody will thank you. Don't waste your time working for that pack of bastards,' by which he means the SS staff.

In one letter he is angry that Gerda is being treated on a par with other SS wives and even the female guards. 'Always bear in mind their degree of education,' he writes. 'Dear Podgy, we are miles above this crowd. When Koegel and others put you on the same level as the female guards in view of their education and their wives' background, don't be surprised.' As time passes, these letters take on a menacing tone. He asks his wife why she hasn't written – 'Is it too much to have to write to me?' And what about getting him a coat for the Leningrad winter? Has his wine bill been paid?

Some time in the middle of 1941 Dr Sonntag started killing. Whether Gerda Weyand knew her husband was murdering people in cold blood is not clear, but Doris Maase, on night duty at the *Revier*, witnessed him entering the building carrying a syringe. When he was injecting a patient for medical reasons he would ask for her assistance. On these occasions he did not. 'We heard him enter a room and the next morning we found a corpse in that room.'

By the summer of 1941 the death toll of Ravensbrück prisoners – exhausted by slave labour, weakened by disease, beaten, or frozen to death – was rising steadily. Now, for the first time, planned executions were taking place. Sonntag was injecting a lethal substance, probably petrol or phenol. Once again there is no evidence that he was acting under direct orders, but it seems most likely that he was, and that they came from Himmler.

During the spring of 1941, Himmler had moved fast with his plans to extend the euthanasia programme to the concentration camps. His request to the T4 head, Philipp Bouhler, for use of his staff and facilities to kill off useless mouths had been readily agreed. As early as April 1941 male prisoners at Sachsenhausen were being selected for gassing, and plans being laid to include other camps in the programme. In the meantime, doctors in Himmler's other camps were receiving instructions to start killing useless mouths – the insane and incurably ill – by the use of injections.

Another prisoner who witnessed the injections was Bertha Teege, the communist, who, as 'camp runner', had the chance to see more than most.

> I was asked one day to go to the punishment block with the guard, Zimmer. We were told that a prisoner had evacuated her bowels. Zimmer said: '*Die Sau muss weg*' – The swine's got to go. I was ordered by Zimmer to take the woman to the hospital. There she was put on a bed. Next morning she was dead. I saw her corpse. She was killed by an injection.

One day a young prostitute on Hanna Sturm's carpentry gang said she could not work any more as 'her head would burst'. She told Hanna that Sonntag had called her in and taken a vaginal swab, telling her it was for a VD test. He ordered her to turn round, saying 'Your time has come', and injected her in her upper thigh. Within hours the woman was dead. 'I showed the body to a Polish prisoner doctor. It was completely deformed. She said the girl was injected with petrol.'

Sonntag's behaviour at this time struck several prisoners as ever more sinister, not only because of the murders but because of what he was telling people. It was as if he was bursting with a secret. One prisoner who went to him about this time with an injured foot remembered how 'in a moment of drunkenness' he confided to her boastfully that he spent his days signing death certificates, but 'one day the day will come when we'll kill everyone'.

On another occasion he ordered his personal secretary, Erika Buchmann, to go around the blocks and list all of the green and black triangles – the criminals and asocials – who had tattoos. 'I had to see the tattoos myself and tell him what kind they were – snake head etc. I did this for him on Sundays. I asked him two or three times why he wanted it. He grinned and said: "You can always use nice little pictures."'

Erika said later that she never told other prisoners at the time about these tattoo lists; the hospital prisoner staff rarely spoke of what they saw. If an informer overheard, they would lose their positions. In any case, they were not equipped to grasp the meaning of what they were witnessing. When Sonntag asked Erika to list the prisoners' tattoos, it was as if he was dropping a hint of what was to come. But it was not until after the war, during the Buchenwald trial, that she first learned that the SS used the tattooed skin of murdered prisoners to make bookmarks, wallets and other emblems.

By the end of the summer several women on the brick gang had succumbed to Sonntag's killing spree. Most had collapsed under the strain of shovelling sand or throwing bricks; they were no use for work any more. One day Olga walked back with the brick-throwers carrying in her arms the skeletal body of a woman, so slight that it could have been a child's. Olga approached the hospital, probably hoping to find Doris Maase, but was confronted instead by Dr Sonntag, who had seen her coming through his office window.

Whatever spark of humanity had once led Sonntag to treat Olga's hands and give her gloves, the sight of Olga – a Jew – now seeking mercy for the exhausted figure lying in her arms had quite a different effect on Sonntag. Olga's plea was enough to trigger in him an uncontrollable rage and he burst out of the hospital shouting 'Jewish pig' and 'Jewish bitch', and lashing out.

He kicked Olga, knocking her and the woman she was carrying to the ground.

According to her friend Maria Wiedmaier, Olga was severely beaten by Sonntag himself. She was taken away by guards and sentenced to another stint in a solitary cell in the bunker. How long she spent in the bunker this time is uncertain, but Maria Wiedmaier said it was several weeks.

Olga's letters, as usual, provide a clue about the timing of events. Back in May of 1941 she wrote to Carlos: 'One survives on hope from autumn to spring and then thinks ahead again to the next winter. How long yet? That is the only question that burns in front of you.' After May, however, there are no more letters to Carlos or to Leocadia until September, which suggests that Sonntag's assault upon Olga and the fragile woman in her arms happened some time in June. She almost certainly spent that summer in a dark solitary cell in the camp bunker, unable to write or receive any letters and quite alone.

There is no record of who the woman was whom Olga had carried to the hospital, or what became of her. But she is remembered today as the skeletal figure lying in Olga's arms in *Tragende*, the statue which looks out over the Ravensbrück lake.

*Chapter 8*

# Doctor Mennecke

For three weeks in the summer of 1941 Ravensbrück seemed enchanted. The guards withdrew and locked the gates behind them. Everything fell quiet. Prisoners could hear birdsong. Bertha Teege, recently promoted to chief Kapo (*Lagerälteste*), said it began when one of the asocials started to drag a leg, unable to move it. Within hours scores more were lame. 'The women seemed to be paralysed,' Bertha informed Langefeld. As the paralysis spread the SS panicked, fearing polio.

The prisoners weren't afraid. Legs were swelling due to the new night shifts in the tailor's shop, said some. Others saw it as hysteria. Max Koegel blamed the doctor's experiments. He was heard swearing at Sonntag, accusing him of infecting the whole camp.

At one o'clock the next morning Bertha Teege was woken and handed keys to the kitchen and *Strafblock*. The camp was now in quarantine, she learned, and she was in charge – 'That's how panic-stricken the authorities were.' Transports of prisoners in and out were stopped until further notice and inmates confined to barracks. No SS personnel were to enter the compound until the mystery plague was gone.

Over the next few days a curious peace descended. The 'paralysed' asocials were put together in a single block, which was cordoned off, and everyone warned to steer clear. One prisoner, however, had no intention of avoiding the afflicted. Milena Jesenska, the hospital clerk who had so brazenly rejected Sonntag's advances, had befriended many of the sick prisoners when they came to the *Revier*. Now she wanted to help them, and nobody stood in her way.

By the summer of 1941 Milena Jesenska was probably the most charismatic woman in the camp. Afflicted by arthritis and kidney disease, at first sight she looked older than her forty-three years, but her spirit was unbowed. Her flame-red hair still grew thick and long and her eyes flashed with the look of someone who had never obeyed a rule. Grete Buber-Neumann said she had a confidence that seemed to protect her from SS blows. Cringing or fear invited blows, but at *Appell* Milena always took her time to line up, angering the duty guard who might move to slap her, but then would catch her eye and back off.

Milena also gathered admirers. 'In the camp the weak were often attracted by those who radiated strength,' said Grete, who, though not weak, was emotionally scarred, and was herself drawn to Milena. This enchanted period saw their friendship blossom into affection and – for Grete – into a profound and lasting love.

Each day Grete followed Milena out to the 'plague block'. They would sit on the step and talk in the August sun. Here Grete heard of Milena's early years in 1920s Prague, of her well-to-do Czech family – her cultured mother and her father, a professor of oral surgery at Charles University. She learned about a younger Milena, the provocative writer with an anarchic charm who asked her readers in an early piece of journalism: 'Have you ever seen the face of a prisoner behind bars? Freedom lies on the other side of the window. Heaven lies on the other side of the window. On the other side of the door there is only reality.'

By 1922, Milena was mixing with the Czech-born German-Jewish writers drawn to Prague's café society. She met Franz Kafka, and read his work, which was little known. Their affair began in 1922, the year he started writing *The Castle*, in which a man called K arrives in a village ruled by a sinister bureaucracy that resides in a nearby castle.

It was Kafka's *The Metamorphosis*, however, that Milena talked of most to Grete; she had translated the novella into Czech. She told Grete the story of Gregor Samsa, the misunderstood commercial traveller, who in Kafka's story is transformed into a huge beetle and is kept hidden by his family under a bed, as they are ashamed of him. In her version Milena embellished parts, particularly the story of the beetle's illness, 'and how, with a wound in his back infected by dirt and mites, he is left to die in miserable loneliness'.

Milena's affair with Kafka, intense and tortured, couldn't last. Throughout their time together the novelist was sick with tuberculosis, and in 1924 he died. From then on, Milena threw herself into journalism, and her fight for social justice. Like so many around her, she devoted herself to communism, until in the mid-1930s she became one of the first amongst her peers to pay heed to reports reaching Prague of Stalin's purges.

By 1937 Milena, now twice married, with a daughter, had thrown away her Communist Party card, though her loathing of fascism was growing stronger every day, as the German invasion loomed. By the time Hitler's forces marched into the Sudetenland Milena's anti-fascist writing was so strident that her arrest was inevitable, and along with the majority of Prague's intelligentsia, she was rounded up by the Gestapo.

In the camp a shared disappointment with Stalin's dream drew Milena and Grete together, but they had more in common than political disillusion. Grete was enthralled not only by Milena's exotic past, but also by her manner. Milena had quickly understood that it was Grete, not she, who had the most extraordinary story of all, because at the age of forty-one Grete Buber-Neumann had already been imprisoned by the world's two most monstrous dictators. Milena, said Grete, was 'wonderfully skilled at asking questions and was able to flesh out the memory of things I had long forgotten. She was not content to hear about the events, she wanted to see the people I had met on my long march through the Soviet prisons.'

And the more the women talked, the more Milena saw that when 'it was all over' the two of them should write their own book. 'Her idea was for a book on the concentration camps of both dictatorships: millions of human beings reduced to slavery in the name of socialism and in the other in the name of profit and glory of the master race. It would be called: "The Age of Concentration Camps".' That conversation took place in 1941, before the Auschwitz gas chambers were built, and before the outside world had any serious inkling of Stalin's Gulag.

For Grete, however, Milena was not only a soulmate but also an ally. More than a year since she had arrived from the Gulag, the camp's communists were still blackballing Grete, and now, by her account, they spurned Milena too for daring to mix with this Trotskyist traitor, Buber-Neumann, who spread lies about the Soviet Union.

That feelings should run high in the summer of 1941 is no surprise; in June Hitler had finally torn up his pact with Stalin and marched into Russia with massive force – Operation Barbarossa. A wave of optimism now swept over the communist prisoners, convinced that the Red Army would fight back and they would all be freed before long. Milena and Grete were not so sure. According to Grete, their scepticism provoked further attacks from hardliners who called them 'class enemies'.

Although certain communist apparatchiks did indeed turn against Milena in the camp, the broader community of Czech prisoners – many like her were writers, or else dancers, musicians, artists, often women she had known for years – loved her for her charm and her courage, whatever their political differences. In October 1941 a Czech resister called Anička Kvapilová, formerly head of the music department of Prague city library, arrived at Ravensbrück. Standing in shock and despair outside the *Revier*, she looked up and saw a smiling face turned towards her and other horrified newcomers, awaiting their medical examination. As Anička recalled: 'The woman stopped for a moment on the steps of the *Revier* block, smiled down at us and said in Czech: "Welcome, girls".' Anička hadn't known Milena in Prague, but knew her reputation and guessed this was she. 'Her hair was shimmering red. In the midst of all that inhumanity this was the first human thing that happened.'

During those enchanted weeks in the summer of 1941, other prisoners enjoyed their freedoms too. The political prisoners went for walks and got in touch with Jewish comrades or visited the sick. The communist Jozka Jaburkova wrote a collection of fairy tales for her friend Tilde Klose, who was sick with TB. In the Jewish block, Olga spent time on her mini-atlas.

As acting chief guard, Bertha Teege allowed the prisoners to take advantage of the quarantine. 'The Jehovah's Witnesses got out their illegal bible,' she recalled, 'the asocials were singing for all their worth, the professional criminals were bickering, the gypsies were dancing, doing acrobatics, having fights and being friends again in the same breath, and the Poles were visiting each other.'

The SS were content to let their valued prisoners run the camp. Such was the SS's confidence in women like Bertha Teege, and other co-opted prisoner staff, that guards simply walked away, in the sure knowledge that things inside would be run efficiently and the camp kept under control. Such a demonstration of trust shows how successful the SS had been to date in delegating the day-to-day running of the camp to prisoners themselves.

Since the communist takeover the previous year, more and more political women had been co-opted into useful jobs. Prisoners now not only ran the blocks, they staffed the kitchen, served meals in the SS canteen and ran the SS nursery. Others worked in the *Effektenkammer* and several prisoners worked in the *Revier* as nurses, midwives and technicians. Nor was it only Germans and Austrians who secured good jobs: Polish medics worked in the *Revier* radiography room, and Czechs staffed the lab.

The fastest rise in recruitment had taken place in the camp offices. As prisoner numbers grew, so had the camp bureaucracy, and Koegel needed office staff. Given that typing, shorthand, bookkeeping and filing were women's work, there were many in Ravensbrück qualified to fill such posts. Women who once typed speeches for male council members or kept the books for a trade union were now typing lists of arrivals or invoicing local farms for prisoners' services.

Near the commandant's headquarters a writers' office, *Schreibstube*, was staffed entirely by inmates. If they wished, these workers could use their privileges to good effect: they could tip off Blockovas about names of new arrivals, or warn of forthcoming ration cuts or VIP visits.

These *Schreibstube* prisoners were highly privileged. Working beside the SS, they were required to wash more often than ordinary inmates, and were better clothed and fed. All such prisoners lived in Block 1, where conditions were better and where many valued prisoner staff – Blockovas, Stubovas, *Revier* workers and others – also lived. With contacts in the offices, Blockovas were also securing new influence and power, and by the summer of 1941 none carried more authority than Rosa Jochmann, the Austrian trade union leader, now Blockova of Block 1.

Although Rosa had initially taken some persuading by Käthe Leichter to do the Blockova job, she had come to see the benefits. At this time 'the whole camp was in the hands of the prisoners', she said later. Such was Rosa's sway that when on one occasion a young woman guard ran sneaking to Langefeld with a minor complaint about Block 1, Rosa went to Langefeld and complained about the guard, saying she had overstepped the mark, so it was the guard who was reprimanded. Rosa Jochmann 'could do no wrong', according to several prisoners. So successful had she proved at running Block 1 that it was now always chosen as the show block; outside visitors – top Nazis, diplomats from neutral countries, industrialists, members of the German Red Cross or officers of the Wehrmacht – would be shown inside Rosa's block to see just how civilised a concentration camp really was.

By the autumn of 1941, however, the camp's most powerful prisoners were the joint *Lagerältesten* (chief Kapos) Bertha Teege and Luise Mauer, both German communists. Bertha had held the post since January 1941, but by the summer, such was the workload that the two women were sharing the job. Often seen at Langefeld's shoulder, or darting down the Lagerstrasse to deliver her messages, the women were invariably remembered later as a double act.

At first sight the rise to power of Bertha and Luise is hard to explain; nothing in their background marks them out from other ordinary German communist prisoners. Bertha, the daughter of a furniture maker, worked as a bookkeeper before the war, then joined the communist opposition and married a communist member of her local parliament. She was a mother of two. Luise Mauer, a dressmaker, also married a communist politician and worked for the party as a courier. Luise had a daughter. The women's stories of arrest and imprisonment were also similar to many others', and on arrival at the camp they made little impression.

And yet, in Langefeld's eyes Bertha Teege and Luise Mauer were obvious recruits. Communists could follow orders, and since the 'coup' the two had proved reliable workers. Both of these women were able; in their late thirties, both had suffered years of imprisonment and separation from their children before they even reached the camp: their resistance had been thoroughly crushed. Luise Mauer had then been further demoralised in the camp by long stretches on the most gruelling work gangs.

Entering the camp a year later, Bertha Teege took one look at the punishments meted out to difficult prisoners and made her mind up fast about survival. Soon after arriving, Bertha saw inside the bunker where several bodies were frozen onto the stone cell floors. 'Hospital workers were called in to "scratch the dead bodies off",' she recalled, adding that she then understood: 'You'd better not show your horror or you are imprisoned yourself.'

Early in 1941, when the first execution was carried out, Teege was brought in to help, which she readily did. The victim was a Pole called Wanda Maciejewska, sentenced to death for 'terrorism' carried out in Poland. The task was to escort Wanda to the location, near the bunker, where the shooting took place. The next job was stripping the corpse, which was taken to the Fürstenberg crematorium by the camp hearse. Teege carried the dead woman's bloodied clothes back to the *Effektenkammer* to be washed and reused.

By August 1941, such was Langefeld's confidence in Bertha Teege that when the SS walked out over the polio scare, she handed her the camp keys. Three weeks later it was time to return them. The plague ended as abruptly as it began, caused perhaps by mass hysteria or by a deliberate stunt set up by the asocials to create panic. A new panic was about to break out, and this time the cause would be real.

Throughout the early autumn of 1941 – Doris Maase said it began in July – Dr Sonntag was drawing up more lists, but nobody knew why. Rumours came from the *Schreibstube* secretaries that he was acting directly on orders from Berlin. Those selected were mostly the old and the sick. Teege and Mauer led the women to the bathhouse, where they were ordered to strip and parade naked in front of Sonntag. Then they returned to their blocks and more women were called to the bathhouse. Many had syphilis or gonorrhoea. Some from the Jewish block were called. Prisoners with TB were selected too, including the Kapo of the 'celebrities' work gang. No one knew who would go next.

Uncertainty was one of the worst things; the smallest changes caused anxiety. Since the invasion of the USSR in June there had been more uncertainties than ever. Rations had dwindled; there were rumours that bread might run out. The canteen shop had next to nothing for sale and the prisoners' mail was about to stop, or so it was said.

Overcrowding caused further uncertainty. More prisoners were pouring in – mostly Poles, but also German politicals and asocials – pushing the numbers up towards 7000. And each week women had to move blocks to accommodate them, which tore them from friends. Some were even sharing mattresses. Showers had been cut back to once every four weeks. There was one blanket each, instead of two, and winter was coming.

The women on Sonntag's lists were to be released, some said. Releases were certainly occurring: to prevent more 'plagues' a number of TB sufferers were told they were to be released, including three communists, Lotte Henschel, Tilde Klose and Lina Bertram. The *Revier* secretary, Erika Buchmann, was released in the summer, apparently on one of Himmler's whims. In July Doris Maase walked free.

Prisoners working in the *Effektenkammer*, however, knew nothing of any releases relating to Sonntag's lists, and they would have been the first to hear, because the freed women's clothes were always collected from storage in advance. On the other hand, to get back your own clothes didn't guarantee release, as *Effektenkammer* staff also knew. The Polish resister Wanda Maciejewska, shot in January, had been brought to collect her clothes and told to put them on just before her execution – a charade intended to disguise the imminent killing.

By the third week of November Dr Sonntag had selected more than 250 names for his lists. On 19 November a man in a suit arrived from Berlin. Nobody knew who he was, but Emmy Handke, a secretary in the *Revier*, learned he was a psychiatrist. Someone in the *Schreibstube* heard he'd been booked into a hotel in Fürstenberg.

It was nearly nine months since Himmler had written to Philipp Bouhler, head of Hitler's Chancellery, asking whether he could use the 'personnel and installations of "T4" for the concentration camps'. The personnel were the German psychiatrists and doctors used to select the disabled for the 'euthanasia' killings; the installations were the gas chambers installed in the castle sanatoria for the purpose. Himmler's interest in using the T4 gas chambers sprang largely from the growing need to free up space in the camps. With the new drive to use prisoners as slave labour for the war industries, there was more need than ever to eliminate prisoners incapable of work – the useless mouths.

Within weeks of his letter to Bouhler, the Reichsführer had been given the go-ahead to use the T4 resources. However, this new series of gassings was supposed to be directed not out of the T4 offices within the Führer's Chancellery, but out of Himmler's own Concentration Camp Inspectorate, located at Oranienburg, on the northern edge of Berlin. Hence a new cover name was invented for the killings: Sonderbehandlung 14f13. *Sonderbehandlung* – 'special treatment' – was the SS and police euphemism for killing. At the camp inspectorate the code '14f' was used to denote prisoners who died in the camps. Under subdivisions '14f14' meant executions and '14f8' suicides. The new '14f13' denoted death by gassing.

The adapted 14f13 programme had been launched in spring with a trial run at the male camp of Sachsenhausen, right next to Himmler's Oranienburg inspectorate. In April 1941, a medical commission arrived there to start selections. Given the leakage of information about the Grafeneck gassings five months earlier, the secrecy surrounding the Sachsenhausen operation was tight, but thanks to letters written by one of the medical commission, certain details have survived.

Friedrich Mennecke, a T4 psychiatrist, wrote each day to his wife Eva, telling her about his work at Sachsenhausen. He was staying at the Eilers Hotel in Oranienburg, in a 'big and pleasant room', while his colleagues from Tiergartenstrasse 4 commuted to the suburb each day on the Berlin S-Bahn. His work was 'very, very interesting' and he enjoyed afternoon coffee and cake with the commandant. After four days Mennecke and colleagues had 'processed' between 250 and 400 prisoners.

A few weeks later those processed by Mennecke at Sachsenhausen were taken to Sonnenstein, near Dresden, site of another gassing centre, also hidden inside a sanatorium. This was another turning point in the escalating Nazi murder programme: the first time prisoners from a concentration camp were killed with gas. A satisfied Himmler directed his 14f13 staff – and colleagues at T4 – to start selecting prisoners at other camps for transport to gassing centres.

Over the summer, however, protests broke out again among the public, and the gassings paused. It was a new gassing centre in a mental institution at Hadamar, near Limburg, that revived the unrest. It lay inside a converted Franciscan priory, and gas chambers had been installed in one of the wings, but once again the cover-up had gone wrong. In June 1941 the bishop of Limburg wrote:

> Several times a week buses arrive in Hadamar with a considerable number of victims. Schoolchildren of the vicinity know this vehicle and say: 'Here comes the murder box again.' Or the children call each other names and say: 'You're crazy, you'll be sent to the baking oven at Hadamar.' You hear old folks say: 'Don't send me to a state hospital. When the feeble-minded have been finished off the next useless eaters whose turn will come are the old people.'

It had also been impossible to disguise the large number of urns suddenly piling up at crematoriums all over Germany. Shocked relatives learned that a loved one, usually a patient in a mental hospital, had unexpectedly died; it had not been possible to preserve the body due to the risk of infection, so the body had been burned. In many cases urns reached the wrong family, and some received two urns. Most horrifying, especially to Catholics, was to know that their loved ones had been cremated at all.

During the spring and summer of 1941 a form of silent protest began across Germany. Families placed identical condolence notices in the newspapers, expressing their disbelief at the 'incomprehensible' news they had received of a loved one's sudden death. Lawyers acting for families of patients still in asylums said families were 'being made fools of' by the 'monstrous programme' and by the 'flimsy camouflage' used to cover things up. Those responsible had 'lost a sense of the difference between right and wrong', wrote another Catholic priest.

On 3 August 1941 came the most serious protest yet. Count Clemens August Graf von Galen, bishop of Münster, took to the pulpit to condemn the murders: an 'unproductive life' was no reason to kill. By this time articles about the killings and the cover-up had begun to appear in the foreign press, most notably the *New York Times*.

The protest had come at an awkward time for Hitler. On 2 June 1941 German forces had marched into Russia and the Führer's attention was focused on Stalin's Red Army. Domestic unrest was therefore a distraction. Nevertheless, not wishing to provoke wider protest just as his more ambitious killing projects were maturing, Hitler said in August that he would stop the domestic euthanasia killings. Public protest quickly subsided and he could concentrate on the overarching task: defeating Stalin and annihilating Russia's three million Jews.

Himmler's own SS murder squads, the SS *Einsatzgruppen*, Special Action Groups, sent in behind the German forces, were given the task of launching the murder of Russia's Jews, and over the summer the Reichsführer went out to the captured Russian lands to supervise. The main method used was mass shooting. At first Himmler's orders were to shoot only the men – perhaps he felt that his killer squads were not yet sufficiently 'hardened' or 'accustomed to their own atrocities', as one biographer put it, to shoot women and children. By the end of July, however, Himmler's orders were that Russian-Jewish women and children must also be shot.

On a visit to Minsk on 15 August the Reichsführer asked to observe a mass shooting. He stood by a trench and watched groups of Jews and partisans – men and women – shot, then fall forward into a ditch in front of him. One soldier said later: 'After the first salvo Himmler came and looked into the ditch, remarking that there was still someone alive. He :: "Lieutenant, shoot that one." Himmler stood beside me while I did it.'

If Himmler had ever had any reservations about including women in his new gassing plans for concentration camp prisoners within Germany proper (the 'old Reich'), after Minsk he had none. In the early autumn of 1941 he authorised the resumption of selections at concentration camps under the new 14f13 killing plan, and Ravensbrück was to be included.

The 'stop' order on the euthanasia murders that Hitler put out in the summer was never what it seemed. The killing of handicapped German adults in the sanatoria gas chambers was largely halted, but only to appease the Church, and 'euthanasia' went on at other institutions by other means, usually lethal injection. Children were poisoned or starved.

Meanwhile, Himmler was able to take up spare capacity in the T4 sanatorium gas chambers and use it for useless mouths from his camps. By November 1941 Dr Mennecke, the T4 doctor who selected the first 14f13 prisoners at Sachsenhausen, had received new orders to proceed to Ravensbrück. He arrived at the camp amid great secrecy, but we know that the date was 19 November 1941, because it is the date of his first letter to his wife, sent from Fürstenberg. He'd travelled by train, there were fleas in his hotel bed, the walk to the camp was a long one, and it was foggy.

Friedrich Wilhelm Heinrich Mennecke, the son of a stonecutter, was born near Hanover in 1904. At the outbreak of the First World War he was ten, and waved goodbye to his father, who even at forty-two was called up to the front. Three years later Friedrich saw his father return home, severely wounded and badly shell-shocked. Disabled and broken, he died at fifty, leaving an impoverished wife and two children.

On finishing school Friedrich was unable to go on to university, instead taking work as a commercial traveller. Only later, with help from other relatives, did he pursue his medical ambitions. A second-rate student, but a committed Nazi, he specialised in psychiatry and in 1939 became director of Eichberg State Mental Hospital, where he met and married Eva Wehlan, a medical technician ten years his junior. In February 1940, during the launch of the T4 euthanasia programme, he was asked to attend a conference in Berlin. He and ten to twelve other doctors were required to select 'lives not worth living' in mental asylums. As all the others 'unhesitatingly agreed' to do the work, so too did Mennecke.

When in 1941 the T4 work was extended to include the concentration camps, with its new code 14f13, his skills were called on again. There is reason to believe that for Ravensbrück secrecy was particularly tight, perhaps because Himmler still feared that gassing women on German soil might be a step too far and would need special camouflage. Not only was Mennecke himself instructed never to mention that he was working at Ravensbrück, but the name of the camp was even omitted from SS paperwork relating to the new 14f13 programme.

An official Nazi document dated 10 December 1941, one of the few 14f13 papers to survive, contains instructions to SS commandants about how and when selections for gassings are to proceed. It is addressed to the commandants at Dachau, Sachsenhausen, Buchenwald, Mauthausen, Auschwitz, Flossenbürg, Gross-Rosen, Neuengamme and Niederhagen. The letter states that 'medical commissioners will shortly visit the above-named camps for the purpose of examining prisoners'; further visits would take place during the first half of January 1942.

The letter goes on to give detailed information about how camp doctors should carry out preselections ahead of the medical commission's visit. A specimen form is enclosed 'to be completed at this stage'.

The omission of Ravensbrück from the list of camps addressed is doubly extraordinary given that by this date one visit by 'medical commissioners' had already taken place there, and another was about to begin. It must therefore be assumed that for secrecy's sake, the information and the enclosure were passed to Max Koegel by hand at an earlier date, by one of the camp inspectorate staff. This intense secrecy caused confusion at Ravensbrück, and obscured the true course of events after the war. Even today many details of this early phase of the Nazi genocide would be undocumented, had it not been for the fact that Dr Friedrich Mennecke recorded in minute detail what happened in letters – sometimes two a day – written to his wife.

Mennecke's first letter from Ravensbrück (addressed 'Fürstenberg in Mecklenburg, Wednesday November 19th 1941, 7h 15 p.m.') sets the tone. As if actually talking to Eva – and he will be talking to her, literally, any moment – he starts:

> *My dearest Mummy!*
>
> *I just arranged for the phone conversation, I wonder: will it be happening soon? I'll tell you everything on the phone, but at least for the sake of completeness, I write you this letter as well. I ordered roast venison for dinner, but will now first drink a toast to you. Cheers! There is such heavy fog today, you can't see for a hundred metres. The Tommies won't be able to attack in this weather.*

He recounts his day, which started in Berlin at Tiergartenstrasse 4, where he had breakfast with the bosses, including Doctors Paul Nitsche and Werner

Heyde, 'who were very, very friendly' and 'send you their greetings'. Nitsche and Heyde also briefed Mennecke on future plans, telling him that he'd be going to Buchenwald after Ravensbrück, and after that he was booked for Gross-Rosen, a men's concentration camp further east. 'This will take about fourteen days, because in a KZ you can finish 70–80 a day,' he tells Eva, referring to the remarkable speed with which gassing victims could be selected at the camps, as compared with the hospitals and asylums where he has worked before.

Mennecke set off to start his work in Ravensbrück. Before he caught his train he ate bratwurst, '50 grams meat' (a reference to meal vouchers), with potatoes and cabbage. At Fürstenberg he went first to his hotel, then to the camp.

On entering the main gate Mennecke was introduced to Koegel, who told him there were only 259 prisoners to examine, which meant 'only two days for two men'; Mennecke's colleague Curt Schmalenbach was to join him, though Mennecke was obviously irked at this – 'I can do it all on my own.' Mennecke tells Eva that if he gets finished by Saturday he'll go straight to his next stop at Weimar, which means Buchenwald. 'There seem to be more there,' he says, meaning more prisoners, 'so we'll be working in a threesome.'

'I had coffee with the "Adju" [the adjutant] – in the officers' mess – and we discussed our work schedule [the selections] and had a beer.' Koegel recommended that Mennecke change hotels because of the bugs and so he moved to a better one, though in the nearby café 'there are many disgusting soldiers'.

Signing off – apparently the phone call had now happened – Mennecke mentions the offensive in the East: 'Let's hope we'll advance quickly. People here reckon the war will be over next summer. Hopefully. You go to bed and sweet dreams, sweet dreams. Most heartfelt kisses, lots, lots, lots, from your faithful Fritz Pa.'

On Thursday 21 November, Mennecke starts his first day's work at Ravensbrück. The same obsessive details pour out to Eva as he writes a timed running commentary: 'I'm sitting down for lunch of lentil soup with bacon, omelette for dessert.' In this letter we learn a little more about his work. He has had a meeting with the SS doctor Sonntag and SS Sturmbannführer Koegel, in which 'it became clear that the number of people in question [i.e. to be killed] needed to be expanded by another sixty or seventy'. Sonntag had evidently interpreted the criteria for a useless mouth too narrowly, an error that Mennecke must now put right by increasing the numbers, which is a nuisance – he'll have to stay on until Monday.

Nevertheless, Mennecke is happy with how things are going, which is 'swimmingly' – not least because he doesn't have to do much at all. Sonntag brings in the 'pats' (patients) and briefs him on their behaviour, 'so it runs flawlessly'. All he has to do is fill in boxes on the forms: 'The headings on the forms are already typed and I just have to fill in the diagnoses, main symptoms and so on.' And Mennecke is glad to say that, after a call to Dr Heyde in Berlin, he has seen off Schmalenbach, who won't be coming after all.

After lunch came a pleasant walk with Koegel and Sonntag – 'we visited the cattle sheds' – and later he joined Sonntag again for dinner in the officers' mess, which was three kinds of sausage. Before turning in, he writes: 'I'll go for a little walk now, mailing this letter, so that it's delivered tonight. I hope you're as well as me. I feel wonderful. Take more heartfelt kisslets from your lordling and embrace your faithful Fritz-Pa.'

As the days pass Mennecke's letters pile up, along with the ever grosser details of his meals, carousing, free vouchers, travel arrangements, hotel rooms, black market dealings and other minutiae, mixed in with his descriptions of signing women off for death. The reason for these running commentaries may derive from a sense of historic mission. Some of the letters contain phrases like 'He who writes lives' or 'They [the letters] should bear witness to these greatest of all times'. The letters certainly show with what ease he was able to blank the backdrop of the camp from his view: after two years ticking boxes to authorise his 'mercy killings', Mennecke was so accustomed to his own atrocities that he could no longer even see the 'pats'.

Sometimes he calls them 'portions'. He certainly never refers to them as women. We know he was capable of insulting women, as in one letter he calls his sister-in-law a Bolshevik because she 'boozes and whores a lot', but the 'pats' excite no such reaction, and when he has filled in their details they simply become 'sheets' to be handed in, on time, to Berlin. Nor does Eva show any interest in the 'pats'. In her replies to 'my dear Fritz Pah', Eva asks 'how much did you get done today' or 'when will you be done with it?' and chats about her own meals and the mice upstairs.

Though Mennecke barely noticed the 'pats', the 'pats' had been carefully watching Mennecke. On the evening of his arrival, Emmy Handke, in the *Revier*, was asked to produce the files of all patients. 'We had to get out all the personal files of the Jews, the professional criminals, the incurably ill and those with syphilis.' Over the next few days, groups of these women were taken to the bathhouse, where Dr Mennecke sat holding a pen at a table piled high with forms while Dr Sonntag stood by him.

Each woman was ordered to strip and walk past him naked. Emmy learned later that he had asked some of them questions: 'For example, to the Jews, he said: "Are you married?" and "Do you have children from this union?" etc.' Another *Schreibstube* secretary, Maria Adamska, heard that the women had to parade naked in front of the commission at a distance of perhaps seven yards. There was no real medical examination.

According to Emmy the women with syphilis and the prostitutes were in the first group. Others said it was all those with genetic defects and the incurably sick amongst the Jews who went first. All agreed that the first women to be called were those on Sonntag's lists.

Soon there was a new alarm: prisoners observed that the names of those called out were no longer confined to women on Sonntag's lists. Healthy women from the Jewish blocks were asked to parade before the commission, among them Käthe Leichter and Olga Benario. Sonntag had never shown an interest in such women. Käthe reported back to Rosa Jochmann:

> She said a lot of Jewish women from Block 11 had to stand naked along a 500-metre line before the doctors. But the doctors didn't really look at them. And there was one doctor who came up to Käthe and said to her: 'Frau Dr Leichter, what is your qualification?' and she answered: 'Philosophy and political economics.' And the answer from the doctor was: 'You will need your philosophy.'

Jehovah's Witnesses came next. Some were taken to the bathhouse straight from beatings on the *Bock*. The commission also started examining women with suspected lung disease from the camp hospital; the Berlin doctors told them they were 'going away for treatment'. To the horror of the communist group, Lotte Henschel, Tilde Klose and Lina Bertram were told to parade – the same three comrades who had been promised release on the grounds that they had TB. Everyone who was sick seemed at risk of selection.

Clara Rupp, who was working in the *Revier* by that time, was so terrified that she couldn't sleep. 'We noticed that anyone sent to the hospital for anything at all was suddenly diagnosed with some genetic disease or perhaps tuberculosis.' Usually this was a fabrication. 'In order to get rid of as many people from the camp as possible the authorities raised the number of sick people by any means. We understood at once that this was a fraud, and warned our comrades not to go to the *Revier*.'

Some of the SS nurses seemed to understand too. One said to Clara: '"When these transports get rolling the camp will be empty soon." We asked her what she meant and she replied: "I can't tell you the truth but I don't want to lie to you."'

The asocials sensed a new horror. No longer were black triangles being listed because they had syphilis or gonorrhoea; the selections were being used as a means of random punishment too. For example, those who had agreed to do beating for Max Koegel were spared selection by the commission, but Else Krug, the Düsseldorf prostitute who had refused Koegel's order to beat Jehovah's Witnesses, was now called up. As she paraded naked before Friedrich Mennecke, Koegel's warning – 'You'll have cause to remember me' – must have rung in Else's ears.

The first that Mennecke knew of the expanded selection criteria was when, much to his annoyance, his T4 colleague Schmalenbach turned up to muscle in on the job after all. Worse still, he brought another T4 colleague, a Dr Meyer, their presence explained by the new instructions they brought: the number of prisoners to be selected was now 2000 – more than six times Mennecke's original target of 320. Even Mennecke was taken aback by the new quota, telling Eva: 'We will have more to do here than was foreseen: about 2000 forms!'

His surprise – astonishment, even – is telling; after two years as a loyal cog in the T4 machine even Mennecke could see that he was being taken for a ride. Throughout the 'euthanasia' gassing programme he had dutifully made his diagnoses of lives not worth living according to the criteria, but those criteria had changed. Not only had he been shifted to select concentration camp prisoners, instead of the handicapped in sanatoria that he was used to, but the guidelines stating which prisoners to choose were now being expanded every few days.

From the moment he arrived, the numbers Mennecke was told to target had begun to rise, at first from 259 to 328 – almost certainly on Himmler's own orders. Calculating that – like his murdering soldiers in Russia – Mennecke would by now be 'accustomed to his own atrocities', Himmler then upped the figure to 2000.

Given that there were 6544 prisoners in the camp at the time, the new target meant that nearly one third of Ravensbrück women were to be 'mercifully killed'. Mennecke now saw that his diagnoses were a waste of time: the numbers were fixed in Berlin, and this annoyed him. Berlin didn't care how the 'sheets' were chosen, he moaned to Eva. It was 'chaos', he complained. 'Who is in charge in Berlin?'

Nevertheless, Mennecke buckled down. He and Schmalenbach and Meyer were quick to get on with the work, starting a competition to see who could fill the most 'sheets'. Mennecke told Eva the other two 'finished only twenty-two forms by 11 a.m. while I myself had done 56 by noon'. At least they could save time by simply waving the Jewish 'pats' through. Here too there were new instructions. Not only had the target been raised, but the three doctors had orders from Berlin not to bother with examinations of Jewish prisoners, as Mennecke confirmed at his post-war trial.

Charged in 1947 at the Nuremberg Medical Trials, held in Frankfurt, Mennecke gave evidence that was almost as frank as his missives to his wife. He detailed, for example, how in November 1941 he was suddenly instructed to select prisoners on 'political and racial grounds' in addition to the 'medical' grounds invoked for 'mercy killing'. From that moment on Jews were not medically examined but just added to the selection list for being Jews. The court sentenced Mennecke to hang, but he died in his cell. His wife had visited him two days earlier, and it was widely held that she passed her 'Fritz Pa' the means to kill himself.

The night before Mennecke left Ravensbrück for his next assignment at Buchenwald he took the time to dine with Dr Sonntag's wife, Gerda. He wrote to Eva that evening telling her they had enjoyed beef cabbage and potatoes in the officers' mess. This was followed by a dinner of meat, bread and tea and lastly two pieces of cake in the market café, before bed. Reminding Eva that he was leaving the next day, he said it was up to the camp staff themselves to find the outstanding 1500 'pats'. It had not been possible for him to complete the job, not least because Berlin had called Schmalenbach and Meyer away again before the work was done.

The forms already signed by Mennecke had been sent back to Berlin with his notes. Attached were photographs of each prisoner, with scribbled remarks on the back, as if to remind him who was who. A handful of these photographs survived, and the scribbles suggest, contrary to the impression of his letters, that sometimes he did take an interest in the 'pats'. On one photograph he noted: 'Anna Sara Jewish, Czech, Marxist functionary, has a ferocious hatred of Germany, had relations with the English ambassador.' On another: 'Charlotte Sara born in Breslau, divorced, Jewish, Catholic, nurse, tried to disguise Jewish origins and wears a Catholic cross.'

After the medical commission left Ravensbrück, the prisoners faced other fears. In November 1941 three more Poles were shot, a mother and her two daughters, and four more Polish executions followed in early December. The shots rang out across the camp and soon afterwards the bloodied clothes appeared in the *Effektenkammer*.

Every woman in the camp wondered if she would survive the winter. Those on the outside work gangs found their limbs swollen black with frostbite. In a letter to Carlos in December Olga wrote: 'I only wish that with the necessary strength of mind and physical condition I will be able to go through the winter that is approaching. The question is only whether this will be my last.'

All news from the front suggested the war was going to go on and on, a prospect that filled everyone with despair. Out east the Red Army was holding the line at Rostov, Moscow and Stalingrad, and on 7 December America joined the war, following the attack on Pearl Harbor that day by Japan.

The women in the Jewish block already had reason to fear the longer war. In October 1941 Hitler had ordered the deportation of all German Jews; trains for the East were leaving from Hamburg and Berlin. Letters to Jewish prisoners talked of whole families disappearing. And with news of the Jewish deportations came the announcement that no more German Jews could emigrate, sponsored or not. For Olga this meant that release to Mexico or anywhere else was now a pipe dream.

And yet, despite the despair, the sight of wounded German officers coming back from the front, and the troubled faces of the SS comrades posted to replace them, reminded the prisoners that the tide might at least be turning in the East. Olga still worked on her mini-atlas. Her latest maps showed Stalin pushing the Germans back at Rostov, and at Leningrad. On one page, she had a diagram from a newspaper showing the latest position of forces around Moscow; on the back of the cutting, the death notice for a German soldier was dated 10 December 1941.

Olga's letters to Carlos at this time were not all pessimistic:

> *Very often I cannot help laughing when I think of the surprise you will have when you see the woman I have become. But one thing I have learned here is to know the true value of everything that is human, of the heights to which the human soul can raise itself... Do you have any new picture of Anita? She will soon also be able to write to us herself.*

In the same letter, however, Olga admits that the effort of believing in a better future is now often too much for her: she finds herself building 'castles in the air about our future together'.

By December there was still no news about the fate of those selected by Mennecke, and nothing had been done to choose the extra 1500 prisoners needed for his lists. One reason for the inaction may have been the departure from the camp of Dr Sonntag, who was posted as doctor to the front at Leningrad. In his place came the young woman doctor Herta Oberheuser, presumably too junior for such an important role as selecting for death. But the respite did not last.

A week or so before Christmas the pretence that a camp doctor was necessary to select for the lists was abandoned and Max Koegel was told to produce the names himself. His method was to delegate: he told his Blockovas to do it.

Koegel took the unprecedented step of gathering the Blockovas together to announce what was to happen. Rosa Jochmann described the occasion as 'an *Appell* for Blockovas'. It was certainly an unusual event – perhaps unique – and it caused considerable foreboding, which quickly changed to disbelief and horror when the women understood what he was telling them to do. 'Koegel told us,' said Rosa, 'that we had to point out all the women who were sick or couldn't work, because they were going to be sent to a sanatorium. He nodded his head towards the bunker and said: "If you fail to do this you'll end up there, and you know what that means."'

Before the commandant stood about twenty women, the camp's most privileged prisoners, almost all of them beneficiaries of the political takeover of Kapo jobs earlier in the year. They faced an impossible choice. Koegel already had their cooperation, and was evidently confident that with a little subterfuge he could win them over to select for the gas chamber too. Looking on was Johanna Langefeld, with her two trusted *Lagerälteste*, Bertha Teege and Luise Mauer. These two had their own instructions: they were to collect the names from the Blockovas and pass them on to Langefeld, who in turn was told by Koegel that she was in charge.

Precisely how the Blockovas reacted we will never know; survivors among them were the only witnesses, and precisely because they were there, and played a role, they were bound to have to juggle with the truth. Some admitted to handing over names, others rejected the suggestion, and some attempted to justify handing over names on the grounds that it was better they did the selecting than the SS.

Nanda Herbermann, the Catholic writer, and Blockova of the asocials, said she chose ten to twelve sick asocials because she believed at the time that they were truly bound for a sanatorium. Rosemarie von Luenink, a Stubova, said that she and her Blockova refused to select anyone. Minna Rupp, the Swabian communist Blockova who had tormented Grete Buber-Neumann on arrival, also denied handing any prisoners over.

Grete did not deny selecting names – she was Blockova of the Jehovah's Witnesses at the time – but said she did so on the basis of Koegel's assurances. 'An order came down to us to give names of congenital cripples, bed-wetters, amputees, mental defectives and sufferers from asthma and tuberculosis. The SS assured us that they were being transferred to a camp where the work was easier.' Grete's statement, however, is uncharacteristically clipped. And it is hard not to wonder why it was, if she really suspected no sinister intentions, that Grete, along with Milena, had been fighting so desperately to have Lotte Henschel taken off the original selection list.

Lotte Henschel was one of the three German communist prisoners who in the early autumn had been promised release because of TB, but who were subsequently selected by Walter Sonntag. Lotte, whom Grete first met in 'the Alex', the Berlin jail, before coming to Ravensbrück, had since grown close to both her and Milena. Milena had befriended Lotte at the *Revier*, where the young German communist also worked, and it was here that Milena observed Lotte falling sick. Knowing at this time that TB patients were being released, Milena devised a ruse to get Lotte out of the camp by swapping Lotte's sputum sample for one that indicated TB. But the trick had gone horribly wrong, because when Sonntag started compiling the first selection lists he included TB sufferers.

Milena, with Grete's encouragement, tried in vain to get the decision on Lotte reversed. 'Milena tortured herself with self-reproach,' said Grete later. 'She had more sputum samples made – which of course were negative – and pleaded with Dr Sonntag to have Lotte discharged [from the hospital] given her miraculous recovery.' Walter Sonntag – just before he was posted to Leningrad – had eventually agreed, and did indeed remove Lotte from the list. 'Only the fact that Dr Sonntag knew Lotte, who had worked in the *Revier*, saved her from death,' said Grete, though of course Grete doesn't tell us whose name was put on the list instead.

The Lotte Henschel story later had a further twist. According to Lotte herself, it was probably Gerda Sonntag, Sonntag's wife, who was really decisive in saving her life. Lotte had worked in the *Revier* when Gerda Weyand was still employed as an SS doctor, before she married Walter Sonntag. At that time Gerda was considered decent and had been friendly with Lotte.

After the war Gerda, like her husband, faced war crimes charges, particularly in relation to the death transports, and in her defence denied all knowledge of them. Lotte gave evidence against Gerda, even though she'd saved her. The fact that Gerda had helped take her off the selection list, said Lotte, was evidence that she knew the truth about the transports. Furthermore, 'If she [Gerda Weyand/Sonntag] had really objected to the crime she would not just have saved me, she would have saved the others' – a reference to the other two communists with TB who were to have been released, Tilde Klose and Lina Bertram. 'And she would have left the camp and left her husband. But she didn't. She stayed there and supported him.'

Lotte Henschel's case is not the only evidence that the Blockovas knew – or had good reason to know – that selection for the lists meant death. Even more damning is the testimony of prisoner secretaries, responsible for the death registers and other paperwork. The highly educated Polish countess Maria Adamska was valued enough by the authorities to be given the post of secretary in the camp's political office, which was responsible for registering all camp deaths.

Until the end of 1941 there had been no need for the camp to have its own registry. Deaths were recorded in the tiny public registry at Ravensbrück village hall. In December 1941, however, a new registry called 'Ravensbrück 11' was created and came under the direct orders of the commandant. Maria Adamska observed later that the registry was created at precisely the time that the order came to produce new lists of sick and disabled.

Another secretary, an Austrian inmate called Hermine Salvini, produced even more evidence of what was coming. Hermine, who worked in the camp's 'welfare department', dealt with the prisoners' correspondence with next of kin. At the time the lists were compiled she was asked to draw up hundreds of forms giving false reasons for cause of death. According to Rosa Jochmann, Hermine told the other Blockovas what she had been told to do. 'She told us that in the offices they had been told to make 1500 copies of a form with the following words: "You are herewith informed that 'blank' has died at Ravensbrück as a result of a blood clot."'

Rosa was one of those who said later that she knew from the start that Koegel was lying about the sanatorium, and she discussed what to do with others. 'We understood that the situation was very serious. I talked about it with my political friends and we decided not to select anyone.' Though she doesn't say who the 'political friends' were it seems probable that Rosa would have talked it over with Käthe Leichter, just as she talked over everything else. After all, it was her old friend from Vienna, with whom she'd fought so many campaigns for women's rights, who had first told Rosa to take the job of Blockova, as she could 'do some good', even as an arm of the SS. To Käthe, called already to parade before the 'medical committee', the situation two years on must have looked very different. Rosa went to Langefeld and told her she wouldn't select. 'Langefeld said nothing,' said Rosa. 'She seemed to understand.'

Bertha Teege and Luise Mauer also made statements after the war claiming to have refused the orders, though of all the group, the testimony of the two *Lagerältesten* is perhaps the most contradictory. In one statement Luise explained that she and Bertha 'were instructed to register all prisoners unable to work', which implies that their job was to supplement the lists supplied by the Blockovas with their own selections. Luise says in a further statement that she and Bertha were 'relieved of the duty and that Langefeld agreed they would not be punished if they refused'.

On another occasion, however, Luise gives a more ambiguous account. She says that she and Bertha first consulted with the other Blockovas and went to Langefeld to ask to be released from the duty. This time, says Luise, 'Frau Langefeld was angered by our refusal and threatened to punish us unless we got on with it.'

Bertha Teege says nothing on the subject of making lists, but she says elsewhere that she was looking forward to being released from the camp in January, when Himmler was expected to make a further visit. Teege's predecessor as *Lagerälteste* had been released a year earlier, and she had taken the job expecting to be released 'just as Babette Widmann was'. In any event, the lists were certainly made, whether by the Kapos, the guards, or probably both, but by Christmas there was still no sign of Mennecke.

Christmas 1941 was remembered for the bitter wind that howled around the camp, and an exceptionally hard frost, but there was no snow. During the Christmas Eve night shift in the sewing shop the guard on duty allowed each national group to sing a carol, and the Germans started with 'Stille Nacht'. At first the Poles refused to join in, then they changed their minds and sang, but as they reached the words 'Take my hand, O Christ child', tears broke their song and they had to stop.

On the way back to their blocks, the Christmas Eve night workers passed a Christmas tree erected by the guards on the Lagerstrasse; it even had candles. And in the SS houses Hanna Sturm, the Austrian carpenter, was putting up Christmas trees for the officers and their families. That night prisoners passed out tiny gifts to each other. Some had made stars and mangers out of straw. Olga's Christmas gift to Maria Wiedmaier was her miniature atlas.

*Chapter 9*

# Bernburg

In early January 1942 snow fell almost constantly, lying six inches thick on the roofs of the blocks, but the skies cleared on the day that Fritzi Jaroslavsky arrived. She had travelled alone by train from Vienna, with just a single male guard. Fritzi was cheered by the blue skies. Just seventeen, she had spent twelve months in a Gestapo jail for helping her father's resistance cell.

In the New Year of 1942 more and more foreign resistance prisoners started to arrive at the camp, following a new German drive to root out insurgents in countries seized by the Reich. Fritzi's father, Eduard Jaroslavsky, a social democrat and factory worker, was one of thousands of Austrians who, three years after the *Anschluss*, were still operating underground. Fritzi took helping for granted. Many friends were doing the same. Her role was 'very ordinary – nothing'. She collected secret messages from a launderette near the office where she worked as a secretary; the launderette served as a 'letter box' where messages arrived for her father's cell. 'The manageress called me up from time to time and said, "Your washing is ready," and I knew that a message had come and I was to go and collect it. I'd take it to my father.'

Early in January 1941 the Gestapo arrested the manageress and seized her laundry phone book, with names of the entire cell. Fritzi spent the next year in a Viennese jail. In June 1941 her mother visited her, and broke the news that her father had been guillotined in Berlin. 'My mother was asked if she wanted his ashes back and told she'd have to pay. She didn't have the money.'

The guard who accompanied Fritzi on the train from Vienna to Ravensbrück told her he had also accompanied her father when he was taken for execution. He was nevertheless quite kind to Fritzi, reassuring her that there was nothing to fear where she was going; she would probably work in the fields. At first, the camp seemed no more horrifying than the Gestapo prison. Much to her astonishment, other Austrians were ready to welcome her. They'd known she was coming: prisoners working in the *Schreibstube* had spotted a teleprinter message from Gestapo HQ in Vienna, and the news had been passed to Rosa Jochmann.

The communist network learned of her arrival too – fresh from the Austrian capital, Fritzi was a potential source of information – so Olga Benario herself, with Maria Wiedmaier, came to find her in the admissions block. 'I was told two important prisoners wished to speak to me,' said Fritzi, talking in her apartment in Vienna. A youngster in the camp, at eighty-five she remains a youngster today by survivors' standards. 'I was told to go outside, as they wanted to talk to me on the Lagerstrasse. I was led out and saw two figures standing by the edge of a block. It was quite possible to talk but we took care nobody could hear. They asked if I had news from Austria.'

Fritzi's memory of Olga and Maria at work, gathering information, gives a rare glimpse of how these former Soviet intelligence agents – Jew and non-Jew – were working together, still trying to use their skills. 'They made an impression on me,' she said. 'They seemed to know a lot, and it was clear they'd been there a long time. I was in awe of them of course. I was very young.'

'How did they look?'

'One of them smiled and told me I had friends here. I think that was Olga. But mostly they wanted to hear what I knew, and it wasn't much. You see, I'd been in prison for twelve months.'

Even so, Fritzi was able to talk of the underground arrests, and of the Jewish deportations from Austria, which she heard about in jail. On the train she'd heard passengers talk about the Allied bombing raids in the Ruhr and the Russian fight-back outside Moscow. 'And I told them about my father's work and what had happened to him. It was nice for me. I had the impression they would look after me.'

A few days later, Rosa Jochmann fixed for Fritzi to move to Block 1, sleeping right above Rosa herself. Fritzi knew she was lucky to be out of the admissions block, where there were 'women of all sorts', but here in Block 1 she found women who understood each other. They could talk about people at home. 'It was more like living with friends. It was easy to tell who was who in the camp. Those from other blocks didn't look as clean or as well fed as us in Block One.'

Rosa was able to organise all sorts of things for the prisoners; they even had coal sometimes to burn in their stove. For Fritzi she fixed a job in the

*Schreibstube*. 'I suppose she mothered me in a way. Yes, she always took an interest in the young ones.' Everyone in Block 1 behaved and nobody stole, although once a woman was caught stealing bread from a cupboard and someone informed a guard. 'The girl was given twenty-five lashes and sent to the bunker, where she died.'

When they took their black coffee in the morning or their soup in the evening it was Rosa who served it in the day room. 'She let us talk quietly,' said Fritzi. 'About the day's work, or the news from home.' Some of the German women had husbands or brothers at the front and some had lost family or friends in the recent bombing.

Fritzi's table head was Anni Wamser, another German communist, who had the job of dividing the bread and putting it on the prisoners' shelves. Maria Wiedmaier was on the table too, and so was Rosa's German friend Cäzilie Helten – Cilli for short. Rosa and Cilli were rarely apart in the camp, said Fritzi, and they lived together openly as a lesbian couple in Vienna after the war.

Through Rosa, Fritzi soon met up with Austrians from other blocks. Frau Lange was the wife of a man who had worked in her father's underground cell. She was Jewish, though she'd been arrested for resistance. Fritzi would see her on the Lagerstrasse and they talked a little. 'Everyone was desperate for any news about the outside world, but if anyone asked about my father I'd start to cry.'

A Tyrolean woman, Fini Schneider, about thirty years old and also Jewish, took Fritzi under her wing. Fritzi looks back fondly on the friendships she formed in those first weeks: they were the 'Austrian family'. She often saw Rosa Jochmann walking nearby with Käthe Leichter, 'talking intently'.

Himmler visited the camp about this time, which Fritzi remembered because a rumour went around that the Reichsführer offered to release Rosa but Rosa refused to go. 'We heard she'd told him she was needed in the camp and didn't want to leave.' I asked if Fritzi thought that was true.

'It could be true. But people didn't like to talk about it.'

Bertha Teege, the *Lagerälteste*, had eagerly awaited Himmler's January visit, hoping to be released. 'The political women were nervous, wondering who would be lucky this time,' she recalled. But the 'Reichsheini', as Bertha called Himmler, 'was in a bad mood'. First he was enraged by an unshaven SS man, then he erupted in a fury about the slow rate of output in the sewing shops. Before he left, Himmler visited Block 1 and engaged in 'short banter' with Rosa Jochmann – "'Why are you here? You'd better reform" – and that was it, he was gone without releasing anyone.'

There is no mention in Himmler's diary of the January visit, though a diary note mentions a phone call from Max Koegel: 'Tuesday 13 Jan 1942, at 12 noon, SS-Stubaf [Sturmbannführer] Kögel telephoned Himmler to say the Jehovah's Witnesses had mutinied again. The women refused to do war work, so given 25 and 50 lashes. Sleep by open windows without mattresses or bedclothes, punished by withdrawal of food.' This protest marked a new phase of protest by a breakaway group of 'extreme Jehovahs', as they became known because they interpreted any task at all as war work. In this case they refused to unload straw: the straw was for the horses, the horses served the Wehrmacht, and the Wehrmacht was fighting the war.

However, the Jehovah's Witnesses' protest alone would certainly not have brought Himmler back to Ravensbrück. During the first week of January 1942 he was in Russia again, and on his return to Germany he had much to do. He was involved in the issue of the 'Final Solution of the Jewish question', which was to be discussed at an urgent meeting, to be chaired by Reinhard Heydrich, at Wannsee, a Berlin suburb, on 20 January. Heydrich was by then the chief of the Reich Security Head Office (RSHA) and Protector of Bohemia and Moravia.

It was probably the Soviet counterattack just outside Moscow in the autumn of 1941 that finally prompted Hitler to formalise his ideas on how to murder Europe's Jews. In the first days of the war, it had been thought possible that the Jews could be removed to Madagascar or elsewhere in Africa, but this had long since been ruled out, and now that the Soviets were fighting back, Hitler's hopes of herding the Jews east into seized Russian lands had also fallen away.

Nobody knows when Hitler formally decided on mass murder. The Führer had always pledged to exterminate the Jews, but until now no solution had emerged. The mass shooting used to kill Soviet Jews had proved inefficient and bad for army morale. On the other hand, gas had worked well in the 'euthanasia' programme, which proved that mass murder of innocent civilians was technically feasible and that German officials and German bureaucracy were ready to adapt to get it done.

By the summer of 1941 the T4 gas chambers had killed at least 80,000 Germans. Although Hitler had announced that the programme was curtailed, some of the sanatoria gassing centres in Germany had been adapted to kill unwanted prisoners at Himmler's concentration camps, under the promising 14f13 programme. And by December 1941 – before the Wannsee conference had convened – gas was already in use to kill German Jews deported to a new camp called Chelmno, established at Łódź in Poland, where it was done by pumping carbon monoxide into the back of mobile gassing trucks. Moreover, a number of T4 personnel had been sent out to Poland to explore how the gassing methodology used for the euthanasia programme in German sanatoria might be further adapted to kill Europe's Jews.

Such matters would inform the discussions at Wannsee, and though Himmler was not needed at the meeting itself, as the man nominated by Hitler to oversee the mass murder he would have wished to be close by. Developments at the women's camp had a bearing on the subject tabled at Wannsee. Just as Wannsee was being convened, the first gassing of women prisoners was about to happen, and it made sense to visit Ravensbrück to inspect the preparations.

Personal reasons probably also brought Himmler to the area at this time. We know that his mistress, Hedwig Potthast (Häschen), was pregnant with the couple's first child, which was due in mid-February. As was his habit, Himmler therefore probably combined his inspection of Ravensbrück with a visit to Häschen, either at his Brückenthin estate five miles away or perhaps at the nearby Hohenlychen clinic. Arrangements had been made for the baby to be born at Hohenlychen, and the chief doctor there, Karl Gebhardt, had agreed to deliver the baby himself.

On 5 January 1942 news that the medical commission was back at Ravensbrück sent a stir through the camp. Fritzi recalls that soon after her arrival people started saying something dreadful was going to happen, 'but nobody knew what'. Rosa Jochmann in the bunk below was on edge. 'I could see that many of the older women were worried. There was a lot of discussion.' On the Lagerstrasse the Austrian group, and particularly the Jewish girls, were talking about it. Fritzi recalled:

> Fini Schneider wasn't worried. She knew she was going to be transported somewhere but she told me she was going to a better place. She was such a pretty young woman. I can see her now, smiling at me on the Lagerstrasse. She was always happy and optimistic, but perhaps she was trying to hide her fears from me.

On his return to Ravensbrück Mennecke was suffering from corns, as he told his 'dearest baby' in a letter written on 5 January: 'My day today was as follows. At 9.30 I had breakfast and went to the city to run some errands; at the post office I put a stamp on the newspaper I sent to you, bought some postcards, because postcards and writing paper have become very rare! Then I bought two packs of corn plaster.' A car now took him to the camp to start work on the 'new files'. He was ravenous, 'so now I'll eat first. Yummy!'

After a six-week absence, Mennecke found changes. Sonntag had left for the eastern front and a new doctor called Gerhard Schiedlausky greeted Mennecke with the news that his wife had just had a baby.

Schiedlausky had one of those 'beautiful houses' in the SS enclave while Sonntag was 'surely freezing bitterly in Leningrad', Mennecke told Eva. With the Russian counterattack near Moscow now under way, there was an ugly anti-Russian mood in the officers' mess. Mennecke loathed the Russians too: 'Russian people are born and raised right in the dirt. A single [Russian] human life means as little as in any lower order of animals.'

Chatting with an SS major called Vogl, who had just lost a leg at the battle of Rostov and was on his way to the nearby Hohenlychen clinic, meant he didn't start work till 2.20, 'and so could only finish 30 files'. He reported by phone to Nitsche and Heyde, but they didn't mind and were 'very nice, asking how you've been'. Mennecke told Eva he was supposed to bring the current files to Berlin on 15 January. 'I go to Gross-Rosen for mid-January' – referring to his next round of selections at Gross-Rosen men's camp. The letter ended: 'I was back at the hotel at 5.15 p.m. I put on my best clothes, bathed my feet and took my time to care for my corns.'

The next day Mennecke saw 181 'pats' – 'All Aryan with numerous criminal convictions. Now there are 70 Aryan and 90–100 Jewish women left' – and he hoped to be through all the files in time to reach Berlin by early Wednesday. 'It's painful to hear about the Russian advance in the Crimea. Let's hope it will be all right.'

On 8 January Mennecke's letter to 'mummy' started with the usual description of dinner, after which he went for a stroll in the snow. His night was disturbed by noise in the next room, where 'a group of SS officers with their girlfriends drank one bottle of wine after another'.

On 9 January at 9.50 he was 'reporting' in again: 'Daddy presents himself before you as a completely clean piglet. What a nice feeling to have rinsed off the dirt of four weeks – but nicer when Mummy does it!' He went 'fishing' for some more 'sheets' to document, then the next day he went to the nearby Hohenlychen SS clinic where he met a man who said he'd sent the 'stuff well packed in a wooden box' – probably meaning black-market liquor.

By 12 January Mennecke was preparing to leave. 'My dear Eva-Mutti, My last letter for you from Fürstenberg, I begin at precisely midnight in my pyjamas.' As for his last day's work, 'the sheets are neatly put into alphabetical order and packed up. I said goodbye to the commandant and paid the bill for lunch (1.05 marks) and gave away my vouchers for today and yesterday.' His bags are packed too. 'Oh yes! Daddy knows how to do this too. I even think I can be proud of it this time, as everything fits in just smoothly, I am keeping the uniform on and all civilian clothes in the suitcases.' With that, Friedrich Mennecke left Ravensbrück for the last time.

*

On Sunday 1 February rumours intensified. The *Effektenkammer* staff had received a pile of fresh civilian clothes, no one knew why. There was more talk of who was on 'the list'. *Schreibstube* secretaries spoke of a *Sondertransport*, special transport, a word they'd seen on documents, but nobody knew what it meant. Fini told Fritzi that she knew her name was on the list. 'That's what she believed,' said Fritzi. 'I was very scared by this, but Fini told me not to worry about her. She believed she was going to a sanatorium.'

Frau Lange was also on the list, or so it was said, as was Käthe Leichter. But Käthe wasn't worried either, or if she was, she didn't show it and was quick to tell others that all would be well. Any who thought they were on the list were terrified, but friends tried to reassure them, repeating new rumours that they were to work in a munitions factory. Everyone was reassuring everyone else, but no one felt reassured.

In the hospital it was already clear that none of the sick or crippled were to be spared and all black and green triangles expected to be picked, but lists were changing all the time, there was still hope. Some talked of escape or revolt, but Teege and Mauer passed on an order – probably issued by Langefeld – that they should all keep calm. Langefeld herself is rarely mentioned in the testimony about these terrifying days, except as a figure watching from afar, often confused with her deputy, Zimmer.

Fritzi remembers that Rosa Jochmann was far from calm. Sleeping on the bunk below her she saw Rosa's growing agitation. She also saw her seek out Käthe Leichter to talk. Rosa herself said later that Käthe talked of making a film about it all. 'No one will believe us,' said Käthe, 'so we need to make a film to show everyone that this really happened. And you'll see, even when it is all over no one will believe us.' Rosa commented later: 'And at this time the gassing hadn't even started, but Käthe knew the gassing would happen.'

On the evening of Tuesday 3 February, the prisoners stood for *Appell*, but there was little doubt that the departure of the *Sondertransport* was imminent. By lights out, many expected it to leave the very next day. When the prisoners had been counted at *Appell*, the list of names was returned to the office and given to Zimmer as usual, but instead of giving the list to one of the clerks to read out for typing, she read out the names herself.

A Polish prisoner, Ojcumiła Falkowska, who worked in the staff canteen, got the first solid news about the list because she saw it. Zimmer had been in the canteen for her evening meal. 'I was told to give bigger portions to a particular group of guards,' said Ojcumiła. 'The guard Zimmer was not very careful and left the list of names on the table, so I seized the opportunity and glimpsed it. I checked that no Polish names were on the list and saw that mostly they were prisoners from the *Strafblock*.'

The SS drivers, von Rosenberg, Huber, Karl and Doering, as well as the transport chief, Josef Bertl, were eating in the canteen and talked about the next day's transport. 'They won't need anything where they're going,' said one. Ojcumiła was ordered to give the drivers bigger portions too, 'to reward them for their loathsome task'.

When the night watch had completed its final rounds, the blocks were quiet but few were sleeping. Meetings were taking place on bunks to discuss what to do, while prisoners moved about from block to block to say farewells. Rosa Jochmann visited Käthe Leichter.

Inside the Jewish block, Rosa found terror. The Viennese group – Marianne Wachstein, Modesta Finkelstein and Leontine Kestenbaum – were all expecting to be taken, along with Herta Cohen and other German-Jewish asocials accused of infecting German blood. Only a small group of Jewish political prisoners, including Rosa's friend Käthe Leichter, were apparently still in doubt. 'About ninety per cent of Block Eleven were convinced they would die,' said Rosa later. 'But Käthe said: "Look at them all, they're really crazy. We're too strong to be killed off. We'll be taken to the mines to work or something."' Rosa never knew whether Käthe said this to make it easier for those left behind, or because she really believed it. 'I will never know what Käthe really meant. It was the most awful farewell ever.'

That evening Bertha Teege briefed the communist leaders about what was to happen – she had probably learned from Langefeld. Those selected would be sent in the early hours of the morning to the bathhouse for a further medical examination. The Jewish block would definitely be called up along with others.

With this firm information, Bertha and Maria Wiedmaier decided that Olga should be told, and they went to the Jewish block to find their comrade. When they told Olga of the plan to assemble the prisoners in the bathhouse in the small hours, she answered at once: 'This means the end.' Bertha and Maria tried to reassure her. Maria recalled: 'Every one of us insisted that it still could be just a work assignment, but Olga said: "No, this is an extermination transport [*Vernichtungstransport*]."' Maria Wiedmaier recalled: 'Olga said that if it "looked like certain death" she would try to escape.'

At 2 a.m. the only light shone from the guardroom where Jane Bernigau, a night guard, awaited instructions. Then came the order from Langefeld, or possibly Zimmer, telling Bernigau to go to the bathhouse. Bernigau was carefully chosen for the task that night: aged thirty-three, she was just back from training at Mauthausen, and was in line for promotion. Once inside the bathhouse Langefeld – or again, possibly Zimmer – told her: 'Prepare the women for transport.'

The prisoners were woken by shouts, and many were ordered to move. The alert came earlier than expected and caught them unawares. The first to be marched out of their block were the Jewish women, but not all of them were called. Among those left behind was Olga Benario. Neither was this particular group taken to the bathhouse at first, but to the *Strafblock*. Eugenia von Skene, a *Strafblock* inmate, said the dog-handler Edith Fraede brought the women into the block on Zimmer's orders. A large group of *Strafblock* prisoners were themselves called up and all of them together – Jews and *Strafblock* women – were marched across the camp to the bathhouse, near the gate. Here Jehovah's Witnesses and asocials joined them.

Inside the *Revier* mayhem erupted. Those who were able to move – asthmatics, women with TB, delirium or venereal disease – were herded outside, clutching crutches and spectacles. Those who couldn't were left in bed or slumped on the floor to await collection. At the bathhouse Langefeld (or Zimmer) checked a long list of names. Bernigau and colleagues were told to strip and body-search the prisoners, who were given civilian clothes to put on. 'This consisted of dress, jacket and underclothes. Their old clothing was taken to the laundry for cleaning and handed out to newly arriving prisoners,' said Bernigau. Within ten minutes lorries drew up to the gates.

All this time the other prisoners had orders to stay in their blocks and not look out, but *Revier* staff saw drivers waiting by trucks. Milena Jesenska peered out of a window in the *Revier* as the signal was given to load the sick women. Grete said later: 'Milena told me how she saw the patients brutally dragged from their beds and dumped into the straw in the bottom of the trucks. From that moment on she knew where those trucks were headed.' The only prisoner left in the *Revier* was Lotte Henschel, the friend of Milena and Grete, whose name had been scratched from the list at the last minute. 'All in the isolation room of the hospital were sent to the transport except me and one dying Polish woman,' said Lotte.

Emmy Handke also watched from the *Revier* and noticed that young girls 'in perfect health' were taken as well as the old and the invalids. 'I even had to help some of the women onto the truck. They were taken off by the SS and we were left stiff with fear that something sinister was about to happen as we watched them – paralysed women, like cattle, thrown into the lorry with all the rest.'

Luise Mauer and Bertha Teege, the prisoner Kapos, helped load victims too. 'Bertha and I carried a lame prisoner from Block One on a stretcher to the camp gates where a truck was waiting,' said Luise. The deputy commandant, a man called Meier, hit Bertha on the side of her face for helping the stricken prisoner.

Even now other prisoners found the chance to catch a last word with departing friends, and the victims tried to pass scribbled messages, mementoes, or just words to be delivered to their families. Fritzi remembers seeing Fini, sitting in the back of the truck, waving to her and smiling. 'Even then she thought she was going somewhere better – I'm sure of that.'

Maria Apfelkammer, the *Effektenkammer* worker, watched her German communist friends Tilde Klose and Lina Bertram – the other two TB sufferers who, with Lotte Henschel, were to have been freed – taken to the trucks. She also watched another communist friend leave: Mina Valeske could barely walk, but managed to hobble to the truck, using her stick.

Rosa Jochmann came out to wave off comrades. 'There I saw Käthe walk along the Lagerstrasse in the cold under the stars. "Rosa," said Käthe, "if it really is that I never come home again please look after my three boys."' Rosa knew that by 'three boys' she meant her husband and two sons. 'And I saw my dear friend Käthe Leichter loaded on. I still don't know if she thought she was going to die.'

The entire camp – guards and prisoners alike – stood in silence as the backs of the trucks were slammed down, fastened with chains and driven off.

The next day camp life continued, but prisoners noticed women who had simply disappeared. Rosa Jochmann peered inside the Jewish block and 'the whole block was gone'. Many bunks in the Jehovah's Witnesses' block were empty. 'The Jehovah's Witnesses could all have saved themselves. All they had to do was sign a paper saying they gave up their faith. But from 1000 only five did this.' The *Revier* was empty too – apart from Lotte. Half the *Strafblock* had gone.

Precisely how many prisoners left that night, or who they were, has never been established. The prisoner secretaries were best placed to find out, because they had to deal with the paperwork. Maria Adamska said that as soon as the lorries left she was told to retrieve the records of certain prisoners and that the largest number were Jews, along with the old and sick. Their files were taken to the new camp registration office and left there for some days, before being returned to the political department and locked in a steel case. Rosa's impression that the Jewish block was emptied out was mistaken, as dozens, including Olga, had stayed put.

Nor did anyone know where the women had gone or what had become of them. Koegel's orders to the prisoner secretaries that night were simply to write *Sondertransport* (special transport) or *Sonderbehandlung* (special treatment) on the files of those who had left; or, in some cases, just 'transferred to another camp'.

The following day none of the prisoners were any the wiser, as Koegel was able to tell Himmler when he met him three days later.

*

Unlike Himmler's January visit to the camp, the Reichsführer's next meeting with Koegel is recorded in his diary. A note for 7 February 1942 states: 'Visit of RFSS Himmler to SS-Ostubaf [Obersturmbannführer] Koegel and Professor de Crinis.' Professor Max de Crinis was a leading T4 psychiatrist.

The diary entry is intriguing on two counts. First, unusually, it doesn't give the meeting place. As Ravensbrück is not specified, it may have happened on Himmler's private train, which he used to move around at this time. More likely, however, is Hohenlychen, the SS medical clinic. Karl Gebhardt had agreed to deliver Hedwig Potthast's baby, and we know that 'Häschen' was due to go into labour at any time. It is possible therefore that Himmler once again combined his killing business with a trip to see her. Hohenlychen was a quiet place to talk and Gebhardt was certain to be discreet.

The subject for discussion, 'Jehovah's Witnesses', is also curious. No doubt Koegel had complaints about the religious women – he always did – but it seems surprising that three days after the 4 February gassing transport, the Jehovah's Witnesses should be a priority for Himmler or even for Koegel, and if they were, why involve Max de Crinis?

De Crinis, an Austrian, was the *éminence grise* of Nazi euthanasia, and probably the major medical intellect behind the T4 gassings. Friedrich Mennecke said at his trial that de Crinis was present when T4 doctors met in February 1940 to agree the outline of the euthanasia plan. De Crinis also moved in the highest Nazi circles, and was particularly close to Reinhard Heydrich.

What Himmler discussed with de Crinis is impossible to say. However, given de Crinis's detailed knowledge of the 'euthanasia' gassings, it makes sense to assume that killing Jews came up. The linkage between the programme to murder the handicapped (T4), the murder of unwanted mouths in concentration camps (14f13), and now the decision, taken just three weeks earlier at Wannsee, to gas all Europe's Jews is sharply symbolised by de Crinis's presence at this meeting. All three killing programmes constituted a stage in the evolving Nazi genocide, and the methods involved in all three – particularly the use of gas – were similar. Even now de Crinis's T4 colleagues were out in Poland advising on how their experience could be adapted to killing the Jews in the proposed new death camps. And no doubt de Crinis was able to offer advice about more gassings closer to home, including the next gassings of Ravensbrück women.

One key priority for the local gassing was the continued need for secrecy. An advantage of carrying out the Jewish killings thousand of miles to the east was its distance from the German public's view, but the gassing of the Ravensbrück women had taken place at one of the T4 gassing centres inside

Germany itself. In view of past protests near these centres, it was of paramount importance that no one must know.

That no news had leaked of the Ravensbrück operation must therefore have gladdened Himmler and de Crinis. Church leaders had looked away, the people of Fürstenberg had taken no notice of the trucks that left the camp, and, as Koegel was able to report, nobody – certainly not the prisoners – knew where the trucks went. The secret of the Nazis' first mass gassing of women had been well kept – except that even as the three men were meeting, in Ravensbrück itself, the secret was, literally, spilling out.

A day or two after the women left, the same trucks that took them reappeared and pulled up outside the *Effektenkammer*. The backs were thrown open and out tumbled a pile of clothes, jumbled up with other items – crutches, slings, dentures, spectacles, walking sticks. Prisoners who sorted through this tangled pile found the clothes and personal belongings of the departed women. Once again, the *Effektenkammer* was first with the news, and the news was that the women must be dead.

It was not the clothes that proved it. As part of the cover operation, before they left the camp the women had been told to remove their usual prison clothes, with the numbers that might identify them, and to put on random, unidentifiable, civilian clothes. But along with this jumble of returns were items that had belonged to the women and were familiar to their friends in the camp: slings, crutches, spectacles – items their owners could not do without.

Maria Apfelkammer was appalled when she pulled from the pile the walking stick that had belonged to her friend Mina Valeske, the same stick Mina had used when Maria watched her hobble to the departing truck. It even had Mina's name and camp number inscribed on it. Her distinctive spectacles came too. Luise Mauer recalled: 'Our friend Frau Türner from Block One hadn't been able to walk without her crutches. Now her crutches were here, so it was impossible that Frau Türner was somewhere in a nursing home. And why should the dentures have returned when their owners were still alive?'

Luise said that a Jehovah's Witness who unloaded the truck told her that a list of those removed was returned with a cross against each name. In the *Revier* the prisoner-midwife Gerda Quernheim recalled receiving back artificial legs and trusses. 'We all recognised them and knew at once that the owners could no longer be alive.'

Even the guards appear to have been taken aback. Emma Zimmer asked the commandant why the clothes had been returned. They were camp property, he told her. 'I believed him but had my doubts too,' she said later. 'I felt by 1942 that everything was not quite in order.'

The guard Jane Bernigau said that the purpose of the transports was unknown to the guards at the time, but that after the lorries had left they 'continued to think about it'. A few days later, when the clothes returned, the camp staff could see that it was 'a transport of "candidates for death" [*Todeskandidaten*]', said Bernigau, adding: 'From the SS chiefs came utter silence.'

Rosa Jochmann said there was no doubt what had happened:

> Within half an hour of the lorry returning all the people in the camp knew about it and everyone knew the women were all dead. There was a cruel silence. The women didn't talk to each other – even the prostitutes. Usually on Sundays there was a singing hour when the women sang together, but that Sunday everyone was silent. At roll call everyone was obedient. The Blockovas didn't need to shout.

About four weeks later, the rumour spread that the trucks were coming to take people away again. Now everyone saw that the *Sondertransport* of 4 February was only the start. At this point speculation spread about the women's destination. Some rumours said that it really was a new concentration camp. But Eugenia von Skene overheard an SS man saying the new camp was in heaven.

The most persistent rumour was that they had been taken to a place called Buch, a suburb of Berlin, and a centre of medical research. Luise Mauer heard that the women had been taken to Buch to be used in medical experiments. Others said they'd been taken to be electrocuted. Hanna Sturm asked the camp doctor about the destination of the transports. 'He said the prisoners would be distributed to sanatoria in Buch.' Maria Adamska said: 'We heard from SS men that the women had been taken to a hospital in Buch and they had been killed there by electric shock. One of the SS men had seen this with his own eyes.'

At some point one of the women, possibly several at once, had the idea that the prisoners next chosen to go should hide messages in their clothes to say where it was they had gone. Assuming the same routine, they could scribble notes on scraps of paper saying where they went and what they saw. Concealed in their clothing, tucked into a hem perhaps, when the clothes were returned their comrades would know what to look for.

For the next departure the secrecy was twice as intense. The SS had learned from earlier blunders. This time they stripped the women of all personal items such as wedding rings and artificial legs beforehand, 'so we knew who would be going', as Eugenia von Skene said. Yet the secret message plan still went into effect, with several volunteers. As the prisoners were searched head to toe before they left the camp, inmates who worked in the bathhouse concealed tiny scraps of paper and pencils in places the women could find before they left.

The second transport took more Jewish women, as well as a large number of green and black triangles. Nanda Herbermann said: 'Many of my prostitutes from Block Two were among them – usually they were infirm, or weak and couldn't do a full day's work.' Luise Mauer said that this time the green and black triangles were taken away – 'minus the floggers', by which she meant the criminals and prostitutes who had agreed to carry out the beatings on the *Bock*.

One woman who refused to beat was Grete's friend, the Düsseldorf prostitute Else Krug. Else had been imprisoned in the *Strafblock* ever since refusing to beat Jehovah's Witnesses back in the summer. Now she was listed for the second *Sondertransport*. She volunteered to conceal a message. Rosa Jochmann recalled that a beautiful and clever Jewish girl called Bugi was selected this time, and she too volunteered. Careful note was taken of what they were wearing when they left.

Sure enough, a few days later the truck came back, and a quick search found Else and Bugi's clothes. According to Maria Apfelkammer, Else's message was the first to be found. Maria doesn't tell us what her letter said, but she evidently wrote the name Buch. Maria recalled: 'We all felt that the women had been murdered, but there was no concrete proof until a letter from the prisoner Else Krug was found sewn into her jacket when her belongings came back from Buch.'

When they found Bugi's message it did not mention Buch. On a tiny piece of paper, hidden in her skirt hem, Bugi wrote: 'Driving through Bernau. Now we are in Dessau. Everywhere the houses look nice' – and there the writing stopped. Bernau was another suburb of Berlin and Dessau a town to the southwest of the capital. Another message came back from an Austrian woman. Luise Mauer recalled that it was hidden in a sleeve and read: 'Arrived in Dessau. Told we now to bathe and will be given new clothes and assigned jobs.'

These messages were inconclusive about the destination. Else's had confirmed the suspicion about Buch, but some of them also mentioned Dessau, which was some way past Buch. Whatever the messages meant, they were seen as confirmation of death, and as news of them spread, the camp was enveloped in 'the same cruel silence as before', said Rosa Jochmann.

Meanwhile prisoners working in the offices had seen concrete evidence. Maria Adamska recalled that when letters from relatives began to arrive for those sent away on the trucks, the staff, under SS supervision, had to take the files out from the steel box again in order to reply. Inside each file they found a death certificate, with cause of death given as one of a number of illnesses.

The place of death provided was always Ravensbrück. The date would vary but was always in the future – in other words, several weeks after the women had been taken away. Emmy Handke said it was *Schreibstube* prisoners themselves who filled in the bogus cause of death. She recalled that staff had been busy for weeks filling in the actual certificates. 'There were four different reasons for possible death: heart weakness; infected lungs; heart circulation problem, or it could be written: "all medical efforts to save the person were in vain". Prisoners who had to fill in the certificates were allowed to choose which illness they wanted the woman to die of.'

The prisoner secretaries also prepared letters to be sent to next of kin, notifying them of the death and giving the false reasons, the false date and the false place of death. They also told the next of kin they could receive their loved one's ashes back in an urn in return for a small payment; it had not been possible to see the body for fear of infection.

The following weeks brought several more *Sondertransporte*. Maria Adamska said they left every fourth day until the end of March, but some said they went on till May. The best estimate is that there were ten in all, each taking around 160 women – a total of some 1600 killed. After the first ones, it grew harder to predict who might come next – there seemed to be little pattern. Nanda Herbermann says 'all sorts' were taken in the end. Nearly all had been doing forced labour until the day they left. Most would have lived for another twenty years:

> The people taken were not only sick with tuberculosis or prostitutes infected with syphilis. No, there were also healthy people amongst them, people who, perhaps due to the unbearable existence in the camp, had suffered an attack of nerves or a heart attack brought on by all the torment. There were others who had worked alongside the rest of us for years but were just not particularly robust.

At two or three in the morning the command went out to report for transport, and the screaming began. 'People who had previously suspected nothing now suddenly learned with horrifying certainty what awaited them – this screaming will ring in my ears today. And the way they were loaded up! Insults like "you rotten pigs" or "infected rabble" were shouted at them as their last farewell.'

It was probably some time in March that Olga's turn came: her close comrade Maria Wiedmaier was sure that Olga left on the third transport.

It was Maria who first learned from Bertha Teege that Olga was on the list and went to tell her, but Olga had already guessed.

> When I met Olga ten minutes later she instantly knew what was going on. She was composed, and tried to calm me down. She spoke of Carlos, of the party, of Anita. I tried to convince her that she was not going to die, that she would see Carlos and Anita again. At last I understood that it was best if I just listened to what she had to say. I had to promise her I would take care of Anita. She had a little photo of Anita that she took with her.

Maria said it was on a Monday that Olga left, at two in the morning as always. Bertha Teege and 'some of the comrades' went with the group from the Jewish block to the bathhouse. 'Olga promised: "If it comes to the point where they're going to kill us, I'll fight back."'

Olga too had promised to hide a note in her clothes. A few days later the truck came back, and Olga's last letter was found. It said: 'The last town was Dessau. They make us undress. Not badly treated. Goodbye.' Four weeks later a list appeared in the *Schreibstube* of those 'Transferred to another camp', and Olga's name was on it. 'This was the last thing I ever heard of her.'

By April there was already more concrete proof of death. Several of the women's families had by now received the notices from the camp with the lies about place and cause of death, and several had taken delivery of what they were told were their loved ones' ashes. Some of these relatives wrote to other family members, also in the camp – a sister perhaps, or a cousin – who had not been selected, stating that they'd received the ashes of the deceased and asking for more information.

Urns were even sent as far as Vienna. In late March, Käthe Leichter's 'Aunt Lenzi' – who had always acted as go-between for letters between Käthe in the camp and her husband and two boys in New York – had received a letter from the camp authorities with news of Käthe's death. The short note informed Lenzi that Käthe had died on 17 March, and with the note came an urn that held her ashes. Aunt Lenzi wrote to a family friend, also in New York, asking them to break the news to Otto and the boys, as the news was better given in person. Aunt Lenzi herself was shattered. She wrote to her cousin:

> All our hopes, and all the happiness of our lives sink into the grave with our beloved Käthe. Now I have to perform the last task of burying the urn with her remains. How different this end is from the one I had imagined – of being reunited with good Katherl. Her last letters were always full of unselfish love and worries for our well-being. Now this voice has been silenced for ever.

Aunt Lenzi added that she hadn't been told how Käthe died, but would pass the information on when it came. What came were of course the usual lies – Käthe had died 'of heart failure'; the place of death was Ravensbrück. Franz Leichter remembers that when he and his brother and father were first told the news they believed the story of the heart failure for some time, knowing no better.

Countless others – relatives of imprisoned communists, Catholics, Jehovah's Witnesses, prostitutes, down-and-outs, Jews and non-Jews – all over Germany were also receiving letters about the death of an imprisoned loved one along with urns full of fake ashes. Rosa Menzer died of 'cancer of the uterus', her family were told. Ilse Lipmann died of 'a stroke'.

Ravensbrück officials often had no idea who to inform about asocials, as the addresses of relatives were usually unknown. If they were Jews, the entire family would probably by now have been deported. But the rule said next of kin must be notified, so letters and personal effects were sent to local police forces, who were told to pass them on. The personal effects of a Jewish woman called Sara Henni Stern consisted of a few coppers. When the local police couldn't find a relative, they were advised to claim it for the German Reich. Julius ten Brink, who had been pleading for the release of his sister Mathilde for three years, received an urn with a package of possessions, listed as 'one coat, one pair stockings, one vest; three pairs pants'.

While all the official letters sent to bereaved families during the 14f13 charade were grotesque, the letter sent to the family of Herta 'Sara' Cohen stands out for historical reasons too. Herta Cohen was the Jewish woman arrested in 1940 for having sex with a Düsseldorf policeman and infecting his German blood. She was among those loaded into lorries to be gassed in the spring of 1942. A few weeks later the Düsseldorf police received a letter signed by the Ravensbrück commandant, Max Koegel. The police were to find Herta's sister, inform her of Herta's death 'from a stroke', and tell her that if she wanted her sister's ashes she should first establish that there was space in the local cemetery. The family should then send a letter confirming the space, along with the correct fee. If the letter hadn't arrived at Ravensbrück within ten days the urn would be disposed of.

While this bureaucratic sham adds yet more tragic detail to the story, it is another part of the Cohen letter which gives it historical importance. The letter signed by Koegel about Herta Cohen's case provides what may be the only documentary proof that the Ravensbrück transports were part of the 14f13 gassing programme.

It was almost certainly Himmler himself who ordered SS officials never to use the secret 14f13 code on any Ravensbrück correspondence; given the particular sensitivity over gassing women, the Reichsführer wanted secrecy increased. In Herta's case, however, the precaution was overlooked. Perhaps because the letter was addressed to a police force, it was considered safe to note the code, or perhaps there was simply a slip. For whatever reason, at the top right-hand side of Koegel's letter, next to the date (13 March 1942), is printed the telltale code '14f13', which signalled to anyone in the know that every word about Herta's death 'from a stroke', so carefully typed out below, was a lie: Herta had been gassed.

By early summer the screams in the night ceased, as the transports came to a halt, but the prisoners were still none the wiser about where or how the women were killed. Throughout the rest of the war, many in Ravensbrück continued to believe the rumours that the transportees of 1942 had been killed in a hospital or sanatorium at Buch, near Berlin. Even at the first Hamburg trial in 1946 some women spoke of Buch as the place of death. To this day there is much that is not understood about Buch, particularly in relation to Nazi medical experimentation at the hospitals there. It cannot be ruled out that some of the victims were trucked to Buch, either for experimentation or in transit, before being taken on for gassing elsewhere. Soon after the war, however, new evidence emerged about the location of the gassing.

When Hitler reorganised his euthanasia programme after the Church protests in the summer of 1941, two gassing centres closed, but two new ones soon opened. One of these was located in a former sanatorium in Bernburg, a pretty German town south of Berlin, on the banks of the River Saale. During the war there had been no cause for the Ravensbrück prisoners to think of Bernburg, or any other 'euthanasia' centre, as a possible destination; afterwards, when the story of the T4 programme began to emerge in the Nuremberg medical trials and elsewhere, the connection was made. Evidence came out that in 1940 Bernburg's sanatorium was fitted with a gas chamber, disguised as a shower room. In this room, which measured 14 square metres, more than 8000 people were gassed. Adjoining the gas chamber was a crematorium with two ovens, a dissecting room and a mortuary.

The victims arrived in big grey buses, but sometimes they came by train. Nurses led them to a room where they were asked to undress and examined; any with unusual physical or mental features were marked on the back with a red cross. In groups of up to 100, the victims were led to the shower room. Here they waited for water to come out, but instead gas poured out of the showerheads and they died, usually after a long and painful struggle. Once dead, the bodies with the red crosses were dissected in the mortuary.

The evidence showed that the first victims were brought here from nursing homes, but later came prisoners from concentration camps. On hearing this, a group of German Ravensbrück survivors, led by the communist Maria Wiedmaier, decided to investigate further, hoping to find out at last what happened to their comrade Olga Benario and other communists sent on the same transports.

The group, mostly members of the 'VVN' (Victims of Fascism) organisation, all recalled the secret messages that their friends had smuggled back, many of which had said: 'Last stop Dessau'. A glance at a map showed that Dessau was the stop before Bernburg, so the VVN women wrote to the mayor's office in Bernburg to ask for any evidence that prisoners from Ravensbrück had been gassed there too. The office replied that all documents relating to the gassing had been destroyed before the end of the war. Correspondence found at Gross-Rosen and at Buchenwald detailed transports sent from those camps to Bernburg, but the Ravensbrück files were all burned.

The man who could have solved the mystery was Irmfried Eberl, director of the Bernburg killing centre at the time of the gassings. Eberl was due to stand trial in 1948 but committed suicide before the case began. He knew his death sentence was assured: following his work at Bernburg, Eberl was the first commandant of Treblinka, the Jewish death camp in East Poland.

Over time the Ravensbrück survivors learned more about Bernburg. In another trial, one of the Bernburg doctors revealed that women were gassed there as well as men. 'When the female prisoners arrived they were already undressed,' he said. 'From our room we took them directly to what was called the shower room, where they were put to sleep with carbon monoxide.'

In 1967 the Ravensbrück guard Ella Pietsch spoke before a German inquiry about Bernburg. In 1941 and 1942 Pietsch was a guard in the camp's straw-weaving workshop, where prisoners were suddenly called out alphabetically and told to leave. This riled her, as it left her weaving shift short-handed. 'There were always two to six who didn't turn up the next morning,' she said. So put out was Pietsch that she asked an SS officer where the women had gone, and was told 'to a new camp'.

Guards were forbidden to ask such questions, but Pietsch persisted. 'I learned that the new camp was the camp of Bernsdorf in the region of the Halle. They gassed people there.' The day after making this statement Pietsch corrected herself, saying: 'The name of the new camp was not Bernsdorf, it was Bernburg.' Evidently an SS officer had let the secret slip.

Many families of those killed at Bernburg never learned the truth; many had no idea how to find it. Ten years after the war, however, Lina Krug, Else's mother, was determined to learn more. Like others, Lina had learned that her daughter had died of heart disease in a concentration camp, but the news made no sense. For one thing, she still didn't see why her good Catholic daughter, who had left home all those years ago to seek work, should have been taken to a concentration camp. Doubting the story of her death, Lina therefore wrote in 1950 to the VVN survivors' organisation asking if they knew why Else had been arrested and how she died.

As a communist body, the VVN was unused to receiving inquiries from the families of prostitutes, but Else was an exception. The story of the Düsseldorf prostitute's courage was well known in the camp, as was the manner of her death. The VVN survivors therefore wrote to Lina Krug, informing her that Else wore the black triangle of an asocial. This told Lina, perhaps for the first time, that her daughter had become a prostitute. The VVN were also able to tell Lina that her daughter's courage was 'exemplary'. Else had stood up to the SS on several occasions. She had refused to beat comrades, and for that she had been sent to her death.

Soon after the war, Käthe Leichter's husband and two sons, Franz and Henry, visited Vienna and learned the truth about her death. They also learned that not long after receiving the news about their mother, Aunt Lenzi – the go-between – had been sent to Auschwitz and gassed.

Fritzi Jaroslavksy, the Viennese resister taken to the camp as a teenager, had never learned the fate of her friend Fini Schneider, who befriended her in the camp. She last saw Fini smiling bravely at her from the back of a truck. She had always assumed she must have died, but never really knew.

When we met in Vienna, I showed her a list of names of Austrians whose ashes had been returned to relatives in Vienna, and a cemetery list showing where the ashes were buried in a Viennese cemetery. On the list was Fini's name, as well as Käthe Leichter's. Fritzi took the list in her hand, and stared at it in silence for some time. Then she said she couldn't understand how the ashes had got back to Vienna. Her mother had had to pay for her father's ashes when they were returned. Who would have paid for Fini's ashes? By then all her family were dead.

No urn or official notice announcing Olga's death ever arrived in Rio, and it was not until the end of the war, when Carlos came out of prison, that he learned for sure that Olga had died, although he must have guessed as much, as her letters stopped in February 1942. If an official notice was sent to Olga's mother in Munich we will never know, as Eugenia, along with Olga's brother, Ernst, was deported to Theresienstadt concentration camp in 1942, where her mother died. Her brother was later gassed at Auschwitz.

# PART TWO

*Chapter 10*

# Lublin

The German police came for Maria Bielicka in the middle of the night, when she was asleep at her parents' Warsaw home. She was nineteen. It was January 1941, and for the past eighteen months – since the Nazi invasion of Poland – Maria had been helping the resistance in and around Warsaw by delivering underground newspapers. Then one of her group betrayed her. A woman she knew was tortured into talking.

'The police just beat down the door, walked into the flat and ordered me to go with them. So as they stood there I got dressed and my mother quietly went to the kitchen and packed my school briefcase, full of things I might need in jail: cold meat, sanitary towels and a loaf of bread. That's a Polish mother for you.'

Maria talked to me at her flat in London's Earls Court in 2010. She said she had rarely spoken of the camp before. When she first came to live in England after the war nobody believed what she had to say. 'Nobody here even wanted to know about the camps.' Since then she had 'got on with life', working for Barclays Bank. Now, aged eighty-nine, Maria wanted to talk. She had been diagnosed with pancreatic cancer and had not long to live.

She pulled out a photograph of her father, arrested by the Soviets for his part in the fight for Polish independence in 1917. Her mother sold everything and took Maria, a toddler, with her to Moscow, in order to bribe the Soviets and get him out of the Russian jail. 'And she succeeded! How to fight for Poland was passed on through generations. My parents met smuggling secret books.' She points to a crowd in the background of the photograph. 'And that's the Russian Revolution going on.'

I asked if her mother had not cautioned her against joining the resistance when the Second World War broke out, and she smiled. 'You must understand that for a century and a half Poland was wiped off the map. Our mothers raised us to understand that the country must never be annihilated again. They raised daughters to believe that resistance was a role for young women as much as men.'

When Hitler's blitzkrieg against Poland began on 1 September 1939 it swiftly became clear that Hitler was set not just on military victory but on killing Poland as an entity and absorbing it into Germany. Behind the tanks came SS Death's Head units, under orders to sweep up, by stripping Poland of all possible leadership, as well as burying its history and cultural identity. In every town, city and village that lay in the path of German armies, schools, universities and town halls were closed and often burned, while teachers, priests, doctors, community elders were rounded up, tortured and shot.

Among those targeted were women as well as men. Whatever reticence the Nazis felt at first about brutalising German women, there was little restraint in Poland. In fact, so violent was the treatment of women during the German assault that after the war, even those later taken to Ravensbrück would recall what happened to them in Poland in these first days more vividly than anything that came later in the camp.

Stanisława Michalik was captured at her home in Terespol and taken with her brother, a priest, to the local Gestapo office. Here she found the town's stationmaster, the headmaster of a primary school and 'all the city's intelligentsia'. For days she listened to the screams of the men being interrogated, and saw them return, broken and bleeding. Men were told to cut off their hair and eat it. Then came her turn. 'They couldn't get anything from me, so they ripped my clothing off and laid me on a block, as two held me down the others beat me on the breasts, and all over with rubber clubs. When I passed out they poured cold water on me and beat me again.'

Stanisława saw her brother pass by, his cassock ripped to shreds. Many other women were brought in, including a friend from Terespol, a corpulent woman. 'She was terribly beaten, until her beaten flesh began to fall off. The pus literally ran off her body in streams, so the entire cell was filled with the stench of decomposing flesh.' The Gestapo torturers were often ethnic Germans, called *Volksdeutsche*, who lived in the Polish regions and made willing collaborators.

Women prisoners might sometimes be spared physical abuse, but instead were forced to watch at close quarters what happened to men. One woman watched a doctor she knew reduced to a 'bloody scrap'. Jadwiga Jezierska, a sociology student imprisoned in Warsaw's Pawiak jail, saw the Gestapo chief shoot a man, then tell women prisoners to go and look at the body. 'He took off his clothes and paraded naked in front of them.'

As the German advance moved deeper into Poland, Lublin, 100 miles southeast of Warsaw, braced for the onslaught. It was among the teachers and their pupils of this university city that some of the strongest resistance was now born. When the news spread that St Adalbert's bookshop in Lublin's old quarter was on fire, students ran to fight the blaze. Wanda Wojtasik, a wiry seventeen-year-old, shouted orders to others to form a human chain and to pass the books on to the next. Krysia Czyż, just fifteen, had the idea of taking the books for safety to the vaults of the nearby monastery. From then on both girls were active in the underground. Wanda distributed leaflets, while her new friend Krysia helped at a children's bomb shelter, once using her scout's ingenuity to tie an umbilical cord during an emergency birth, with a shoelace.

Secret cells were organised by the students' own teachers, and by parents. Krysia's mother, Maria, took a senior post as a major in Lublin's Home Army, the AK (Armia Krajowa). During the First World War her mother had served in a field hospital with 'the legions' – the armies that brought about an independent Poland in 1918 – and she passed on all she knew to Krysia. Krysia's father, Tomasz, a teacher, joined the secret teaching programme in which teachers held clandestine lessons for children whose schools were closed. Teaching became a form of covert resistance, a way of ensuring that however many died, Poland's history and culture would live on.

Michał Chrostowski, a radical intellectual, hosted a salon for Lublin's musicians, writers and artists. His two daughters, Grażyna, aged eighteen, and Pola, aged nineteen, were in the flat when Hitler's forces reached the city, making plans for an underground newspaper: *Polska żyie* – 'Poland's Alive'. Pola, dark and tall, was a journalist, while Grażyna, with fair tumbling curls, had turned to poetry and art.

Such resisters stood no hope against Himmler's local police chief, Odilo Globocnik, who by early 1940 was smashing all Polish opposition and sending the men to the first Nazi concentration camp on Polish soil, established at Auschwitz, in Silesia. Amongst those taken there was Michał Chrostowski. Soon Pola and Grażyna were arrested too, and taken for interrogation 'under the clock', as prisoners called Globocnik's police HQ, with its seventeenth-century clock. Other women were rounded up in distant villages and then brought to Lublin across the snow in sleighs, driven by Germans in sheepskin coats.

By May 1941 Krysia and Wanda were also captured and imprisoned in

Lublin Castle. Grażyna and Pola were kept there too. Nazi judges heard spurious charges against them and then passed sentences of death. From time to time a name was shouted out and a woman was called for execution. On 21 June 1941 both Grażyna's and Pola's names were called, along with eighteen others, but as a guard led them away to be shot the prison's commandant passed by. A Silesian who spoke Polish, he angrily ordered the women back to their cells, saying this was not a day for such things; the German invasion of the Soviet Union was under way.

The women passed the time waiting for their names to be called or watching out of a window where men – often a brother, father or husband – were lined up below to be taken to Auschwitz. Or they composed poems and drew portraits of each other on paper smuggled in by friendly Polish guards. Grażyna wrote in a note to an aunt: 'Write if you know something about Papa, he left on the 22nd to a camp.' Krysia too smuggled out secret messages to her mother, who sent messages back.

Some of the girls' messages, so tiny they could be rolled into nothing and hidden in a palm, have recently come to light and are displayed in a Lublin museum, 'Under the Clock'. Krysia's daughter, Maria, found the tiny notes hidden in her grandmother's old sweet tin. A handful of portraits are also displayed on the museum walls, including one of Krysia Czyż, drawn by Grażyna in the castle prison, her spectacles perched on a freckled nose. Drawings by Krysia are here on the museum walls too, including several maps, meticulously drawn, showing countless routes home to Poland, from Ravensbrück.

In September 1941 a train left Lublin for Germany packed full of women prisoners. As they climbed into comfortable passenger carriages, they felt happy for the first time since the start of the war, believing that change must be for the better. Zofia Stefaniak remembered: 'We were all pleased to leave the castle. We didn't know what was next but it was a change and it felt peaceful.'

They were leaving at a pivotal moment in the war to the east, and the signs of what was happening were all around, although they couldn't read them. On the truck taking them to the station they had seen vast crowds of Jews herded into Lublin's caged-off Jewish ghetto. On the edge of town they saw a massive construction site at the suburb of Majdanek; they had no idea that Majdanek would soon be the site of a new concentration camp.

Whatever the future held, these Lublin women felt that at least their lives had been spared. They were going to Germany, but what could be worse than what they had been through? Why transport them hundreds of miles to their death? If they were to have been executed it would have happened at the castle, of that they were sure.

On the station platform, relatives tried to pass last-minute packages. It was only when the speed picked up that the girls understood they were leaving Poland, with no idea if they'd find a way back, so they threw hurried notes out of carriage windows – to a mother or a sister – hoping the finders would send the messages on. Above the noise of the train, Wanda shouted to Krysia: 'We've got to hold on, do you hear? We've got to come back.' Grażyna held on to Pola. She told a friend that from this moment on, she would never leave Pola's side.

Within a few hours the bombed-out skyline of Warsaw came into view, and here more carriages were attached, containing women from Pawiak jail, among them Maria Bielicka, the girl with the school briefcase, packed by her mother. 'Later my mother sent another package on to Pawiak jail. It had my winter coat and ski boots, which I was able to take with me when we left for Germany on the train.'

It was dark when the train pulled out of Warsaw, Maria recalled. 'We sang to cheer ourselves up, and I remember one of the tunes delighted the guard, so we had some fun at his expense. When we were passing through Łódż we sang "Hitler hangs by his tie" and the guard still smiled because he couldn't understand. We always found little things like that to keep us going. Girlish pranks you could say.'

As the train moved on, word spread from the Warsaw women that they were heading to a place called Ravensbrück. Others from Warsaw had already been taken to this place, and some had managed to smuggle information about it back to friends in the capital. They passed through Poznań. Someone threw another letter out of the window. 'We are heading into the unknown.'

As they cross the German border, leaving Poland behind, Krysia is asleep but wakes to hear a friend cry: 'Dear God, let me die in Poland.' Grażyna composes a poem as Wanda tries to see where it is exactly they are going. On the second night they pass slowly through Berlin, which is totally dark – the dark of the blackout.

At dawn on 23 September the girls wake from a half-sleep to find the train is pulling through woods and passing a glistening lake. Soon they see freshly ploughed fields where men and women are labouring. Almost in the middle of a field, the train pulls to a halt. There is a platform and a tiny station: Fürstenberg. A moment of silence, then shouting and screaming breaks out as 'huge blonde giantesses' appear on the platform below, with snarling hounds.

The noise gets louder, the giantesses throw open doors and pull the women to the ground, and down they tumble, suitcases and bags all around them. 'Ranks of five, ranks of five.' The snarling hounds are unleashed. Wanda, Krysia, Grażyna, Pola, Maria, everyone lines up, but someone at the back stumbles and cries out. Nobody moves. The stumbler is kicked. Silence reigns. It is a dreadful sort of silence that they don't yet understand, but will go through again and again. 'Why can't I lash out at these hideous women with my bare fists?' Wanda asks herself.

Even the knowledge that they are all together doesn't help. On the contrary it makes the humiliation more unbearable. Wanda thinks: 'What the hell. I'll go for the one that's nearest and hang the consequences.' The black cape comes nearer. 'But what if she strikes me or Krysia? I'll look her straight in the eye.' The guard averts her gaze and passes on. As they march to the camp, the women pray under their breath. They stare at the woods and the lake and at the giant, sullen sheds in perfect rows, and as they get closer they notice symmetrical red flower beds around some of the barracks, and lines of small trees.

Waiting on the Appellplatz with their bags, they watch files of women in camp stripes, marching, carrying tools. The biggest shed sounds and smells like a kitchen. Skinny figures come dashing, hands to their mouths, signalling to the new arrivals that they should eat whatever food they have in their bags, as it will be taken from them. The arrivals signal back and offer their extra food. The skinny ones look terrified. They shake their heads, hissing 'Bunker, bunker' – but the new arrivals don't know what it means.

As they wait in the heat, some sit down on bags and are set upon by guards. They wait until late afternoon, and through the evening. At four in the morning they are still waiting and are finally taken into the bathhouse. Male officers watch as they strip. 'They came close to us, tall with their bayonets, and they laughed,' Maria Bielicka remembered. 'They enjoyed it. Of course they enjoyed it – to look at our young bodies – but I don't think it was sexual, it was more about power.'

Maria describes what happened to an older, obese woman amongst them, whom they knew as Granny Fillipska:

> After her shower she tried to put on a vest, which was far too small. She had an enormous bosom and these men just roared with laughter as she struggled. She was very bulging, you know, and one of these men came up to her with his bayonet and played with her breasts, lifting them up to see them swing. They all roared with laughter again.

Like those before them, the Polish girls were now shaved. 'Is that you, Wanda?' said Krysia. 'Is that Grażyna?' Grażyna's curls had all gone. 'We looked like clowns, some with dresses to their ankles, some to their knees,' said Maria.

In wooden clogs, they tripped out, trying to stay upright. More prisoners passed, who did not seem to notice the newcomers at all. 'They don't seem to have faces,' Wanda said to herself. 'Oh God, if you have a care in the world, grant that we keep our faces in this dreadful place.' Krysia was obviously thinking the same thing. She grasped Wanda's hand. 'They all look exactly alike,' she whispered.

Zofia Kawińska said all she could remember of the arrival was the din of the constant screaming of the giantesses. As they waited outside again, a handful of Polish prisoners came up and spoke to one or two of them, whom they knew from Warsaw. 'Prepare yourselves. Stand firm,' they told the newcomers. Maria Bielicka recognised a friend from Warsaw called Maria Dydyńska. 'Maria looked terrified to see us and that frightened me – as if she knew something.'

Another figure rushed out at them and hissed: '*Sondertransport*' – special transport. Sinister whispers echoed: '*Sondertransport, Sondertransport.*'

At first, nothing special seemed to happen to this *Sondertransport*. After the 'bath' they were given red felt triangles stamped with a black P. Almost all foreign arrivals were designated political and a letter printed on the triangle denoted nationality. The Warsaw-Lublin women were given numbers from 7521 to 7935. Wanda made sure her number was next to Krysia's; they were 7708 and 7709. The new arrivals were marched in ranks of five to two quarantine blocks, set back behind a wire. Quarantine had been normal practice for several months, amid SS fears that arrivals from Poland would bring typhus.

Increasing overcrowding had made cleanliness harder to maintain, so extra rules had been introduced: the soles of shoes were checked for specks of dirt, a lice-checking gang was formed. As the Poles were seen as dirty the new arrivals had to scrub their block several times a day with a brush made of rice stalks.

To begin with the cleanliness was a thrill. At Lublin Castle fleas had massed in black heaps, but here there were white sheets and every woman had her own utensils, as well as a cloth for cleaning them. One of the quarantine Blockovas, a *Volksdeutsche* called Hermine, constantly harassed the women, but at least her bullying produced order, which they hadn't known for months.

There was no work in quarantine. Days passed sitting around in the block. They had been stripped of everything by now – snow boots, sketchpads, pencils – all taken away on arrival to be labelled and stored. Crosses were yanked from necks. Those with toothbrushes could keep them. And if they had them, sanitary towels were allowed; the knitted ones, supplied by the camp, had run out. But most of these women had stopped menstruating long ago, with the shock of the first imprisonment.

Now they lived in boredom, doing nothing, sitting in the 'day room' squashed on benches, or on the floor. They made up games and listened to the rhythm of the camp – the sirens, the tramp of feet, the shouts of '*Raus! Raus! Achtung!*' and the howling of dogs. In the mornings and evenings they got half a beaker of coffee, which Wanda and Krysia guessed was made with acorns or from some part of a turnip. The bread had the consistency of clay and was mixed with wood shavings. The midday meal was a bowl of potatoes in their jackets with mashed swede or mangel-wurzel.

When the 9 p.m. siren rang for sleep, and Hermine drew the curtain around her Blockova's cubicle, the girls lay close and whispered about their families, wondering what was to come. Prayer was forbidden. The wake-up siren sounded at 4 a.m. The quarantine blocks were counted indoors, but through the windows the women glimpsed women pouring from other blocks, standing for hours, often in rain. Krysia called these 'deathly parades'. 'But at least they can look up at the stars,' said Wanda.

From time to time the girls saw grey figures flit past the block. Suddenly these same grey figures would appear from all corners and run towards something and pick at it, stuffing their mouths. Or they sank on all fours and licked the ground, then ran back to where they came from. These figures always seemed to be alone. Krysia and Wanda called them – ironically – *Goldstücke*: 'gold coins'. As the *Goldstücke* wandered around, other prisoners passed them by and sometimes pushed them out of the way.

Every group arriving from now on would describe similar figures in the camp as their numbers steadily grew, but the Poles seem to have been the first to view the *Goldstücke* as a category. The guards had another name for them: *Schmuckstücke,* by which they meant useless, dirty 'pieces'.* In fact these prisoners were simply the poorest of the poor in the camp. Denise Dufournier, a French prisoner who arrived in 1944, described the *Schmuckstücke* as 'the most wretched, dirty, and ragged'. Always holding out empty mess tins, 'they resembled the poor of every country in the world'.

A year ago, the SS would have cleared the Lagerstrasse of any such women; now they were mostly ignored. A collection of *Goldstücke* or *Schmuckstücke* always hovered at the kitchen block when the *Kesselkolonne*, the soup-gang, started its round through the blocks. The women were waiting for a spill, which often happened because these kettles – vast iron pots – weighed a ton and the carriers struggled to keep them upright on the barrow, shouting to the *Goldstücke* to keep away or they'd spill the lot, and they'd all be in the bunker.

Sometimes the *Goldstücke* came up close to the quarantine wire, and the

* *Schmuckstücke* was also ironic. *Schmuck* means jewellery, or trinket, so *Schmuckstück* is a piece of jewellery. *Schmuck* is also Yiddish for 'poor man', which might explain its use here too. Guards more often just called prisoners *Stücke* – simply 'pieces'.

Lublin girls recoiled. 'Look at that,' said Krysia the first time they appeared. 'She has given up the fight,' said Wanda. And they prayed to God that whatever happened to them, they would never become like that.

A few days after their arrival, the Lublin and Warsaw girls see a quite different group of women appear behind their quarantine wire. Krysia, Wanda and the others hear talk that these are Polish friends, who have been in the camp a long time already. They have come to greet the new arrivals and to seek news from home. This contact breaks all the rules, but Hermine must have been bribed or received orders to let them approach the wire, because the Blockova says nothing.

These long-established Ravensbrück Poles seem strange and foreign at first. The new girls call them 'elders' or 'old men', as some have grey hair. Most have numbers as low as 2500, which means they've been in the camp nearly two years.

The fresh intake are suspicious of the 'old men' and feel superior to them. These early prisoners were arrested just for living in disputed parts of Poland, near the German borders. They weren't in the resistance, they didn't fight in the war. They've been here so long their skin is grey. Some have hair growing on their faces. And their accents are unfamiliar, they use mysterious words when talking about the camp – *Sandgrube*, *Bock*. And they speak German, the language of the guards.

But over the quarantine weeks, as the 'old men' return, suspicion subsides. They seem to have good advice for the new intake: 'Always save half your bread till the evening.' 'Never drink the water.' 'Pick out your lice.' Later the 'elders' bring bits and pieces they have 'organised' – the camp word for stolen or smuggled. A year ago the Poles were at the bottom of the social heap here, unable to organise anything, but by the time of the *Sondertransport* of September 1941 their position had started to change.

Exactly when these first Polish prisoners began to claw their way up the Ravensbrück ladder is hard to pinpoint, but it may have been thanks to a Polish countess and her fairy tales that their fortunes first changed. In early 1941 a group of Poles joined a gang of German asocials working in the vegetable cellar. During the long night shift they sat on top of mountains of swedes, peeling until each had filled twenty-five buckets – the quota the kitchen required for the next day's soup. It was hard to keep awake, but no rest was allowed until they were done.

One day a group of the Poles began reciting poetry and telling stories. They captured the ear of every peeler, and as they spoke the buckets filled at double speed. One Polish teacher told fairy tales in the dialect of the Tatra Mountains, but the most popular storyteller was a countess from Poznań, Helena Korewina. Her Polish myths and legends filled the buckets faster than ever. Noticing how fast a nearby Russian gang was peeling, the storytellers projected even louder, enticing the Russians over simply by the sound of their voices, and speeding things still further.

Even the guards seemed to listen, and word of the storytelling reached Langefeld, who was looking for a Pole to act as her interpreter. So fast had the Polish population grown that it almost outnumbered the rest of the camp, but most spoke no German and couldn't understand orders, which were often beaten into them instead. Langefeld preferred to be understood, and hearing about the Polish storytellers she called Helena Korewina to see her, appointing the countess as her interpreter.

By the time the students from Lublin and Warsaw arrived, the Polish countess had not only impressed Johanna Langefeld, but won the German blacksmith's daughter's trust. On Korewina's suggestion, Langefeld appointed several Poles as block leaders, as well as secretaries in camp offices. Korewina herself was one of the most powerful prisoners in the camp.

The moment the four-week quarantine is over the women are forced outside for morning roll call. Krysia says it's too cold to look at the stars. One of the girls puts a towel under her dress for warmth. A guard sees and smacks her in the face. Now it is they who are stared at. As the newest in the camp they excite a kind of jealousy, as if something of the outside world still clings to them. Other prisoners try to touch them.

After roll call the group are back in the block, queuing for coffee, but they haven't yet learned to eke out their bread, and the 250 grams shared out the night before has already gone, so there is nothing to eat before work starts.

Out on the Appellplatz again, for labour roll call, they learn they are *Verfügs*. As a *Sondertransport*, the new Poles are banned from working outside the camp, although no one tells them why. So they have to join the line of the *Verfügbare*, literally availables or leftovers, though to the Poles it appears to mean rabble – prisoners who have to pick up any work left over when all better jobs are allocated.

So as other gangs leave the camp gates, heaving kettles for lunchtime soup, the Poles join up with the *Verfügbare* and a *Kolonka* (short for *Kolonnenführerin*, forewoman) calls out their numbers. Certain *Verfügs* seem to fix with the *Kolonka* to get the plum jobs, but the new arrivals get to clear cesspits, shovel mud or throw bricks. The overcrowding has brought new rules for the gangs. Bricks, tossed from person to person, are counted so that a certain number is put in each cart; the amount of sand that goes on a shovel is checked, even if hands are bloody and raw.

There are those who know the ropes and those who don't – the new Poles don't. On the brick-throwing gang, for example, if one woman faints the others are not allowed to move her, so the bricks have to be thrown right over her to the next in line. But the German women, who are now experienced, throw fast, and if the Polish newcomer doesn't catch it, the brick falls on the legs of the one who passed out.

The Poles have also yet to learn how to catch the bricks but avoid the sharp edges. Soon Wanda's hands are a mass of bleeding flesh – so bad is the pain that she lets them drop and watches the blood drip down. 'What's going on?' Wanda lifts her hands to show the guard. After lunch break – watery soup in the block – the same guard quietly pulls her out of the line and sends her to carry baskets for a day or two.

At 7 p.m. the siren sounds and they rush to queue again for swede soup. At 8.15 it sounds for bed and at 9 for silence, except that now a guard with a dog comes poking at the bodies to see who has put on extra clothes. Culprits are turfed out onto the floor and are set upon by the dog. The guard leaves for the night shouting out: '*Alles in Ordnung.*'

In the block the girls try hard to understand the rules, if only so as not to break them. Clearly, German property is sacrosanct, so a scratched cup means a report, and probably a beating. Initiative brings the cruellest punishment. A woman makes toe warmers out of scraps against frostbite. She gets twenty-five lashes, even though now she can't work. Another alters a dress to fit her better. She is whipped. And all rules must be followed at once: on the order you leave the block 'like fleeing a burning building' or else you get a dousing, which in winter means frozen clothes all day.

But the rules have no logic. They multiply by the day. The cleanliness they welcomed at first is enforced not for hygiene but as a crazed obsession. For example, the women are told to wipe glasses with a dirty apron because the clean dishcloth might leave white fuzz. And the rules on folding blankets have now run riot. Not only are bedclothes folded and refolded, but so is everything. Much of Sunday is spent folding beds, blankets, towels, dish-cloths, napkins, into ever more intricate triangles.

Yet enforcement is entirely arbitrary, depending on the whim of the Blockova. One has a rule that says windows must be left wide open all night, so the women wake up to find hoarfrost on the ceiling, dropping onto beds and melting. Sometimes they have to yank frozen hair off their pillows. Another Blockova likes to spot-check knickers for extra padding. To do so she suddenly locks the dormitory door and forces everyone to march in front of her holding their skirts up their back.

Another goes wild if a prisoner tries to improve the look of her hair. Often punishment is given to teach a lesson, as the camp is now so big that not all offenders are caught. So a seventeen-year-old suffers two weeks in the bunker simply because she tried to trim her fringe. The cell is freezing and her legs turn gangrenous, so she is taken to the *Revier* for amputation, but surgery comes too late and the girl dies.

By the winter the new arrivals' shaved scalps are beginning to sprout new hair. Grażyna Chrostowska, the Lublin poet, tries to make a hairstyle with her tufts, but a guard spots this and Grażyna is shaved anew as a punishment. The largest number of new rules are designed to stamp out friendship, or in camp-speak, association. The Poles, as a group, are particularly guilty of friendship and association, so they are told there can be no meetings, and one day that they can't exchange looks through a window. They can't shake hands in greeting, or speak to each other without permission.

But Halina Chorążyna, a chemistry professor from Warsaw, knows ways around these rules, and on Christmas day she defies the ban, calling the girls together to sing Polish Christmas carols. 'But don't sing out loud,' she whispers. 'Sing inside your heads.' They sing in silence, mouthing words in unison, and somehow it works. Halina has only been in the camp as long as the young girls, but she is already an 'old man' in terms of wisdom. Like many of these girls' mothers, she fought in the First World War.

Each day, under Halina's direction, the women decide to do something, however small, to help each other, perhaps a smile for someone like Grażyna, who worries about her sister Pola, who is sick. Friends notice that neither girl has smiled since learning that their father died. Or another day Halina might say: 'Befriend another who seems alone.' On the bunk below her, Stanisława Michalik finds a new arrival, a Polish farm girl, who is in great distress. On her first night she confides in Stanisława that she is pregnant, and terrified about what will happen.

The next day the young Pole is taken to the *Revier*. Later that night she returns to the block and weeps in Stanisława's arms, saying the baby has been 'cut out of her'.

By the winter of 1941 everyone in Ravensbrück knew that babies were being aborted in the *Revier*. The rules were that babies must not be born here. In the early days those arriving pregnant were so few that they were simply sent off to give birth in a hospital at Templin, a nearby town. Two years later, however, the number of pregnant women had multiplied, due almost entirely to the arrival in Germany of thousands of Polish slave labourers.

Since the invasion in 1939 Hitler's forces had rounded up Polish men and women, to work on German farms and in factories. In 1940 Himmler issued a decree ruling that any German woman who had intimate relations with a Polish man must have her head shorn in public, and then be led through the streets 'as a warning to others'. But the stigma of public humiliation did not stop the contacts, and pregnant German women – as well as Polish slave labourers made pregnant by German men – were brought to Ravensbrück and forced to have abortions. All were given the red triangle of political prisoners, but to distinguish them from other 'true' politicals, the other camp women labelled them, cruelly, *Bettpolitische*, bedpoliticals. Like the Jews who were rounded up for having sex with Aryans, these women were also accused of committing *Rassenschande*.

The abortions were usually carried out by one of the new camp doctors, a former naval surgeon called Rolf Rosenthal. Every prisoner who worked in the *Revier* recalled his butchery. Hanka Housková, a Czech prisoner nurse, recalled how on one occasion Rosenthal cut out a five-month foetus from a woman's body with a medical saw. Dr Bozena Boudova, a Czech pharmacist, heard groans from the operating theatre one day and saw a dead baby with its bloody umbilical cord in a bucket.

Rosenthal was assisted in his work by the prisoner Gerda Quernheim, known as 'the little ferret'. Quernheim, born in Oberhausen in the Ruhr Valley, was thirty-four when she arrived at Ravensbrück in the spring of 1941. An experienced nurse and midwife, she had been arrested for carrying out abortions, which outside the camp were illegal: good German Aryans were supposed to do everything they could to raise the birth rates, not lower them. Illegal abortion would nevertheless not normally lead to a concentration camp, but Quernheim had compounded her crime by insulting the Führer during her trial.

When she first came to Ravensbrück Gerda was assigned to the delousing gang, to shave heads, but it was when she joined the corpse gang, which collected bodies and took them to a collection point for onward transport to the Fürstenberg crematorium, that her attitude first attracted attention. Helena Strzelecka, a Pole on the same gang, recalled going with Gerda to the bunker to collect the body of a Jehovah's Witness from a cell. 'Actually it was just a skeleton,' recalled Helena, 'lying in water.'

Under Mandl and Binz the horrors of the bunker had mounted and water torture became common. There was a tap in Cell 64, known as the death cell. Prisoners who passed out after beatings were laid on the floor and the water was turned on. They were left there lying in the water so long they sometimes froze to death. This was what had happened to the Jehovah's Witness. 'The guard Hasse, was playing with the keys and making fun of the dead woman,' said Helena. 'When they put her in the coffin Quernheim said: "Oh you stupid Jehovah's Witness. Now you'll go to your Jehovah." The dentist then pulled the gold teeth out. They went in large quantities to Berlin.'

Within a short time Quernheim was selected to work in the *Revier* alongside the camp doctors. In return she was allowed to eat in the SS canteen, which was when Doris Maase nicknamed her 'the little ferret'.

When the new woman doctor, Herta Oberheuser, arrived, she co-opted Quernheim to help with lethal injections, which Oberheuser had continued to administer after Sonntag had left.

The German prisoner Klara Tanke, another *Revier* worker, recalled that in early 1941 a transport of Dutch prisoners – mostly communists – arrived and amongst them was a dentist in her twenties, suffering from jaundice. Klara recalled: 'She asked me for a pill to soothe her pain. I couldn't help her. The Dutch woman complained to Oberheuser, who said: "I will give you an injection to give you peace." Quernheim went off to fetch the syringe from the medical room and Oberheuser then administered a lethal injection. The body was taken to the room where corpses were kept.'

Klara also saw Dr Oberheuser give a lethal injection to an eighteen-year-old woman from Bremerhaven, which was her home town. The woman was injected for 'bed-wetting', said Clara. Again, it was Quernheim who fetched the syringe.

When Rolf Rosenthal learned that Quernheim was a trained midwife, he instructed her to help with abortions, which in the camp were legal because the prisoners were 'lives not worth living'. Quernheim's crime had now become a duty: she helped Rosenthal induce labour, and then killed the foetus either by strangling or by drowning in a bucket. In return she earned more privileges, wearing a clean white apron and sleeping overnight in the *Revier*.

Ilse Machova, another Czech *Revier* worker, described how Quernheim disposed of the bodies at night by placing them in cardboard boxes, taking them to the camp boiler and throwing them into the furnace. Prisoners also saw her walking to the boiler in broad daylight, usually carrying a bucket. In the words of the prisoner nurse Hanka Housková:

> We often caught sight of Gerda Quernheim's pail, covered with a woollen cloth, that she carried back and forth daily, containing the dead newborn infants. Once she carried two pails. On another occasion, we convinced ourselves that we heard the cry of a newborn child coming from her pail. After this cry we ran out to the corridor. Dr Rosenthal came along and asked what we were doing and chased us back to work.

The identities of the mothers and dead babies were not recorded, and after the war the surviving bedpoliticals rarely wished to talk, such was the shame they still felt. The story of Leni Bitterhoff, however, as she told it to an investigating police officer, was among the few Nazi police files that survived.

In 1939, after a tip-off, police opened a file on Leni, a farmer's daughter from Kleve, in northwest Germany. Leni lost her husband on the eastern front in 1941. According to her police interrogation, it was while her husband was away that she visited a friend who worked in an inn, and there met a Polish worker called Michał, whose wife also worked there. He smiled, but 'I didn't return the smile.'

When, two years later, they met again on the street they stopped to talk. A week later Michał visited Leni's flat, where he kissed her. 'Also the Pole touched me immorally during the fondling, which I did not resist.' She went on: 'After prompting [by the police] I admit that we had sexual intercourse during this meeting.' There were further visits. The couple had sex, and 'I have to admit I gave the Pole coffee and bread on two occasions.' Once she went to the cinema with Michał and his wife, and afterwards 'they went home to their place and I went home alone'.

Leni did not hear from Michał again for some time, though she sent him a Christmas card, by which time she knew she was pregnant with his child. 'I knew that Michał was the father. I did not have sex with other men.' Michał gave her a bracelet, 'which I hereby give to the police'. In return for the bracelet, Leni gave Michał a little handkerchief. 'I owned the handkerchief and did not buy it especially for Michał.'

She told Michał about her pregnancy, and he promised to divorce his wife and marry her. But Leni was soon brought to Ravensbrück, where the baby was aborted, probably by Rolf Rosenthal.

In the winter months of 1941–2 the Polish *Verfügs* were given pickaxes and told to break up the frozen sand, chopping out a square, before moving it to another place. After a big snowfall, the gang was sent to pull barrows out from the edge of the lake, where they were half-submerged in mud and ice. They filled them with snow and pushed them up the muddy hillside to the SS houses at the top, then dumped the snow and came back down, watched by guards with dogs.

Wanda saw that Krysia couldn't make it. A huge hound was straining to maul her the minute she fell, so Wanda walked behind her and didn't see that she was crying until they reached the top. It was then that the barrow slipped from Krysia's hands and a guard fell on her with a horsewhip. Instinctively Wanda stepped in and put up an arm to shield her, shouting to the guard: 'Can't you see the child is all in?' The guard looked at her, astonished, and walked away. From that moment on Wanda vowed never to leave Krysia's side.

After six months in the camp, the Polish students were learning how to get round some of the rules. For example, the rules against friendship were drawing the women closer, into ever smaller, safer groups, and forcing them to show their friendship in new ways. In the blocks, late at night, or perhaps at mealtimes, the school-age Poles attended lessons organised for them by older women, often teachers, so that they would not be behind in their studies when they went home.

Zofia Pociłowska, a sculptor, started making tiny little gifts for her friends, chiselling with broken sticks on anything she could find. One day, someone outside the block organised a knife for Zofia. Now she could sculpt much finer objects, like a crucifix on a piece of coal, or a Mother Mary on the end of a toothbrush, the size of a thumbnail. Overnight, Zofia became the most popular woman in the block. Everyone wanted a sculpture of their own, which they could admire and hide in a crack in the wall. The most sought-after sculpture of all was a ring engraved with the prisoner's camp number.

Grażyna composed more poems and 'gave' them to her friends – though she had no paper, so to record them safely she composed at roll call, standing in the centre of her rank of five and thinking up lines that were passed along to those closest, and each remembered a line or two – 'Rambling bird, passing birds, why are you flying here? This is no path for you; it is a camp, a place condemned and forgotten by God' – as the count went on. Janina Iwańska, another friend from Lublin, could remember the whole lot. Sometimes they managed to organise scraps of paper to write the poems down.

Then came a move to stamp out Polish friendships another way, by splitting up the Polish group and sending them to different blocks. Wanda and Krysia's new block was 'full of prostitutes and thieves of every nationality, coarse, screaming harridans' who 'spat on our sheets and stole our few treasures', as Wanda recalled it later. Two weeks later the girls were transferred to Block 11. Here women, many of them Gypsies, performed what Wanda called ugly and inhuman acts of lesbian love.

Sitting in her Kraków apartment, overlooking the central square, I asked Wanda about the 'inhuman acts'. A portrait of Pope John Paul II stared down on us from the wall, and Wanda stared too, saying nothing. She asked if I had travelled all the way to Kraków to ask her that. But there was a time when Wanda Wojtasik was haunted by the 'inhuman acts' of lesbian love as much as she was by other acts the camp was known for. In her memoir, published in 1948, she said that Block 11 was where she 'lost her innocence' and where this thing called 'LL' – lesbian love – acquired 'a grotesque human reality'.

It would take Wanda ages to get to sleep. 'At first I couldn't believe what was happening and watched wide-eyed, torn between curiosity and despair.' Wanda managed to shield Krysia from seeing some of what took place.

Krysia, she says, was 'a quiet, pretty, graceful girl, not only innocent but also naive and credulous'.

Wanda wondered, however, 'whether one day we will be like that too'. A note was pressed into Wanda's hand by a Gypsy called Zorita, who was tiny and very thin. 'If you want to, come to the corner of Block 12,' it said.

> Zorita had seemed like a gentle girl, with great black velvety eyes. Only now did I understand the meaning of those inviting glances. My first reaction was to laugh. So I was to play the man, was I? But it was horrible, and sad. I wanted no part in it. But sometimes I would accidentally catch Zorita's eye, and what I saw there made me frightened. I recoiled at first and felt pity.

Propositions came 'thick and fast'. Wanda found herself in demand as 'woman and as man' as lesbianism 'spread like a plague'. She would have none of it, she said, but it destroyed her faith in the innocence of even simple human gestures. And Krysia saw, 'of course she did. How could she not see those awful scenes when they were actually being enacted by our own bedside? She cried for a long time that first night and never again came to say goodnight to me in bed, at least not in the same way as before.'

Other Polish women, asked today about the lesbianism they encountered, talk more easily than Wanda Wojtasik. Most say they were propositioned at some time. And some talk, like Wanda, of a time when lesbian sex seemed to explode in a wave of promiscuity throughout the camp – but only amongst the Germans, Gypsies and the Dutch, they insist, never among the Poles.

'There were these women,' said Maria Bielicka, 'and it was a shock to all of us students as we knew nothing of these things. We were brought up so very strictly.' But it was not as dramatic as some made out, suggests Maria. 'It happened rarely at night as women were too tired. Mostly at weekends. But discreetly. They kissed. Licked each other. Touched each other. Whatever they normally do. There were many couples. It was their kind of friendship but not one that we could understand at that time. And in any case we had more important things to worry about.'

In the early spring of 1942 the women were worried they were beginning to starve. The bread allowance was cut from 250 to 200 grams and the soup got thinner. A disastrous harvest had affected supplies across the whole of Germany and all prisoners' rations were cut. Wanda tried to protect Krysia from hearing the 'morbid, drooling' conversations starting up around them as 'gaunt-faced women, eyes glistening, hallucinate about food'. It would start with a conversation about a trip to the theatre and end with 'Where did you eat afterwards?' and details of their imaginary feast would spill out.

The newcomers were starting to grow hair on their faces, hands and legs, and their expressions were grey and dull, except when the talk was of food. Irena Dragan saw a woman catch a bird that flew through the rafters, and eat it raw.

Now there were *Goldstücke* inside the Polish blocks. 'There were some in every block,' says Maria Bielicka. 'When the food came you'd see them. They would always be pushed to the end of the queue and never managed to have anything at all. And the room leaders would always go for them. And they were in all classes, all nationalities. I knew one who was quite well off before the war but the change was so colossal she could not adapt. She was a landowner's daughter.'

'What became of them?'

'They wandered out of the block one day and disappeared – probably picked up and taken to the punishment block.'

'Did anyone in your transport end up like that?'

'No, we were a strong group. They were one here, one there,' and she points around the corners of her Earls Court flat. 'And the difference was that when we arrived in the camp we arrived with nothing. Everything was taken from us except perhaps our glasses or sticks for the very old. And they carried on taking things. But after six months we had started to get something back again.'

Some time in early 1942 Maria Bielicka was picked out of the *Verfügbar* lines by Langefeld herself and sent to the bookbinding workshop. The camp was so self-sufficient now that it was binding its own ledgers and records. 'She walked down the queue of women asking if anyone had ever learned bookbinding. I had once done a term of it at school, so I put my hand up.' Working here, Maria was out of the cold, and she picked up news from Czech friends working in the nearby *Effektenkammer*.

Others were getting better jobs too. Another Polish *Verfüg* was assigned to one of the rabbit hutches, where the job was to clean out cages and collect angora fur that they could sometimes organise. Several Polish women, including Wanda and Krysia, were taken out of the *Verfügbar* and sent to the straw-sewing and weaving shop, which made straw shoes used as warm overshoes for camp staff, and also for soldiers in the Waffen-SS. The work was unpleasant and the manager of the workshops, a tailor called Fritz Opitz, was a brute. The women choked on dust as they sat at tables plaiting and pulling at large bundles of straw, which cut into their hands. But at least they were inside a barracks, with a better chance to survive.

Nobody had any doubts that the better jobs for the young Poles derived in part from Helena Korewina's influence. It was six months since the *Sondertransport* had arrived, and in that time Korewina, the Polish countess-interpreter, had won Johanna Langefeld's trust. The two were rarely apart. 'Langefeld was full of affection for Korewina,' recalled another woman in the chief guard's office. 'Langefeld depended on her absolutely and followed her judgement. One time, when fifty-two teams of outside workers had to be organised, Langefeld told Korewina: "You do it, and tell me what you've done." It was like that. Needless to say the *Kolonki* [gang leaders] on the work teams were largely Poles.'

The Polish women with fluent German were also taking more and more positions in the offices and blocks. Maria Dydyńska sat in the Gestapo office, where she saw the prisoner transport lists and typed official correspondence that went to Berlin. The Polish dancer Ojcumiła Falkowska was working in the canteen. Poles were now working in every part of the camp, from the clothes store to the kitchen; they even cleaned SS houses. In the blocks, Polish Blockovas were now enforcing the SS rules.

But, also like their predecessors, few doubted that cooperating was the right thing to do.

The Polish military instructor Maria Moldenhawer even congratulated the Germans for their 'honesty in finally seeing the worth of the Poles, who, as workers, compared with the asocial German women, who were depraved types, inspired trust in the camp authorities'.

Through her influence, by Easter 1942 Helena Korewina had even secured Langefeld's agreement that the Polish prisoners be reunited in adjacent blocks. Most remarkably, she enabled the creation of a *Kunstgewerbe*, arts and crafts workshop, where young Polish artists could work, painting, embroidering and sculpting little artefacts. The workshop was based at the side of the straw shoe-making barracks, and, under Langefeld's orders, was given special protection by friendly guards.

According to Zofia Pociłowska, many of the girls who worked on the shoes, including Krysia, Wanda, Grażyna and others, were transferred to the art workshop in the winter months of 1942. How Helena Korewina persuaded Langefeld to agree to an art workshop is impossible to say. Perhaps she showed the chief guard the exquisite miniatures the girls were already making out of nothing, and Langefeld saw a way to help them.

How Langefeld persuaded Fritz Opitz, head of the sewing workshop, to allow the art workshop is not so hard to explain: Opitz took the artworks for himself and sold them. 'He even ordered objects especially for his girlfriends. So we made what he wanted and the guards came and packed them away,' according to one survivor's account. And other guards turned a blind eye, knowing that they would be given a beautiful portrait, or a painted doll. Grażyna's portraits soon hung in the SS houses, and officers' wives flaunted exquisitely embroidered slippers.

Another of the Polish student group, Wojciecha Buraczyńska, remembers how Helena Korewina used to visit the art workshop and watch them at work. 'Korewina was always elegant, even in her camp stripes. I don't know how, but some people were.' The Poles knew by this stage that Langefeld was to some extent protecting them. 'We had always known she was our ally. She let us leave earlier from roll call if it was snowing, and she never made us stand there longer than necessary. We knew she wasn't 100 per cent SS.'

As she spoke, Wojciecha hunted for her copy of Grażyna's last poem. It was about a sunflower, she said. Sunflowers grew outside the block, and through the window they could see their bobbing heads. She pulled out sheaves of papers, letters and drawings, including a sketch of herself as a teenage girl – 'Grażyna drew that in the Ravensbrück art workshop.' And Wojciecha found a tiny object and laid it in the palm of her hand, holding it under a light. It was a crucifix, carved out of the very end of a white toothbrush.

*Chapter 11*

# Auschwitz

Wojciecha Buraczyńska was not the first to observe that Johanna Langefeld was 'not 100 per cent SS'. Like the Poles, Grete Buber-Neumann, the former communist who later worked closely with Langefeld in the camp, came to see her as a woman torn in two by her conflicting instincts and beliefs. On the one hand she fervently believed in the ideals of National Socialism, dreaming of the day when the Führer would make Germany proud and great again. She also admired Himmler to the very end, certain that the Reichsführer SS had no idea of the crimes his thugs committed in his name.

Yet Johanna Langefeld never gave up her religious faith, said Grete, and found it increasingly hard to reconcile her Lutheran values with the SS order of terror, in which she was forced to play a part: 'So she came to the camp every morning praying and begging God for strength to stop evil from happening. What a disastrous confusion.'

Despite her confusion, however, Langefeld's life at Ravensbrück in the early spring of 1942 seemed settled. She had made her own apartment, overlooking the lake, a happy home for Herbert, now fourteen, who was attending the local school in Fürstenberg along with other guards' children, and played with them along the lake shore. And despite her disputes with Max Koegel, Langefeld could tell herself that at least Himmler still recognised her abilities, particularly her skill in keeping 5000 prisoners in line.

Just as important for a smooth administration, Langefeld had managed the growing ranks of female guards with success, and kept them happy. An efficient group of prisoners, mostly Germans, Czechs and Poles, were helping to run the camp.

In the spring of 1942, Langefeld even hit on the idea of setting up a hair salon for the staff, which made her popular with all. The German-Czech prisoner Edith Sparmann was amongst the very first to hear of it. One day on the Lagerstrasse, prisoners were asked if any had trained in hairdressing. Edith, then working in the *Effektenkammer*, said she had, and was ordered to the chief guard's office.

> At first I didn't understand, so they told me they were setting up a hairdressing salon at the camp, so that the guards wouldn't have to go into Fürstenberg each time. I said they'd need brushes and scissors and curlers and curling tongs and driers. They asked me to work there. I remember it became pretty well known on the Lagerstrasse that this was happening, and prisoners from my block said to me: 'So you've got yourself a big career.'

The salon was constructed in an old workshop on the other side of the camp wall from the bathhouse, where new arrivals had their hair shaved. Three prisoners worked there all day. There was plenty of work, as most guards had an appointment at least every two weeks. 'They liked to come to the camp salon', said Edith, 'because it was cheaper than the one in town – and just as good. The Olympia roll was all the fashion at the time' – she lifted her hand to her forehead in a flourish. 'It was a single roll swept back from the crown.'

Edith got to know the guards well because they came so often. She remembered Dorothea Binz, though Binz was not one of her regulars. And she remembered Maria Mandl:

> Everyone knew who Binz and Mandl were. When they ran the bunker they preferred to beat people themselves rather than have someone else do it.
>
> Binz used to scream at people, but in the salon she didn't shout at us. She was just like a normal client in a hairdressing salon. She didn't really talk to us prisoners, only to say what she wanted doing – Binz had an Olympia roll too, but longer than the others. Shoulder length. She was very blonde. She was naturally blonde. Many dyed their hair but Binz didn't need to.
>
> And she would chat to other clients there at the same time. She'd ask what shift they were on or what they were doing in the evening. To us they were like normal clients too.

I asked Edith what sort of hairstyle Johanna Langefeld preferred, but she said that neither Langefeld nor her deputy Edith Zimmer ever came to the salon. She didn't have her hair done – it was just pulled back in 'a messy bun', said Edith.

On 3 March 1942 Heinrich Himmler paid another visit to Ravensbrück. His desk diary states that he arrived at 11 in the morning and stayed for three hours. His main purpose that day was to talk to Koegel about a problem that had cropped up at Auschwitz.

Following the Wannsee meeting six weeks earlier, plans to start exterminating the Jews had advanced quickly. Death camps were being opened at Belzec, Treblinka and Sobibor, all in central Poland. A new department (IVB4: Jewish Affairs – Evacuation Affairs) of the Reich Security Head Office (RSHA), under the direction of Adolf Eichmann, was organising the exterminations and was about to send its first 'official' Jewish transport to Auschwitz. Twenty thousand Jews from Slovakia were due to arrive in only three weeks' time.

On the face of things Ravensbrück was not involved in such arrangements. The camp was not designated as a Jewish killing centre, or death camp, and in any case, under the new plans, any Jews arriving at Ravensbrück in the future would themselves be moved on to Auschwitz.

However, at this late hour two facts had been drawn to Himmler's attention. First, that among the Slovakian transport bound for Auschwitz were 7000 women. Second, that Auschwitz was not equipped to accommodate women. The camp had only ever held men, until now mostly fighters in the Polish resistance, or Soviet prisoners of war. Clearly there was no room for the 7000 Slovakian women Jews at Ravensbrück, and, in any case, Jews were no longer permitted on German soil.

At the last minute, therefore, Himmler ordered Rudolf Höss, the Auschwitz commandant, to evacuate an area of his camp used for Soviet prisoners of war, of whom few remained after mass executions, and set it aside for the arriving Jewish women. The area was divided from the men's section by a wall and electrified fence.

It is perhaps surprising that Himmler should go to the trouble of separating women from men at Auschwitz, given that under the new Wannsee plans all Jews were in future to be exterminated by gas. But not all of those arriving were to be gassed on the spot. Auschwitz was to play a dual role in the Final Solution: slave labour as well as extermination. Jews would be spared the gas chamber as long as they were deemed fit for work.

And while they were in the camp, it was of paramount importance that the sexes didn't mix, and possibly spawn more unwanted lives. The separation of the sexes was also a useful part of the camouflage devised to ensure that arriving Jews would not guess their fate. In Himmler's view, placing women and men in separate sections would seem to them more normal, more in keeping with a regular slave-labour camp, which was what they'd been told Auschwitz was.

And not only should the Auschwitz women prisoners be separated, but they should be guarded by women. This too would seem more normal, not only for the prisoners but also for the guards. So it was in order to recruit women guards for Auschwitz in time for the first Jewish arrivals that Himmler visited Ravensbrück on 3 March 1942. He told Koegel that he expected him to supply the entire corps of guards for the new Auschwitz women's section. In addition 1000 of his prisoners must work there as Kapos. They had to be ready by 26 March, just three weeks' time, so that they were in position by the time the Slovakian transport was due to arrive.

Himmler also told Koegel that as nobody at Auschwitz had any experience of guarding women, the entire administrative responsibility for its new women's section was to be placed under Ravensbrück's authority, and the camp would, from now on, train all Auschwitz's future women guards. Himmler wanted Johanna Langefeld to take charge of the new Auschwitz women's section: she was the most experienced woman guard he had.

The changes meant huge upheaval at Ravensbrück, but Koegel naturally followed Himmler's orders. Langefeld was dispatched to Auschwitz to reconnoitre the camp, returning a few days later. In the early hours of 26 March she set off again by train, this time taking with her 1000 prisoners to work as Kapos and a small troop of women guards.

We have little information about the guards who left for Auschwitz that day, but of the fourteen named later by Langefeld, several were notorious brutes. Margot Drechsel took a leading role in the roundups for the Bernburg gas chambers and Elfriede Vollrath, a Fürstenberg woman, was known as a beater, as was twenty-three-year-old Elisabeth Volkenrath.

The guards who left for Auschwitz, however, were vastly outnumbered by the 1000 prisoners sent to serve as Kapos. Among them were about fifty Jehovah's Witnesses and a score of political prisoners, mostly German communists, including Langefeld's favourites Bertha Teege and Luise Mauer. There were also a very large number of 'criminals' and asocials. It is surprising that such a large number of Kapos were thought necessary at the new Auschwitz women's camp. However, given the shortage of trained women guards a decision had clearly been taken – probably by Himmler himself – to let these already brutalised and desperate Ravensbrück prisoners keep order and do so in any way they chose.

Again, details are scarce about who these women were. There were certainly several notorious names on the list, including Philomena Müssgueller, the Munich brothel-keeper and *Strafblock* terror Kapo, and another hated prostitute called Elfriede Schmidt. However, given the large number, most must have been picked at random. For example Agnes Petry, the penniless Düsseldorf prostitute, caught up with Else Krug in the first '*Asoziale*' round-up of 1938, was among the group.

Else was now dead, transported a few weeks earlier to the Bernburg gas chamber for refusal to beat fellow prisoners. Now Agnes was on her way to Auschwitz to guard other prisoners facing the same death, though neither Agnes, nor any of the others on the train in March 1942, could possibly have known what their new camp would bring.

Apart from the Poles, who knew of the place because relatives had been sent there as resisters, few prisoners in Ravensbrück had heard of Auschwitz in March 1942. Even Langefeld herself appears to have known very little. On return from her visit she told Teege and Mauer that she had seen male prisoners 'in terrible shape', but that was all. According to Grete Buber-Neumann, so little-known was Auschwitz at the time that several Ravensbrück women volunteered to go there as Kapos in March 1942 thinking conditions might be better. As the train moved east, passing the ruins of Polish towns, at least one woman changed her mind and managed to escape.

Though little is known about the way the Ravensbrück women were chosen for their work at Auschwitz, we know a great deal about what happened when they arrived, largely thanks to Bertha Teege and Luise Mauer, who both left vivid accounts.

Their train pulled up at Auschwitz around mid-morning on 26 March, with just a few hours to spare before the first transport of female Jews arrived. At first the Ravensbrück women saw nothing to startle them. The landscape around the camp was more desolate than they were used to; instead of Ravensbrück's woods and lakes, they saw grey, empty plains, pitted with bombed-out villages. And the camp itself was far larger in scale, its brick-built blocks starker than the painted wooden barracks they were familiar with. As they entered the gates the women's section was deserted.

The first order they received – to stand to attention on the Lagerstrasse – was no surprise. In fact they stood for four hours while the woman who had escaped was hunted down, brought before them and flogged.

It was mid-afternoon when the Jewish women eventually arrived from Poprad in Slovakia. It happened that just as 999 women had arrived from Ravensbrück, so the first group of Jewish Slovakians numbered 999 too.

'The Slovak women were well-fed, educated, well-groomed people with extremely extensive luggage,' recalled Bertha Teege, who was so accustomed to seeing Jews as the desperate wretches Ravensbrück had made of them, that now she could hardly believe her eyes. She was told that the Slovaks had brought luggage because they had all seen the notices back home telling them they were going for Labour Service for three months and that they should bring clothing, linen and food up to a maximum of 50 kg. 'In fact,' she wrote later, 'everybody brought the best they had and everybody was firmly convinced they would be used for work.'

One of the Jewish women dropped a bag and oranges spilled over the Lagerstrasse. 'My eyes popped out of my head,' said Teege, who had not set eyes on an orange for years. She reported the incident to a senior SS man, Hans Aumeier, and was told: 'Stuff your oranges, arsehole.'

The Slovak women were stripped, a process the Ravensbrück prisoner guards were familiar with, but the difference here was that none of their possessions were recorded. 'Our first thought was why are all the prisoners' possessions jumbled up? Later the women will surely have to get their stuff back.' Clothes were also thrown on a big pile, and the food they brought set aside. The Slovakians were then made to stand naked ready for the 'bath', described by Luise as a tub eight metres wide in which all 1000 women had to take a bath in the same water.

The gynaecological examination, brutal enough at Ravensbrück, was performed here by the coarsest of Ravensbrück's prostitute asocials, who were told to probe not for disease but for hidden jewellery. Some of the Jewish women were as young as fourteen and many were virgins, a fact that delighted the watching SS, who looked on, yelling obscenities. An SS doctor arrived on the scene and said he didn't believe these young Jews were all virgins and he would find out for himself.

Clothing was handed out, but instead of the clean stripes of Ravensbrück, these Slovakians received torn and filthy lice-infested men's uniforms, taken from Russians who had occupied their blocks before execution. The women were crammed into the vacated blocks in such numbers that many had no bed, and certainly no bed linen.

Bertha Teege wrote later that she and her friend Luise Mauer were 'innocent' about all this – 'After a few hours in Auschwitz we had no idea what it all meant.' It would take years before historians established what these events meant: the arrival of the Slovak Jews on 26 March 1942 was the first 'official' Jewish transport, sent to Auschwitz by Adolf Eichmann, the man charged with implementing the Final Solution.

And yet, although the German communist prisoners had no idea of this, they seem to have had a sense of being close to the epicentre of some as yet unknown monstrosity. 'March 26th 1942 – I will never forget the date,' wrote Bertha Teege later. And though 'innocent', these two Ravensbrück prisoners were not perhaps as innocent as they made out. At Ravensbrück they had been attuned to Nazi methods. Both had witnessed how Jews were treated there, and both had witnessed – and helped Langefeld organise – selections for the 14f13 death transports.

So the women were more used than most to certain signs. In particular they were used to the masquerade put on by the SS to disguise what they were doing. Just two days after the Slovaks' arrival, Bertha Teege was working in Langefeld's office when she was handed a box of 700 letters written by the Slovak women to their loved ones at home. All had been given pencil and paper and promised that the letters would be sent. Teege was told to burn the letters in an oven, which she did, under supervision.

Over the next eight days more transports arrived from Slovakia, and in the following weeks more huge transports arrived from Slovakia and other parts of Poland, so that by the end of April there were 6700 prisoners in the new Auschwitz women's section. This figure was higher than the number in Ravensbrück itself – by April 1942, some 5800 – and as the numbers rose Teege and Mauer observed more signs of their likely fate. Conditions were so appalling that the once well-groomed women were now covered in black lice and marked with scabies boils.

Teege and Mauer's descriptions of the women's section are echoed by the Auschwitz commandant himself, Rudolf Höss. In his memoir, written while awaiting execution, he devotes several pages to the women's section, which appears to have fascinated him, almost more than any other part of the camp. Conditions there were atrocious, he says, and far worse than in the men's camp, due largely to extreme overcrowding in the female blocks. From the start the prisoners there had been 'piled high to the ceiling'. The meagre sanitary facilities were soon overwhelmed and women relieved themselves wherever they could. A prisoner sent on an errand from the men's camp reported that conditions in the women's blocks 'passed all imagination and everything was black with lice'. Women were dying of typhus or killing themselves first.

According to Teege and Mauer, conditions on the women's labour gangs were also worse than anything they had seen at Ravensbrück. Male dog-handlers guarded the workers, and SS men patrolled on horseback with submachine guns. Escapers were shot and the officers put in reports 'to impress the commandant and get a day off in Katowice'. Bertha Teege knew this, as her job was to file the reports. Often the workers got nothing at all to eat, as the bread was mouldy and the excuse given by the 'bandit SS guards' was that it was 'booty from France', and all they had.

The women of the first Slovakian transport were sent out to work demolishing bombed houses in the area. 'They were supposed to raze them to the ground,' Bertha recalled, 'hitting walls with long and very heavy iron rods.' There were many injuries and deaths and the returning gangs were a terrible sight, with women coming back bitten, beaten, and often carrying bodies of their dead.

Teege and Mauer found out 'little by little' about the 'facilities and methods' used here, and understood that the SS had deliberately created these conditions in order to ensure that the women housed in the camp would die. 'You never got rid of the horror,' wrote Bertha, 'and in addition there was the constant prospect that you yourself might become one of the victims one day.'

Höss, by contrast, blamed the horror of the women's camp on the prisoners themselves. 'When the women had reached the bottom they would let themselves go completely,' he said. 'They would then stumble about like ghosts without any will of their own, and had to be pushed everywhere by the others, until the day came when they quietly passed away.'

Höss wishes us to believe that to him these 'stumbling female corpses' were 'a terrible sight'. There was nothing he could do about it, he said, and blamed staff shortages and Langefeld herself: 'To have put these swarming ant heaps into proper order would have required more than a few female supervisors allotted me from Ravensbrück. The chief female supervisor of the period, Frau Langefeld, was in no way capable of coping with the situation.'

However, as Teege and Mauer were also fast beginning to see, those women who didn't do as the SS wanted by passing away were murdered outright. Shootings had occurred from time to time at Ravensbrück, but such killing – always out of sight – was usually done singly, and bore no relation to the mass murder that was practised here, as Luise learned when a friend invited her to look through a spyhole punched in a barracks wall. Here she saw fifteen to eighteen women lying dead, some holding children in their arms. The SS were firing at the dead and the living indiscriminately.

According to Bertha Teege the Auschwitz prisoners had no idea about the gassing. This was plausible, because at this early stage of the slaughter the camp had just one gas chamber which had barely been used and was half hidden underground, with grass growing on top. When killings happened nobody was supposed to be around, but Bertha Teege went to investigate one day and heard screaming.

After about two weeks in the camp, Luise Mauer was called to Langefeld's office and instructed to make all prisoners 'vanish' from the Lagerstrasse. She did as she was told, and on returning to the office found only her friend Bertha still there. Everyone else, including the SS, had left. Half an hour later about 300 women, children and men, young and old, healthy and sick, some walking on crutches, approached down the Lagerstrasse, flanked by SS men with dogs. They drove the prisoners into a tunnel, a sort of subterranean passage leading into what looked like a giant silo with ventilation shafts. Two SS men in gas masks emptied cans into the shafts. The air filled with dreadful yelling and screaming, the children's most prolonged, and subsiding into whimpering. After fifteen minutes all was silence. 'We knew that 300 people had just been killed,' said Luise Mauer. The killing she had witnessed was probably the first mass gassing at Auschwitz.

One hour later Johanna Langefeld appeared at the office looking pale and distraught. She was even more distressed on finding Teege and Mauer there, and asked if they had seen what happened. When they answered yes, Langefeld told them she hadn't known that people were being killed here. She said: 'For God's sake don't tell anyone what you have seen, or you will be gassed yourselves.'

Almost at once she made a protest to Obergruppenführer Oswald Pohl, head of the SS Economic-Administrative Main Office, who happened to be inspecting the camp soon after the event. Speaking later to US interrogators, she said: 'I took the first opportunity to raise the state of affairs with Lt General Pohl.' But Langefeld is vague about the nature of the state of affairs that she raised. From her subsequent comments it seems highly unlikely that she mentioned the gassings specifically; more likely she questioned administrative arrangements, and complained that she was not being consulted about decisions that affected the women's camp.

As chief women's guard, Langefeld firmly believed that she should have sole authority over the women's camp, and that male SS officers should stay away. If this principle could have been established, she believed she might have influenced events for the better, as she felt she had done at Ravensbrück. Pohl, however, was 'not sympathetic' to her complaints, she said later.

Convinced of her command of the rules, Langefeld made a further protest, this time to HQ in Oranienburg. Her account to the US investigators stated that she asked HQ to confirm that 'in the SS rules, in matters concerning women, the female chief guard sets the policies'. HQ agreed with her, she said, but the local SS – i.e. Rudolf Höss – overruled the decision, thus further undermining her authority at Auschwitz. As a result she asked to be sent back to Ravensbrück, but the request was refused, and from then on she was engaged in a full-blown power struggle with Höss.

Langefeld refused to take orders from the SS man, Hans Aumeier, whom Höss had placed in charge of her, and Höss himself refused to allow any SS man to take orders from her. Meanwhile, as Höss again describes, conditions in the women's camp grew worse, particularly as the women guards became increasingly depraved.

The problem, says Höss, was that while at Ravensbrück, these women guards had been 'thoroughly spoiled': 'Everything had been done for them [at Ravensbrück] to persuade them to stay in their jobs at the women's concentration camp, and by offering extremely good living conditions it was hoped to attract new recruits.' At Ravensbrück, 'their work was not particularly onerous as there was no overcrowding yet', whereas at Auschwitz the guards had to work 'in the most difficult conditions'. 'From the very beginning,' Höss claims, 'most wanted to run away and return to the quiet comforts and the easy life at Ravensbrück.' That being so, Langefeld began to lose control of her own guards, who 'ran hither and thither in all this confusion like a lot of flustered hens'.

In the midst of the chaos, the Jehovah's Witnesses, who also arrived from Ravensbrück to work as Kapos, went on hunger strike and declared: 'Hitler and his vassals are the devil's instruments.' Several were hanged, but Höss chose some who did not join the protest to work in his villa. He wrote later that these religious German women, whom he nicknamed the 'bible-bees', were a welcome change from other prisoners: 'My wife often said that she herself could not have seen to anything better than they did.'

It wasn't long, says Höss, before morals collapsed even further. One woman guard 'sank so low as to become intimate with some of the male prisoners, mostly the "green" male Kapos'. The woman habitually had sex with these Kapos, who in return provided her with jewellery that they stole from the mountain of valuables taken from the arriving Jews.

What Höss does not tell us is that not only were his own SS officers profiting from the same trade, so was he. He was also conducting an affair with an Austrian woman prisoner, Nora Hodys, originally from Ravensbrück, who worked in the jewellery depot. She helped him smuggle jewellery out of the camp. An internal SS inquiry was started and then quickly dropped, but not before it emerged that Höss had had a room fixed for him and Hodys to meet in one of the women's blocks. According to evidence given to the inquiry, Johanna Langefeld made the arrangement, though what she had to say in this regard is not recorded.

Langefeld did, however, confirm that her own ability to influence events in the women's section was undermined by the more and more dissolute behaviour of her women guards. There is ample evidence of drunken debauchery involving the Ravensbrück guards, particularly in the Auschwitz staff canteen. As Langefeld herself put it later: 'A large number of the female guards came under the influence of SS men with whom they had entered into close relations.'

Teege and Mauer admitted that 'domestic affairs' in the women's section were now 'out of control'. In the clothing store, where Philomena Müssgueller worked, guards and Kapos 'lined their own pockets'. As for their own living conditions, there was a 'lack of everything', and in their own privileged block there was 'even a window in the door for male guards to look through'.

At the same time these two political prisoners were increasingly asked to take on the role of women guards. Bertha Teege said this was because the real female guards at Auschwitz were 'too lazy' and even refused to stay on for the final roll call, so she had to take it herself.

Soon it was these two communist prisoners who were called on to preselect for the gas chambers. This was a task they had first been given at Ravensbrück in December. On that occasion they were told the prisoners were going to a sanatorium – a lie they had chosen to believe. At Auschwitz they heard the same lie, and were told that doctors would make final decisions, 'but we knew now the sanatorium was the gas chamber,' and both women tell us they refused to make the selections. 'We were quite frank about it with Langefeld,' said Teege, who adds that Langefeld understood their reasons and did not report their insubordination. Instead she made sure the real guards did the preselecting.

Teege and Mauer say they began to try to warn the block leaders about the gassing, urging them to persuade those who were sick to pretend they were fit for work, but their efforts rarely succeeded. 'We ran through the blocks ahead of the doctors and asked the elderly to at least pretend to be working, but all they did was say they were aching all over.' The dilemma for them both was that they could not tell the prisoners that those chosen were going to the gas chambers – 'to do so would risk forfeiting our own lives'. Once, Mauer went down with typhus and was nearly sent for gassing herself because the selectors made no exceptions for sick non-Jews.

Another job given to the couple was dealing with camp children. One day a four-year-old boy was handed over to them and they were told to find his mother. They did find his mother, and witnessed a 'moving reunion'. The following day both mother and child were gassed.

All this time Langefeld, Teege and Mauer developed an ever deeper hatred of the male SS, particularly Hans Aumeier, Höss's man, who would come over to the women's camp, drunk and cursing, to harass them and to further damage Langefeld's authority.

On 17 July 1942, a very hot day, four months after the Ravensbrück women arrived, Auschwitz was preparing for a visit from Heinrich Himmler. He arrived with a large entourage and demanded a detailed tour of the camp. First he briefed Höss on his decision to accelerate the gassing of Europe's Jews: from now on, Eichmann's programme for the transport and extermination of the Jews would intensify month on month. The death camps at Belzec, Treblinka and Sobibor were already in operation and more gassing centres were planned.

Construction of a vast new complex at Birkenau, two kilometres from the Auschwitz main camp, had just been completed and new gas chambers were already working there. Inspecting the Birkenau camp that day, Himmler told Höss he went 'weak at the knees'. At the same time he told him to step up the gassing there at once – a demonstration of how 'a man must overcome his weakness to remain hard', wrote Höss.

Himmler inspected not only the killing facilities but also the slave labour factories, and he agreed with Höss on a new system whereby useful workers would be sorted from the rest: in future prisoners arriving by train would be selected on a ramp immediately on arrival, and sent either to the gas chamber or to the factories.

The July visit was also a chance for Himmler to indulge his special interest in agriculture; he asked to see the Auschwitz cowshed, where he tasted a glass of milk. Then he asked to see the women's section, which was about to be transferred to Birkenau. This visit was Langefeld's chance to protest in person to the Reichsführer about the state of women's affairs in the camp, and she had prepared to present five 'deserving' prisoners, brought with her from Ravensbrück, in the hope that he would grant them early release. She was kept waiting, however, while Himmler watched women being flogged. A trestle table had been prepared for the purpose.

According to Bertha Teege, who helped prepare the victims, ten women were lined up for beating before Himmler that day, including five Jehovah's Witnesses, half starved from their hunger strike, and five Jews of various nationalities, 'who were well built, mark you'. Seven of these prisoners were eventually flogged, but all were made to wait naked all day, until the moment came.

'Towards the evening the gentlemen arrived in their cars, a retinue of curious hangers-on behind them,' recalled Bertha Teege. 'Himmler gave a brief glance at the parading prisoners, had the naked women presented to him, before spending the bulk of his time here watching the floggings.' At the end he issued an order that in future the lashings should no longer be given by a guard but by a prisoner, as was done at Ravensbrück. 'Sad to say, a few brutalised whores – there is no other name for these females – volunteered with great enthusiasm,' said Teege.

Himmler and his retinue then approached the lines of prisoners, and Langefeld came forward to propose the release of her women. According to Teege and Mauer, Himmler addressed the candidates for release individually, asking them why they were in detention. Mauer explained that she was a communist, and her husband had once been a member of the state parliament for the German Communist Party.

Himmler asked: 'Are you still a communist?', to which Mauer answered yes. 'What are your views on National Socialism?' Mauer replied that she had been in prison for so long she had few positive opinions. Himmler told her that she should become acquainted with National Socialist rule, and would be released after a one-year trial, working as a cook for the SS. Others were released on similar terms, though Bertha Teege was freed quicker.

Questioned by Himmler, Teege pledged to 'endeavour to fit in as a citizen' and was told she could go home to her family in Berlin straight away, under police supervision. 'He shook our hands and left.' A few days later she was accompanied by a guard to the gate. She ran without stopping to the train station.

Johanna Langefeld's account of that day includes a further exchange with Himmler. The exchange is telling, both for the light it sheds on Langefeld and her priorities, and also because it illuminates the peculiar workings of Himmler's mind.

Their exchange concerned the question of her authority in the camp. Her growing concern, it seems, was the manner in which the SS was manipulating the female Kapos she had brought with her from Ravensbrück, and using them against her. To illustrate the point, Langefeld explained that she had recently adjudicated on a disciplinary matter involving a Jewish prisoner called Gorlitz, brought before her on a charge of stealing apples. When Langefeld looked into the matter it had become clear to her that one of her women Kapos, an asocial, had told Gorlitz to steal the apple while at work. Langefeld cleared the Jewish woman and punished the Kapo, but the Kapo complained to Hans Aumeier, who in turn accused Langefeld of protecting a *Judenweib*, Jewish woman. This interference was unacceptable, said Langefeld.

Himmler promised to look into the matter, then walked off along the line of prisoners, stopping in front of a tall blonde German asocial to ask her: 'How come such a beautiful woman as you can be an asocial? Why didn't you marry, have a family and get children?' Aumeier now interrupted, saying this was 'the bitch' involved in the incident just discussed with Langefeld. Himmler looked at Aumeier and hissed at him: 'How dare you call a woman such an ugly swear word?'

According to Höss, however, Himmler did not let the matter of the women's section lie there. Before he left the camp he gave specific orders that the women Kapos be given more power, not less, thereby further undermining Langefeld's authority in the women's section. In Höss's opinion, these women Kapos were 'truly repulsive creatures' who 'far surpassed their male equivalents in toughness, squalor, vindictiveness and depravity'. Himmler apparently agreed, and told Höss to make better use of them. Höss says Himmler observed the 'green' and 'black' women – presumably during the floggings – and seeing their 'desire to vent evil over other prisoners', he decided that these women were 'particularly well suited to act as Kapos over the Jewish women'.

With his tour of the camp now complete, Himmler sped away from Auschwitz, never to return.

*Chapter 12*

# Sewing

As the new enlarged gas chambers started to function at Auschwitz-Birkenau, Helmut Kuhn, a Fürstenberg joiner, was still making coffins for Ravensbrück's dead. A horse-drawn hearse driven by Herr Wendland, of the Wendland Trucking Company, carried the coffins across town to the Fürstenberg crematorium. In each coffin was a metal tag, with the name and number of the dead prisoner inscribed on it.

At his joiner's shop Herr Kuhn made all sorts of things for the camp. Today his son Erich still lives above the old workshop across the lake. 'Not only coffins. We made doors, shelves, bunks. I used to go with my father to measure up and install.' Erich Kuhn says he didn't see much. 'Everybody was concerned with themselves in those days. We just did the job and left.' But he remembers seeing prisoners walking through town. 'I once heard that people from town spat at the prisoners, but I didn't believe it. Most people looked quickly away.'

An old order book lies on the table and he leafs through the pages reading: 'SS ... Order for doors ... 301 Reichsmarks. We did a good job. Some doors are still standing today.' But the coffin work tailed off in the middle of the war because the camp built its own crematorium. Only the *Prominente*, important prisoners, had coffins from then on, he says. 'They didn't bother with the rest.'

From its first beginnings, Ravensbrück had evolved in a home-grown kind of way. As the only women's camp, it was less bound by central directives than male camps. Perhaps because it was smaller, and more peripheral – at least to start with – Ravensbrück developed stronger local ties.

In 1942 the camp's links with its local community were evident on many fronts. Prisoners were working on local farms, picking beets or potatoes, while others were hired out in small numbers to workshops in town, under locally negotiated contracts. Watching from his Fürstenberg schoolroom, Wolfgang Stegemann saw the women march by in their grey stripes. There were children of guards and of SS officers in his class as well. 'They all walked down from the camp in a group. We didn't talk much to them. We were jealous as they got better food.'

Wolfgang's father had a laundry in town, where twenty prisoners worked, washing clothes – military clothes and prisoners' clothes. 'My father sometimes smuggled a piece of bread into the clothes. I didn't understand how it could be done but I didn't ask questions. Nobody did.'

The straw shoes made by the prisoners were sold locally. And for a while the *Kunstgewerbe*, the prisoners' art workshop, sold toys for local schools. Even Himmler sometimes took an interest. On one visit he stopped and watched the women at work, much admiring an ornamental chariot carved out of wood. Guards came later and packed it away, and everyone knew it was going to the Reichsführer SS.

It was through the guards and their families that the camp developed the strongest local links. By the summer of 1942 the demand for new women guards was growing, not only because Ravensbrück itself was expanding but because the camp was now training guards to work in the women's section at Auschwitz too.

Recruitment reached out far afield, but locals still applied – girls like Irma Grese, a dairyman's daughter from a nearby village. Grese, a troubled nineteen-year-old whose mother had committed suicide when she was twelve, had hoped to work as a nurse but settled on camp work instead. The attractions were obvious – the uniform, the free accommodation – and new perks were now being offered, including an on-site hair salon and free tickets to the cinema in Fürstenberg.

The guards themselves were the best advertisement for the job. Dressed in their mouse-grey jackets, culotte-style skirts, caps and leather boots, they walked along Fürstenberg's high street, the envy of local girls. From January 1940 they wore eagle patches on their left sleeves and caps to show they were employees of the Reich. Dog-handlers walked about showing off their large German shepherd dogs too.

'I think it was the uniform that attracted them most,' says Ilse Wiernick, the daughter of a Fürstenberg schoolteacher. Her family had relatives in Himmelpfort, a local village. 'There was one guard from Himmelpfort and I remember one day she came back in uniform to visit and the villagers all adored her and told her how beautiful she looked.'

By now many had formed relationships with SS officers, and there had been several pregnancies. One of the female guards gave birth to a baby boy in the camp, Ilse remembers, but she didn't marry and wasn't allowed to keep her baby; he was sent away to be raised by her sister.

The camp was very close so any changes across the lake were bound to be quickly picked up in Fürstenberg. In the summer of 1942 the Dachau-based textile giant Texled opened vast new workshops on the site, and the town's small sewing factories were closed, so trade was lost. Officials from Siemens, the electronics company, had taken rooms at the Fürstenberg Hotel and were said to be planning a factory at the camp, though what that meant for the town, nobody knew.

Meanwhile, Herr Wendland's work was expanding; his horse-drawn hearse was making more and more journeys. By the middle of the year he had purchased a motor-drawn vehicle to take the load, and Herr Kuhn's order book for coffins was full too – the new demand not unconnected to the sound of shots that rang out through the woods in the early evening. An hour or so later an SS man called Artur Conrad came with friends to drink in a town centre bar. He boasted of his expertise: the *Genickschuss* – a shot from a 7.65 mm pistol to the base of the head, followed if necessary by a shot to the heart.

As sinister rumours spread, some older women pleaded with the young not to take the jobs as guards, says Ilse Wiernick. They tried to persuade Margarete Mewes to give up the job. Mewes, the mother of three, had worked at the camp for nearly three years, but she didn't listen. 'When she got home from work she couldn't look after her children and just lay on the bed.'

Ilse's own family had a maid called Elli Hartmann who also went to be a guard, 'and my mother tried to stop her,' says Ilse. 'She asked her if she really thought it was the right job for her. But Elli said she could earn more and so she went. I remember she got engaged to an SS officer who left for the front. Elli was a nice person. Her husband came back and they went to live in the West.'

Rumours of what happened at Ravensbrück reached outlying villages too. Dorothea Binz used to return from time to time to see her family in Altglobsow. Her mother was often drunk and had washed her hands of her, but her schoolfriend Ilse Halter remembers her own mother trying one day to persuade Dorothea to reconsider what she was doing. It was one of Dorothea's days off, and Ilse's mother, respected in the village, called her to their house. 'She wanted to find out what really happened at the camp. There were so many stories about the place and my mother wanted to know the truth,' said Ilse, who was present when Dorothea came.

Dorothea told my mother the rumours were untrue. She said: 'But Frau Schumann, you must understand that there are criminals and prostitutes in the camp and women who misuse religion. They are not educated.' My mother made out she was satisfied with what Dorothea said, but I think she was just afraid. My father was not in the party but my mother was more neutral.

It was then I realised that Dorothea was a liar. I looked at her and was astonished how her face had changed since she went to work there. It was harder. Wizened somehow. I often think of that.

For the prisoners, Johanna Langefeld's departure from Ravensbrück in March signalled the first major change of 1942 – a change for the worse, particularly for the Poles. It was only thanks to Langefeld that the Poles had been given any status at all, and allowing them to take useful jobs around the camp had 'reduced the impetus to interfere on the part of the guards', as Maria Moldenhawer put it.

Langefeld's replacement as chief guard was the twenty-three-year-old Austrian Maria Mandl, whose position as chief guard of the bunker went to Dorothea Binz. Mandl loved to 'interfere'. Her special amusement at roll call was the hunt for curls. She would stride slowly along the ranks inspecting heads, and if she found a curly lock she would beat the woman around the head or kick her to the ground. Or, depending on her mood, she sent the offender to be shaved and then made her parade in front of others with a placard hanging from her neck: 'I broke the rules and curled my hair.'

Maria Bielicka saw Mandl kick a Jewish woman to death at roll call. 'She had done something wrong and first she was slapped then kicked.'

But a strange thing happened after that. I had a friend who had a job cleaning in the guards' hostels. One of the senior guards had a piano in her room. One day my friend went in and heard the most beautiful music. The woman who was playing was lost in a world of her own – in ecstasy. It was the same guard who had murdered the Jewish woman a few days earlier.

The appointment at Ravensbrück of a new chief woman guard was however unrelated to the more fundamental changes in the camp regime taking place in the spring of 1942 – changes ordered by the Reichsführer SS himself, that would from now on tie the camp more firmly to the central SS machine. Once again Maria Moldenhawer's commentary is astute: 'At this time we got the clear impression that harsh directives were coming from the central authorities. The camp authorities carried out these orders ruthlessly, in contrast to the home-grown torment we had known up until then.'

The first of these new harsh directives were felt in the camp shortly after Himmler's March visit. Though the immediate purpose of the visit was almost certainly to agree the allocation of Ravensbrück guards to work at Auschwitz, the Reichsführer's broader concern at this time was by all means possible to extend the use of concentration-camp slave labour. Following the defeat near Moscow and other reversals in the East, hopes of an early victory against Stalin were shattered. As war was now sure to continue for some time to come, the need for munitions was urgent, but workers were in short supply.

The outcome was that more and more Ravensbrück women, along with prisoners in all concentration camps, were to be deployed as slave labourers making military equipment, clothes and arms. With this new priority in mind, Himmler had toured the workshops in March and flown into a fury on discovering that the women harnessed to the weaving treadmill were still only working an eight-hour shift. Eleven-hour shifts were introduced, as well as night shifts in the sewing workshops and stringent production quotas.

In his discussions with the commandant, Himmler also revealed that talks had begun with the German electrical giant Siemens, and with officials of the Luftwaffe, to enable Siemens to install a factory at Ravensbrück to make electrical parts for fighter planes. The plan had wide-ranging implications for the prisoners: soon the women would be deployed as slave labour in one of the key areas of arms production. The deal also had implications for the company of Siemens & Halske, as it then was, cementing its already close relations with the Nazi regime. Its plant at Ravensbrück made Siemens one of the first major German companies to install a factory at a concentration camp, and the first of all German companies to exploit women slave labourers.

Founded in 1847, Siemens & Halske had started as a family firm, but by the 1930s it was the country's biggest electrical company, and to preserve its market dominance it collaborated with Hitler's Third Reich, securing lucrative arms contracts. Several senior company figures, including Friedrich Lüschen, who invented the first telephone cable, joined the SS, and one of the directors, Rudolf Bingel, became so close to Heinrich Himmler that he was invited to join his circle of friends – the Reichsführer's favourite German industrialists.

In the run-up to war Siemens, which was based in Berlin, lost thousands of workers, called up to the front. To make up the shortfall the company took more than 3600 Jews as slave labour. Hoping their work for Siemens might spare them from deportation, the Jews worked hard, and Siemens found them invaluable, especially the women, with their nimble fingers well adapted for precision work. By early 1942, however, the shipment of Germany's Jews to the new gas chambers in Poland was well under way, and Siemens required another new workforce, so the prospect of cheap female labour at Ravensbrück could not have come at a better time. Moreover the camp was ideally located: out of the firing line of Allied bombers, it had excellent communication links and was convenient for company headquarters in Berlin.

Within a week of Himmler's March 1942 visit to the camp, Oswald Pohl, his economic chief, wrote to Siemens promising 6000 women workers from the camp. Work on building the plant was to start in early summer.

In the meantime, Ravensbrück became aware of other new slave-labour directives issued by Himmler, some of which were implemented sooner. One of these directives, set out in a letter to Pohl, involved establishing brothels at the male camps, in which Ravensbrück women would work as prostitutes. After visiting the quarries at Mauthausen men's camp, where emaciated prisoners were dying like flies, Himmler had hit upon the idea of reinvigorating the slave labourers with the lure of coupons to visit a brothel. To Himmler's mind, the availability of sex would 'encourage the men to work better'.

Soon after the order was issued the Ravensbrück doctor Gerhard Schiedlausky began selecting women according to certain criteria. Those chosen were told they would be released after six months at the brothels. Most of them were German black triangles, classed as asocials and imprisoned in Ravensbrück precisely because they were prostitutes. Now these same women might win early release by working again as prostitutes in the male camps.

'The women chosen had to be pretty, with good teeth, and with no venereal infections or skin disease,' recalled Schiedlausky. The first to leave were twelve prisoners assigned to brothels at Mauthausen, four to Dachau, fourteen to Buchenwald and twelve to Flossenbürg. Edith Sparmann recalls the women arriving at the *Effektenkammer* to collect clothes. They didn't have to take their own clothes, but could choose whatever they wanted 'in order to look their best', and were accompanied by women guards.

Of all the new 'central directives' imposed on Ravensbrück in the first half of 1942, the most hated were those that set new hours and quotas for the sewing shop. This workshop, in the industrial area at the back of the camp, had long been one of its most dreaded workplaces. The noise of machines was deafening and the air always thick with dust. Stretching down the room were conveyor belts, with lines of women sitting alongside at sewing machines, making uniforms for the Waffen-SS as well as clothes for the camp prisoners.

At any moment the shop-floor boss, an Austrian called Gustav Binder, nicknamed Schinderhannes after a notorious Rhineland outlaw executed in 1803, might come raging out of his office and throw a stool, or perhaps a shoe with needles still protruding, that would catch a woman on the face.

After Himmler's visit the ordeal intensified. The factory barracks were enlarged, the prisoners worked eleven-hour shifts, and for the first time there were two shifts – day and night. There were new quotas too, which the Ravensbrück textile bosses – Fritz Opitz, the manager; his deputy, Josef Graf; and Binder, the shop-floor man – were required to enforce. All were qualified tailors, trained at Texled's Dachau headquarters. One of the four biggest SS enterprises, Texled was professionally run, used the latest equipment and relied almost totally on camp slave labour so was highly profitable. Oswald Pohl located the main Texled sewing shop at Ravensbrück because garment making was 'women's work'.

Fritz Opitz, the boss, set out in late April for the Texled HQ at Dachau to take instructions on the new quotas. Opitz, however, though a master tailor, could barely read or write, so Graf, recently invalided back from the Russian front, and Binder worked out the schedule. Binder sat at a sewing machine and sewed each section of each garment himself, while Graf stood by with a stopwatch. In this way they worked out the minimum time it took to sew, say, a cuff or a seam.

They set the quota at two and a half minutes per shirt, which meant a minimum output of 180 garments each shift, given precisely fifty-seven women on each of the ten belts, working for eleven hours starting at 7 a.m. and finishing at 6 p.m. The night shift would start at 7 p.m. and finish at 6 the next morning, and all prisoners had a half-hour break in the middle. Binder then 'trained' the women to work the quotas, and he began with the night shift. With windows blacked out at all times, the women sat at their machines, their feet clad in special cotton slippers, ready to press the pedals.

'Tonight we are going to produce 180 shirts,' says Binder, who stands next to the first woman on the line and counts out the seconds on his chronometer as she sews her section of shirt. When she fails to meet the target, he hits her across the face and she falls off her stool. The other 600 or so workers tremble and watch Binder, his face flushed, shaking, pouring with sweat. He has a rustic complexion and a thick neck. He pulls the woman back to her seat and she sets her machine running to try again while he takes up his chronometer. After two, three, four more failed attempts, the woman has been battered so hard she can barely sit up, but on the fifth attempt she succeeds. Binder does this for each of the women on the line.

And for a while the quota is met, so Binder delegates supervision to deputies and retreats behind the swing door leading to the office where

Graf sits, and where a prisoner plots production on a graph, based on the count of shirts, trousers and jackets at the end of every shift. If the lines climb, Binder and Graf can report with pride to Opitz that the quotas are achieved and Opitz can report to Dachau. These men are not answerable to the SS commandant, and though they carry whips they don't wear SS uniforms, because they pride themselves on being tailors, not mere SS guards.

But it is always touch and go, as the timings are so precise that the belts must run continuously, so it is essential that the cutting supervisor, the German prisoner Maria Wiedmaier, a communist and Ravensbrück old-timer, keeps the sewers supplied with fabric. It is also essential that broken needles or snarled threads are dealt with swiftly, so another prisoner, a Czech called Nelly, has the job of running round the machines changing threads and broken needles. She has to move fast so that the sewer can finish her garment section before the next one comes along the belt.

And as each sewer adds to the work of the one before, there can be no pause, apart from the half-hour stoppage. Extra toilet breaks are allowed, but on a rota basis: a guard who has all the 600 prisoner numbers on a list calls out the numbers one by one throughout the shift, but never reaches the end, so that some numbers go uncalled for days and the woman may have to urinate where she sits. And this is punished, often with standing to attention out of doors for up to four hours, often at night in the freezing cold, and after April, shoes and winter clothes (socks and jackets) are taken away and the women wear just thin cotton.

But a belt will often stop suddenly in the middle of a shift when a woman falls asleep at her machine. Binder has timed the tasks by his own performance, unaware that a half-starved prisoner will take twice as long and soon lose strength. The instant he hears the belt stop, Binder is out of his office and hurling scissors at the sleeping woman. If he misses he stands over her, grabs her by the hair, lifts her up and smashes her face down onto the machine until her nose pours blood.

Binder and Graf sometimes come onto the shop floor together, both drunk. They pick out an elderly woman, accuse her of some crime, then start to beat her, and throw her across the table so that she falls to the floor on the other side. On one such occasion a young woman, maybe a niece or a daughter, tries to help the older woman, but the drunken tailors grab her and Binder kicks her in the stomach with his metal-shod jackboots. Now she too falls, clutching her stomach and screaming. As work resumes, the girl is left lying there. Eventually she is removed to the *Revier*, from which word comes that she has died.

It is in the final hour of the night shift, when the women should be looking forward to a rest, that the worst fear spreads. Everyone knows that the garments are being counted; they know what will happen if they miss the quota. So when all the machines finally stop and silence falls they turn their eyes, 600 sets of them, towards Binder's door. Suddenly Schinderhannes comes charging out of his den, face scarlet, eyes glaring, fists clenched, shouting abuse. All eyes follow him as he rampages from one woman to the next, grabbing their hair and smashing heads against sewing machines, until he himself is completely exhausted.

The whole workshop will be punished for missing the quota – probably by having to stand to attention for several hours before returning to blocks for sleep, or by a new, higher quota that is even more impossible to achieve.

Some machinists managed better than others. When Grete Buber-Neumann joined the sewing shop she noticed a young Ukrainian girl who occasionally looked across from her machine and smiled. During the midnight break the girl, Nina, taught Grete Russian folk songs that they sometimes sang together as they worked – the machines were so loud that nobody could hear. And there was one supervisor called Siepel, a Hungarian, who tried to help by going around showing the women how it was done. The women learned to love him, only to find one day he had left for the front.

One day the prisoner supervisor, Maria Wiedmaier, took Grete aside and offered her a better job in the workshop office. Maria had the power to do this now, as she was so favoured by Binder for helping him reach the quotas. Many of the German communists had a servile attitude to the SS, said Grete. The work seemed to give these prisoners a purpose, and they 'put their heart and souls into war work'. Perhaps this is not too surprising, as the German prisoners also had loved ones at the front, and families at home in bomb shelters.

Maria Wiedmaier worked so hard that Graf was heard to comment one day: 'What would I do without her?' Binder thought so highly of her that he even called her as a witness at his trial. He clearly still felt pride in his work at Ravensbrück, boasting in court of his famous '140 pairs of trousers a day'.*

'And is it true that the same task was carried out in the same way, according to the same rules, in the same two and a half minutes, every day?' asked Stephen Stewart,† the chief prosecutor. '*Jawohl,*' said Binder.

After Binder was sentenced to death, his wife made an appeal saying it

* Some German prisoners were reportedly paid one Reichsmark a day for their work in the sewing sheds: enough to pay for a little fish paste or perhaps some shrimps, which by then was just about all that was for sale in the prisoner shop.

† Stephen Stewart was born Stefan Strauss. He fled Austria for England just before the Anschluss.

was he who was under pressure, not the prisoners: they kept on trying to sabotage the work. The prisoners had 'maliciously damaged hundreds of clothes so that it was impossible for my husband to fulfil the quota'. Could the court spare his life for her sake, and the sake of their two children? But Binder was hanged, along with Graf and Opitz.

There was, however, an element of truth in what Martha Binder said. One of the unintended consequences of Himmler's decision to harness prisoners to the war effort was the incentive it gave for sabotage. There had been no point in sabotaging sand shifting, or coal unloading, but damaging the garments to be worn by German soldiers was worth the risk.

Most prisoners in the sewing shop were far too exhausted, too terrified of the consequences, or both, to even consider sabotage, and workers on the conveyor belts were far too exposed to risk it. In the cutting area, however, under less stringent supervision, Katarzyna Kawurek put properly cut pieces of uniform in the waste, which infuriated Binder. 'He could never match the right number of items in each pile,' said Katarzyna, 'but he never guessed that anyone might be putting them in the waste.'

And it was precisely Binder's own stupidity that made the sabotage possible. His insistence that the same procedures happened 'in the same way, on the same day' applied also to the way he checked finished clothing. Every day the same parts of a garment were checked and others overlooked. So Wiktoria Ryczko, who sewed buttons onto the uniforms, observed that although Binder always checked the strength of the sewing, and women got hit on the head and face when it wasn't strong enough, he never checked the positions of the buttons. So she sewed on her buttons securely, but in positions where they wouldn't do up.

Another Pole, Krystyna Zaremba, discovered how to waste thread by making deep cuts through whole spools. 'The more damage we did the better we felt, and it helped us survive the horrible days in the camp.'

The most effective sabotage was in the fur workshop, which opened in early 1942. Arctic conditions during the Soviet winter of 1942 had crippled German soldiers with frostbite, and Ravensbrück now became the main workshop for warm army clothes. Angora rabbit fur, farmed in the hutches outside the camp gates, was already used for making caps and gloves, but a far larger source of fur was now available. In December 1941 Himmler ordered the confiscation of all fur owned by Jews, and also ruled that 'fur of all kind, sheep, hare and rabbit, must be made available for the Waffen-SS factories at Ravensbrück, near Fürstenberg'.

The order also stated: 'It is important also to examine the items to make sure nothing is hidden or sewn inside' – a reference to the vast amounts of hidden cash and jewellery concealed in the pockets and linings of the clothes.

By early 1942 sumptuous coats, mufflers, hats and gloves bought in some of the most fashionable stores from Paris to Prague poured into Ravensbrück. 'It was a kind of history lesson in German conquests,' said one of the fur workers. 'Sometimes we had the whole of Europe lying on our work table. We could read the labels from every city.' There were 'beautiful furs, embroidered as if from a museum'.

The SS were likewise impressed, particularly the general manager of the textile factory. Fritz Opitz 'took the money and gold from the clothing and fur coats of Jewish women and children and lived like a king', wrote Maria Wiedmaier. 'Drunk on his riches, he barely hid his debauchery, then afterwards there were orgies with the women guards in the rooms of the SS.'

Another woman, Maria Biega, remembered seeing Opitz 'laden with Jewish furs' as he thrashed a worker, a Polish grammar school teacher, across the face 'so that her blood spilled all over the fur-shop floor'. Graf, the sewing shop manager, joined in, beating the woman with a rubber truncheon.

The fur-shop night shift was considered the most gruelling of all, but it was best for the saboteurs: with SS eyes on the loot there was less attention to quotas. The furs were hand-sewn, which created more chances to spoil garments than on the machines. The workers, many of them young Poles, were supervised by an asocial prostitute who walked along the table 'lifting our chins up with her foot if we started to nod off'. According to Irena Dragan, one of the fur-shop Poles, the prostitute's legs were covered with boils and open sores.

The fur was not always so sumptuous, and often arrived stinking and vermin-ridden, having been packed away for months. And for some of the workers the horror of this was too much to bear. One young woman asked Irena to poke her with a needle so she could 'wake up from the nightmare'. But others were carefully sewing loose stitches, knowing the anoraks would fall apart. Sometimes they put notes inside them telling the soldiers they were fighting a losing war.

Women often worked together, agreeing to destroy the finest fur by cutting it into tiny pieces, which they called poppy seed or macaroni, 'but we had to be very careful because of German women working with us', said Irena. Others worked in groups of up to twelve, taking advice from veterans like Halina Chorążyna, the Warsaw chemistry professor, who calculated how to give the anoraks special treatment by piercing the fur in such a way that it would fall apart.* They packed a well-made anorak on top, with the sabotaged ones beneath, so as not to be spotted.

One day there was an order to make anoraks for the Luftwaffe chief,

* Chorążnya also organised to sabotage the knitting, splitting thread so holes would appear in soldiers' gloves and socks. Maria Bielicka described her as 'like a little mouse. Sitting there. A very strong little mouse. She organised everything.'

Hermann Göring himself. They were to be made of selected silver fox fur. 'We'd given the fur special treatment so that from the outside the anoraks looked very good.' But when the prisoners beat the fur – which they always did before collection, so as to soften it – it fell apart a little too easily. 'The Germans were furious, but they thought they had made a mistake in beating such delicate fur, and somehow we got away with it.'

On occasions when they didn't get away with it the punishments were harsh, 'but it didn't stop others from doing it again and again,' said Krystyna Zaremba, though by the summer the night shift had started losing some of its most courageous saboteurs.

Stanisława Michalik remembers the blood-red sunrise on the morning of 18 April 1942. 'Even today when a day like this dawns I feel terribly sad.' Wanda Wojtasik remembers it was a 'beautiful sunny day' and that soon after morning roll call, and certainly after the night shift returned, a guard entered Block 11 and called out a series of prisoners' numbers. The women called were to go *nach vorne* – out front, near the office buildings. Neither Stanisława, Wanda nor Wanda's best friend Krysia were on the list, but several of their close friends were, including the sisters Grażyna and Pola, and others who had been in Lublin Castle.

Many of the Polish survivors said later that when this first summons came they had no idea what was going to happen to those called out. The call *nach vorne* could have simply meant a punishment or a 'report', said Wanda Wojtasik. It was unusual for so many names to be called at once, and there was a certain nervousness that all the names came from the *Sondertransport*, but most thought that if those called were to be shot it would have been done directly on arrival, not after keeping them alive for six months. Nevertheless, the word *Sondertransport* had always sounded sinister and had never been explained to the women. And among the group were many who, on arrest in Lublin, had been brought before Odilo Globocnik's puppet police court and then supposedly sentenced to death.

This spurious legal process, which usually took place in the country of arrest, appears to have been triggered in certain cases where a captured man or woman was considered by Nazi occupiers to be particularly dangerous or to have played a significant role with a paramilitary resistance group.*

The choice of those to be 'tried', however, was itself often random; among this *Sondertransport* were women who didn't know if they had been sentenced

* Undercover agents working behind the lines for Allied forces – agents of the British SOE (Special Operations Executive) for example – were also sometimes, though not always, sentenced to death, then sent on to camps.

or not. Later it was learned that some of them simply had the words 'Fanatical patriot, not to be returned to Poland' written on their files. In any case, there was no conceivable logic to explain why the women on this first list had been called out and others not. In fact, throughout the life of the camp nobody ever found any logic to explain why some women were called for execution on a particular day while others, who might have expected it, never were.

Some of the women in the block even had cause to hope that those summoned were about to be released. In January that year a group of ten resisters had been called out from a different Polish block and sent back to Warsaw to be freed – or so it was said. Maria Bielicka, who was in that block, remembered the events clearly because among the group was Władysława Krupska, the woman who had first betrayed her.

By April, however, when this new summons came, neither Maria nor any of the other *Sondertransport* women had yet learned that the group sent back to Warsaw in January had in fact been shot. They only found this out some weeks later when more Poles arrived from Warsaw and told the prisoners what had happened, including the heartrending story of their near-escape.

On the way to Warsaw the lorry carrying the ten prisoners had broken down and the women were left unguarded briefly while the driver went for help. Several wanted to escape but Władysława Krupska persuaded them not to, saying they were bound to be caught, and would not then be freed. On arrival in Warsaw all the women – including Władysława – were shot.

Whatever confusion reigned amongst their comrades, it seems that the women listed for 18 April had little doubt what would happen. As the day went on, more were called. Stanisława Młodkowska was sewing on buttons next to one of them, Zofia Grabska. Zofia had just returned to work after several days in the *Revier*, where she was treated for swollen legs and arms. 'She was looking in a little mirror she'd somehow got hold of, and she was complaining that her family would no longer recognise her as she had got so thin and pale,' Stanisława recalled.

> At that moment the guard, Erich, came into the sewing room and read out Zofia's number and told her to go out. Zofia stood up on trembling legs and looked at me piteously, and with a sad smile, threw the little mirror on the table and went up to the guard. As she was going out she forgot to take off the cotton slippers that belonged to the sewing room, for which the guard kicked her on the legs.

Grażyna also knew what was to happen. The night before, friends had got word from contacts in the *Schreibstube* that she might be called at morning roll call. Grażyna herself was on the night shift, so when she was sleeping, her Lublin friend Janina Iwańska went through her clothes and hiding places searching for scraps of paper on which her poems were written, so if she was searched she would be 'clean' – and also to save the poems. Two days earlier she had written her 'Sunflower' poem; it was the 'scream of unbearable longing we all felt', said Wanda Wojtasik.

Grażyna had had a premonition, said Wanda. 'She had been telling her friends that she was soon to die.' Wanda recalls that most of the girls 'refused to believe the worst – but not Grażyna'.

'Why Grażyna?' I asked.

'Grażyna was different. She always thought she was about to die. She was one of those who had very little will to live.'

What is most puzzling, perhaps, about the 18 April summons is why the camp's old-timers – the Poles and others who had seen it all before – didn't appear to know what would happen. And if they did – as they surely must have – why they didn't say.

By this time all camp veterans, especially those working in the offices, knew that *Sondertransport* and *Sonderbehandlung* were Nazi euphemisms for killing. At least five Polish women had been executed at the camp already, and as the veterans knew, by identical procedures. In each of these cases a special courier had arrived by Berlin the day before to deliver the order for execution into the hands of the commandant. And in each case, elaborate camouflage was used to make the women think they were to be freed, or sent to another camp.

Perhaps these veteran Poles were protecting the younger women from what they knew for fear of frightening them. They may simply not have known what to say, as there was nothing they could do. In any case, well before 18 April all the signs that a mass execution was about to happen must have been there for the old hands to see. So large were the numbers this time that a special execution squad had been formed, among them Artur Conrad. In the SS canteen Conrad had even been boasting he'd get extra food.

In case of any lingering doubt, a special courier arrived from Berlin the day before to deliver the execution order to the commandant with a list of fifteen names. As Maria Adamska, the Polish office worker, herself admitted, from now on any suggestion that the girls were going to another camp was an 'elaborate charade'. But it was one that the whole camp was forced to watch, and in which several prisoners played a part.

The *Effektenkammer* women's part was to collect the girls' clothes, so that everyone could pretend they were going home, and yet there was no order to return their luggage, as would happen if they were really going home. The women in the kitchen were ordered to make food for the journey home, but the tiny amounts they prepared wouldn't do for a journey; they were sent to the bunker instead.

The bunker chief Dorothea Binz, along with her prisoner assistants – three Jehovah's Witnesses and the Polish dancer Ojcumiła Falkowska – were waiting at the bunker entrance to receive the women. Ojcumiła, who had worked until recently in the SS canteen, had been sent to the bunker for smuggling bread, but instead of being locked up had been hired by Binz as her interpreter. Ojcumiła said later that as soon as she set eyes on her Polish comrades at the bunker door she knew what was going to happen to them. 'I knew they were going to be shot when they appeared in civilian clothes without luggage.'

But even Ojcumiła resisted giving any warning to the girls, probably because she was strictly watched by Binz, but also because she too wouldn't have known what to say. Instead, she played her part in the charade by following Binz's instructions, showing the women to their cells and giving them a lunch of the usual soup.

Then the 'formalities' began, as Ojcumiła put it. Binz checked the women's identities and read the death sentence, Ojcumiła translated. 'After lunch a lorry came and I and the Jehovah's Witnesses had to load the lorries with the right number of coffins.' Ojcumiła explained that at this time there was still one coffin per person but, to economise, later there would be two bodies per coffin.

> The *Lagerführer* [commandant] came with an employee of the political department and the head of the bunker, and with my assistance as interpreter, a final check of identity was made. The *Lagerführer* all the time held all the papers he had firmly in his hand. From where I stood I could see papers for every prisoner, sometimes with photographs.

Throughout the afternoon the women were kept in their cell, while the rest of the camp continued the usual routines. At 4 p.m. coffee arrived for the prisoners, but before they received it Dorothea Binz went into an outer room alone and prepared some sort of potion. Ojcumiła saw her through a door as she mixed it in the coffee.

Ojcumiła was given the job of serving the girls the spiked coffee and was told to encourage them to drink. 'I tried to find out what the liquid was. It was transparent and had no smell. I couldn't read the label on the bottle.' On a later occasion, when Binz mixed the dose for another group, Ojcumiła plucked up the courage to ask what it was. 'Since Binz trusted me by now, she said it was a tranquilliser. She told me that before they used the tranquilliser prisoners had shouted slogans and protests as they faced the execution squad.'

Once the coffee was drunk, things moved like clockwork. At 5 p.m. a police van drove up. The convicted, as Ojcumiła described them, were drowsy by now and had to be led to the van. Here Ojcumiła's account concludes, as she and the three Jehovah's Witnesses were locked in a cell and could see no more. But when she emerged from the cell, she did see the women's coats, handbags and shoes, which had been left behind. 'So my conclusion was that they were taken away with bare feet.'

This fact was certainly borne out by other witnesses. Although the SS had tried hard to hide the women during the day some prisoners caught a glimpse as they were led away. According to Grete Buber-Neumann, shortly before evening roll call, orders went out for the Lagerstrasse to be completely cleared. All the prisoners were ordered back to their blocks, with doors closed, and no one allowed by the windows. But women working in the hospital and the kitchen observed the Polish women being led out from the bunker and across the camp square, barefoot and in dresses, 'like medieval penitents'.

Then, as they left the camp gates, some of the women 'turned and waved cheerfully, in the hope that some of their friends could see them'. Wanda Wojtasik, who was also in a position to see, did not recall the waving but did see Pola Chrostowska, Grażyna's sister, look back towards the blocks: 'Pola pointed a finger up to the sky.'

The actual place of death was kept secret, though there are clues. The guard Ella Pietsch, working in the headquarters building, remembered that as she was chatting at the end of her shift with her friend, another guard, Grete Hofbauer, 'a truck carrying prisoners together with SS guards in steel helmets and carrying rifles went by the window'. The truck went along by the lake. 'Hofbauer said that the prisoners were going to be shot.'

At his trial, one of the SS officers, Heinrich Peters, said he was ordered to assemble a squad of men for an execution about this time, and recalled that the women were taken to the spot in a closed car. Peters said the women were tied to a stake and shot. He drew a sketch showing a sandy area in the woods outside the wall towards the rear of the camp.

In any event the shooting was within earshot of the camp. We know this because we know what happened in the finale of the 'charade', as Maria Adamska described it. In fact, Maria herself tells us what happened next.

Although the Lagerstrasse had been cleared while the women were led away, shortly after the evening siren the prisoners were ordered onto it again for evening roll call. 'At 6 p.m. roll call the prisoners heard a volley of shots. Then nine single revolver shots rang out.'

Grete Buber-Neumann confirmed the sequence of events. 'We stood there in our thousands and waited as usual. Everything was silent. And suddenly, from the other side of the wall, sounded a rattle of shots, followed, a second or two later, by several single shots.'

Grete, who was standing with the German political prisoners, was in a position to observe the Polish prisoners. 'Opposite us stood the women of the Polish block, their lips moving in silent prayer. The camp walls caught the evening sun as usual, and a host of crows settled down again on the roof of the *Kommandantur*.'

*Chapter 13*

# Rabbits

On the morning of 27 May 1942, SS-Obergruppenführer Reinhard Heydrich, Protector of Bohemia and Moravia and head of Hitler's security police, took a seat in his open-topped Mercedes-Benz and set out for work at Prague Castle. His driver pulled up at a tram stop, where Jozef Gabčik, a member of the Czech resistance working under the direction of the British Special Operations Executive, stepped out in front of the vehicle and tried to open fire, but his gun jammed.

A second assassin, Jan Kubis, threw a bomb at Heydrich's vehicle, which blasted through the car's right fender, embedding shrapnel, glass, wire and fibres from the upholstery into Heydrich's spleen. Rushed to hospital, he received emergency surgery, carried out by local doctors because Himmler's top surgeon, Karl Gebhardt, flown out especially, had been unable to get there in time to operate. After the surgery, Heydrich's condition appeared to stabilise but soon deteriorated.

As his temperature soared, gas gangrene infection spread around his wounds, and produced suppurating black swellings. Gebhardt failed to halt the infection, and despite morphine, Heydrich writhed in agony, dying in acute pain on 4 June. The doctor's report said the cause of death was lesions in vital organs 'caused by bacteria and possibly by poisons carried into them by bomb splinters ... agglomerating and multiplying'.

Heydrich was a key figure. Hitler sought revenge. German forces were already losing ground on the eastern front; now this attack struck at the heart of the Nazi machine, suggesting vulnerability. Mass execution of suspects started all over the protectorate, but Hitler demanded symbolic sacrifice from the Czechs themselves, and called on the local Gestapo to 'wade in blood' as they sought Heydrich's killer.

On 9 June a false lead led the investigators to believe that the assassin was hiding in a small village fifteen miles from Prague called Lidice. Ten trucks filled with security police rolled into Lidice and every man in the village was rounded up, lined up against a barn wall and shot. All buildings were set alight and razed to the ground, killing those left inside. Surviving women and children were taken to a nearby sports hall where children were parted from mothers, babies torn from their arms and taken away. A few of the children, deemed to show Aryan features, were sent for adoption by Germans, but the rest vanished. A few days later, the 195 Lidice women were loaded onto cattle trucks to be transported west, destination unknown.

The rest of the world learned swiftly of the Lidice atrocity, but nobody heard of the other repercussions of the Heydrich killing, which happened behind the walls of Ravensbrück concentration camp, about 500 kilometres north. In the middle of June prisoners there were astonished by the spectacle of an entire village of terrified and dumbfounded peasant women – young girls, grandmothers, mothers, aunts, neighbours, friends – sitting on the Appellplatz in front of the kitchen.

Vera Housková, a Czech political prisoner, remembered:

> They were holding on to their small bundles of belongings, which they'd been allowed to take with them – curtains, a pot of lard. They sat there, terrified, looking at us – striped silhouettes in the distance. They had lost everything – their country, their husbands, their village and their children – though they didn't know the full truth. They didn't know why this had happened to them or why they were here. They knew nothing. At least we knew why we were here.

Camp guards had been told that these women were complicit in Heydrich's death and set about brutalising them in the worst possible manner. One of the Lidice women gave birth in the camp hospital soon after arrival. 'It was a little boy who arrived in good health and his mother heard the baby and saw him enter the world with a happy face,' said Vera Housková. 'A few hours later the doctors announced to the mother that the baby was dead and they brutally beat the mother. She was a mother of ten children, eight of which had already died in the tragedy at Lidice.'

Other events linked Ravensbrück to Heydrich's death. As the manhunt for the assassin intensified, so the doctors who failed to save Heydrich's life came in for attack. Hitler accused Karl Gebhardt, director of the Hohenlychen SS clinic, of not making use of a new class of drugs, sulphonamides, when treating Heydrich's septic wound.

For some months, Germans had been suffering unprecedented casualties on the eastern front, where thousands died of gas gangrene caused when wounds pierced by shrapnel and other debris became infected, just as Heydrich's had. Whether to use new brands of sulphonamides on soldiers, rather than operate immediately at field hospitals, had been debated fiercely by Nazi doctors for many months, especially as the Allies now had a 'miracle drug', a newly formulated type of penicillin that was saving their soldiers' lives.*

Gebhardt had studied the science on sulphonamides and was convinced that the drug was no penicillin. Now, as he faced accusations from the Führer of failing to save Heydrich's life, he came under pressure to change his view. It was Himmler who found a way forward. He ordered Gebhardt to carry out experiments that would test the value of sulphonamides in treating gas gangrene once and for all. The experiments were to be held under the auspices of Ernst Grawitz, SS chief physician and president of the German Red Cross, but Gebhardt was to direct them, and Himmler would provide the guinea pigs: young healthy prisoners from his camps.

By 1942, Himmler had started to see medical experimentation as a key purpose for the concentration camps. Here was a chance to use human guinea pigs, and to achieve bold scientific innovation that the conservative medical profession outside the camps would never envision. To this end Himmler had established his own circle of experts – nature healers, industrialists, fringe medical practitioners – united under the guise of an institute called 'Ahnenerbe', 'Ancestral Heritage', which raised money to support some of the Reichsführer's more radical medical projects.

Karl Gebhardt had no interest in Ancestral Heritage or its eccentric ideas. His clinic had an international reputation to uphold. Founded in 1902 by the German Red Cross as a sanatorium for child tuberculosis sufferers (among them the young Dorothea Binz) the Hohenlychen clinic grew into a vast and elegant lakeside health spa, which under Gebhardt had been converted into a centre of medical excellence, specialising in sports medicine and innovative surgery. The clinic came into its own during the 1936 Olympic Games, complete with a swimming pool, sports hall and masseurs. Now the clinic treated Germany's war wounded, and was favoured by top military and SS men.

Although Gebhardt had no interest in the gas gangrene experiments, he found it hard to refuse Heinrich Himmler. The two men went back a long way; they had grown up together in Munich, where Gebhardt went to school with

* Pressure to find a miracle drug increased when the Allies started dropping leaflets over German lines, announcing that their soldiers were being treated with sulphonamides and penicillin.

Heinrich Himmler's older brother Gebhard. And nobody could refuse a request from the Reichsführer SS, who had soon provided Gebhardt with his first guinea pigs: a group of male prisoners from Sachsenhausen. The men were brought to Ravensbrück for the tests, as the camp was convenient for Hohenlychen. Cuts were made in their leg muscles, small quantities of bacteria inserted to create infection, and then sulphonamide was introduced and the results examined. The tests proved inconclusive, but Himmler wanted more.*

Gebhardt, and his deputy, Fritz Fischer, would both assert at the Nuremberg doctors' trial in 1947 that the idea of using women as the next guinea pigs was nothing to do with them. Gebhardt even claimed that he was ill in bed when the decision was taken to use women. The first he knew of it, he said, was when Fischer came to him in a panic and said 'contrary to his [Gebhardt's] stipulations and instructions a woman had been presented for the next tests. What should he do?'

Angered by the news, Gebhardt rushed off at once to consult with Himmler, who happened to be 'visiting some relations in the neighbourhood'. Himmler told Gebhardt that it was he who had decided women should be used, as the experiments so far had been 'quite harmless'. Furthermore, the women he had personally selected were ideal for the purpose: healthy young Polish girls from Lublin. And he reassured his old friend by telling him that because these girls were under sentence of death they could be offered a reprieve and freed, in return for undergoing the tests. As Gebhardt told the court, he then 'gave in' and ordered the experiments to begin upon the Polish women.

What Gebhardt didn't tell the court was the identity of the relations Himmler was visiting in the neighbourhood, who were almost certainly his mistress, Hedwig 'Häschen' Potthast, and the baby boy, Helge, who was born at Hohenlychen on 15 February. After, the birth mother and child were staying at Brückenthin, Himmler's nearby estate. Here they were safe from the air raids over Berlin and close to their doctor. Not only had Karl Gebhardt delivered Helge at Hohenlychen in February, Himmler had made Gebhardt Helge's godfather, to further seal family ties.

At Ravensbrück in early July 1942, prisoners saw new equipment being installed at the operating theatre, and everyone was ordered to keep away. Soon after a lorry arrived, with a load of wooden crutches. Some said a branch of the Hohenlychen sanatorium was being set up at the camp, to care

* Hitler backed the experiments on concentration camp prisoners, saying they 'ought not to remain completely unaffected by the war while German soldiers are being subjected to almost unbearable strain and our native land, women and children, are being engulfed under a rain of incendiary bombs'.

for wounded officers. Nobody noticed that Sachsenhausen prisoners had been brought there for operations, so strict was the guard.

On the morning of 22 July, seventy-five of the youngest and fittest women from the Lublin transport were called to the Appellplatz. Some were called from the blocks, having just come off the night shift, others from the sewing shops or other work gangs. Stefania Łotocka was working in the fur room when she and others were told to go *nach vorn*. They lined up in fives. A moment later Koegel walked over with 'a short, fat SS officer with red hair and lots of medals'. This was Karl Gebhardt. With him was a tall slim man, very fair, with large blue eyes. This was Fritz Fischer, his assistant.

The Ravensbrück camp doctors were also present, Rolf Rosenthal and Gerhard Schiedlausky, as well as the tall blonde Herta Oberheuser. Nobody had ever had anything good to say about Oberheuser. The thirty-year-old, born in Cologne, was a skin specialist and had volunteered for Ravensbrück to see extreme skin diseases but she had never shown any interest in helping prisoners, shouting at them 'you horse, you cow, don't come near, you have lice' – or similar. The chance to work alongside Gebhardt was her big career break, though to the prisoners lined up on the Appellplatz it was obvious that Oberheuser was the lowest in the medical pecking order. 'As she put on her obscene kittenish airs the others ignored her completely,' recalled Wanda Wojtasik.

The Poles had to lift their skirts and the doctors stooped to inspect their legs. They 'mocked and abused' them as they did so. 'We couldn't understand why they wanted to look at our legs. Perhaps they had some new work planned and strong legs were needed. We were mystified,' said Maria Bielicka. The women were sent back to their blocks and heard no more, but rumours multiplied. Some said that they were being chosen for an exchange and would be sent on a transport to Switzerland. Others that the SS was preparing for a mass execution.

Four days later the same group of seventy-five were rounded up again and told this time to report to the *Revier*. Wanda Wojtasik's group were the last to get in line, and she joined the end of the last rank of five. The same doctors were present. Koegel checked the names from a list and 'with a theatrical gesture' pointed at the prisoners and gave the list 'to the fat man'. Herta Oberheuser called the names of the first ten, who had to stay behind, and the rest were sent back to their blocks.

Wanda was picked out last from the very back of the lineup. 'All I could think was that this time I was on my own. Krysia was not going with me.' The legs of these women were examined more closely and six of them, including Wanda, were told they were to stay the night in the infirmary. The remaining four were sent back. One of them, Zofia Sokulska, a law student from Lublin University, was rejected as too skinny. Maria Bielicka was rejected too but never knew why.

Those dismissed were terrified about what it might mean. 'We could see no pattern,' said Maria Bielicka. 'Nothing made any sense.' The *Sondertransport* women were used by now to the idea of imminent death. Since the executions of 18 April, calls had come once or twice a week, usually at morning *Appell*, and at the evening roll call came the volley of shots.

But this was different. 'We talked about it all night,' said Wacława Gnatowska. 'If there was going to be a mass execution why do it in stages like this?' The skinny lawyer Zofia Sokulska – known as Dziuba – who had better contacts around the camp than most, had heard that experiments were planned, though she didn't want to frighten others, so didn't say.

The next day the six who had stayed at the *Revier* suddenly reappeared on the Lagerstrasse, walking – staggering – to their blocks. They had clearly been drugged. Wanda Wojtasik seemed drunk. Friends from the Lublin group flocked around her. 'What did they do to you? Is that all? Do you feel all right inside? What about your head?' Wanda retorted: 'Well of course while I was inside they extracted my fifth screw,' and someone replied: 'There! Didn't I tell you they'd come out with a screw loose?'

But the bravado stopped at the next roll call, when Wanda passed out, overcome by the morphine. That night she lay close to Krysia and asked: 'What will they do to us next? At least it's me and not you.'

Four days later guards come for the same six and take them back to the *Revier*, where they are made to wait. Wanda looks at Maria Gnaś, who is sickly green. Maria whispers: 'What are they going to do to us?'

'Exterminate us,' says Wanda.

Maria shrieks: 'No! It can't be true.'

The women are ordered to undress and step into a warm, soapy bath. This is such luxury that they splash about and can't help enjoying the warm clean water, but when they are shown six beds, made up with crisp, clean sheets, they begin to feel the deepest dread. They lie talking, chattering, about anything. Memories. Tired of wondering what will happen next, Wanda closes her eyes and is woken by a sudden scream to see a nurse leaning over Maria Gnaś with a razor. Wanda leaps out of bed but the nurse explains she isn't going to hurt Maria, only shave her. Why shave their legs if they mean to kill them?

One by one the women are injected, and wheeled out on a trolley to the operating theatre. Sinking under the anaesthetic, Wanda repeats over and over: 'We are not guinea pigs; we are not guinea pigs.'

When Wanda wakes again she is back in the bed, her legs in plaster. On the plaster of one leg are written the letters 111 TK. The other five have similar markings. None are in pain now, but by evening all are writhing, screaming and groaning. Maria Gnaś sees someone at the window and asks the nurse in German: 'He's coming for me. Can you see outside the window? He's there coming for me.' Maria Zielonka shouts: 'Oh Jesus. Jesus.' Wanda shouts back at her friends: 'Shut up or I'll squash you flat.' Their ravings frighten the German nurses in the next room, so much so that when the next prisoners are chosen, the doctors look for non–German speakers.

Now Wanda sees someone at the window. It is Krysia, who has managed to sneak a look in as she returns from night shift. Wanda manages a smile, and painfully rolls back her blanket to show her leg in plaster. Krysia leaves.

Over the days that follow, the women's legs swell up so that the plaster cuts into their flesh right up to the groin. Oberheuser comes in, bends over Wanda's legs and sniffs, makes notes and takes some blood. The girls are returned to the operating theatre and the plaster removed, but they can't see who is doing it because someone has tied sheets over their heads. They can feel the scraping though, and hear the pus dripping out into tin bowls. They sense that things are being extracted from the wounds before the dressings are put on and plaster replaced.

Back on the ward, the women see brown stinking fluid seeping from the plaster of the girls on the nearby beds. They can't sit up far enough to see that their legs are also leaking the same liquids, but they can smell it. They all have a raging thirst. At midday nurses pass through with the usual meagre camp food, but at night the women are locked in. Shutters are closed because of the air raids. There is no water and nobody to help. They cannot move. Swarms of flies buzz around the rotting flesh. They drift in and out of consciousness.

The days pass and more friends outside come up to the window. Someone brings an apple, another a boat carved out of a toothbrush. Jadwiga Kamińska, one of the Lublin group, is organising the support. 'Anything to keep their spirits up,' she tells the others in the block, and the Poles in the kitchen are asked to smuggle out bits of extra food.

Then Jadwiga herself is called up for the *Revier*, as are six more from the block. Wanda and the others try to reassure the newcomers as they lie on clean sheets and await the anaesthetic, and after the operation Jadwiga smiles and says she has no pain. Wanda nods. Within hours Jadwiga too is writhing in pain.

Night falls, the shutters are closed, and older guinea pigs busy themselves to tend to the newer ones. A nurse has left a couple of bedpans and a bucket of water. Hopping in the dark from one bed to another, Wanda takes the bedpans around, but soon they are full. She offers the new guinea pigs water from the single bucket until all that is gone, then heaves herself back on her bed, leaving a trail of brown pus.

One of the new girls won't wake up, so a nurse is called and she alerts the duty doctor, Rosenthal, who lurches in drunk, his shirt only half buttoned over his hairy chest. He takes a needle from the nurse's hand and sticks it into the pillow. Laughing, he lurches back out again. Not long after this another nurse comes back and gives the comatose girl an injection, which revives her and she wakes up.

After three weeks, nine guinea pigs have had surgery, and they are all taken through to another room, laid on tables and their bandages removed. They can see their own wounds for the first time, and each stares in disbelief at the swollen lumps of flesh and the incisions on the tibia, so deep they can see bone. One woman pulls out a piece of glass, another a wooden splinter two inches long.

For hours they lie here, sweating, with their wounds exposed. Suddenly nurses cover the guinea pigs' heads, tight this time, to keep their torturers concealed, but Wanda sneaks a look and sees Gebhardt, plump hands folded behind his back. She also sees Fischer, wearing a blood-stained coat – he must have come straight from an operation.

The doctors pick up and examine labels stuck to each of the girls. There are several other officers here – Wanda counts eleven. One that she doesn't recognise looks particularly important, and others seem in awe of him. She has no idea that this is Ernst Grawitz, chief SS physician and head of the German Red Cross. One by one, all eleven lean over the women examining and sniffing excitedly at the putrid wounds.

We are more like rats, she thinks. But she is still able to tell herself that at least they may now be spared execution by agreeing to be rats.

At their post-war trial Gebhardt and Fischer gave their own accounts of the same inspection. Following the inconclusive tests on the Sachsenhausen men, the doctors had taken the decision to insert a larger amount of bacteria into the women's legs, with more dirt, glass and splinters to ensure that infection spread further. The wounds were scraped out, cleaned with hydrogen peroxide, and then treated with different sulphonamide drugs, or other drugs, or nothing, and suitable labels placed on the legs. Gebhardt had still not expected the tests to yield anything, but at least their failure this time could not be blamed on the limited amount of bacteria used.

When he examined the women, Gebhardt had found, as he expected, that the results were once again inconclusive. Despite the extensive infection, no proof had emerged that one woman had fared better than another with any particular drug.

Ernst Grawitz, however, the 'important doctor', thought the injuries inflicted had still been far too mild to prove anything. The wounds were mere flea bites, he protested. 'How many deaths have there been?' 'None,' said Gebhardt. So Grawitz ordered Fischer to shoot the subjects in the leg next time and then inject the bacteria. Only this would create the reality of battlefield wounds.

After Grawitz left, Gebhardt and Fischer decided not to shoot the next group's legs. Instead they planned to intensify the bacteria again and ensure even greater infection by cutting the supply of blood to the wound.

A few days after the doctors' first inspection Wanda and the other original guinea pigs were ordered back to their blocks. They could barely walk. On arrival they were cared for by friends, but many familiar faces were missing – while the guinea pigs had been in the *Revier*, more *Sondertransport* women had been shot.

Krysia nursed Wanda. Friends offered food. Alfreda Prus, a quiet, gentle girl, a student at the university of Zamość, near Lublin, threw Wanda her daily bread ration. Then on 20 September Alfreda and several others were ordered *nach vorne*. Because it was morning, the time when those selected for shooting were usually called, Irena Krawczyk was so sure she was about to be shot that she shivered violently and could not dress. Marta Baranowska, her Polish Blockova, helped her to muster her last strength and go.

Instead of marching them to the bunker, the waiting room for execution, the guards led the women to the *Revier*, where they were greeted by Dr Herta Oberheuser, sitting on a table in a black cloak, one leg crossed over the other. When taken to the ward, they found their Polish friends now occupying two rooms, lying prostrate with legs bound in thick bandages, greenish and foul-smelling.

The 'old' victims tell the new ones they feel better already, but everyone hears the wailing from next door. The next day this group are also sedated. Alfreda Prus, the student from Zamość, begins to sing crazy songs of hot nights and palm trees.

Stefania Łotocka wakes to find her legs grotesquely swollen. She can only see her foot, which has an enormous sore covered with blisters full of colourless fluid. The rest of the leg is covered in thick white dressing. She feels her temperature rising, and with it an excruciating pain. There is a buzzing and thumping in her ears. Have they amputated her legs? And there is a terrible thirst, but nobody cares, until Jadwiga Kamińska, operated on earlier, and now slightly stronger, drags herself out of bed and with a face twisted in pain, hops to help the latest victims. Jadwiga has taken over from Wanda as the guinea-pig nurse.

In the morning Herta Oberheuser appears, to draw blood from the ear and finger for testing. She stands back, noting what she sees. Her face is a mask, her eyes glassy. She shows no shadow of pity and leaves wounds undressed for days, so the women feel they are rotting away inside the plaster, but when at last the dressings are changed it is the worst torture of all.

The Hohenlychen doctors usually do the dressings, and the women's faces are as always covered with a sheet. But before they cover Stanisława Młodkowska she notices that the nurse holding the sheets in place is Gerda Quernheim, the midwife baby-killer. Abruptly, Stanisława feels bandages being roughly torn off and wounds opened even wider as a doctor takes something out, and it feels as if he is raking around in the wound with a sharp instrument, squeezing the leg. She passes out.

On return to the ward Stanisława is groaning and Jadwiga Kamińska bangs on the door to get help. Eventually Dr Oberheuser comes in, lifts Stanisława's blanket, shakes her head, goes away, returns and injects something, so she begins to revive. Soon Stanisława is strong enough to worry about what is happening to her friend Alfreda Prus. The girl from Zamość lies quiet. On her small face Stanisława sees only enormous eyes, bright with fever. Whenever she moves, Alfreda breaks into hiccups.

Friends are now appearing more and more often at the infirmary window. Word has got out that Alfreda from Zamość is in a dreadful state. By a miracle someone hands a spoonful of jam in a mug to Stefania Łotocka and Stefania now tries to persuade Alfreda to eat it, as she remembers her mother telling her it helps stop hiccups. Alfreda refuses the jam. 'It won't help me anyway,' she says. 'I shall die whether I eat it or not.'

For four days the women are delirious with fever and are regularly taken to the operating theatre, each time for more injections. They cry out for water, with lips so parched they bleed. Eventually Oberheuser orders water to be brought and the women drink thirstily, but it makes their cracked lips sting. The water has vinegar in it, which gives them a greater thirst, as Oberheuser knew it would.

On the fifth day the injections stop. A big commotion erupts in the next room, where Weronika Kraska gives out a terrible moan and makes a loud rattle. Weronika, whom few had worried about because she seemed so strong, is complaining of a stiff neck. Dr Schiedlausky is on duty and says there is nothing to be done for her, so the ward is shut down for the night.

Jadwiga Kamińska hops into the other room and returns to report that Weronika looks strangely stiff and horrible. The code on her leg is E11. Jadwiga and some of the stronger ones are beginning to realise that the codes must specify a bacterium of some sort, and some have been given a stronger dose than others. A stiff neck could mean tetanus, which will kill Weronika, although she is still fighting it.

By morning Weronika is dying. She knows it herself. She can barely speak and water has to be poured into her locked jaw. Summoning a last ounce of strength, she manages to utter words through clenched teeth about her two small children. As her words fade, there is a harsh rattle in her throat and her face contorts. She gives out a final, terrible scream, unlike anything human that anyone has heard. Her face twists in a fearsome grimace and her head coils around on her stiffened neck.

Gerda Quernheim runs in with a needle, and inserts it, gently, releasing Weronika from her misery. Her face softens and the tension in her body eases swiftly. The hospital falls silent.

News of Weronika's death spreads fast around the Polish blocks, while inside the *Revier* the girls are now worrying about Alfreda Prus, who grows paler by the minute. Her code is K1, and someone says she seems to have gangrene. Still hiccuping, she keeps saying: 'I'm dying. I'm dying.'

Outside, everyone waits to hear news of Alfreda, and Eugenia Mikulska, who comes from the same town of Zamość, runs to the infirmary window as soon as she can. Before the war she trained as a nurse with Alfreda's sister. Alfreda turns and sees Eugenia's face smiling encouragement. The next day Eugenia returns to the window and Alfreda lifts a hand and says: 'Remember me to our friends in Zamość.'

Soon afterwards Alfreda is taken away for a new incision, and when she is returned to the ward her wound is bleeding heavily. Her straw mattress turns red and a pool of blood collects beneath the bed. A camp nurse seems to take pity and gets a mug of coffee for her from the officers' mess, but this of course does no good, so the nurse calls Oberheuser. Oberheuser clearly knows that Alfreda is close to death, as she tries to inject her with something to stop the bleeding. The doctors don't seem to want her to die yet. Perhaps the experiment is not complete.

Complete or not, next morning two nurses come and take Alfreda away. When she is carried out on a stretcher she turns her head towards Stefania, her companion on the next bed, and smiles and says: 'You see, I told you I was going to die.'

A moment later the others hear more terrible, inhuman screams – this time from Alfreda Prus. So piercing are Alfreda's screams that other guinea pigs tell each other the whole camp must have heard her die.

*Chapter 14*

# Special Experiments

I found Zofia Kawińska in her tenth-floor flat overlooking the cranes of Gdansk shipyard. She was one of the second group of victims of Himmler's sulphonamide experiments. A tiny, bent figure, she walks with difficulty, and has since the war. I ask if she still suffers pain from the experiments. 'A little,' she says, as she offers tea and biscuits.

She stoops to show the scars on the sides of her legs. 'They put the bacteria in, and glass and bits of wood, and they waited.' She looks up and fixes me with deep brown eyes, as if trying to see if there is any chance I understand. 'But I didn't suffer as much as some. Everyone in Poland came home with wounds.'

Zofia came back to find she had lost her father at Auschwitz. He had been arrested at the same time as her, at their family home in Chełm. 'The last time I saw him was on the lorry to Lublin Castle. We shared a loaf of bread my mother gave us,' she says, looking across at the cranes, eyes welling with tears.

Her memories of the camp emerge in a series of sharp images.

She remembers Binz. 'She had a little dog that she caressed. Binz loved that dog, but liked to beat people. The guards were not educated women.'

She remembers the cold more than the hunger. 'We made fur gloves for the pilots, but our feet were like blocks of ice. They took our shoes away in the spring.'

And when she talks of the experiments she remembers the smell of rotting legs. 'We were locked in with it, you see, and we couldn't open the windows. It was worse than the smell of rotting corpses. Our own legs. It was Oberheuser who locked us in, because we weren't allowed to see the important doctors. The important doctors didn't want witnesses because they knew they'd be shot for it.'

'What was Oberheuser like?'

'When it started, before we were too sick, I remember she came in and we asked her: "What have you done to our legs? We won't be able to wear stockings now."'

'What did she say?'

'Nothing. She smiled, a strange smile.'

After we had talked for some time longer, I asked Zofia if she had ever lost her faith in Ravensbrück. She paused and looked away. 'No. I have no less faith. You see we came to the camp with an iron will to survive.' And she clenches two tiny fists on the tablecloth and darts another look – again, as if to see if I can understand.

After hesitating a moment, she got up and fetched something to show me: a small silver medallion with an image of Christ. It belonged to a close friend who died at Ravensbrück. Zofia had kept it with her always. In the camp she hid it in a hundred hiding places, burying it in soil, hiding it behind planks in the walls, but she always found it. Even when she left the *Revier* she found it again, hidden somewhere in the block. It was a miracle that she didn't lose it, she says. 'It protected me.'

On 7 October 1942 another group of guinea pigs were called up to the infirmary. Maria Plater-Skassa saw autumn leaves falling as she was marched out. Genowefa Kluczek was woken that morning by the Blockova, Marta Baranowska, who climbed up with tears in her eyes to her third-tier bunk bed, saying: 'Get dressed, child. Come with me. Be brave.' Pelagia Maćkowska still half-believed that the promise of return to Poland if she agreed to the operation might be true. She'd see her husband and sons again. Both had been sent to Auschwitz, as members of the Polish underground.

Everything happened as before. The new guinea pigs lined up, avoiding each other's eyes, skin earthy grey, brushed with fine down. All delighted in having a bath until one of them started to cry, remembering her children. They were told to parade naked in front of a doctor, probably Rosenthal, who sat on a stretcher with a cigarette in his mouth, surrounded by German nurses. He was paying no attention to them.

As the new patients settled into their beds, they pleaded with Jadwiga Kamińska to tell them what had really happened to their friends Weronika Kraska and Alfreda Prus, but Jadwiga didn't want to tell them in front of Maria Kuśmierczuk, one of Alfreda's closest friends, who was lying on one of the beds. Maria, who knew Alfreda from school, had surgery a few days earlier and had the same code as Alfreda – K1 – marked on her leg.

Dr Rosenthal examined Pelagia's arm for a vein to inject. '*Gut, gut,*' he said.

She woke up two days later hallucinating. Her mother's face was leaning over her, and she shouted out: 'Why aren't you helping me, Mother?' Her leg was a bluish-black log. As before, the women heard others' screams before screaming themselves. And as before some of the girls got hiccups and some got stiff necks.

Although procedures were the same, the accounts of this later group suggest that the doctors' demeanour had changed. Eager at first to work on Professor Gebhardt's experiments, now they all seemed bored. Observation of the guinea pigs had been left in Dr Oberheuser's lowly hands.

Oberheuser comes around the wards every morning, sometimes to take blood, but usually for no reason. A camp nurse called 'the duck' always accompanies her. The prisoners call her the duck because she waddles, and another is called the rat. The nurses all pull faces at the stink, but Oberheuser 'seems used to it and just smiles, looking so pleased with herself,' says Pelagia.

It is the day for dressings again and Stefania Łotocka peeks out from under the sheet and sees the doctors amusing themselves. On the left of the table stands Fischer. In his right hand he has a gleaming metal hook. On the right side stands Oberheuser, holding a large kidney-shaped bowl. She is wearing a white, rather transparent silk blouse, through which her pink underwear can be seen. She has gold bangles on her arms and rings on her fingers. They stand there smiling at each other and Pelagia sees they are flirting.

When Pelagia's dressings are changed she hears the sound of metal instruments from under the sheet, and she hears Oberheuser saying: '*Gleich, gleich*' – 'Wait, wait.'

Back on the ward, Zofia Kiecol has hiccups and Kazia Kurowska, a sturdy country girl, lies unconscious, her grey-black legs swollen to four times their normal size. Maria Kuśmierczuk, Alfreda's school friend, and the one with the markings Alfreda once had, is also dangerously ill.

To everyone's surprise this group is suddenly given better food. 'So the doctors don't want us to die quite yet,' someone says. But the smell of food, mixed with the stink of their legs, makes them retch. Zofia vomits and hiccups incessantly. Zofia and Leokadia Kwiecińska, who lie next to each other, are friends from the sewing workshop. Zofia used to ask Leokadia every day: 'What do you think. Shall we get back to Poland? If only we could get back. Who will look after my girls if I don't get back?'

Now Leokadia watches the nurses take Zofia away. And they take Kazia too. But Maria Kuśmierczuk, the one with the same K1 code as her friend Alfreda, is still miraculously fending off the infection. Only nine of their group of twelve remain. 'But we must hang on,' someone shouts out. And they look at Maria, who was written off just a few days ago, but is still fighting for her life.

Dziuba Sokulska, the skinny lawyer, is told by Oberheuser that she'll be better any day, and sure enough she is, and is sent to roll bandages on the other side of the hospital. And Stanisława Jabłońska has new strength too – enough to tell stories to the others, to give them something to think about, apart from rotting flesh.

More friends turn up to visit at the window. Everyone in the camp now calls them *Kaninchen* – rabbits. Those outside pass bits of food or crusts to the Poles who have contacts with the *Revier*, saying, 'This is for the *Kaninchen*,' and the gifts are smuggled in. At first the girls tried to discourage the name, but, as rabbits, they are famous. The guards call them rabbits too, so now the prisoners' vocabulary is official.

It is not only by collecting food that others in the camp can help the rabbits. Prisoners are also collecting information. On bandage-rolling duties, Dziuba Sokulska is in touch with a Polish doctor, Zofia Mączka, from Kraków, who works in the *Revier* as a radiologist. Like all the prisoner nurses and doctors, Zofia is banned from the experiment wards, but she spies through keyholes, listens at doors and watches through windows, gathering information that she passes on to Dziuba. The doctors come and go in their cars from Hohenlychen. Each time they come they bring bacteria in little vials, which are labelled, and which Zofia sees later, lying around. She sees tubes of paper, covered with pus, which are used to insert the bacteria into wounds, and this tells her which patient had which dose.

Blood and urine samples are analysed in the lab by medical students, some of them Polish prisoners, who pass on what they learn. With all this information, Zofia learns that Weronika Kraska was infected with a lethal dose of tetanus well before she died, and that Alfreda and Kazimiera Kurowska were infected with gas gangrene bacteria in such massive quantities that their bodies could not put up a defence.

Zofia is able to monitor Kazia Kurowska's death through a keyhole over several days, as the gas gangrene destroys her right leg and begins to infect the entire right side of her body. In the end the nurse, Gerda Quernheim, ends Kazia's life with a morphine overdose.

Some weeks after the operations began, Zofia Mączka found a way to keep records, which she hid somehow with the help of friends in the sewing workshop. One day she would use the records to convict the murderers, she told Dziuba. Dziuba wanted to tell the world now, to stop the evil, but Zofia saw no chance of that. Soon after this, however, Maria Bielicka was presented with just such a chance. Maria had been rejected as a rabbit and was still working in the bookbinding workshop in the autumn of 1942. The workshop was next door to the *Effektenkammer* where three Czech girls worked, and they and Maria Bielicka became friends.

Maria learned that the Czechs often sent the clothes of executed prisoners back to their families. The system was always the same. The clothes were brought down from the storage and packed up in a box, which was sealed by the SS guards. The guards never checked, but just looked at the label on the box and sent it off. The bereaved family received a separate letter from the commandant that informed them their daughter had died of natural causes.

The Czech girls said it was possible to smuggle out letters with the clothes. Once or twice they had even fooled the guards by sending back clothes of girls who were not executed, with notes hidden inside. 'Everyone was trying to help the Poles at this time,' said Maria.

> Everyone was shocked by these experiments, and terrified the same might happen to them, so they asked me if I would like to send some clothes home, so I could smuggle out a message to my parents about what was happening. Both my parents were in the Polish underground in Warsaw. I thought this was a big opportunity to tell them about the camp.

With this in mind Maria and some friends drew a big map, showing where the camp was, and the layout. 'We wrote about the experiments and the executions, and everything we could, and the Czech girls put the letter in the bundle with my clothes. I told them to send everything except my overcoat and my snow boots – just in case. The guards sealed the box and stamped it with official SS stamps and sent it off.'

Later in the war both of Maria's parents were captured and shot, so she would never have known their reaction to receiving the package, had it not been for a friend who lived close by in Warsaw and who was present when her parents opened it.

'Imagine what they thought at first,' said Maria. 'They thought I must have been executed. But my friend told me that when they found the letter they were full of joy that I had been so clever to do it!' Maria hoped her parents would pass the information on to the Polish underground and that it would reach the outside world. 'But, you see, for us in the camp it was a victory anyway. Of course we wanted to tell the world about the crimes, but the joy for us was that we'd also fooled our enemy. It was a little victory. Actually this was quite a big thing. Sometimes it was smaller things. But these were the things that kept us prisoners going.'

*

By the end of October some of the women had been in the ward for two months. Beds once white were now grey and sticky. Stefania Łotocka tried to pull her blanket up tight around her neck so that the stink of her leg did not escape, but it didn't work. Her matted hair formed a sort of coxcomb on top of her head.

They had been mutilated; now they'd been abandoned. Even Oberheuser rarely walked through the ward. Swarms of flies fed on pus, and white bandages were covered with black maggots. They would be killed by the filth, if nothing else, thought Stefania as she watched the cockroaches in the cracks of walls.

One morning Oberheuser walked onto the ward, brisk and important, announcing that they were all to be cleaned up and given clean nightdresses. The professor was coming again. Though he wasn't due until 2 p.m. the women were prepared hours ahead, laid out on special boards in the surgery 'like bodies in a mortuary'. Each wore a ragged nightdress and had been given a card to balance on her front, on which codes were written in fine Gothic flourishes. As the hours passed their wounds ached and bled. Oberheuser rearranged the cards from time to time: AI AII, CI CII, DI DII, EI EII.

It was late afternoon when Karl Gebhardt turned up with his doctors. All of them were drunk. Gebhardt, in boastful mood, showed off his *Kaninchen* to the rest, who marvelled at the sight. 'Look here,' he said, proudly pointing at swollen legs and festering wounds, and as he explained something behind his hand, everyone roared with laughter and a dozen eyes looked on, making mental notes. According to one woman, Gebhardt's appearance that day was 'fat with a pale, pudding-like face and small eyes. Dressed in civilian clothes – a navy-blue sweater.'

Each time the chief surgeon came up to one of the women, Fischer and Oberheuser hovered at his elbow trying to impress with their report, and as he nodded Oberheuser 'beamed with satisfaction', her face 'excited and red'. Quickly bored with Oberheuser and the patients, Gebhardt left.

Like his staff Karl Gebhardt had obviously lost interest in the cases; the results, yet again, produced nothing new. Grawitz, the director of the experimental programme, had not even turned up this time. In any case, the man who promoted the sulphonamide experiments in the first place, Heinrich Himmler, had found more absorbing experiments to follow.

By late October 1942 Himmler's enthusiasm for medical experimentation was burgeoning. Instead of cures for battlefield wounds, he was asking Sigmund Rascher, another favoured doctor, to find ways to revive sailors and airmen pulled out of freezing seas. Himmler had been reading about methods used by coastal communities in past centuries to save shipwrecked crews in the Baltic. Country folk often knew excellent remedies, he told Rascher in a letter, such as teas brewed from medicinal herbs.

Himmler went on: 'I can also imagine that a fisherman's wife might take her half-frozen husband to bed with her after he had been rescued and warm him up that way.' He urged Rascher to try the same, and told him to use Ravensbrück prostitutes, sent to work in the Dachau brothel, for the 'human warmth'. At first Rascher rejected the idea, saying that it wouldn't work, but Himmler insisted and as Rascher was another close friend, and a devotee of the Reichsführer's Ancestral Heritage projects, he came round.

Since the establishment some months earlier of a brothel at Buchenwald, staffed by Ravensbrück women, a brothel had also been set up at Dachau, and Ravensbrück women had been sent to work there too. From among these women Rascher was given four 'prostitutes' for his tests.

One of the women, however, Rascher rejected on the grounds that she was too Nordic. He wrote later that she 'showed unobjectionably Nordic racial characteristics: blonde hair, blue eyes, corresponding head and body structure'.

> I asked the girl why she had volunteered for the brothel. I received the answer: 'To get out of the concentration camp, because I was promised that all those who would volunteer for the brothel for half a year would be released from the camp.' To my objection that it was a great shame to volunteer as a prostitute, I was told: 'Rather half a year in the brothel than half a year in the concentration camp.'

Rascher said the woman had also given him an account of 'the most peculiar conditions' at Ravensbrück, and this account was confirmed by the others.

> It hurts my racial feelings to expose as a prostitute to racially inferior concentration camp elements a girl who has the appearance of a pure Nordic and who could perhaps by assignment of proper work be put on the right road. Therefore, I refused to use this girl for my experimental purposes.

Content to use the other Ravensbrück women, Rascher prepared for the experiments, keeping Himmler informed of progress. First, eight male prisoners were placed in a large tank of near-freezing water and left there until they passed out. Each of the men was removed from the tank, unconscious, and placed between two Ravensbrück women lying naked in a spacious bed. The women were told to nestle as close as possible to the moribund man. All three were covered with blankets. The result was that the men quickly revived. Once the subjects regained consciousness they did not lose it again, but 'very quickly grasped the situation', as Rascher put it later, and 'snuggled up to the naked female bodies'.

The rate at which the men's body temperature rose was about the same as if they had been warmed by packed blankets. 'But in four cases the men performed an act of sexual intercourse with the women.' The chilled men's temperature rose faster after intercourse. Experiments using only one woman instead of two showed an even faster re-warming, perhaps, according to Rascher, because inhibitions were removed and the woman snuggled closer to the man. In none of the cases was the re-warming of the man any more effective than if they had been placed in a hot bath. And in one of the cases the man had a cerebral haemorrhage and died.

In early November a man called Ludwig Stumpfegger turned up at Hohenlychen, and any hopes that the Ravensbrück experiments might come to an end were dashed. The access to female material for experimentation had tempted Stumpfegger to come and do some tests himself: he wanted to break bones and see if they would grow back together again. Stumpfegger, another Himmler favourite, proposed the experiments to Gebhardt. Gebhardt knew Stumpfegger well – they had worked on the German medical team at the 1936 Berlin Olympics – but he claimed later that he opposed Stumpfegger's tests on the grounds that such experiments had already been done.

But Stumpfegger had Himmler's approval. The Reichsführer had recently carried out a tour of convalescent homes for wounded soldiers, and believed more could be done to mend broken bones. He proposed to Stumpfegger that he experiment on young Polish prisoners at Ravensbrück.

On 2 November a sixteen-year-old Polish dancer called Basia Pietrzyk, the baby of the Lublin transport, became one of Stumpfegger's first victims. Basia was a slight, graceful figure whose dark hair and black eyes had earned her the nickname 'Pepper' in the Polish block. During her operation Stumpfegger chiselled pieces of bone out of her right and left tibias before plastering over the legs up to the groin and scribbling on the cast the code 1A, to signal the start of his series of experiments. He took the pieces of Basia's legs away in his car to Hohenlychen to study them.

Once again the operations were conducted in supposed secrecy, but once again the secrecy misfired. Not only was the Polish radiographer Zofia Mączka able to observe as before, but now she was even brought in to participate, as it was she who was ordered to take the X-rays before and after each operation.

Over the next weeks, as more and more Polish women were called to the *Revier*, Zofia recorded three different sorts of operation: bone-breaking; bone grafts and bone splinters. The breaking lasted up to three hours, during which the shinbones of both legs were smashed with hammers on the operating table. The bones were set – either with or without clamps – and the wounds sewn shut and put in casts. After a few days the casts were removed and the bones left to heal without the cast. In other operations a whole fibula or tibia was just taken out.

Operations on muscles began at the same time, also at Stumpfegger's instigation. In these the victim would be recalled several times. First a piece of muscle was excised from the shin and thigh, and in later operations larger and larger pieces were taken.

Izabela Rek was called to the *Revier* and entered to see five of her friends already undressed, lying with their faces turned to the wall, with thermometers in their anuses. She was soon the sixth to lie there. After an operation on one of her legs (she had operations on both) Dr Rosenthal picked up a knitting needle from a nearby table and tapped an area of exposed bone, while Izabela looked on.

With the new series of experiments under way, the sound of bones being smashed and splintered, and muscles grafted onto bone, came from the operating theatre every day, accompanied by Herta Oberheuser's whistling, especially if Dr Fischer was around.

When Maria Grabowska was wheeled up to the theatre door to await her operation, she heard the sound of drilling from inside. She waited an hour, and Oberheuser opened the theatre door, 'her white overall soaked in blood'. Maria was left with pain so acute that it felt as if her shinbone had been pierced with a nail and drilled, which was near enough what had been done to her. It was so unbearable that she felt her heart contracting.

Eugenia Mikulska is held down by nurses as the doctors cut into her shin, even though the anaesthetic has clearly not worked. Days later, when she summons the strength to look at her leg, she sees the bone completely uncovered from just under the knee to her ankle, with folds of green flesh all around it. Sent for new dressings a few days later, she waits outside the operating theatre and hears her friend Jadwiga Dzido screaming from inside, so Eugenia tries to run away but finds her legs won't carry her and she falls. A nurse comes up and asks: 'Why are you running away? You know you've got to go in there like her and he'll cut you up too.'

Before Rosenthal begins on Eugenia, he notices her small foot and high instep and asks if she is a ballet dancer. 'No, I'm a nurse,' she says. 'Oh, *Krankenschwester*, *Krankenschwester*,' he repeats, as he cuts away the living muscle. When Eugenia gets back to the ward she shouts out, 'There is no God' but Jadwiga Dzido is shouting far louder. 'Give me a sword, give me a sword, I must defend myself. All Poland is bleeding and I am bleeding,' she cries over and over again.

Jadwiga is delirious. She is also haemorrhaging badly. Blood is flowing from her mutilated leg, which is locked in an iron splint, so Eugenia forces herself out of bed, hobbling and falling, to reach Jadwiga. On the third attempt she gets there and, propped up on Jadwiga's mattress, she makes some kind of tourniquet for her friend's leg. But Jadwiga looks nearly finished. Oberheuser comes in soon, and the look on her face shows she thinks so too.

The next day, Jadwiga is still delirious and fading, so Eugenia, who is mending, hops through to the other room to tell other friends about Jadwiga Dzido. When she turns again, to go back to her bed, she stops at the door in horror. Oberheuser and Gerda Quernheim are standing over Jadwiga holding a syringe that is about to slide in. 'And I kept thinking: "You must not kill her."'

Eugenia and others now shout out: 'Don't kill her. She's not going to die,' and Oberheuser and Quernheim look over towards Eugenia. There is silence. Oberheuser pulls Gerda Quernheim's hand away from Jadwiga and they walk off.

Eugenia looks at Jadwiga, now thinking the only hope is that she will come out of her delirium. Miraculously, almost at that very moment, she opens her eyes, looks at Eugenia and says, quite normally: 'Where am I? What is happening?'

When supper comes Eugenia persuades Jadwiga to eat, and she does. Four years later Jadwiga Dzido becomes one of four Polish rabbits to give evidence at the Nuremberg doctors' trial.

The rabbits' accounts not only detail the butchery they themselves were subjected to but also throw light on other atrocities going on inside the *Revier* at the same time; in particular their reports reveal how the Ravensbrück doctors were increasingly and habitually using injections to kill.

That doctors and nurses in the camp were reaching for syringes to murder mutilated Polish rabbits was obviously no surprise to prisoners working in the *Revier*. Ever since the days of Dr Sonntag, the use of injections to kill the sick had been commonplace and the new medical team – Schiedlausky, Oberheuser and Rosenthal – thought nothing of murdering a patient by injecting her with phenol, Evipan or even petrol. All had been told this was an efficient means of getting rid of useless lives.*

* Murder by lethal injection was commonplace in all concentration camps and was still widely used to kill lives not worth living in German sanatoria under the so-called euthanasia programme.

Nevertheless, it is clear from the rabbits' observations that in the autumn of 1942 the practice of murder by injection was being stepped up. For one thing, the prisoner nurse Gerda Quernheim now seemed to be authorised to carry out injections and was doing so at will. The Polish radiologist Zofia Mączka thought Quernheim might be killing her victims 'to liberate them' from their suffering, although she added: 'This was the danger – she lost internal control over whom to kill and whom not to kill.'

Other *Revier* staff believed that Quernheim knew exactly who to kill and was deliberately murdering prisoners in partnership with Rolf Rosenthal. In the early days Rosenthal and Quernheim worked together on abortions, and this continued, but by mid-1942 they were spending more of their time killing patients, using lethal injections, which prisoners noticed they seemed to enjoy.

It had become the practice to place prisoners to be injected in a small *Revier* room called the *Stübchen*. The Czech prisoner nurse Hanka Housková recalled walking into the *Stübchen* during the period of the medical experiments:

> A little Gypsy girl lay on the bed. Gerda Quernheim and Dr Rosenthal were bent over her. The child called to me for help and as I came toward her I saw Gerda Quernheim with a syringe in her hand injecting into a vein. Dr Rosenthal held the child's hand with a piece of rubber tubing. The child wept and struggled. Dr Rosenthal shouted at me to get out, as I would get in their way, or did I want an injection too? After a while I could still hear the child crying, Dr Rosenthal and Gerda Quernheim went back to her, and then came unpleasant giggling.

Afterwards the Gypsy's body was brought out, with blue spots on her body.

Milena Jesenska was keeping the closest eye on Quernheim and Rosenthal. In order to count the killings she made it her habit to open coffins that were placed each morning in the *Revier* yard. In late 1942 she began to notice bodies of those who had obviously been killed overnight. On these bodies were 'marks of hypodermic needles, smashed ribs, bruised faces and suspicious gaps in their teeth', she told Grete Buber-Neumann. The only prisoner allowed to move about the *Revier* at night was Quernheim, and it soon became apparent that Rosenthal was joining her in there and the two had sex. Then they often murdered a prisoner – 'not only for the perverse pleasure of it,' said Milena, but for profit. Milena was convinced that during the day the couple selected their victims – usually those with gold teeth or gold crowns – which were removed before the women were killed, and Rosenthal sold the gold.

Others were also aware that murder by injection had grown commonplace.

'I often saw Gerda Quernheim with a syringe going into the *Stübchen*,' said the Czech doctor Bozena Boudova, whose job it was to make up the lethal solutions. Nor was Quernheim the only one who helped the SS doctor with the killings. 'One knew that not only the doctors were giving the injections, but also prisoner nurses themselves.'

Since the early autumn prisoners noticed another pattern in the injection murders: the victims were often Jews. Hitler had by now ordered that Germany was to be '*judenfrei*' – cleared of Jews – by the end of 1942, and Himmler likewise ordered that each of his camps on German soil must be *judenfrei*. One by one the camps were sending their Jewish prisoners east, mostly to Auschwitz.

During the Bernburg gassings, which were wound down in early summer 1942, Ravensbrück was largely cleared of Jews, but more had then arrived, rounded up with other incoming groups. Some were foreign – including eighty-two Dutch Jews brought in over the summer months. In the autumn, as the camp prepared for a final Jewish evacuation, orders had obviously been given to doctors to hasten the death of as many Jewish inmates as possible – ahead of the clear-out – in order to save on transport costs. Magdalene Hoffmann, a senior nurse, noticed the Jewish women were put to the hardest labour, such as digging graves: 'They were often sick, with swollen legs, but treatment by SS doctors and SS nurses was forbidden. At this time these Jewish women began to be given a lethal injection of Evipan, and Gerda Quernheim assisted.' Hoffmann said she herself was ordered by Rosenthal to give injections to all Jewish women suffering from dysentery, and all of them died. In the first days of October the last remaining 522 Ravensbrück Jews were deported to Auschwitz.

By November 1942 the medical experiments had moved into another phase and the horror in the *Revier* deepened further. First, a second round of bacteria experiments was carried out on the Poles. Soon after other nationalities were brought to the experiments ward: random women – Ukrainians, Czechs, Germans – some young and some old. Nurses called these women 'the lunatics' but nobody seemed to quite know why they were there. The Poles tried to befriend them.

Amongst the group was a Russian woman who was black all over with frostbite, but she wouldn't speak. Also brought in was a frail little woman who cringed and trembled violently when anyone even tried to go near her. This woman was Yugoslavian, the rabbits discovered, and they learned that her husband was shot before her eyes.

And there was an old German – a 'green' – who it turned out used to be an opera singer.

She must have been a great beauty in her day, they all said. And on a good day she sang an aria or two for the others and handed out her bread. But mostly she was in a bad mood and shouted out loudly: '*Hitler kaputt*' or '*Heil Hitler*' and hid under the bedclothes and laughed.

Later, one by one, the young amongst the so-called 'lunatics' were taken away and the word was that they were going for 'special experiments'. These special operations were carried out by Stumpfegger, assisted sometimes by Fischer, and involved the amputation and removal of entire limbs. The victim was killed outright on the operating table by lethal injection and the limbs packed into operating sheets and taken to Hohelychen for further use.

One of the first 'special experiment' victims was a Ukrainian girl whose name was Hania.

Hania told the Polish girls she had been brought to Germany as a forced labourer and had been made to stand for hours on a damp cold factory floor, which had inflamed her hip joints and prevented her working, so she had been brought here. She was a strong girl, nevertheless, and refused to be sedated by Rosenthal, fighting him off as the Poles watched on. When he came with his needle she struggled so hard to get away from him that Rosenthal had to call the German nurse, Dora, to help him, but Hania fought them both off.

She held on to the sides of the bed to stop them putting her on the stretcher, and as she levered herself with all her strength to push Rosenthal away, Rosenthal lost his temper and leapt forward hitting Hania in the face as hard as he could and grabbing her hair shouting: 'Ukraine, Ukraine.'

Still she resisted, so Rosenthal grabbed her by the neck of her nightdress and threw her on the stretcher. The nurse, Dora, had backed away by now, watching in horror, and she turned and ran out.

Hania was now crying and screaming for her mother as she was tied down and wheeled away. Hania never returned. But Dora returned to the ward some time later and told the Lublin girls she was ashamed of being German and didn't want to work here any more. Dora soon left the camp. Shortly after, a second Ukrainian woman had an entire collarbone removed.

As if the scene at the camp infirmary were not already macabre enough, prisoners now noticed Fischer and other doctors getting into vehicles, carrying whole limbs, barely hidden under blankets, and driving off towards Hohenlychen. A few hours after Hania was taken away, Zofia Mączka, the radiologist, observed Dr Fischer in the Hohenlychen car holding a leg wrapped in a sheet.

Once again, Karl Gebhardt, the chief surgeon, would try to deny at his trial that he had any involvement in these operations, referring at one point to 'these Ravensbrück prisoners, with whom I am always being reproached,

I don't know why'. He also claimed that Stumpfegger alone had taken the 'special experiments' on, as a follow-up to his splinter operations, and directly on the orders of Himmler. The Reichsführer had heard about research done by a Russian doctor in Kiev involving transplanting whole limbs, or pieces of limbs, and wanted Stumpfegger to copy the technique, but Gebhardt claimed to know no more.

As Stumpfegger had committed suicide at the end of the war, and as all his 'special experiment' victims were dead, there might have been no knowledge of these cases at all, without the testimony of Zofia Mączka, and other prisoners.

However, Fritz Fischer's testimony also proved crucial in the trial, as under cross examination he admitted to having taken part in at least one of the 'special operations', saying he had opposed the operation 'on medical and humanitarian grounds' but was ordered to perform the surgery by Gebhardt, and therefore had no choice.

The operation involved a young male German patient at Hohenlychen who had lost a shoulder blade and collarbone due to a tumour, so a plan was devised to give the patient a shoulder blade from one of the Ravensbrück 'lunatics' and graft it on, 'giving him a good chance of survival'.

The shoulder blade was to be taken from a woman's shoulder, which was not functioning quite normally, due to a previous amputation of the hand. Originally Stumpfegger was to have performed the amputation, but Fischer was called in at the last minute to do so.

The court heard that Fischer amputated the shoulder blade at Ravensbrück, killed the victim with a lethal injection, drove to Hohenlychen with the shoulder blade wrapped in a blanket, and passed it to Gebhardt. Asked by the judge if the limb belonged to a man or a woman, Fischer said he didn't know: 'the subject' had been covered during the operation.

At Hohenlychen, Gebhardt sewed the shoulder blade onto the sick man, helped by Stumpfegger and one other. The man later died. During the course of the trial, the victim's identity was never established, and the court heard simply that the shoulder blade 'was removed from an insane female inmate of the camp'.

Throughout the winter more 'insane' women were brought in to the experiment wards. One of these women – a Czech – cried out so loud one day that the Polish rabbit Stanisława Czajkowska, just returning from an operation, awoke from her anaesthetic asking: 'What is happening? What is happening?' The Czech woman's cries spoke of 'untold despair, pain and revolt', she remembered later.

Someone then told the Poles that the Czech woman had been brought to Ravensbrück from a Czech village called Lidice, which had been razed to the ground by the Germans. The rabbits found a way to communicate with the Czech woman and learned from her that during the assault on Lidice, her home was burned to the ground with all her children inside. The children had called to their mother to help them but the Germans refused to allow her to go to them.

Hearing this, the rabbits were overwhelmed with pity and tried to befriend the woman. They had no idea at the time how much they and the Czech mother had in common. The destruction of her village and killing of her family, along with their own mutilation at the hands of SS doctors, were both the direct result of Reinhard Heydrich's death.

*Chapter 15*

# Healing

The last thing Stefania Łotocka remembered, before she was first anaesthetised, was the sight of copper-coloured leaves blowing past the infirmary window. Waking fully many weeks later, she saw snowflakes settling on the same pane. It was early December and she was starting to recover. The rabbits' ward seemed peaceful for the first time since it began. Even Krysia, the bespectacled schoolgirl, had stopped weeping.

Krysia was one of the last group of Lublin prisoners called up for the bacteria operations; afterwards there were no screams, only weeping. Stefania, in the next bed, listened to Krysia night after night. The teenager grew delirious and her leg swelled up so much it seemed it might burst any minute. Even then she didn't scream, but wept, 'like a little child who had been wronged, calling to her mother to save her,' said Stefania. 'I took hold of her hand, hanging limply from the bed and kissed it. And to my surprise Krysia stopped weeping.'

The experiments were not over. A few women were still undergoing repeat surgery. But rarely were new Polish rabbits called up, and those done with had now been abandoned 'like forgotten war wounded'. Left to nurse themselves, they carefully squeezed the pus out, picking out foreign bodies like so much flotsam and jetsam – broken china, a strip of felt, pieces of glass, splinters of wood.

They helped each other too. When Izabela Rek choked and turned blue in the face, her friends prised open her mouth with a fork and yanked out her tongue. And the Poles in the camp outside had now set up an aid committee; each rabbit was assigned a Polish 'mother' to look after her. Usually the 'mother' worked in the kitchen or canteen and had access to extra rations that were smuggled into the *Revier*.

The women noticed their young skin was healing; severed flesh fastened by plaster was drawing together of its own accord. In mid-December Eugenia Mikulska's appetite came back. Someone tapped at the window and passed her a bowl of buttermilk, which she gulped down. 'It was like a small miracle,' and she dared to think that the worst was over. Irena Krawczyk discovered she could stand on her operated leg – 'a moment of joy for my ward companions and for me – it was one of the biggest experiences of my life'.

The women even talked about how they'd manage the train home to Poland on crutches. Others said they'd be lucky to reach their block, never mind Poland. The block seemed a world away from the *Revier*. Whenever anyone opened a window, an icy blast blew through, and they all strained to breathe the air, 'like an elixir'.

Izabela Rek began to dream of getting back to her block. 'It'll be like going home,' she said. They all understood what she meant, although they also knew about the terrible things still going on out there. Executions had never stopped.

One of the women close to the *Revier* window saw a girl bashing at the doors of the *Effektenkammer* and screaming for her mother. That morning Kazimiera Pobiedzińska's mother had been called *nach vorne* and sent to the store to collect her clothes. The teenager learned what had happened and rushed to the *Effektenkammer*, but her mother had already been shot. There were rumours that Johanna Langefeld – recently returned to the camp – had tried to help.

After just six months as chief guard at the Auschwitz women's section, Johanna Langefeld returned to Ravensbrück in October 1942, and resumed her old job as *Oberaufseherin* there. The reason for her transfer is intriguing. At the time of Himmler's July visit to Auschwitz there had been no question of her leaving. On the contrary, although Langefeld herself had requested a transfer, on the grounds that Höss refused to accept her authority, that request was refused. For his part, Höss had asked Himmler to replace the troublesome Langefeld, but Himmler told him she must stay.

According to Höss's memoir, after Himmler's July visit to Auschwitz the situation in the women's section went from bad to worse, and this was largely due to the new powers bestowed on the Kapos by Himmler himself. On the day of his July visit, the Reichsführer had specifically ordered that they be encouraged to 'vent their evil on prisoners', particularly the Jews. After this, says Höss, as the Auschwitz women's section expanded, 'these unscrupulous Kapos took over, setting up a system of prisoners' self-rule'.

In the first days of October the Kapos' brutality came to a head in a manner more atrocious than even Höss or Himmler had envisaged. A small village called Budy, four miles from Auschwitz, had been turned into a subcamp. Here 400 women, many of them French-Jewish intellectuals, teachers and artists, as well as non-Jewish Russians and Ukrainians, lived in a deserted school, and worked to drain a swamp. The women were guarded by scores of the Ravensbrück recruits. Conditions were appalling; each day SS male guards goaded the female Kapos to beat up the Jewish prisoners. One of the Kapos, the former prostitute Elfriede Schmidt, first sent to Ravensbrück in 1939, was having an affair with one of the SS guards and was the ringleader of the 'beaters'.

In the first days of October 1942 there was a riot at Budy and a massacre. An SS officer, Pery Broad, described what he saw in notes taken at the scene:

> On the ground behind and beside the school building dozens of maimed and blood-encrusted female corpses are lying helter-skelter, all of them wearing only shabby prisoners' shirts. Among the dead some half-dead women are writhing. Their moans mingle with the buzzing of huge swarms of flies that circle over sticky pools of blood and smashed skulls, and this produces a peculiar kind of singing that initially baffled those who came on the scene.

Höss came to inspect. 'The Budy bloodbath is still before my eyes,' he wrote. 'I find it incredible that human beings could ever turn into such beasts. The way the Kapos knocked the French Jewesses about, tearing them to pieces, killing them with axes and throttling them – it was simply gruesome.' Broad suggested that the massacre was staged by the Kapos to cover up their beatings, which had gone too far. Another possibility was that the women prisoners, believing they had a chance of escape, as they were outside the camp walls, launched a desperate revolt at Budy and their revolt was put down.

Whatever the cause, the slaughter caused a scandal among the SS. Although by now more than 1000 were dying each week in the gas chambers at Auschwitz-Birkenau, the unplanned killing of 150 women outside the camp gates at Budy was deemed unacceptable within SS ranks because it showed order had broken down, and it had broken down amongst the women. Höss needed scapegoats and six of the women Kapos present at Budy were summarily executed.

Langefeld may not have been at the camp when the massacre took place; she later claimed she was away recovering from an injury at the time. It is notable, however, that her removal as chief guard at the Auschwitz women's section, and her return to Ravensbrück, happened just days after the Budy massacre. According to Danuta Czech, author of the *Auschwitz Chronicle*, the Budy massacre occurred on 5 October 1942. On 8 October 'The SS-

Oberaufseherin of Auschwitz and Ravensbrück concentration camps were exchanged. Langefeld returned to Ravensbrück after arguments/disagreement with Rudolf Höss, Auschwitz commandant. Maria Mandl came to Auschwitz.'

Fear of mutiny in the concentration camps ran deep, and Budy may well have finally persuaded Himmler to give in to Höss's protests that Langefeld was wrong for Auschwitz and should be replaced by a woman more suited to the task. That woman was Maria Mandl, who was already known in Ravensbrück as 'the beast'.

Back in the camp in October 1942 Langefeld found that much had altered. In her absence Max Koegel had been posted to the death camp at Majdanek and a new SS team had taken over. The new commandant was Fritz Suhren, formerly of Sachsenhausen. A slim, dapper figure – fair and freckled – Suhren, aged thirty-four, was born near Oldenburg in Lower Saxony and had worked as a textile merchant. He was known in the SS as a backroom boy, who liked to do things by the book. A new Gestapo chief called Ludwig Ramdohr had also arrived. His first task at Ravensbrück was to investigate SS corruption, particularly looting in the fur workshops, so he was loathed by prisoners and SS alike. The camp was bigger – swollen by the arrival of slave labourers from the East. Everywhere the compound was being churned up by digging and building, as gangs of male and female prisoners constructed new barracks for the industrial sector at the back and new accommodation barracks near the south wall.

Most striking for Langefeld must have been the presence just outside the walls of the Siemenslager, as the new Siemens plant was called. In her absence, a state-of-the-art factory, surrounded by electrified barbed wire, had shot up on a tract of high ground about half a mile beyond the south wall. Finished in just ten weeks, the plant had taken a lethal toll on the hundreds of prisoners from men's camps, many of whom had recently been brought here from Buchenwald especially to construct the Siemenslager. In order to meet the Siemens deadline, they were driven and beaten far past the point of desperation as over the summer they cleared trees, dredged ditches and heaved masonry. The deadline was met, but 300 of the builders were dead, and a further 300, too enfeebled to do more, were sent to Dachau on a sick transport.

When the first women started work in the barracks on 25 August 1942, Siemens & Halske joined three other major German manufacturers – IG Farben at Auschwitz, Steyr-Daimler-Puch AG at Mauthausen and Heinkel at Sachsenhausen – in using concentration-camp slave labour. So pleased was the company with its new Ravensbrück factory that Rudolf Bingel, the

Siemens member of Himmler's circle of friends, wrote to the Reichsführer SS thanking him warmly. Himmler's kindness towards Siemens inspired him with 'particular joy', wrote Bingel, who promised to render service to Himmler at any time.

By the time Langefeld was back in October, about 200 women were already employed at Siemens and the sight of the Siemens gang marching out of the camp gates each morning, then turning left towards the Siemens hill, was already familiar to everyone at Ravensbrück. At lunchtime the women marched back again for their soup, before leaving again and returning at the end of the day.

Most women were thrilled to be offered work at the new plant. After months of hard labour pushing and pulling carts 'like a horse', the sight of the bright, clean, heated factory 'took my breath away', said Rita Sprengel, a German communist. Inside her *Halle*, as the factory barracks were called, were row after row of clean tables with shining machines where the women would wind thin copper wire onto spools, sitting on adjustable chairs with a back and armrests. 'Of course,' said Rita, 'the comfort was not created for the sake of the prisoners.' She understood that without these aids the spool winders would have performed less efficiently, and in any case the wires must be kept at room temperature in order to be pliable enough to wind round the spools. Nevertheless, such comforts were a joy and 'delayed our end'.

Furthermore, the discipline at Siemens was at first less harsh. Although there was an SS woman guard on duty inside each *Halle*, responsibility for keeping order was shared with company managers, most of whom had come from Siemens's Berlin headquarters and had no direct experience of concentration camps. As a result the women guards felt somewhat restrained and, inside the factory barracks at least, were less ready to beat, although in their frustration some guards would lash out even harder as soon as the women were outside. Waiting with others to march back to the main camp one day, Georgia Tanewa, a nineteen-year-old Bulgarian, tried to read an old newspaper, used to wrap machine parts stacked on a shelf. 'I forgot for a moment where I was, when a guard suddenly thumped me and smashed in my face.'

Pleased with the first output figures, Siemens at once took on more women. The young were picked first, as long as they had good eyesight and could pass certain tests. One of the Siemens civilian *Meister* (foremen), Richard Lombacher, explained the tests to Rita Sprengel as he marched with the women to work.

> He said he used pliers to see if the women could bend thin wire. Or his people would call out a whole block of women and make them hold their hands out. Then the *Meister* walked along the rows, looked at the prisoners

to see if they were young and agile, and checked their hands to make sure they didn't tremble. They looked for smooth dry skin and lean straight fingers.

Siemens also snapped up women with administrative skills, to work as secretaries and bookkeepers. One of the very first prisoners they took on was Grete Buber-Neumann, who was given a top job working for the Siemens plant director himself, Otto Grade. Having started at Siemens as a labourer apprentice at the age of nineteen, Grade, now thirty-eight, had worked his way up the company ladder, to win a major promotion, and pay rise, when he was appointed to run the Ravensbrück plant. Working in Grade's office, Grete was quickly able to observe the qualities that had won him the job: he was assiduous at calculating to the last Pfennig whether the prisoners were working hard enough to justify their 'wage'. 'Each prisoner's output was carefully measured and payment was by result,' she recalled.

Of course, as Grete explained, Siemens did not pay the 'wage' to the prisoner, who was paid nothing at all. The money the prisoners might have earned was paid direct to the SS from whom the women were rented as slaves. Under the terms of their contract, Siemens paid the SS about forty Pfennigs for each hour worked. Even so, the company wanted its money's worth, and it practised a system of incentives. If the prisoner wound more than her quota of spools she received a coupon worth up to one Reichsmark, which could be spent at the camp shop; if she fell below the quota, Grade ordered a guard to box her ears. If that didn't work, he sent a report to the main camp labour office saying the woman was useless and should be replaced. As a result she was sent back and probably put in the bunker, or given twenty-five lashes, or both, and a new worker would be sent out the next day.

Any rejected prisoners were noted on Grade's monthly report, an account of prisoner turnover that was sent to Siemens's Berlin headquarters. The report would list such a woman as 'unsuitable' or 'sent back by main camp office'. Grade had no qualms about making such reports, said Grete. He was a slave driver and would have been an ornament to the SS. His main motivation in this was his fear of being sent to the front. 'If he proved to be an efficient manager by keeping output high, Siemens could seek an exemption for him and Grade wouldn't be called up.'

By the end of the year Grade was obviously doing a good job, because the Siemens plant was expanding again and from her window in the director's office Grete was able to observe a gang of male prisoners carrying out the work. So appalling were conditions for the builders that several men tried to escape. 'In the short period of my work for Grade I heard of five executions "while attempting to escape", and that was just from one work gang.'

*

Grete only worked at Siemens for a short period, because not long after Johanna Langefeld came back she demanded that Grete go and work for her instead. Such was the influx of Russians since she'd been away that Langefeld needed a Russian-speaker in her office as well as a good stenographer. Grete was both. Moving into Langefeld's office, she was in a position to observe the *Oberaufseherin* more closely than ever; she noticed that after her return from Auschwitz Langefeld was 'in a bad state'.

'She had all sorts of neurotic habits,' said Grete. 'Before she spoke she would always have to clear her throat once or twice, and she was endlessly stroking her dress straight, or shaking a non-existent lock of hair out of her eyes. Sometimes she would stop in the middle of a sentence and stare out of the window for minutes at a time.'

As chief guard, she was obliged to attend floggings once again, a duty she evidently hated as much as ever.

What seems to have disturbed Langefeld most on her return, however, were the latest horrors perpetrated by Dr Rosenthal and Gerda Quernheim, which Grete described to her. Grete heard in detail about the growing scandal because every evening Milena Jesenska returned from her office in the *Revier* to the mattress she shared with Grete in Block 1, and described what she'd seen. On one occasion Milena heard the cry of a newborn baby behind a door, and opened it to find a healthy newborn 'wriggling between its mother's legs'. Quernheim was absent from the *Revier*, and a healthy full-term baby had been born alive – a rare occurrence – but soon the baby's cries ceased as Quernheim drowned it in a bucket. Then in early December Quernheim herself had become pregnant with Rosenthal's baby, and Rosenthal had aborted the foetus.

As the year drew to an end Milena was also ever more convinced that Rosenthal, with Quernheim's help, was killing prisoners and selling the gold from their fillings. 'Horror-struck', Milena pleaded with Grete to tell Langefeld, hoping that she might intervene. Grete 'screwed up her courage' and passed on what Milena told her to Langefeld, who screamed at the top of her voice, saying: 'These SS doctors are just as great criminals as the camp commandant and his men.'

Grete asked, hesitantly, 'If that's what you really think, why do you stay here?', to which Langefeld replied that she had to stay 'to prevent the worst'.

And yet, as Grete also observed, Langefeld had no qualms, even now, about drafting new lists of Jews to be sent east, though she now knew better than anyone what would happen to them. Since Langefeld had last worked at Ravensbrück Jews had been entirely 'cleansed' from the camp and sent to Auschwitz, so the Jewish block here had been shut down. Nevertheless small numbers of Jewish women – either singly or in groups – still randomly arrived, caught up perhaps with other transports. They too were then sent straight to Auschwitz, so that Ravensbrück had now become a sort of transit camp for female Jews.

Langefeld now had the job of filling out these Jewish transport lists, and as she read out the names, 'her face was distorted and her voice full of hatred,' said Grete. Langefeld told Grete one day, 'Auschwitz is the most horrible place that the mind of man can conceive of,' but she didn't mention the crimes committed against the Jews, saying, 'I can never get over the fact that the Jehovah's Witnesses I took there came to their end. But at least Teege and Mauer were saved.'

On return from Auschwitz Langefeld still seemed to admire the Führer, as well as the Reichsführer SS, but at the same time she made no secret of her hatred for the SS under them, and the new crowd at Ravensbrück seemed to her worse than the last. The SS now blamed her for everything that went wrong. In the winter two Poles working in the kitchen escaped by hiding in refuse bins that were loaded into a lorry and taken away. One was captured, brought back and put in the bunker, while the other was reportedly shot dead crossing a frontier. Ramdohr blamed Langefeld for lax security in the kitchen, which was 'ruled by filthy Poles'.

Langefeld was a 'strange woman', said Grete, 'who could show a warm heart'. When a Gypsy came to her for help – a woman she had known since Lichtenburg – Langefeld spoke to her 'consolingly and with great kindness'. Grete also noticed that Langefeld, unlike any SS man, was open to persuasion, and that could be useful. On one occasion an asocial was brought into the office, reported for stealing a turnip, which, if proven, meant the bunker.

'Did you steal the turnip?' Langefeld asked the woman.

'*Frau Oberaufseherin*, I was so hungry, really I was,' came the answer, with broken sobs.

'But if everyone stole turnips there would be none left for anyone else,' said Langefeld, and sent the woman from the room.

Grete appealed to Langefeld, saying that the woman, whom she knew, would never survive the bunker, and she was not a bad person. 'Frau Langefeld considered the case a moment as her face twitched nervously. With a sudden gesture she tore up the report and threw it in the bin.'

Langefeld still maintained her greatest sympathy for the Poles. On return from Auschwitz, she was particularly concerned about the *Kaninchen*, whose plight had by now won sympathy across the camp.

Towards the end of 1942 prisoners were told they could receive food parcels from their families for the first time. The news caused elation. Until now only certain favoured prisoners had been able to receive parcels from their families, and food had never been permitted. The idea was Himmler's. If prisoners were to work to bolster the war effort, they needed better food; it made sense to let families help provide it. Himmler, as usual, had put his personal imprint on the order. The contents of the parcels were to be eaten within two days or would be confiscated (perhaps to prevent vermin). Any SS who stole from the parcels would be sentenced to death.

The first the Polish rabbits knew of the parcels was when friends started sneaking little luxuries to them. A Czech friend brought Maria Grabowska a little sugar, which she sprinkled on her bread. In mid-December Pelagia Maćkowska had received her own food parcel from home – including a warm pullover, knitted by a sister. Oberheuser and the nurses came to admire the treats.

Not only did the parcels contain luxuries such as home-made bread, cakes and sugar, they also contained hidden letters and perhaps a photograph of a child not seen for years. Now the rabbits' thoughts of home revived again, especially as Christmas was coming.

On Christmas Eve the soup was served early on the wards as the German staff went off duty to celebrate. The talk turned to Christmases at home. A tap came at the window, and suddenly a friend called Halina was amongst the women, kissing them, her cold frosty cheeks against theirs. Only after Halina had gone did they find that she had left behind her a little cake made of bread, margarine and jam. On top was a jam rabbit. The rabbits were delighted by such a clever gift on Christmas Eve, but excitement set off their fevers. Pelagia struggled out of bed in her white plaster 'boots' to take water around, but as she moved her boots suddenly turned red and she heaved herself back to bed, crying out and leaving bloodstains across the floor.

By the New Year, several of the rabbits were deemed well enough to return to their blocks, including Stefania Łotocka, who was given her clothes and a pair of crutches and told to walk back. Somehow Stefania managed to stagger out of the *Revier*, but outside the door the frosty air hit her and she fainted and slipped to the ground. Fearing a guard would pass at any moment and kick her, she lay curled round her crutches thinking, 'I'll just try to make myself as comfortable as possible lying here' when a figure appeared above her, grasped her gently under the arms, and carried her to her block. The 'figure' was Rosetta, Blockova of the Polish block. The warmth of Rosetta's body revived Stefania as she lay in her arms.

In mid-January came the announcement the Polish rabbits had longed for: Herta Oberheuser informed them that there would be no more experimental operations. A day or two later, the commandant, Fritz Suhren, came in person to confirm the news and to deliver another announcement: two women, Maria Gnaś and Maria Pajączkowska, were to be freed. He spoke with glazed eyes, 'as if we were not in the room, and then he was gone'. They all stared at the two Marias, whose wounds had barely even begun to heal, and everyone, including the two girls, could see there was no chance of them going home. One of Langefeld's clerks then came with papers stating that the women were freed and 'should go straight home to Lublin'.

'But we can't even walk,' said Maria Pajączkowska anxiously.

A few days later both were taken away – apparently freed, but Dziuba Sokulska soon heard otherwise. Dziuba made contact with a Polish friend in the *Schreibstube* who said she'd seen a piece of paper with the women's names on, and beside each was a cross. The cause of death in both cases was given as pulmonary embolism, but everyone knew they had been shot.

When Dziuba broke the news to Block 15, silence fell, the same ominous silence Wanda had once struggled to explain. 'We were silent because we were overwhelmed by our humiliation and the utter physical weakness that plagued us.' There had never been any intention to send them home. The SS doctors wanted the two rabbits dead because alive, they were evidence of their crimes.

The grief poured out. Why the two Marias had been singled out first for execution, no one could think, and so no one could guess who would die next. With this came the fear: it could be any of them, at any time.

Dziuba Sokulska was the first to suggest a protest. Ever the lawyer, she said it should be done in orderly fashion, starting with a brief letter to the commandant, asking for an explanation. They sent their protest. Suhren did not reply. His silence, however, only fuelled the women's disgust and spurred them on.

The early protests were small – more like individual acts of defiance – and were barely noticed, but they signalled a changing mood. For example, Eugenia Mikulska, struggling on her crutches in the *Revier*, saw Oberheuser and Fischer looking in her direction and laughing as she lost her balance. 'I managed to support myself on my crutches enough to turn my back on the two criminals. They obviously understood my gesture of contempt, for they went away.'

The SS knew the rabbits had growing support around the camp, so they started to spread smear stories, saying that their families in Poland had all received vast sums of money as rewards for their daughters' suffering, that fathers, brothers, husbands had all been promised early release from prison.

The few who might have believed the lies soon changed their minds when they saw the broken figures of these once lithe and healthy girls come stumbling out of the infirmary, trying to return to their blocks. When the rabbits themselves heard what was being said about them, the talk of protest action grew more heated. Once back in the block there was a great deal of time to talk and plan. They could not go out to work, and remained inside assigned to knitting and sewing.

'The sight of so many disabled women in one block had an effect on us and we suddenly had a growing sense of our own power,' recalled Wanda Wojtasik. Groups of rabbits even started to venture out to breathe the air, and on sunny days they gathered in a sheltered spot against the block wall. Pelagia Maćkowska remembered the 'painful sight' of these young girls, 'their shoulders unnaturally stiffened by their crutches, leaning against the back wall of the block and their thin pale faces turned towards the warmth of the sun for salvation'.

The worst tensions sprang from the continuing executions of Poles. No more rabbits were killed at this time, but other Polish women were picked out once or twice a week. A messenger would come and call numbers and the women would stand and walk away. That evening the shots would be heard.

In February 1943 two groups of eight were called on consecutive days, and by the time the volleys sounded on the second evening the entire block was in ferment. Arguments broke out, as ringleaders amongst the rabbits called for action, while others, often older and worried about repercussions, asked: 'And what do you propose? You all went off to be cut up without complaining.'

Among the rabbits a new recklessness took hold, and some talked of hunger strikes, or a mass protest on the Lagerstrasse, even escape. The more cautious in the block – again, usually the older women – said mass protest on crutches was laughable, and as for escape, this was impossible. But the younger ringleaders argued back, saying they weren't going to die for nothing, and their voices grew in number as more victims left the infirmary and came 'home' to the block.

The sister-in-law of Maria Gnaś, one of the murdered rabbits, really did escape. Somehow she got over the wall and walked away into the fields beyond. She was in some kind of trance, so people said. Captured at once, when Suhren asked why she tried to escape, her reply was: 'I don't want to be shot.'

Everyone became obsessed with how she got over the wall. Several said they would rather escape and be shot than go like sheep to the slaughter. Others said they would commit suicide before they were experimented on again. And though many were still in a pitiful state, all were slowly convalescing, helped by the parcels, which gave them both physical and moral strength.

By January Krysia too had returned to Block 15 and was mending fast, with Wanda's care. The two shared a mattress, as before, and on the next bunk were the Iwańska sisters Janina and Krystyna, also from Lublin. Together the four mulled over the various choices – escape, suicide, hunger strikes – and then Krysia came up with her plan for 'telling the world'. They should smuggle information about the doctors' crimes to people outside. If they could only get a report of these atrocities to the Polish underground, the underground would signal it to London. Once it reached the Polish government in exile, it would find its way to the powerful people.

The women were well aware that everyone – at least in Poland – already knew about concentration camps, that people were dying there. But they also felt sure that no one could ever have dreamed that experiments were being done on healthy young women, who were then being shot. If the powerful people knew this – Krysia meant the governments in London and Washington, the International Red Cross, the Pope – they would surely speak out and it would be stopped, she said, and the others agreed. So they discussed how to get the story out, and it was probably Janina Iwańska who came up with the idea of writing in secret ink.

All four were trained scouts, and all four had learned about secret writing, using lemon juice, milk or onion juice as invisible ink. But what were they going to use for ink? Krystyna suggested urine. Her mother had once told Krysia that it had been used for secret writing in her own army days in the First World War. 'But what do we use for paper?' someone else asked. 'And how do we smuggle our letters out?'

Maria Bielicka had smuggled information out some months earlier through her contacts in the *Effektenkammer*, hiding notes in clothes parcels, but Maria was in the Warsaw group; none of the Lublin girls knew of her smuggling or had contacts in the *Effektenkammer*. Their only communication with the outside world to date had been the monthly official letters in German, censored by the SS, in which they could say little more than '*Ich bin gesund und fühle mich wohl*' (I'm well and I feel fine).

'So let's write between the lines and in the margins of the official letters,' Krysia suggested. As this was something else her mother had done, she would know to iron the letters to show up the secret writing. Krysia solved the next question too: to tip off her family the invisible writing was there, she would give clues in the German writing.

As children, she and her younger brother Wiesław used to read the adventure stories of the Polish writer Kornel Makuszyński. A favourite was *The Demon of the Seventh Form*, in which the hero sent information in letters, concealed in code. The key was the word made up by the first letter of each line. Krysia's idea was to make a reference to Makuszyński in her next official letter home. The family were bound to smell a rat, and her brother would get the hint.

The girls agreed that the plan might work. All four would write each letter together and nobody outside the group must know. When the next day came for an official letter home, they found a hiding space in the attic of their block; the space was already used by smokers who organised cigarettes from the stores. Here they prepared their first secret letter.

First they wrote their visible sentences in German, and in them Krysia reminded Wiesław how they used to admire the ingenuity of *The Demon of the Seventh Form*. She arranged the lines in the letter so that the first letters of each line made the words '*list moczem*' – 'letter written in urine'. Then dipping a stick in urine, she wrote in the margins: 'We have decided to tell you the whole truth.'

The first secret letter was to be brief, so there followed just a few sentences about the medical experiments. At the end, Krysia wrote, 'More letters will follow' and gave a code word for the family to use in their next official reply, to show they had received the secret message. The first letter went off, but part of the code that signalled the secret contents was rubbed out somehow by the time it reached Krysia's family, so the trick very nearly failed.

Wiesław Czyż, Krysia's younger brother, remembers well the arrival of the first secret letter at their home in Lublin. As always when a letter arrived from his sister, his father, Tomasz, read the contents out loud to Wiesław, then aged fifteen, and his mother Maria. Till now the family had tried to read between the official lines for any hint about Krysia's well-being, but the formal language was always the same. Then one day in early 1943 a letter mentioned a story by Makuszyński. 'It seemed out of context,' says Wiesław. 'But as I was still very young the story was fresh in my memory, and straight away I remembered that the high point was a tale of children sending secret messages hidden in texts. So I quickly guessed what she was trying to tell us. Krystyna was a quiet girl but smart, and always full of bright ideas.'

Wiesław and his parents deciphered the code, but due to the missing letters they read the instruction as *list mocz* – wet the letter – instead of *list moczem* – letter in urine. So the family sprinkled water on the letter, which revealed the secret writing, but only in time to decipher it and then it disappeared. Guessing their mistake, they rushed out and took the letter to a trusted chemist to ask how to reveal text written in urine. He told them to apply a hot iron. This they did and the words appeared again.

'It was an extraordinary thing to get this information from my sister straight from a concentration camp,' said Wiesław. 'There were only three people at this operation with the iron, my mother, father and me. You are speaking to the only living witness.'

I asked if the family were worried by the risks Krysia was taking.

'Yes,' said Wiesław, 'but nobody questioned it. We knew she was doing what she had to do – keeping up her resistance. It was instinctive. It was what we all did. It's hard for you to understand today, but you see, resistance was all that kept us going at that time. We were living under a cruel and brutal power. The only thing that mattered to us was mutiny.'

After this first letter, more arrived, packed with more information about the camp, though all these years later Wiesław could not remember the details. He did recall that their mother, as a major in the Lublin 'Home Army', was able to pass on the reports to her underground chiefs in Lublin: 'By sending the messages Krystyna knew that she would immediately be linked up to the wider Polish resistance network because of her own mother.'

Wiesław knew that the commanders in Lublin had sent the information on by signal to stations in Warsaw, who in turn passed it on to stations in Sweden, from where, the family hoped, the messages might even reach the Polish government in exile in London, though whether this ever happened, nobody had ever found out.

Was Krystyna particularly courageous? Not especially, said Wiesław.

> She was just a normal girl like the others. The only thing you might say about Krystyna was that she had a special innocence. You see, she was particularly young. At the time of her arrest all she had known about was her schoolwork, and her patriotism. Her friends were the same. But she was younger somehow. More innocent.

His sister never talked about the letters after the war: 'When Krysia returned home in 1945, all she wanted to do was to forget, and to get back to school. She refused to speak about the camp ever again.'

When I spoke to Wiesław in 2008, Krysia was still alive and living with her daughter, Maria, in Lublin. Maria might know where the letters were, thought Wiesław, but Krysia herself had now lost her memory and was unable to talk.

Krysia's daughter, Maria Wilgat, said she knew nothing of the surviving letters and knew little about the camp, as after the war Krysia had never spoken of it to her either. But Maria did offer to help. Twenty years after the war her mother had agreed to write an essay about the secret writing, as it was special to her. 'This was the only story she wished to tell,' said Maria, and she sent me a copy of the essay.

The letter writing began, wrote Krysia in her essay, in order to tell the world of 'the shameful acts of the German doctors' and in the hope that if the world spoke out about it, the Germans might halt their crimes. 'Several of us died as a result of these operations, many were crippled for life and all of us, regardless of the degree of damage done to our health, suffered mental torture that cannot be forgotten.'

From the start the project was undertaken with the utmost seriousness.

> After we received a sign from my family that the first secret letter had been deciphered this dangerous game absorbed us completely. We began to

> work on improving and expanding our correspondence. The first improvement we made was to stop writing between the lines. Instead we used the inside of the envelopes of the camp letters. This way we gained some extra space, because we could write more densely on clean paper. It was also safer. In the first period of our correspondence we put a successive number on each envelope so that our families in Poland could know if they were receiving all the letters we had written.

In order to send longer letters, the girls had the idea of sending part of each letter to each of the four families, who had to meet in secret to join them up and read them. A sign was given to show what had been done. These joint letters were 'less personal', as they were to be read out to other families. All four agreed the facts that went in and the letters were usually composed by at least two people. The system was also improved by asking the families to conceal their 'receipt' signs in the food parcels they were now sending – a thread of a certain colour left in the package, or the number of a received letter inscribed on a food tin.

'Once we realised what the methods in the camp were for checking food parcels [SS women inspected them in front of the prisoners] we even got secret notes from our families, usually concealed in toothpaste tubes. This accounted for the frequent reference to toothpaste in our letters.'

Later the girls received food packed in pages of books. 'In this way our families managed to smuggle to us *Pan Tadeusz* and Zeromski's *Forest Echoes*,' said Krysia. After a while the group expanded, adding four more who included Dziuba Sokulska, the Lublin lawyer, and the young Warsaw student Wojciecha Buraczyńska. There was a further group who knew about the letter-writing and assisted, but did not write letters themselves.

For Krysia the letter-writing became a mission to which she now devoted herself, planning what and where to write and how to divide the letters, devising signs and working out how to hide the evidence before climbing into the attic late at night and silently squatting to collect the urine – she doesn't offer details – and to write. Furthermore, the facts had to be as accurate as possible, checked and double-checked, as this was first-hand evidence of atrocity; no time or space was wasted complaining about conditions or giving general descriptions of the camp.

In her essay, Krysia quotes from her own letters, apologising to readers for failing in some places to include all names, or getting them in the wrong order. 'There was room only for the briefest description of operations,' she explains. She also apologises for the fact that some of the women named in the letters as alive were already dead, but this was because they were executed a short while after the letter was written. Looking back at her own letters, Krysia is struck by their childlike qualities. 'We must remember that they were written by young girls. Our age and lack of perspective accounts for the way the events are described and for the interpretation of the facts.'

She has even censored the letters she chooses as illustrations for the essay, to remove 'irrelevant detail' or 'optimistic postscripts'. These were little phrases inserted to give a positive view of the camp – 'we wanted to cheer up our parents after reading the contents of the letters, which brought such dreadful news'. Other bits and pieces she quoted had also been self-censored, and it was obvious from the essay that somewhere most of the original letters must have been preserved.

In 2010 Krysia's daughter, Maria Wilgat, told me that her mother was now critically ill, with little time to live. So Maria had been spending more time in her mother's house and had taken the chance to look around. She had discovered secret letters and other documents hidden in her grandmother's old rolling pin, and in a carved-out hole in a chopping board. When we met again Maria produced the secret letters – all twenty-seven of them, some just crumbling parchment, barely legible, and in various shapes, including triangular. Some were obviously the backs of envelopes and others had words round the edge of other words. All were lovingly preserved.

The earliest letters were mostly long lists of names of the executed women and of those operated upon, some with black crosses against them, which the four families meeting in Lublin must have pored over, before passing on bad news. There were also detailed accounts of operations, dates and more names. On 24 March Krysia wrote:

*Up to January 16th 1943, 70 persons were operated on altogether. Out of this number 56 were from the Lublin September transport, 36 of these operations began with infection (3 without incision) and 20 bone operations. In bone operations, each incision is opened again. No more new operations since Jan 15.*

Then follows an almost complete list of surgery dates, with the women's camp numbers: 'Infection operations August 1st 1942: Wojtasik Wanda 7709, Gnaś Maria 7883, Zielonka Maria 7771 ...' Here too are the names of the doctors, who at that very moment were still operating and hiding behind sheets.

*Apart from Professor Gebhardt, operations are also performed by his two assistants, Fischer and Stumpfegger.*

*As a sign that you have read this letter, send me a blue thread in a parcel ...*

> *You can send a note hidden in the double bottom of a tin. Write at least once, describe the political situation. I am waiting for that! Message continued in letters from Wanda and Janina Iwańska.*

In several letters Krysia writes how eager she is to know if their messages are reaching London and the rest of the world.

Reading on we found some of the 'silly postscripts' Krysia had written to cheer up her parents. 'We are not doing badly. We are all together,' she wrote in one letter. 'All is fine with us. We get up early so I am grateful to papa that from childhood he got us used to that.' In another letter: 'We have the chance to wash and the cold water is healthy and really quite pleasant.'

Later, reading the letters more carefully, I found several that Krysia didn't mention in her essay. One begins:

> *Mama dear, from yesterday I am depressed and I cannot stand it, so I have to write to you my thoughts and imagine we are close and that I can feel you near to me. I feel how nice it is and I start to cry. Sometimes it is so bad I have to talk to you in my head or write, or I have to start thinking about something else because otherwise I collapse.*

Another letter, the date of which has faded but which was probably written at the end of March or in early April, has an entirely different tone; it talks of how the first real camp protest began: 'The first protest against the lawless acts ... On March 12th 1943 five healthy women were again taken for operations. They put up resistance. No physical force used against them. One of them, Zofia [Dziuba] Sokulska strenuously protested.'

Krysia had told her parents in an earlier letter that since 15 January 1943 'nobody has been taken for an operation', but by the time they received that letter, the information was already out of date. In the first days of March the *Revier* was said to be preparing for more operations, and anger reached boiling point again. Five women already cut open once or twice were recalled, among them Dziuba Sokulska.

Events in Block 15 unfolded fast. As Wanda Wojtasik put it later: 'Suddenly we had the suicidal courage of those who knew they could act as they chose today, because they would be dead tomorrow. Wordlessly we all reached the same conclusion at the same moment: enough was enough.' Dziuba, once again, made the first stand. Summoned to the *Revier*, she asked Dr Oberheuser to explain the reason for operations on healthy prisoners. Oberheuser ignored her. Dziuba now told her that she had had two operations and would refuse a third. She walked out of the sickbay and back to the block, where word had already arrived of what she had done and there was great excitement at her courage.

At almost the same time, another of the five recalled women, Zofia Stefaniak, was lying in the *Revier*, still recovering from a previous operation. With three holes drilled through her leg, she had stayed longer than others and had witnessed some of the worst of the later atrocities, Stumpfegger's work. So horrified was she by now, that when Zofia heard that she was to be operated on yet again, she found sudden strength to clamber down from bed, heave herself over to the window and leap out.

'I was so frightened of the operation that this time I had to escape,' Zofia said. 'I thought this time they would cut my legs off. I had just seen a Russian girl with her legs cut off. So I just jumped out onto the grass.' Zofia escaped after evening roll call, so nobody saw her. Somehow she made it back to Block 15, and only then did she hear that Dziuba had also refused. They hid her in the attic.

The refuseniks now waited for a response from the SS, but none came. It was as if the entire SS staff were pretending the experiments had never happened. 'They act as if we are nothing to do with them,' said Jadwiga Kamińska.

A standoff ensued, until next day a second list of five names came from the *Revier*. Nobody responded. Inside Block 15 someone, probably Jadwiga, suggested a protest march, and this time the idea was not laughed off. 'If the commandant wants to pretend there have been no medical experiments in the camp, let's go and stand in front of him and show him,' said one of the ringleaders. 'Our attitude was that if we were going to be murdered let's be murdered for a reason – not cut up first,' Eugenia Mikulska recalled.

Someone else suggested it would be better to march to Langefeld's office, not Suhren's, as she might at least listen. They should take a petition that each of them should sign, said Dziuba Sokulska. Halina Chorążnya, the chemistry professor, offered to draft a brief statement for one of them to read. Jadwiga Kamińska and Zofia Baj were elected as the marchers' spokeswomen. They would march the next day. Everyone was to go to show unity. Those too badly injured to walk would be carried by the stronger. Others would go on crutches, or hobble as best they could.

Testimony about the date is conflicting, but Krysia states in her letter, in her characteristically matter-of-fact tones: 'On March 14th all the women who had had operations gathered before the *Oberaufseherin*, demanding an explanation as to what grounds there were for performing operations on political prisoners, and whether they were envisaged in special sentences.'

It was probably mid-morning when the marchers set off, as that was when the Lagerstrasse was quiet. The women lined up slowly outside the block and their procession began. 'It seemed a long way for us – 300 metres or more. And the ground was very rough,' Wojciecha recalled.

Pelagia Maćkowska remembered the scene like this: 'A column of crippled women, some leaning on crutches, others on walking sticks or carried by healthy companions, moved slowly in the direction of the camp office. I shall never forget that sight.'

At the head of the column were the most disabled of all. 'I was at the head of the group and the silent procession of young cripples walked behind me,' recalled Mikulska. The column moved the entire 300 metres in total silence, except for the clicking of sticks on the Lagerstrasse. Each woman took one step and then gathered herself for the next. It seemed to take an age.

The first few metres were the most dangerous, for surely the guards must appear, but no attempt was made to stop them, or to interfere in any way. Gangs of prisoners returning early from work simply stared in astonishment. Others, inside the barracks, looked out through windows, but still no guards appeared.

'We reached the main square, where the camp office was, without any obstacles,' said Pelagia, though they were aware of eyes watching from inside the *Kommandantur*. The procession arrived, and someone called the column to halt. The two who carried Eugenia Mikulska moved out to the front and put her down.

'In front of the *Schreibstube* they put me on the ground and went back to the ranks standing about fifty metres behind. I couldn't stand, so I knelt on my sound leg and stretched the operated one out in front of me, as I couldn't bend it.'

Once all the marchers were gathered in position, their spokeswomen, Jadwiga Kamińska and Zofia Baj, approached Langefeld's office. As they did so, a single woman guard appeared, and they informed her that they wished to see *Oberaufseherin* Langefeld. The guard went back inside and for some time nothing happened.

'We were prepared for the worst,' recalled Eugenia. More time passed. 'All was silent around us. There was not a soul in the camp roads.' According to Pelagia: 'We waited in deep silence and we all stared fixedly at one place.'

When Langefeld still failed to appear, Jadwiga Kamińska read out her short statement of protest, in a quiet voice, in front of the office: 'We, the Polish political prisoners, categorically protest against the experimental operations performed on our healthy bodies.'

Still Langefeld did not appear, and nor did Suhren, nor anybody else. So the women continued to stand there, staring ahead. The flame-coloured salvias were out, and the midday sun was beating down. Jadwiga read the statement again, in the same quiet voice: 'We, the Polish political prisoners, categorically protest against the experimental operations performed on our healthy bodies.'

There was still only silence.

After a while, according to some of the women, a German office worker emerged and told Jadwiga and Zofia that the *Oberaufseherin* 'knew nothing of the operations', they 'must be a figment of the prisoners' imaginations'. The new call-up for rabbits to go to the *Revier* had simply been a request for them to have temperatures taken. They should all now behave and go back to their barracks.

Krysia, however, recorded in her letter home that Langefeld's message was quite different. The chief guard informed the marchers, through her official, that she had referred the matter to the commandant, who would respond himself. Most protesters also remember that Johanna Langefeld did, briefly, appear before them outside. 'She came out and looked at us for a moment,' said one. She 'looked embarrassed', said others. 'She looked paralysed somehow and awkward, as if in pain,' said another. But all agreed that Langefeld said nothing, turned around and quickly went back inside.

Grete Buber-Neumann, now Langefeld's personal secretary, is disappointingly silent on this episode – perhaps she was not in Langefeld's office that day. But she tells us enough of Langefeld's mood to suggest what 'paralysed' her, as she looked out at the massed ranks of rabbits. Around this time, Langefeld had told Grete that she had been having bad dreams.

> One morning she entered the office tired and depressed. She had had a dream, which she wanted to tell me, so I could interpret it. In the dream, bombs were landing in the camp, and foreign tanks came and conquered Ravensbrück. I said without hesitating: 'Frau *Oberaufseherin*, you are afraid that Germany will lose the war,' and I added, after a moment: 'And Germany will lose the war.'
>
> For this I should have been thrown straight in the bunker. But she just looked at me in horror and stayed silent. From this point I knew that this woman would never harm me.

Grete tells us that Langefeld's position at this time was in growing jeopardy. She already stood accused by the SS of sympathising with Polish prisoners, and Suhren had been gathering other evidence against her, with Ramdohr's help. Grete goes to some lengths to tell us that Langefeld was increasingly 'torn' in the early months of 1943 between right and wrong. And Grete herself takes considerable credit for shifting Langefeld's perspective to see things from the prisoners' point of view. 'I had not only shaken her conviction in a German victory, but I had also made her see the concentration camp system through the eyes of its victims,' she says.

Grete's influence upon Langefeld was no doubt significant. However, as Langefeld's secretary, her own position was also compromised at this point. Her eagerness in retrospect to claim credit for 'turning' Langefeld may well have helped her gloss over the fact that, sitting in Langefeld's office, she was by now the most privileged prisoner in the camp.

And however torn Langefeld was, she had done nothing since her return from Auschwitz to stop the murders and atrocities committed at Ravensbrück. Even now, faced with the rabbits' protest, she simply passed the buck to the commandant, as Krysia reported. Suhren had no idea what to do; there were no rules on his desk saying how to crush an uprising of women on crutches. So with one eye on the crowd outside his window, the commandant picked up the phone to seek instructions from Berlin.

The protesters, meanwhile, were in pain and could not wait for an answer, so their leader gave the signal that they should return to the block. Eugenia was still balancing on her plastered leg. Later she recalled: 'My companions again came up to me and lifting me up, carried me back to the barracks and put me to bed.' All the others turned around and made their way back. 'We felt we had put up resistance, we were a united group with a kind of strength,' said Pelagia Maćkowska.

Protests were not over, however. The next day, still lacking a response from Suhren, the women resolved to write again: 'We have not been told and would like to know if these operations are envisaged in our sentences, whose contents we do not know. We request a hearing or an answer.' The letter was delivered direct to Suhren.

A response of sorts came – not from Suhren but from the *Revier*. As if to prove the claim that the summonses had been a 'misunderstanding', a message went round, requesting the women to 'volunteer' to attend the *Revier* 'to have their temperatures taken'. Nobody did. The five called up earlier for new operations were not recalled, and the protests spread.

No doubt emboldened by the rabbits' uprising, and by the lack of an SS response, a group of 'healthy' Polish prisoners now made their own 'energetic protest', as Krysia put it. Again the authorities 'did not apply repressions or use force', she wrote in her letter home.

The protest by the 'healthy' Poles was a near-mutiny staged three days later. The incident was sparked when, just before the start of evening *Appell*, nine women, all from Warsaw, were suddenly called and ordered to report to the *Effektenkammer*. Clearly this meant execution. Perhaps because of the febrile atmosphere following the disabled protest, or because the women were part of a particularly strong group, this announcement raised unusually high emotion. Friends of the victims, angry that they had not even had time to say goodbye, broke ranks and moved spontaneously towards the *Effektenkammer* to try to glimpse the condemned women one last time.

Helga Gallinat, one of the guards, got wind of what was happening and came chasing after the prisoners, yelling and hitting out at them. The women astonished Gallinat by hitting back and nearly lynching her. Other guards went to her help and were also attacked. As uproar erupted, and Langefeld's

Polish interpreter, Helena Korewina, asserted her considerable authority by setting off the siren calling the night shift to work. As the siren rang out, thousands of night-shift workers flooded the Lagerstrasse, the disturbance subsided and the camp sank back into order.

But everyone knew Ravensbrück had been minutes away from mutiny. The mood was now all the more inflamed, and Fritz Suhren had more proof to use against Langefeld, as the riot showed she was plainly no longer in control.

It was another incident, however, soon after the near-riot, that tested Langefeld's loyalties and Suhren's patience to breaking point. Once again the rabbits were involved. Grete Buber-Neumann, who on this occasion was at Langefeld's side, gives a detailed acount. According to her, Langefeld was particularly horrified by the rabbits' plight because they had been lied to by the promise to send them home in return for agreeing to operations; instead the 'used' victims were being shot.

It was not, however, until one day in early April that the reality of this deception hit Langefeld. On this day, as Grete worked with the *Oberaufseherin* in her office, a memo came from the Gestapo office asking for ten Poles with numbers between 7000 and 10000 to present themselves *nach vorn*. Grete saw the memo and knew what it meant, as of course did Langefeld. A messenger fetched the women from their blocks. Grete recalled:

> I sat at my typewriter and looked through the window. As the group were brought across the square I noticed that two of them were on crutches.
>
> 'Frau Langefeld,' I called out. 'They are going to shoot the rabbits. They are coming now.'
>
> Langefeld sprang up, gave one glance out of the window, picked up the telephone receiver and demanded to speak to the commandant.
>
> I sat there listening anxiously.
>
> 'Herr *Lagerkommandant*,' she said. 'Do you have permission from Berlin to shoot the rabbits?'

Grete didn't hear Suhren's answer. Langefeld hung up and turned to Grete, telling her to go out and send the two prisoners on crutches back to their block.

After four years as chief guard at the women's camp, and six months at Auschwitz, Johanna Langefeld had finally chosen between right and wrong, shaken off her indecision and acted to save two Polish prisoners' lives. Grete, knowing that Langefeld was disobeying SS orders, and therefore at considerable risk to herself, carried out her boss's instructions and told the rabbits to return to their block.

Two weeks later, Grete was in the office again and watched as Langefeld took a brief call from Fritz Suhren. On this occasion, Langefeld listened in silence, replaced the receiver and left, saying nothing.

As a result of her decision two weeks earlier to halt the execution of the crippled women, Johanna Langefeld had been dismissed. Himmler himself had approved the decision. For this – and an array of other 'crimes' concocted against her – she was to face charges of breach of discipline before an SS court. In early April 1943 Johanna Langefeld left Ravensbrück for the last time.

# PART THREE

*Chapter 16*

# Red Army

Valentina Samoilova, a medical student in Kiev, was celebrating the end of the term eating ice cream on the banks of the Dnieper River when Hitler's forces crossed into Russia in June 1941. 'Then the sky lit up and orders came to mobilise,' she remembered. 'At first we sang songs and then came the sirens and the boys said goodbye to the girls. That night we saw planes on fire in the skies and wounded horses in the streets. We had to work to clear the area of bodies. We could see everything coming to an end.'

It was the same story across the Soviet Union. War broke out just as students were finishing exams. Anna Stekolnikova, a trainee teacher from Oryol, south of Moscow, was celebrating the end of term when the voice of Molotov, the Soviet foreign minister, burst out over a speaker system, saying war had started.

> We were all told to gather at our college, where we were taught to set off incendiary bombs. Then the boys left for the front and we never saw them again. Then suddenly we all had to leave. It was 2 July 1941, and the order came for all medical staff to evacuate the hospital. The students amongst us had just finished exams, but everyone was called up.

In Odessa, on the Black Sea, trainee women doctors and nurses were given military uniforms, assigned to a marine medical division and sent to treat the wounded in trenches at the front, which was closing on the city. 'We didn't think twice about it. We were little more than children but we loved our country and wanted to defend it,' says Maria Vlasenko, an

Odessa nurse, who was wounded in the trenches by shrapnel in the eye and leg.

When the harbour city of Odessa fell in November 1941, Maria and her medical division retreated with the troops to the Black Sea beaches, to board ships to Sevastopol and defend the Crimean Peninsula. Sevastopol already lay in ruins, and there was little hope of halting the German advance, but Stalin's orders were to fight to the death. 'There are no Soviet Prisoners of War, only traitors,' he told his forces who were pushed back to the tip of the promontory, where they were trapped by the Germans, sea on all three sides. Ships took senior Red Army officers off to safety but the nurses and doctors were left on the Crimean clifftops, tending the wounded.

> We were told we would be rescued by ship or by submarine, but none came for us. We moved to the very last bay – Sandy Bay – where the wounded lay all around us. We dragged them close to the cliff so they could be hoisted off onto rescue ships, but they still didn't come.
>
> We used everything we had to help them – old sheets or shirts. For splints we chopped up a stool. We used alcohol instead of morphine. But we knew we were cut off. We were isolated there with our wounded on this promontory, which was about to collapse. Bodies were falling into the water where they bubbled and burst. The sea was turning red all around us. Then the peninsula was hit by a bomb.

As Maria Vlasenko talks, other members of her family arrive at her small dwelling in a dusty village on the Black Sea coast. They sit cross-legged on the floor and listen. They haven't heard her story before.

Maria and others like her are among the most anonymous Ravensbrück victims of all. Western survivors would recall the 'disciplined' Red Army women who came to the camp, but nobody knew much about them, and once the Iron Curtain came down, these women disappeared entirely from view. Moreover these survivors were also anonymous in their own country, where they were terrorised into silence.

It was Stalin himself who instilled the terror. When Soviet survivors returned to the motherland after years of suffering in German camps, Stalin proved true to his word and treated his own soldiers as traitors simply because they had been captured and hadn't fought to the death. This also affected many of the 800,000 Soviet women who had volunteered or been mobilised to work in intelligence units, as signallers or as doctors and nurses. The very fact that they had been in a foreign country and mixed with foreigners – albeit foreign prisoners – meant they were contaminated by fascism.

Back home in Odessa, Maria Vlasenko and most of her comrades were interrogated by SMERSh, the Soviet army's wartime counterintelligence service. At best they were then blacklisted and denied work permits. At worst trumped-up charges were invented and suspects tried in secret Soviet courts. Comrades were tortured, bribed or blackmailed into denouncing comrades, then the 'guilty' were sent to Siberia or shot.

After Stalin's death in 1953 the atmosphere eased and some of those exiled to Siberia were able to return, but fear of persecution persisted and accounts of the Nazi camps were still heavily censored. It was only after German reunification in 1990, when for the first time Berlin offered small sums of compensation to those in the old Eastern bloc, that victims began to declare themselves in order to claim their cash, though by this time most were dead.

Since the end of the Cold War, the Russian authorities have also given limited access to their archives, throwing more light on the extent of Stalin's persecution. The documents include papers relating to secret post-war trials. For example, in 1949, at Simferopol, in the Crimea, five Red Army women – doctors and nurses – were tried for 'collaboration' with the 'fascists' in Ravensbrück. During the trial one of the accused was 'turned' and gave evidence against her friends. Another hanged herself in her cell. The remaining three were found guilty and sent to Siberia.

Maria Vlasenko knows of the trial. Her friend Lyusya Malygina, one of the Red Army doctors, was one of those found guilty of collaboration and sent to Siberia. But she won't discuss it – 'It was a dark story.' Her friend Ilena Barsukova lives near by, and may know more.

'Malygina was a beautiful woman, and very brave,' said Ilena Barsukova. 'She saved many lives in the camp. And she tried to save us all from capture too.'

When the Red Army doctors and nurses were cut off in July 1942 on the tip of the peninsula, a volunteer was required to swim with a message from the head of the Crimean forces, General Ivan Petrov, to officers across the bay. 'The message was for Stalin,' said Ilena. 'It was Lyusya Malygina who volunteered. She protected the secret document somehow and carried it as she swam. We thought it meant we could still be saved.'

As the Germans drew closer, however, the women realised that they'd been abandoned and the only option to avoid capture was to jump into the sea or scale the cliffs to caves down below. 'We tried to drag the wounded down into the caves too, but most were now dead so we climbed down and hid. We were there five days with no food. The Germans were right above us and knew we were starving. So they dropped ropes.'

At the top the Germans were waiting. 'We took off our boots and let the water out,' said Ilena Barsukova. 'Then we learned that seventy-one of our commanders had been taken off by submarine, so they wouldn't fall into enemy hands. It was only then that we cried.'

The captured doctors and nurses, along with the remaining male troops, were marched fifty kilometres back up the headland towards a staging point at the town of Bakhchisaray. There was no water on the march and temperatures soared to 40°C. Locals offered help, but anyone who tried to drink from a pond or reached to grab an apple from a tree was shot. The trail was 'drenched in blood', and everyone was afraid of what would happen next. News had spread fast of the German slaughter of captured Red Army soldiers. 'I saw a man reach down to his boot, pull out a knife, and cut his own throat,' said Maria Vlasenko.

The Red Army women knew of the rape and butchery of women in other captured units. German troops were fed propaganda describing uniformed Soviet women as 'disgusting men-women' and declaring: 'This is what Bolshevism has done for women.' These were 'depraved creatures' who had 'betrayed their families'.

At Bakhchisaray they started shooting the Jews. The captured soldiers, doctors and nurses were lined up in front of a big anti-tank ditch with a plank across it. Germans stood all around with guns and dogs, then prisoners were picked out and marched forward. 'It was always the Jews,' said Ilena Barsukova. Scenes like these had been enacted all over captured Soviet territory ever since the invasion began.

The men were called first, but only because they were easier to identify. 'I remember one who pleaded: "I am not a Jew. I'm a Ukrainian," and then he was told to drop his pants. They said, "Ah, you're not a Jew," so they let him go,' said Ilena.

With the women, the Germans could not be so sure, so they sought other prisoners to help identify the Jews among them. Non-Jews informed with a nod, or pointed with a stick. 'Perhaps there were scores to settle,' says Ilena Barsukova. 'Perhaps those informers were offered beds or food if they helped. We never knew.'

Rosa Markova was one of the first to be informed on, and she was told to step forward. 'She didn't look like a Jew,' said Ilena Barsukova. 'She wore her hair in a braid. But they picked her out anyway.' Semyon Adler was next. Then a third woman, Anna Brin, stepped out. 'I think she just saw they were taking the other Jews so she decided to go with them. We said to Anna: "You don't have to go. You haven't been picked out." But she insisted.' These three then took each other's arms and walked together to the plank, where they were shot in the back of the neck and fell into the ditch.

From Bakhchisaray they marched to Simferopol, another forty kilometres to the northwest. It was even hotter now. Of the women's division, only

200 were still alive, and many were wounded. Those who collapsed were shot.

The women were now marched in a different line from the men, and as they moved forward they heard whispered instructions passing from one to the next. They came from a 'leader' up ahead. At first the instructions were simply 'have courage'. The leader was 'old and knew a lot'. She would look after them, it was said. Someone even knew her. She was a teacher from Odessa. She had fought in the civil war.

'Be strong,' came another message. 'Look after each other. Believe in a Soviet victory.' More information followed: 'She speaks languages. She understands what the Germans say.' And then people started whispering her name: Yevgenia Lazarevna Klemm. 'We were very young and knew nothing at all,' said Ilena Barsukova. 'But already we felt stronger, you know. We knew that this Yevgenia Lazarevna was experienced and would tell us what we should do.'

At Simferopol they were crammed into a small jail where the heat and filth bred infection. In the yard Yevgenia Lazarevna mingled with the women and they saw her for the first time: a tall woman of about forty, with brown-blonde hair. '*Devochki!* [Girls!],' she would say. 'Those of you who don't know me, I am Yevgenia Lazarevna Klemm. How are you girls? You'll be all right. You are Red Army girls. We are prisoners of war. Remember that.'

'And we believed her,' said Ilena Barsukova. 'We didn't know what "prisoners of war" meant but we thought somehow it might mean the world outside would help us, so it gave us hope.'

Yevgenia Lazarevna chose doctors as her helpers. Maria Vlasenko's leg was infected, so a helper came to dress the wound, but a guard saw and shouted at Maria to get up and he hit her. Klemm's helper shouted back in German 'Don't beat that woman, can't you see she's wounded?', so the guard pulled her bandage away and beat her all the more, knocking out her teeth. 'Then the guard went away and came back with soup and a piece of bread and said "*Essen*" [eat] and went away again.'

Soon the women were once more marching west. After a day or so they were put on cattle trains. 'We peeked through holes in the wagon and saw a big sign saying Kiev. It was my home,' recalled Tamara Tschajalo, who trained in medicine at Kiev.

Many hours later they pulled up at a garrison town called Slavuta, where they were marched to a sprawling camp run by the German army for captured Soviet troops. It was filthy. The women fell sick with typhus, diphtheria, syphilis and TB, and several died. 'They made us cut our hair to get rid of the bugs,' said Ilena Barsukova. 'We had to boil our clothes in pots. It was the typhus that terrified the Germans so they kept away. Yevgenia Lazarevna told us that if we could just live through it for three weeks we would survive, and that was true. If someone was sick she made sure there was always a friend to hold their hand.' The doctor, Tamara Tschajalo, nearly died at Slavuta, but Yevgenia Lazarevna nursed her back to life. 'She told me she was immune from typhus as she'd caught it during the civil war.'

Yevgenia Lazarevna now had several helpers. Among them was Lyusya Malygina, the doctor who swam across the bloody Crimean Sea, and another was a doctor called Lyuba Konnikova. Lyuba was Jewish, but nobody had picked her out so far, and nobody had informed against her. 'She was a hot-tempered one,' remembered Maria Vlasenko. Ilena Barsukova remembered that Lyuba had 'nerves of steel'.

At Slavuta, more Jews were shot. Another of the Odessa women, Nadia Nakonechnaya, remembered how her Jewish friend Anna, a doctor, was given away by a fellow doctor called Yusefa. 'These two had always been in conflict back at the hospital in Odessa,' said Nadia. 'Anna was sure that Yusefa would tell the Germans she was a Jew.'

Another Odessa survivor, Zoya Savel'eva, spoke of a dungeon, 'a big black hole', somewhere at Slavuta. 'The Jews were put in this hole for weeks and kept there in darkness. There was no food and nobody knew what was happening to them or if they were dead yet or not. One day the dead women's uniforms were thrown back into the cells, for the other girls to pick over, in case they were of use.' By now all the women's uniforms were stained and ragged, but Yevgenia Lazarevna told them it was important to keep them on, to show they were prisoners of war.

The next stop was Rovno, near the German border. Here Raisa Veretennikova was picked out and shot for her curly hair. Disgusted by the traitors in their midst, the women were now fighting amongst themselves, but Yevgenia Lazarevna said the treachery must stop. 'We are all Soviet Army girls. Take care of each other and we will survive this.' Some weeks later – it was now late autumn – the women were piled into cattle trucks again.

The next time they stopped it was December 1942. The women had been on the road for five months. Temperatures were minus forty. Still wearing their Red Army uniforms, they were lined up in ranks of five. They didn't know it yet, but they were in Germany, at Soest in Westphalia. Here they found other Red Army women, some of them signallers or intelligence officers, others, like themselves, doctors and nurses who had also served at the front – at Kiev, Stalingrad, Rostov and Leningrad. Maria Klyugman, an experienced surgeon, had operated at the front at Cernigov.

Valentina Samoilova, the ice-cream eater from Kiev, had been posted as an army medic to Stalingrad, where she helped her unit defend a bridge outside the besieged city. Surrounded during the final desperate defence, she and her comrades had camouflaged themselves by smearing their bodies in river mud, but the bridge was lost and all were captured. Valentina was shot in the leg and left for dead, but the Germans took her body, still smeared with mud, and threw her on a freight train piled with corpses. At the next depot a crane lifted the bodies off and Valentina was picked up on a giant hook. 'And then I wriggled and someone saw I was alive. They said: "Look he's alive" – because they thought I was a boy – but a German doctor came and found I was a girl, so I was put on the train west. It was snowing and very cold and eventually we arrived in Soest.'

It didn't take long to realise that the camp at Soest was different from all the others; there was a sports hall and a huge railway junction nearby. The guards were Gestapo, not soldiers. The site had recently been turned into a marshalling yard for thousands of slave labourers brought from the East. Each day streams of Russian civilians and Ukrainians poured off the trains and were marched to the sports hall.

Many of the civilian women had been swept up at random by Nazi units passing through eastern Ukraine. Evdokia Domina was harvesting when she was scooped up by German soldiers and put on a train. 'My mother didn't even know I had gone.' Alexandra Dzyuba and her friends were lured into their village hall, where the Germans had promised a film show, but when they went along all were arrested. 'My father took a horse and tried to follow our train to snatch me back at the next station but the Germans beat him back with their guns.'

In the sports hall German employers – factory *Meister* – moved amongst the captured women with whips, picking who they wanted, some for farm work, but most to work on munitions. Watching these selections, the new arrivals did not realise at first that they too would be ordered to make enemy munitions. To date the Germans had killed all Soviet prisoners or locked them up in the worst conditions. Recently, however, the urgent need for workers had led to a change in policy, and Red Army captives were to be used for slave labour too.

'When they tried to take us off to work we didn't understand at first and the first fifteen who were chosen just started to go,' said Tamara Tschajalo. 'Then Yevgenia Lazarevna got word to them not to move. "Stand firm," she said. "We must not do this work." And they came back and stood together with the rest of us in line. Now we thought we were bound to die, but we were prepared.'

Tamara remembered Klemm's words: 'She told us we were prisoners of war, and under international law the enemy had no right to make us work in the war factories. This advice was sent amongst the women and we obeyed. The Germans threatened us with beating and took us to the Gestapo chief, who made us stand in cells for three days. But we didn't complain and sang our battle songs.'

When Yevgenia Lazarevna's turn came to go before the Gestapo chief she told him, to his face, that he had no right under the Geneva Conventions to force prisoners of war to make arms for their enemy. All along the journey from the Crimea, she had talked to the women about how soldiers had suffered in the past. She herself had served as a Red Cross nurse during the First World War and knew the rules, agreed since then under the Geneva Conventions, about how prisoners were to be treated.

'Remember you are prisoners of war, girls,' she told the women again and again, insisting that they kept their uniforms intact as best they could, as this was the only proof they had of POW status. 'You have rights,' she told them, but she must have known this wasn't true. Stalin had refused to sign the Geneva Conventions, and as far as the Germans were concerned, the Soviets had no rights at all.*

And yet Klemm may have judged that even the Gestapo would think twice about shooting dead 500 uniformed women, doctors and nurses, standing on German soil. In any case, it must have been clear to her that many of these women would refuse the order whatever happened. Lyuba Konnikova knew little of the rules of war, but she knew she hadn't marched all the way from the Crimea 'just to make guns to kill my comrades at the front'. So when the *Meister* first appeared in front of her Lyuba picked up a piece of metal and threw it at one of the German guard dogs, but the guards said nothing. Klemm told Lyuba later 'not to show her anger', Maria Vlasenko recalled. 'She always cautioned the fiery ones.'

And she cautioned the woman from Stalingrad too, though she didn't yet know Valentina Samoilova's name. Valentina remembered:

> We were called out in groups into some sort of sports hall and they said to us: 'You go to this factory, you go that way.' So I asked this man: 'Is your factory for military work?' And the factory owner said: 'Yes.' So I told him: 'We are military prisoners, we will not work in munitions,' and for half a day they all tried to get us to do so but we refused. We thought we'd all be killed.

* Klemm would also have known of the 1907 Hague Convention, which the USSR had signed and which protected POWs and limited their use as forced labour. However, both Hitler and Stalin in equal measure made a mockery of 'rules of war', whether signed or not signed. Germany had signed the Geneva and Hague conventions, but German forces slaughtered an estimated 3.5 million captured Soviet troops.

Even Valentina, caked in mud, had kept her uniform intact, and when her turn came to appear before the Gestapo chief, he stared at her for some time. 'I was pale-skinned with blonde hair and he asked if I was a German girl. I said, in German: "No, I'm Ukrainian." He asked me: "Why don't you work?" I said I was a good worker but would not work in a German military factory. He kicked me so hard that I fell to the floor.'

In the sports hall Valentina noticed that someone among the Red Army women was giving signals about how they should all behave:

> A woman I didn't know approached me and said I should keep calm. She was older. I heard she was from Odessa. This was Yevgenia Lazarevna, but at the time I didn't know her. I listened to her advice. She said: 'You are very young. We do not need victims, we need fighters.' She said I should wait for a signal from her before doing anything more. We had to move as one, that was her message.

Yevgenia Lazarevna's authority swiftly spread beyond the Crimea group to all the Red Army women present. If they were to protest it must be 'as one', recalled Valentina:

> She told us we mustn't 'break the circle'. That was the expression she always used. Nobody must 'break the circle'. We must stand together and then we'd be all right. And suddenly we had the feeling that maybe we would not all be killed after all. That was the start of our organisation. And we sang our Soviet songs: 'We will fight for Stalin.' This silenced the Germans. They didn't know what to do. They seemed to have no orders. Their orders were to make us work, but now that we refused they were shocked. They didn't dare shoot us.

Three nights after the protest began the Germans withdrew the orders to work in munitions factories. The Russians were marched to a waiting train and herded into cattle wagons. Buckets were placed inside; the wagon doors nailed shut and covered with barbed wire. They travelled for five days and five nights, stopping only briefly at stations where water and bread was handed in through apertures. At night it was pitch-black inside, but in the daytime cracks let in shafts of light that slanted across the bodies, huddled up against each other for heat. Temperatures outside rarely rose above freezing. Many of the women were sick with typhus and TB. No one knows how many were dead when the train rolled up at Fürstenberg station. It was 23 February 1943 and Valentina was twenty-four. The girl they had hooked off the Stalingrad corpse train arrived at Ravensbrück on her birthday.

*Chapter 17*

# Yevgenia Klemm

For a second there was pitch-black stillness. Suddenly from outside came a bashing at wagon doors, which were thrown open and bodies steamed in the freezing night air. The women looked out into lights, but before they could move, figures in capes jumped into the wagons, took hold of their arms and legs, shouting and kicking, and hurled them outside. Everywhere there were dogs. Some said there was snow on the ground. It was certainly clear and cold. Valentina Samoilova remembered:

> From the train we marched, five in a row. I was weak and someone put out a hand. I thought it was to help me but it was to hit me. 'Russian pigs! Russian bandits!' Nobody could understand why they were being beaten. We hadn't learned yet that this was just the way they behaved. It was as if they expected something from us. Perhaps it was because we were still in uniform.

That each woman should preserve her uniform, even in these conditions, seems remarkable, but nothing was dearer to them than these simple khaki clothes – skirts or trousers and jackets, piping on the shoulder to identify a medical or signals battalion, and a red star on a green cap to identify them as Stalin's own soldiers.

Word was passed down the line that they should fall in, and the column started moving, but it was so long that those at the back had no idea what was happening at the front. There were even brighter white lights up ahead; they'd never seen such lights in the Soviet Union and they were dazzled.

Valentina remembers being forced to run towards the light, and then she realised she was running towards giant gates. Those who fell were shot. Everything seemed so big. The women with the black capes were giants.

Inside the camp gates an SS officer shouted orders and pointed towards a building, but few of them understood German. Suddenly they were pushed forward to scramble through open windows. 'So we thought, what is this place we are entering through windows, but we couldn't think for long because the next thing we were ordered to undress and to put our uniforms in a pile. Everything we held dear was taken from us.' But Valentina held on to her Komsomol (Communist Youth) card by clenching it between her teeth. 'Then they looked us over and poked at us and made us lie down.'

Each woman was examined all over, hands thrust inside them, searching, as the SS looked on and shouted: 'Filthy bitches, Russian whores.' Among the SS officers standing there was Fritz Suhren and his deputy Obersturmführer Edmund Bräuning. The camp's most senior officers had come to the bathhouse in the small hours to hurl abuse and stare at these Soviet women who had come from Leningrad, Stalingrad and other cities that already spelt humiliating defeat.

Ludmilla Voloshina says the SS laughed when they found jewellery hidden in a woman's vagina, but everyone knew they'd made it look like that. Some remembered being given pills to swallow. Valentina spat hers out.

Then came the shower, and after that they were drenched in a slimy disinfectant then rinsed. Hair was chopped – not shaved, but roughly chopped with scissors so that it stood up in tufts. They looked for their uniforms but they'd gone. The SS laughed and told them their uniforms were burned, so they had no choice but to put on the striped camp clothes. 'I looked at the others with their tufts of hair and they looked like flowers on a stem,' said Valentina. 'And someone said, Valentina, you look like a flower too. We were very young.'

As the women marched to their blocks they were beaten and kicked. Yekaterina Boyko said:

> One tall blonde took her belt off and hit me over the head and a dog bit me. I fell over and woke up wet and didn't know why this was happening. We lined up and they shouted a number at us and the woman with the number was standing next to me, so I said that is your number, but it was too late as they started beating her and they beat her till she fell unconscious and I stood and watched, boiling inside.

Looking back, Maria Vlasenko thinks: 'It was as if we might have horns.' The Ravensbrück SS had certainly been prepared for trouble, which was why

Suhren brought the Red Army women into the camp at night and forced them to climb into the bathhouse through the back windows, so that no one would see them in their uniforms, which he then tricked them into taking off.

Suhren's ploy was almost certainly carried out on orders from above. As the Germans' confused reaction to the Red Army women's protest at Soest showed – and as Yevgenia Klemm had hoped – there were some in Nazi circles who were sensitive to the dangers of ignoring the Geneva Conventions when it came to this group of women POWs. Nobody had baulked at massacring male Soviet POWs, especially as it happened away to the east. But these female uniformed combatants – medics to boot – were on German soil and any violation of their status as POWs would be harder to explain, should Geneva choose to take an interest.

To date, Himmler had easily rebuffed questions about his camps from the Geneva-based International Committee of the Red Cross and the ICRC had declined to get involved, arguing that the prisoners were civilians and therefore not covered by their mandate. The presence of these Red Army women, however, might draw more searching questions from Switzerland. Himmler didn't want that, so Suhren was instructed to disguise who they were by removing their 'war status'.

By the time the women reached Ravensbrück, the only evidence of that 'war status' was their uniforms, so Suhren made sure these were removed on arrival at the camp.

However, Suhren then made an interesting concession – also as ordered. When the Red Army women were given numbers to sew on (theirs were in the 17000s) along with the red triangles that classed them as political prisoners, they might have expected to wear the simple letter 'R' to mark them as Russians, like other Russians in the camp. Instead, the Red Army women were given the letters 'SU', Soviet Union, which at least allowed them to continue to claim that their special status had been recognised and they were still being treated as prisoners of war. Certainly the rest of the camp would always call the women with the letters SU 'prisoners of war'.

Despite attempts to conceal the Red Army's arrival, prisoners on night duty in the offices saw everything and spread the word next day about how the Soviets entered the camp moving as one, with heads held high. They were obviously under the command of a powerful leader, everyone said. Not only had they arrived in uniform, but some were still bloodied from the front.

The Soviets were put in a special barracks, apart from the rest of the camp, ringed by barbed wire. Their block was guarded by the newly formed 'camp police' – the *Lagerpolizei* (LAPO) – made up of inmates, armed with whips and truncheons. The Soviets were also to be kept in quarantine for twice as long as anyone else. The whole camp eyed their quarters. For ordinary Russians, brought here as slave labourers, the presence of these 'official' Russians caused nervousness. Some tried to smuggle in messages of praise for Stalin, giving their camp numbers and offering help.

For the communist leaders in the camp – Czechs, Germans, Austrians and others – the arrival of the Red Army was momentous, and plans were made for making contact. 'They came from a country that carried hope,' said Dagmar Hajkova, one of the Czech communists. Another Czech, Helena Palevkova, volunteered for delousing duties, hoping to be able to greet her Russian comrades.

And it was not only prisoners who were impressed. Johanna Langefeld, still in her post when the Red Army arrived, was overheard admiring their 'discipline' and said the behaviour in the bathhouse of the commandant and his men was 'contemptible'. Langefeld also said the women were clearly controlled by a high-ranking leader, but as far as we know neither she nor any SS officer ever found out who that 'leader' was, or learned that she had no rank at all.

I first heard Yevgenia Klemm's name while sitting on a bench by the Schwedtsee, outside the Ravensbrück camp walls, in April 2008. A woman wearing a thick woollen hat pulled over her ears was throwing red roses into the lake below in remembrance of lost comrades. She was here to commemorate the liberation. She didn't wish to talk, but when I asked who the Red Army leader was in the camp she looked at me and said: 'Yevgenia Lazarevna Klemm. She was the reason we survived.' Then the woman turned away. It would be hard to find out more.

Red Army survivors alive today were too young to know Yevgenia Klemm's detailed story, and the older generation were dead, their official testimony censored, as I learned from Maria Vlasenko, one of the Odessa nurses. Maria pulled out a newspaper article she'd written in the early 1970s describing her experience in the war. It might be interesting, she said, 'but they cut a lot out'.

What had they cut? I asked.

'The truth,' she answered. 'When we wrote about the camp we couldn't say anything that might suggest the fascists were not evil all the time. We couldn't say we had Sundays off or that we had a spoon of jam at weekends. We couldn't write about our real suffering. We always had to be standing up to it and being brave. Any weakness was cut out.'

Nobody experienced post-war censorship more painfully than Antonina Nikiforova, another Red Army doctor, who arrived at Ravensbrück in March 1944. Antonina worked as a pathologist in the *Revier*, and collected material in the camp that she hid and hoped to use in a book. After the war, however, SMERSh confiscated her materials and her manuscript, which even today cannot be found in Russian archives.

Yet Antonina never gave up. Soon after her first manuscript was confiscated she asked all her comrades to write to her with their memories. With the help of these letters she began writing again, but her work was still censored. She carefully preserved the letters, however, though refused to allow anyone to read them until after her death, which came in 1994. They have only recently found their way to the Ravensbrück camp archives, waiting to be read. From four large boxes the voices of Red Army women whose accounts seem lifeless in official texts come spilling out – chatting, mourning, reminiscing, lying, accusing, laughing, and telling stories that dart back and forth, like the letter from Anya Munkina, who had lost an arm at the front, and had a special job in the camp mopping floors. Gladdened to hear from Antonina after the war, Anya writes:

> I am crying for joy, I'd like to meet and hug you and talk of the concentration camp. Your work was terrible – I think a lot about you, especially in that dungeon, you and a corpse in front of you and you are working without any mask. During the day everyone goes in her direction and me I grab my mop and clean the courtyard and try to find a piece of beetroot or a potato. In the evening in the barracks it was cosy – every woman trying to warm the atmosphere with her heart. I listened to the newspaper readings by Yevgenia Lazarevna. After listening to her voice it was nice to fall asleep, if a bit frightening. Soon I was separated from my friends and sent to Bergen-Belsen. That was a real lice-ridden hole where I contracted typhoid and dysentery. I had no hope of seeing the sun again.

Ilena Vasilievna (who gives no surname) tells Antonina: 'I bear no grudge that you don't remember me – there were many of us. You helped me and two other Polish girls to leave for work. That is why I'm still alive.' Digging deeper, there are more mentions of Klemm. 'She cured my typhus by rubbing me with bark.' One letter from a cousin of Klemm's said that after the war, when she returned to Odessa, Yevgenia Lazarevna didn't want to talk about the camp ever again. 'She was nervous when it came up, so I tried to avoid the topic. But I heard her once saying that at the camp they put rubber pants on people and beat them. And there were things a thousand times worse than that.'

With Antonina's names and addresses, it was possible to find more women who'd known Yevgenia Klemm and to learn something of her life. She was born in Odessa, probably around 1900. Her father was thought to have been a Serb, her mother Russian. Some said she was Jewish, others not. As a schoolgirl she developed a passion for history and trained to be a history teacher in Odessa. In the early 1920s she joined the Bolshevik revolution by serving in field hospitals, mostly on the Polish front, which was where she nursed a wounded Latvian called Robert Klemm. They fell in love and on return they married, but soon after Robert died of TB. There may have been a son, but nobody was sure.

In the 1930s Klemm became a teacher trainer at the Odessa Pedagogical College and won the highest accolades. Her pupils adored her. Olga Khohkrina explained why:

> In class she painted pictures for us of the past with her descriptions, and would produce marvellous materials so we lost ourselves in history. I remember a lesson she gave on greater Russia and she was using materials on the Tartars and the Cossacks to such effect that she had pupils in tears. There was a lesson on the Mongolian invasion when she described things in such a lyrical way that her pupils were open-mouthed. She would tell us that knowledge gave strength and understanding. She had an ability to inspire love and respect. It was a gift.

'What was she like?' I asked.

> Very humble. She gave the impression of having no interest in material wealth. She would often invite her pupils to her flat and warm them with a cup of tea. It was very cold and she was very poor.
>
> And I think she was an idealist who wanted to play her part. She told me when she was a nurse in the civil war she had fallen sick with typhus and nearly died. When the Second World War broke out there was no need for her to volunteer again, as our teachers were all evacuated to safety, but she joined up again.

I wondered what sort of communist Klemm might have been. 'The romantic kind,' said Yevgenia Vladimimova, another former pupil:

> I think that as a young woman she was probably attracted to the cause in a devoted but humanitarian way. Like so many young Russian men and women she probably became intoxicated with the Bolshevik dream. She would have seen it as a way to build a better world. I think a lot of people saw it like that at first. I remember hearing that when Lenin died she played Liszt for hours.

During the first weeks in Ravensbrück, Yevgenia Lazarevna's gifts were badly needed. Women in the rest of the camp were impressed by the Soviets' discipline, but inside the block many were sick with typhus.* The SS took several to be shot, to prevent infection. Others were simply terrified. One of Antonina Nikiforova's correspondents wrote:

> I found the camp so eerie with its black streets, the female guards in black cloaks and their wild dogs and orders, with all the people dressed in striped clothing and mostly with shaven hair that I am not even going to try to describe it on paper. Our terror – my terror – consisted at first in the fact that we did not know the language and didn't even know what *Konzlager* [concentration camp] meant.

At least the journey had ended. On arrival in the block Tamara Tschajalo found a space on a mattress next to Yevgenia Lazarevna and immediately fell asleep. And they were together under one roof where they could try to heal their wounds. Yevgenia Lazarevna went amongst them late at night, showing what position to lie in to ease the pain. She also chose helpers to tend to the needy, among them Alexandra Sokova, a poet and teacher, and Maria Klyugman, the surgeon from Kiev. It was significant perhaps that at least two of Klemm's helpers, Sokova and Klyugman, were Jews, as was Lyuba Konnikova, and there were several other Soviet Jews who had remained unidentified to the SS.

The treachery of the last six months was not forgotten. The SS had already removed their spies: the Red Army women who had pointed out Jews to be shot on the journey were put to other dirty work. But much bitterness remained. One woman writing to Antonina said: 'I don't see Lyusya any more and I don't want to see her, the same goes for Vera Bobkova, especially when I think how they grabbed the clothes of the Jews in Slavuta after their death.'

In the block Klemm urged the women to heal these wounds too. 'Don't let the fascists divide us. That's what they want. Keep clean and tidy, it is possible even in the worst conditions. We are civilised people.' Some women still had periods. 'We were given nothing – not even underwear. It was a great problem for some girls but soon none of us had them of course. We washed a little bit with icy water, that's all,' said Ekaterina Goreva.

The Red Army women were cut off from the camp outside, so Klemm tried to gather information. Messages smuggled in through the Polish Blockova brought contact with the camp communists. Czech doctors, sent to the block to identify typhus sufferers, made themselves known to her. The

* Though killer disease was widespread in the camp, prisoners rarely complained of colds or flu. When fleeing the Germans on the Eastern Front, Ida Grinberg, a Red Army doctor, slept on branches of fur trees laid on the snow. 'We didn't get colds then either.' Ida also observed that men were usually much weaker physically, 'and I believe they had a weaker will than women'.

Czechs explained who else was here – the nationalities and numbers – how the camp was organised and what slave labour was done. They even smuggled in a German newspaper.

At night Yevgenia Lazarevna gathered the girls around her in groups and read the newspaper to them. Interpreting the Nazi news, she said the Red Army was breaking through outside Moscow and German casualties were high. She told them what she learned about the camp: they were to be fenced off for several weeks, but then they would have to work. Women here sewed clothes for the German army. There was a big factory making electrical components for weapons – the Siemenslager.

Klemm said that while in quarantine they must all learn German. 'Girls,' she said. 'For now we're surrounded by wire, but one day the Germans will take the wire down and then you will have to mix with women of other nationalities. You need to learn their language. This will help you in the struggle to come.'

All German-speakers were asked to raise hands and Klemm organised the block into eighty groups of three or four prisoners, each with a leader, and each leader took the day's lessons from Klemm. Among the crammed bunks the learning began. 'And she would tell Vera Bobkova, "Vera, keep in mind that the German sentence is built like this and that," and Vera would whisper what Klemm had said to her small group,' Ilena Barsukova recalled.

Klemm also befriended the younger women, some as young as sixteen and seventeen. She asked where they came from and what they had been through, and whether their parents were alive. 'We will stay together, girls. You are with me.' She remembered their stories. And she would know at once who were the daughters of commissars or kulaks,* or whose father might have served under the tsars, and she understood the different camp 'families' as they were already calling themselves – the Moscow family, Leningrad family, Odessa family.

Sometimes she'd ask the girls about their favourite recipes and tell them hers. And then she'd read a poem that Alexandra Sokova had written and talk about it. Or she'd talk to them about the women who had been prisoners under the tsars and how they'd suffered and survived. 'She told stories of the past so we would forget the present,' said Tamara Tschajalo.

Lyusya Malygina, the doctor who dived into the Black Sea, organised a group to look after Klemm herself. Older than most, her legs were swollen, and her bout of typhus years ago had left her partially sighted in one eye. Her helpers dressed her sores and made space for her in the washroom. Some said these women were an elected committee, but most said they simply wanted to

* Kulaks were prosperous peasants; many of them were liquidated in the 1920s and 1930s during the Bolshevik drive to collectivise farms.

take care of her and help. 'She was the mother I missed,' said Tamara Tschajalo.

As their quarantine time drew to an end and the women tried to see beyond the wire, they noticed a new building rising behind the wall: a giant chimney. They saw how a wagon, pulled by six women, would pass by each morning piled high with bodies. And they saw new arrivals marched towards nearby quarantine blocks. They made up nicknames for the guards, 'black ravens' who all had 'extremely beautiful clothes' with belts and shoes 'of finest leather'. One guard in particular would come up to the block to shout at them. Lyuba Konnikova, 'the fiery one', called this guard 'the beautiful blonde'.

Prisoners outside still peered towards the Soviet block and saw the shorn heads of the women, 'always held high'. Sometimes they heard them singing. Looking back later many survivors would say – in fact many would insist – that the Red Army women wore uniform while in the camp. Perhaps the growing disorder outside simply served to emphasise the order of the Red Army when they first arrived.

The winter of 1942–3 was hard and long, leaving the women exhausted and diseased. Early in the year longer shifts were instituted. On 20 January 1943 Richard Glücks, the new chief of Himmler's camp administration office, wrote to all commandants requiring them to 'exhaust every opportunity to maintain the prisoners' ability to work'. The dearth of German labourers had reached crisis point. Although slaves were being herded from the East, they were not enough. Even Ravensbrück prisoners deemed too old or sick to work were now to be used to knit socks for soldiers.

Himmler had promised industrial chiefs that he could fill the shortfall in labour with concentration-camp workers. A network of new satellite camps was planned, each with a factory where prisoners would work.

Ravensbrück, designed originally for 3000, now held 18,000 women, and more were arriving every day. Not only did they come from the East, but numbers from the West were mounting too. In April more than 200 Frenchwomen arrived and were given numbers in the 19000s.

More barracks went up, but no amount of building could keep pace; each time more women arrived everyone was packed tighter. Where sand wore away, cinders were spread on the walkways. A new painting gang was formed and shabby blocks painted green. The sewage system overflowed, and a new prisoners' plumbing gang was formed, as well as a new delousing gang. All over the camp, placards declared 'Lice = Death'. Prisoners were regularly forced to stand outside naked, even in the snow, while clothes and blankets were burned and blocks fumigated with gas.

When Langefeld was sacked, her favoured Blockovas – experienced hands, who knew how to keep control – were thrown in the bunker, including Grete

Buber-Neumann, who was given several weeks' 'dark arrest'. With these women gone, Ramdohr, the Gestapo chief, asserted his own form of control by posting spies to penetrate deep inside the barracks. According to the German communist Maria Apfelkammer, Ramdohr would walk straight into a block and ask: 'Is anyone interested in their freedom?', at which point one or two women would break ranks and follow him – his new *Lagerspitzel* (camp spies). 'Then we never spoke to them again,' said Maria.

These new *Spitzel* would never be posted back to their own block, however; instead they'd be sent to another and do their spying there. Prisoners working in the camp office would know who the spies were, as they'd have to adjust the paperwork. They'd try and warn women in the new block, but the camp offices were penetrated too, so this was dangerous. *Spitzel* informed on people for anything, particularly organising. With the growing overcrowding, organising thrived, as there were shortages of everything – straw for mattresses, bowls for soup, and even clothes.

By early summer 1943 the camp had entirely run out of striped prison clothes. Dead women's clothes replaced them. Each week trucks arrived from Auschwitz delivering the clothes of the Jews, removed before they entered the gas chambers. These garments were given to new Ravensbrück arrivals, so that when Grete Buber-Neumann eventually emerged from the bunker she noticed prisoners 'strolling up and down the camp streets dressed in coloured clothes of all kinds and not in stripes. The Gypsies in particular were as bright as tropical birds, with all sorts of coloured scraps.' She also noticed that 'the regulation step the SS had taken so much trouble to teach was disappearing too'.

For the prisoners the worst effect of overcrowding was the increased torture of *Appell*. Whereas once they rose at 6, now it had to be at 4 just to get through the count, which could last three hours or more. And such was the size of the camp that the new chief guard would often appear down the Lagerstrasse on a bicycle, black cape billowing behind her. This was the 'beautiful beast'. The Soviets would soon find out her name was Dorothea Binz.

At about the time of her promotion, Binz paid a visit to her home village of Altglobsow driving a horse and carriage. The villager Ilse Halter remembers her appearing on the main street, her black cape flaring out behind her, with a dog and a whip. 'She thought she was very grand,' said Ilse. 'I think she came back to show us all how well she had done. People were scared of her by now.'

'Why were you scared?' I asked.

'Because they all did such terrible things up there,' and Ilse paused. 'You know what they did? You have read about it? They threw babies into the air to shoot them' – she made a throwing gesture with her arms.

I asked where Ilse had heard that. Did she believe it?

'I think so,' she said. 'Oh yes, I believe it.'

In mid-April 1943 the wire around the Red Army block was taken down and the women were marched outside for their first *Appell*. 'It was 4 a.m. It had been snowing. We lined up outside in ranks of ten and tried to stand close to each other like a flock of sheep does in cold weather,' wrote Tamara Limakhina, one of Antonina's correspondents.

The Soviet women were then lined up again for the labour-gang selections, and feared they might be posted to Siemens to do munitions work, but like all newcomers before them, they were sent to the *Sandgrube*. If these Soviets were to be put to useful work, their strength and spirit must first be broken, and the best place for that was the sandpit. On the first day Nina Kharlamova slipped and her trolley, full of wet sand, stuck in the mud and tipped over, so a guard set about her with a truncheon until she filled the trolley again. But it again stuck and tipped over, and this time Nina was kicked and beaten to the ground.

The Soviet women worked longer shifts than other prisoners and were not allowed to enter their block until after the evening *Appell*, so that after twelve hours' labour they had to stand outside in the cold and rain until after nightfall, their wet clothes clinging to them.

When they were let back in, Klemm and the poet Alexandra Sokova were waiting for them. As older prisoners, they had been put to work as knitters inside the block. Yevgenia Lazarevna found scraps of rag to wrap Nina's sores and blisters, and told the women to look out for each other: 'Don't put yourselves in danger. Look for small things you can do to help us all. If a guard is eating breakfast, steal a newspaper and bring it back.' And she told them not to believe the Germans when they told them they had lost the battle of Stalingrad. 'She knew before any of us that we won,' said Nina Kharlamova.

The Red Army doctors were left toiling in the sandpit for many weeks, but some of the other Soviet women were soon sent to the sewing shops, where they encountered Gustav Binder, whom they called the Giraffe. 'Suddenly from machine to machine there is a whisper: "Giraffe is coming," and every woman now trembles, turns pale, and shivers low over her machine,' wrote Tamara Limakhina, recalling the scene for Antonina Nikiforova.

> There is complete silence. You can only hear the noise of the machines. Then on the threshold emerges this tall SS with the long neck of a giraffe. Having slowly scrutinised all the working women he goes to the table where there is a pile of finished items and he takes a pair of trousers and starts scrutinising them and all the women's hearts are beating like a bird's

in a cage and in everybody's head there is a thought: now he is going to beat up someone. Then he screams '*Kolonnenführerin* [squad leader], what's that, what's that?' pointing to the item.

A little woman with a pale, sickly face, slowly but steadily, without betraying her fear, is moving towards the table. Nobody can protect her. Everybody knows she is going to be beaten up. Maybe until she is half dead. 'What's that?' And he stares with this face red from hate into the face of the woman. 'What's that?' and he starts beating her with hands and with boots with metal studs. She tries to protect her face and save herself, but this enrages this beast even more, and red from rage and with foam on mouth he incessantly beats her on her back, face and chest. The woman is suffocating like a corpse and she is lying on the floor and bleeding from her nose and mouth and then he grabs her stool and by this time nobody was sewing any longer. Everyone was standing and with hate and terror stared at this beating up. In their heart there were tears of hate and impotence and humiliation and inner pain. And then there was a scream from the floor, a heart-breaking scream from the woman who could not resist any longer, and the beast, completely startled, stops and puts the stool down. He looks around at everyone scrutinising, gives her a last kick and then shouts: '*Arbeit schnell*.' And leaves. Those were the frequent scenes. And we, the girls who fought at Stalingrad, could only look on.

Often Binz appeared outside the sewing workshop as the women queued to leave and lashed out at them – particularly the Red Army women – shouting: 'Russian swine, you march your Russian march, now you march for us, you Russian pigs.' One day she lashed out at Ilena Barsukova, the Odessa nurse. 'She hit me over the head and back but I didn't cry. I forced myself not to cry – not there outside the workshop. Then when I returned to the block Yevgenia Lazarevna was waiting for me. She had already been told. She knew. And as soon as I saw her, I started crying. And then everyone started crying. She cried too.* She told me in future to avoid the SS eyes. And then we got together in a group and planned how to do small pieces of sabotage by sewing up openings in the arms or cutting away an elastic so the garment would tear but in a way nobody would notice, which was easy with the white camouflage coats.'

Soon after that, one of the Moscow family wrote a poem about Binz. Anna Stekolnikova kept a copy, and she pulled it out of a drawer in her tiny flat at the top of a Moscow apartment block, where it had been hidden for

* Ilena Barsukova's is a rare description of women crying. 'I saw very few tears in the camp. For some reason people didn't cry,' said Anna Stekolnikova.

seventy years. Anna said the poem was written by a friend called Lydia Gradzilowa, and she read it out.

> 'A beautiful blonde'
> You are so beautiful,
> With shining blue eyes and locks of hair,
> But if we could, we would tear the insides of your soul
> And strangle your bloodthirsty heart.
> Do you remember the girl you were whipping, Jacqueline?
> How you stamped on Wanda, the Polish girl?
> How you tortured the Russian girl Veronicka? You and the dog.

I asked Anna if Binz was actually called the Beautiful Blonde in the camp, and she said: 'Beautiful bitch, more like. But she was beautiful – tall and elegant.'

'Was she a sadist?'

'We knew she hated us Russians. She treated Ukrainians differently, but if you were Russian you'd had it. Yes, I think she was a sadist, a real sadist. Her eyes almost shone when she beat people.'

One day, however, Binz spared Anna's life by calling off her dog.

> I'd been digging sand at the bottom of the lake and we were coming back to the camp in ranks of five and someone asked me a question and my lips moved. Binz saw and shouted my camp number and called me out to stand on the little mound outside the hospital for several hours. It was always windy there and terribly cold, so the girls in my barracks kept food for me, but then Binz came over with her dog and the dog bounded up at me with its paws and knocked me over. And I fell and it began to go for me but Binz pulled it back. It was as if she had pity on me and she shouted to me: '*Weg*' – on your way. Soon after the dog died, and Binz buried it right there where it died in front of a block and planted the grave with flowers.

Olga Golovina shook hands with a young woman's strength, then told more stories about Binz, and the Moscow family.

'In the block we always stuck together, but it was hard,' she said, tipping cigarette ash onto a dusty pot plant. Her voice was husky, her hair blonde and permed. Olga was in intelligence. Her mission was to drop by parachute behind German lines. She had never parachuted before and had no training. To lessen the impact on landing she had bark strapped to her feet. She pulled out photographs of Red Army friends. 'In the block we all had nicknames. I was Pushkin because of my curly hair. And then there was the Cat, and

Vera Samoilova was the Bear, because she was grumpy. Alexandra Sokova was *Graf* [count], because for some reason she'd come wearing trousers and because she was so serious. We met in the evenings.'

Olga's job at one point was to haul the giant *Kesselkolonne* (soup wagon) from the kitchen to the block. One day as they struggled the cart tipped over and poured boiling coffee over her friend Nadia's legs, scalding the skin, but Nadia kept on walking all the way to the block, knowing that if Binz heard they'd all be in the bunker. On another occasion she and the other girls pushed the wagon into a pile of bodies, stacked like logs. 'And they all fell down.'

She mentioned Lyusya Malygina: 'You must write about Lyusya – so beautiful and brave, Lyusya saved many lives. She worked in the hospital and swapped names to save us from the death lists.' Did Olga know about the Simferopol trial? I asked, referring to the trial in which Lyusya Malygina and others were accused of collaboration by Stalin's secret police. She nodded, and asked me what I knew.

I showed her a letter I had found in Antonina's boxes. The letter was written by Maria Klyugman, the Red Army surgeon, another of the accused. The letter is the only written record of the trial to have come to light; in it Maria names the accused and their accusers, and three others.

Olga asked to see the letter, read it and seemed shaken. It had always been rumoured that something like this happened, she said, 'but no one knew for sure.' She went for another smoke.

'But there were no traitors in the camp,' she said when she returned to the room. 'Not that I knew of. In the camp we were strong, you see – we Soviet girls,' and she recalled one October revolution day when Lyusya Malygina 'jumped down from her bunk and danced', and a French woman sang an aria. 'Yevgenia Lazarevna would always come round and say: "Happy holiday, girls." She always encouraged us to celebrate in any way we could.'

In autumn 1944 Rosa Thälmann arrived in the camp. She was the wife of the famous German communist Ernst Thälmann, shot dead in Buchenwald in August that year. 'So Yevgenia Lazarevna said: "Let's bake her a cake." And we really did. We were given 25 grams of margarine at the weekend and a spoon of jam and somehow we mixed it with bits of bread and made this cake and decorated it with flowers that we stole from the grave of Binz's dog.'

In the summer of 1943 Suhren made a new rule that on Sundays all prisoners must march, not stroll, down the Lagerstrasse in order to restore discipline and order, lost since Langefeld's departure. The Soviets – banned until then from appearing on the Lagerstrasse on Sundays – were also instructed to march.

'Our own beautiful blondes saw it as a chance to show off,' said Olga, laughing. 'They ironed their dresses by putting them under their mattresses and made themselves look smart. They even washed their hair using coffee. Then we all marched out as if on military parade and everyone stared.'

Dagmar Hajkova, the leading Czech communist, gave a more dramatic account in her post-war testimony. The march happened on a very hot day, she said. 'The whole camp's surface was covered with black cinders. It was as if the camp was wrapped in a mourning veil. Several thousand women in striped rags, with wooden shoes or on bare feet, were marching in ranks of five in thick clouds of black dust.'

The women were told to sing German songs. Some Czechs tried to sing Czech national songs instead, but the guards stopped them so they were silent. 'Only the proletarians [asocials] carried on singing,' said Dagmar, 'mostly popular songs about blue eyes, red lips and kisses. It was a sorry picture. All young girls, almost unlike human beings – greasy, barefoot or in wooden shoes, their steps stumbling due to tiredness. It wasn't a real march at all. Some were limping. Everyone was longing for the end.' Then suddenly a roar broke out across the camp and everyone turned to see the 500 Soviet women march to the main square, lined up according to height and marching in ranks of five in perfect military parade step.

> Standing on the kitchen steps the commandant and his staff were watching, stunned. From the camp square, thousands of eyes of imprisoned women from all European peoples were watching the Soviet women too. When they arrived in the centre of the square, they all began to sing a Red Army fighting song. They sang with clear and loud voices, one song after another. They walked into the centre of the square, young faces, shaven heads as a sign of shame, but with their heads up high: and everyone froze on the spot. They walked on as if they were parading on Red Square in Moscow, not in a national-socialist concentration camp.

What Dagmar Hajkova says happened next seems like wishful thinking on her part. The other prisoners made a guard of honour for the Soviets, she claims. 'Thousands of hands applauded them. The Red Army soldiers sang the Partisans' Song, and now the whole camp joined in.' Olga Golovina had talked more simply of the Soviet girls 'showing off'.

Nevertheless, the SS were taken aback and didn't react for some minutes. 'Binz stood and waited for the signal,' said Hajkova. 'They hadn't experienced such daring behaviour. It took them a while to chase them back to the barracks. We weren't allowed to leave the barracks again that Sunday. But we didn't receive a mass punishment. The SS didn't report this event to Berlin. They didn't want them to know. And we never had to march on a Sunday again.'

*Chapter 18*

# Doctor Treite

The Red Army women need not have feared being sent to the Siemenslager. Under the terms of their imprisonment they couldn't work outside the walls; nor could they do munitions work, as they were likely to protest. Siemens didn't want troublemakers at their plant, which by the summer of 1943 was performing exceptionally well. So pleased was the Siemens boss Rudolf Bingel with output at Ravensbrück that in 1943 he donated 100,000 Reichsmarks to Himmler's 'circle of friends'.

Since the factory opened a year before it had tripled in size, and more than 600 women now worked twelve-hour shifts, including a night shift. They made copper coils, switches, microphones, telephone equipment and condensers, which poured off conveyor belts to be sent to the finishing shop and then packed up and loaded onto railway wagons. The women had little idea what these parts were used for. 'We thought, is this for a plane or for a gun?' said the Bulgarian inmate Georgia Tanewa.

A railway network had been laid through the woods, linking the Siemens plant to a jetty on the lake and to the main line running through Fürstenberg. Plans were also being made to link the plant to a young offender institution for delinquent girls which was situated close by, in an area of woodland known as Uckermark. Run by the judiciary police, not the SS, the Uckermark Youth Camp, as it became known, held up to 400 adolescents said to be morally or sexually depraved. Prisoners in Ravensbrück said the girls had mostly committed petty offences: many had just been thrown off trains for not having a ticket. Young and strong, they were bound to make good slave labourers, so Siemens had struck a deal to build a factory outpost at the Youth Camp too. After a year at Ravensbrück the Siemens management and SS were working hand in hand. Important men in civilian clothes appeared at the plant, including the top Siemens director Gustav Leifer, another member of the SS, who visited Fritz Suhren in his camp headquarters, while Suhren had visited the Siemens headquarters in Berlin. Otto Grade, the Ravensbrück plant director, was on excellent terms with Suhren, and was often seen around the main camp. Working under him were scores of Siemens civilian staff – technicians, managers and instructors.

Not everything at the plant had run smoothly. The management had clamped down on contacts between civilian staff and prisoners. An Austrian-Czech communist, Anni Vavak, employed at Siemens, had tried to talk to the civilian staff to alert them to the atrocities. 'I absolutely wanted to get in touch with these civilians,' said Anni. 'I wanted these German workers to pass on what I told them so people in Germany would know what happened at the camp.'

A handful of the senior managers seemed decent. One Siemens man used to hide a newspaper under his table so the prisoners might find it, and another civilian offered to post prisoners' letters. However, most Siemens civilians were 'coarse' and were 'repulsed' by the prisoners, so Anni had failed to win any over. Most were also convinced Nazis. The head of the *Spulerei* (winding department), Lombacher, was 'both a Nazi and a sadist', and he was not alone. Even the kinder ones changed their behaviour after new directives from the Siemens management, barring all contacts. One such directive came into Anni's hands, 'which I screwed up in my fist and told myself that the political prisoners rose way above this rabble'.

Anni didn't say what the notice said, but we know the company thinking on fraternising from another management note, which is on file. Frustrated at a stoppage caused by a shortage of parts, the manager complained: 'It is incomprehensible that prisoners should in a sense be paid for warming themselves and resting in our nice clean production facilities. Feelings of sympathy are inappropriate in these cases and everyone must constantly suppress them in himself.'

Siemens managers had also complained about 'feelings of sympathy' shown by Hertha Ehlert, one of the first women guards at Siemens, who liked to give food to the prisoners, and had therefore been removed and sent by the SS to work at the death camp of Majdanek in Poland. Ehlert was replaced at Siemens by Christine Holthöwer, who was known as a beater, and a spy for Ludwig Ramdohr.

As the Siemens camp grew, new guards were recruited from Siemens's Berlin staff. Lured here with promises of more money and food, some were homesick and hated the place. 'I wanted to go back straight away,' said one woman, 'but they said I had signed so I had to stay. It was hard at first. For the first eight days I couldn't swallow a thing. But then you get hardened to it.'

The declining health of the prisoners, caused by the appalling camp diet and overcrowded blocks, meant a high turnover of Siemens workers, but there was nothing to be done about it, as under the contract between Siemens and the SS, the SS had sole responsibility for the women's food and accommodation. As one Siemens official put it: 'As the housing and food were assured by the camp all measures on our part were superfluous.' Nor did Siemens have to care about workers' health: under its contract with the SS the company had the right to strike off its lists any sick women, along with any unsuitable women who had misbehaved or failed to meet the quota. Otto Grade, the plant director, made sure the number of rejected prisoners was always noted on his monthly reports to Berlin, as well as the number of new replacements.

The workers' health was also damaged by the long march to and from the factory that they underwent four times a day. The distance from the gates to the wire of the Siemens plant was less than a mile, but for the prisoners it felt far longer. With ill-fitting wooden clogs they marched first across the wet sand or bog beside the lake, then plunged into woods and up the steep hill as feet sank into soil and slid on wet leaves. In snow and ice the women slipped and fell.

The Siemens workers left the camp – after standing for *Appell* – with only their coffee for breakfast. 'We reached Siemens frozen and began working with stiff fingers, stomach always empty, head sleepy,' said Anni Vavak. To make matters worse, when the prisoners arrived, the civilians were often eating their breakfast. 'Under our eyes, knowing we were starved, they took out all their delicious food, which we didn't even know the name of any more,' recalled Minny Bontemps, another Siemens woman.

On return for lunch the women just had time to grab a bowl of watery soup of swedes and two or three potatoes, but the push for quotas meant that the guards would chase them out before they'd eaten, driving them back up the hill shouting: 'Hands down, gobs shut, idiots, filthy good-for-nothing bitches!' At the end of the day, the exhausted women walked back again, and as dark fell the Siemens night shift set off, working through from 10 p.m. until 6 a.m. without even a slice of bread.

Siemens women suffered severely from boils, swollen legs, diarrhoea and TB, but the long hours of repetitive tasks, and constant pressure to meet the quota, produced an illness of its own: nervous twitching. 'After three months the women were a bundle of nerves and couldn't go on,' said Irma Trksak, an Austrian-Czech prisoner. 'Many started wanting to dig sand or even empty ditches.' Those with these nervous twitches were soon listed as unsuitable and quickly removed from the lists.

Selma van de Perre (née Velleman, and known in the camp as Margareta van der Kuit),* a Dutch prisoner who arrived at Siemens the following year, said many women at the plant had nervous breakdowns. 'It was one of the dreadful things – the madness. I have often seen it – it started like this' – and she made her eyes flicker and twitch. 'Then the strange laughing started.'

One of those afflicted was a young Dutch woman called Jacqueline van der Aa, who arrived with her mother Bramine. Mother and daughter came from a high-class family; they had been arrested for helping the Dutch resistance, said Selma. 'They were perfectly all right when they arrived. Jacqueline was beautiful, with gorgeous long hair, but she was shaved – the only one of our group. She cried and cried.' A few months after starting at Siemens, Bramine died of typhus after drinking the water out of one of the taps at the plant. Then Jacqueline began to show signs of nerves. 'I noticed it was often those from good families who couldn't cope. They weren't used to the conditions,' said Selma, who remembered many other cases including a woman called Benno Hoenicke. 'She was a solicitor in the ministry of food before the war. I remember she stole my bread one day. Then she started twitching. It was a phenomenon. I could always see the beginning of it.'

I asked what happened to them. 'Oh, the guards noticed quite quickly and they were sent back to the camp and killed.'

As Selma observed, the killing of the 'mad', and of other 'useless mouths', had never halted. Lethal injection had continued in the *Revier*. After the big transports which took women to their deaths at Bernburg in early 1942, smaller selections were held from time to time; trucks came in the night and took away up to fifty women for gassing, probably at Auschwitz.

Details of these smaller death transports, which became know as black transports – or *Himmelfahrt* ('heaven-bound') transports – are sparse, but Gerhard Schiedlausky, the camp doctor, revealed at the Hamburg trial a little of how they worked. The black transports were disguised as 'euthanasia' under the same 14f13 order that governed the Bernburg gassings. The camp doctors gave a medical report on those selected, he said, and the prisoners themselves were required to take an intelligence test to see if they were 'mad' or not.

In the spring and summer of 1943 more and more important men in civilian clothes appeared on the Ravensbrück Appellplatz. These were *Meister*

* Selma was Jewish, and on joining the Dutch resistance took on the name and identity of Margareta van der Kuit, a non-Jewish baby who had died at birth. The number of Jewish prisoners at Ravensbrück who never revealed their true identity cannot be known, but probably runs into the hundreds.

from Heinkel, Daimler-Benz and other arms manufacturers, come to select workers. Learning of the success of the Siemens operation – and encouraged by Himmler – they too were hiring slave labour for their munitions factories. Unlike Siemens, however, most of these industrialists were loath to site their factories so close to a concentration camp; they built them at 'satellite' camps or 'subcamps' located some distance from Ravensbrück, though drawing their workers from the mother camp.

The Polish student Maria Bielicka was chosen to work at the first Ravensbrück satellite camp of all. In March she was called out with scores of others to stand on the Appellplatz as *Meister* walked up and down staring at them. Then, with about fifty others, she was taken 400 miles south to Neurolau, near Karlsbad in Bohemia, where the women made bowls for soldiers in a porcelain factory. Soon Siemens had built a subcamp at Neurolau too, and Maria was making parts for Messerschmitt aircraft. 'It was very hard. I remember losing skin, as we had to put parts into scalding ovens.'

The departure for Neurolau caused a stir throughout the main camp. Krysia mentioned it in a secret letter home that said: 'On March 25th several dozen Polish women were sent to Karlsbad, a china factory.' In the same letter she reported: 'On April 30th five more Poles were shot.' She also asked for a French dictionary, as a large group of French had arrived.

Among the French group were Micheline Maurel, a literature teacher from Toulon, and Denise Tourtay, a student from Grenoble, both captured in random sweeps to catch resisters. As soon as their group was out of quarantine they too were made to stand on the Ravensbrück Appellplatz as the *Meister* looked them over. Then they waited eleven hours with no food, until doctors arrived to examine their hands and feet, for reasons they didn't understand.

'They chose us just like we were cows at a cattle market,' recalled Micheline. 'They even made us open our mouths to look at our teeth.' Then it was '*Schnell, schnell*' and they were screamed at and beaten into running to the station, where they were piled into cattle trucks and taken to Neubrandenburg, about fifty kilometres to the north – 'a forsaken and forgotten outpost where nobody will ever find us'.

The introduction of the subcamps was the latest step in Himmler's plans to transform his camp empire into a hub of arms production. The armaments minister Albert Speer would say later that Himmler was simply trying to grab more power and money – 'to build a state within a state' by shifting production to his camps. The Reichsführer certainly wanted to get his money's worth.

As with Siemens, the cost of renting out slave labour for the satellite camps was carefully calculated between industry and SS. The difference was that with the satellites so distant from the main camp, the companies provided the accommodation and the food, and the cost was deducted from the hire for the prisoners.

So detailed were the contracts that in a deal agreed between Ravensbrück and the company Filmfabrik Agfa a clause said that the SS would provide the women's clothes while the company would provide headscarves. Sometimes there was room for flexibility; for example, if a higher output was required, the women were to be provided with better food. And as in the case of Siemens, once a woman was deemed by the managers to be too exhausted, 'mad' or sick for work, the contract stated that she was automatically sent back to the main camp and the SS replaced her with someone else.

The appearance of the *Meister* on the Appellplatz in the first half of 1943 heralded probably the most significant change in the daily life of the camp since it opened four years earlier. From now on prisoners might be ordered to line up outside at any time and driven off to destinations unknown. Women returning from their daily work gangs to their blocks would find that friends, sisters, mothers and daughters had vanished from the camp, often never heard of again.

As some prisoners quickly discovered, however, there were advantages in working at the subcamps too.

For some time the rabbits had been looking for better ways of smuggling their letters out. Since the mass protest of March, Karl Gebhardt's doctors had switched to experimenting on dogs – the butchered animals were seen being taken to and from the *Revier* – and the experiments on Polish women seemed to have stopped, 'whether because of the protests or the publicity given to them, we don't know', wrote Krysia. But the women still had a great deal they wished to tell the world, and the space for their invisible writing was limited, especially for Krysia, who had started giving a running commentary on events in the camp, and naming war criminals.

'The hospital is run by Dr Rosenthal, Dr Schiedlausky and a woman Dr Oberheuser,' she wrote in tiny writing on the back of an envelope in April 1943. 'It is a place of crime; children born in the camp are killed. People suffering from nervous shock or mental disease are killed by injection – from our transport, Teodozja Szych (7908).' On another letter she squeezed words around the edge of the envelope: 'They have built a crematorium outside the walls of the camp, so there will be no proof, like at Katyn.' This was a reference to the massacre of 20,000 Poles in a forest near Katyn in 1940, which, as it later emerged, was the work not of Germans but Russians.

From all her letters it is clear that what Krysia feared most of all was the imminent execution of all the rabbits, 'so there will be no proof' of the experiments. She urges her family again and again to tell the world, and in

May 1943 she proposes a new way to do it: 'Something that would help protect us is a broadcast on English radio. The only thing to stop them is the disclosure of the secret to the world. We shall keep going until the end for certain, if they want to keep us alive. Sign, pencil in parcel.'

Krysia's reference to 'English radio' shows she knew, by May 1943, that such a broadcast was possible. Almost certainly, the secret letter writers had learned about a clandestine radio station called 'SWIT', meaning Dawn, which broadcast from England to the underground in Poland and elsewhere in the world. Dawn Radio was set up in October 1942 by members of the Polish underground who had escaped to England, and was linked to – though separate from – the Polish Service of the BBC. Its purpose was to provide underground cells in Poland, which were mostly cut off from each other, with a means of communicating, as well as giving them a link to the outside world.

The station gathered news from Poland delivered either by Polish couriers who had got out overland or sent by coded signals via a Polish outstation in Sweden, which then signalled the reports on to the Polish government in exile in London. After passing through British censors, the Dawn Radio scripts were driven to a recording studio at Milton Bryan, near Bletchley Park, the government decoding centre in Buckinghamshire. The SWIT operators then broadcast the reports back to Poland daily. Other world news was also broadcast to keep the Poles in touch with developments in the wider war.

Krysia's knowledge of 'English radio' had almost certainly come from Polish women newly arrived at Ravensbrück. Before their arrest they had listened to broadcasts on SWIT, and passed on what they learned to friends in the camp.

In a further letter home in July, Krysia also announced that the rabbits had discovered a better means of getting their own information out 'to the world'. In early summer two of them had been assigned to make a trip once a week to a subcamp about twenty kilometres north of Ravensbrück at Neustrelitz. Their task was to collect special food parcels left at Neustrelitz for SS officers at Ravensbrück, and to bring the food back to the camp. During their visits the women discovered that next to the Neustrelitz subcamp was a prisoner of war camp (Oflag) full of Polish officers. Over the weeks they managed to make contact. The men, who as POWs could post letters via the International Red Cross, offered to post the rabbits' letters for them, using the Red Cross mail. In the first instance they sent the women's letters to another POW camp inside Poland, from where their families could arrange to collect them.

To explain the arrangement, Krysia wrote home on an envelope in the usual way, giving details of how to collect the letters, and saying:

> The boys sent a list of women operated on, those shot, and poems of Grażyna Chrostowska. They are reliable fellows. We owe a lot to these boys. In addition to helping us in the most important thing, sending out letters, they have also procured some Polish books for us. Send news from Poland in notes hidden in toothpaste tubes.

Over the coming months the boys from the Oflag forwarded several long letters, and the women started receiving letters back, as well as books and much more. Zofia Pociłowska, one of the instigators of the plan, explained how it worked:

> The first time we made contact they saw us and said 'Are you Polish girls?' and so then it started. They saw we came to Neustrelitz each Monday and they started leaving things for us in hiding places, like behind the toilets. And we left letters for them and told them everything that was going on and what we needed. I even got a pair of glasses. And yes we got books – wonderful books.

There was a boy called Eugeniusz Swiderski – Niuś for short. 'He was the go-between. Sometimes we even met up, but usually we would leave our letters in a jar in a hole behind a toilet, and when we came back there'd be letters for us.' Zofia then hid the letters inside her clothes and prayed she wouldn't be searched on re-entering the camp. One day the women found that Niuś had left them the sacrament – little pieces of bread consecrated by a priest.

I asked Zofia if she wasn't afraid.

> We weren't so afraid – we were young. All we were thinking about was we wanted the world to know what was happening to us. Sometimes we even wrote down everything that was happening and buried it in the camp, hoping it would be dug up later. I had a kind of faith and optimism that I wouldn't be caught, that was why I wasn't afraid. And I don't think the guards even suspected for a minute. We told no one we were doing it because of the spies.

I said I'd heard there was a love affair between Zofia and Niuś, and she laughed. She said she met Niuś years later in Warsaw at a meeting organised by one of the survivors. 'No, it was not a love affair. People teased me though. We called him Apollo.'

By the end of the summer of 1943 Ravensbrück had spawned twenty more subcamps and the Appellplatz was regularly transformed into a slave labour market. According to Lotte Silbermann, a waitress in the SS canteen, Fritz Suhren 'produced a feast' each time the managers came to the camp.

> Binz and Bräuning and the rest would always be there. Large amounts of food and drink were consumed with lashings of wine, champagne and schnapps. Before the managers started to pick the prisoners they had always been drinking hard in the canteen. We were always afraid on these occasions about them getting drunk and drinking to the brotherhood and eyeing up the waitresses.

All this time the Red Army women observed the slave market and wondered when they'd be chosen. If they were, they agreed they'd refuse munitions work just as they had at Soest. When a guard entered the Red Army block one day and called out the names of several doctors they feared their turn for the subcamps had come, but the women were told to report to the camp hospital. Instead of working as slaves themselves, they were to work to keep the slaves alive.

Although prisoner doctors had worked in the *Revier* from the earliest days, they had not been allowed to work as doctors. Now, however, doctors in concentration camps were in demand, whether prisoners or not. The reason was simple: the urgent need for prisoner labour to build more arms had focused SS minds on the fact that the camps killed inmates simply through atrocious conditions. As the supply of slave labourers from the East was expected to dry up, given the reversal in the war, Himmler had ordered in December 1942 that 'the mortality rate [in the camps] must absolutely be reduced'. So at the start of 1943 edicts went out to commandants to improve hygiene and build more and better blocks. Not only must camp conditions be improved, but hospitals too, and the number of doctors increased.

The idea of Himmler trying to improve the health of his prisoners seems on the face of things absurd. At Auschwitz new crematoria with extra gas chambers had been opened at Birkenau, the camp's extermination plant. By the end of April, the new Ravensbrück crematorium was in use; the sight of the chimney rising over the camp's south wall was clear evidence that an increase in killing was about to start.

Yet the rise both in killing and in working was consistent; the rules were simply clearer than before. As long as prisoners were fit for work they were to be kept alive. As soon as they were useless they must die, so as not to waste resources on feeding and housing them. The principle did not apply to the death camps – Sobibor, Treblinka, Belzec – whose sole purpose was the killing of Jews. Yet such was the need for slave labour by 1943 that more and more of the Jews sent to Auschwitz were also being diverted from the gas chambers and put to work if deemed useful enough.

Doctors were now held directly responsible for keeping more prisoners alive. Richard Glücks, head of Himmler's camp inspectorate, had even written directly to all SS doctors in early 1943 complaining that far too many were dying – of 136,000 arrivals in the camps the previous year, 70,000 were already dead. 'With such a high rate of mortality we will never achieve the number of prisoners required [as workers] by the Reichsführer.' On 27 April 1943 Himmler issued a further instruction calling for a reduction in death rates; in future only the mad should be killed, or, as his order read, '... only those suffering from mental illness must be selected by the medical commission in the context of the operation 14f13. All other prisoners unable to work (those with tuberculosis, the bedridden etc) are in principle excluded from this operation. The bedridden must be given work they can do lying down. The Reichsführer's order must be scrupulously obeyed.'

Keeping more prisoners alive obviously meant more doctors, and as SS medics were increasingly being sent off to the front, it made sense to use qualified prisoners instead, which explains why the Red Army medics were suddenly called up. But the Red Army doctors in Ravensbrück were not so sure they should take the work; it wasn't only the Poles who saw the *Revier* as 'a place of crime'. Lyuba Konnikova declared that she would refuse. 'I didn't want to do it,' she said later. 'We knew that in the *Revier* people were beaten, maimed and killed with injections. We knew that Rosenthal and Schiedlausky kicked people with their boots.' Yevgenia Klemm told them, however, that there were also good reasons to take the work: they could use their skills to save lives and smuggle out medicines. In the hospital they would make contacts across the camp and gather intelligence.

And conditions in the hospital were improving rapidly in the summer of 1943. In response to Himmler's edict more medicines were available and the *Revier* had expanded from two blocks to six. Soon after the Red Army women started work there, the hated doctors Schiedlausky and Oberheuser left Ravensbrück, and Dr Rosenthal was dismissed and later put on trial, accused of having had sexual relations with the prisoner midwife Gerda Quernheim, on whom he had carried out at least two abortions.

At the end of August a new doctor arrived at Ravensbrück. It was said he preferred to cure than kill.

Percival Treite had none of the usual traits of a concentration camp doctor; he wore a white coat instead of an SS uniform and carried a stethoscope rather than a whip or a stick. At thirty-two years of age, he was a fair, slender figure. He didn't hit or kick his patients and rarely wasted his breath on verbal abuse. Treite even had a correct and businesslike air about him – more suited to the faculty of medicine at Berlin University, where he had just completed his medical studies, than to the *Revier* of a concentration camp. He also seemed to be interested in practising his skills.

Treite's demeanour was as much to do with his family background as his professional training. For an SS man, he had an unusual family tree: when asked to trace his roots for the SS genealogical record, an English branch showed up. His upbringing was also unusual: raised a Salvationist, he marched from his earliest days with the army of God.

It was Percy's German grandfather, a devout Baptist called Carl Treite, who forged the family's English ties. In the 1890s, living in northern Germany, Carl fell in love with a young Englishwoman, Louisa Foot, from Southampton, whom he met while she was staying in Germany as a children's governess. As Carl would later say, 'God then led me across to England', where they married, and the couple settled in Lewisham, in south-east London, and came under the influence of William Booth, founder of the quasi-military Salvation Army. Booth wore a uniform to preach to the poor outside the Blind Beggar pub, and soon Carl Treite was also urging London's down-and-outs to 'suffer for the Lord'.

Eager to take the message back to his homeland, Carl and Louisa, now with three small children, including Percival senior, returned to Germany, where Carl's sermons on the virtues of discipline and the sins of alcohol were at first reviled. By the time he died, however, the Salvation Army had branches in many German cities, and Percival Treite senior settled in Kiel, where he became a Lieutenant Colonel and founded the German Salvation Army's first brass band. The young Percy and his sister Lily marched with the band and followed every tenet of the faith, which, before Hitler, included pacifism and a belief in the sanctity of human life.

By the mid-1930s Percy's mother and his sister had left Nazi Germany to live in Switzerland, where an uncle founded another Salvation Army mission, but with a medical career in mind Percy stayed behind in Berlin. Having joined the Nazi Party and the SS – admittedly belatedly – he went on to specialise in gynaecology at the University of Berlin. A first-class surgeon – he had 'good hands' – Treite then travelled widely, studying under eminent professors, spending time in Prague and in Bern. By 1943 he was close to securing a professorship in medicine in Berlin, but before he could complete his practical surgical experience in order to qualify, he was ordered to take up a post at Ravensbrück. The appointment was a setback in his career, but he took up his job with enthusiasm and reorganised the *Revier*.

Treite immediately established an infectious diseases block for typhus, scarlet fever and diphtheria, as well as a block for skin diseases and one for dysentery. He even requested a pathology lab and mortuary to be built under the main *Revier* block, arguing that it was important to know the causes of death. A system of bandaging stations out in the blocks was an attempt to curb the growing problem of swelling legs and boils and to reduce the queues at the main *Revier*.

To rationalise the use of hospital beds, Treite set up a system of *Bettkarten*, bed cards. Those lining up to see a doctor might be given a *Bettkarte* for a number of days. At the end of every bed hung a temperature chart with arrows pointing up or down so it was clear when the patient was well enough to go back to work. A system of pink cards was another innovation: women too old or frail to carry out hard labour could apply for a pink card, which allowed them to work in their block. The system formalised the status of 'knitters' already permitted to work in their blocks, and also fulfilled Himmler's latest instruction that instead of being killed, bedridden prisoners be found useful work.

Within a few weeks of Treite's arrival the *Revier* had been transformed. A new *Oberschwester* (head nurse) called Elisabeth Marschall took charge, and the team of camp nurses, dressed in brown uniforms and white scarves, were told to smarten up. Treite ordered that all the nurses be taught basic hand-washing techniques and wear a thermometer on a string round their neck.

Even Milena Jesenska, in the *Revier* office, was impressed. Treite befriended Milena from the start; recognising the name, he discovered that her father was the same Professor Jan Jesensky under whom he had studied oral surgery at the University of Prague. Soon Treite was treating Milena too, who fell so sick in the summer of 1943 that she was sure she was going to die. 'After her illness she examined her face in the sickbay mirror and announced that she looked just like the little sick monkey belonging to the organ grinder who used to pitch his cart outside her house in Prague,' said Grete Buber-Neumann, who since her return from the bunker had again shared a mattress with Milena in Block 1.

In August Milena's Czech friends gave her a magnificent birthday party in one of their blocks, 'as if they too thought it would be her last'. A table in the Blockova's room was laden with presents. 'All those who loved her were there – the Czech dancers, writers, and musicians – and they had made gifts such as little handkerchiefs embroidered with prisoners' numbers and tiny hearts made of cloth bearing the name Milena. Already very weak, Milena was moved to tears.'

Shortly after this Milena told Treite of her illness. According to Grete:

> He immediately treated Milena with the greatest civility and examined her and diagnosed an ulcerated kidney, saying he would operate, which he did with the greatest skill, and for a while she regained some strength. She felt confidence in him when he told her that during his student days in Prague he had attended her father's lectures and he transferred his respect from the father to the daughter.

Under Treite the *Revier* quickly became the most international place in the camp. The Czech nurse Hanka Housková was taken on as the 'miracle interpreter' because she spoke six languages. Soviet doctors worked on several wards, while Czechs ran the pharmacy. The X-ray room had Polish radiographers, and Yugoslavs worked in the pathology lab. On the prisoner staff too were a Belgian midwife and a French nurse. Even the *Oberschwester*, Marschall, spoke French.

Treite was always scouting for new talent. Sometimes he would walk onto the Appellplatz when a new transport came in and shout for doctors to raise their hands. If a woman impressed him, as happened with Zdenka Nedvedova, he would wait until she was out of quarantine, and then walk over to her block and have her brought to the *Revier* before her transfer to a subcamp.

Zdenka Nedvedova arrived in August with one of the first groups of prisoners to be transferred to Ravensbrück from Auschwitz in order to work in a new subcamp. The daughter of an eminent Czech musician and philosopher, she too had studied at Prague, where she qualified in child medicine. She was arrested in 1940 for anti-fascist activity and sent to Auschwitz, with her husband, who died there of TB.

Although inmates knew a lot about Auschwitz by now, the appearance of the Auschwitz prisoners on the Ravensbrück Lagerstrasse stirred horror. Many had survived a recent typhus plague, which had devastated the Auschwitz women's camp. 'Even the SS guards watched us silently, shaken by our appearance,' Zdenka said later. 'We were thin and bald, with enormous frightened, absent eyes.' For Treite, however, the fact that Zdenka had survived typhus made her a better prospect for his hospital: she would be immune and could work with infected prisoners.

For Zdenka, Ravensbrück came as a pleasant surprise. Above the camp walls, she saw treetops. Inside the camp looked clean. 'It was very different from the bareness of Auschwitz. I thought: this is not a camp, this is a sanatorium.' In quarantine the Auschwitz women were astonished by the running cold water and food 'provided in reasonable quantities'. They were even more astonished to learn that in Ravensbrück old women knitted woollen socks in their blocks, and there was a hairdressing salon and a fashion boutique for the women SS. At first sight, there seemed to be fewer of the horrific medical practices she had seen at Auschwitz – such as sterilisation experiments – happening here.*

Most incredible of all, to Zdenka, was the camp *Revier*, and when she saw the prisoner doctors' accommodation she couldn't believe her eyes. Treite had not only revamped the hospital itself, he had insisted on the best conditions for the prisoner staff. Hygiene in particular was to be of the highest standard, especially as these women were to work alongside him. Zdenka recalled:

> Bedding was regularly washed and medicines seemed to be in good supply. I got two sets of underwear and a proper dress, and we could even have a hot shower. And we all looked smart in our dark blue outfits with white mottling and short sleeves, while the SS doctors wore white coats and the sisters, white headscarves. The hospital was heated and we slept on clean camp beds and had a washroom and our own nice dining room and a small garden where we could sunbathe naked in the summer. This was a momentary joy.

Not all the prisoner doctors responded in this way to their luxurious quarters. For some the gulf between their privileges and the misery outside was too much to bear. The revulsion of Lyuba Konnikova at the contrast evidently showed on her young face, as *Oberschwester* Marschall accused her of insolence, calling her a 'Bolshevik cow' and gave her the filthiest work. Refusing even to acknowledge that at just twenty-four years of age Lyuba could be a doctor at all, Marschall told her to mop floors in the dysentery block and empty bedpans, and once she'd done that she had to take the *Oberschwester* her lunch.

While Lyuba's reaction was understandable, when she reported back to Yevgenia Klemm the older woman urged her not to lose hope. The compromise forced upon the Soviet doctors would bring benefits, said Klemm. Just by working in the *Revier* they had already saved lives and managed to smuggle medicines out for use in the block. Maria Klyugman had even had the chance to sew up one of the Polish rabbits' legs, performing an operation under anaesthetic and removing large bone splinters from the wound.

More important, perhaps, was the intelligence the Soviet doctors had

*In fact, mass sterilisation experiments had been due to start at Ravensbrück in the summer of 1942. On 10 July 1942 Rudolf Brandt, on behalf of Himmler, wrote an officially secret letter to Carl Clauberg, the sterilisation expert, asking him to go to Ravensbrück 'to perform sterilisation of Jewesses according to your method'. Clauberg didn't come, however, choosing to experiment (for the time being) at Auschwitz instead.

gathered and brought back to Klemm. Through the hospital network, Maria Klyugman was now in regular contact with Maria Wiedmaier, the German communist leader, who smuggled her newspapers, and Maria Petrushina, one of the 'Moscow family', had secured a job with the plumbing gang, which along with the '*Sturmkolonne*' – as Hanna Sturm's carpentry gang was now known – was the best informed.

Klemm's increasing knowledge became the lifeblood of the Soviet block, as Zoya Savel'eva explained:

> She could tell us what was happening at the front, and who was about to arrive in the camp. She came to talk to us at night: everyone would clamber around her and she would pull out a whole newspaper as if by magic, and explain the contents to us. Sometimes she read the cards. The girls would run to her and say, 'Come on, Yevgenia Lazarevna, show us the future,' and she would laugh and do it.
>
> Did she believe in the cards? I asked.
>
> 'Perhaps. She believed in many things,' said Zoya. 'She was not a straightforward person. She believed in God.'
>
> 'But she was a communist?'
>
> 'Yes, that too. But mostly she believed in knowledge. You have to understand that knowledge was everything to us. We knew nothing, but Yevgenia Lazarevna had the knowledge and the belief. She told us we would survive and get back home, and how it would all unfold.'

And however torn some of the doctors were at having to work for the SS, the prisoners themselves were delighted.

Another change that struck Grete Buber-Neumann when she emerged from the bunker that summer was that the *Revier* had lost its terrors – largely because prisoner doctors were working there. Though some of the women 'shamelessly' favoured the sick of their own nationality or political group, 'most did their best with great devotion in extraordinarily difficult circumstances,' said Grete. Inka, a Czech medical student, had treated Grete for an attack of boils. Grete had feared to go to her at first because she was a staunch communist 'and was bound to consider me the scum of the earth', but Inka was 'friendliness itself' and treated Grete with great care.

'The conditions she worked in were appalling. She had no proper room and the bandages were piled up all around her as women queued up between the mass of bunks.' So well did Inka and Grete get along that Grete returned several times, partly to hear Inka's gossip about the camp communists, and one day Inka told Grete that there was a new communist leader in the camp called Yevgenia, who in Grete's words 'gave everyone the party line'. Grete never met Yevgenia Klemm. Had she done so her prejudices might have been dispelled.

Of all the prisoner doctors recruited into Treite's *Revier* in the summer of 1943, it was Zdenka Nedvedova who became the most popular of all. 'Zdenka, where is Zdenka?' was now a familiar cry around the *Revier*, and it was one that went out on the night when a new French arrival collapsed in her block. The number of French had been rising during the year, and in October Germaine Tillion arrived with a group of fifty women from Paris. Germaine fell sick at once, and could not eat or speak. Her Blockova took her to the *Revier*, where she waited, slumped on the ground, until a doctor in a white coat, whom she later learned was Percival Treite, came along and nudged her with his foot – not brutally, but to make her get up. 'And looking at me with a distracted air he said: "*Kein Scharlach – raus*" [no scarlet fever in here – out],' and she was sent back to her block.

Germaine's Blockova made contact with the Czech prisoner doctors, and in the night they took her to Zdenka – 'she had a young, serious face and white hair' – who diagnosed diphtheria. The women exchanged no words, but the Czech doctor treated the French ethnologist – Germaine was a well-known expert on African tribes – with a serum.

Germaine was admitted to the diphtheria ward of the infectious diseases block. Later she would reflect on how lucky she had been to go there at a rare moment when lives could be saved. 'And one could see the power of small groups of courageous women who were able to save a life of another without even exchanging a word with the person they saved, because they probably didn't even speak the same language.'

Throughout these weeks arrivals from more and more countries continued to pour in. They included a contingent from Norway, among them the fifty-year-old Sylvia Salvesen, not a doctor herself, but the wife of a well-known Oslo physician. Whereas Zdenka, arriving from Auschwitz, had been pleasantly surprised by her first sight of Ravensbrück not long before, the same scenes horrified Sylvia, arriving from prison in Norway. Giving evidence at the Hamburg trial in December 1946, her account of her first impressions was so vivid she held the court spellbound:

> This for me was like looking at a picture of hell. Why should I use this word? Not because I saw anything terrible happen at that time, but because for the first time in my life I saw human beings that I could not judge if they were men or women. Their hair was shaved, they were thin, unhappy

and filthy. But that was not what struck me most. It was the look in their eyes. They had what I would call dead eyes.

Sylvia was lining up with other new arrivals for the 'medical' when a trolley brushed past bearing a body wrapped in a white sheet. The sheet pulled back and she saw the face of a seventeen-year-old Norwegian who had arrived with her. The girl had died of typhus. This place was like 'no other hospital on earth', she thought, resolving to try and do something to help, when a man in a white coat approached, and she found the courage to speak up, asking if she might be given work.

Treite stopped in amazement and said, 'What impudence,' but Sylvia said: 'I am not impudent, I am Norwegian and I am a doctor's wife. And while I am here I would like to help.' In this tall, elegant woman, with large blue eyes, grey-white hair and impeccable German, Treite recognised a prisoner of some breeding. He ordered her to report to the *Oberschwester*, who gave her a job bandaging wounds.

On checking her husband's credentials, Treite discovered that Dr Harald Salvesen was physician to the ousted King Haakon VII of Norway, and the family had strong connections to the British aristocracy. Furthermore, it soon became apparent that Sylvia had contacts high up in Germany too. A glamorous young woman came to visit her one day accompanied by Gestapo officers; the rumour among the SS guards was that the visitor had been given permission to come by Himmler himself.

Pedigree influenced Treite's decisions on other appointments. Not long after Sylvia arrived, a Swiss prisoner in the TB block – Block 10 – was sent to Treite for diagnosis. Her name was Carmen Mory, and he asked: 'Are you the daughter of the Swiss doctor Mory?' She replied that she was. Treite told Carmen, a journalist, that her father had treated his mother in Switzerland twenty years before, and, seeing that Carmen had worked once for the *Manchester Guardian*, he mentioned his English connections too. Treite treated Carmen for her sickness and later used his influence to secure her a job as Blockova of Block 10, one of the new *Revier* blocks.

Even the Russians' background was of interest. When Antonina Nikiforova, the Red Army pathologist, arrived a few months later Treite was impressed with her dissection skills and asked who had taught her. She had trained in Leningrad, she replied, and when she named her professor, Treite asked: 'Was he a Jew?'

Treite encouraged this coterie of like-minded intelligent women to gather around him, and he liked them to help with his work. 'Treite often came into the operating theatre and said he felt like operating,' said Zdenka. 'He would observe a woman waiting to give birth, and without any warning he then performed Caesarean sections, and deliveries using high forceps and other instruments.' He sometimes invited Sylvia Salvesen into the operating theatre just to watch him at work. 'I thought it might interest you, Sylvia,' he once said to her.

To the rest of the prisoners, the women who staffed the *Revier* were an elite. Nelly Langholm, a young Norwegian who arrived at the same time as Sylvia Salvesen, said that the ordinary working-class Norwegians had little to do with those who worked in the *Revier*. Sylvia, a fellow Norwegian, and friend of the Norwegian king, lived 'in a high-class part of the camp' and never went to the Norwegian block.

'Except one day she came with a big box of chocolates,' Nelly recalled. 'I was lying on the third mattress of the bunk and I remember the smell of those chocolates. But she didn't offer us any.' I asked why Sylvia would have brought the chocolates if she hadn't meant to offer them round, at which Nelly scoffed, and said that Sylvia probably 'just wanted to show us she had got them'. True or not, Nelly's explanation revealed how the deepest class hatreds could survive in the camp, even within a small national group. 'I think she got them from some high-up visitor,' said Nelly, 'and my friend Margrethe was so angry she went up to her and slapped her face.'

The *Revier* women certainly enjoyed a certain protection under Treite; after the SS staff had left the *Revier* for the day the prisoner staff might even find a chance to meet and talk. One such discussion took place in the early autumn of 1943, when according to the Czech communist Synka Suskova, a bitter row broke out involving Milena. 'The conversation turned to sharing news from the war outside and guessing whether the Americans or the Soviets would reach the camp first, and which country offered people a better future.' Synka recalled two Poles – non-communists – 'saying they expected freedom from the Americans, while we Czechs saw freedom being given to us by the Soviet Union'.

> Pela [one of the Poles] said, 'For us Poles, Hitler is better than Stalin,' to which Hanka Housková replied, 'But that's incredible,' and we all agreed and protested. 'Who annexed Europe and murders and exterminates everywhere he goes? How could you say something like that here, when you can see so clearly what Hitler is?' Then we started shouting, as we were enraged, when Milena got up and separated us. She was pale, and evidently sickening again. 'Enough. Stop it,' she said. 'If the *Oberschwester* and the doctors hear there will be trouble.'
>
> And someone else then said: 'Milena, how can you talk like that? Is that the most important thing?' Milena said: 'Here and now it is,' and she

spoke matter-of-factly. Hanka then said to her: 'Milena, you can't remain neutral. You must say which side you are on. You can't stand in the middle.'

'Oh,' said Milena, quietly. The older partner, she was trying to calm the young Hanka down. 'Side? Side? Why do you have to be one or other side of the barricade? No, Hanichka. You don't understand a thing.' But Hanka didn't want to be quietened and ran out into the corridor, shouting: 'I don't understand! What is it I don't understand? It's you I don't understand. Milena, I don't understand you. Who do you belong to? Which side are you on? Tell me. Tell us. Who do you belong to?'

Lyuba Konnikova had always known exactly which side she was on. Whatever changes Treite might have made for the good, Lyuba saw only the mounting horrors; if the *Revier* had been reorganised to save lives, why were patients in some wards left to die? So crammed were the patients in the dysentery ward that those on the upper level, too sick to move, had to lie in their own excrement until it flowed onto those below.

Lyuba was not the only one to be revolted by what she saw in Treite's *Revier*. Maria Klyugman had seen different horrors. As a skilled surgeon she was given dog bites and battered flesh to mend. Women beaten on the *Bock* were brought in with burst kidneys or haemorrhaging. Treite, however, was never in the *Revier* to sew up these beaten women because he had attended the beating: like his predecessors, one of his duties was to take the victim's pulse and tell the SS officer how many more lashes the woman could stand.

During the course of 1943 the manner of the beatings worsened and a new sort of *Bock* was introduced. Women were put in special rubber pants in case they urinated and told to lie face-down on the table, which was indented like a trough, edged with wooden rods, and had iron stirrups for the legs, placed below knee level. Two inmates, usually green or black triangles, put the woman into the stirrups and fastened a leather belt that went around her shoulder blades. As the beating began they held on to the rubber pants, pulling tight as an SS man or another prisoner beat her with a leather riding whip. Near the end of the beating the woman would always pass out. Then the green triangles would lift her off the contraption and push her through the door where others were waiting their turn, fainting and urinating in terror.

The new beating procedures would all have been approved by Himmler. In evidence later the camp staff all said that Himmler insisted on approving every individual beating and the manner in which it was done. A document unearthed in the papers of the SS Administration Headquarters by war crimes investigators in 1945, entitled 'Flogging of Female Prisoners', showed this to be the case. It confirmed a verbal order issued by Himmler in July 1942 stating that 'orders for punishing female prisoners should be reported to him for approval'. The orders 'must be numbered in red pencil in the right hand top corner consecutively'. In order 'to save time' Himmler also wanted the names and numbers of each woman to be flogged printed on a separate list, so he could notify his approval of the flogging by referring just to a number. In 1942 the flogging was to be done 'with strokes to follow quickly after each other with a single-lash leather whip, the strokes being counted. Undressing and baring of certain parts of the body is strictly forbidden.' From the evidence of Maria Klyugman in the *Revier* and countless flogging victims, by 1943 Himmler had updated the procedures, ordering that the beating should be done on bare buttocks.

While Maria was kept busy sewing up her patients, Lyusya Malygina, a gynaecologist, had the job of assisting with abortions carried out on the *Bettpolitischen* and of examining the women selected to work in brothels at the male camps. Before they left she checked them for syphilis and was told to improve their appearance, by dyeing their hair and disguising their sores.

Nor was it only the Russian doctors who recoiled at what they saw in the *Revier.* Zdenka Nedvedova was increasingly revolted by Treite's experiments, with which she had to help. One day Treite told Zdenka to collect cockroaches, found scuttling around the *Revier*, which she had to boil up and then feed the juices three times a day to patients suffering from swollen legs. The experiment was pointless and dangerous, and when Treite wasn't looking Zdenka would pour the liquid away and serve up water instead.

In another experiment Zdenka had to collect the urine of pregnant women and inject it into another group of pregnant women, but this time Treite caught her cheating. He raged and shouted, and threatened to send her to the bunker with twenty-five lashes, but Zdenka stood her ground, saying that as a student at Charles University she had been trained to have respect for patients. Treite relented, 'perhaps because he was taken aback by my fearlessness', she said, though she realised it was more likely that to report her would have disclosed his secret scientific work to the camp authorities. It was clear to Zdenka that Treite's operations and experiments were mostly done with a view to his professorship at Berlin University and he certainly didn't want Ramdohr to find out.

The prisoners all knew that Treite was terrified of the Gestapo chief. When Ramdohr demanded narcotics to help with his interrogations, Treite had strongly disapproved – or so he said – but was too great a coward to refuse.

Sylvia Salvesen was also increasingly horrified by Treite's *Revier*. Not long after her arrival she saw inside the *Idiotenstübchen* – or 'madhouse'. It was perhaps as a result of Himmler's April order that only the insane should in future be selected for death – or, as he put it, 'selected in the context of operation 14f13' – that Treite had decided to set aside a special room for the 'mad'. Perhaps it was also part of Treite's attempt at reorganisation, given the growing number of 'idiots'. When, periodically, trucks came secretly to take them away, it was practical to have all the women in one place.

In any event, Sylvia and other prisoner staff, sleeping in the *Revier*, were often woken by the screams that came from the room, which was at the side of the mortuary; it had a stone floor and was without beds or bedding. Another prisoner doctor, a German woman called Dr Curt – 'a pitiless brute' – was responsible for the women and when the screaming broke out would go in and sedate them. On one such night Dr Curt called on Sylvia to help.

'Armed with a broom handle, she went off,' said Sylvia, who asked her what she was going to do with the broom handle but was told to shut up. Dr Curt was back a few moments later, saying: 'The lunatics have run wild', and she asked Sylvia and another prisoner nurse to go back into the room with her.

> We opened the door and I shall never forget the sight that met my eyes. Six women – if they can be called women – were fighting hand to hand. There were two mattresses full of excrement and dishes of old food on the floor. The women were practically skeletons, wearing only dirty vests with sores and bruises all over their bodies. A lovely young girl, a Russian peasant, with fair plaits, sat terrified in a corner screaming. It was her howls that had woken us. She sat there like a fair, hysterical Madonna.

Sylvia had seen the girl before, because Dr Curt had thrown her in there two days earlier, insisting that she was insane. In fact, she had tried to kill herself with a knife in the bathhouse soon after arrival, and had first been sent to the ordinary *Revier*. There she had started singing in bed one night, so Dr Curt threw her into 'this unbearable hole'.

> Seeing the Russian girl again, screaming in that horrible little room, sent Dr Curt wild, and she attacked her with the broom handle until blood flowed from her nose and mouth. I tried to get hold of the broom handle but was given such a bang on my neck I almost fainted. Eventually Dr Curt got hold of the Russian girl and pushed in the syringe. She rushed out, and tried to slam the door in my face. I think she meant to lock me in with the lunatics.

It was the offer of SS payments in return for their work that finally convinced Lyuba Konnikova that she, for one, could no longer tolerate the camp hospital. In the second half of 1943 the SS began offering a few Pfennings to the hospital prisoner staff to encourage them to work harder. Already the French and Poles were refusing the payments, and when the Red Army doctors learned that they were to be bribed too, Lyuba stormed out of the *Revier* saying she would refuse to take it.

The Red Army doctors had always been uneasy about their hospital work. Although they took some comfort in the fact that they were not making enemy munitions, it was clear that their skills were being exploited to keep the enemy's munitions workers alive and now they were being paid to do it. Most other Red Army doctors and nurses then also refused the bribes, and Yevgenia Lazarevna supported them, saying: 'Girls, we must show the fascists we can't be bought by their marks.'

When news of the Soviet refusal reached Ramdohr, he ordered that they be punished, and the punishment he chose was to send them to subcamps and force them to make German arms. Lyuba Konnikova was the first to be sent, but on reaching the subcamp of Genthin, where women helped make ammunition, Lyuba refused to do it. She was kept in a dark cell for two weeks and then brought back to Ravensbrück, where she was beaten on the *Bock* and tortured by Ramdohr, but still she refused to work on munitions, so she was shut in the *Strafblock*.

Yevgenia Lazarevna Klemm was told the news by her contacts and informed the Soviet women at their Sunday meeting in the block. Several of the women remembered what she said:

> Today we have learned that our friend Lyuba has received twenty-five lashes. Never before have prisoners of war, doctors above all, been ordered to work in war factories, working against their own country, forced to work towards the death of their brothers. Today they have given this punishment to a Soviet doctor, a prisoner, who courageously refused to make arms for the enemy. Our Lyuba, our comrade.

Klemm then proposed that the block send a letter to Lyuba, to be smuggled into the *Strafblock*, along with a poem composed for her by the poet Alexandra Sokova. There was quiet applause.

*Chapter 19*

# Breaking the Circle

From the moment he arrived at Ravensbrück, Ludwig Ramdohr had developed his own style of terror. The camp Gestapo officer liked to work alone, and had little to do with other members of the SS. Though nominally an SS officer, he rarely wore the uniform, preferring a dark flannel suit. He interrogated prisoners in his office and any torture that he wished to carry out was done there, perhaps after the regular SS beating, which happened in the bunker nearby.

Ramdohr's job was to make people talk. He carried a leather strap, made to his own specifications, which he used to thrash women across the face. He also forced prisoners to lie stomach down on a table, then with the woman's head hanging over one edge, he would grab her hair and plunge her head into a bucket of water until she nearly drowned, repeating the action several times.

If a woman still refused to talk he might have her fold her hands while pencils were inserted between the fingers. Then he would press down on her hands so hard that the fingers broke, if she didn't pass out first. He kept his favourite torture devices under lock and key, including a coffin with closing ventilation holes and claws – metal teeth of some kind – that penetrated the body.

More often though he simply used his leather whip, and if she still remained silent he resorted to beating the woman with his bare hands and thrashing her head against his office wall. Ojcumiła Falkowska, the Polish dancer, said even Binz looked shocked on one occasion at the amount of blood on Ramdohr's walls, saying such beatings were not authorised by the commandant. Ramdohr didn't care what the commandant thought; he was answerable only to his Gestapo bosses in Berlin. In fact Ramdohr was loathed almost as much by other SS as by the prisoners: when first appointed to Ravensbrück he was told to uncover corruption amongst the staff, particularly the wholesale looting in the fur workshop. Ramdohr also claimed credit for exposing the 'appalling conditions', as he put it, in the *Revier*.*

Ludwig Ramdohr had not always been a committed National Socialist. Born in 1909 in the central German city of Kassel, he first joined the German Social Democratic Party (SPD) rather than the Nazi Party, and his career began with a regular police investigation unit, not Himmler's SS elite.

As a boy Ludwig had apparently never shown signs of cruelty. Petitioning for clemency after Ramdohr was sentenced to death, his friends and family claimed he was squeamish about causing animals pain. 'When he buried his mother-in-law's canary he tenderly put the little bird in a box, covered it with a rose and buried it near a rose bush,' said a family friend. The judge had no time for such petitions. He had heard evidence that the adult Ramdohr liked to lock defenceless women in underground boxes – especially dungeons filled with water and crawling with rats.

Ramdohr's speciality, however, and surely his most valuable weapon, was his personal network of camp spies.

Spies had never been hard to recruit. An extra slice of bread, or a better job, and women could be found who would tell Ramdohr anything he wanted – true or not. Those who worked well were given chocolates or other delicacies stolen from the prisoners' parcels. His favourites might gain a fur coat – especially if they granted him sexual favours too.

Once recruited, the new *Lagerspitzel* stayed on Ramdohr's books or faced the torture table herself. One woman was so badly beaten after trying to escape his clutches that she slit her throat, and was saved by Dr Treite. Any women beaten by Ramdohr came under instant suspicion as spies themselves. After the war allegations spilled out about who had worked for him. At his trial he claimed to have created a shadow 'political movement' in the camp, to destabilise and trick those movements that already existed, like the communists.

In the second half of 1943 Ramdohr was at the height of his powers. Inside the main camp he claimed to have fifty to eighty spies, and was recruiting in the new subcamps too. The sheer size of the camp meant that Ramdohr's intelligence was needed as never before, simply to maintain control. Furthermore, as munitions work became more important spies were needed to report on saboteurs.

* In evidence, Ramdohr said later that Milena Jesenska had come to him and revealed the crimes of Rosenthal and Quernheim including lethal injections and abortions. 'On searching the sickbay, I myself discovered a human embryo in alcohol which, according to Quernheim's statement, was her own.' It was a result of Ramdohr's investigation that Rosenthal was dismissed and Quernheim put in the bunker.

As part of their contracts, the factory managers insisted that the SS provide not only healthy workers but reliable ones too. Making munitions, they could do far more harm than just spoiling soldiers' clothes: they could tamper with ammunition, botch fuses or fit triggers the wrong way. At the Siemens plant workers had been ruining spools by cutting the fine wires, or misplacing orders for new parts. There were particular fears about women in this regard. 'It is not easy to control women because they are better deceivers than men, and because when they escape they are better at hiding and finding ways of surviving on their wits undetected,' said one manager.

Such concerns were exacerbated by the growing lack of good women guards. As the camp expanded, and its satellite network grew, recruitment drives were carried out, but most new female guards were conscripts. 'They were very young, impressionable, and very poor, and many pleaded to be sent home as soon as they arrived, though mostly they adapted and stayed on,' recalled Grete Buber-Neumann. According to Lotte Silbermann, the SS canteen waitress, one group, conscripted from the production line at Filmfabrik Agfa in Wolfen, seemed particularly ill-suited to the work.

> These recruits arrived with their clothes in a terrible state. They had to wait with us in the canteen while their new uniforms were fetched, and as they waited they often behaved worse than the worst street prostitute. I had to stand and watch while one of these new guards, who was going to be in charge of us, lay on the table and was given the full treatment by an SS officer.

Lotte remembered one particular recruit called Ilse Hermann who was interested in nothing but finding a husband and forced her to save the best food in the canteen to serve up to her 'suitors' amongst the male staff. Hermann also made Lotte write out marriage ads to put in the papers.

Rudolf Höss, commandant of Auschwitz, whose camp still drew its women guards from Ravensbrück, also noticed a decline. 'The original female supervisors were far and away superior to those we got later,' he wrote in his memoir, because, in spite of recruiting by Nazi women's organisations, 'very few candidates volunteered for concentration camp service'. Instead, the armaments companies to which prisoners were sent to work were obliged in return to provide their own civilian employees as guards.

Needless to say, stated Höss, 'they didn't give their best workers', but after just a few weeks' training at Ravensbrück they were 'let loose on the prisoners'. Before long they were thieving, having sex with male prisoners, and 'an epidemic of lesbianism' broke out. On outside work parties, where control was difficult, all women supervisors had guard dogs, but they would set them on prisoners 'for fun'. These offending guards were thrown in the bunker or punished with twenty-five lashes, just like the prisoners. 'I have always had the greatest respect for women in general,' Höss lamented, 'but in Auschwitz I had to modify my views.'

Höss also complains that Ravensbrück kept the best of the women for itself, though what an Auschwitz commandant meant by 'best' is hard to say. At least two Ravensbrück women had done well at Auschwitz. Irma Grese, the farmer's daughter, trained at Ravensbrück in 1942, was now a chief female overseer at the Birkenau extermination annex. Maria Mandl, who arrived at Ravensbrück at the start, was appointed chief woman guard at Auschwitz in 1942, taking over from Langefeld, and soon became the most powerful woman in Himmler's empire. Mandl – the woman overheard by Maria Bielicka in Ravensbrück, 'lost in a trance' playing the piano – went on to found the women's prisoner orchestra at Auschwitz.

By the early autumn of 1943, Ramdohr was determined to extend his spy network still further. One group he had so far failed to penetrate were the Red Army women, whose unity had largely proved impossible to break. With the decision to send some to work in the subcamps, he saw his chance. If the women were scattered around far-flung outposts and cut off from their leader, whoever she was, their unity would be easier to crush. He certainly had spies in all the subcamps by now.

Earlier in the year the RAF had bombed a major Heinkel aircraft factory situated at Rostock, on the Baltic. A replacement factory was constructed nearby on the edge of a small lagoon at Barth, on the northern tip of Germany. In the autumn of 1943 Heinkel managers started coming to Ravensbrück to recruit women for the factory. A number of Red Army doctors and nurses were called *nach vorn* and selected. Valentina Samoilova was sent in the winter, as she told me in her spacious apartment in the centre of Kiev.

We talked first of Stalingrad, where Valentina had fought to hold a vital bridge in the final days of the siege. 'One day the Germans held the bridge, one day it was the Soviets. It was like that. It was a very bloody fight,' said Valentina, now eighty-nine. Then she talked of Barth. Along with the other Red Army doctors working in the *Revier*, Valentina had refused to take the SS bribes, she said, and knew at once she would be punished. 'We had contacts in the office and they told us we were going to this place called Barth.'

Other Red Army women were sent there too, including Lyusya Malygina, Maria Klyugman, Tamara Tschajalo and another doctor called Zina Avidowa. Before the group left there was a secret meeting with Yevgenia Lazarevna Klemm to agree a strategy.

Yevgenia Lazarevna told us we should protest if we were ordered to make munitions just as we did at Soest, but we shouldn't protest so much that we were shot. She said what she always said: 'Stay together. Don't break the circle. Remember that.' And we talked about how we would stay in touch with her by smuggling messages back, wherever we went.

The women were put on a train, which headed not to the Baltic coast but almost due south, which was unexpected.

After two days or so we were taken off at Buchenwald. So we wonder, what are we doing here? Then we're called down from the train and an SS officer goes along our line and picks out ten of the best-looking girls and brings them to the yard, and a man – a German prisoner – comes up to us and tries to be friendly and says, 'Hello, I'm a German communist,' but we think this is provocation. So I tell him: 'Get lost.' Then he starts laughing with an SS officer. And then another prisoner comes up and throws us a piece of bread, and inside is hidden a small note.

While the second prisoner talks to the guards we read the note. It's a warning to us, saying: 'You have been brought here to work as prostitutes for the SS officers.' So I step out of the line and tell the SS officer I would rather die than that. No single SS man is going to come close to me. And the others say the same. But they didn't believe us. They didn't yet know what they were dealing with, so they took us to a room. It was big. And we were told to take our clothes off. There would be lots of men coming, they told us.

We looked at each other and then an SS man comes up and touches my breast and says how beautiful I am, and I spat at him and pushed him away. We all say again we would rather die than let anyone touch us. So they beat us up for that. Then they put us back on the train and we went back in the other direction.

Several days later the train reached another small station and halted again. Bars were cranked open and women stared out. On the ground were the Ravensbrück 'crows', but this was not Ravensbrück. The air was different; they guessed they were close to the sea, as the wind smelled of salt and silt. This was Barth, on the northern tip of Germany, by a Baltic lagoon. As they marched, it began to snow and they were harried into a run. It was 23 February 1944, Valentina's birthday again. She was twenty-five.

'Girls, look, it's an airport,' someone whispers. Approaching the lights of the small camp, they make out a tall electric fence, watchtowers and barracks, and then, not far away, a vast flat space – an airfield. Snowdrifts are whipping up around a hangar. So it's true, they tell each other, they've been brought here to build German warplanes. They are marched into a squat brick barracks. It is freezing cold, there is no heating, and they sleep in three-tiered bunks under a single blanket.

Next morning, at *Appell*, they are standing outside in the snow when an elderly German in civilian clothes calls out numbers from a list and says in Russian: 'You are about to do important and responsible work. The management will give food bonuses for those who'll do good work. You might even go home on holiday. But we will punish careless work very severely.' He raises his finger and barks, in a military fashion: 'Right about face, at the double, march.' Nobody moves.

The Yugoslavs and Czechs refuse first. A young Czech simply steps out of line and makes a short statement, saying that she and her group 'will not make bombs to kill our families'. The guards set upon the woman, kicking and beating her until she falls to the ground. Two Yugoslav girls go to her aid, but dogs are set upon all three. They are badly mauled, and dragged off leaking blood across the snow. One is certainly dead, maybe all three.

Now it is the turn of the Soviet group. They have done it before, they can do it again. 'Nobody must break the circle.' Those were Klemm's words and they repeat them under their breath. There's safety in numbers, they tell each other, and standing alongside the Soviets is a big group of Ukrainians, mostly captured labourers, but some partisans who have also just arrived. The Red Army girls spread the word down the Ukrainian lines: they too must refuse to work making the enemy's planes. The Ukrainian girls signal that they too will refuse. So when the order comes to move forward, the whole line stands stock-still, as if frozen solid in the icy wind.

Now comes the commandant. A fat man in his sixties, angry at being brought out into the snow, he bellows until his glasses steam up, and he's red in the face, looking for ringleaders. Maro Lashki, one of the Georgians, catches his eye. He shouts at her to step out of the line and stand to attention. She refuses. He shouts: 'You are an officer. A soldier. Show some respect to another officer.'

'I see no one to respect,' she says. 'Russian pig!' he yells, and lashes out at her, then kicks her several times with his jackboots, until she lies limp and is also dragged away from the group.

It is Valentina Samoilova's turn to be picked out, probably – as happened at Soest – because she stands out as tall and blonde. The commandant asks her why she refuses to work and she says: 'This is an armaments factory.'

'Yes. So?'

'We are members of the Soviet military and we refuse to produce weapons to murder fellow soldiers. According to the Geneva Conventions you cannot force us to do such work.'

Now the fat officer goes red with rage and howls like an animal: 'Oh, so you remember the Geneva Conventions, then I'll beat you until you forget them.' He starts to beat on her wounded breast. 'And you'll even forget your own name when I've finished with you.' But he soon tires of this, and walks off leaving the fifty-four Soviet POWs to stand where they are on the yard in the sub-zero temperature until they change their mind.

Evening comes and lights are turned on in the barracks. Groups of forced labourers – men and women – walk past and ask: 'Who are these people?'

'They're Russians. They're refusing to work,' says someone. 'Bravo, Russians,' say the workers, and a piece of chocolate lands at a girl's foot. She bends to pick it up and is smashed in the face by a guard.

The women are still standing as night falls. It is near minus 20. The girls have thin cotton clothes. Each tries to lean close to the person next to them for warmth, but as soon as a girl moves, a figure like a ghost in a black raincoat appears. A whip hisses and burns the face.

Morning comes and they are still standing there, although several have collapsed by now and the snow is falling on them. Then Ludwig Ramdohr appears. The Gestapo chief must have been alerted about the protest at first light and sped north to deal with it. He walks towards the stricken figures and orders that they all be stripped nearly naked and left to stand there again as temperatures plummet further.

After several hours more, the German civilian boss returns, and walks up to Valentina, pokes her in the chest and says: 'Her.' Then he points at three others nearby, including Lyusya Malygina. He lights a cigarette and tells the other protesters that the lives of these four are in their hands. He doesn't raise his voice. 'If you still refuse to work the four will be shot before your eyes,' he says.

The four are taken away and put in a bunker, expecting to be shot, but the women outside can't allow it – 'Yevgenia Lazarevna said don't get shot.' They debate what to do and then agree that they might all be shot. They must do the work after all, they decide, and they march to the hangar. But all of them know that part of the agreement with Klemm was that if they were forced to work, they would open another front, and sabotage the German planes.

'So we made planes that blew up in the air,' says Valentina.

Of all the subcamps opened in 1943, Barth was surely the most desolate, perched on the northern tip of Germany on a stretch of coastline lashed by storms and often flooded. The little town itself was never hospitable. Local history books tell how it was punished over the centuries by invaders, ravaged by cholera and the Black Death, and visited by witches. Three witches were even burned at the stake here in 1693.

For the prisoners, Barth quickly became a hell worse than Ravensbrück itself – a kind of mini-hell, smaller, more isolated, more brutal. The daily routine was much the same as at the main camp, but everything was harder: it was colder here, and roll call more of a torture. The food was of even poorer quality. One Russian recalled the day the soup arrived so thick with maggots that the whole camp came out in protest.

The routine was relentless, as there was no work but the endless factory shifts; twelve hours a day of tedium, soldering small springs while *Meister* moved among them with stop watches and a guard sat at the end on a table with fist clenched ready. Others were assigned to work with metal lathes with no goggles; the fine swarf either gradually turned them blind or the acid vapour gnawed at lungs and hands, or both.

After a while, Ravensbrück was remembered as lavishly equipped by comparison. There was green paint on the barracks at the mother camp and trees all around, but here the landscape was grey or black and the barracks black brick. At the main camp it was now and then possible to organise a comb or maybe a woollen vest from the stores, but here there were no stores. Prisoners got a bowl and spoon, but if they lost them there were no spares, so women foraged in rubbish and bins for rusty tins to put their soup in or go without. The women walked around with their bits of cutlery tied around the waist with string.

There were more locals around in the subcamps, moving around on the outskirts or even working alongside the prisoners, and sometimes they helped by smuggling bits of food, or in other ways, but mostly they walked on past.

The camp of Neubrandenburg, twenty-five miles to the south, where the new French arrivals were taken at about the same time, was run on much the same lines, but the French fared worse, as none had been battle- or famine-hardened like their Slavic comrades. Micheline Maurel was teaching in a school in Lyon when Valentina Samoilova was fighting at Stalingrad, and within days of arriving at Neubrandenburg she was thinking not of protest but simply of staying alive. Micheline's friend Denise Tourtay, the student from Grenoble, had a weak heart and could not keep up with the work, so her soup ration was withdrawn and she was beaten so badly at the subcamp that she could no longer work or even stand. Within weeks she was critically sick with dysentery, and then typhus, and died in the Neubrandenburg *Revier*. 'She was the first of our convoy to go,' wrote Micheline. 'She was only twenty years old.'

Blockovas were chosen for their cruelty. At Neubrandenburg a Blockova called Charlotte Schuppe loved to swat at the French with a soup ladle and wake them in the morning with a bucket of ice-cold water. At Barth the

Soviets all remembered a German Blockova called Julie Wolk, a beater who stole food from prisoners to give to her favourites and who would torment the women for nothing.

Guards here seemed little different from at Ravensbrück at first, and they soon had nicknames – the Hangman, Baba Yaga, Squinty Eye. And yet as a group, these guards were more slovenly, and there was special barbarity about the way they did things. One Russian saw a guard beat a woman on her glass eye until it fell out. Micheline Maurel saw an SS man feeding his dog with sugar lumps while nearby, at the water trough, two women guards held a prisoner's head under water until she died.

At first there seems to have been no all-powerful Binz figure to oversee these women, though later at Barth there was a guard called Blondine who held sway of some sort, probably because the prisoners knew she worked for Ramdohr. She was young, with 'a sporty physique' and 'big hair'.

The subcamp prisoners also suffered more than their comrades back at Ravensbrück in that they had been parted from their leaders, who were often older women and likely to remain in the main camp. The Red Army women were cut off from Yevgenia Klemm, though as Valentina explained, they tried their hardest to keep in touch.

Back at Ravensbrück Klemm had got to hear about the Barth protest and smuggled out a letter with the next prisoner convoy from the camp. By now, new prisoners were coming out to Barth all the time, as the sick and exhausted were sent back, often in the same trucks. 'We were never out of touch for long, and this helped us. She could still advise us what to do,' said Valentina.

This first letter told the Barth girls they were right to have decided to work, but resistance must go on by carrying out concerted sabotage. 'And she said we must teach others to do the same, but we must not be fanatical. And we must stay together,' said Valentina. 'This was always Yevgenia Lazarevna's advice, and it was good advice. I was taught the same as a child. If you are together, nobody will break you.'

The women then met in secret in their block to plan the sabotage. For example, women on one conveyor belt would agree to connect the wires on the engine parts the wrong way round. Women on another conveyor belt would solder connections so that they fell apart. 'It was always risky, of course, because a factory supervisor might carry out spot checks,' said Valentina. 'Sabotage meant we always stood with a foot on the gallows.' But the supervisors were often distracted and the female guards often bored, or flirting with these same supervisors.

German civilians, sometimes communists themselves, were employed at the factory as skilled workers, and some tried to help the prisoners. Contacts with these men were not easy, but in slack moments it was possible to meet up in the lavatories, perhaps, or walking back to the blocks, when messages could pass.

It was one of these civilians who taught Valentina to sabotage planes so that they 'blew up in the air'. He told her he knew how to make a bomber stall in mid-flight by drilling holes in the wings and filling the holes with metal shavings. The wings doubled as fuel tanks, so the shavings would soon clog up the fuel pipes, causing the engine to stall. Valentina then collected metal shavings, found lying around the factory floor, and hid them in a tiny box that she inserted into her vagina until a moment came when she could pass them over to the civilian worker.

Whether planes really blew up we don't know, but the belief that they did clearly gave the Red Army women a certain strength. When Ramdohr came down to investigate they refused to confess. At Barth there was no cell bunker, but Ramdohr tried everything to get them to talk. Just for 'acting suspiciously' women were pulled out of the line and forced in midwinter to stand in baths of freezing water, and then more water was poured on top of them by other prisoners using buckets. If the other prisoners didn't do the pouring they knew they'd get the same treatment.

Sometimes an example was made of someone. Lydia Rybalchenko, another of the Red Army women, was taken one day to an underground cellar, dug out under one of the brick barracks. The cellar had room for just two people to stand and was filled with water. Lydia was left standing with water up to her neck for several hours, but still she refused to talk and was pulled out. 'She told us there were rats swimming near her eyes,' said Valentina.

At this time Ramdohr was not only investigating sabotage at Barth; at the subcamp of Genthin a young Red Army woman called Vera Vanchenko, an intelligence officer, had been spoiling bullets meant for German guns. Vera had worked out how to insert the bullet ignition into the cartridge case upside down, and had shown every woman on her shift how to do the same. Once the dud cartridges had been passed to the next room, where the bullet head was pressed on top, it was impossible to see that any sabotage had been carried out. What Vera did not know was that spot checks were to be carried out on the ammunition before it left the plant. The batch chosen for the checks was theirs, and when every one of the bullets failed, Vera was identified as the ringleader and taken back to Ravensbrück for interrogation by Ramdohr.

According to a prisoner in the next cell, she was taken ten times for interrogation. Each time she refused to give names and each time was returned with more broken bones. The final time every bone in both her hands had been broken. Then Vera Vanchenko was hanged. After the Genthin case an order went out that all saboteurs were to be hanged. Now Yevgenia Klemm sent another note warning the women not to risk their lives.

At Barth, Ramdohr recruited more spies. Guards were ever harder to recruit, but spies came cheap and were the best defence against sabotage or slack work. A senior official in Albert Speer's armaments ministry believed there were other ways to make women work. 'Psychology, this is the secret,' said Karl Saur. 'These women ... must first understand that there is no hope at all of liberation. Then out of pure boredom and despair they will turn to work.' At Barth, however, the absence of hope had led thirteen women to attempt escape, and several others died on the wire.

In Barth it was Blondine's *Spitzel* that caused the most despair. It wasn't long before the guard with 'big hair' was appointed to run Ramdohr's network there. Everyone knew she was recruiting her own informers right inside the blocks, so women felt there was no place they could feel secure. In the Russian block the hated German Blockova Julie Wolk worked for Blondine, which was dangerous, says Valentina, 'because Wolk watched everything we did. Instruments used for sabotage – bent knives, old screws – now had to be hidden more carefully. No planning could be done inside the block itself.'

It worked like this, says Valentina. 'Wolk also began to pick off prisoners as her spies in the block. Everyone knew when this happened because a girl would be called away by Wolk and taken into Blondine's room. When the girl returned her behaviour would be different. Things had obviously been said that scared her, and from then on she'd keep her distance from us.' At least five were recruited in this way, including one or two Red Army girls, and there could have been more. 'But this just made us want to sabotage more.'

Whenever Ramdohr appeared in person everyone suspected a tip-off from Blondine. Always raging about sabotage, he would assemble the workers and demand that those responsible own up. If nobody confessed he threatened to pick out the ringleaders himself and throw them in the cellar or shoot them there and then. On one occasion nobody confessed and they all stood there expecting one of Blondine's spies to walk out and pick someone out, but instead a woman called Vera Sintsova, who had nothing to do with the sabotage, stepped forward and confessed to it all. It was suicide, and Ramdohr shot her in front of everyone with a single bullet to the back of the head.

Soon the prisoners opened up 'a second front', says Valentina, who talks as if she was fighting some kind of insurgency behind the lines. The new resistance effort was run from inside the infirmary at Barth, which was quickly filling up with prisoners suffering from diarrhoea, scabies, dysentery and typhus. The Soviet doctors – Maria Klyugman, Tamara Tschajalo and others – had no medicines to use. Young Russians and Ukrainians with TB would convulse with coughing spasms, but all that Klyugman and Tschajalo could do was hold out jam jars as they spat blood. Other prisoners were brought in injured by Allied bombs that had fallen close to the plant.

Gradually the doctors found the means to smuggle in medicines by making contacts with civilians and with prisoners of war in nearby camps, and by getting messages to the main camp asking for medicines to be sent with prisoners on the next incoming truck. Trucks were taking prisoners back and forth almost daily now. Managers were always complaining that the infirmary was overflowing and the sick weren't replaced fast enough. Then Blondine would come into the infirmary and choose the ones to go. 'This one, this one,' she would say, and would tell them they were going to a rest camp. Nobody believed her: the word from Ravensbrück was that when the sick got back they were sent off again to be gassed at Auschwitz or some other place. The Red Army doctors tried to smuggle women out of the *Revier*, or swap women at the last minute, 'but they knew spies were watching all the time'.

Valentina's story had reached a period near the end of the war when the Red Army front was drawing close, planes were flying overhead and the prisoners had more reason for hope than ever. Together she and Lyusya Malygina began to distribute leaflets around the camp telling the prisoners that victory was near. In the final weeks civilians were often more willing to help, she says, by smuggling in paper and pencils for example. 'We now knew we were going to win, it was just a matter of time.' Ramdohr soon learned about the leaflets and appeared at the camp again in another rage. No one confessed, though many were close to breaking point.

Then Zina Avidowa, one of the doctors, could stand no more and ran into the wire. Valentina was taken by surprise. It was so near the end. Zina was thirty-five years old and a mother of three. Her eldest son was in the army. 'Zina's patriotism was so strong,' says Valentina.

> But then she started behaving strangely. One day she just couldn't work in the hangar any more. She said: 'My children and family are in Leningrad. I can't make weapons that will kill them.'
>
> We had been holding her back. We persuaded her to be calm. We thought she had taken our advice and that she would not kill herself. Then the next day we were standing there and the siren started up and just as everybody started to go to the barracks she ran towards the fence. The fence was seventeen metres from the barracks and was electrified. We were never supposed to go within ten metres of it. We all saw it happen. Everyone was running after her. She shouted back at us …

Valentina's voice trails off. 'Zina Avidowa was not the only one,' she says.

> Almost every day people were throwing themselves on to the fence because it was so hard for a person to cope with the pressure. Everyone had their breaking point. She had been quite normal. She even shouted goodbye. She was left on the fence all night. We all saw her on the fence at the morning *Appell*. Still there. Then after we were taken to work, they took the body away.

I asked Valentina what Yevgenia Lazarevna thought of these suicides. 'She was against it of course,' she replied. 'We discussed it many times before we left. She would say we should never do it in any circumstances. She sent more notes saying suicide shows our weakness to the enemy.'

The women redoubled their defiance. One day they managed to smuggle in some red fabric and made a red flag, which they hung from a block. This time, when Ramdohr came, he erected gallows in the camp square and strung two nooses up. He picked out Valentina and Lyusya Malygina and took them to the dark cellar where they were locked up with the rats and the water level rising around them.

'We were sitting there I don't know how long,' says Valentina, who becomes hard to follow at this point. 'It was very dark. There were things coming towards us.' Then she halts and starts talking about other things, about her youth and her patriotism, and I have to ask her what happened next, but no answer comes at first. Other prisoners' accounts describe how when these two were taken away to the cellar the rest were told that no one was to eat until Valentina and Malygina confessed. Everyone saw the gallows being erected and feared the worst.

Then Valentina starts talking again and says that she and Lyusya were taken from the cellar to the camp infirmary, where they were looked after by their friends Tamara Tschajalo and Maria Klyugman. She doesn't explain at first what it was that brought about their release, but then she says an American bomb dropped nearby, injuring scores of people. Doctors were needed in the hospital, so she and Lyusya were released and told to help the injured. The gallows with two nooses were removed.

Valentina's story becomes confused. She says Lyusya was given an important job in the camp after these events; she was made the top Blockova. I ask Valentina if it is true that Lyusya Malygina became an informer for Blondine, an accusation I had read in post-war papers, found in the Russian archives.

'I never believed that,' says Valentina. 'They gave her an important job in the camp and they hoped to get information out of her. But she was a loyal person. Malygina was never a traitor. I knew her as I knew myself. She was a beautiful girl with big dark brown eyes.'

*

Some time later, after meeting Valentina, I came upon Blondine's version. Blondine was in fact Ilse Hermann, one of the impressionable, home-sick Agfa factory girls seen arriving at the camp by Lotte Silbermann, the canteen waitress. It was Hermann who asked Lotte to write her marriage ads.

Immediately after the war Hermann, like countless other women guards, had escaped arrest and by the 1950s was living safely in East Germany, behind the Iron Curtain. By the early 1960s she must have thought she had got off scot-free, only to be arrested by the Stasi, the East German secret police, who had begun their own Nazi war crimes investigations and trials, fifteen years after the end of the war.

Scornful of the paltry number of convictions secured by the West, the East German trials were partly devised to score a Cold War propaganda coup against the 'fascists', but also to bring to account some of the thousands of Nazi war criminals who by then were hiding out in the East.

After charging Hermann with crimes against humanity, the Stasi inquisitors questioned her about Ramdohr's *Spitzeltätigkeit*, spying activities. Fifty pages of interrogation with the Agfa factory girl painted a chilling portrait of how an ordinary young woman was snatched from her job threading film, then won over with chocolates into terrorising women prisoners in a backwater of the Nazi hell called Barth. After hearing Valentina's account, Blondine's had a special power to shock, as it mirrored what Valentina had said almost every step of the way.

It is not clear exactly when Ludwig Ramdohr began to court Hermann's attention, but probably when she was about to be sacked for bad behaviour at another subcamp. She feared going back to the Agfa factory, and told her Stasi interrogator that Ramdohr was very nice to her. He gave her a cigarette and chocolates, and this surprised her because she'd heard what a brute he was from others.

When he asked her to spy on the prisoners at Barth she immediately agreed. She was told that the Soviet women needed to be 'stamped out for causing the war'. Ramdohr's first concern was about the sabotage going on in the Heinkel factory; he suspected the Red Army women were masterminding it, but he needed proof. Hermann told her interrogators how she went to Barth and quickly recruited helpers – her two roommates, as well as a German communist called Julie Wolk.

It was simple to pick off informers from amongst these worn-out prisoners. 'I didn't have to pay them,' she said. Likely recruits were invited to Blondine's room, where Wolk, who spoke Russian, did the talking. Blondine also watched other guards and the SS themselves. 'I had to keep my eyes open and I had to watch who sat next to who in the canteen.' She made reports and sent them back to Ramdohr by post. Ramdohr had given Hermann a cover name, which had a capital letter and a number. Everything was to be 'top-secret'. He would then come down and punish the culprits, though Hermann said she didn't know how.

From the reports of his spies, Ramdohr learned that the resistance at Barth was being masterminded in the camp hospital. Maria Klyugman and others were trying to smuggle medicines in, and to swap the numbers of sick prisoners selected to go back to the main camp with the numbers of those already dead. Blondine's task was to report on this too, based on what her spy in the hospital told her.* She knew where these trucks were going because she had the job of selecting the 'finished' women. And she knew they were gas-chamber fodder or Belsen fodder, as she put it – 'I knew that the women returning were going for extermination.'

Hermann's account shows just how effective the Red Army's 'insurgency' in Barth was becoming. It was certainly worrying Ramdohr, so he told Blondine to recruit more spies. Her interrogators asked her to identify informers, suggesting names such as Klava, Hawa, Shura and Vlaja, but she couldn't remember them.

Before long it became clear to Blondine and Ramdohr that the prisoners were getting information about the advancing Soviet front. Somehow they were spreading leaflets giving news of how close the Red Army was. 'He said the Bolshevik influence was taking over the whole camp.' Now Blondine secured new informers whom she met 'in a cinema', and more chocolates arrived from Ramdohr.

Hermann's interrogators reverted again to establishing the identities of her informers. They produced statements for her to read, made by the former Red Army prisoners at Barth, including Maria Klyugman, Tamara Tschajalo and Valentina Samoilova herself. The statements, taken in Moscow and sent on to the East Germans, were intended to help in their investigation, and were included in Blondine's Stasi file.

At one point, according to the interrogation transcript, part of Valentina's evidence was read out to Hermann. In the passage cited, Valentina accused the former guard of recruiting agents and provocateurs at Barth. It appears from these transcripts that several – perhaps as many as twelve – Soviet women were at one point working for the Germans. For example, she [Hermann] tried to recruit the former Soviet prisoner Lyusya Malygina. Hermann's informers 'were offered better food in return for their

* The spy in the hospital was the Swiss prisoner Carmen Mory, who had by this time been transferred from the main camp – where she had been Blockova of Block 10 – to spend the last months of the war as one of Ramdohr's spies at Barth.

services,' Valentina had stated, according to the Hermann interrogation transcript.

The Stasi interrogators clearly had reason to believe that Hermann had succeeded in recruiting Malygina. Then further revelations in Hermann's interrogation file gave the story yet another twist, raising questions as to whether it might in fact have been Valentina Samoilova herself who worked for the Germans and not Lyusya Malygina.

When the former guard was shown photographs of Lyusya Malygina and asked if she remembered her as an informer, Hermann said she didn't remember Malygina at all. She was asked several times if Malygina was one of those who agreed to collude, but again denied knowing her. However, when shown Valentina's photograph, Hermann at once volunteered the information that Samoilova herself might have been the Red Army informer "Valya" – short for Valentina.

These revelations in the Stasi documents were unsettling, especially as they contradicted everything that Samoilova had said about Lyusya Malygina. 'Malygina was never a traitor, I knew her as I knew myself,' she had told me. One explanation was that the testimony of the former prisoners was manipulated by the Stasi to support a pre-fixed case. Another was that both Valentina and Lyusya Malygina were so terrorised by Ramdohr, particularly as he erected the gallows, that in the very last weeks of the war, even these two strong spirits had indeed turned informer.

In our meeting I had asked Valentina if she was interrogated about collaboration with the fascists after the war, and she told me she was, though she was never charged. 'They could see I had the scars, so they couldn't accuse me of being a coward,' she said. 'Look: I have only one breast, you can see for yourself. I proved with my blood that I was innocent.' She pointed to her breast, and the wound she had received at Stalingrad. Then she left the room, and returned carrying a box spilling over with medals, awarded to her by Stalin after the war.

All these years later, it is impossible to establish exactly what lay behind the allegations on Blondine's file. Yet the essence of the Barth story seems clear. On the outer periphery of Himmler's empire, cut off from Yevgenia Lazarevna Klemm, the Red Army's circle had fallen apart. At Barth some of the strongest spirits were broken, many by hunger, disease and despair, others by Ludwig Ramdohr and Blondine.

But the story did not end there. When Stalin's secret police set out after the war to accuse Soviet prisoners returning from Nazi camps of 'collaboration with the fascists', they probed and blackmailed survivors in every way they could, trying to turn them against one another. In interviews with survivors I came across scores of examples of such intimidation – of friends being pressured into betraying friends and of survivors who had been accused, tried, sent to Siberia and, in at least one case, shot.

Of these cases the most notorious centred on the so-called doctors' trial at Simferopol in the Crimea.

Exactly what evidence first led to the Simferopol charges will probably never be known. Requests to Russian archives for the official trial transcripts remained unanswered. However, thanks to the letter that Maria Klyugman wrote in 1959 to Antonina Nikiforova we have a rare insight into how Stalin's courts worked and of the tragedies caused.

Charged at Simferopol with Maria Klyugman were Lyusya Malygina, Anna Fedchenko, Valentina Chechko and Lena Malachova, all Red Army doctors and nurses at the camp. Maria's letter begins by giving a bare account of her own story.

'I was born in 1910 in Cernigov, then my parents moved to Kiev. I came from a big family. In 1931 I went to the medical institute in Kiev.' She describes her medical career, her work at the front as a surgeon, her capture and her experience of Ravensbrück, where, along with several others, after some months she worked as a doctor in the *Revier* at the main camp and at Barth. After the war she worked again in Kiev and Moscow as a doctor, until in 1949 she was arrested by the Interior Ministry and taken to jail in Simferopol to face trial at the Military Tribunal of Tavrich Eskoje.

'We were accused of helping the fascists liquidate people,' wrote Maria. 'I was accused of having injected people with lethal doses of pentothal [an anaesthetic] and of having infected prisoners' legs with bacteria. Of giving women in the bathroom precious stones to hide in their vaginas.' For these crimes the tribunal sentenced the women to twenty-five years in a Siberian camp. The trial took sixteen months, and while the women waited the verdict one of them, Lena Malachova, hanged herself in her cell.

Maria then named three of the accusers, all of them comrades from the camp: doctors and nurses. The first of their group arrested – Valentina Chechko – was the first accuser. Under interrogation Chechko 'started accusing herself and us of having liquidated people'.

Two fellow nurses, Vera Bobkova and Belolipe Tskaya, also testified against them: 'They came several times to Simferopol as witnesses.'

Maria said she had spoken out against the charges in court: 'I told Chechko she would have to live with the consequences of making the daughter of Malachova an orphan. For that I had four weeks in solitary confinement. In December 1950 I was taken to a camp near Lake Taischet in the Irkutsk region.'

Red Army survivors today say they know of no good reason why the accusers should have betrayed their comrades who had been so courageous in the camp. Chechko 'lost her head' under interrogation. Bobkova was frightened into making false accusations and was under pressure from her husband to say whatever the SMERSh wanted. There is no doubt that many Soviets were jealous of their women doctors and nurses who were deemed to have special privileges in the camp. Antonina's post-war correspondents occasionally give their views. Tatyana Pignatti wrote of her admiration for Maria Klyugman whom she saw 'at the operating table in the burning fires of Cernigov', but she added that in the camp some girls had suspected Klyugman of giving a fatal injection to one of their comrades who was dying from typhus, apparently to release her from the pain. The accusation was not true, wrote Pignatti; the injection was done by an SS nurse – 'but it is so hard to get clear of the mud'. In the camp Klyugman did nothing wrong, 'but the girls didn't like her for her pride'.

As for Lyusya Malygina, she and Vera Bobkova had been the best of friends in the camp, 'but Vera was a witness at the trial and Malygina was convicted'.

Pignatti could make no sense of it, saying to Antonina: 'You must have seen how a storm brings all the dirt to the shore. Life clears away these people as the sea clears away the dirt.'

*Chapter 20*

# Black Transport

The 'glamorous' woman who appeared at Ravensbrück to visit the Norwegian prisoner Sylvia Salvesen in the late summer of 1943 was a Norwegian student called Wanda Hjort. Blonde, blue-eyed and just twenty-one, Wanda had been visiting Norwegian prisoners at the male concentration camp of Sachsenhausen, near Berlin, for nearly a year. The prisoners there knew her as 'the potato-cake girl' because she brought them, home-cooked by her mother, in her backpack.

The idea of a foreigner, especially from an enemy nation, turning up at the gates of a concentration camp to visit prisoners seems beyond belief. No German civilian dared go near, and the International Committee of the Red Cross was banned. The only visitors were German dignitaries, and even they were not allowed past the show block. And the story grows all the more extraordinary in that Wanda was herself a prisoner of the Nazis: she was living in Germany along with her family under a rare form of house arrest.

Wanda's unusual status came about as a result of her father's arrest in Norway three years earlier. After German forces invaded and then occupied the country in April 1940, Johan Hjort, an eminent Norwegian lawyer, attacked the legal basis of the occupation. At the time, thousands of Norwegian resisters were being rounded up and sent to concentration camps, but Hjort was taken instead to a German prison from which he was soon released and placed under house arrest.

Hjort had powerful relatives inside Germany. Most influential was his sister's husband, a man called Rudiger von der Golz, who was Joseph Goebbels's lawyer. When Hjort was jailed, his brother-in-law struck a deal:

Johan Hjort was allowed to live under house arrest, provided his family lived with him. The idea was almost certainly dreamt up by Himmler himself. Through his studies of ancient Germanic customs, the Reichsführer had discovered the practice of *Sippenhaft*, whereby Germanic tribes made all clan members answer for the crimes of any one of them.

Wanda, charismatic and exceptionally strong-willed, was furious at the news that she was to be imprisoned – albeit only under house arrest – in Nazi Germany. At the time of her father's arrest she was already working with the resistance, visiting captured Norwegians held in the Nazi camp of Grini, on the mountain slopes outside Oslo. She refused to go to Germany at first, but concern for her father caused her to change her mind, and with her mother, younger brother and sister Wanda went to live at a small estate near Potsdam, called Gross Kreutz. Once in Germany she set about looking for ways to continue her work with prisoners and began to trace the whereabouts of Norwegians held in concentration camps.

Despite the house arrest, and a Gestapo guard, the Hjorts lived with a degree of freedom. As long as she didn't roam too far, Wanda could take suburban trains. One Friday morning, accompanied by her younger brother, also blue-eyed and blonde, she set off for the closest camp, Sachsenhausen. On reaching the gates, fair curls spilling out under a scarf, she approached a sentry and said in her best school German that she'd like to leave her parcels for the Norwegian prisoners.

'The sentry was young like me. He looked at me suspiciously and asked me to fill in a form, saying he'd have to ask his boss, but then he gave me a smile and I smiled back.' The sentry asked Wanda where she was from and she said Gross Kreutz, the name of the estate, which he seemed to hear as Rote Kreutz, or Red Cross. Unaware of any rules saying such visits weren't allowed, the guard permitted her to leave the packages. She asked if she could return the following week to collect the boxes, and the guards said yes, as they had no rules against that either. From then on Wanda Hjort appeared each Friday at the Sachsenhausen gates.

At each visit she saw abuse heaped on terrorised, skeletal men. They were obviously starving. If there was one thing that must be done for them, she decided, it was to make sure that somehow they received proper Red Cross food parcels.

The Nazis had recently made an apparent concession to the International Red Cross on the question of parcels for prisoners in concentration camps. Himmler agreed in early 1943 that Red Cross food parcels could, in theory, be sent to certain categories of prisoner. The ICRC had even set up a 'parcels service', as had the national Swedish, Norwegian and Danish Red Cross societies. However, by the SS rules, the Red Cross were required to have the name, number and camp of each recipient, which had to be printed on the parcels, or else they would not be given out. Furthermore, the recipient must sign a receipt. In a tiny number of cases the Red Cross had these details – perhaps because families had passed them on – but only Himmler's SS knew who was in which camp, and requests for such information were always refused by Ernst Grawitz, head of the Nazi German Red Cross. That made the 'parcels service' almost meaningless from the start.

Wanda Hjort, however, saw a way to make it work. She set about tracing as many Norwegian inmates as she could, in order to build up a database of names and addresses. Word of her visits spread among the Norwegian prisoners in Sachsenhausen, who found ways to smuggle information to her, leaving names and addresses under stones, or whispering in Norwegian as she passed by the wire.

She then began making contact with the prisoners' families in Norway. The Hjort family was barred from posting letters, and everything was censored, but when Wanda experimented by taking letters to the local post office near Gross Kreutz and asking to post them to Norway, she found the postmistress had no instructions to refuse and they went in the ordinary mail. Soon a flood of letters came back, not only from the families she had contacted, but from others who had heard of her work and were desperate for news of missing men and women; their names were now added to her database.

Wanda also sought out other Scandinavians operating covertly in Germany, including a group of Norwegian pastors working with Norwegian seamen in the port of Hamburg. She gave them the names and numbers she had collected and they passed them to the Norwegian Red Cross, which was now able to send parcels to the prisoners.

All this time Wanda was learning from her contacts at Sachsenhausen of other camps, unknown outside Germany, where other Norwegian nationals had been sent. Ravensbrück kept cropping up, but the women's camp was not on the suburban lines and by early 1943 the railway tracks around Berlin were often bombed so it was hard for her to reach.

In the summer of 1943 Wanda received a letter from Norway asking if she had come across 'Aunt Sylvia'. The letter was signed Uncle Harald. It had passed through the censor. At first she was unsure who Uncle Harald might be, but after she spoke to her parents it became clear that he was the Norwegian doctor Harald Salvesen, whose wife, Sylvia, was in Ravensbrück. There was a distant family connection, as the professor's brother was married to one of Wanda's many aunts, but Wanda had never met Sylvia or Uncle Harald.

Now she had a new reason to reach Ravensbrück, and resolved to take

Sylvia a package. The railway line had reopened. The journey was still risky and long, but Wanda reached Fürstenberg station. She made her way on foot to Ravensbrück, through flurries of snow and icy wind from the Havel River. Near the gates came a now familiar sight: stooping figures in striped clothes, bare feet inside wooden clogs. Knowing that they were women gave Wanda a particular shock. Some were pulling huge road-rollers as guards cracked whips. Others were labouring in fields.

Wanda approached a sentry at the gate, but this was not Sachsenhausen: there were no smiles, and although the package for Sylvia was accepted, Wanda was quickly sent away. But she had to return, and the only way would be to approach her Gestapo minder and say she wished to visit her aunt. She knew it was quite likely that the request would go to Himmler himself, which was hazardous: not only would he probably refuse, but the request itself might draw attention to all her secret work. On the other hand, if it would take her into the women's camp, Wanda was willing to pull strings, even the Reichsführer's.

She had requested a favour of Himmler before. Soon after arriving in Germany she had felt so miserable she wrote directly to him asking for permission to be sent home. She received a reply, couched in the politest terms, saying she could return if she agreed to renounce all political activity, but Wanda could not accept and stayed on in Germany. The request to visit her aunt in Ravensbrück, however, was granted.

'*Die Salvesen, nach vorn, aber schnell*' – 'Salvesen, out front, be quick' – was the first Sylvia knew of her visitor. She was given soap and told to wash, then ushered into a room near the commandant's office. A guard told her to speak in German and not to say a word about conditions in the camp. Before her in the room stood a group of SS officers, and a pretty, well-dressed young woman in civilian clothes.

As Sylvia eyed the SS men, warily expecting their commands, the woman turned towards her. 'I was looking into a pair of smiling blue eyes, and a young voice said in Norwegian, "Good morning, Aunt Sylvia",' at which the guards repeated that they must speak only in German.

Wanda's main fear was that Sylvia would suspect some sort of trap and deny all knowledge of her. After all, they had never met. She continued, 'Mother sends her love,' and saw Sylvia look puzzled, so she explained: 'Mother has just heard from Aunt Ellen. She's been to see Uncle Harald, and they're all well at home.'

The mention of these names led Sylvia to realise that Wanda must be the daughter of Johan Hjort, who was a distant relative. She had heard before her own arrest that he had been put under house arrest in Germany. Seeing that Sylvia didn't remember her name, and this would look odd to their German minders, Wanda said: 'My name is Wanda. It's such a long time since you saw me, Aunt Sylvia, that perhaps you've forgotten my name.'

'Yes, you've changed a lot,' replied Sylvia, who now began to grasp how imperative it was that she convey a sense of what was happening in the camp. Wanda helped by saying: 'Mother told me to ask whether you needed anything we could send you.' Sylvia looked nervously at the Germans and said: 'I don't know if it would be allowed, but perhaps a pair of pyjamas and some underclothes.' Wanda explained a little of her own circumstances. When she asked her 'aunt' if she was sleeping well, Sylvia said yes, 'considering I sleep with between four or five hundred other women'. Here the guard said: 'Nothing about the camp.'

After trying to convey a little more with hints and looks, Sylvia bent down to fix her wooden clogs and whispered, 'It's really terrible here,' but she didn't know if Wanda heard. As Sylvia left she was horrified to see Ludwig Ramdohr standing behind her, 'devouring' Wanda with his eyes. 'Perhaps she seemed to me younger, purer and more lovely than she really was – but to me she had come as a messenger from a world I had almost forgotten, like a ray of hope in the darkness.' Then Wanda was shown out and was gone, leaving a parcel with bread and real butter. 'Never have I tasted anything so delicious,' recalled Sylvia.

What she learned from Sylvia had been scanty, but Wanda had made a vital contact inside Ravensbrück and soon found out more of other camps. As her own knowledge grew, however, so did her frustration that the world seemed to be ignoring what was happening in the camps. Speaking in her Oslo apartment, she explained:

> Nobody who saw what I saw would have been able to ignore it. Each time I went I felt guilty about how little I could do. There was I, well fed and well clothed, watching this terrible suffering. I thought that anybody who actually saw this would surely feel the same. And it was because of that guilt that I kept going back. I am still haunted by what I saw today. And I still feel guilty today.
>
> The only reason I got away with what I did was because I was young and naïve and nobody took me seriously. But then I also realised that because of this I had a responsibility to try and find out everything I could and tell the world.

In the autumn of 1943 Wanda decided to seek help from the Berlin delegation of the International Committee of the Red Cross. Taking the train, she found the committee's delegation to be housed in a luxurious villa situated in the prosperous suburb of Wannsee.

> I rang the bell, quite nervous, thinking they wouldn't listen to me. But I had to tell them what I'd seen with my own eyes. The Red Cross would have to intervene. That was what I had to say, because it was the truth. In my innocence I felt sure they couldn't possibly know how terrible it was, or they'd be trying to help and telling the world themselves.

From the earliest days of Nazi rule the Geneva-based International Committee of the Red Cross (ICRC), guardians of the Geneva Conventions, had been unwilling to act against atrocities in the Nazi concentration camps and opposed even to telling the world what it knew. Members who inspected some of the camps before war broke out were duped into judging conditions as acceptable; others appeared to encourage Hitler in his wider work. Carl-Jacob Burckhardt, one of the most prominent committee members, and an eminent professor of history, visited the early camps and was also invited on a tour of projects across the Reich. After it he wrote personally to Hitler thanking him for his 'magnificent hospitality' and saying how impressed he was with 'the joyous spirit of cooperation' and 'social thoughtfulness' he had encountered. He signed the letter: 'Your deeply devoted, deeply respectful, deeply grateful Carl Burckhardt'.

Later, as evidence of atrocity mounted, the twenty-three-member committee – all of them from Geneva's oldest and wealthiest families, philanthropists and mostly Protestants – opted for 'quiet diplomacy' which took the form of ingratiating letters to Ernst Grawitz.

The hands-off policy remained in place throughout the euthanasia gassings, the growing Jewish persecution, the roundup of asocials, Gypsies and homosexuals, and the founding of a women's concentration camp.

Once war broke out the ICRC took the narrow legal view that assisting civilians held in concentration camps – or death camps – was not within its mandate which was to assist uniformed prisoners of war. There were to be no Red Cross parcels for concentration camp prisoners and nor was there much attempt to inspect. Any proposal to do so was rejected out of hand by Berlin.

What was indisputably within the ICRC's mandate, however, and enshrined at successive meetings of the entire Red Cross movement, was the duty to 'protest against horrors of war' and do all in its power 'to mitigate murderous aspects'. In other words, even where it felt unable to act, the Committee was empowered, indeed mandated, to at least speak out. On this, by any view, it had failed, its failure all the more shocking given how much it knew by then. As the world's chief humanitarian body, with contacts on the ground and in every capital, the ICRC had received more evidence of the unfolding catastrophe than any other single organisation.

The most appalling evidence of all had started pouring into the ICRC's headquarters since the Final Solution agreed at Wannsee in January 1942. Reports from the World Jewish Congress, the Polish underground and other resistance movements, diplomats, escapees, churches, the press and national Red Cross societies painted a graphic picture of genocide. So overwhelming was the latest evidence, particularly from Poland, that the Allied leadership – hitherto sceptical about Jewish claims – had decided to make a joint declaration stating there was no longer any doubt that Hitler had begun exterminating Europe's Jews, which was 'cold blooded' and 'bestial'. A similar declaration by the ICRC, protectors of the Geneva Conventions, could have given strong, independent moral authority to the Allied protest, giving courage to others – even in Germany – to speak out.

At a crisis meeting held in November 1942 the Geneva Committee had a historic opportunity to issue such a declaration. On the table was a motion to make an unprecedented public appeal, revealing to the world what it knew, and calling for a halt. Those in favour argued that the most fundamental principles of humanity were being violated. Margaret Frick-Cramer, a lawyer and the first-ever woman member of the Committee, declared that not to speak out would be cowardly. Others, however, repeated arguments that had paralysed the Red Cross Committee from the start.

Carl Burckhardt, who had written fawningly to Hitler in 1936 and was now the Committee's de facto president, given the illness of president Max Huber, argued that 'work behind the scenes' and 'a few judicious letters' would achieve more than public appeals. After a long debate, the proposal for a public appeal was dropped. Only Margaret Frick-Cramer remained in favour, declaring that by its silence the Committee was 'abandoning the moral and spiritual values on which it had been founded'. She warned that doing nothing at this juncture would be a 'negative act' and would threaten the very existence of the ICRC.

Nevertheless, the policy of silence was agreed, as anyone who appealed to the body from now on was soon to learn.

When Wanda – an uninvited visitor – first knocked on the door of the ICRC's elegant Wannsee villa, she was determined that they should hear what she had to say, and felt sure that once they knew, they would act to stop the horror. She was asked to take a seat and wait, and eventually shown up sweeping stairs into a large room.

> They were all sitting round – all men in dark suits and all looking up towards me – staring. I said I was Norwegian and had been in touch with prisoners in the concentration camps. I noticed they were all quite young. They seemed to listen carefully. When I had finished talking they were silent for a moment or two.

The silence presumably meant that the men in suits were lost for words. Even the most senior among them, a delegate called Roland Marti, had failed to gain access to a single concentration camp, never mind to hand out food as this young woman had. And some of the places Wanda told them about, they had never heard of. She had even found out about a camp called Natzweiler, in Alsace, its existence so secret that it wasn't listed on Nazi documents, but she knew about it from prisoners at Sachsenhausen. Natzweiler had the designation NN – *Nacht und Nebel*, Night and Fog – which meant that all the prisoners there were intended to disappear.

Then Roland Marti spoke. 'He told me that they knew about the problems of the camps and were in touch with the Norwegian representative in Geneva. He said they were interested in any information I had, but they couldn't make it public and didn't want to know anything about how I had acquired it.'

Poignant though Wanda Hjort's appeal to the Red Cross men was, an even more startling appeal, also from a young woman, had reached the Red Cross's Geneva offices that same summer. This appeal had been written inside the camp of Ravensbrück itself and secretly smuggled out.

It was now eight months since Krysia Czyż and her fellow rabbits had embarked on their own campaign to tell the world about the crimes at Ravensbrück, and their methods had since grown more sophisticated. The rabbits knew that the information was reaching their families in Lublin because the secret signals came back – a blue ribbon, or a scratch on a tin – but could never be sure that it had been possible to send the information on, as they hoped, to those in London and Geneva who had power to raise the alarm.

Even long after the war it remained difficult to establish exactly how much intelligence information, signalled by the Polish underground to London about all concentration camps, had reached its destination. When the communists took power in Poland in 1945 much of the wartime underground material was destroyed, and thousands of Polish resisters rounded up and arrested.

Nevertheless, many wartime secret signals were salvaged thanks to a decision to preserve Polish underground files in London, and today they are still kept at the Polish Underground Movement Study Trust, based in a terraced house in the London suburb of Ealing. Amid the countless documents lies a file containing coded signals sent to London via Sweden. In this file is a message, dated July 1943, detailing the facts of medical experiments at Ravensbrück.

The most important surviving document is a coded telegram, a terse seven-line summary of Krysia's long letters. Krysia's mother, a major in the Polish Home Army (AKA), had evidently sent on the information in her daughter's letters to the Home Army in Warsaw. From there details were passed to a

Polish cell in Sweden, where a Polish signaller, code-named Lawina, tapped out a message for London. The resulting telegram reads: 'In the concentration camp for women in Ravensbrück, from July 1942 to July 1943 the German doctors, under Professor Gebhardt, were forcibly performing experiments on Polish women, namely surgical operations on legs, muscles and bones, as well as infecting with tuberculosis, tetanus and gas gangrene.' The message states that there were seventy-seven victims, of whom five had already died.

This single sheet of faded, flimsy paper is testimony to the courage of the Lublin students, whose smuggled letters told the outside world of one of the most shocking Nazi medical atrocities of the war, and disclosed it just weeks after the events. The telegram – probably not the first to have arrived about the rabbits – even named the Nazi responsible for the atrocities: Karl Gebhardt.

The related correspondence, however, shows how 'the world' they had hoped to prompt to act instead ignored them. Horrified by the 'atrocious' and 'unthinkable' practices at Ravensbrück, Polish government officials in London wrote at once to the ICRC in Geneva and to the Vatican, calling on both 'to intervene against this massacre'. The experiments were 'not only against the morality of Christian beliefs but against medical ethics, which allows only animals to be used for experimental purposes'. Moreover, the experiments breached the Hague Convention of 1907.

The Polish correspondence then describes Geneva's response:

> Regarding experiments at the concentration camp Ravensbrück, where several hundred Polish women are being held, the Ministry of Foreign Affairs has taken steps to induce the International Red Cross to examine the case for intervention, but did not receive a positive result. The ICRC has explained that the German authorities do not allow their representative to visit this type of camp, and insist that such camps are not subject to the rules of the Geneva Convention of 1929.

With that excuse Geneva refused not only to intervene with the Germans, but also to publicise what it had learned, or to take up the matter with Allied governments, or with the new War Crimes Commission that by then was actively gathering evidence in New York.

The Red Cross reaction is doubly shocking given that they were informed not only of the atrocities but of the name of their perpetrator, Karl Gebhardt, a man they knew full well to be a close associate of Ernst Grawitz, president of the German Red Cross, and the most powerful medical figure in the Third Reich. As the Committee must therefore have understood, Grawitz, their main interlocutor in Berlin, and the man refusing them entry to the concentration camps, was also the man who had authorised the medical atrocities described by the Polish telegrams.

Within weeks of Krysia's revelations reaching Geneva, Grawitz authorised new experiments. Throughout the early summer of 1943 the Polish women in Ravensbrück had found reason to hope that they were over, but no one could be sure, and when ten rabbits were suddenly summoned again and told to report for work at a subcamp, everyone recognised a trap. A tip-off had come from friends in the *Schreibstube* and the women therefore refused to appear.

Dorothea Binz then came in person to the block and ordered the women out, but again they refused. Each in turn spoke out, telling Binz they knew they were to be experimented on again and would refuse to leave the block even if it meant execution.

According to Dziuba Sokulska, the Lublin lawyer who had led the earlier protest and who was named on the list of ten, Binz then 'gave her word of honour' that the women were simply being sent on a labour transport and they should go to her office to confirm their details. 'We decided to go, but on condition that we would run if we saw any threat to take us by force,' said Dziuba later.

While they stood in front of Binz's office, near the *Revier*, the women were warned by Polish friends that SS men and guards with dogs were on their way. 'We could hear motorbikes arriving and dogs barking from the other side of the wall. We started to run along the camp like hunted animals to show all the prisoners what was happening. When we got back to our block we stood still among the others to hide.'

Binz now brought reinforcements. As well as SS officers, she had with her a group of prisoner policewomen, who dragged the ten women to the work office, 'biting and punching us until they had dragged us as far as the bunker'. The fresh assault on the rabbits, horrifying enough, was made worse by the brutality of these fellow prisoners, working as 'police'. Of all the women who took SS jobs, this newly formed group was naturally the most despised by ordinary inmates. As the ten rabbits were dragged off and locked in bunker cells, the 'police' barricaded prisoners inside Block 15, which had its windows blacked out, without food or electricity. Any who wished to disassociate themselves from the ten could be let out of the stifling block, said Binz, but none did. Even the Czech Blockovas and Stubovas pledged their support, and for four days the block was locked down, surrounded by the prisoner police. 'Bribed by an extra bowl of Judas soup they carried out their duties with great zeal,' said Stanisława Młodkowska, one of those locked up.

Inside the bunker one of the threatened ten rabbits, Bogna Bąbińska, had the idea that they should commit suicide in protest against medical experiments, and Dziuba agreed, but others were against and they gave it up. After twenty-four hours the first five in the bunker were taken to another cell and questioned one by one by an SS doctor, one they didn't recognise. In a bizarre charade, given the previous atrocities, the doctor asked the women if they would agree to a 'small operation'. All refused, saying they had already been operated on. The SS man then told the women it wasn't true. Even when they showed him their scars, he continued to deny it, saying the scars were not from operations at all.

Five more SS officers and doctors came in, overpowered the Polish women and held them down as they kicked and screamed, before gagging them and pouring ether on their faces until they passed out. When they woke next day they found their legs, dirty and black from dust and dirt, had been butchered again as they lay there on the cell beds. All were moved to the *Revier* and locked up on a ward. Helena Piasecka was particularly badly mutilated; a liquid had been injected into the bone marrow so that the leg looked as if it was crumbling. When Helena tried to walk on it some weeks later, the shinbone snapped.

Winter was approaching, and once again the killing was stepped up. Whatever orders had been given earlier in the year to kill only the 'mad' had been superseded by new commands to save on feeding useless mouths, especially those who wouldn't last through winter. In Ravensbrück the killing spree was first apparent in the *Revier*, where lethal injections became common again, ordered by Treite, as Sylvia Salvesen observed when her friend Emma Brundson, a Norwegian Red Cross nurse, was taken ill. She had been suffering from cirrhosis of the liver and Treite had shown sympathy at first, attempting an operation to save her.

Sylvia, still hoping her friend would live, was called one day to the *Stübchen* to find Emma lying 'crumpled up in the bed as if someone had struck her brutally'. She was 'dead but still warm'. Sylvia pulled up the sleeve of Emma's jacket and found a deep injection with blood and mucus running from it. A prisoner nurse told her she had seen one of the camp nursing staff leaving the *Stübchen* carrying a hypodermic syringe.

Treite called Sylvia in to see him. 'Emma is dead, Salvesen,' he said. 'It is better that way. Don't you agree?' Sylvia had counted twelve women murdered by injection in the *Stübchen* that day. 'Emma was the thirteenth.'*

* *Revier* workers noticed that Treite's patients were also dying because of simple mistakes during operations. Treite was using more and more untrained assistants. One gave a patient an anaesthetic one tenth of the correct solution and the other gave a solution ten times the normal strength. Both patients died. Bozena Boudova also noticed a rise in demand for lethal serum: 'I saw Dr Treite in the pharmacy filling a syringe with this solution.'

By the end of the year the death rates were rising not only in the *Revier* but throughout the camp. A woman in the sandpit who could no longer work was shot and killed on the spot. Tuberculosis was rampant; many in the sewing shop were afflicted, but it spread especially fast at the Siemens camp. Prisoners said that the five stretchers kept at Siemens and used to transport sick women from the plant to the main camp were not enough. Richard Mertinkat, a new civilian manager, was shocked by the 'pitiable' and 'lamentable' state of the women's health. 'Siemens could have intervened to insist on better food and decent barracks for the women. But these good gentlemen of Siemens didn't bother counting the number of dead.'

Rita Sprengel, a secretary in the *Spulerei* hall, recalled: 'Many women had to be struck off the lists as incurable. Many died before they were even struck off the lists – usually of tuberculosis.' Under the Siemens contract each woman struck off the lists must be replaced with a healthy one, but these were in short supply, and such was the overcrowding that even when new transports of fresh workers were brought in there was nowhere to put them.

Since September 1943 Jews had even started arriving again. Some were of 'mixed race', sent on from Auschwitz to work. Others were so-called 'protected' Jews – those from countries allied to Germany or from neutral countries that had opposed the gassing of their nationals. By early January huge numbers were expected from France. The need for space grew ever more acute, so the SS took more radical measures to dispose of useless mouths.

Treite announced that no bandages were to be issued to elderly women with leg sores, and no medicine given to those with TB. The camp's old hands, recalling the gassing transports of early 1942, read the signals and knew that more concerted murder 'by letting a certain amount out through the chimney' was almost certainly being planned.

Since 1942 the removal of useless prisoners for gassing had continued with the 'black transports' or *Himmelfahrt* ('heaven-bound') transports in which from time to time lorries had taken away small groups of so-called lunatics as well as other 'useless' prisoners, probably to Auschwitz.

Block 10's Blockova, Carmen Mory, knew as early as December 1943 that another far larger black transport was now planned, and she heard that it too was bound for Auschwitz. Mory often had good information, perhaps as an acolyte of Treite's, but more likely because she had recently become one of Ramdohr's spies.

Women at the subcamps knew about the plans too. In the Neubrandenburg *Revier* prisoners were quite openly being selected for death, and in January

1944 Micheline Maurel, the French literature teacher, had a near escape. After eighteen months at Neubrandenburg, Micheline's health had collapsed and she was admitted to the subcamp's small *Revier*, suffering from high fever and suppurating sores. She was pleased to be out of the snow, and soon made friends inside the little sickbay.

In the next bed a young Polish patient called Irenka was recovering from typhoid fever, which had left her paralysed in one leg. Also here was a group of young Russians who wandered from bunk to bunk exchanging recipes, then broke into spasms of coughing and spat blood into jars. A Red Army prisoner doctor teased Micheline about her 'capitalist toes' (they'd been pinched by high heels). And even though they didn't understand French, everyone listened to Micheline's poems, written on scraps of paper provided by the friendly Blockova, an old hand of such long standing that she carried a number in the 3000s.

Towards the middle of January Micheline saw the Neubrandenburg chief guard enter the *Revier* followed by the prisoner doctor and the Blockova. 'She pointed at the sick women saying, "This one, this one, that one." She looked at me covered with sores and turned away in disgust, but she pointed at Irenka's bunk and said, "That one," then she left.'

The Blockova explained to those chosen that they'd be sent to a convalescent camp. 'You won't have to work any more.' A covered truck came that night. 'The little tubercular Russians, the lame Irenka and quite a number of others were loaded up. The tarpaulin was fastened and the truck departed, skidding a little in the snow.' Afterwards the Blockova sat on Micheline's bed and began to cry. 'Irenka. Poor Irenka.' Micheline asked why she was sad, as Irenka was going to a better place, to which the Blockova looked at Micheline 'hopelessly, without replying'.

Back at the main camp attempts were also made by the SS to disguise what was about to happen. According to Carmen Mory, Treite sent for her and told her that her block, the TB block, were all to be sent to a convalescent home, but Mory already knew it was a lie, and that 1000 names were down for the *Himmelfahrt* transport yet, including women who were fit to work, as well as TB patients, epileptics, women with syphilis and other diseases, many of them 'anything but incurable'.

With this intelligence, Carmen went to talk to Treite again. 'I asked him if it was true that this transport was heading for the gas chambers of Auschwitz. Treite told me I was mad. There were no gas chambers in Auschwitz, he said.'

At about the same time, Germaine Tillion, the French ethnologist, secretly observed Dr Treite as he personally selected an infant for death. Germaine was lying in the infectious diseases ward, still recovering from diphtheria, when to her surprise Treite came in. The SS rarely entered the ward for fear of infection, but Treite showed no fear and went over to a cot where a two-year-old Jewish child lay. The boy – a Dane, presumably separated from his parents – had arrived with the recent transport; one of Zdenka's helpers had been caring for him. Treite picked the child up gently to examine him. Believing he was unobserved, Treite 'showed affection to the child and even gave the little boy an apple', but next day the boy was gone, and Germaine later learned that Treite had written his name, that very day, on the list for Auschwitz.

Around the main camp it was soon common knowledge that a transport was due for Auschwitz, so when news emerged that all holders of pink cards, regardless of age, would be selected, panic broke out and prisoners who had begged for pink cards clamoured to give them back.

So certain were the rabbits about the transport's destination that they decided once again to tell the world. This time their revelations were smuggled out before the crimes described had even been committed. Krysia wrote home on 28 January announcing that 'Transports of the sick are being organised, their destination is most probably the gas chambers.' Once again she pleaded for the information to be passed on so that it could be broadcast.

'The list has already been drawn up,' she wrote. 'There are 1000 persons on it.' She even gave the categories to be killed, including Jehovah's Witnesses, Jewish children, women with venereal disease, and a large number of working women too, including the exhausted. All nationalities were on the lists, including French, Russians and Poles. 'It is impossible to get anybody off the list,' said Krysia, though many were trying.

In the final days each nationality tried to save their own. Sylvia Salvesen pleaded with Treite's secretary to strike all Norwegian names off the list or paste white paper over them, writing other names on top, but the secretary wouldn't do it and told her to speak to Treite himself.

> I went to Treite and begged him to spare them. He fobbed me off saying that he had nothing to do with it and it was the *Oberschwester* who decided. So I went to her and she asked me what work the three did. I said they knitted. 'All the knitters are to go whatever happens,' she said, and told me to go away. From that moment on nobody wanted to knit.

German communists clubbed together with Austrians and Czechs and warned trusted party Blockovas what was to happen. They managed to take fifty pink-card communists off the lists. 'Difficult decisions had to be made about who to save and who should go instead,' recalled one of the Germans, Hildegard Boy-Brandt. When the Germans in the *Revier* asked Treite to remove names, he replied that 800 had to go whatever happened, and suggested they try to replace some with 'asocial elements'. 'This was a terrible responsibility,' said Hilde.

> People came with names of other older women or names of idiots, or criminals, and asked the doctors to swap them. So we did this gruesome thing, and the only thing to say on our behalf is that we rescued some valuable human beings. Had we not done so there would have been even bigger misery. But still it isn't possible to describe how this made us feel. There were many desperate scenes in the hallways of the *Revier*. Many Gypsies were among those selected and their relatives would come along and ask to go with them. And we thought, good heavens, we can't let these healthy human beings leave! But they begged so heartbreakingly: 'Please let me go' – let me go with my daughter, aunt and so on. When the whole process came to an end we were in a very bad state.

Time was running out to complete the list, as the transport was due to leave at the end of January, so Treite and Marschall scurried to fill in gaps, sometimes by just picking people from a transport of new arrivals. 'Dr Treite appeared to be doing the selections against his will, but Marschall appeared to be enjoying it,' said Sylvia Salvesen. Carmen Mory watched as Treite and the prisoner Eugenia von Skene discussed how to complete the list that was still one short because a Czech had just been removed. 'So Treite said, "Let's pick one of the old criminals," and he went along to the records room, picked up a file, read out the medical history of a syphilitic German woman and said, "She'll do."'

Terrible scenes unfolded on the Lagerstrasse. Germaine Tillion recalled: 'One day a woman we called Vercingétorix [after the Gallic chieftain] was selected as she stood right next to me.' The following day Germaine looked out of a window of Block 27 and saw a woman coming out of Block 28 fighting with a guard. 'She held her arms above her head like someone on a Greek vase.' Germaine's friend Anise Girard saw a very young Russian being pulled along by camp policewomen 'literally torn apart by despair'. Another Russian, Marina Smelyanskaya, was seen by friends running towards the Red Army barracks screaming out that she'd been selected for the black transport. Olga Golovina recalled pulling Marina inside the block and dyeing her hair with carrot juice 'so she looked less like a Jew', said Olga. 'Then we hid her in the attic of the block. At night she came down and slept between me and Katzia Goreva. Just before dawn she went back up into the attic.'

In the *Revier*, the Red Army doctors got word that as many as ten Soviet names had been put on the list at the last minute, including Zoya Savel'eva. Now it was Zoya's turn to run screaming into the block, and as news reached Yevgenia Klemm that other Red Army women were on the list she resolved to act. The women of the Soviet block were called together, and a protest against the selections began.

'First we lined up in the block and marched out towards the front of the camp. We carried our sick along with us and went together,' said Olga Golovina. 'We shouted: "We don't want our sick to be transported."' Some said the Red Army women were then chased back to their block, where they barricaded themselves in, 'and we all stood there shoulder to shoulder refusing to respond to the numbers they called out,' said Leonida Boyko. SS men with guns as well as women guards managed to break down the doors. 'They beat us and slapped our faces.' Leonida went on:

> They finally managed to drag out the 'named' women as the rest of us started chanting for the head of the camp. He finally came and asked, who speaks German? 'I do,' said Klemm. 'You can't treat us like this, we are prisoners of war. There are recognised conventions on proper conduct for prisoners of war. Not one law in the world allows you to kill and burn alive sick and weak human beings. We are protesting against this black transport.'

Fritz Suhren seemed taken aback, then ordered the women out of the barracks 'before I shoot you like dogs'. At this the women came out, but called a three-day hunger strike to continue their protest. Most of those on the list were taken away, but Zoya Savel'eva stayed hidden at the top of one of the bunks.

The Soviet protest failed to halt the transport, but it certainly helped to cause a delay: the departure was put back by eight days. The destination of the transport may also have been altered due to the protest, because now the SS began to tell the prisoners that the transport was going to Lublin, and not to Auschwitz at all. 'I give you my word of honour as an officer that the transport is going to Lublin,' Treite told Carmen Mory. At Lublin the women would be 'cared for by the Polish Red Cross'.

A German woman berated Suhren on the Lagerstrasse, telling him she had lost six of her sons at the front, 'and now you are going to gas me'. Suhren gave her his 'word of honour' that the departing women were simply going to a better place at Lublin in order to be replaced by younger workers. 'You'll even be able to write to your families and tell them where you've gone,' he said. What neither Treite nor Suhren declared was that the better place was Majdanek concentration camp, on the edge of Lublin, still working in January 1944 as an extermination camp.

On 3 February 1944 about 900 selected women were finally gathered together on the Lagerplatz. Most had no idea that they had been chosen for the black transport, or why. A French schoolteacher from Brittany, Yvonne Le Tac, was collected that morning from her work gang – filling mattresses with straw – and made to march with the others to the station. Yvonne was never told why, but it was probably simply because she had grey hair; she was sixty-two years old. Those who couldn't walk were carried by stretcher. Rita Sprengel recalled that several of the Siemens women were 'sent to Lublin with the sick transport'.

Some women passed out on the way to the station. Two prisoners helped to load them, and when these prisoners came back they said the women were loaded up sixty to each cattle truck with no food and no buckets or WCs of any sort. The trucks were sealed and the trains moved off in the snow, towards Majdanek.

Krysia's report on the transport was posted to her family in Lublin a week later. From what she wrote it seems that the prisoners in the camp were still not certain that Lublin really was the destination, nor does it appear that Krysia yet knew about Majdanek. Her report stated:

> On 3rd Feb 44 an international transport of 945 women – elderly, ill and generally unable to work, left allegedly to Lublin (to be checked). There were 110 Polish women (many names we didn't know). They added Russian Red Army women, some disabled from the war. The Red Army women tried to protest but were threatened with decimation. Some of the women were sick, but many were healthy. Many had TB but would have been curable. We managed to get some off the lists. They left, 30 to each freight train. We know of 40 who passed out on the way to the station.

Krysia named one of the Poles on the transport as Kiryłło Rozalia (no. 7702), who had asked before she left that her family in Lublin be told. Krysia gave Rozalia's address, adding: 'She was ill but curable.'

In the weeks that followed, more news reached Ravensbrück about the fate of the departed women. Two guards who had travelled with the prisoners returned soon after and reported that the journey had taken at least three days and the train had to stop several times due to heavy snow. When the wagons were opened at Majdanek, scores were already dead, some of them frozen to the wagon floors. How many died on the journey nobody knew, nor did they know what became of the survivors.

Later came more news, sometimes from survivors of the transport who found themselves sent back again to Ravensbrück. One prisoner learned what happened to her mother from one of these same returnees. She said:

> The worst of all for my mother and the other women was the journey. All through the journey snow had blown into the carriages. When the trains had to stop the women had to march on foot in the deep snow. There was nothing to eat. After a long and awful march they arrived at Lublin. My mother was at her end. They killed her straight away with an injection.

Still more reports arrived stating that after some weeks in Majdanek survivors of the train journey were taken on to Auschwitz, where most disappeared and were presumed to have been gassed. A small number deemed still fit enough for work survived and worked at Auschwitz; one or two of this group were also returned full-circle to Ravensbrück. These women were able to confirm that most of their comrades taken on the Majdanek train had indeed then been gassed at Auschwitz.

During this time news had come of a different kind concerning the Majdanek transport. New prisoners were still arriving each week from Poland, among them more members of the underground. These women told friends in the camp that they'd heard a broadcast on English radio about a transport of women from Ravensbrück being sent off by train to be gassed. The broadcast went out on the underground radio station known as SWIT – Dawn Radio.

The news of this broadcast taking place sent a thrill through the camp, particularly among the secret letter writers. In her letters home, Krysia Czyż had pleaded for her information about 'these criminal acts' to be broadcast on English radio, and here was the first evidence it had happened. As German intelligence was known to monitor such radio stations, some of the Poles believed the SWIT broadcast might have contributed to the SS decision to delay the transport, and to the change in destination from Majdanek to Auschwitz, in order to mislead the outside world.

The precise date of the broadcast isn't known, and nor has the transcript been unearthed. However, a small number of SWIT transcripts, filed away as secret after the war, have recently come to light in British archives. Amongst these are others concerning Ravensbrück, including one transmitted two months after the Majdanek transport. The Ravensbrück material is based as usual on information smuggled by the rabbits, and was transmitted from the SWIT studio in the Buckinghamshire village of Milton Bryan to Polish underground cells, listening in secret.

On 3 May 1944, at 19.10 hours, SWIT broadcast ten items of news.

Number three on the list was headed: 'Roosevelt's Telegram: "Roosevelt in his telegram to the President of the Polish Republic stated that the determined fight of the Poles against the invader was an inspiration to all Nations fighting for a better world."' Other items concerned Spain's neutrality and new reports of 'destruction by the Germans of Polish culture'. Item number eight is headed 'Vivisection in Ravensbrück':

> In the concentration camp for women in Ravensbrück, the Germans are committing new crimes. The women in this camp are being submitted to vivisection experiments and are being operated on like rabbits. The authorities have made lists of all women who had to submit to such operations. It is feared that these records are being kept for the purpose of murdering these women so as to obliterate all traces of their crimes. These fears are substantiated by the fact that the camp is surrounded by trenches and mounted machine guns. At present there are close on 3000 Polish women in the Ravensbrück camp.

The report goes on with a 'Warning to Criminals':

> For the fate of the women in the concentration camp of Ravensbrück all Germans are responsible: SS officers and doctors of the administration of the camp. The prime responsibility therefore falls on the Commandant of the camp Hauptsturmführer Suhren; his Adjutant, Obersturmführer Bräuning; Kriminalassistent Ramdbehr [*sic*] and the chief woman guard Binz. All these we are warning solemnly that if any mass murders are committed, or if the vivisection experiments continue, they will be held responsible – they and their families. We have established their identity and we are finding out particulars about their families. May they remember that their days are numbered. We shall find them even if they were to hide under the earth. None of the hired assassins of Ravensbrück will escape justice. We shall wreak such vengeance that future generations will remember it. These crimes shall be avenged with a red-hot iron.

# PART FOUR

*Chapter 21*

# Vingt-sept Mille

On 1 February 1944 a crowd of women gathered on a station platform on the outskirts of Paris waiting for a train. It was cold, but the women were dressed in woollen coats or ski costumes; some even wore furs.

Denise Dufournier, a young Parisian lawyer, carried a rolled-up blanket taken from her prison cell, tied with plaited cord. Her friends Suzanne Hugounencq and Christiane de Cuverville carried kitbags made of canvas ripped from a mattress. Some women had packed their bags with lace pyjamas, powder compacts and eau de cologne, smuggled into Parisian jail cells by their families. Denise and her friends packed sausage, cheese and bread to eat on the journey. The three had become friends over months of imprisonment in the Paris prison of Fresnes. Now they stood on the platform guessing when they'd be back home.

The Allied landings were expected in May at the latest, so they'd definitely be back by Bastille Day, 14 July, said Christiane. A general's daughter, she had joined a resistance cell at seventeen without telling her parents; when her mother found that Christiane was arrested she marched into the Gestapo's Paris headquarters declaring, 'My daughter is not a terrorist. I want her back.'

Neither she nor any of the others were given a chance to tell their families they were leaving for Germany. Denise had lost both her parents when she was very young, and after living out the first phase of war with her brother Bernard, a French diplomat, in neutral Portugal, in 1942 she suddenly decided – against his advice – to return to France and join the resistance. Along with several other women here on the station platform, she worked with the Comet Line, an underground escape network that guided stranded Allied servicemen out of France, usually over the Pyrenees. She was arrested in the summer of 1943.

Though anxious, the mood was not gloomy. The women were pleased to be out of French prisons, and the worst they expected in Germany was hard labour, which they hoped would be in the open air. Anyone observing the group might have thought they looked more like a happy band leaving on a camping expedition than a group of prisoners going to a concentration camp. Most knew next to nothing about the camps, and those who did certainly didn't believe they'd be taken to such a place.

An opera singer from Orléans struck up with a Scottish ballad and even the '*groupe de comtesses*' maintained their esprit de corps, although several recoiled in horror at seeing a crowd of French prostitutes gather on the platform. The women had been arrested for infecting the Gestapo with VD, the countesses said.

As they waited, more women arrived. Geneviève de Gaulle was here, niece of the Free French leader. An elegant, reserved young woman, Geneviève was working on an underground newspaper in Paris when arrested, though of course the General knew nothing of it. Convent girls barely out of school, mostly resistance lookouts or couriers, stood beside older sisters who had cycled up to 50 miles a day delivering secret messages. Several members of the *Prosper* resistance circuit were here; the circuit had been run from London by SOE, the Special Operations Executive, but had been infiltrated by the Germans and decimated.

A group of French Red Cross nurses were here, a teacher from Normandy, a librarian from the Quartier Latin, and an eminent grey-haired art historian called Emilie Tillion. She had been arrested with her ethnologist daughter, Germaine, who had been taken off to Germany the previous October, though Emilie had no idea where she had gone.

Some on the platform had been warned of the risks they ran before embarking on resistance work. Cicely Lefort, a British SOE woman who landed in France by moonlight in a small Lysander plane, was told by her bosses back in Baker Street that she'd be shot if arrested. Most, however, knew little of the risks, and several, caught up in random Gestapo sweeps, had no idea why they were even here.

When the train locomotive arrived it pulled wagons, not carriages, and on the wagon doors were written the words: 'Men 40, horses 8'. Sixty women were loaded into each truck. A guard put a tin pot in the middle, then slammed the doors shut, locking each wagon with a bar and a lead seal fixed on top. Denise, Christiane and Suzanne, squashed together at one end of a wagon, heard Geneviève de Gaulle and her group strike up in song – '*Ce n'est qu'un au revoir mes frères'* – and then everyone sang the Marseillaise. Through chinks in the door they glimpsed railwaymen on the tracks and threw farewell notes. Cicely Lefort scribbled her husband's address in Brittany – he was a French doctor – with a note saying: 'Leaving for Germany. C'.

As the train moved towards the German border, it pulled up from time to time and soldiers opened doors to empty buckets. The women were thirsty, and struggled in the darkness with hands, arms and legs that were jolted and jarred. The smell grew nauseating. Over the border a German officer with a riding whip ordered everyone out. Denise observed that he 'didn't dare meet our glance for fear of seeing our confidence in our certain victory'.

Soup was offered at the next stop and soldiers shouted '*Arbeit, Arbeit*' and laughed, and the women laughed too. 'We still thought we were heading for Silesia to work, then we turned north so we thought, no it can't be that,' said Christiane.

Two more days, then at 2 a.m. on 3 February someone shouted: 'We've arrived.' As they tumbled out half dazed, the women stared at the guards and the dogs in utter disbelief. The French women's description of their arrival has a different tone to many other prisoners'. Though they were shocked by the brutality, what they remember most today is their inability to believe what they saw. 'The reality was so brutal and so hard we could hardly grasp it,' said Denise Dufournier. Some survivors said later they genuinely thought they had been brought here by mistake. Others say they simply refused to see what was in front of them. 'There was a healthy smell of resin and the air felt salty on the lips,' said Denise. 'Just to breathe the Baltic sea air was good,' said Michèle Agniel.

The women recall being 'half in a dream' as they trudged to the camp gates, and many stumbled and fell. 'Our bundles so carefully prepared but too hastily packed hampered us a lot,' said Denise. At the gates they passed 'without transition from pitch darkness into a blinding light'. Then someone said: 'Oh we've arrived at a concentration camp.' Others said: 'No! Are you mad? It can't be true.'

'Inside the gates we saw this "*stupeur des visages*" [stupefied faces]. It was obviously a place of death. We had a sense of entering an abattoir. Really it was like that. But we never thought we were going to stay here,' said Anise Girard. 'You see,' said Christiane de Cuverville, 'we were "*jeunes filles bien élevées*" – well brought-up young ladies – and we thought, this cannot be for us. It is a mistake. Someone will come along soon and take us on somewhere else.'

Walking on inside the camp they saw strange half-starved creatures like figures from the Middle Ages, carrying vats, and so now they began to think they'd all gone mad. 'Eat your food, they'll take everything from you,' said a figure darting forward.

In the bath they were stripped. 'And then the young ladies had to stand "*nues devant leur mère*". It was the worst. In those days the humiliation for French girls to be naked in front of their mothers was something terrible.' As heads were shaved the guards ransacked bags for eau de cologne. 'They searched us with toothbrushes between our legs,' said Amanda Staessart, a Belgian who was there with her mother.

After the shower they were taken to a temporary block for the rest of the night, crammed in with 'strange half-starved creatures', and some of the women were so terrified by the skeletons that they shouted to the guards to 'keep these monsters away' while others offered the skeletons their last bits of food. French prisoners who had arrived a few months earlier got word that friends or relatives were amongst the new group and tried to get messages to them. Germaine Tillion, who had arrived in October, heard that her mother, Emilie, was here.

At daybreak a woman with a vat of beet soup appeared, but the French women refused to believe the food was really for them either. One shouted: 'Come on, we can't eat this, let's eat our own and have a picnic,' so they made a picnic, sitting on their kitbags out in the snow, eating the left-over cheese and bread from their bags. They looked around to see who'd dare stop them, but so amazed were the guards and camp police that nobody did. Prisoners passing by whispered '*Französinnen*' and stared.

Inside their quarantine block, the French still refused to believe that anything was real, and told each other they'd be out of there as soon as the authorities learned their mistake. Meanwhile, the women told stories and recited poems and played their guessing game about the end of the war. They made up names for the '*Aufseherinnen*' – or '*officerines*', as the French called the guards. 'We'll live if we don't eat the soup,' said Christiane, who already had stomach cramps from the raw swede. Someone looked out of a window and saw prisoners kneeling sharing out a bit of bread, and what looked like women dressed as men walking on the path. The Blockova called them '*les Jules*'.

And if the mood was down, it only took one of them to say, 'Girls, I dreamt of shoes last night, which must mean we'll be returning soon,' and in a flash the rumour would go round that they'd be out by Bastille Day, and everyone would cheer and laugh.

'Yes we always tried to laugh,' says Christiane. 'You see, because we couldn't believe, it helped to laugh. I remember when my hair was shaved and someone said: "*Mais dis donc*, hey, Christiane – it suits you,"' and she laughs. 'The other groups were far more serious. The Poles were very serious. I remember the day soon after we arrived and the Polish Blockova was ordering us to clean up because Himmler was coming to inspect. But we French refused to budge. So she was very angry and she said: "Himmler is coming and the whole camp trembles but you French just laugh."'

The inspection by Himmler that made the French laugh is not noted in his official diary, but the German prisoner Klara Tanke remembers the Reichsführer's visit some time in the early months of 1944 because he ordered her release 'after four years, six months and fourteen days in the camp'. He was looking for women to work in his Berlin office, which had lost staff in the recent bombings. Klara recalled: 'He picked out eight big blonde women and I was one.'

The timing of Himmler's inspection almost certainly coincided with another visit to Häschen, who was expecting a second child. He was much in need of a break from the pressures of the war, particularly on the Russian front. According to Felix Kersten, his masseur, the Reichsführer's health had not been good since January. After a treatment session, Kersten noted on 15 January 1944 that Himmler was 'depressed in mind as well as in health'. From Kersten's account, he was most depressed about matters of propagation – both animal and vegetable – which were not working out as he had once hoped.

Despite the mass killing, Russia's population was still growing at the rate of three million a year. It was 'like the hydra in the Greek myth. If you cut off its head, seven more grow in its place.' Furthermore, Himmler complained, the Russians had developed a new breed of corn that could withstand extreme cold, and this had enabled them to reclaim more land to the north and to grow more corn for feeding their troops.

It was not only the broad strategic issues of propagation, according to Kersten, that were troubling Himmler; more localised breeding questions were on his mind. For example, too few SS officers were marrying and producing children. The Reichsführer SS had also requested a report on how best to produce boys rather than girls. If Germany's women spent too much time in bomb shelters there would be little procreation at all, he told Kersten.

Himmler's comments show how by early 1944 even he had begun to accept – in private, at least – the limitations, perhaps even the madness, of the Nazi project. He had also begun to concede the possibility of defeat, speaking to Kersten of the need to put out feelers to the Americans and British, who 'would soon realise the danger of Russian predominance on the continent' and seek a separate peace with Germany. Himmler had even asked Kersten to go to Sweden to seek out possible negotiating partners in Washington and London, and to reward him Himmler had given his loyal masseur his own estate not far from Ravensbrück, as well as a handful of women prisoners – Jehovah's Witnesses – to work on the estate as slaves.

Despite these private doubts, however, in public Himmler, like his master, displayed absolute certainty in a German victory. In a series of speeches made to party officials and to his SS generals at Posen over the winter of 1943–4, he glorified the Führer's achievements, particularly his success in 'eradicating the plague of Jews'. In this area Himmler claimed that he had, indeed, been able to control propagation. He even explained, in unprecedented detail, why it had been necessary to take the 'difficult decision' to kill Jewish women and children as well as the men; it was done, he said, in order to prevent a new generation of avengers:

> We come to the question: how is it with the women and children. I have resolved even here on a completely clear solution. That is to say I do not consider myself justified in eradicating the men – so to speak killing or ordering them killed – and allowing the avengers in the shape of the children to grow up for our sons and grandsons. The difficult decision had to be taken, to cause this *Volk* to disappear from the earth.

Yet even as he talked of victory, Himmler was hedging his bets. He had started to gather hostages and hold them in his camps as bargaining chips, ready for when his secret peace negotiations began. Some of those chips were held at Ravensbrück.

The gulf between theory and reality was as clear to see at the camp in early 1944 as anywhere else in Himmler's empire. The Reichsführer had ordered death rates reduced to keep good workers alive, but instead the rates were rising and a new crematorium furnace was being built to cope.

Himmler's dietary theories were being confounded at every turn. He had recently issued new rulings on nutrition with a view to improving production. Up to 50 per cent of vegetables added to the prisoners' soup were to be raw, and added shortly before distribution; the amount of food at midday should be one and a quarter to one and a half litres of soup – not clear but pureed. Himmler had also insisted that the prisoners should have time and 'calm' to eat, so that digestion could happen properly. However, as was clear from the camp's emaciated bodies, the raw root vegetables were wreaking havoc, causing scabies and sores. As for the mealtime calm, so crammed were the blocks by now that there was never room to sit. The Siemens workers marched back from the factory for lunch barely had time to eat at all.

Other orders issued by Himmler and designed to improve camp hygiene, and hence production, had also proved futile. Prisoners should have time to wash their hair, supposedly to help prevent lice, but washing of any sort was almost impossible, and anyhow the recycled clothes coming from the gas chambers invariably had lice already breeding in the hems. Coupons were still on offer as an incentive for good work, to be spent at the prisoner shop, but the shop was empty and the coupons had sparked a protest because prisoners objected to being bribed.

Two further incentives Himmler dreamt up were free tobacco and a visit to a brothel. Neither applied to Ravensbrück: women were banned from using tobacco, and it was women from the camp who provided the incentive in the brothels. In early 1944 he ordered brothels to open at three more men's camps, with prostitutes as usual supplied by Ravensbrück.

Yet even the standard of the prostitutes was falling, as Himmler had obviously observed because he called for measures to improve their appearance. In the early days, he could rely on Ravensbrück to produce a steady stream of professionals for his camp brothels, not least because German asocials were often brought here straight from working brothels and knew what was required. Nowadays, however, even the German asocials arriving there were of 'poorer quality', which was not surprising, as they were often no more than homeless women snatched for loitering on the streets of bombed-out German cities. Himmler therefore ordered that the SS try them out before they were hired.

But far greater problems were looming. For example, what was the camp to do in future with the growing number of women who ceased to be of any use? The last transport of about 900 useless mouths had left Ravensbrück on 3 February to be taken to the Majdanek death camp, but Soviet forces were now approaching Majdanek and the death camp was about to be closed down.

And what was Ravensbrück to do about the rising pregnancy rate? It was no easy task to sift out pregnant women before they arrived, and the doctors simply couldn't abort all the babies, especially as the chief abortionist, Rolf Rosenthal, was now in prison. Rosenthal had been sentenced to eight years after making the prisoner-midwife Gerda Quernheim pregnant – at least twice – and then carrying out abortions to terminate her pregnancies. Himmler had reviewed his plea for clemency, and knew the disturbing details.

In his appeal, Rosenthal tried to explain his relationship with the prisoner Quernheim, saying that while at the camp his marriage had fallen into difficulties, as he and his wife could not bear children. According to Quernheim, whose evidence Himmler also read, the couple became intimate when left alone at night in the operating theatre. On these occasions she would offer him a cup of tea, 'because he would tell me his wife never cooked dinner and failed to care for him'. Rosenthal, she said, had been particularly kind to her the evening she learned her mother had been injured in a bombing raid.

When Gerda found she was pregnant there was no choice but to abort, and so Rosenthal carried it out. Gerda, however, was upset by the termination. Longing to keep the foetus, she preserved it in alcohol and kept it in a bottle in the Ravensbrück *Revier*. Surely no single image could better symbolise the tragic absurdity of the Nazi attempt to control the process of reproduction, though whether Himmler saw it that way seems doubtful.

Himmler did, however, consider that there were mitigating factors in the case and reduced Rosenthal's sentence from eight to six years, to be spent in the Dachau police cells. Quernheim was soon sent to Auschwitz to work again as a midwife, but first she spent a term in the Ravensbrück bunker.

On his way back to the gates, Himmler liked to inspect the bunker, which for some months had served not only to punish prisoners but as a useful place for him to hold his secret hostages and other prominent captives who might in the future be of use. In March 1944 the *Prominente* included the mistress of a former French prime minister, an American pilot, a Polish countess and a German cabaret dancer.

The pilot had parachuted from his stricken plane, and having landed nearby, was brought to the camp. Christiane Mabire, an elegant Parisian, had been private secretary to Paul Reynaud, the last French prime minister before the war. The dancer was Isa Vermehren, famous for her cabaret shows for German troops. Isa was arrested for being rude about the Führer, though it was only when her brother, a German diplomat, defected to Britain that she was brought to Ravensbrück.*

Most prominent of the *Prominente* was probably Helmuth von Moltke, great-grand-nephew of the Prussian war hero Helmuth von Moltke senior. An Oxford-educated lawyer, and leader of a German resistance group, the 'Kreisau Circle', von Moltke junior had long been a thorn in the Führer's side, though Himmler must have known he was no serious threat. The worst that von Moltke had done was to try to stir Germany's conscience by campaigning for non-violent resistance and for implementation of the Geneva Conventions in the camps. He had also leaked information on Nazi war crimes to friends in the British Foreign Office, offering to go to any lengths to assist them, but they rebuffed him, asking for deeds not words.

Also held in the bunker was a mysterious British major, Frank Chamier, who refused to give Isa Vermehren his name, identifying himself only as 'Frank of Upwey 282', which would turn out to be his home telephone number.

* Once in England, Isa's brother Erich had begun to broadcast against Hitler on the BBC and also wrote propaganda leaflets which were dropped over Germany by British and American planes. 'As a result of this,' Isa said, 'I was arrested and put into Ravensbrück. My father and mother and another brother were also arrested and went to Sachsenhausen.'

Of the Ravensbrück hostages, the Polish countess Karolina Lanckorońska was of most value to Himmler at this point. A renowned art historian, she had been teaching at the University of Lwów, in Poland, when the Soviets invaded in 1939. Horrified by the murder of several fellow university professors, she at once joined the Polish resistance, first against the Soviets, then against the Germans, until she was captured and sent to Ravensbrück. However, it was not what Karolina had done, but who she knew, that was of interest to Himmler. When she was arrested, not only did the Italian royal family write directly to the Reichsführer SS appealing for her release, but so, in the strictest secrecy, did the head of the International Red Cross in Geneva, Carl Burckhardt, a long-time friend of the countess's. Karolina was even, according to some, the love of his life.

Given the ICRC's refusal to accept a role in helping the Jews and other camp prisoners, Burckhardt's appeal for a personal friend was incriminating, and he removed his letters from the ICRC files after the war. Some of Himmler's replies, however, have survived, and show Burckhardt appealed to the Reichsführer over Karolina at least three times. In the summer of 1942 he wrote asking Himmler where Karolina was being held, to which Himmler replied saying he would find out. In autumn 1942 Burckhardt even asked Himmler for a meeting to discuss her case. This intervention showed special hypocrisy on Burckhardt's part, given that at precisely that time he was advising his Red Cross colleagues, at their landmark meeting in November 1942, to remain silent about those in the camps.

As a result of Burckhardt's letters Himmler obviously realised Lanckorońska was a valuable hostage, and from the moment she reached Ravensbrück he made sure she was treated exceptionally well. Her cell was fitted with the best white linen, and decked with fresh flowers. She was to be known in the camp under the pseudonym 'Frau Lange', and allowed to order books from the SS library and to roam around the bunker and the garden beneath her cell, chatting to inmates and guards. It was thanks to this last privilege that Karolina, a colourful and controversial character, was later able to give a picture of life in the Ravensbrück bunker.

Amongst the first prisoners she encountered were two clairvoyants who had been punished for predicting the future for SS clients, and in a nearby cell was Gerda Quernheim, who appeared to Karolina to be a 'gentle and well-mannered girl' who 'at the first sight of my food parcels took a great fancy to me and told me absolutely everything she knew'. Quernheim even answered Karolina's questions about the abortions, admitting that it was a 'nasty subject'.

Karolina also met two German guards, one of them imprisoned for stealing prisoners' clothes from the *Effektenkammer* and the other for lesbianism, which Karolina said was 'widespread among the German women in the camp'. The same lesbian told Karolina about Ramdohr's special prisoners, locked up without light or food, and she gossiped about the bunker guard Margarete Mewes, who had three children, 'each by a different father', and about Dorothea Binz, 'the real power in the camp', but only because she was having an affair with Suhren's deputy, Bräuning. The two of them were often seen holding hands when prisoners were beaten on the *Bock*, said the woman, adding that the silk underwear hanging out to dry beside the bunker belonged to Binz, who had stolen it from a prisoner, and she knew which prisoner, but would not tell. Another of the bunker guards was 'built like a Valkyrie' but was sympathetic and helped Karolina to smuggle food to the dungeon prisoners and to the two clairvoyants.

Quite often Suhren used to pop in and ask if there was anything else the countess wanted, offering to order books for her from the SS library, though Karolina said she preferred Wordsworth and Tacitus to the camp's Nazi tracts, so the commandant arranged for her to order those in.*

Walking in the small flowerbed outside, Karolina observed the Fürstenberg spire and wondered how it was that her 'beloved German culture had been so degraded'. Her musings were always spoiled by the smell from the chimney, which the German lesbian later told her came from burning hair.

Out in the garden she chatted about the classics to Christiane Mabire, often watched over by Dorothea Binz, lounging in a nearby deckchair. Lanckorońska's observations of Binz strike a different tone to almost every other prisoner. To the countess she posed no threat, seeming almost lonely, and adopting a subservient manner towards Himmler's 'Frau Lange'. She would chat about this and that, and told the Polish countess one day that she was a cook by profession, lived locally and was twenty-two years old.

Not only did Karolina have no fear of Binz, her dog did not frighten her either. It seemed to Karolina to be a sad and scrawny mongrel, and not the monstrous hound described by other prisoners. It always seemed hungry when Karolina passed, and flung itself at her, sniffing persistently at her pocket in the hope of finding some food. 'Isn't it nice to see how much he loves you,' said Binz one day, with a smile.

* When Karolina's copy of Tacitus arrived, Binz informed her that the commandant had confiscated it because it contained 'Catholic prayers'. Puzzled, Karolina asked to see the book, which was in fact Petrarch's sonnets. She explained to Binz these were not Catholic prayers but love poems, and she was allowed to have the book. 'So ended what I am sure was Binz's only encounter with Petrarch,' commented Karolina later. 'Presumably the phrase "Madonna mia" gave rise to the error.'

We don't know if Karolina ever met Himmler on his visits, but she describes his 'bleak eyes, staring down from behind their pince-nez', from a portrait on the wall in the bunker office. While she was in the bunker, he ordered a box of his prize tomatoes to be sent daily to her cell.

As he left the camp, Himmler would have observed the prisoners assembled for *Appell*. He may well have noticed how international Ravensbrück had recently become – letters stamped on prisoners' triangles denoted twenty-two countries represented. He must also have noticed a very large number of yellow stars.

Fifteen months earlier, Himmler had boasted to Hitler that Germany and all its concentration camps were *judenfrei* – free of Jews. But theory and practice conflicted again, because lined up on the Ravensbrück Appellplatz were now at least 400 Jews: the mixed-race women from Auschwitz and the 'protected' Jews – nationals of Germany's allies or of neutrals – who had been spared the gas chamber, at least for now. The majority of the 'protected' Jews were of Hungarian, Romanian and Turkish origin, and had been living in the Netherlands or Belgium. Not only were Jewish women from these countries standing there on the Appellplatz, but so were their children – the very 'avengers' whom Himmler claimed in his Posen speech had 'disappeared'. One of these 'avengers' was Stella Kugelman, a four-year-old child with big black eyes.

Stella remembers little of her arrival at the camp, except that it was night, and her mother, Rosa, collapsed as soon as she stepped off the train. Stella also has only fleeting memories of her life in the camp itself. Paradoxically, however, she knows a great deal about her first four years, before she arrived at Ravensbrück, because she has her mother's diary, in which Rosa described almost every day of Stella's life from the day she was born until the Gestapo came.

Rosa Kugelman (née Klionski) was Lithuanian, and her husband Louis Kugelman, a Spaniard – both were Jews. Rosa and Louis both lived in London during the 1920s, where they met. Then they moved to Antwerp, where Stella was born one month before the outbreak of war, on 29 July 1939. Eighteen months later the Gestapo came to the door – the first event in her life that Stella remembers. She recalls a car driving up 'and police telling us to pack our things and go. I remember it was a bright sunny day.'

First the family were taken to a camp in Belgium, where Rosa and Stella were separated from Stella's father. He was sent to Buchenwald, while they were taken by train to Ravensbrück. Stella thinks she remembers saying to her mother in the train: 'Let's run away.' Her mother was already very sick with TB and too weak to attempt escape, so she stroked Stella's long black plaited hair and tried to smile.

It was the sight of the dogs on arrival at Fürstenberg that made Rosa shriek, thinks Stella. And when the truncheons hit her mother on the platform she collapsed and was immediately taken away, but Stella didn't know where.

Left alone, someone must have taken her hand and led her on, she thinks, because somehow, later, she was in a block. Her plaits had been cut off. There were other children there, and many were very sick. Older women looked after her. And Stella remembers that when her hair grew back, a French woman combed it.

*Chapter 22*

# Falling

'R*aus raus, Franzosensäue. Links rechts, links rechts,*' shout the guards, but the French can't march. Only Christiane the general's daughter can keep in step; most don't even try. As they leave quarantine the women are herded down to their new blocks at the back of the camp. '*Links rechts, links rechts.*' A straggler is kicked. 'It's the maquis down here,' says Denise as they approach Block 27. Some call this line of blocks – 27 to 31 – the slums. With peeling paint and broken windows, they stand so far back in the compound that they are built on sand.

As they enter, the women recoil. Arms blotched with sores reach for the evening soup. In quarantine the French had at first refused the soup. Four weeks later they grab bowls along with the rest. Suzanne's bowl is snatched. She complains to the woman serving, a Pole, who answers in French: 'So what are you going to eat with then?' Suzanne is shoved aside. 'Typical Slav,' says Denise. 'Just because she's been here four years already and we haven't.'

Someone shouts at the thief, a Russian, who shouts back, '*Ne ponimayu, ne ponimayu.*' The French girl throws herself at the Russian, shouting, '*Ne ponimayu* yourself, you brute,' but someone else explains that '*Ne ponimayu*' means 'I don't understand'.

'This is not so funny,' says Christiane. A Stubova tells Suzanne to go and look in the bins for an old tin discarded from a prisoner's food parcel. 'So others get food parcels?'

The French stare and the other slum-dwellers stare back: 'A bowl for a piece of bread?'

'*Du Scheisse Französinnen*,' shouts someone in the crowd. 'A nice welcome,' whispers Christiane, not noticing that a woman dressed as a man is watching her with hungry eyes. These are the *Jules* they heard about in quarantine. The Belgian Amanda Staessart takes her mother's arm, promising they'll stay together. Their numbers are consecutive, so they can't be split up.

Denise exclaims, 'Look at that' as she catches sight of another group of repellent creatures, but these speak some sort of French. They are what the *jeunes filles bien élevées* call *les volontaires* – French women who had 'volunteered' to come and work in Germany. The *volontaires* had been brought to Ravensbrück too, accused perhaps of a 'crime' – stealing bread or having sex with a German – or more likely to be used for slave labour in the subcamps. 'So we are in with the French gangsters too,' says Denise.

In the next block – Block 26 – the women are also lining up for soup when a guard comes in; she is young, pretty and blonde, and carries a stick. 'She looks OK,' says one of the French girls, then the guard shouts, '*Ruhe du alte Sau, ruhig toi, cochon*' – 'Quiet, you old pig, quiet, you pig' – and the pretty pale face snarls and her stick comes down on one of the French 'volunteers'. The girl had tried to style her hair in a knot on top of her head.

'*Französin*?' She nods. 'Who is this?' asks the blonde guard, turning to her interpreter, a prisoner, who gives a name then explains in French, trembling, that hair must be pulled back and flat, and anyone who disobeys will be beaten to death. Observing the effect of these words on the French faces, the guard turns and leaves. The Polish Blockova shouts: '*Achtung, alle ins Bett*' – 'Attention, everyone in bed.'

So tightly packed are the bunks that to climb to the third tier you clamber like a monkey. At night it's impossible to reach the lavatories without walking over hundreds of others, and many don't bother, as is obvious from the stench.

Denise, Suzanne and Christiane share a single mattress. There is one blanket between them and they lie in the mould left in the straw by the night workers who slept here in the day. Christiane's nose nearly touches the roof. If she straightens an arm she touches the French peasant in the next bunk who is shouting for her daughter.

The next they know is the Polish Blockova shouting, '*Raus, raus, Achtung*,' and the siren screaming for morning *Appell*.

So large is the camp now that the waking siren has been brought forward to 3 a.m. It takes a strong hand to beat these women out of bunks, washrooms and outdoors by 3.30. The 959 new French arrivals line up to be counted with their comrades in arms: Paris, Montluc, Fresnes, Dijon and Toulon, standing motionless under the stars. Their triangles are red, for political prisoners, and their numbers run from 27030 to 27988. But they have not been given their 'F' for French, as the Poles have been given a 'P' and the Russians an 'R', or, for the Red Army, 'S.U.' This is deliberate, they say. The Germans want to crush French national pride. But the group is so large it soon gets its own name and becomes the *vingt-sept mille*, referring to the numbers given to this transport, all in the 27000s.

'The bitches,' one of the French girls whispers as guards appear wrapped in thick black capes, their blonde curls impeccable even at this hour.

It is cold and getting colder. Christiane is tall enough to see right down the Lagerstrasse over the heads of 18,000 others, lined up in an infinite throng of ghostly figures. Annie de Montfort has a shaved head, bare to the sky, and sparkling with a thin covering of frost. The red flame of the crematorium chimney lights up the end of the Lagerstrasse.

'*Die Nase nach vorne, Franzosensäue*,' yells a guard – 'Noses to the front, French sows.'

'*Les vaches!*' retort the 'volunteers'.

Guards thump those who stamp their feet for warmth. A blast of freezing air cuts through the women's thin clothing, then a whisper passes down the line, 'Stand firm, *les Françaises*,' but someone is missing and the count starts all over again as a row of bodies collapses, one by one, 'like ninepins felled by some invisible ball'. Among those down is the librarian from the Quartier Latin.

The missing woman is finally dragged out. Everyone watches her defend herself with flailing limbs against a corpulent figure with a red armband who grabs her by the hair, turns her over, pulls out a whip and gives her four lashes on her back. The woman no longer moves. Is she dead? The figure disappears into the darkness.

'It's Thury. Thury? Is she a guard? No, she's another prisoner.' The women are horrified to find they are guarded by prisoners too. An Austrian, Elisabeth Thury is head of the 'camp police'. '*La vache*,' say the French, staring at Thury.*

From another direction comes a 'crow' on a bicycle, and as she pedals she sees a woman stick out her tongue at her. It is an old French peasant woman, and she's yelling in a Pyrenean dialect that not even the other French can

* Elisabeth Thury, a social democrat and journalist, had been arrested in Vienna on the first day of the war for anti-Nazi activity. At Ravensbrück, she had been picked for work sorting out the filing system in the camp clothes store, and graduated to head of the camp police in 1943. Isa Vermehren, the bunker hostage, said Thury was 'power-hungry and vulgar' and her 'blows were feared'. She had 'a big head, grey hair in a men's style' and sometimes conducted a camp choir 'with savage sentimentality'. Others said Thury managed to protect prisoners from a certain amount of SS violence.

understand. The crow dismounts and kicks her, and she falls. '*Alte Sau. Franzosensau.*'

A desk is erected on the Lagerstrasse where Binz sits to check the count. Eventually, returning to their block, the *vingt-sept mille* are stiff and silent, and the sobs start. An old woman implores Denise to rub her hands very gently as they hurt so. Amanda Staessart notices that her mother's hair has gone quite white.

No sooner have they drunk their 'coffee' than the women are marched out again to join the *Verfügs*, casual workers, for the labour roll call.

The Parisian trio are set to shovelling sand. Denise suggests they try to build sand castles to help distract them, and as they walk back at the end of the day they feel fit enough to march around the block 'for no other reason than to show off'. Other prisoners observe the French in astonishment, murmuring: '*Französinnen.*'

There had always been 'slums' of a sort in the camp – blocks more cramped and dirtier than others, usually towards the back, and occupied by asocials, Gypsies and others at the bottom of the heap. In early 1944 the slum area was so big it became official; blocks 27 to 32 were cordoned off behind barbed wire. Block 27, built for 200 prisoners, now held 600, and more were arriving every day.

Most Russians and Ukrainians were brought to the slum blocks, as well as the Jews who were arriving again at the camp. All the French were brought here automatically. There were no exceptions: the French countesses, teachers, generals' daughters, 'volunteers' and prostitutes were all '*Franzosensäue*'.

Suhren had made sure to put Poles in charge of them as their Blockovas and Stubovas, thinking that they detested the French for leaving Poland undefended in 1939. Four years ago it was the Poles who had been at the bottom of the heap, hated and despised, but over time many had prised themselves out of the slums, and it was the French who were hated now – perhaps even more than the Poles ever were.

The real camp aristocrats at the top end of the camp kept away from the slums because of filth and disease, and also because of vigilante gangs.* Even the guards had largely withdrawn from the area, leaving it in the hands of the prisoner police. Inside the blocks though it was often the powerful *Puffmütter* (brothel madams), like 'Clap' Wanda, who ran things.

Anja Lundholm, a German prisoner sent to Ravensbrück in 1944, wrote

* One such gang was the 'Holy Ghost–Kommando'. According to the prisoner Joanna Baumann, the five-prisoner gang 'dealt with prisoners who stole from others or betrayed them'. For example, a prostitute from Dortmund who made others do her heavy work was beaten up.

later about a woman nicknamed Clap Wanda, who had worked in a military brothel before the war and was famous in the camp for infecting a whole troop of German soldiers with gonorrhoea. But Wanda had not been arrested for spreading disease, but because she strangled her newborn son, threw him in a bin and called out: 'Here's your present, my Führer.'

Characters like Wanda were useful to the authorities as informers, and also for helping pick out women for the brothels. She was told to look for new arrivals who were 'healthy and well-fed'. According to Anja Lundholm, Clap Wanda herself was 'flabby, with a bloated face and repellent appearance, always surrounded by a clique of submissive women – all German black or green triangles whom she bossed around'.

Submissive women of the kind that Wanda might take under her wing were arriving every week at the camp, usually more German 'asocials' made homeless by the bombing. One such was Lydia Thelen. Arrested by police in 1943 for loitering in the waiting room at Cologne railway station, she told interrogators that her husband had served in the Sudetenland offensive and was now away serving in France. She said that their apartment had been destroyed in the Allied bombing and everything she had was lost. She lived on money from the war damages office. But the city police suspected Lydia of prostitution. They said she was a danger to the *Volk* and sent her to Ravensbrück, where she died in October 1944.

At night Clap Wanda would gather her clique around her to tell stories, Anja Lundholm recalled. 'Wanda liked to be entertained by stories of love, sex or tragedy,' and Anja herself became one of those storytellers. She was so good at it that Wanda rewarded her with bits of food, which made Anja hated and envied by others in the block.

The French general's daughter, Christiane de Cuverville, who lived alongside such characters in Block 27 and lives today in the exclusive 16th district of Paris, visibly shudders as she remembers women such as Clap Wanda. 'Yes, there were women like that – *quelle horreur*.' It was *la pagaille* – bedlam – she says, and then she folds her long legs under her, laughs and talks about the *Jules*.

'The first time I was propositioned by a *Jules* she offered me a piece of chocolate. They had trousers and jackets and walked around with cigarettes in their mouths looking for a fight or for sex. Block 27 was impossible – *affreux*, dreadful. This crowd you can't imagine – the Russians, the Gypsies, and the criminals from German jails, *les Jules, les Charlies*.'

After the first few days in the sand the Parisians' hands hardened as their skin turned grey – their clothes, their mess tins, mattresses, full of sand. Many of the sand gang now had diarrhoea because their stomachs simply couldn't digest the raw swede soup, which according to Denise Dufournier was 'a yellowish liquid giving off a noxious smell'. Cystitis spread too, because there was no water to drink – only the 'black stuff called coffee'.

Within weeks almost all the French of the *vingt-sept mille* transport were covered in boils and several had succumbed to TB. Those who said on arrival that they wouldn't get lice were scratching sores.

Some believed that if they could just get work indoors things might improve. Everyone knew those chosen for Siemens were better fed to eke more work out of them, but they didn't look much better off, coming off the night shift 'like ghosts at dawn'. For the three Parisians, Denise, Christiane and Suzanne, the idea of making German munitions was the worst horror of all, so they kept their heads down and stuck with digging sand.

Others simply couldn't bear the torture of *Appell*. One morning a woman standing close to Amanda Staessart collapsed. When a guard set her dog on the stricken woman, Amanda cried, 'What are you doing, you brute?', so she was sent to the *Strafblock* and put to work shovelling excrement from the latrines, along with the Countess Yvonne de La Rochefoucauld.

The countess had been working in the *Revier* as a nurse when she was given an order she didn't understand, so she shouted back, 'The English are coming, so you'd better learn English. The Germans have lost the war.' She might have got off with a punch, but Carmen Mory, Ramdohr's informer, overheard and reported her. The French said Mory looked like a figure from Hieronymus Bosch.

The freezing winter melted into a cold, wet spring. Water poured through the roofs of the slums, and at work, sodden sand caked on women's feet. Denise, Christiane and Suzanne began to hate the sand and the lake. Their legs had broken out in boils, but they wouldn't go to the *Revier*. They had seen the doctor – a new man, called Orendi – when they first arrived, and would never go back. He clearly loathed the French. When they went for their inspection on arrival he had made them undress and stand outside in the freezing cold 'as if it were the most natural thing in the world to undress in a public place, in the open air, in temperatures below zero,' wrote Denise. The SS dentist, Martin Hellinger, checked teeth for gold 'so he could recover it later'.

All the French women's periods had stopped, and some noticed symptoms of early menopause. Gynaecological tests were carried out to see who had venereal disease, and the same instruments were used without cleansing for each woman, so many caught diseases from others. Some were made to swallow a substance that made them break out all over in septic spots.

Older women and the very sick went back to the hospital, nevertheless, in the vain hope of treatment. 'Where do you work?' Orendi would ask them, and if the woman had a job at Siemens or in the sewing shop she might get an *Innendienst*, a permit to work indoors.*

Usually, however, at his *Revier* 'surgery' Orendi just walked past the sick or kicked the patients out. '*Es ist für das Reich. Sie müssen arbeiten gehen, krank oder nicht.*' ('It is for the Reich. You must go to work, sick or not.') On other days, he walked past the queue of sick, turned and grinned, drew his gun from his holster and pretended to take aim and fire. He laughed and shouted: 'It would be better if I just shoot a few.' The women screamed and he shouted again: 'Why not? You'll die anyway.'

When Amanda Staessart was taken in sick from the latrine gang she heard that her mother was in the *Revier*.

> Someone said: 'Come and see your mother, she is very bad.' So I was taken to her and she said I'll get better if you give me a little milk. And then she died. I stayed with her. I stayed for hours. A nurse came and told me: 'Take your mother away.' I had to drag her to the washroom.
>
> Yes, I did it myself. I had to drag her. I don't know how I did it. And I stayed with her in the washroom until the truck came. It was a truck with thirty dead bodies on it. And they put my mother naked on top and took her away.

Every nationality in the camp seems to have noticed how quickly the French began to fall. Some said they had only themselves to blame. The Czechs grumbled that if only the French had learned to wash they could have prevented the scabies, the swollen legs and the boils. The French were afraid of washing in cold water, said one Czech woman, 'but we Czechs had known nothing else before the war'. Even when they fell sick the French would pretend it wasn't happening, and claim that they were suffering from a lack of vitamins.

A Red Army doctor, Ida Grinberg, noticed the French 'were very emotional and shouted a lot'. Others said the French spent too much time trying to beautify themselves by putting grease on their faces, or making bows out of rags or arranging their clothes in stylish ways. The Russians remembered that they often managed to look 'quite chic'. Some of the old hands noted

* Such was the level of sickness at Siemens in February 1944 that Richard Trommer, the head doctor, paid an unprecedented visit to the plant, though his intention was not to treat the sick but to weed out the weakest-looking women before important visitors arrived. Two days after Trommer's inspection a high-level delegation from Berlin came to inspect the Siemens works.

that the French had no organisation, no leadership. In any case, they had no time to organise before their health began to fail, and then it was too late.

The French had no support on arrival: no French Blockovas to watch out for them, no one in the kitchen to slip them extra food. They had no influence at all; they had arrived too late, when the good jobs had gone. And anyway, they didn't want the Germans' jobs and spurned other prisoners for working for the SS, like Countess Karolina Lanckorońska, who became Blockova of Block 27.

After several months in the privileged bunker, Karolina Lanckorońska had requested to return to the normal camp, believing that her place was with the other Poles, but instead she was sent to rule over the French. At first she looked forward to meeting other women of 'high culture', as she knew the French to be. Instead, she complained, she found 'a rabble of women who refused to do anything to help themselves'.

Each morning a gang from every block went to the *Brotkammer* (bread store) to collect the block's bread, but the French could never get there in time. 'One had to literally throw them out of the block or we all went hungry,' said Lanckorońska, though she conceded that the containers were heavy and the French prisoners were weak. 'But there was nothing to be done about it.'

Furthermore, the French 'set out to cause trouble'. Getting them out for roll call was 'a hideous affair' because French 'agitators' deliberately confused the count by whispering 'Form ranks of nine, form ranks of eleven' when they knew perfectly well it was supposed to be ranks of ten. Binz would turn up and say to Lanckorońska, '*Natürlich die Französinnen!*' and she would order two hours' standing punishment, 'which meant another few cases of pneumonia'.

No prisoners in the camp observed the new French arrivals more intently than Germaine Tillion, the French ethnologist, and her friend Anise Girard, who had both spent four months in the camp by the time their compatriots of the *vingt-sept mille* arrived. 'When they first entered the camp the sight was so optimistic and gay that it gave us hope – they were a ball of oxygen,' said Anise Girard. 'But at the same time we were full of dread. They arrived thinking the war was over. They were so unprepared. It was tragic what happened.'

By early 1944, however, Germaine and Anise were arguably even worse off than the newcomers. In February both were assigned to a mysterious new block, Block 32. It lay in the very back of the camp, near the slum blocks, but was even more isolated, set right back against a rear wall. About 300 women were selected without warning for Block 32 and told they would have to obey an entirely new, draconian, set of rules.

No contact was allowed with those in Block 32; there was a no-go area around it and it had its own cordon of barbed wire. Prisoners there were not allowed outside the camp walls and forbidden to send or receive mail. None of them knew it, but they had been designated as NN – *Nacht und Nebel* – which meant they were supposed to literally disappear into the night and the fog, and nobody would ever know where.

The Norwegian visitor Wanda Hjort had first discovered the existence of this sinister category in 1943 when she heard that Norwegian prisoners held at Natzweiler in Alsace were designated NN, and she passed the information on to the International Red Cross. But nobody knew that in January 1944 an NN block was opened for women at Ravensbrück.

Hitler passed the so-called 'Night and Fog' decree in December 1941, and intended it to terrorise and deter resisters in western European countries. In the first years of Nazi occupation, resistance ringleaders were executed, but Hitler thought that created martyrs. Under the NN decree, dangerous resisters were to be sent to concentration camps instead, and executed in secret, their names and whereabouts never to be made known. In this way, Hitler intended that their families and friends would suffer as well, by living in perpetual uncertainty.

Some time in the winter of 1944 the same order was applied to a small number of Ravensbrück women, mostly prisoners from France, Belgium, the Netherlands and Norway, as well as a few Yugoslavs and Poles. Also held in the NN block were the Red Army women and the Polish rabbits.

Neither Germaine nor Anise understood why the rules of their imprisonment suddenly changed. 'It all seemed random,' said Anise. 'Why did they shave one head and not another? Why shoot one woman one day and another the next? We never knew. In the end we understood that there was no logic to anything they did. Our stories were not much different to other French who arrived.'

Germaine's mother, Emilie Tillion, who had arrived with the *vingt-sept mille*, was not designated NN, though she and Germaine were in the same resistance cell. It had horrified Germaine to learn her mother had arrived at Ravensbrück, and now she couldn't cross the no-go area to see her.

At first the NN women were afraid. 'We realised they wanted us to stay inside the walls so that we were available for execution,' said Anise. But then nothing much seemed to happen, and they found there were advantages to being NN. The prisoners were all 'political' and well motivated, able to keep an orderly block – 'We didn't need to be told how to queue for food.' And those kept inside were spared the hardest labour. Germaine Tillion even found time to continue her ethnological research: instead of studying African tribes she started to study the camp.

'What you must understand about Germaine is she had *une énorme tête* [a terrific mind],' said Anise, who first met Germaine on the platform of the Gare de Lyon as both were waiting to leave for Germany.

> I came onto the platform and I saw this small woman with a very large bag – like a bag of potatoes. She told me that inside was her thesis on African tribes. She was planning to work on it in Germany, she said, but of course she had no idea where we were going, so she said she would find out and she pointed at one of the German guards. She said: 'Look, Anise, I'm going to show you how to behave towards a savage. I'm going to ask him where we're being taken. Germans love nature and animals. I'm going to show him a pretty photograph of a sand fox and see if he'll talk.' She took the photograph up to the German. Naturally he knew nothing and said go away – she spoke abominable German. But he loved the sand fox. And he wasn't bad. He even offered to take a letter to my mother and I found later he had done it.

Anise had planned to escape that day. 'I had made sure I had good shoes for running and a ticket for the metro. I could have done it.' I wondered if she regretted not trying.

> To escape you have to have a lot of courage. Leave the group and take risks. And I was afraid they would take my brothers. I knew if you escaped they took your family. But, yes, I have a sense of guilt for not doing it. And then there was Germaine too. I was big and strong. She was very small. She was not someone for escaping. She was a thinking person, not a runner.

So Anise helped Germaine carry her papers onto the train, and when they were in the NN block she helped her again. After suffering from diphtheria on arrival, Germaine had a limp. 'So she leant on me. That's when they started calling us Don Quixote and Sancho Panza.'

Germaine's research on African tribes was confiscated immediately on arrival, but her studies of Ravensbrück were soon absorbing her instead. Early on she noted that the most frail and isolated prisoners were more *déracinées*, rootless, than any she had seen in Africa. The gap between the haves and have-nots – the *Schmuckstücke* – was wider than the gap between the Queen of England and a London street urchin.

Soon Germaine began to collect figures about arrivals and departures and tried to count the numbers of the dead – 'and the living dead,' said Anise. She quickly grasped that this was a place of slow extermination. She knew that the departure of the Majdanek transport on 3 February had been deliberately timed to make room for the new shipment of the *vingt-sept mille* that arrived later the same day. 'We were the new stock,' said Anise.

Germaine also heard that black transports were continuing to leave the camp. The room in the *Revier* called the *Idiotenstübchen* was regularly being emptied. Trucks came for the 'idiots' at night, but no one knew where the trucks went or who the idiots were.

Several prisoners working in the *Revier* were by now collecting information about the black transports too. They spoke of women being thrown on lorries half naked, their number traced in purple on their backs. The destination of these transports was more mysterious than ever. Majdanek, destination of the last major death convoy, had now been evacuated.

After the uproar caused by the Majdanek transport, the convoys were being arranged with much greater secrecy. So well hidden were these smaller black transports that even today, little is known about where they went. A German nurse, Schwester Gerda Schröder, who arrived in April 1944, said in evidence later: 'I knew that the mentally deficient went on transports and that they were exterminated, and I believe that the place of extermination was not far from Ravensbrück'. The camp informer Carmen Mory gave evidence suggesting that some of the black transports never even left the camp.

On the night of one February black transport, Mory was being held in a cell in the bunker, and overheard guards talking. 'From my window in the bunker I could see the crematorium chimney, which suddenly began to smoke,' she said. She heard an SS man talking to a woman guard about the smoke and saying: 'They're killing off the women from the *Idiotenstübchen*.' The guard asked how they went about it. The SS man replied that every evening a lorry went to the *Idiotenstübchen* and women were chosen and driven to the crematorium. There they were killed 'in some way' and burned.

It came as news to Mory that the women had been killed right here at the camp. She sought to verify it when she returned to her block, and asked another prisoner, her fellow informer Giolantha Prokesch, what had happened. According to Mory, Prokesch confirmed much of the story and also told her that before the victims were taken away a medical commission had arrived to make selections: 'The victims were first of all checked by a medical team, including Dr Treite, his boss Dr Trommer and a psychiatrist from Berlin. For over six hours the doctors selected sixty names, placing a black cross against each.'

Prokesch told Mory how during ten days in February a lorry had come every evening and taken away seven or eight idiots; sometimes it had come twice in one evening. When Mory asked how the women died, Prokesch said she had been told that the first groups were beaten to death and then burned.

But Suhren was worried that the beating made too much noise, so the rest were killed first by injection and burned. Lists of the victims were promptly destroyed.

By April the French were dying faster than any other national group. Germaine Tillion would say later that the reason was simple: they couldn't eat the food, so they lost their strength, and with it the will to live. Karolina Lanckorońska observed that there was something 'hideous' about the way the French suddenly started to die.

> They perished without a struggle. No death throes. Often in their sleep. Increasingly often at dawn. Just before roll call. A neighbour would come running with the news. 'Madame X has died.'
>
> 'When?'
>
> 'When I don't know. I know we were chatting together at dawn. I got up and now I've just found her body, already cooling.'

*Chapter 23*

# Hanging On

It wasn't until early April that the Mecklenburg sun provided any warmth, and even then it was not felt at the Neubrandenburg subcamp until late in the day. 'We still shivered for hours in the morning in sleeveless dresses as we stood in the wind,' recalled Micheline Maurel, 'but it was warm and clear later. And the sky, Neubrandenburg's one real beauty, was superb.'

The sunniest place was behind the delousing barracks. Crouching here, just where the heat of the wall met the warmth of the earth, Micheline's friend Odette remarked: 'Yes really, I think I'm getting used to this. I think now that maybe I could even hang on for two months if need be.'

Close by, the women found mushrooms, which they picked and crunched together with sorrel and dandelion, and ate, imagining lashings of olive oil. Russians watching on were puzzled about the French delicacy, so they rooted up the lot, and when the French went back for more there were none left – the Russians had been selling them in exchange for bread.

The talk of two more months was spread by new arrivals who said it might be as short a time as that before the Americans and British landed in France.

By the spring of 1944 prisoners were pouring into Ravensbrück in astonishing numbers. In March alone, 4052 women entered the camp – three times the rate of the previous year – raising the population to 20,406, the size of a large town. Poles rounded up ahead of the Red Army advance still comprised the largest group, and if proof were needed that the Soviets were getting nearer it came with the arrival in March of prisoners from Majdanek concentration camp, near Lublin. So close was the Red Army to Lublin that

Hitler ordered the camp to be evacuated and prisoners transported further west.

In April another big convoy arrived from Paris, 400 strong. Once again the newcomers brought hope that the British and Americans were to land any day on the continent – another 'ball of oxygen'. Knowing that Allied armies were closing in, both to the east and the west, gave some prisoners new strength to hang on.

Micheline Maurel remembers that the kindness of a stranger helped her find strength. One evening, when the prisoners were being served soup with semolina – which, unlike the cabbage soup, she could drink – a woman came up to her and said: '"Micheline, I think this is a soup you can eat. Here, take mine too." She emptied her bowl into mine and went without food that day.' The woman knew Micheline's name, but Micheline didn't know hers, just that she was 'a French prostitute – a group that kept to themselves'.

A stranger helped Denise Dufournier to 'hang on' too. Twice Denise had escaped selection for a subcamp, but the third time her luck ran out; she was called for the required medical inspection, which she was bound to pass. As she awaited the results at the *Revier*, a Belgian prisoner nurse whispered to her: 'It isn't every day that one does a kind act, but I'll strike your name off the list. It will be the first time I've done such a thing.' The nurse, not long in the camp, added: 'But don't say a word because it could be very serious for me.'

Denise worried about the morality of dodging her turn, as someone weaker might be sent instead. But she didn't worry for long, and returned to join her friends, Suzanne and Christiane, shovelling sand – which suddenly didn't seem so bad: at least they weren't making German guns. More important, the Belgian nurse had taught Denise that there were loopholes in the system. Even in a concentration camp, it was possible to break the rules.

Women who had been there far longer than Denise observed that by the spring of 1944 it had never been easier to break the rules. Overcrowding meant that order was falling apart: there were too few guards, new conscript recruits were easier to fool, and during air raids – which happened often – the entire SS scattered in fear.

Prisoners were taking more risks. In March two more Poles escaped, this time from an outside work party. Later they sent a postcard to the commandant wishing him 'further success in his work'.

In a letter home in early 1944 Krysia Czyż told her family of 'changes for the better'. 'Before you could go to the punishment block for anything – or to the bunker – but nowadays you can get away with a lot. And there are many more things that you can get on the side,' she said, although as always there were never enough medicines for her mutilated friends. 'Could you send Propidon for Nina's leg.'

Despite the welcome change, Krysia had new fears. Her letters in early 1944 show her anxiety that with the advancing Soviet front all communication with Poland – legal and illegal – would soon be severed. As early as January she was thinking of new ways to keep channels open once the Red Army had reached Lublin. Perhaps Niuś, the 'postman', could find a replacement, she wrote on 28 January. She was sure her next letter would be her last. 'If you can please send calcium as milk powder. For confirmation you've got Niuś's address, send us toothpaste. We think about you all. I'm kissing and embracing you with all my love and saying goodbye.'

It was at the *Verfügbar* roll call that Denise Dufournier and her Parisian friends first tried breaking the rules. With the rise in the camp population, the number of casual labourers often outstripped demand, and some days the girls could engineer things so that they had no work to do at all.

They also contrived how to shift to better work gangs. Most sought-after were the gardening and the removal gangs, but these were hard to get, and if they didn't keep their wits about them the trio were chosen for the worst gangs, such as refuse removal or coal-barge unloading, whereas lice-picking and corpse-carrying were already sewn up, so they stood no chance of being picked for those. Most dreaded of all was the fuel gang, which involved entering a huge cellar piled to the ceiling with coal, climbing to the top and shovelling as avalanches fell on heads below.

The Parisians soon learned tricks to avoid the bad squads too. One ploy was to hide in the ever-longer line of the sick outside the *Revier*, or among the Siemens night workers, who were too exhausted to notice as they waited to return to their blocks to sleep. Or else the girls would wrap their heads in scarves stolen from the clothes store and stagger as if old and crippled, until the gang leaders chose stronger women.

Another trick was to hide in amongst the growing number of 'pink cards' – the women allowed to work in their blocks. At labour roll call these women now had a special place to stand, and the very weak were allowed to sit on stools. According to Denise Dufournier there were even 'sham' pink cards who faked a disability and when selection was over 'picked up their stools and skipped away'.

One day the Parisian *Verfügs* were selected for the gardening squad. Armed with forks and hoes, they found themselves digging outside the house of Edmund Bräuning, Binz's lover, and they watched his sons head off to Fürstenberg School, carrying tennis rackets and books.

The removal squad was best of all for getting around, and when they were assigned to it they didn't let anyone dislodge them. The whole camp was on the move nowadays, with prisoners switching blocks, secretaries moving offices, and guards transferring barracks, always to make space for new arrivals. The removal gang was therefore much in demand, moving bunks and stoves, filing cabinets and bedpans – anything and everything that could fit in their wooden handcart, which they pushed back and forth in endless journeys. Often it seemed they were pushing the same items round in circles and back again, several times a week, but at least it meant they could see new places, which they'd never dreamed existed.

At the top of the camp, they saw inside blocks 1, 2 and 3, where the privileged inmates lived 'like the Queen of England', as Germaine put it, with a mattress to themselves, neatly folded sheets, a pillow each, and two blue and white blankets. In the *Schreibstube* they saw the well-fed prisoner secretaries who lived in the same privileged blocks, wearing striped uniforms that looked immaculate compared with the Auschwitz cast-offs given to the 'street urchins'. Under new rules all prisoners wearing the clothes of the dead were obliged to have a large black cross daubed on their backs, to deter more escapes.

Moving on to the camp kitchen, the removers saw gleaming machines and kitchen workers who 'seemed to have contempt for anything but pots and pans', but one of them, Katya, took a liking to Denise, and asked if she'd teach her French. They passed the dog kennels, which were overcrowded too, especially as the number of dog-handlers was increased – another move to stop further escapes.

Most marvellous of all was the sight of the *Bekleidungswerk*, clothing store, which Christiane dubbed the Galeries Lafayette. The store contained possessions taken from prisoners on arrival. There was everything one could wish for, said Christiane: underwear, shoes, silver, books, medicines, often of French or Polish origin, all of which could be readily 'organised' by prisoners working there.

The removers' last stop was usually the main *Revier* barracks, where they would often bump into the corpse cart, just starting its round. The corpse gang first loaded bodies from the *Revier*, before moving off to the bunker and then to other blocks, collecting more bodies, which they stacked like a pile of logs outside the crematorium that lay just beyond the camp wall, beside a hill of ash.

Within weeks, the Parisian removers had observed the camp from every angle. One day they were even sent to move furniture into a new guards' barracks, where they caught a glimpse of life for newly conscripted women. These new barracks were nothing like the well-appointed apartments offered to earlier volunteer recruits; in layout they were similar to those lived in by the prisoners, with two rows of three-tiered bunks. In one barracks the French saw bunks crammed almost as close together as theirs, and tables littered with stale bread, half-smoked cigarettes and curling tongs.

The next time the squad were sent to the guards' barracks their task was to move cupboards so that even more conscripts could squeeze in. This time the French girls took delight in ransacking the German women's possessions by opening cupboards and throwing the contents – 'common clothes and cheap perfume' – all over the floor.

Who these German guards were is impossible to say, as most of their camp identity cards were destroyed in the last weeks of the war, but a card belonging to Elfriede Huth survived, and shows she was hired to work at Ravensbrück as a dog-handler in June 1944. Huth's home address was Holzhauser Strasse 36, Leipzig, and – remarkably, given that Leipzig was flattened by Allied bombs – the building still stands today. Leonore Zimmermann, aged eighty-eight, comes to one of the apartment doors and remembers Elfriede Huth's friendly smile.

'Oh yes, Elfriede was a pleasant girl – not remarkable in any way – but always friendly. She was chubby with blonde-reddish hair – and she used to stop at our flat to pass the time of day on her way out to work. She always asked if we needed anything from the shops. Her father was a carpenter – but quite hard up I remember.'

Leonore says Elfriede worked as a seamstress for a Jewish fur trader before the war, then in 1942 Leipzig's Jews were force-marched through the streets and out to the death camps at Treblinka and Auschwitz. 'We all saw them leaving,' says Leonore, who is sure that Elfriede would have seen them leave too. 'We didn't know where they were going though – but we had our suspicions.'

With the fur traders gone, Elfriede took in sewing. Her records show that her next job was as a supervisor in one of the city's munitions factories, which employed Ravensbrück slave labour. From here she was conscripted for Ravensbrück. After a few days' training as a dog-handler she started work.

The removal gang were not the only prisoners to scorn the conscript guards who appeared at the camp in 1944. Krysia Czyż told her family that the new guards were less and less well qualified:

> A skilful gang leader can often win them over. Many complain now about the job and the food and they talk to us because they are afraid. You can't imagine how the guards try to flatter the Polish cook so they get more food. They steal asparagus from the garden and apples from the orchard. They fight for better work gangs and the guards in the workshops steal slices of bread given at midnight to the prisoners.

Prisoners overheard the guards talking about how they'd lost their homes in the bombing, or a father or brother or husband at the front. Guards even arrived pregnant, recalled Edith Sparmann, the prisoner hairdresser, who saw one pregnant new recruit pick out a Jewish prisoner at *Appell* and kick her senseless. Afterwards the same guard came to Edith and demanded that she do her hair.

'Sometimes they would just come and find me and ask me for a hairdo,' Edith said. 'But I told this girl I refused to do her hair. I told her I didn't like what I'd seen, and she should think about how what she had done would affect the unborn child, and the physical and moral wellbeing of that child. She was very upset and began to cry.'

Lotte Silbermann, the canteen waitress, noticed that the behaviour of the SS men was worsening too. Nowadays there were always drunken orgies after the execution squad – Pribill, Pfab, Schäfer and Conrad – came into the canteen for their bonus food, which was usually a giant schnitzel, wine, schnapps, and cigarettes, 'as much as they wanted'.

The prisoners serving them were terrified, said Lotte, who recalled an occasion when the executioner Pribill came behind the counter and took a small revolver 'and put it at the back of my friend Lottie Guttmann's neck and said: "Shall I pull the trigger?" They went away and carried on drinking in another room. They opened the window and one after the other threw up on the grass outside. The Jehovah's Witnesses had to come and clear it up.'

Edmund Bräuning, Suhren's deputy, held his own orgies in the canteen and his favourite women guards were always there – particularly Rosel Laurenzen and Dorothea Binz, who were 'fierce rivals for his affection', said Lotte. 'And we had to witness everything. They smoked, drank and ate only the best. We had to fetch the drinks discreetly so the other SS men wouldn't notice. That's why we covered everything with cloth.'

One Sunday morning Bräuning went to the bunker to collect a group of male prisoners who were held there as they waited to be hanged. Bräuning led the men to a green wagon, then climbed up himself, at which point Binz appeared. 'Binz came running out shouting out: "Wait for me, wait for me, I want to come and see it."'

The SS *Kameradschaftsabend* – comradeship evening – was held once a month. Suhren would open the evening with a few mumbled words, 'but he couldn't speak, and the master of ceremonies for the rest of the evening was Bräuning, but he soon got completely drunk, going from one table to another always followed by Binz, because she was so jealous – and Bräuning was married and father of three children'. Most of the leading SS men brought their wives to these occasions, but not Bräuning.

After a short time everybody was drunk and lost control. 'We, the waitresses at these occasions, were subjected to disgusting things. And Suhren would stop the party, but the other men went on drinking till morning.'

After their day's work the French removal squad retreated as usual to their slum blocks, where by early summer lawlessness was growing and a Ukrainian gang of 'street urchins' had staked out territory beside a pile of cabinets that lay rotting in the sun. Inside the blocks the straw was sticking out of the mattresses, making the bunks 'look like a sty', but to cheer things up, the *groupe de comtesses* put red rags up at the broken windows. There were advantages to the worsening conditions, even here.

Such was the crowding inside the blocks that no guard could fit between the bunks, so there were rarely any checks and the French girls could safely keep a store of treasures – a scarf, a potato from Katya, a pencil – in their mattress. Before they went to sleep they sat cross-legged, one in front of the other, picking out lice from the scalp in front, which they crushed with their nails while relaying gossip.

The older French women also began to organise, and a group of intellectuals emerged, including Emilie Tillion, Germaine's mother, who gave talks from her bunk on the history of French art and culture. Meanwhile, Annie de Montfort (born Arthémise Deguirmendjian-Shah-Vekil; her parents had fled the Armenian genocide in Turkey in 1915) held seminars on the history of Poland. In 1919 Annie had founded the French-Polish society in Paris and under Nazi occupation had co-founded – with her husband Henri de Montfort – a clandestine magazine, *La France continue*, which led to her arrest. The French intellectuals joined forces with like-minded Poles to create an 'international association' inside the camp, aimed at promoting cultural ties between every prisoner group. The chaos allowed the women to build a greater sense of community than ever before, said Maria Moldenhawer, one of the organisers of the new association. The 'delegates' from each country made plans to continue their work after the war, 'but due to the deaths of some of the most outstanding individuals in the group, and for other reasons, this was not possible'.

Evidently – contrary to what Suhren believed – by no means all the Poles disliked the French, although as a national group they still puzzled other prisoners. Even the Francophile Maria Moldenhawer seems to have been unable to make up her mind about them. Some of the French were 'the worst street types', she said, whereas the French political prisoners, 'coming from a nation that had not known captivity, often, very audaciously, though unwisely, opposed the authorities' orders and with a great deal of bravura'.

Maria Moldenhawer may have been thinking of Jacqueline d'Alincourt, one of the *groupe de comtesses*, who in the early summer of 1944 had the 'audacity' to oppose the authorities' attempts to send French prisoners to work in brothels.

In the summer of 1944 Himmler's three new camp brothels were up and running, but the shortage of good recruits had become acute; the pool of German asocials arriving at Ravensbrück were now almost all too decrepit for the job. In December the Poles had protested over attempts to recruit them,* as had groups of Russians and Ukrainians. Such were the horrors now circulating about what happened in the male camp brothels that few were tempted, even if it meant getting away from Ravensbrück, and nobody believed the lies that they would be released after six months.

A woman who returned in 1944 after just six weeks in a brothel told Anja Lundholm of a horror of rape and abuse. 'Every morning the prostitutes had to get up and let themselves be cleaned by female guards. After the coffee the SS men would come and start to rape and abuse the women. It would go on for sixteen hours a day, and only two and a half hours for lunch and dinner.'

Friedericka Jandle, an Austrian working in the *Schreibstube*, had a Viennese friend in the office who volunteered. 'She believed she'd be released if she agreed. I tried to stop her but she told me, "I have nothing to lose." Six months later she returned. She was finished. Totally used up. Destroyed. She said she wished she'd listened to me.'

The new French arrivals, however, had not yet learned the truth, so among the *volontaires* and the prostitutes brought from French brothels, the SS found ready recruits.

'At first they didn't understand, these women,' said Jacqueline d'Alincourt. Just nineteen when she arrived – tall, elegant and of aristocratic stock – Jacqueline was horrified to discover that she shared her block not only with 'brutal Russian peasants and thieving Gypsies' but 'an entire brothel from Rouen'. 'They were uneducated,' she told me.

> They had nothing to hold on to – no religion, no values. I remember one of these poor creatures lying on her mattress saying: 'Why am I here, why am I here?' We in the resistance, we knew why we were there. We had a superiority of spirit, you understand. We had the desire not to die in

*According to Wanda Wojtasik, when the Poles of Block 15 were lined up and asked to volunteer there was 'thunderous silence', until one stepped forward to boos and hisses. Wanda led a delegation to protest to the commandant, who 'gaped at us and didn't know what to do', eventually cancelling the protestors' parcels. Meanwhile, Irena Dragan and nine others – mostly rabbits – cut off the hair of the volunteer and beat her up. 'I took the scissors,' said Irena. Four of the beaters were given twenty-five lashes for 'punishing' the volunteer.

> Germany and to see France again. But these creatures had no idea why they were there. It was a question of spirit.
>
> So we political women got together and decided to make a list of everyone who had volunteered to go. And we told them not to take this work. We said: *Non! Ce n'est pas question de ça!* [There's no question of that.] We were very severe. And we watched carefully what they did.

I asked Jacqueline, meeting in her apartment near the Arc de Triomphe, if she ever knew the names of any of the French prostitutes – those from Rouen perhaps – but she looked astonished at such a suggestion and said no. 'They didn't write their memoirs, these women,' she said. 'And after the war they were certainly not invited to join any of the associations of deported women. They were not in the resistance.'

The French prostitutes in Ravensbrück are as thoroughly forgotten as the Germans; not a single published French memoir mentions the name of any of the French prostitutes there, or of the *volontaires*, though there were probably thousands. The resisters' testimony may recall acts of kindness or even acts of courage from 'a prostitute', but even then, none thought to ask or remember the woman's name.

The only known exception is a schoolteacher called Marie-Thérèse Lefebvre. She remembers meeting a prostitute called Simone (not her real name) who arrived in Ravensbrück in mid-1944. Like Marie-Thérèse, Simone was sent to the subcamp of Zwodau, where she was put on laundry duties, and smuggled extra garments to prisoners to keep out the cold. We only know this because one day she gave a warm vest to Marie-Thérèse, who was so grateful that she spoke a few words to Simone and the two women discovered they were both from Le Havre. Marie-Thérèse recalled:

> I asked her why she was here, and she said she was not arrested for prostitution but because she'd been hiding American pilots in the brothel where she worked. There was a room above the cabaret where the Americans were hidden, while the German officers were with women in the next room. And she told me she'd fallen in love with one of the pilots, who had promised to come and find her when it was all over.

After the war, Simone had no wish to tell her story back in Le Havre for fear of being reviled as a prostitute. Yet as we now know, prostitutes played a vital role in resistance work, particularly with escape lines. Allied airmen were often hidden in brothels as they escaped from France, particularly in port cities like Le Havre and Rouen, and in the city of Toulouse, not far from the Pyrenees. Such women took as many risks as any other resistance women, yet none has ever been recognised. Some even met their future husbands this way.

Soon after she returned to France after the war, Marie-Thérèse bumped into Simone again in Le Havre and Simone told her that her American pilot had come back to find her. 'She told me the American had asked her to go with him to America and marry him. What should she do? So I said: "You must go, of course. Go to America and start a new life!"' Papers held by the Le Havre town hall show that this is exactly what Simone did. In the summer of 1946 she married the serviceman whose life she saved, and went with him to America to live.

In April 1944 the numbers rose again, with about 4000 new prisoners registered and the recorded monthly death rate at the main camp put at ninety. Among recent arrivals was another group of evacuees from Majdanek, including more Red Army doctors and nurses, as well as 473 Gypsies transferred from Auschwitz. There were Italian partisans, Slovenians, Greeks, Spaniards and Danes, as well as three Egyptians and seven Chinese who, perhaps for reasons of marriage, or travel, or because they had volunteered to help the anti-Nazi resistance, found themselves swept up and brought to Ravensbrück. Two more British women had also arrived. A nanny, Mary O'Shaughnessy, was working with a family in Provence when she was arrested for helping hide Allied airmen. And a woman called Julia Barry, of Hungarian descent, was arrested on the Channel Island of Guernsey for sending signals to London about German troop movements.

By the end of the month the camp held a total of twenty-one nationalities and a babble of competing languages sounded on the Lagerstrasse; hardly anybody understood each other; the guards certainly didn't understand the prisoners, or the prisoners the guards. The inability of guards to understand what prisoners said may explain why in the middle of 1944 prisoners started being hit more and more often across the face.

Soon after she arrived Mary O'Shaughnessy was called outside her block by a woman guard who spoke to her in German, 'which I did not understand, and then she punched me violently on either side of my face, breaking some of my teeth. She then came back to me again as I was still standing up and hit me across the face with her fist, breaking my nose. I have seen many of the prisoners smacked across the face with whips by SS women.' Mary added that the striking of prisoners by male and female guards 'was too common an occurrence to be worthy of note at the time'.

It was the growing number of children in the camp that changed the atmosphere the most.

By early summer 1944 it was a common sight to see children at roll call, 'sometimes dressed like dolls', said Maria Moldenhawer. Some of them came with the recent Gypsy transport from Auschwitz; others were children of the 'protected' Jews – sixty-four in total – who had arrived from Belgium and the Netherlands. During the week the children stayed mostly in their blocks, but on Sundays they played outside, throwing stones, perhaps, or chasing each other around. Guards sometimes joined in. Or else the children would lie with their mothers, watched sadly by other mothers who were longing for their own children back at home.

Micheline Maurel, a published poet, wrote poems for mothers to help them bear their sorrow. One woman who had left two babies behind in France asked her to write a poem about her love for them, and wept over the words. Another young mother was found in tears, clutching another of Micheline's verses and yearning for her daughter.

Some grieving mothers adopted orphans in the camp and became their 'camp mothers', dressing them up in pretty clothes and jewellery, organised from the store. The French prisoner Odette Fabius adopted an orphan Gypsy girl with jet-black hair, whom she shared her mattress with. A Belgian woman called Claire van den Boom adopted Stella Kugelman, the dark-haired child who arrived from Antwerp in January, though Stella had several other camp mothers too. Later she remembered at least four.

In the early summer of 1944 Claire took Stella to see her own mother, who had been in the hospital since they arrived, and was now dying. 'It was a grey day, like this,' says Stella, who lives today on the outskirts of St Petersburg. Her small, simple apartment is full of dolls.

> I remember Claire came and picked me up one day. And she asked me, 'Would you like to see your mother?' and she carried me out of the block to another block where behind a window my mother was sitting. I could see her. She looked the same to me, but she had fluffy hair.
>
> And she'd made two little toys out of scraps of foil. We couldn't speak through the window, but she smiled. Of course I didn't really understand what was happening but I was very happy.
>
> I saw her one more time. This was different. Someone came to get me – perhaps it was Claire again – and took me outside onto the Appellplatz and we stood, and she said: 'Look, your mother is over there.' This time I couldn't see anyone who looked like her – a silhouette maybe.

Stella thinks now that the last occasion was just set up so that her mother could see her little girl for the last time, before she died. 'I have a memory of Claire saying later: "You know your mother has been burned."'

Claire was sent away to a subcamp, and another camp mother, called Rosanne Lascroux, looked after Stella for a time. Stella liked Rosanne. 'She was from Paris.' Later Rosanne jotted down her memories of their friendship, and Stella was sent a copy, which she read out.

> Claire was Stella's main camp mother. She loved the little girl and was with her all the time, but she couldn't stay with her because she was sent to work in the mines in Silesia. It was then that Stella began eating and sleeping in our bed.
>
> I remember well how we washed her face and curled her hair. She never cried and it seemed that she understood everything.
>
> She was exceptionally intelligent for her age. I talked to her in French and I could understand Spanish. Once she declared to me that she never wanted to see the Germans again as she knew they killed her parents.
>
> Like all the children she was scared of the guards, especially Binz and the policewoman, Knoll,* who was always shouting angrily at the children.

Stella says she has no memory of most of these things. Almost all of what she knows about herself in the camp, she has been told by others.

She reads out a brief note that her mother wrote from the camp to a friend, Herr Lepage, in Belgium. Herr Lepage kept it, along with Rosa Kugelman's rosary, and gave them both to Stella long after the war. The letter has clearly been smuggled out, as it is not on the formal camp paper. The postmark says Fürstenberg, and at the top Rosa has written her number, 25622, and Stella's number, 25621.

Stella reads it: 'I send you my greetings. I hope my letter will find you healthy. You will find a packet with this letter and I ask you a great favour' – but the rest of the letter has been damaged and is impossible to read. Stella doesn't know what the packet was, or what favour her mother asked. But the date of the letter shows that it was written just before she died, on 14 July 1944.

* The hated Kapo Käthe Knoll had by now joined the camp police.

*Chapter 24*

# Reaching Out

By early summer 1944, Bernard Dufournier was beginning to lose hope of finding Denise. It was nearly a year since his sister's arrest and he still had no idea where she was. With both parents dead, he perhaps felt especially responsible for his only sibling, and pulled every string to find her.

As a diplomat Bernard was well connected; he had even managed to raise Denise's case with the acting president of the International Red Cross, Carl Burckhardt, who wrote back saying he knew nothing of Denise's whereabouts, but: 'We are in touch with the German Red Cross and if we hear anything we will let you know.'

Given what is known today of Carl Burckhardt, the ICRC and the Holocaust, that two-line reply to Bernard Dufournier is chilling. Clearly he was correct not to make a special plea on Bernard's behalf, yet Burckhardt had used his own unique position to appeal direct to Himmler for the release of his friend Countess Karolina Lanckorońska. Far more disturbing is Burckhardt's readiness, even then, to refer so confidently in writing to the German Red Cross as a serious body that the ICRC could do business with.

By the summer of 1944, under mounting international pressure to get off the fence, the ICRC was trying harder to send parcels to concentration-camp prisoners, but the attempts were again easily blocked by Himmler: only 250 parcels had arrived at Ravensbrück, all of them ransacked by the SS. The only camp the ICRC delegates had been allowed to inspect was the so-called model camp of Theresienstadt. Here German Red Cross minders took their Swiss visitors to see show blocks and to talk to tutored inmates, ensuring that glowing reports went back to Geneva HQ.

Meanwhile, the ICRC was being inundated with pleas for help from terrified relatives all over Europe. The approach of D-Day had exacerbated fears that once the Allies landed, Hitler would retaliate against his prisoners, even slaughtering them. Relatives who wrote to Geneva asking for news, however, all found the same: Geneva could tell them nothing at all.

As families tried to reach out to their missing relatives, so the women in Ravensbrück were increasingly trying to reach out to them. It was clear to all in the camp that Hitler's days were numbered and that liberation was within sight, but the women had never been so afraid.

New arrivals from Poland brought good news about evacuations from the eastern camps ahead of the advancing Soviet front. And yet these same prisoners also spoke of further atrocities enacted by the Germans before the camps were evacuated. A Pole who arrived from Majdanek had witnessed the shooting in November of 17,000 Jews in a single day. Gypsies arriving from Auschwitz described the burning down of their entire Gypsy camp and the murder of 20,000 men, women and children.

The prisoners understood far better than the world outside that when Hitler felt the end was coming he would massacre them too, or hold them hostage. And if this happened they would be on their own, as nobody knew they were here.

Every national group sought news from its own war front, listening to the guards or trying to glimpse a German newspaper. Ojcumiła Falkowska, the Polish dancer, had a new job cooking for German officials evacuated from Berlin and relocated to temporary offices in the Ravensbrück woods. Here she heard snatches of the BBC news as the Germans tuned in, and she passed on what she learned.

Those lucky enough to receive post from their families looked for clues in censored letters. Micheline Maurel had written to her father in Toulon every month since arriving in 1943, but never heard back. Then in May 1944 she received an envelope postmarked Toulon, but found when she opened it that the censor had snipped out so much that just a corner remained, and on it one word: 'Papa'.

Two food parcels then came from home for Micheline in quick succession. The first had been torn open before it reached her, and all that was left was a small tin of meat spread and some chocolate bars. She shared the meat with her friends, and hid the chocolate bars in a bag beneath her mattress to eat the next day, but by then the bag had gone. In the next parcel came six eggs, only one left unbroken, so she and her friend divided it in two and ate it raw.

Others had heard that it might now be possible to receive Red Cross parcels if the International Red Cross knew their names and numbers. A group of Poles had managed to smuggle their names and numbers out through yet another group of friendly POWs whom they met on an outside work gang. Parcels had come, with their names on, but like all parcels they were rifled before the women got them. Guards were seen eating the Red Cross chocolate and smoking American cigarettes.

Most women, however, knew that even now nobody had any idea where they were. With the fronts advancing, even their official mail would soon be cut off and their families would simply think they'd disappeared. That was their greatest fear, so while they looked for news, prisoners also looked for ways to preserve their stories. Many tried to bury precious items with notes or photographs around the camp, in the hope that one day someone would find them, or else they told their stories to a friend, hoping the friend would survive if they did not.

Milena Jesenska had entrusted her story to Grete Buber-Neumann long before she realised that she was going to die. Throughout the winter of 1943–4 Milena's health had continued to fail; then in April she was diagnosed with an ulcerated kidney. Dr Treite operated again, but it was too late. One day Milena said she wished to get up and go to her office in the hospital, to snatch a last look at freedom, just visible through the camp gate, but she was already too weak to move. Then her other kidney failed. 'Look at the colour of my feet. They're the feet of a dying person,' she told Grete. 'I shall go on living through you.'

With her Czech friends around her, as well as Grete, Milena died on 17 May 1944. She was given a coffin, and when the corpse squad came, Grete was allowed to accompany the body through the drizzle to the crematorium. Here, male prisoners, both green triangles 'with faces like executioners' assistants', lifted the body out and said to Grete: 'Don't be frightened of grabbing her, she can't feel anything any more.' Dr Treite later wrote to Professor Jesensky, saying he could arrange for Milena's ashes to be sent to Prague.

No prisoners had better reason to fear they would disappear than those held in the NN block. Hitler's express intention was that these prisoners would 'disappear into the night and the fog'. Yet paradoxically – perhaps because they understood they would probably not survive – these women did more than any to preserve their stories and the story of the camp itself. Many of the NN women – Red Army, Yugoslavs, Belgians and Dutch – were gathering information and trying to analyse it. Germaine Tillion was continuing to treat her inquiries as if they were a piece of ethnological research.

Over the months, Germaine had secured a camp-wide network of informants. She could not have done this without her helper Anise Girard, who served Germaine not only as a physical prop, but as fixer and facilitator. A fluent German-speaker and a communist sympathiser, Anise was able to win the trust of some of the camp's most powerful and knowledgeable 'aristocrats', the prisoner secretaries. Some of these women had been here so long they were almost considered SS, and behaved as such, too busy surviving to leak information. But others observed the SS 'like old rats' and passed on what they knew: lists of arrivals, departures, the dead and the sick. Germaine in turn squirrelled the information away in hiding places whose whereabouts even Anise was not told. 'It was a very big secret, but I discovered one hiding place was under a loose plank in the roof above her mattress,' says Anise.

Before long, Germaine had set up a system whereby the 'old rats' were bringing camp lists to her every day, as were the prisoners on the hospital staff too, all of which she annotated, analysed and then hid.

First she received the number of women counted at the morning *Appell*, as well as the actual camp number given to the latest woman to arrive. One day in June 1944, for example, Germaine found out that there were 30,849 women in the camp and that the latest woman to be registered had received the number 42158. The difference between the two figures was presumed to represent the number of women sent to subcamps, or transferred elsewhere. But as Germaine had no means of gathering information on how many women actually arrived at subcamps, it was hard to be sure.

A second set of lists, one from the *Revier* and one from the office, showed numbers of deaths, but these figures also never matched. On one day in May, for example, a figure of 151 deaths came from contacts in the hospital, compared with a figure of 191 produced by the camp office. Germaine deduced that this difference of forty must represent the number of executions, because the hospital did not register executions – but again, how could she be sure?

What about deaths in the bunker? These were said to be rising again. And the 'old rats' had no lists of the women sent on the black transports. For information on these, Germaine had to rely on rumours from the *Revier*, where it was said that the *Idiotenstübchen* was being cleared perhaps as often as once every two weeks.

By this time Germaine Tillion's reputation as an intellectual had begun to grow and other respected figures in the camp wished to meet her, among them Grete Buber-Neumann. Just as Milena Jesenska had entrusted her life story to Grete before she died, so Grete wanted to pass on what she knew to a trusted confidante, and she chose Germaine.

Just before D-Day, on the top mattress of a bunk, with Anise Girard squeezed between them as interpreter, these two camp 'sages' met. Grete spoke first and spent long hours relating to Germaine what she had experienced of the horrors of Stalin's communism and of Siberian camps. The two then compared Grete's experience with what was unfolding at Ravensbrück. With her communist sympathies, Anise did not believe that Stalin's camps could be as bad as Grete made out. 'But Germaine was convinced that Grete spoke the reality, and retained every word in her head.'

Grete had related her story 'paragraph by paragraph', said Germaine, recalling the meeting after the war. 'And like so many of us, she was haunted by the desire to ensure that what she knew survived.'

None of these groups had been as adept as the Polish rabbits at making what they knew survive, yet in the spring of 1944 the rabbits became haunted by a fear that the world might not have been receiving their information after all. The women had certainly learned that something of their story had reached England already, because Polish comrades newly arrived at the camp had heard reports about the Ravensbrück atrocities broadcast to the Polish underground on the clandestine English radio station Dawn Radio (SWIT).

However, Krysia remained anxious about exactly what information had got out and who might or might not have received it. In one letter she asked her family to tell her 'which envelopes are missing'.

The reason for the sudden anxiety is not immediately clear, but a clue comes in a further letter in which she talks for the first time of the possibility of receiving Red Cross parcels. Krysia, like all prisoners in the early summer, became aware that certain women in Ravensbrück were receiving parcels sent by the International Red Cross in Geneva. She also knew that this could only happen if Geneva already had their names and numbers.

She was particularly interested in the fact that another group of Poles – non-rabbits – had received such parcels. Like the rabbits, these women had made contact with a group of POWs at a nearby Oflag, who had offered to send their names and numbers on to Geneva, presumably via their own Red Cross mail. Krysia tells her family: 'These other women's names have been handed in by the Oflags.'

As Krysia obviously understood, the arrival of the parcels demonstrated not only to the prisoners, but to the SS, that the International Red Cross had a list of certain women who were in the camp. Such a list would clearly be some kind of insurance against 'disappearance'. The question that came to mind was why were the Polish rabbits not receiving parcels? They had sent on information with their names and numbers over a year ago. Had these lists not, after all, been received? Had they not been passed on to Geneva? It is vital that they are passed on, writes Krysia, and she explains why:

> If the names of those who have had operations could be given there [i.e. to the ICRC] it would be a great help to us; it is not a matter of food but the moral significance the parcels have. The parcels are signed for meticulously,

> and if they came for all those who have been operated on it would make some impression on our keepers – it would look as though they [the ICRC] had a list of us there, which could have an influence on our fate. We constantly have the feeling that they will want to liquidate us as living proofs.

Krysia then tells her family to seek further contact with Niuś ('Apollo'), the POW go-between, who could provide another copy of the list, assuming it had got lost. Niuś 'has our list', she writes, and she seems to think that Niuś has the means to send the list straight to Geneva, as the Oflag boys did for the other Poles. Krysia signs off saying: 'If the idea with the parcels is possible to carry out, write "the whims of the girls can be satisfied" or "cannot be satisfied" if nothing can be done.'

There is an added urgency – almost panic – to get an answer because the Red Army have now almost reached Lublin and she thinks the mail really is now about to be stopped. 'Dearest! We predict contact with you is about to be cut off . . .'

Once again, however, Krysia finds that communication has not yet been cut off, because a reply clearly comes back with more positive news, and in April she responds, mentioning a mystery 'cousin in Sweden'. She writes: 'I'm really glad you got the letters from . . . Niuś . . . The correspondence with a cousin from Sweden brought us even more joy.' As Krysia knew, the Polish Home Army used Sweden as a signalling base. Her reference to the correspondence with a cousin from Sweden shows she has now been reassured that Warsaw sent the information to Sweden, which has sent it on to the Polish government in London, which in turn will have sent it to the International Red Cross in Geneva.

At this point Krysia's correspondence with home was finally cut off, but at least now she had the joy of knowing that her information had almost certainly got through to the right place, and parcels should follow. Yet nothing arrived from the Red Cross, either in the summer months or at any time later. Why not?

We know the ICRC had received the information, so that was not the problem. Furthermore, not only had the necessary details of the girls come in from the Polish government in London (and perhaps direct from Niuś as well), but the ICRC's own delegate in the field was now picking up confirmation of the medical atrocities at Ravensbrück and passing what he knew back to Geneva.

By 1944 Roland Marti, and his colleagues at the ICRC's Berlin delegation, were collecting more and more information about Nazi war crimes. Among their best sources were Allied prisoners of war, held in POW camps that were by now dotted all over Germany and Poland. The POWs were increasingly used as slave labourers, and often found themselves working alongside concentration-camp prisoners in factories. They therefore gleaned a lot from these prisoners, and passed on what they heard to Red Cross delegates who, under the terms of the Geneva Conventions, regularly visited their camps.

On one occasion a POW told Roland Marti that Jewish children at Ravensbrück were being sterilised, and another informant spoke of the medical experiments. As a result, in a report written to his chiefs in Geneva on 12 June 1944, Marti said he had just learned that at Ravensbrück the conditions were 'tragic'. In particular 'they are carrying out bone and muscle operations on the legs of Polish women and many can show their scars. As well, at the slightest thing, the women are shot, and recently at least ten Ukrainians have been executed.'

The POWs who passed on the information obviously assumed that it would be acted on in some way, or at least passed to Allied intelligence, but they were wrong. Marti certainly passed it on to Geneva, but he knew it would never be made public. 'This information seems to be certain,' he wrote in a report to his superiors, 'but cannot be used. I pass it to you for your files and it will help perhaps to throw light on the situation.'

Nevertheless, combined with information coming in from the Poles in London, the pressure was clearly building on Geneva to respond in some way over the Ravensbrück rabbits, because in the second half of 1944 the Committee did decide at least to review the case, and one of the questions on the table was whether to send the stricken women Red Cross parcels. Given that they had the women's names and numbers, that was possible and desirable, especially as – in Krysia's words – sending parcels to all seventy-seven rabbits would 'make an impression on our keepers' and 'might influence our fate'.

And yet the decision taken by the Committee was not to send the parcels, almost certainly because making an impression on the women's keepers was quite simply the opposite of what the ICRC was trying to do: preserving 'neutrality' was so much more important. There may well have been those on the Committee who feared too that sending the parcels would offend Ernst Grawitz, head of the German Red Cross. In any event the decision not to send the parcels was one that the woman lawyer on the Committee, Margaret Frick-Cramer, found very hard to take.

So frustrated was Frick-Cramer at the grotesque absurdity of the Committee's position that she proposed – perhaps ironically, perhaps seriously – that the foremost humanitarian body in the world should send the women the means to kill themselves to end their pain. She said: 'If nothing can be done, the wretched victims should be sent the means of committing suicide; this would perhaps be more humane than giving them food.'

While the International Committee of the Red Cross were hushing up the rabbits, however, the Poles of SWIT at Milton Bryan in Buckinghamshire were continuing to do all they could to publicise the women's plight. Not only was news of the atrocities being transmitted from England to Poland, but it was now being sent out in translation on other clandestine networks to France, Germany and other countries too.

On the evening of 19 May 1944 at 19.10 hours, the SWIT staff went on air again with another warning to the German 'war criminals'. After brief news reports on the role of Poles in the latest Italian offensive, and on the 'puppet union of Polish patriots' (the new pro-Soviet Polish government inside Poland), the station announced that 'further gloomy details have been received from the women's concentration camp at Ravensbrück'. Apparently drawing on Krysia's account sent in a secret letter, detailing everyday life in the camp, the station reported:

> The daily routine starts at 3 a.m. After 3 hours mustering in the open, work starts for the rest of the day with half an hour's break for dinner. The work consists mainly of breaking stones on the roads. Women are usually shot in accordance with prepared lists. Recently 176 Polish women were shot. Women are subjected to experimental surgical operations such as sterilisation and injections. When a few weeks ago describing the conditions in this camp we warned the German staff, we also appealed to the free world to voice this warning. The British radio has since taken up this warning to the German criminals by repeating it in a number of languages. In view of the fact that these crimes are continuing we repeat our appeal. The Germans will only react to force and fear, and perhaps a repetition of the warning will stay the hands of the criminal staff and surgeons at Ravensbrück.

Following earlier broadcasts, Polish women newly arrived at the camp reported that they had heard the 'English radio' broadcasts before their arrests. After this latest broadcast, French women arrived at Ravensbrück saying they'd heard the reports on the French service of 'English radio' as well. Wanda Wojtasik, Krysia's Lublin friend, recalled how at first the new French prisoners had not believed what they heard on the radio, and on arrival in the camp asked to see the rabbits for proof.

'At first sight of our mangled legs they rubbed their eyes in horrified wonder. They had not believed the broadcasts, they said. When they saw us they tried to put fingers in the holes in our legs and then they believed it.'

It was probably Ojcumiła Falkowska who first broke the news of the Allied landings to the camp. Ojcumiła said she heard about the landings on the BBC at 5 a.m. on 6 June 1944, while cooking breakfast for the Berlin government evacuees at their temporary camp in the Ravensbrück woods.

According to Karolina Lanckorońska, Dr Treite announced 'in a loud voice' at morning surgery that the Allied invasion had begun. Having made his statement, he clicked his heels and returned to the operating theatre.

At the Zwodau subcamp, a group of French prisoners learned about the landings from their Polish Blockova, whose husband was serving in a Polish regiment of the British Army. The French teacher, Marie-Thérèse Lefebvre, whose home was on the Normandy coast, recalled: 'She called us together and said: "Now ladies, I have some very important news to tell you, but keep quiet about it. The Allies have landed in France."'

At Neubrandenburg the news came just as the RAF bombed an airfield, and the explosions seemed so close that the French women's bunks rattled and shook, and someone joked: '*Mon Dieu!* The Allies have arrived here already.' The next day, the Neubrandenburg women were all marched out to clear the debris from the airfield, and as they laboured the locals stared and the children spat. Suddenly Normandy seemed a world away.

Excitement about the D-Day news did not last long. For most Poles the capture in May of Monte Cassino, taken by a Polish brigade, had caused far more celebration. And the Russians were more interested in monitoring the rapid advance of the Red Army, now moving towards Belorussia.

In the hospital Dr Treite's words were also soon forgotten. 'Many of us had already realised that we would just be too exhausted to hang on,' recalled Karolina, whose French friend Dora Dreyfus was dying from a lung inflammation. Dora heard the news and was cheered by it, 'and we talked of how I would go to visit her in France after the war,' said Karolina. 'But in less than twenty-four hours she was no longer with us.'

Grete Buber-Neumann remembered that the news of D-Day came as 'the first real harbinger of freedom – we were overjoyed'. But if only Milena had been alive to experience it. 'For so many years all our desires had been in common and all our plans for the future made together. Now I wept in my pillow at night.'

The French removal gang rejoiced at the news, but they decided to defer serious celebration until the Allies reached Paris. Like the rest of the camp they were, for the moment, more concerned about food.

Ravensbrück was nearer to starvation than ever before, but at subcamps it was worse, as no food was getting through. At Neubrandenburg, Micheline Maurel stood at *Appell* behind a newly arrived 'fleshy' Czech. 'The idea of that mass of meat in front of me drove me to desperation. My hands were shaking.' Some days the camp kitchens had no food at all and so none was given out. On other days, dehydrated food was handed out, which made people feel sick and suffer even worse diarrhoea. The real aristocracy in the camp was now, without doubt, those few who received food parcels; they stood more erect and had a sheen on their skin. Many shared what they got in their parcels, dividing delicacies like chocolate or cheese 'until they were the size of a nut'.

After D-Day there were more to feed, because the number of new arrivals continued to grow, and the camp began to feel utterly overwhelmed. The clamour for the lavatories and latrines was fiercer than ever, and the plumbing couldn't cope. The women in the *Schreibstube* were unable to keep up with registering so many new arrivals, so that evening *Appell* was abolished and quarantine cut to two weeks to free up more space.

In early July more transports of French women arrived, and not all their news was good: there was fierce fighting in Normandy and the Americans and British were failing to break through. News from the eastern front was mixed too. In the sewing shop there was graphic evidence of slaughter in Poland, with several prisoners reporting that severed German fingers, or even whole hands, were found inside the sleeves of soldiers' jackets brought in for repair and recycling.

A Hungarian Jewish woman also appeared at Ravensbrück reporting that Hitler was beginning an entire new extermination drive, rounding up all Hungary's Jews. The woman, Gemma La Guardia Gluck, had been captured in Budapest, where her name had come to the attention of Adolf Eichmann, the man in charge of the Jewish exterminations. Eichmann identified Gemma as the sister of Fiorello La Guardia, the mayor of New York.

Brother and sister were both born in New York, the children of Italian immigrants, but Gemma had married a Hungarian Jew, Hermann Gluck, and in the 1930s went to live in Budapest. In 1934 Fiorello La Guardia was elected New York's mayor, warning in one of his first speeches that Hitler's intention was to annihilate the Jews. Ten years later Fiorello's sister, aged sixty-three, was spared annihilation because she shared his name.

Learning of her capture, Himmler at once sent orders that Gemma be treated as a hostage, and on arrival at Ravensbrück she was allocated to Block 2, one of the most privileged barracks, where she didn't have to work and where she had her own mattress. In nearly all other blocks prisoners were by now sleeping three to a mattress and bunks were pushed so close together that the women had to walk over dozens of bodies before finding a gap to squeeze down. Bunks were also crammed in all the day rooms, so there was nowhere to eat or talk.

In August more women started turning up from Auschwitz and in greater numbers – usually young Jewish women, spared the gas chambers for slave labour. One August transport from Auschwitz also brought forty-nine French women, the only survivors of a group of 230 non-Jewish women who had been sent from Paris to Auschwitz eighteen months earlier. Among the group was a prominent French communist called Marie-Claude Vaillant-Couturier, who gave the most compelling account of Auschwitz yet.

Her vantage point was unique. In the 1930s Marie-Claude had worked as a photojournalist for the French newspaper *L'Humanité*, and was one of the very first journalists to report on Hitler's camps, secretly taking photographs of prisoners through the wire at Dachau and Sachsenhausen. When war broke out she was arrested for her work on underground communist publications, and found herself a prisoner in Auschwitz. So valuable was Marie-Claude's testimony considered after the war that she was called to give evidence at Nuremberg.

On arrival at Ravensbrück she told the French how their compatriots who had travelled with her to Auschwitz had first been spared the gas chambers, as they were not Jews, but many had weakened fast and were soon being killed instead as 'useless mouths'. First they were deprived of food and water and then, if starving didn't kill them fast enough, they were gassed. Soon Ravensbrück was awash with stories of the Auschwitz horror, and some saw familiar patterns, predicting that before the end, similar atrocities would be enacted here.

It was not only the women who came from Auschwitz, or other eastern camps, who had premonitions of things to come. Louise (Loulou) Le Porz, a doctor from Bordeaux, arrived at Ravensbrück in June, having travelled via the men's camp of Neue Bremm, a Gestapo punishment camp. Here her transport was held over for some days, and during this time the women were often marched past the men's camp, where – deliberately it seemed – they were given the chance to observe the brutality meted out to male prisoners. Among other tortures, the men were shackled to one another naked, and made to jump up and down going round and round a ring while guards whipped them, until they were bloodied all over and dropped. Then they were beaten again, and made to jump some more, until by the end several were dead.

Loulou would say later that she never forgot the shock of Neue Bremm, and that because of what she saw there she always had a dread of what the future might yet hold for those at Ravensbrück.

Soon after arrival, Loulou's group was lined up on the Appellplatz for a selection; that day, factory managers from Leipzig were choosing slave labourers. Loulou's cousin Françoise Couëron, who was arrested with her in Bordeaux, was standing at her side when a man in a white coat appeared and asked if any present were doctors. Loulou did not at first raise her hand – she didn't want to be separated from Françoise, and Leipzig was bound to be better than this. Nor did she like the look of the doctor. 'But I thought, even so, perhaps I could help in some way. So I raised my hand.'

Loulou's first task in the *Revier* was to check arrivals from Auschwitz for infectious disease, and on the list she was astonished to see the name Vaillant-Couturier. Marie-Claude's family were well known in France before the war, not least because one of her uncles was the creator of Babar the Elephant. And she herself had become famous through her photography as 'the lady with the Rolleiflex'.

The serious young Catholic doctor Loulou had little obviously in common with the fervent communist intellectual Marie-Claude. But as they crossed paths in the *Revier* they were able to exchange a few words and quickly understood each other well. Before they had a chance to cement their friendship, however, Loulou had been sent to the *Strafblock* for lashing out at a guard, who had punched her for being outside during an air raid. The guard also accused Loulou of being 'too proud'.

Tall and strong, Loulou was then set to work unloading bricks and coal. 'I remember a little French girl called Raymonde Sauvage, who had no strength left. So I said hold on to my belt and I'll pull you, and she did, but it was extraordinary because I felt nothing at all. She had the weight of a soul.'

As the summer heat beat down ever more intensely, an inexplicable excitement broke out in certain quarters of the camp, particularly among the German political prisoners. It was a sense – nothing more at first – that before the liberating armies arrived, the nightmare might come to a very sudden end.

The German people were growing restless. Life expectancy on the eastern front was less than three months; almost every family had lost sons, brothers or fathers. Bomb damage was crippling the country, and women and children had been evacuated from Berlin. Food shortages were acute, and women were now being asked to clear away rubble in the cities. In Fürstenberg locals talked openly now of what would happen when the Red Army overran the town, and many were already making plans to move.

Behind the wire, the concentration camps were not immune from this general sense of panic and unrest. Talk of an implosion of some sort was rife among the guards and the civilian workers. Air-raid sirens blasted out almost every day, and prisoners were assigned to building ditches around the camp.

Nor was it only the guards who brought news from the German street.

Among the new arrivals were many German prisoners – women who had insulted the Führer or complained about the length of the war, or asocials caught in a roundup. From these women, the German political prisoners were able to glean a great deal, and the best-connected amongst them passed on rumours that many in Hitler's inner circle were restless too.

In the early summer of 1944 Grete Buber-Neumann received a coded letter from a well-connected relative that there was about to be an attempt on Hitler's life. Grete was in regular correspondence with a brother-in-law, Bernhard, who had been a concentration-camp prisoner himself in the 1930s, and knew how to beat the censors. Various clues convinced the women that the army was about to strike against Hitler. Bernhard had clearly got wind of the growing reports in military and diplomatic circles that revolt against the Führer was reaching its climax.

On 20 July 1944 Claus von Stauffenberg walked into a military conference with the Führer at his eastern military headquarters, the *Wolfsschanze*, or 'wolf's lair', and placed a briefcase containing a bomb under the table, as close as possible to Hitler; but a stout table leg deflected the bomb, and Hitler survived, suffering only burns and shock.

In a little-noticed footnote to the affair, at Hohenlychen Clinic, a few miles up the road from Ravensbrück, a baby called Nanette Dorothea Potthast had been born just before the assassination attempt – an event that has some significance in relation to the plot. Nanette was born to Heinrich Himmler and Hedwig Potthast on 3 June. It is not, however, the date of her birth that is of historical interest, but the date and the place it was registered – 20 July, at Hohenlychen – and the fact that the father had to be present. Speculation has always surrounded the whereabouts of Himmler on the morning when Hitler was nearly killed; some have even suggested that his absence from the scene implicated him in the plot. Nanette's birth certificate provides strong evidence that he was at Hohenlychen on that day, attending the registration of the birth of his child.

Himmler would soon have further reason to return to the area. The Reichsführer was put in charge of the investigation into the 20 July plot, and the police operation was based at the SS training centre at Drögen, just five miles from Ravensbrück. The Ravensbrück bunker was even used to hold many of the plotters while they were under interrogation. Prisoners remember a 'great commotion' when the culprits were driven into the camp in cars and all inmates were ordered indoors and told not to look out of the windows.

Isa Vermehren, the cabaret singer, who had been in the bunker's privileged wing for nearly nine months, observed the plotters in their nearby cells as they awaited their fate. The first she saw was Count Wolf-Heinrich von Helldorf, the Berlin police chief, who had masterminded the expulsion of

Berlin's Jews. So angry was Hitler at von Helldorf's betrayal that he forced him to watch his co-conspirators hanged before being hanged himself. One day Isa saw another plotter – the elderly Otto Gessler – in the yard outside. 'He sat on a chair in the sun, more dead than alive, with an expression of endless sadness on his face'.

Soon wives, sisters and daughters of von Stauffenberg and his relatives were arrested and his own wife, Nina, was brought to Ravensbrück. Towards the end of July, one of Hitler's senior generals, Franz Halder, arrived at the bunker along with his wife. Though kept in separate cells, the couple were allowed to meet to say 'good morning' and 'good night'.

During this time Helmuth von Moltke, the other bunker hostage, began to realise that he too was doomed. Though not directly involved in the 20 July plot – he had been held in the bunker since February on unrelated charges of treachery – he knew, nevertheless, that Himmler's investigation would link him to the conspirators. Discussing his future with Isa, he said he was no revolutionary and was against assassination. 'He was smart enough to see that a successful assassination wouldn't have had a better outcome than a failed one,' Isa recalled. 'He was of the opinion that Hitler had to destroy his system himself, in order to leave the other National Socialists no arguments for their defence.'

Von Moltke also told Isa he sympathised with the women prisoners here, but was fearful for their future. 'Hope is not my métier,' he said once.

In the last days of July, Isa was interested to observe 'the three Hoepner women were brought in – all of them dressed in pure Potsdam style'. General Erich Hoepner, who had led the assault on Moscow as part of Operation Barbarossa, was already under interrogation at Drögen. 'The aunt told me she found it quite annoying that this had happened just now, when she and her husband had just received confirmation for a three-week reservation at their favourite sanatorium. And now this, just because of her brother.'

Hoepner's daughter wondered if there might be a way to deliver a pistol to her father, so he could take his own life. He was tried on 7 and 8 August, after which he too was hanged on a wire noose – another execution that Hitler watched on film.

After this, the Hoepner aunt was soon released, but the daughter and her mother were sent to the *Strafblock* for four weeks for further punishment. The mother suffered badly, and next time Isa saw her she was shaved, pale and skinny. 'Rumour had it that her husband had incriminated her heavily under interrogation.'

Frau Hoepner, was, however, able to find friends in the *Strafblock*, among them Loulou Le Porz, the doctor from Bordeaux. By this time Loulou had made firm comrades there, particularly a French woman called Madame

Lelong and a Polish countess called Maria Grocholska. Maria spoke impeccable French and German, so when the Hoepners came to the block she was able to interpret as they met on Loulou's bunk before going to sleep.

Looking back, says Loulou, it was in the *Strafblock* that she made her best *camarades*. In the camp in general there was not so much friendship between nationalities, but in the *Strafblock* there was, perhaps because the block was closed off from the rest of the camp:

> Outside women sometimes had the mark of education, but they had fallen in amongst the masses. In the *Strafblock* one could often get to know their names and situate them somehow. I found out that Maria Grocholska was the daughter of a Polish prince. And Madame Lelong's husband had worked with De Gaulle. Madame Hoepner was adorable too. They were my lice-picking syndicate. They picked the lice out of my hair for me and out of the hems of my clothes. I thought at the time, nobody is ever going to believe this. A countess and two generals' wives picking my lice.

One day the Hoepners left the *Strafblock* and Loulou didn't know where they went. 'But it was like that in the camp. You were always uncertain. Someone would tap you on the shoulder and you didn't know what might happen next.'

In early August uncertainty infected the whole camp. The Poles were waiting desperately for news from Warsaw, where an insurrection was said to have begun, and the French heard news that Paris might be liberated any day, but they couldn't be sure. Denise Dufournier and her Parisian removal gang – some of whom had meanwhile been transferred to the painting gang – were sent off to yet another block, where the overcrowding was such that they were four to a bed and had to crawl to their mattress on all fours, lying flat on their stomachs to eat their soup.

At the end of August another big convoy from France arrived and the women spread the word that Paris was liberated at last. The veterans of the *vingt-sept mille* observed these new French arrivals with fascination. They were cheerful and wore 'ridiculous dresses they'd concocted somehow'. One even had an Hermès scarf, and another a powder compact that she'd smuggled through the showers.

'It was as if a little of our former life had slipped illegally into the camp. A breath of France,' said Denise. 'And we thought – what did our own fate matter if the Tricolour was once again flying over Paris?'

# PART FIVE

*Chapter 25*

# Paris and Warsaw

On 8 August 1944, with American forces just 100 miles west of Paris, three British women were taken from the cells in the city's Fresnes Prison, put inside a truck and taken to the Gare de l'Est. Violette Szabo, Denise Bloch and Lilian Rolfe were shackled around their ankles and put on a train for Germany. In a separate carriage on the same train, handcuffed two by two, was a group of British men.

On the station the women and men had recognised each other. All were members of the Special Operations Executive (SOE), and all had parachuted into France to work with the resistance. Violette Szabo saw Harry Peulevé, a British man she had trained with. Denise Bloch saw her circuit leader and her lover, Robert Benoist, a French racing driver. The agents had been captured in the run-up to D-Day and held by the Germans in French jails. They had hoped to be liberated by the Americans, probably in a matter of days. Instead, along with thousands of captured French resisters held in prisons across France, they were snatched away and sent to German concentration camps in the last days before Allied forces recaptured Paris and took back France.

As the Germans retreated from French soil, the Führer called for all captured French resisters to be sent as slaves to German factories. Daily the exodus gathered speed; in the three weeks after the first D-Day landings 6000 French men and women were taken by train to Germany. The journeys lasted for days, due to Allied bombing of the tracks, and took a dreadful toll. A so-called *train de la mort*, death train, arrived at Dachau in July with

Frenchmen dead. During long delays, they had suffocated in the heat, or killed each other as they struggled to get out.

The train carrying Violette Szabo, Denise Bloch and Lilian Rolfe made slow progress to the German border, as bombing caused many stops. During one long halt, Violette appeared at the men's carriage window, offering water. She crawled down the side of the train, still shackled to Denise Bloch, as the German guards took cover during an air raid. When the train neared the border at Soissons, the stationmaster and French Red Cross nurses tried to persuade the driver to turn back, but were ignored.

At Saarbrücken, in a transit camp, the women encountered Yvonne Baseden, another SOE woman. Six weeks earlier, in the Jura Mountains, her SOE circuit had received the first daylight drop of arms from a US Flying Fortress and hidden the munitions on a dairy farm behind stacks of giant cheeses. When a German patrol approached, twenty-year-old Yvonne hid there too, but was discovered and arrested. With train lines to Paris out of action, she was put on a train direct from Dijon to Saarbrücken. Among her travelling companions was a French countess who had no idea why she'd been arrested, a group of 'squabbling communists' and a 'bossy' British woman who wore the uniform of the French Red Cross.

As these trains left, thousands remained in Paris prisons. Amid fears that the Germans would massacre them all in the final days, resistance leaders called for an insurrection ahead of the Allied liberation. The Swedish consul in Paris, Raoul Nordling, as representative of a neutral country, attempted to negotiate with the Germans for the French jails to be placed under Swedish protection, and he called for a halt to the deportations. By now the city's electricity was cut off, French train drivers had called a strike, and the Gare de l'Est had been destroyed by an Allied bomb. But the trains continued to leave. German train drivers were called in and the trains left from a suburban station, Gare de Pantin.

On 15 August Virginia Lake, a thirty-four-year-old American, stood on a packed bus crossing the Place de la Concorde. A month earlier she had been helping Allied airmen reach safety, but now, along with scores of other women resisters, she was part of a convoy heading for the Gare de Pantin. The French bus driver told Virginia he'd been ferrying prisoners to the station all day long and was sick of it. It was as if every prisoner in Paris was being evacuated that day, he said.

'And the Allies? Where are they?' she asked him.

'They're doing well,' he said. 'They're at Rambouillet,' mentioning a town just forty-five kilometres from Paris.

At the Gare de Pantin, the prisoners were packed sixty to a truck. Red Cross workers passed out parcels and assured them: 'You'll never make it to Germany.

It's impossible. You'll be liberated before then.' As the train rolled out carrying a total of 2200 prisoners including at least 540 women and 168 Allied pilots, a blizzard of notes sailed onto the tracks, to be collected by passers-by.

So frequent were the stops and detours that the prisoners hoped they wouldn't make it to the border. During one stop they were forced out of the train and made to march miles past the bombed tracks. A young French resister called Nicole de Witasse saw a chance to escape and dived into a pile of straw, but was soon found, beaten, and brought back.

Villagers called out: '*Bon courage! Vive la France!*' Once again a stationmaster called for the driver to stop, but it did no good. Soon, peeking through the slats, the prisoners read German signs and wept. Their guards relaxed. Four hours later, the train reached Weimar and stopped. The married women were told they could say goodbye to their husbands, who were sent on to Buchenwald. Soon after all the women were put on a train north to Ravensbrück, which arrived on 21 August 1944. On 25 August, Paris was free.

The sun was hot as the women were marched towards the camp. Through the gates they saw rows of gnome-like women and enormous bottle-green barracks standing on black dust.

They'd been crammed inside trucks for fifteen hours and cried out for water, but were told there was none. 'Typhus, typhus,' said the creatures: the water could not be drunk. A small jug of ersatz coffee was distributed, but there were no cups, so the new arrivals delved in their rucksacks for cups or bottles, or frantically emptied jars of jam or sugar that they'd packed and held them out for a drop of brown liquid. Other prisoners looking on saw the spilt sugar and jam and tried to scrape it off the ground.

As night fell the new arrivals had still not been allocated blocks. The camp was in chaos, and the women were being squeezed down a narrow side alley and pushed up against a line of open latrines. Virginia looked up at the wire behind her and saw a skull and crossbones sign, warning of live current. An overpowering stench came from under her feet: she was standing above the mortuary.

There were hundreds of others squashed into the alley, and they cried out in different languages: Dutch, Romanian, Hungarian, Greek, Serbo-Croat and many more. As night began to fall all these prisoners were pushed on further into the camp. Ahead they saw what looked like the top of a giant tent.

A new group, some dressed in fur coats, pushed their way through the alley, then slumped exhausted to the ground and lay moaning. Others – mothers with children – sat on expensive leather suitcases and stared in disgust at those around them or wailed. The word went round that these were Poles. The French stared at the Poles and the Poles stared back. One or two could speak each other's language. The Poles had come from Warsaw, the French learned, and the Poles learned that the French had come from Paris. Paris was about to be liberated, the French said. Warsaw was burning, said the Poles.

At the beginning of August, as the French had been waiting for the Americans to liberate Paris, the Polish resistance army saw their chance to rise up and seize their city, but the revolt had been crushed. Himmler's SS divisions moved in and set the city on fire, slaughtering as they went. A sixteen-year-old girl called Krystyna Dąbrówska was here in the alley; three weeks earlier she had watched her home in Warsaw go up in flames. Krystyna's father, a doctor, escaped through the sewage system; her brother was shot. She and her mother were then herded onto a train and sent west along with thousands of others to work as Hitler's slaves.

On her first night in Ravensbrück Krystyna eventually found a place to sleep, after descending some steps and curling up where it was warm. When she woke in the morning she found she had slept in the morgue. Others on Krystyna's transport from Warsaw slept their first night in the giant tent.

The tent seemed harmless enough when it first appeared in the middle of August, its clean white canvas flapping in the breeze. Denise Dufournier and the painting gang watched it go up, amazed. Was it to be a circus, perhaps, or an exhibition centre? they joked. Nobody expected prisoners to live in it. In fact, it was an old army tent and Suhren claimed later that he had found the last of its sort in Germany – such was the demand for them in other overcrowded camps. When the tent arrived Suhren even helped bang in the pegs himself.

The tent was put up on a piece of waste ground between blocks 24 and 25. In winter it was a swamp and in summer a rubbish tip, infested with flies. Then word got around that this was a temporary measure to put a roof over the heads of new arrivals, and there was certainly a need for that, as every inch of space inside the walls was now used up. In most blocks women slept three to a mattress, but in the large slum blocks as many as seven squeezed onto two adjoining mattresses. The day rooms were packed with prisoners lying on tables, benches or on the floor. In the Gypsy block the women crouched on the basins 'like perched hens', said Sylvia Salvesen. The mortuary was always so full that dead bodies were piled up in the washrooms of the blocks until the corpse cart came to take them away.

The surge in arrivals had been overwhelming and had begun to accelerate long before the Warsaw women arrived. As the Russians drove on across Poland, Hitler had ordered that every Nazi camp and prison that lay in their path must be emptied: no prisoner of the Reich must fall into enemy hands.

As a result thousands of prisoners had been put on trains west to camps further behind German lines, all of which now overflowed with new arrivals. Although the Russians were still miles away from southern Poland, evacuation transports from Auschwitz had already started, and the Polish ghettos were being cleared too, some of the Jews held in them sent on west.

At the same time throngs of German prisoners were still reaching Ravensbrück – housewives heard doubting Germany's victory, prostitutes found wandering the ruins of Dresden, more *Bettpolitische*. Then came the latest transports from France, ahead of the Allied liberation. And evacuees from the concentration camp of Vught, in southern Holland, were also expected soon.

All summer long Fritz Suhren had tried to make more space, building new blocks, squeezing more in here and there, but by mid-August the camp infrastructure was crumbling. He didn't even have the staff to process arrivals. Under strict camp rules no prisoner could be admitted without filling out forms and being issued with a number, which was why the French and others had had to wait in alleys before they could be processed.

Then, when the Warsaw influx began, the camp bureaucracy finally collapsed. The tent alleviated things, but it was not big enough to accommodate an entire city's womenfolk. In the space of a few weeks between August and October 1944 more than 12,000 Warsaw women and children would be put on the road to Ravensbrück.

By the end of August Suhren had refused to admit more. Those awaiting registration were kept in a vast seething mass outside the gates, exhausted, hungry and sick. The ground on which they sat and lay was soon a field of mud, excrement and human detritus.

The camp Poles were eager to glean whatever news they could from the new arrivals, and Krysia Czyż and Wanda Wojtasik, now strong enough to walk, had been assigned to guard new anti-aircraft ditches, dug outside the camp walls as bomb shelters, which gave them a chance to observe the Warsaw women, whom they found in a desperate state. After ten hours in cattle wagons, the newcomers had been left in the sun without food or water. Krystyna and Wanda took buckets of clean water for them, asking: 'What news of Warsaw?' The answer kept coming back 'There is no Warsaw. There is nothing left.'

Whole families arrived, and soon children were everywhere, running off into the woods, or trying to get food from SS villas. Still more kept coming and each transport appeared to bring with it more and more paraphernalia. Women sat with heaps of possessions piled around them, packed in suitcases, boxes or giant trunks.

Asked why they had brought these things the women said they had been told by the Germans to 'bring everything' and they had also been promised safety. Others had looted the riches themselves. Inmates of an entire civilian prison arrived along with nuns from several convents. Some women brought pet dogs and Grete Buber-Neumann noticed one woman with a canary in a cage. As the squalor worsened the SS feared the spread of disease, and more effort was made to get the women inside, so they could at least be disinfected and await their registration in the tent. But given the numbers involved, and the amount of baggage to be processed, the usual shower and disinfection procedures were impossible.

In the first instance the women were quickly searched for valuables before being sent to the tent, and seeing this many then tried to bury what they had in the ground, or to hide jewellery and other valuables in orifices. Most luxury apparel and jewellery were eventually stripped off the women by the guards, but such was the quantity of goods that whole piles of personal effects were left outside the bathhouse.

'There were badges and brooches and images of Our Lady and the Polish eagle, powder boxes, watches and evening dresses, prayer books, pots and pans, silver spoons, whole lengths of expensive material, mirrors, eiderdowns and violins, beautiful silk underwear and peasant kerchiefs – all higgledy-piggledy,' said Karolina Lanckorońska. Prisoners passing by stood staring in astonishment at the finery, and many helped themselves.

When the first group were herded inside the tent, they were told that this was Block 25. Like any other block, it was assigned a Blockova and two Stubovas – both of them Polish camp veterans. The tent was cordoned off and strictly patrolled by camp police, as if what happened here was all a secret, but the tent was to become the worst-kept secret of all. Soon brown liquid started oozing from under the flaps, and at night came screams and moans.

One of the tent Stubovas, Halina Wasilewska, made sketches of the structure and notes of how it looked, keeping a grid of who arrived and when. The original tent, she said, was an army tent about 10 by 40 metres and 3 metres high, held up by a pair of central posts, which meant that the walls kept drooping lower and lower. There was no lighting and no source of water. With no access to latrines or lavatories, wooden boxes were put around the tent perimeter, with buckets inside. The first 900 occupants arrived on 23 August. Problems began at once because they had not been taken to the bathhouse first. They were all filthy and lice-infested and had to lie in the same clothes they had worn in the cattle trucks and outside the camp gates.

The women were ravenous, but food distribution was almost impossible, as camp utensils were not provided, so they had to eat from their own dishes if they had any – often just jars or tins – but with no chance to wash anything, the pots turned rancid from the food left on them.

Only after two days were the women taken off to the bathhouse for a shower, and now any last belongings they had managed to cling to were taken away, and they were put in cotton camp dresses. But then they were sent straight back to the tent and forced to sit or lie on the same stinking straw. Every day the SS guards would come to carry out random searches for more valuables, snatching the last rosaries, photographs and wedding rings. In mid-September the days were still hot and stuffy but the nights were starting to grow cool. Rain started to pour through open sides and the wind pulled the tent poles so that the structure swayed and the whole tent very nearly collapsed.

Although the tent was supposed to be a no-go area for the rest of the camp, other inmates stared at it with growing disgust, saying: 'They're for the corpse squad', though many others tried to help. When the word spread that the women inside were starving, prisoners from the kitchens and the offices tried to get inside to give out soup and bread. The Austrian prisoner Anna Hand was horrified by what she found. 'The strong snatched bread from the weak and many prisoners got none at all. There were 1000 women in there, crammed like sardines in a space so small that many could only squat. Some were already being trampled to death.'

All this time, at the gates, more women from the Polish capital continued to arrive, along with transports from other places too. A group from the Łódź ghetto were put in the tent, along with the latest arrivals from Auschwitz. It was still the Warsaw women that flooded in fastest; the city now seemed to arrive area by area, as if methodically snatched from the flames and transplanted here. It seemed that the whole of Warsaw had been scooped up – rich and poor, educated or not, women from old people's homes, children from orphanages, teachers, countesses and more; all milling around, trying to find mothers, sisters or children separated on different trucks or, more likely, killed in Warsaw's flames.

The behaviour of some of their Polish compatriots horrified the political Poles. Wanda and Krysia observed that many wanted to please the Germans, believing that they really had been brought here for their own protection. 'They seemed to have no understanding of their predicament,' said Wanda. With the latest contingent came wagonloads of goods looted by the Germans from ransacked houses, churches and offices in Warsaw. So lavish was the haul that special warehouses were opened just outside the walls, and prisoners assigned to sort it out. One woman recognised her own curtains from her apartment in Warsaw.

The sight of the Warsaw women caused more and more consternation among other prisoners, particularly the Russians. Antonina Nikiforova stared in disbelief at the fur coats and the cases full of gold.

> They had brought everything because Hitler had promised them houses. They had put themselves under the protection of the fascists and thought they had nothing in common with us, so they looked at all of us with disdain.
>
> I saw nuns with big flowing black robes and gold crosses shining on their chests ... They lay down on the ground, their arms over the cross, refusing to take them off. But soon all the camp understood how you take off the robes and crosses of the devout. The SS pulled them up with a kick and tore them off. A few days later you couldn't tell them apart from the other prisoners. Only once or twice you would notice a woman raise her eyes to the heavens murmuring a prayer, and we knew this was a 'sister'.

In the later transports from Warsaw came more and more women with young babies and children. The sight of women with babies in the camp enraged some of the SS men. Sara Honigmann, a Polish prisoner, saw a group of Warsaw women standing near the bathhouse one morning. One of them was carrying a baby. 'The deputy camp commandant strode over to the young woman, grabbed her baby from her arms and beat it against the camp wall. The mother collapsed on the ground weeping.' After this another SS officer remonstrated with the first, who drew his gun, and the commandant himself had to settle the disturbance.

Karolina had won permission from Dorothea Binz to walk among the crowds, and she found many women so distressed about what had happened to them that they couldn't even answer questions. Often they'd been forced to leave children behind, or seen them killed. One woman told Karolina that she had left behind two children as the Germans had snatched her away without them. Another whispered to Karolina that she had seen the same woman's son blown up by a bomb.

For Suhren the arrival of the children presented another logistical problem. Since the winter of 1943, when the special Jewish group arrived from Belgium and Holland, the camp had always held a few young children, and more had arrived with a Gypsy transport in July. But for the most part, careful screening prevented young children from boarding the trains that headed for Ravensbrück because they were no use for work.

The groups of Jewish prisoners now being transported here from Auschwitz were the most carefully screened of all: any very young children would certainly have been picked out on first arrival at the Auschwitz ramp and sent for gassing, probably by Josef Mengele, the doctor best known for his experiments on twins.

In September a sixteen-year-old girl called Pola Wellsberg, a Polish Jew, arrived at Ravensbrück. She had faced Mengele at Auschwitz just two weeks before. Imprisoned first in the Łódź ghetto, her parents and four brothers had all been sent to the Chelmno death camp, but Pola and her younger sister, Chaya, survived because they were sent to a ghetto factory to make soldiers' shoes. When the ghetto was emptied in August 1944 she and her sister were taken to Auschwitz, where everyone from Łódź was lined up before Mengele. He pointed to each of them so that one group, chosen for the gas chamber, formed to his left and the other, chosen for work, to his right. Pola and Chaya were sent left, 'but I was pulled out at the last minute,' says Pola. She was judged fit for work, which was why she was sent on to Ravensbrück.

Regina Minzburg was also at Łódź before being sent on to Auschwitz, where she too was selected to live – 'We were on our way to the gas chamber when they suddenly decided to pick out 500 more to work. I was fourteen but they thought I could work.' But most of the Warsaw women had undergone no such preselection. These women often came straight from their homes with their goods, chattels, grandparents and children – and many of them were pregnant too.

Faced with this ever-growing crowd – many of them women who couldn't possibly work – Fritz Suhren's options were limited. At other camps thousands had been turning up from Warsaw too. The commandant of Stutthof Camp, which was overwhelmed by new arrivals, received an order from Richard Glücks, head of the camp inspectorate, on 14 August 1944 that Warsaw women with children under fourteen should not be admitted to the camp – they should not be 'recorded on the lists'. The order almost certainly meant that the Stutthof arrivals were taken off and shot. It seems highly probable that a similar order was sent to Fritz Suhren.

Suhren's other solution to the overcrowding was to send for a bigger tent. According to Halina's report, the new one was about 20 metres wide by 50 long, twice as wide as the first, and its sides more than three metres high, with a two-peaked roof. The second tent had a gutter and a light, but it had no natural light, so it was darker, especially as the electric light was feeble and barely lit up one end. The gutter leaked with the first rains. It leaked more or less in the middle, forming, on top of the groundwater below, a permanent puddle of about 100 square metres. Halina reported the leaking gutter several times, but it was never repaired.

From the start there was not enough straw for everyone in the second tent, and still nowhere for the new arrivals to wash, or to cleanse their dishes. A lavatory was sited outside, but it wasn't possible to go there except in groups, escorted by a guard. Soon the lavatory broke down. With about 100 under-twelves now living in the tent, the conditions became unspeakable. Twenty buckets were put inside, which were emptied into pits dug right behind the tent that quickly began to overflow.

By early October the nights were damp and cold. There was no medical help for the sick. The tent staff brought water from other blocks to wash the children, but it was almost impossible. There were more and more children and the fights for space increased. Within days of the new tent going up at least two women had given birth.

Every night the other prisoners heard dreadful high-pitched screams coming from the tent. One morning a prisoner was seen emerging and crouching just outside. Anja Lundholm saw the figure resting her head against a wooden pole.

> Her long hair was in disarray, spread over her head and shoulders. It was probably once blonde hair, but was grey with dirt. In her skinny arms the woman held something, but we couldn't see what it was. Slowly, carefully, she lifted her head, and saw us staring as we walked past with the kettle. She nodded and reached out her bundle towards us, smiling with an elated look. It was a baby. Rather, it was a baby's dead body.

*Chapter 26*

# Kinderzimmer

Karolina Lanckorońska was one of the first to notice how many of the Warsaw women were pregnant. Some of those pregnant were already mothers, and came with other children. Others were expecting their first child. Some gave birth outside the camp gates. Karolina asked Binz if she might give out milk to the pregnant women and Binz – perhaps a sign of pity – said yes 'on the grounds that they are not criminals like us'.

The presence of so many pregnant women among the thousands who arrived from Warsaw was no more surprising than the presence of children. These women were a cross-section of Warsaw's population, so many would naturally be in various stages of pregnancy. There had been no chance to screen the pregnant out before putting them on the trains. And yet the high number of pregnancies was especially striking. Karolina noticed large numbers vomiting. Many of these women were not sure yet that they were pregnant, but feared they might be, because during the German onslaught on Warsaw they had been raped.

Many women in the crowd spoke of rape, as Karolina and others heard when they walked around. One woman waiting at the gates screamed all night, every night. When Karolina asked what troubled her, the woman told her that her home had been ransacked, and she'd seen her daughter raped by Vlasov's forces. Andrei Vlasov was a Soviet general who defected to the Germans, and who on Himmler's orders led rogue Russian brigades into Warsaw, where they raped thousands of women, nuns and schoolchildren among them.

On arrival at Ravensbrück many of the pregnant Warsaw women were put inside the tent, but they were terrified of what would happen next. Eighteen-year-old Stasia Tkaczyk, two months pregnant, easily hid her pregnancy and took the chance to get out on a work gang leaving for a subcamp. Those closer to giving birth were unable to leave.

Nor was it only the women from Warsaw who were arriving pregnant. The screening of new arrivals in general was less thorough now, and pregnancy amongst other newcomers more common. A Breton woman who gave birth on the Lagerstrasse became infected and bled to death. Women were also more likely than before to fall pregnant at the camp itself; prisoners had more contact with men, particularly in the subcamps where German civilians and male POWs often worked alongside the inmates.

Nevertheless, it was the arrival of the Warsaw women that raised pregnancy rates to unheard-of levels. According to the office staff, one in ten of the Polish women arriving at the gates by September was pregnant. As a total of 12,000 women arrived from Warsaw by early October, this meant as many as 1200 babies were likely to be born in the camp over the next nine months.

The need to respond to the growing number of pregnant women in the camp was obvious to the SS; they could see the women all around and hear the sound of babies crying as well as anyone. In October women started going into labour at *Appell*, in the bathhouse and in the tent. When Leokadia Kopczynska felt contractions and collapsed at morning *Appell*, the guards, instead of kicking her, allowed her friends to take her to the *Revier*.

Perhaps it was Leokadia's collapse at *Appell* that prompted Suhren to call through to Richard Glücks at the Central Camp Inspectorate (IKL) for further instructions, or perhaps the new instructions had already come. In any case, we know what the new orders were from what happened next: for the first time in the history of the camp, permission was given for babies to be born. A room in the *Revier* was designated, with midwives to assist.

'I was taken to the delivery room in the *Revier* and straightaway gave birth,' Leokadia remembered. A Polish midwife cared for Leokadia, and asked her to name her baby. 'I said call her Barbara,' and the midwife held the baby under a tap and said: 'I christen her with this water and give her the name Barbara.'

The decision to allow the birth of babies at Ravensbrück was an extraordinary policy reversal. One of the camp's most important rules had always been that birth was banned. At first, women found to be pregnant were sent elsewhere to have their babies, which were taken from them to be raised in Nazi children's homes. Later, when numbers of pregnancies rose, abortions were carried out. Any baby born alive was murdered. At the same time everything was done to prevent any chance that the women sent to concentration camps might reproduce. Women were kept entirely separate from men in the men's camp, and male SS officers punished severely for any contact with the prisoners. And not only was birth banned, but the women at Ravensbrück were used as guinea pigs for experiments in sterilisation.

The sheer number of pregnant women arriving at the gates in October forced a change in this policy. There were simply too many babies to abort. Already Percival Treite was spending half his time performing abortions, and the camp had no facilities for more. It was probably in early October 1944 that Treite announced the change to the *Revier*. His instructions to prisoner midwives and doctors were to make all necessary preparations for the delivery of babies.

Amongst the first to be told was the Czech prisoner doctor Zdenka Nedvedova, who was put in charge of making arrangements. Given that Zdenka was an able child doctor, trained at Charles University in Prague, the expectant mothers could not have been in better hands. Treite seemed at first genuinely to encourage a professional approach, and there were signs that he supported the whole idea.

When the go-ahead was given, the nurses and doctors set to work. 'We got a free hand on preparing things,' Zdenka recalled. Within a short time a clean and well-equipped delivery room was ready, with enough spotless linen and warm water available, as well as paper for nappies, good lights, and other essentials. Nearby was the operating theatre, which was made available if necessary.

Whether Barbara was in fact the first baby born is not clear from the testimony. According to Antonina Nikiforova, the Red Army doctor, the first baby to be born in the new delivery room was not a Pole, but a Russian called Victoria. Sylvia Salvesen, the Norwegian, who was working as a *Revier* nurse, agreed that the first baby was a Russian, but said it was a boy called Nicholas. The news of the birth spread around the camp, causing great elation. 'People were all telling each other: "A child has been born in Ravensbrück called Nicholas."'

Sylvia Salvesen gave evidence to the Hamburg court in December 1946. 'Nicholas was treated like a prince,' she said. 'He was wrapped in beautiful clothes, given by the women who had arrived at the camp with baby clothes, and hadn't yet had them taken away.'

More births 'miraculously' followed. Zdenka considered it a miracle that sick and malnourished mothers gave birth to babies with a healthy weight of 3 kilos or more. One Warsaw Pole, Hanna Wasilczenko, collapsed at *Appell* after standing for three hours, and came to the *Revier* and gave birth to a 4 kg baby, called Witold Grzegorz. The Austrian prisoner Ilse Reibmayr, enlisted as a midwife, said 'it was a miracle' that the midwives in the *Revier* could actually bathe the mothers.

> We did it in a big basin kept in the surgery. We undressed them completely and put them into this basin. With a cloth we washed, soaped and rinsed them thoroughly from head to toe. We did their feet and they got a white nightgown. We were able to order white frocks from the sewing workshop, where everybody wanted to help. The way the women were suddenly allowed to lend a hand was wonderful. Everybody was sewing nappies and dresses for us. The expectant mothers were prepared for birth as if they were in the best sanatorium.

The prisoner medics were still concerned that despite the good birth weight the babies would be sickly, but for the first days of their lives they developed quite normally. In fact the poor nutrition, which meant high water content in the tissue, made the babies quite puffy and therefore particularly adorable. 'They looked gorgeous,' said Ilse Reibmayr, 'but of course we knew it was an illusion.'

Illusion or not, most wanted so badly to believe it that they raised no suspicions. In fact, reading the testimony, it is striking how little any of the prisoners involved feared the consequences of what was happening, or wondered why it was that births were suddenly being allowed. Sylvia says the women did wonder 'What does it mean?', but they simply told themselves that the SS were doing it for 'good propaganda' as the war came to an end – 'showing they were normal'.

In any event, for the camp's prisoner medics there was no time to think further: they were too busy trying to help. As Sylvia Salvesen went on to tell the court, after the first baby, more and more arrived: 'One, two, three … twenty or so in the early days, and at first they were still very well-treated.' To begin with the mothers were even allowed to stay close by, although they were not allowed to see their babies at night, when the maternity room was locked and nobody was allowed in.

At the start Treite allowed a glass of milk for mothers immediately after birth, and for a while he even turned a blind eye when the kitchen smuggled oatmeal into the *Revier* to mix with the milk. Nor did he object when his staff rushed off to attend emergency births elsewhere in the camp.

'We worked day and night,' said Sylvia. 'I was never without a pair of scissors and thread in my pocket. With these two things the life of a woman and child can be saved.' One night she and Zdenka were called to the bathhouse, where a young Polish woman was giving birth on the bare floor. 'We had to leave the mother. We rolled the child up in a blanket and took it back with us to the *Revier*.'

The miracle of the births, however, didn't last, as Sylvia went on to tell the Hamburg court. 'I remember a doctor telling me that two babies had died one night because there was no nurse with them at night and they had turned over and couldn't breathe.' At this point there was an interruption in the court proceedings as one of the defendants' lawyers, Dr von Metzler, raised an objection to the way Sylvia's words had been translated. The lawyer said that the translation was misleading, as it implied that the babies had been 'deliberately killed' because they had been unable to move, whereas the witness had not said this, just that they 'could not breathe'.

The chief prosecutor, Stephen Stewart, tried to clarify the matter, telling the court: 'The witness said, if I may repeat it, that the child turned round at night and because there was no nurse present it died, whereas the interpreter in German said it had no room to move and therefore died.' Stewart went on: 'Is that satisfactory, Mr von Metzler?' and at that moment all eyes turned to the man who evidently believed the illusion too; because whatever error the translator made, everyone in the court – von Metzler, apparently, excepted – knew already that of course the babies born in Ravensbrück were to be deliberately killed, simply because in Ravensbrück a baby could not live.

Himmler knew this. The Reichsführer had long taken an interest in the rearing of young babies, even to the extent of giving his own instructions on the supervision and feeding of Aryan babies born in his special SS *Lebensborn* maternity homes. For example, in early 1944, to comply with new food rationing, Himmler had issued orders that the *Lebensborn* babies be fed on porridge made with water instead of milk.

Himmler also took a close interest in the rearing of his own children, particularly the two by Hedwig Potthast. In early October 1944, despite his busy schedule, he found time to spend a whole day with Hedwig and the children, who had moved to a home in Berchtesgaden, in Bavaria, the Nazi leaders' Alpine retreat. Next day Himmler confided in Martin Bormann, Hitler's private secretary, that he had accepted no telephone calls but had devoted himself to 'hanging pictures, doing things about the house and playing with the children the whole day long'. The little boy, Helge, was now two years old, and the little girl, Dorothea, four months. According to a letter written at the time by Gerda Bormann, wife of Martin Bormann, and one of Hedwig Potthast's neighbours in Berchtesgaden, Hedwig and Heinrich's new baby girl was 'ridiculously like her father' and had grown 'big and sturdy and is so sweet!'

Within days of the first births at Ravensbrück, Treite received orders to stop the offerings of extra milk and porridge from the kitchen, so from then on the feeding mothers received only the usual diet of watery cabbage soup and a slice of bread. Very quickly none had any milk to speak of in their breasts and the babies began to starve.

The deliberate starving of babies was a long-established Nazi technique of killing. Baby starvation was first carried out during the euthanasia killings in 1939, when physically or mentally handicapped babies were deliberately left to die. Hermann Pfannmüller, a Nazi doctor and early exponent of infanticide by starvation, stated in 1939 that starving was a 'simpler and more natural' way than poison or injection. He devised a method whereby the baby's food was not suddenly withdrawn, but rations were slowly reduced. This was the means now practised at Ravensbrück: although the mothers had very little milk, they were encouraged to continue to try to feed, even with just a few drops.

As soon as they realised that they were unable to feed their babies adequately, a kind of mania broke out, as the mothers pleaded and screamed for help to save their children. Some found ways round the problem for a while. Leokadia Kopczynska says that as soon as she found she had no milk she traded clean water from the kitchen in exchange for her daily bread. 'I filled a bottle with the water and tried to feed her.' But of course her baby wanted milk, not water, and refused to drink, became dehydrated and lost weight.

As Ilse Reibmayr explained, the pregnancy itself had already drained the mothers. The Warsaw women had suffered appalling privations travelling to the camp, and many were forced to live in the tent or engage in hard physical labour, as well as being fed on starvation rations throughout. 'The foetus had to find nutriments from an organism that was at the limit of life, and the women themselves suffered from starvation that made them mad.' When the mothers needed to produce milk, of course, they could not. For many this was a first baby and they had no experience of what to do. 'Some perhaps got drops of milk but most got nothing,' said Ilse, and the mothers became even more desperate, shouting, 'Save my child, save my child.'

After about two weeks the number of babies in the *Revier* had grown to more than twenty, and no more could be accommodated, so the 'delivery room' moved to Block 11, where a so-called *Kinderzimmer*, babies' room, was constructed at one end of the barracks, with the help of the Fürstenberg joiner Helmut Kuhn. Treite recruited new midwives specifically to work in the *Kinderzimmer* and to 'care' for the babies. He took some trouble about whom he chose, among them a young French woman called Marie-Jo Wilborts.

At the outbreak of war Marie-Jo and her parents had hidden British soldiers who were left behind after the evacuation of Dunkirk in their Normandy house. All three were captured; Marie-Jo's father was taken to Buchenwald and in the summer of 1943 she and her mother came to Ravensbrück. At first Marie-Jo worked in the Siemens plant, but in September 1944 she was called to the *Revier*, where she hoped to do useful work. 'So my friends cleaned me up and made me look the part,' said Marie-Jo, talking in the front room of her house in Antony, a suburb of Paris, where photographs of her children and grandchildren filled the shelves.

When she entered the *Revier* Marie-Jo was shown to a room where Treite and Marschall were sitting at a desk. 'He was blonde, slim, not bad-looking and wore a white coat. *Oberschwester* Marschall also wore a white coat. Treite had read my file already because he said, "I see your father is a paediatrician. Well you will be home to see him very soon," but I already knew my father had died in Buchenwald.'

They took Marie-Jo to the new *Kinderzimmer*, inside Block 11. It was a boarded-up area – about 4 by 2.5 metres – in the middle of the block, with a single window and two bunk beds. At this time the mothers were still giving birth in the hospital, but their babies were brought straight to the *Kinderzimmer*, where Marie-Jo's job was to help lay them out on the mattresses of the bunks. Along with three other prisoners – a Dane, a Dutch woman and a Yugoslav – she had the task of caring for them as best she could. Zdenka, the Czech child doctor, visited every day. An SS nurse, 'Sister Helen', had overall charge.

The babies were placed across the mattresses, lying head to toe, five one way and five the other, said Marie-Jo, with a gesture – 'like sardines'. But in contrast to the set-up in the hospital when the babies had first been born, there were very few blankets for them now. Sylvia Salvesen, who also visited, said: 'We had to more or less steal rags to wrap around them. We had perhaps one little rag for every baby.' The nurses used rags for nappies too, which they washed out as best they could in the block washroom, but it was impossible to get them dry. Sometimes mothers would try to wash their babies' rags in the watery coffee they were given in the morning, and they tried to dry the cloth on their stomachs when they came to try to feed.

At first the mothers were allowed to sleep in the same block as their babies – alongside the sick – but after a week they had to return to their own blocks, and came to visit their babies and attempt to feed them four times a day, waiting in a corridor outside until the appointed time. However, given that they had been sent back to work, the visits were difficult and the mothers lived in terror of missing their time.

Like those before them, these mothers had almost no milk, but still they came each day and queued outside in the corridor, sobbing as they waited to see their babies and try to feed them. 'The pretty little face the mother had known at first was soon transformed into the face of an old person,' said Marie-Jo, 'the body covered in ulcers and sores. The mother was powerless to do anything.'

A French woman prisoner in Block 11 described how she would hear mothers come to the *Kinderzimmer* to see their babies, and try to identify them amongst all the others. 'They would count them off, in all languages. They stood at the bunk saying: "One, two, three, four, five – that's where I left him, or her, so that's mine." And in all the languages came the same expressions of despair.' A mother described placing her hand on her dead child. Another remembered picking up a dead baby by mistake. 'I remember the feeling of contact with the frozen face. It is a feeling I will never forget.'

The rule remained that at night the babies should be left alone, and they were always locked inside the *Kinderzimmer*. Sister Helen, the SS nurse, insisted that a window be left wide open, even in the winter. Hanna Wasilczenko, the mother of Witold Grzegorz, was horrified when she heard that the babies were left alone at night, so she stole the *Kinderzimmer* key – apparently with Zdenka's help – and broke in one night to see her baby boy. 'It was a dreadful sight. At first it was quite dark but when I managed to turn on a light I saw vermin of all sorts jumping on the beds and inside the noses and ears of the babies. Most of the babies were naked because their blankets had come off. They were crying of hunger and cold, and covered in sores.'

In these conditions the babies lived for a few days or perhaps a month. Vitold Georg lived for sixteen days before dying of pneumonia. After thirty days, the first 100 babies born were all dead. 'They died without crying. They were simply dead,' said Marie-Jo. Back in the *Revier*, Zdenka informed Treite of the conditions in the *Kinderzimmer* and pleaded each day for milk for the babies, suggesting he should come and see for himself, but he never did.

As the deaths continued to mount it was *Oberschwester* Marschall, rather than Treite, whom the prisoners increasingly blamed for the growing horror. She had long incurred a particular loathing in the *Revier*. According to Sylvia, who knew her better than most, Marschall was one of those 'that had accepted without question that all these women in the camp were a burden on the fatherland. Germany was everything to her and the Führer was going to make Germany rule the world.'

At the same time, said Sylvia:

> The *Oberschwester*, with her rounded figure and attractive face, her plump well-kept hands and neat uniform, had a mask of amiability and could give the impression of an elderly and good-natured nurse. I surprised her once, finding her with the baby Nicholas in her arms – a Russian, so one of Germany's deadliest enemies too. But there she was prattling to the baby, who of course understood nothing but the friendly tone of her voice. Nicholas smiled and the Matron Marschall smiled back at him.

Some time in October 1944 word got out that Marschall was storing large quantities of powdered milk in her personal cupboard in the *Revier* – milk stolen from prisoners' Red Cross parcels. The news caused outrage among the midwives and the nurses. Every inmate knew that when Red Cross parcels reached the camp they were ransacked by the SS, but it was Zdenka Nedvedova who found out that Marschall herself was hoarding dried milk, as well as semolina flakes and porridge in quantities that would have saved many babies.

As this news spread, Zdenka plucked up the courage to ask Marschall to give the milk to the dying babies, but Marschall refused. She even refused to come to the *Kinderzimmer* to see things for herself, saying that Sister Helen was in charge. According to Marie-Jo, Sister Helen loved the newborn babies and used to come quite regularly at first to make sure things were done properly. 'She had a tiny white headscarf and used to say how pretty the babies were, but as they became thin and lined, they started looking like little old people. We told her once the rats were attacking them and we asked for poison to keep them down. So she just laughed and left the room.'

In late autumn 1944 a small amount of milk powder was given for the babies. Zdenka and the nurses were overjoyed, but the quantity provided was so tiny that it almost made things worse. Furthermore, there was no means of doing the feeding. Nobody making up the Red Cross parcels had thought about feeding babies, so they did not send teats. The women managed to smuggle two bottles and one teat from the camp's clothing stores, but that was all. There were now at least forty babies to feed.

Zdenka had the idea of stealing Treite's plastic surgical gloves, 'so we cut them and made the fingers into teats,' said Marie-Jo, 'and when the mothers came to feed we just had to make them wait'. Ilse Reibmayr said that when the mothers learned there was the chance of powdered milk they 'became like animals' and when the small amount was produced 'they battled and fought and screamed. It was not their fault. They were forced to watch their children getting weaker; they were forced to watch them die.'

I asked Marie-Jo how she and the other baby nurses managed to carry on, and she gave a sad smile. 'You see, we believed – we hoped – that we might save some of them. We thought the war would be over soon and so we had to try and keep these babies alive until then.' She picked up an old ledger smuggled out of the camp, and said she was going to show me 'something terrible'. It was the birth book, which Zdenka had compiled. It recorded every birth and death in the *Kinderzimmer*.

Each time a baby died a procedure had to be observed, Marie-Jo explained. First, she or Zdenka had to take the body to the morgue, which was underground, and 'atrocious' – 'You know the Germans were indoctrinated. They saw us all as vermin.' When they had passed through the morgue they had to fill out a form, showing the baby was dead. 'Zdenka then took the pieces of paper and wrote the names in the book, before taking the forms to the camp office.'

She turned to the birth book and traced her finger across a page, showing the names of babies born. There were 600 names in total born between the months of September 1944 and April 1945. Of these, she explained, forty survived, 'but most of those were taken to Belsen in February 1945, where they also died'.

Zdenka had managed to smuggle the book out at the end, and she had also smuggled some of the forms. Green forms were for the dead babies, blue for those deported. 'But not all died,' said Marie-Jo. 'Babies were born right up until the end, and we did save some. We saved three little French babies. There were little Polish babies and Russians who lived too.'

*Chapter 27*

# Protest

After the shock of arrival, waiting for hours in the stinking alley, the French women who came from Paris in late August spent ten days in quarantine blocks. With them were the five British SOE women, as well as the American Virginia Lake, who had all arrived on the same trains. Crammed in with 600 others of various nationalities, the group were bawled at 'by servile German and Polish women anxious to preserve their privileges', as Virginia Lake remembered the quarantine Blockovas.

Some among the new French arrivals tried to boost morale, urging the group to stay strong. One young French woman, Jeannie Rousseau, told them they'd soon be free. 'Do you know that feeling of delivering good news? It was like that,' she said, looking back. 'We had come straight from Paris with news that the war was over.'

Even in quarantine Violette Szabo was already talking of escape, as her SOE training had taught her. All the SOE women were trying to stay in the background, hiding their identities, trusting nobody, keeping their aliases. They knew that if the German police identified them as secret agents or 'commandos' they could expect to be shot, but if they could merge into the crowd as ordinary French resisters they stood a greater chance of survival.

One of the British group, Yvonne Rudellat, was recognised on arrival in the camp by a group of French women from the *Prosper* resistance circuit, whom she had worked with in France. Her friends could see that Yvonne was unwell – her hair had gone quite white. They tried to make contact and offered help, but she pretended not to know them, saying she had a different name. On leaving quarantine they were sent to shovel sand. Guards hosed them with water, so they shivered in sodden summer clothes. Lilian Rolfe, another of the SOE girls, could barely hold her spade. The others noticed she was 'easily discouraged' and already physically extremely frail.

Old-timers watched the group with dread. They knew that paradoxically the newest arrivals were probably worst equipped to survive the camp. Such was the chaos, and so fast were conditions collapsing in September 1944, that it had never been harder for newcomers to gain a foothold. Physical stamina had never mattered more. As the Polish military instructor Maria Moldenhawer – five years in the camp – would later recall: 'Ravensbrück was by this time divided into two worlds: there were those who had been a long time in the camp and had had time to better themselves, and those who arrived now and struggled pathetically to keep their heads above water.'

Marching back and forth to work, the Paris arrivals stared in disbelief at the corpse carts, the beggars squatting around the kitchen block and the crematorium furnaces billowing smoke.

Most astonishing to the group was the scene on the Appellplatz, where a fat SS man on a bicycle circled round lines of women every day, lashing out with a whip. This was Hans Pflaum, the new slave labour chief. They learned to call him the cattle merchant, and this was his cattle market, where he selected prisoners for the satellite camps. There was talk among the group that they too would be sent to satellite camps soon; most hoped for the chance, thinking anything would be better than this.

The Ravensbrück satellite network had nearly doubled over the past year. By October 1944 the women's camp was sending slave labour to as many as thirty-three subcamps scattered over a vast area of Germany.

Once on the periphery of Himmler's camp empire, Ravensbrück had grown in importance and was now crucial to Germany's fight back, supplying labour to some of the most valued arms factories in the Reich. Some of the satellites were so far away that they'd been placed under administrative control of men's camps like Buchenwald, Dachau and Flossenbürg, but Ravensbrück still supplied the female labour and the guards. It was to serve these subcamps that the French women had been brought here, along with all the other slave labourers now pouring in.

In mid-September the camp filled with another transport of fresh slave workers; this group were mostly fair and all wore neat blue dungarees and matching blue headscarves. These Dutch prisoners had come from the concentration camp of Vught. On 4 September, just as Canadian troops were about to liberate them, the women had been driven out of the camp gates and put on trains to Germany. After 'quarantine' in the tent many of the Dutch were selected for a subcamp at Dachau, while others were chosen for the Siemens plant at Ravensbrück.

Of all the Ravensbrück munitions factories, Siemens & Halske had always been the most important. By the autumn of 1944, Siemens employed 2300 Ravensbrück women at their main camp plant, and perhaps as many as 150 civilians, and an unknown number of women slave labourers were working at subcamps too. In September the company was again looking for fresh workers to replace those expended; Siemens had a contract to make parts for the V2 miracle weapon that Himmler had promised would win the war. As always, young women with slender fingers were in demand. For many months Siemens had also been employing teenage girls imprisoned as delinquents at the nearby Uckermark Youth Camp, where the company had built a factory outpost in early 1944.

From the cattle market at the main camp incoming girls of fifteen and upwards were now also being snapped up. Some came to work at Siemens with sisters or mothers, some had lost mothers, and many were torn from mothers on the Appellplatz and then marched up the hill. 'We saw them crying quietly calling for their mothers,' said Anni Vavak, the Austrian-Czech prisoner who was now a senior Kapo at Siemens.

The new Dutch transport also contained nimble hands. Some even had relevant experience, having worked already at a Philips factory near Eindhoven, so they too were selected for the plant. To the Dutch, Siemens certainly seemed preferable to working out of doors, especially as winter was coming, so the astute nineteen-year-old Margareta van der Kuit volunteered.

Margareta's skills were quickly identified by a Siemens *Meister* who promoted her to work for him in a clerical job. Like others before her Margareta tried to tell this German civilian – a man called Seefeld – about the horrors of the main camp in the hope he might help.

> He looked at me and said, 'But you have all done something wrong, haven't you, something illegal. That is why you are here,' as if that justified it to him. So I said, well Herr Seefeld no, we haven't done anything wrong, but he didn't understand. But he was not a bad man. He said to me, 'Well, Van der Kuit, when you are free go to Berlin and tell them I sent you and you will get a good job.'

Also among the Dutch chosen in September for the Siemens plant were Corrie ten Boom and her sister Betsie. The daughters of a watchmaker from Haarlem, the women, both devout Christians, were arrested for their part in hiding Jews. Corrie was fifty-two and Betsie fifty-nine when they arrived in Ravensbrück, and Betsie was in poor health. At first the sisters were pleased to be joining the so-called 'Siemens brigade', as it meant marching out of the vast iron gates and 'into the world of trees and grass and horizons'.

Given the preference for using young women, it is surprising that two ageing Dutch sisters were chosen for Siemens, but the company needed outdoor workers too, and instead of coiling wire under cover, Corrie and Betsie were made to push an iron handcart laden with metal plates along a railway track, for eleven hours a day. When they returned to the main camp in the evening, Betsie, the weaker, could barely walk from exhaustion. After the evening soup, the sisters found a space on a flea-ridden bunk and read quietly from a bible they had smuggled into the camp. As Betsie and Corrie translated the Dutch verses into German, they heard their words passed along the aisles in French, Polish, Russian, Czech and back into Dutch. A group of Catholics recited the Magnificat.

When the Paris women were called to the cattle market some of their group were selected for Siemens too, but an order had come from a Heinkel factory at Torgau, 200 miles to the south, and most of the French were sent there. The women were eager to go, 'especially as everything here seemed calculated to make people die without being killed', recalled Virginia Lake. By early September they were on a train out of Ravensbrück, and praying they'd never come back.

It took three days in cattle wagons to reach Torgau, a pretty town on the Elbe. Marching to their subcamp, Lilian Rolfe felt faint, so a French woman who had befriended her, Jacqueline Bernard, linked arms and helped along. Ravensbrück women were astonished to pass a POW camp where thousands of French men were held. They looked healthy and happy, which cheered the women. 'It won't be long now,' the men shouted. 'We've crossed the frontier. The Allies are in Germany and on their way.' At this news a new surge of joy erupted along the women's ranks. Some said it could be weeks, others that it might be days. Hitler might surrender any day, now he knew that all was lost.

Entering the camp gates, the barracks seemed clean and well equipped. They had a mattress each and there were steam radiators in each block, with running water. Their first night, they even had a blanket each. Next morning the pleasant surprises continued. At *Appell* the commanding officer addressed the women politely, using good French. 'You'll soon have everything you need,' he said. That evening they had fresh bread, sauerkraut and a piece of sausage each. Seeing how thinly dressed the women were, the officer allowed them to stand at the next *Appell* in their blankets. Lilian was taken to the hospital, which even had medicines.

Among the group, however, there was unrest. Torgau was obviously a munitions factory and some of the women were talking of revolt. According to Virginia it was precisely the atmosphere of cleanliness and consideration that made the women 'freshly conscious of their rights'. Lists were drawn up of who was for and who was against a protest. 'Not even the Nazis have the right to make us work in arms factories,' the women said.

Soon Jeannie Rousseau, the woman who back in the quarantine block had told them they would soon be free, had once again taken a lead, telling the women they should refuse to make arms. A spirited twenty-two-year-old from Brittany, Jeannie had perhaps more reason than most to feel this way. Early in the war she had worked as an interpreter for German generals in France. So adept had she been at securing their trust that she was privy to high-level discussions about the German V2 bomb. She even saw inside Hitler's weapons establishment at Peenemünde. She passed on what she learned to British intelligence, who considered her so valuable that in May 1944 plans were made to get her back to London for a debriefing, by taking her off the Breton coast in a small boat. But traitors scuppered her escape and Jeannie was arrested by the Gestapo.

As she called the protest at Torgau, Jeannie still had no idea that the factory there made parts for the V2, but she knew enough to tell the German officer in charge there that she would not work for him. 'I went to this man and said in my beautiful German: "We are with the resistance. We cannot accept work on ammunition." I told him we would work, but not to produce arms,' said Jeannie, who spoke 'beautiful English' too. She lived on the Quai de Grenelle on the banks of the Seine. 'So this officer, he just said: "OK, it can be arranged. If you refuse to work in the factory you can go back to Ravensbrück."'

At this the protest fell apart. Nobody wanted to return to the camp. Lists were drawn up and women put their names down to stay or go. The war was so nearly over that the arms they would make would never be used, said some. Others said that Ravensbrück would kill them if they went back. 'Half-heartedly I signed up for Ravensbrück, but half an hour later someone convinced me it was lunacy and I took my name off,' Virginia Lake recalled.

Jeannie addressed the crowd. 'I stood up in front of them all and I said, look, we have gone through so many difficult years. Now, after all that work, for the first time we can stand up to the Germans. I thought this was our chance. I was there like that in front of them all. You see I was convinced somebody had to do something. Somebody had to stand up. I decided to do it.'

'Why you?'

'Because I was there. Period.' She drew on a cigarette. 'And because I was very young.' At eighty-nine Jeannie, now Jeannie de Clarens, had lost little of her allure, but her voice faltered as she talked of her action that day at Torgau. She knew that many women – including many French – had died in atrocious circumstances as a direct consequence of the protest she led. She knew that comrades blamed her at the time and that some still blame her today.

'It was very childish. I never knew his name, that man. I remember there was this one officer and he was in charge of the factory. And there were 1000 of us standing to attention. I decided it was the time to come out in the open. I said you obviously don't know who we are. We are this and we are that, and I told him what we had done. We ought to be protected by the Geneva Conventions, I said.'

'What was he like?'

> I remember feeling I could talk to him. This is my name, so-and-so, and I am speaking for my friends. We will not do this work. Many remained silent, you know. Many said no.
>
> And I went on and said: 'We will go and pick your potatoes but I won't make your bombs.' It was when I said that that he threw me in the punishment cell, and it was not a very pleasant punishment cell I can tell you. He was flabbergasted. He could not imagine this could happen. And for a long time he didn't know what to do with the others. But he sent me to this cell while he tried to get orders about what to do with the rest. I spent about three weeks there. Every morning I was put under a cold-water spray. And beaten. And then back to my cell. Next morning same thing.

'Did you have any doubts at the time?'

'No, I had no doubts. I knew the chance was there. We never knew at the time we would spend another winter there.'

While Jeannie was in her cell, the munitions workers went to the factory, where they endured terrible conditions. Most made shell cases, which were dipped by cranes into tubs of acid that burned their hands and clothes, and they choked on sulphur. Others worked in sunken caves linked by underground railway tracks. Those who had refused to make arms were sent instead to work in the kitchens and the fields, while the camp director sought instructions about what to do with them. They were far better off than those in the factory, often working in the fresh air.

Virginia recalled that all the Anglo-Americans were there. She didn't know all the English women's real names, because they still kept their aliases, but her descriptions of the women, recorded in a diary, identified three 'parachutists' who clearly included Violette Szabo. 'She was young, charming and attractive. She used to stretch her limbs like a cat as she lay on her bunk not far from mine.'

Denise Bloch was there too – 'She was very much in love with a French automobile champion.'* And Lilian Rolfe, now out of the sickbay: 'We lost patience with her sometimes. We tried hard to make her eat the little food we were given, but she wouldn't because she didn't like it. She appeared to be doomed from the start.'

Virginia herself was the only American-born woman here, but there were two other Americans by marriage. Charlotte Jackson, a Swiss woman, was married to an American doctor who had been working at a hospital in Neuilly, outside Paris, at the outbreak of war, and she was arrested with her husband and son. Also in the group was a French woman, Lucienne Dixon, married to an American engineer who had also been working in France.

The other two British SOE women who had also arrived from Paris in late summer – the white-haired Yvonne Rudellat and a radio operator called Eileen Nearne – also went to Torgau at first, but they didn't stay. Yvonne Rudellat returned to Ravensbrück, probably too sick to work. Eileen Nearne joined the protest at Torgau, but was then selected for a different subcamp near Leipzig and taken away.

The seven British and Americans who remained at Torgau were then sent to work in the vegetable cellar just outside the camp wall, where they made contact again with the French POWs. The men left messages and gifts in a hiding place in the woods – aspirins, pencils, paper and prayer books. The POWs were much better off than the concentration-camp women. One day they provided a banquet from their Red Cross parcels – Kraft cheese, Sun-Maid raisins, Jack Frost sugar. They told the women they had built a secret radio transmitter, and offered to send messages to London. Violette, Lilian and Denise gave them numbers and a code with which to contact their headquarters in London's Baker Street. Whether it was really possible to send the message, they didn't know.

At this time Violette was again talking of escaping. 'Night after night her plan was to be culminated,' Virginia recalled, 'but somehow it never worked, although she spent hours waiting for her chance.' Then in early October the Anglo-American group were told they were to leave the vegetable cellar and feared this might mean a return to Ravensbrück, but instead they were sent to dig potatoes. It was getting colder but they were pleased to be out in the open. The forest turned yellow, red and orange. Then came further rumours

* This was Robert Benoist, the SOE agent who was arrested with Denise in France. Benoist was taken to Buchenwald where he was executed in October, a few weeks after Denise had arrived at Ravensbrück. Also executed at Buchenwald in October were the other eight French section SOE men who had travelled on the same train as the SOE women.

about a return to the main camp, but the orders were to dig faster, the frosts were coming.

While the Torgau potato-pickers dug into frozen soil, another group of French and British women had turned up at the Ravensbrück gates. This was a small transport of just fifty, and among them were Yvonne Baseden, the SOE woman captured in the cheese factory near Dijon, and her older English travelling companion, the bossy woman in the French Red Cross uniform. The woman's name was Mary Lindell, though she was also the Comtesse de Milleville, as she had married a Belgian count.

Such was the chaos at the gates at the time Yvonne and Mary's group arrived that they seem to have wandered into the camp almost unnoticed. It was getting dark and they stumbled across a giant tent. According to Mary Lindell, it was empty and 'piled high with clean straw and blankets'. Someone told them they couldn't sleep in it because a new transport of Polish prisoners was expected any minute, so this must have been the second, bigger, tent, put up in the first week of September. Mary and Yvonne saw it just before it was filled with more prisoners, so it was still clean.

Mary marched in, grabbed an armful of blankets and handed them out to her friends. After making sure Yvonne was warm enough – Mary had taken the young woman under her wing – they all settled down on the ground. It was damp and a mist blew off the lake, but they were all so tired they fell asleep.

An important-looking German officer and a woman guard approached and pulled the blankets off. The officer, who had an interpreter, demanded to know who gave the women permission to take the blankets. Mary jumped up and retorted: 'I did. Who gave you the right to allow women to sleep out in the open like this? We are prisoners of war. These women have been sleeping in a cattle truck for over fourteen days, and I'm going to see they keep the blankets for the night.'

Mary's behaviour must have astonished onlookers, but it came as no surprise to Yvonne, who was already used to her companion's brazen ways. In her forty-five years Mary Lindell had never been one to show fear. At the start of the First World War she volunteered as a Red Cross nurse and organised dressing stations close to the front line. Between the wars she married a Belgian count and raised a family, then in 1939 she volunteered again as a French Red Cross nurse before being recruited by the British escape service, MI9, to smuggle Allied servicemen out of southwest France. Finding herself in a Nazi concentration camp, she now seems to have thought nothing of tearing a strip off an SS commandant.

'She always thought she knew best,' said Yvonne Baseden. 'She was an impossible character and disliked by everyone in normal circumstances. But in the camp you needed someone like that.'

Fritz Suhren, however, was not at all put out by *die Engländerin*, as he called Lindell. But he was interested in the quality of her barathea twill uniform. When she had finished complaining to him, he leant forward and felt the lapel, then he turned to Dorothea Binz, saying: '*Das ist schön.*' Binz felt the woollen cloth too. After more discussion the group were permitted to keep the blankets for the night. The following day Mary continued to protest that she and Yvonne were prisoners of war, but the women were soon sent off for the usual shower. Mary was forced to remove her uniform and was handed a soiled yellow flowery dress in return, while Yvonne took a red skirt and shirt.

A woman with a red arm band, printed with a black 'P', then approached them. 'You are English and so am I,' she said. The woman said her name was Julia Barry, and she was a camp policewoman. She explained that she had been chosen for the role because she spoke several languages. Yvonne and Mary had no idea what to make of her. The camp appeared to be run by the inmates, and one of them, this 'Englishwoman', Julia Barry, carried a truncheon and a whip.

And yet Julia Barry obviously wanted to help. She hid Mary's First World War Croix de Guerre medal, which had been pinned on her uniform, and suggested that Mary should seek work in the *Revier*, as conditions were better there. The SS doctor even had English connections. Julia Barry said there were several other Englishwomen in the camp too, and she described a few. Some were obviously the SOE women, whose identities – despite their use of aliases – Yvonne guessed. But Julia mentioned others who had nothing to do with SOE.

Under interrogation after the war, Fritz Suhren denied there were any British women at all in Ravensbrück. It was one of his many blatant lies: he knew that by September 1944 the camp held at least twenty British prisoners, or women who were British by marriage. And not only had *die Engländerin*, Mary Lindell, caught his attention, so had a woman called Odette Sansom, whom he believed to be related to Winston Churchill.

Odette Sansom, who was French by birth and married to an Englishman, was another SOE agent. When she was captured in southern France in 1942, Odette was in bed with her SOE circuit organiser, Peter Churchill, a very distant relative of the British prime minister. Hoping it might help her, Odette told her German captors that she was 'Mrs Churchill'. Her deception afforded her little protection at first, but on arrival in Ravensbrück in July 1944, Suhren questioned her about her family connections. 'I told him that "my husband" was a distant relative of the prime minister, but I could see he thought I was a nearer relation than that,' she said. Suhren put Odette in one of the 'privileged' bunker cells, with a bed, blankets and SS canteen food. He also visited her regularly to check that all was well.

To be British in Ravensbrück in 1944 was certainly unusual, but it was not unheard-of. The numbers were small because the British Isles were not occupied. Mass deportation never happened. Nevertheless, several hundred British men and women did find themselves in Hitler's camps. Those we know most about were captured while working with the resistance in occupied countries on the continent, either for British intelligence or guerrilla cells such as those organised by SOE.

Less well known are the hundreds of ordinary British men and women who simply happened to be on the continent when war broke out and were then captured. Many British women – nurses, nuns, governesses – were captured in France, Belgium and the Netherlands, where they were living and working, perhaps married to a Frenchman. Those captured and sent to Ravensbrück had often helped a local underground cell and had been rounded up like any other resister.

The stories of the SOE women taken to Ravensbrück were investigated after the war, but most of the other British prisoners at the camp have remained largely anonymous. Hints of who some were and what became of them appear from time to time in the testimony of other survivors, in letters, or occasionally in post-war reports filed by Allied officials who investigated the camps. One such report shows that among the motley British group were a former British golfing champion called Pat Cheramy, who worked on a resistance escape line, a sixty-year-old Scottish nurse called Mary Young and the Irish-born governess Mary O'Shaughnessy, who had an artificial arm and came from Leigh in Lancashire. Two Irish nuns who hid Allied airmen in their convents were also loosely joined to the British group.

There were also women who claimed to be British, but who probably were not. One, a journalist called Ann Sheridan, with Swiss connections, was distrusted by the rest of the group for being 'too close to the Germans'. On the other hand Julia Barry, the camp policewoman, whose claim to be British was also doubtful, was well liked and said by others to have been cheerful, and 'intensely patriotic about Guernsey'.

Born Julia Brichta, her father was a Hungarian Jew and her mother American. In the 1930s she married an Englishman called Barry and went to live in the Channel Islands, where she had made several applications for a British passport, which were always refused. In 1942 she helped British intelligence by sending signals to London about German shipping movements in the Channel, for which she was arrested and sent to Ravensbrück.

Julia's own story emerged in more detail than many others after the war, in part because she gave evidence at the Hamburg trial. As a camp policewoman she might well have faced accusations of collaboration with the SS, but Julia had made good use of her policing role to get around all parts of the camp, gathering vital information as she went. At the same time she became known to the other British women because she was the only one of the group who seems to have tried to keep an eye out for the rest. Leaders are usually easy to identify amongst other national groups in the camp, but the small number of British women seem to have been unusually disunited and diverse. Amongst them only Julia Barry seems to have displayed any 'British solidarity' and tried to follow what happened to them all.

For example Julia quickly heard when Pat Cheramy, the golf champion, was bitten by a guard; Pat even went to Julia 'to show me the teeth marks'. Julia heard about a British woman called Sylvia who was beaten up so badly her face was covered in blood. And when Mary O'Shaughnessy was beaten so hard across the face that her front teeth were knocked out, Julia learned of it. She also learned that after Mary was knocked down for the first time, she stood up and was beaten down again, and smashed in the face so that her nose was broken.

As a camp policewoman, Julia Barry also saw when British women came and left the camp. She knew that the British SOE women had left for Torgau in mid-September, and on 6 October she saw Violette, Denise and Lilian come back. The three returned with the American, Virginia Lake, and a large group of French, all of whom had taken part in the Torgau protest. It was expected that they would now be punished, though nobody yet knew how.

Entering under the Ravensbrück gates was far worse the second time. The women were treated as if they 'already belonged here' and everything was eerily familiar. Even in a month things had got worse. The guards seemed more brutal, pulling hair, beating with sticks and 'seizing our miserable little sacks that we had made of whatever we could'. The food rations were smaller and there was less bread. The morning *Appell* was much worse too. At 4 a.m. in mid-October it was far colder than it had been in early September, and the women had no coats. There was a 'black-haired Gypsy – a witch' who kicked and shoved them out into the cold. After a few days, some of the younger women were issued with coats while the old were left shivering with no coats at all, 'but still we clung on to ours,' recalled Virginia.

The Norwegian prisoner Nelly Langholm remembers meeting Violette in October, when she was sent to work with Norwegians in the fabric store. 'She talked of her little daughter and was so beautiful and cheerful and full of life.'

A guard came and took Violette away, but before she left, she was ordered to remove her number and triangle, 'which made us all very scared, as it only happened when prisoners were going to be shot,' said Nelly.

Yvonne Baseden also saw the women when they returned in October. The three sought out Yvonne in her block, probably on the direction of Julia Barry, and they told her they were leaving for another subcamp. This would explain why Nelly saw Violette take off her number. Prisoners were always given new camp numbers when they went to subcamps. Violette, Denise and Lilian also told Yvonne something of their time at Torgau:

> They said they'd taken part in a protest. They told me they'd met with POWs and given everyone's names, which the POWs had promised to send on to London, so London would know where we were. They were pleased to be leaving to another subcamp. They'd been lucky with the first one and they hoped they'd be lucky again.

*Chapter 28*

# Overtures

If anyone in London had picked up messages sent by the French POWs on behalf of the three SOE women, it would have been Vera Atkins, the SOE desk officer who helped train them and saw them off to France. But after the women disappeared, the SOE signals room in London's Baker Street remained silent.

Soon after Paris was liberated, Vera Atkins travelled over to France by naval gunship, to begin the hunt for the missing. She visited French jails where once the women had been, and saw scratches on cell walls – '*Vive la France*' – and calendars with dates crossed off, but no trace of where they'd gone. Only in one case was there a lead. Cicely Lefort's husband received a note from her in the summer of 1944 giving an address: 'Konz Lager, Ravensbrück, Fürstenberg, Mecklenburg'. Vera had heard talk of Ravensbrück, but when she asked the War Office in London what they knew of the camp, they replied: 'Ravensbrück camp as such is comparatively unknown to us and we have no record of any British civilian internees being in Brandenburg now.'

Had War Office officials wished to learn more about Ravensbrück they need only have walked around the corner, where on 4 October 1944, in a Westminster meeting room, a group of women's leaders were hearing a report, 'delivered to this country by hand' and listed under urgent business, on every aspect of the camp. The Liaison Committee of Women's International Organisations, representing women lawyers, peace-makers, nurses, doctors and others, heard about the medical atrocities – 'the pus is collected in sealed vessels' – and about the perpetrators – 'two professors from Berlin and a camp doctor who is a woman'. They learned about the executions and the torture:

'Women are confined to a dark cell for 42 days and beaten with a metal rod.'

A Polish lawyer, Barbara Grabińska, presented the report but did not reveal who it was who had brought it to the country. It may have been Aka Kołodziejczak, a Polish-American prisoner released in December 1943. Born in the United States, Aka was with her family in Bydgoszcz, Poland, when war broke out and was arrested trying to flee. Her release was probably part of a prisoner exchange, secured through contacts of Aka's father, before the war a businessman in Poland and the US. When she left, Aka promised her comrades to tell the world about the camp, and in early autumn 1944 she passed through London on her way to the United States.

After reading the report, the Women's Liaison Committee sent a telegram to the International Committee of the Red Cross expressing their horror at what they'd learned of Ravensbrück and calling on the ICRC to 'give all possible protection to the women imprisoned there'. The ICRC replied that it had no access to the camp and could not intervene; its rules forbade it even to publicise the women's appeal.

It was now two years since the ICRC chose to stay silent about atrocities in the Nazi camps. It was also two years since the Allied leaders had spoken out forcefully against the 'barbarous extermination' in the Joint Declaration of December 1942, yet those words had not been followed by action to protect the victims. The Allied response had of course been to prepare to defeat Hitler militarily, but it had taken two years to put armies back on the Continent and in that time nearly a million Jews had been gassed at Auschwitz alone and hundreds of thousands of others exterminated.

Greater knowledge of the horror had not made intervention on behalf of prisoners more likely. Throughout 1944 the evidence had become more terrible and more incontrovertible. Advancing across Poland and Ukraine, the Soviets had overrun death camps and found the gas chambers. At Majdanek they found thousands of half-burned bodies and mountains of human hair and shoes. Over the spring and summer of 1944 Adolf Eichmann began the roundup and gassing of Hungary's Jews, which was monitored by Jewish organisations, by Swedish envoys and by the foreign press, and reports sent to Allied capitals. Editors at SWIT, the clandestine radio station, received graphic new reports about Auschwitz, but managers banned their broadcast because 'The information is so terrible it won't be believed.' Churchill believed it, calling the extermination 'probably the greatest and most horrible crime ever committed in the whole history of the world'. Jewish organisations now advocated bombing the Auschwitz gas chambers as the only way to halt the nightmare, an idea which Churchill considered but which Washington opposed on the grounds that nothing should distract from the prime objective: winning the military war.

*

In other European capitals, however, ideas for helping prisoners were being discussed. A few weeks after Vera Atkins had been in Paris searching for her missing agents, the vice president of the Swedish Red Cross flew into the French capital. Count Folke Bernadotte of Wisborg, grandson of King Oscar II, the last monarch to reign over both Norway and Sweden, had failed as a businessman but shown a flair for humanitarian work, most notably in successfully negotiating with the Germans for the release of captured Allied airmen.

So pleased were the Americans that Bernadotte was invited to Paris in October 1944 to meet the busiest and most powerful man on the planet, General Dwight D. Eisenhower. Just five weeks after Allied forces had liberated Paris, the atmosphere at Eisenhower's HQ at Versailles was buzzing and full of good cheer, according to Bernadotte. Eisenhower displayed immense confidence in the gargantuan task that lay ahead as his armies prepared to take back Germany. Bernadotte observed, however, that the general's war plans took no account of the fate of prisoners, a matter that Sweden was now actively discussing.

After visiting Eisenhower, Bernadotte went to see an old friend, Raoul Nordling, the Swedish consul in Paris, to discuss Swedish prisoner rescue plans. Nordling's attempts to halt French deportations ahead of the liberation had been widely applauded in Paris, and he continued to take an interest in the deportees.

Whereas in Britain and the US, prisoners were still a distant concern, France had lost many thousands of its citizens to the concentration camps. In October French newspapers ran interviews with a woman released from Ravensbrück in an exchange. She said women were dying of starvation on a diet of soup and cabbage. Bodies burned day and night in a crematorium. 'Pretty flowers are planted around the blocks to fool the world.'

French families, silenced under Nazi occupation, were now clamouring for information, and through his private network Bernard Dufournier had a breakthrough, learning in October that Denise was in Ravensbrück. A Spanish diplomat in Berlin was sending her a parcel, telling Bernard: 'In my experience the more desired articles are a tooth brush, toothpaste, soap, chocolate, Ovaltine and condensed milk plus vitamins.'

General de Gaulle's niece, Geneviève, had disappeared, and now his brother, Geneviève's father Xavier, French consul-general in Geneva, joined thousands of French who were appealing for information to the ICRC in Geneva. Inquiries from further afield were mounting too. In Brixton, south London, Violette Szabo's father, a cab-driver, had requested news of Violette from the War Office, who told him nothing, so he wrote to the British Red Cross, who passed his inquiry on to Geneva.

Virginia Lake's mother, Eleanor Roush, wrote to the US secretary of state, Cordell Hull, saying that Virginia had disappeared in France while doing 'valuable work for the Allies', and she hoped her case would get 'priority attention'. She added: 'Virginia is a gentile which might be in her favour in view of German standards.' Mrs Roush's inquiry was also referred to the ICRC. But to all these questions Geneva gave the same stock answer: the Committee had no access to the camps and couldn't intervene.

The Swedes, however, were taking a different view. When they met in Paris in October 1944, Folke Bernadotte and Raoul Nordling discussed not only how Sweden might be able to intervene, but also how it might send a task force into Germany to rescue prisoners from the camps.

Sweden's role in any last-minute humanitarian intervention was to some degree self-serving. Neutral from the start of the war, Sweden had found by 1944 that neutrality was not a comfortable cloak to wear. Allied victory was by then a virtual certainty, and the extent of German war crimes was increasingly being laid bare. Acting fast to help prisoners was one way in which Stockholm could begin to answer charges of having failed to play its part in ridding the world of Hitler and his Nazi machine. It might also build bridges with its neighbours. Both Norway and Denmark had been invaded and occupied by Nazi forces, suffering terrible losses, and many in those countries saw their larger neighbour's neutrality as betrayal. Norway in particular had lost thousands to the concentration camps, and Norwegian diplomats were now placing heavy pressure on Stockholm to find a way of getting those prisoners out before even worse atrocities came.

There were other reasons for intervention. Swedish leaders were only too glad to step in where Geneva had failed, and Stockholm was plainly in an excellent position to lead any new initiative. Not only was the Swedish capital a good place for discreet diplomatic contacts, but the Swedes had unique access to information about the concentration camps, provided in large part by the Norwegian intelligence cell started by Wanda Hjort.

By the summer of 1944 the Hjort family, based at Gross Kreutz, near Potsdam, had extended and refined their intelligence-gathering about Hitler's camps. Their group had been strengthened by the arrival of a young Norwegian doctor, Bjørn Heger, and by Professor Arup Seip, rector of Oslo University, both of them held in Germany on the same basis of house arrest as Wanda's father, Johan Hjort. The group had also made contact with the Swedish delegation in Berlin and were sending detailed weekly reports on the camps to Stockholm via the Swedish diplomatic bag.

Since the Allied landings in the summer of 1944 the Norwegian cell had been picking up reports that Hitler planned to liquidate the camps. Arup Seip, who had contacts with the German underground, learned of preparations for blowing up certain camps before the Allied armies reached Berlin.

By early autumn such reports were multiplying and had spurred the Swedes to consider some form of rescue.

If any form of general rescue was to be achieved, however, Heinrich Himmler, without whose knowledge nothing in the concentration camps could happen, would have to agree. Here Sweden again had good intelligence, this time not about what was going on in Himmler's camps, but about what was going on in Himmler's mind.

Felix Kersten, Himmler's masseur and confidant, had for some time been living in Stockholm, returning regularly to Germany to treat his master's ongoing stomach pains. Kersten's purpose in moving to Stockholm had been in part to put out feelers to the West – via Swedish intermediaries – on Himmler's behalf. By the second half of 1944 Kersten's message to the Swedes was clear: Himmler knew the war was lost and was looking for ways to build bridges with Washington and London. Such bridges could only be built, of course, behind the Führer's back.

In his memoirs Kersten later claimed that during a treatment session in September 1944 Himmler declared quite suddenly: 'There has been too much bloodshed.' Himmler believed, said Kersten, that Churchill and Roosevelt would prefer to reach a deal with Germany, rather than let Stalin into Berlin and open the way for Bolshevism to take over in Europe. Obviously the Führer himself would not tolerate any discussion of defeat, but in these secret overtures Himmler wished to let it be known that in future – should the Führer no longer be in power – he, Himmler, would be in a position to discuss a deal.

Kersten's overtures on his master's behalf were rejected out of hand in Washington and London, which continued to insist on total surrender. Churchill said flatly: 'No truck with Himmler.' And yet it was clear to his Swedish interlocutors that Kersten believed his master was serious about getting his message heard, and that in order to show good will Himmler might offer to release some prisoners. The Swedes saw no reason not to exploit such an offer and secure as many releases as they could, even though Himmler's aim of securing a separate peace was going nowhere. The first sign that Himmler might mean business came in the autumn of 1944 when, via Kersten, he agreed to negotiate the release of Norwegian policemen and students.

Other more high-profile prisoner releases were also on Himmler's mind in the autumn of 1944, but these releases were outside the ambit of the Swedish talks. Among these VIPs were three hostages held in Ravensbrück; each woman had a very powerful relative (or so Himmler believed) in either Paris, London or New York.

Since arriving in the camp with the *vingt-sept mille* in February 1944, Geneviève de Gaulle had been treated just like every other French prisoner.

She lived in the overcrowded slum block, Block 27, and shared a mattress with the British woman Pat Cheramy. Pat said later that for a long time the SS didn't even know who Geneviève was – or, if they did, they didn't appear to care. While Germany still occupied France, there was no call to take special notice of the niece of the exiled general, but by the autumn Charles de Gaulle was president in waiting of France, and now his niece was a useful pawn.

Himmler had almost certainly been alerted to Geneviève's presence as a result of the inquiry made to the ICRC by her father soon after Paris was liberated. Within days the Reichsführer had ordered Suhren to improve her treatment and smarten her appearance in the event of her release.

After nine months in the camp, Geneviève had lost half her body weight, and the sight of her standing before him in his office took even Suhren aback. 'He seemed put out to see me in such a feeble state,' she remembered later. 'He asked if I had any complaints about the regime, and the way I had been treated.' Not wishing to single herself out, Geneviève took the chance to protest on behalf of the whole camp against 'the abominable manner' in which the prisoners were treated, and the French in particular.

'My protestations were received with discomfort by the commandant, who gave the following immediate orders by telephone to *Aufseherin* Binz: to have me transferred to one of the privileged blocks; to give me a job in the office of the *Revier*; to arrange a medical examination by Dr Treite.' Despite protesting about being treated with favouritism, Geneviève now found Suhren's entire staff rushing around after her as if there was no time to lose in improving her health. Better soup was offered straight away, while Treite admitted her to the best hospital block. 'This was the first time in the camp that I saw sick people treated well.'

Not until later did Geneviève learn the reason for the hurry. On the day she had been called before Suhren, 3 October 1944, Himmler had offered Geneviève to her uncle, in exchange for a German held in France.

Just two days after Geneviève was called to see Suhren, Odette Sansom – the SS knew her as Churchill – was also offered better treatment. Odette had been kept in a privileged cell since her arrival in July 1944, but the cell, in the basement of the bunker, was damp and dark. She suffered from painful glands and her hair was falling out in clumps.

On 5 October a nurse visited Odette in her cell. As in Geneviève's case there was a sudden urgency to improve her health. She was taken to the *Revier*, where X-rays showed that she had TB. A few days later Suhren came and told her she was to move into a cell on the ground floor. A specialist doctor would examine her inside the commandant's headquarters, where she would also receive weekly ultraviolet treatment to stop her hair falling out and infrared rays for her lungs.

While Geneviève and Odette were being pampered ahead of a possible release, Himmler's third high-value hostage, Gemma La Guardia Gluck, went on receiving favoured treatment in Block 2. Unlike the other two, however, she did not receive any new attention from the SS in October 1944. Perhaps she was not to be part of any deal. More likely, living in the privileged block, her health had suffered less. In any case, whatever deal Himmler had in mind, nothing materialised and none of the three were released. The women themselves had not expected it. Nor were they under any illusion that their own better treatment might herald any early end to the Ravensbrück nightmare; they could see as well as anyone how conditions were worsening every day.

While Geneviève was recuperating in the *Revier*, in October six French comrades were taken from their blocks and shot. A few days before Odette was moved to a better bunker cell, she saw twelve women herded into a cell close by, where they were left with nothing to eat for a week. 'I saw a Russian girl being carried away from the cell by her comrades; she was nothing but skin and bone.' Through her new cell window on the ground floor of the bunker, Odette could see the crematorium flame blaze ten feet high from the chimney every night; she could even hear the roar of the fire. 'There was a considerable amount of black smoke and an unbearable smell. When I had my window open my room filled with black ash.'

Rumours of hostage releases and possible exchanges certainly gave no new hope to ordinary prisoners, who saw no evidence at all that anyone outside was interested in them or was trying to help. On the contrary, by October 1944 the women in Ravensbrück had never felt more alone. For most, parcels had dwindled, all rations had been cut, and mail had stopped. Winter was approaching and the liberating armies were not even close. The summer's hopes that the Germans might give up now seemed absurd. Instead, prisoners from Hungary were flooding in, the tent was fuller than ever, the mortuary was being extended, and a new extension to the Siemens plant was under construction, with fresh workers hired for the plant each day and rejects sent back to the main camp in growing numbers.

In October, Betsie and Corrie ten Boom, the elderly Dutch sisters, had been struck off the Siemens lists and sent back to level ground inside the camp wall. Betsie had started coughing up blood and could only shovel tiny amounts; the guards mocked her by snatching her spade and taunting her as 'Madame Baroness', and prisoners laughed at her too.

To Corrie's astonishment Betsie too was laughing. 'But you'd better let me totter along with my little spoonful or I'll have to stop altogether,' she said, at which the guard lashed out with a whip, leaving raw marks across Betsie's neck. 'Don't look at it, Corrie,' said Betsie. 'Look at Jesus instead.'

*Chapter 29*

# Doctor Loulou

By mid-November 1944 the women who arrived on the last Paris convoy were laying slabs of sod in the snow at a desolate subcamp called Königsberg, 150 miles east of Ravensbrück. The sheltered potato cellar at Torgau, the gifts of Jack Frost sugar, seemed like a dream. Most had given up hoping for the end of the war. 'Instead we hoped for the end of winter, because we could count on it,' said Virginia Lake, who was now keeping a diary.

At Königsberg they were building an airfield, but the sods of earth would not lie flat on the snow; once it iced up the squares became impossible to shift. Some days there'd be a thaw and the sods had to be laid in the water. They floundered in the mud to lay it right. Then it would all freeze over again and they'd be hacking at the ice. In fact, it was an impossible job. Everyone knew that the ground would never be level.

They were famished by now, as well as cold. Just three months after leaving Paris, the women still had a little fat in reserve, though it was fast disappearing. When they marched onto the aviation field, blasts of icy wind pierced their thin clothes. The women robbed mattresses of straw and stuffed handfuls down each other's sweaters.

At Neubrandenburg subcamp, fifty miles north of Ravensbrück, Micheline Maurel had not an ounce of fat left on her, having been here nearly two years. She too was keeping a diary. Her entry of 29 October reads: 'Sunday: My bread ration stolen in washroom.' 13 November: 'First snow, ate nothing.' 14 November: 'Very cold. It's freezing. So sad.' Then her diary stops for good and she started praying to God to let her die. Micheline had constant dysentery and yet was eating nothing. 'I wished I could let myself go and disappear completely. On the spot. I called for my mother. By this time I had no flesh, the skin hung in dry folds over my bones.'

All the subcamps were killing, but Königsberg was new, a 'punishment camp'; it killed fast. In the autumn of 1944 prisoners became aware that Königsberg, along with the new subcamps of Rechlin and Malchow, were particularly abominable places. Women sent here did not work in well-equipped arms factories like those at the subcamp of Torgau. The work was hard labour of the worst kind and the prisoners were clearly expected to work to their last breath and then die.

One look at Königsberg and the women could see that nothing there could long sustain life. The barracks rattled in the wind and the guards seemed mediocre, as if they were dispensable too. It might not even matter to the Germans if the work on the airfield was completed or not. It was just meant to break those who did it.

Even the civilian foreman seemed to grasp this. In the bitterest cold, seeing they were at the end of their endurance, he took pity and allowed the women to make a fire on the airfield. They could spend five minutes by it one by one, but there were those who refused to leave it. 'And though our foreman threatened to strike, he never did – he only stamped out the blaze. That was the worst blow he could have given,' said Virginia.

Real hunger soon gripped Königsberg. A girl fell while hurrying back from the soup wagon and lost all her soup. Everyone knew what this meant; they gave her one, two, three spoons of their own 'because it was giving life'. Eyes grew dull, cheeks hollow, skin turned grey and limbs were no longer round. 'Mina, a beautiful strong young Swiss woman, in two months had become a wrinkled bent and haggard old lady; she had lost her morale and had to be led about like a very young child,' said Virginia.

The tougher Slavs lasted longer. They'd been chosen for Königsberg because they were surplus to requirements in the factories on a particular day, and often such women were quickly moved on. Some at Königsberg specifically came for punishment. The French, and the handful of Americans and British, were here to pay for joining the protest at Torgau. Most of the women sent to the punishment camps had already been exhausted in the sewing shop, or perhaps at Siemens. Their last ounce of strength could now be eked out on digging, clearing and chopping. Amongst the 500 or so women at Königsberg many were from the Warsaw Uprising group, who had already been weakened in the tent.

Many lost their minds first. Before the snows came there was a potato patch at the end of the field and sometimes you could steal potatoes. One day a Polish woman crept there and was seen by one of the guards, who warned her to come back. 'Perhaps she didn't hear or perhaps she was partly mad.

Anyway he shot her in the back and she died right there on the ground,' recalled Virginia.

Those driven out of their minds were put with the hopelessly sick to be shipped back to die. Micheline Maurel recalled some of the French going 'mad'. The Marin sisters ran a little café in Lyon. One of them died at the subcamp and the other 'went mad' and was sent back to Ravensbrück.

Back at the main camp the prisoners often saw the trucks coming in from the subcamps. The dead, the nearly dead and the 'mad' were dumped by the *Revier*, where they were sorted. The first time the French doctor Loulou Le Porz saw this she was standing with her friend Violette Lecoq, a French Red Cross nurse.

> It was night and the electric light suddenly came on. We were by the big gates ... I said to Violette: 'If one day someone makes a film they must film this scene. This night. This moment.' Because there we were – a little nurse from Paris and a young doctor all the way from Bordeaux. There was a lorry that suddenly arrives and it turns around and reverses towards us. And it lifts up and it tips out a whole pile of corpses. We were there because we'd just taken one of our dead to the mortuary. And suddenly we were in front of a mountain of bodies. And if we recount that one day, we said to each other, nobody would believe us. And they didn't. When we came back, nobody wanted to know.

The dead were carted off to the crematorium, while the nearly dead were often sent to Loulou's block, Block 10. Many died in her arms.

Before Loulou even entered Block 10 it was clear to her that this was no hospital block but a type of mortuary. When she first started work, *Oberschwester* Marschall told her:

> 'We don't waste medicines on the TB patients,' and she gave me none. And when I entered I looked around and saw 400 dying or dead women, lying on mattresses, crammed into the block. And here was I, a doctor, with nothing to treat them with. It was an abomination. An anteroom to death.
>
> You see, they called it a hospital block but that was a piece of theatre – a theatre of marionettes, and we who worked there were to be their puppets. They weren't yet using gas, but we knew these women had been selected for death.

The camp hospital had always had a dual role of cure and kill, but in the autumn of 1944, just as some subcamps were being categorised 'punishment camps', a decision was taken to differentiate between regular *Revier* blocks where prisoners might be treated for sickness, and those where they were left to die. The regular blocks were now called workers' blocks. The other *Revier* blocks had no name, but people knew their numbers and knew they were death blocks. At the Hamburg trial in 1946, the prosecution called what happened in these blocks 'neglect killing'. By any name, the deliberate killing introduced in the autumn of 1944 was a new and concerted method of mass murder.

That the TB block was the first death block was no surprise: the Nazis had always dreaded tuberculosis, linked in their minds with dirt and degenerates. And yet, if the purpose was death, why send a prisoner doctor, a TB specialist, to work there?

Louise 'Loulou' Le Porz was a posthumous child: her father was killed in the first days of the First World War. Raised by her mother as a Catholic, Loulou knew she wanted to be a doctor from a very young age, and chose infectious diseases as a specialism, caring for the poor. When the Germans entered Bordeaux in 1940 her father was very much on her mind. A friend, a surgeon in the same hospital, asked if she wanted to help and put her in touch with a resistance cell that collected intelligence for the British on shipping movements in Bordeaux. On capture she spent three months in solitary confinement in the city's Gestapo cells before being sent to Ravensbrück. She was twenty-nine years old when she arrived there in June 1944.

Loulou has no idea why she was chosen for the Block 10 job. 'People said it was all ordered in the camps, but it wasn't like that. It struck me very quickly that in fact there was often no rhyme or reason about the way things happened. Things were quite unpredictable in the camp. You must remember that.' She had her suspicions: she might have received the appointment because Carmen Mory, the Blockova there, wanted to recruit her. There is reason to believe that Loulou was right.

By the autumn of 1944 Mory was probably the most powerful prisoner in the camp. She was also the most feared and had variously been nicknamed *Vulgaris* – common wolf; *Schwarzer Engel* – black angel; and The Witch. Once one of Treite's protégées, her power had grown ever since she was taken on by Ramdohr.

Mory was born near Berne in 1906, her father a wealthy, well-connected doctor. Her mother died when Carmen was three. A talented but precocious child, educated at different boarding schools, she spoke several languages fluently and spent her twenties flitting around European capitals before moving to Berlin in the 1930s and taking up freelance journalism. By 1938 she had been recruited by German intelligence and sent to France to spy on German communist exiles. Arrested by the French, she was sentenced by a Paris court to death, accused of passing secrets of the Maginot Line, but her sentence was commuted and she was jailed instead. When the Germans took France in May 1940, they released her and sent her back to Berlin, but Mory must have fallen foul of her German handlers, because by 1941 she was in Ravensbrück, where Ramdohr found her invaluable.

Even Binz feared her, primarily because Mory's patron was the sworn enemy and constant rival of Binz's lover, Edmund Bräuning, Suhren's deputy. Binz in turn tried to keep Carmen Mory down, sending her to the *Bock* for twenty-five lashes on at least one occasion, and for a while to the bunker. Once she was 'freed' both Treite and Ramdohr supported her appointment as Blockova of Block 10. From Treite's point of view, she was a good candidate, as she had herself suffered from TB and was therefore immune. For Ramdohr, Mory would be more useful as a spy if she held a Blockova's job.

By October 1944 Mory had built up so much power as Blockova that she was even in a position to recruit her own staff. She preferred to hire the French, in part, it seems, to set up a rival power base to the Poles and Austrians whom she detested, precisely because they too had power.* By October 1944 she had secured jobs for three French women inside Block 10, but she wanted to hire more; in particular she wanted to recruit the tall fair French woman who was accused by guards of looking proud and who she knew from the file held in Ramdohr's office was a doctor.

Loulou clearly recalls when Carmen Mory first tried to recruit her; she was lying in the infectious diseases block, recovering from scarlet fever.

> One fine day Mory appeared at the window by my bed and started talking to me. She didn't say much but she was obviously testing me out. I already knew who she was – everyone did. She was very distinctive and attractive in her way – striking, with brown hair, always curled and darkish skin – a little oriental-looking. I said nothing. One distrusted everyone in the camp. One never knew how it might end up. And people said Mory had once been a German spy.

Mory's first attempt to recruit Loulou came to nothing, probably because of the French woman's illness, but by late October Loulou had fully recovered – she was one of a number of prisoners who had such strong constitutions that they resisted sickness, and even the starvation diet didn't set

* Mory particularly hated Elisabeth Thury, who as head of the camp police was the only other prisoner with real power. In interrogations after the war Mory devoted pages to attacking Thury, implicating her in the 'French jewellery affair' – a scam involving theft of prisoners' jewels – in which Thury had got the better of Mory.

her health back. 'So Mory came to me again, and this time she told me she had fixed it for me to work as the doctor in Block Ten,' said Loulou.

One reason Mory needed Loulou was for form-signing in the block. Under the new rules, every *Revier* block – even the death blocks – had to have a prisoner doctor, if only to sign the death notices. Neglect killing had to be officially registered like other deaths, and there were so many such deaths now that SS medics didn't have time to sign all the forms. Mory had recruited another prisoner doctor, a young Swiss woman called Anne Spoerry, who should have been able to carry out the task, but Spoerry, it emerged, was not fully qualified. The daughter of a Swiss textile magnate, she had trained as a doctor in Paris but was arrested for resistance activity before taking her final exams. As a result, SS rules meant she couldn't sign the forms.

Nevertheless, Mory wished to keep Spoerry in the block. The older Swiss woman had grown attached to Spoerry, and the two shared a mattress in Mory's Blockova cubicle. Slight, with cropped brown hair, Anne Spoerry was known by the French as a loner and she unsettled her comrades by following Mory everywhere and taking on a false name, calling herself 'Claude'. The other women believed 'Claude' was infatuated with Mory, though she herself would say later she was 'bewitched'. Loulou, who still uses Spoerry's camp name today, says she mistrusted 'Claude' from the start. 'We saw how close she was to Mory, so we knew it was dangerous to have any contact at all.'

It may therefore have been simply because the younger doctor couldn't sign the death forms that Mory recruited Loulou as well. 'Although there may have been other reasons too,' adds Loulou. 'Mory only ever told half-truths and the rest was whatever she wanted it to be. Perhaps she was impressed with my title: Doctor of Medicine. I found out later that her own father was a doctor in Switzerland – it was said he had killed her mother but one never knew.' Whatever the reason, it was thanks to Carmen Mory that Loulou, an earnest young TB specialist from Bordeaux, found herself working now in the first death block in Ravensbrück.

When Loulou started work in Block 10 there were two French nurses already working there: Violette Lecoq and Jacqueline Héreil. At the outbreak of war Violette nursed soldiers at the front for the French Red Cross, then she joined a resistance cell, and after capture spent a year in solitary confinement at Fresnes Prison. She arrived at Ravensbrück with the *vingt-sept mille*. Jacqueline Héreil, also a trained nurse, had worked for an escape line; she came in May. These three now shared a bunk: Loulou in the middle, Violette below and Jacqueline above, with 'our sick all around us'. They instantly became friends and set about organising the care of those in the block.

Mory and Spoerry's private cubicle was in the middle of the block and curtained off. 'We didn't see them so much at first. They prowled the camp outside or came in and stayed in their cubicle. I don't know what they did in there – what they pleased. In any case it didn't concern us. We had to attend to our sick and our dead.'

Without medicines or anything else, there was little they could do 'except watch the little German who delivered the soup, and make sure she didn't steal it'.

> But of course we had our hands, our eyes and ears. So we used those. We divided up the block, and each morning we visited our patients and listened to them, and talked to them. We spoke no common language – many of our patients were Poles and Russians – but we often found an interpreter. And we had a sort of language of gestures. We told them we were doctors and nurses, and that gave them confidence, though we had nothing to prove it, except Violette, who had a thermometer tied round her neck on a string.
>
> She'd been told by the *Oberschwester* that if she lost it she'd go to the bunker, so she had a pocket full of spare ones too. It made no difference what their temperatures were, as we couldn't give them anything. One day Violette spilled them all and shrieked with laughter, asking what would the *Oberschwester* do with her now? But Marschall never came into the block, so she wouldn't know. None of the SS came into Block Ten because they were terrified of the sick. That was one advantage we had.
>
> And our patients could see we weren't frightened of them, which helped them in some way. Our sick women didn't have to stand for *Appell* because they couldn't. This was another advantage. When the guards came every morning and asked for the numbers, we passed them over at the door.
>
> They were only interested in numbers – always counting us. But we kept our lists of names. Jacqueline used to go round each day and write down the names of every patient, which she kept in a book, where I noted my diagnoses too. When someone died we carried the body to the washroom to wait for the cart, but Jacqueline would always try to get a lock of our dead friends' hair before they were taken away. She kept it carefully with the book to give to the family if we got home.
>
> It wasn't always easy to get the lock of hair because the bodies were piled so high in the washroom by then. The book was taken from Jacqueline just before the end.

By this time, however, Loulou herself had stored countless names of the sick and the dead in her own head. She can recount them even now, with the names of their husbands and children, and their diagnoses. Because although Loulou claims there was nothing she could do, she did a great deal. She diagnosed each woman's condition, and contacted her friend the radiologist so that X-rays could be taken. She also smuggled in medicines with the help of a Yugoslavian pharmacist who received medicines meant for the SS and put some aside for Loulou.

'I could have helped so many more.' She leaned forward and suddenly brightened as she exclaimed that in her block there were women 'of such courage you can't imagine'. There was a brilliant pianist called Geneviève Tillier, '*une femme adorable*', who had a lesion on her thumb. 'We knew she would never play again, but she could easily have been cured.' And there was Anne-Marie Cormerais, who had 'a transverse myelitis of the lung, but no lesion, and could certainly have survived'.

Loulou recalled an 'adorable little *Bretonne*', Simone Jezequel – 'she died of TB in my arms'. And there was a little *Hollandaise*. 'Her brothers came to see me when I returned because they heard I'd been with her, and I remember they cried.' And Loulou got to know the Russians and Poles in the block just as well, though names were harder to recall. She formed a particular bond with a Red Army doctor called Maria Czeniciuk, who was suffering badly with TB. 'We couldn't speak, of course, but we understood each other as doctors.'

The Armenian-born Annie de Montfort was 'a dear friend'; she died of exhaustion, 'and just before her death she asked Violette to collect her furs from storage in the Rue de Rivoli'.* And Loulou had many memories of Madame Van den Broek d'Obrenan, 'a woman of a certain age', who was extremely rich: 'I saw her the evening of her death. She said all she wished now was that her body be taken back to France ... She had come to the camp with her maid who died too, before her mistress I believe.'

Loulou's favourite was probably Mademoiselle Zimberlin, an English teacher from Cluny in Burgundy, who in the resistance had helped somehow with '*les parachutages*' – the reception of parachutists landing from England – but was 'very discreet', so Loulou never heard the details. In fact Marie-Louise 'Zim' Zimberlin, aged fifty-six, had used her English (learned in Scotland) to interpret messages sent by signal from England when parachutists were about to land and then took them to resistance cells around Cluny. Loulou had met Zim in the scarlet fever block.

'She was an older woman and very weak, but her spirit was strong. She hadn't "*baissé les bras*" [given up] so I arranged that she should come into

* Germaine Tillion said later that Annie de Montfort had called for an 'imaginary chauffeur' just minutes before the end.

Block Ten. At least there was shelter from the worst of the camp in there and we could look after her.'

At the end of the day the three French medics would huddle on the top bunk and talk about Zim, Madame de Montfort and the other sick comrades.

> And then we made up recipes and remembered our families. I learned all about Violette's brother Jacques, and Jacqueline spoke about her sister. We had total confidence in each other; but still we didn't talk of what we did in the resistance even then. It was dangerous. One never knew who was listening.

Mory and Spoerry were close by, hidden behind their screen. Sometimes they would hardly see Mory all day, but sometimes she would appear with her whip, and if she felt angry she would lash out at the sick with the whip or her fists, or just cancel their food. She particularly detested the women who soiled their beds, and though the French nurses tried to clean as best they could, there was little they could do: there were only two bedpans for the whole block. As the weeks passed, more and more of their patients were dying of dysentery and other sickness, not just TB.

'Mory terrified everyone,' said Loulou.

> Jacqueline said she even terrified Treite. But I must say she was always reserved with me. I kept my distance and she kept her distance from me. It was very ambiguous. Very bizarre. She never did me personally any harm. When it was my birthday she even signed her name on a card that Violette had drawn.
>
> I never understood why she behaved like this to me, because I had no power in the camp at all, and it was she who had the power. With others she was always very aggressive, particularly towards the Jews. I asked myself why does she behave like that?

Mory and Claude treated the 'mad' women worst of all, says Loulou. The French trio were not allowed in the Block 10 *Idiotenstübchen* over which Mory had sole control, though often she sent Claude into the room to quieten the women. 'Claude would do anything for Mory. I think she was very frightened – of everything in the camp. Some people were so terrified they reacted like that. They became easy prey. And don't forget Mory had power and charm.'

Loulou says she herself was never frightened in that way in the camp. We were talking in the sunny conservatory at her Bordeaux home. I asked her why. 'Perhaps I had seen more of life. I'd seen people die before.' She paused.

'And I had my faith. But I have to say there were days in the camp when I found it hard to pray.'

Loulou had kept the birthday card that Carmen and the others signed: 'For Doctor Loulou, for your smiles and optimism towards all your patients on this scrap of paper we give you a piece of our hearts.' And the card was signed 'Violette, Jacqueline, Carmen and Claude'.

The first *Idiotenstübchen*, described by Sylvia Salvesen, was close to the main *Revier*. The new one, in Block 10, was probably established over the summer of 1944 when the block became a 'death block'. Sylvia saw six women in the original 'lunatics' room'; now there were at least fifty. Treite selected women for the room, but he never showed anyone the records, so an 'idiot's' name was rarely known unless one of the Block 10 prisoner staff had come to know them. For example Carmen Mory recalled that a Belgian woman called Nelly Decornet was put in the mad room, simply because she had a nervous tic.

Treite carried out experiments to find out what sent people 'mad'. In one case he carried out an autopsy on a woman who had killed herself by throwing herself at the wire. The Norwegian Nelly Langholm remembers another sort of experiment, which was probably also conducted by Treite. In her block Nelly befriended a young Polish woman who spoke fluent Norwegian.

> She was called Joanna and in Poland she had studied Norwegian literature and the Norwegian language. She was quite young and very, very clever. So she was delighted to meet us real Norwegians. We spoke about Ibsen and became very good friends. One day she was taken to the *Revier* and she came back again without hair and with a big, big scar. She couldn't speak and she couldn't eat. She was very, very intelligent. I think they made some experiment to find out what makes a good brain, then they took her away to be killed.

Sometimes prisoners would notice a friend going 'mad', and then she would suddenly disappear. Micheline Maurel remembered how this happened to the twins Marie and Henriette Léger. Micheline had befriended the twins, in their early thirties, when they arrived together at Neubrandenburg, probably in the spring of 1944. They told Micheline they had been arrested for writing a book in praise of the French army. 'They were a little odd, and neither could do anything without the other, but they were the most dependable of friends. One of them became mad and was sent back to Ravensbrück. Then the other lost her mind, and she too was sent away.'

It was Henriette who was sent back to Ravensbrück first; we know this because her camp health card is one of the few to have survived, and shows she died on 7 June 1944 of TB, probably in Block 10. Her twin Marie, who could 'do nothing without her sister', was later sent to the Block 10 'lunatic room' and was seen there by Loulou Le Porz, who remembers Marie well:

> She and her twin were the daughters of a notary from Normandy. Then they lived in Fontainebleau. But the girl was not mad. She was a little special in her manner perhaps. If you live in those conditions some people react in strange ways. But it always surprised me that there were not more mental problems than there were in the camp. The resistance gave women a strong character, perhaps it was that.

Treite recalled at his trial that at first the Block 10 *Idiotenstübchen* was split into two, one side for the 'dangerous lunatics' and the other for the rest, but by the time Marie Léger was put inside there were so many 'idiots' that the partition was removed to make space; but the numbers grew, so the room was moved, this time right next to the cubicle occupied by Mory and Spoerry. This did not please Mory, who demanded to be relocated, as the *Idiotenstübchen* impinged on her space, though it was still only three by four metres in size, and the fifty women had to fit in.

The *Idiotenstübchen* had one boarded-up window, no furniture and nothing on the floor. The rations were half what the rest of the inmates had. They were fed twice a day, but much of it spilled. Their heads were shaved. Each morning they were let out one by one to visit the washroom and latrines, marched by a camp policewoman, usually with Mory and Spoerry looking on. Stragglers were whipped and punched. For the rest of the day and night the women were locked up; they had to relieve themselves where they sat or stood. Each morning two or three bodies were taken out and thrown straight onto a cart, and perhaps every two weeks a group of 'lunatics' would be taken off in lorries.

There was constant disturbance. If the noise got loud Mory dragged out the culprits, whipped them and called for straitjackets. Jacqueline Héreil, Violette Lecoq and Loulou Le Porz all recalled how in October 1944 Mory dragged out a Polish woman who was covered in excrement. She dragged the woman to the washroom, where she doused her with cold water for so long that the next day she died. Anne Spoerry helped Mory do all this. 'Claude was always at Mory's boot,' said Loulou.

In her own testimony Mory said it was Treite who ordered half-rations and Treite who ordered the mad women's hair to be shaved. She said she had never wanted to take charge of the lunatics, as it wasn't possible to control fifty women shut up in such a room. That was why she had demanded straitjackets, but there were none to be had. She tried on one occasion 'to tie the women up inside a blanket to control them', but it hadn't worked and they had started to foam at the mouth. In his testimony Treite seemed to concede that Mory had protested about being put in charge of the lunatics. 'She repeatedly asked to be moved,' he said.

I asked Loulou what it was really like in the room, and she seemed to hold back. 'The women were in a terrible state. It was disgusting. A state of total misery you can't imagine. They couldn't leave the room. Others could move about in the block, at least, but the women in the mad room could never leave – only in the lorries that came to take them away. Have you seen Violette's drawings?' She opened the sketchbook lying on the desk, which fell open at 'Vermin and Vultures'.

> You see how big the rats were. They came out at night in the washroom where all the bodies were piled. And we tried to chase them out but they came back very quickly. Once one of our dead came back to life. Someone had taken her away too soon and Violette ran in from the washroom crying out: '*Mais dis donc!* There is a dead woman who is sitting in the bathroom and talking,' There were situations that were so grotesque we had to laugh. But we were not *tranquilles*.

She rubs thumb and forefinger together. 'When the chimney was throwing out its smoke we could feel the dust in the air. You know it was very fine. And we would turn to each other and say: "You see they are amongst us again – our comrades."'

By the end of November 1944 there were sixty-five 'idiots' at any one time, jammed wall to wall, so a truck came and cleared the room again. Loulou remembers a time just after it was cleared when Mory turned up with a group of Slovakian Jews. The women had just arrived and it was obvious what was going to happen, as the guards didn't even bother to put them in camp clothes. 'They were just going to let them die, right here in this room of hunger and thirst. That was the reality by then.'

> It was just not worth while to transport them elsewhere or waste food on them. But Mory made me examine them because there had to be a doctor to sign the forms. So there I was, standing in front of fifty Slovakian grandmothers who were about to die, and I thought I was going mad. What am I doing here? I couldn't talk to them – they spoke only Yiddish. They were all over seventy.
>
> We pleaded to be able to give them food or drink, but we were not allowed. It was cold and they had nothing. We were not allowed to go in the room, and they died one after the other. In a week all of them were

> dead. And I thought why did I examine them? For what? I should have simply written: 'These are grandmothers and are going to be left to die.' This is my most abominable memory. I am haunted by that.

As the weeks passed the disturbances in the idiots' room got worse, and those present remembered several horrors, which in their testimony seem to merge into one great horror, as the pattern hardly changed. According to Jacqueline Héreil one morning the French trio found that the 'mad women' had been attacking each other in the night and one had her face scratched to shreds. In what may have been the same incident, Mory said that when the door was opened one morning women were found strangled; they'd been killing each other. In another incident someone said five were found dead. Mory recalled when she led a 'mutiny', telling Treite 'this could not go on, and conditions should be improved'.

Loulou and the French nurses remembered another occasion when, after a commotion in the 'mad room', Mory called for all the lunatics to be killed. She asked Loulou, Jacqueline and Violette to help her kill them. On that occasion, said Violette, the block was woken by terrible cries in the night. 'We got up, so did Carmen Mory and Anne Spoerry, and when we went in we saw the cries came from a woman, probably a Russian, who was fighting with another among the prostrate bodies. There were sixty-seven women in the room that night. Mory hit them with a leather strap but failed to quieten them.' Mory's version was that Anne Spoerry had come to her one morning and said that a Polish woman, 'Paulina', who had 'Herculean strength', had killed one of the others by banging her head against the wall. Mory went to Treite and said, 'I've found two more dead in the room,' at which Treite laughed and replied, 'Better two less than two more.'

On another occasion, so Mory said, Spoerry took all the other block workers to see another dead body in the mad room. It was terribly mutilated and had marks around the neck. Part of the head 'had been literally scalped, with big blue marks all over'. Spoerry looked at Paulina's hands and under the nails, finding traces of blood. *Oberschwester* Marschall was brought to see and 'thought the situation was as appalling as we did'.

Violette said that Mory went to the French group and asked for their support, saying the lunatics should be killed rather than live in those conditions. 'But we refused to agree.' Jacqueline said Treite then appeared and told Mory to choose the maddest, as he was going to inject them. 'Mory chose them and the women disappeared.'

Loulou remembered nothing of the scalped head or the traces of blood, but she recalled Paulina, who had a 'superb singing voice' and had sung out loud all night. 'She was in a kind of hallucination. A delirium.' The next morning Mory came up to Loulou carrying a syringe with something in it. 'She said: "We can't go on, we must execute her." I said I couldn't do that. She threatened me. Menaced me. At that point Claude volunteered. Anne Spoerry took that syringe and injected Paulina right there in the heart and she died immediately.'

Soon after Paulina died the *Idiotenstübchen* was cleared out again, but this time it wasn't only the 'idiots' who went, but many of Dr Loulou's patients too. As always it was the office workers who found out first that a new black transport was planned, when lists were called for, and secret plans made for a medical commission to come from Berlin to oversee the selections. The selections began in Block 10, and all the prisoner medical staff had to be there too.

There was the usual utmost secrecy about the destination, but this time more questions. It couldn't be Majdanek, where the last gassing transport had gone – it was now in the hands of the Russians. Nor could it be Auschwitz: the gas chambers there had been dismantled ahead of the evacuation. The office workers were simply told to write beside the selected names: 'sent to a new camp'.

Once a list was drawn up, the final selection took place. Violette Lecoq was called to one of the big rooms in the main *Revier* block, where a large table had been placed, behind which stood Drs Trommer, Treite and Orendi, and a 'psychiatrist from Berlin'. Also present, she recalled, were '*Oberschwester* Marschall, Carmen Mory, Dr Le Porz, Jacqueline Héreil, Anne Spoerry and myself'.

Lists for selection had been prepared, and now the prisoners were called by name. 'Thus began a march-past by which with a simple gesture the women were chosen either for transport or for return to their block,' said Violette. Many of the names were well known to the Block 10 staff. The French woman Marie Léger was among them. Loulou tried to persuade Claude to use her sway with Mory to take Marie Léger off the list – she was only on it 'because Mory detested her'. But Claude refused to help.

Julia Barry, the 'British' camp policewoman from Guernsey, was called to guard the women in the *Idiotenstübchen* the morning before they left, and she later recalled that one of them was English. 'When they passed, a young girl spoke English to me. She said she was going away now and would soon be home. I asked if she was an English girl and she said: "Of course." That was all, and I never saw her again.'

According to Violette Lecoq, those selected remained in the block that night, and the following evening at seven 'we started to dress them'. At 4 the next morning, Bräuning and Binz appeared at the block along with the prisoner camp police chief, Elisabeth Thury, and several women guards, who began to round up the women and pile them onto lorries. Violette was ordered to accompany the transport as far as the station, along with Carmen Mory.

At the station Violette saw the women put into cattle trucks 'that contained nothing but a truss of straw', about fifty crammed into each truck, under an armed SS guard. A Gypsy convoy left at the same time. Even then nobody knew for sure where the women were going, but Mory knew more than the rest: she told *Oberschwester* Marschall that she had heard they were going to Linz, in Austria.

In evidence for the trial in Hamburg in 1946 Percival Treite said at first that the women were sent to a health spa at Thüringen. Questioned again, he said: 'We supposed that they went to a psychiatric hospital at Linz, but later a nurse told me that it was a transport for the gas chamber.' Where exactly the gassing took place at Linz did not emerge until SS truck drivers gave evidence in a separate trial, relating to Mauthausen concentration camp. The drivers were questioned about gassings of male prisoners at Castle Hartheim near Linz.

Castle Hartheim was one of the first euthanasia gassing centres, opened in 1939, and had remained operational as a gassing centre until 1944.* One of the SS drivers, Georg Bloser, said he drove women as well as men to be gassed at Castle Hartheim. He picked them up from a local station. 'They were always in a terrible state. When I got to Hartheim the staff there took them away. Sometimes I was taken to a waiting room where they gave me a cup of tea.'

Karl Wassner, a crematorium worker at nearby Gusen concentration camp, also accompanied prisoners to Castle Hartheim, and on one occasion, as he waited, he saw inside the gas chamber. 'I had a glance through the judas window. I could see that the prisoners were already lying down in this inner room. It was the gas chamber and was lit on the inside. I noticed that inside there were many more people than those we brought from Gusen. I was able to observe that there were women amongst them.'

In December 1944, as the Russian front approached Austria, Castle Hartheim was closed on the orders of the Führer, and the institution restored as a normal sanatorium. Those given the task of destroying evidence of the gassing were a group of prisoners from Mauthausen, amongst them Adam Gołembski, who described what the castle was like inside.

From the entrance, he said, you went deeper into the fortress. Eventually you came to a room for photography that led on to a room that 'gave the

* An estimated 18,200 disabled and mentally ill Germans and Austrians were gassed at Castle Hartheim. An early victim was Hans Rosenberg, a first cousin of Vera Atkins, the SOE staff officer, who had been taken to Castle Hartheim in 1940 from a mental hospital in Vienna.

impression of being a bathroom; the door was cast iron, with rubber around the edges and in it was a little peephole'. Inside were six showers. From this room a door led to a further room, where bottles of gas and other gassing equipment were stored. And there was yet another room hidden beyond, which was clearly a laboratory of some kind, as there was a large table. When Gołembski reached this room he found some papers, which appeared to be a report on research done on a body. From this room another door led to the crematorium, with two furnaces.

Once outside again, looking to the left of the entrance, Gołembski found a pile of ashes with bones 'enough to fill sixty bins'. He also found an electric mill for crushing bones left over after the burning. Finally, in the castle garage 'we found clothes of children, women and men – enough to fill four horse-drawn carts'.

How many of the Ravensbrück black transports were taken to Schloss Hartheim is impossible to say, but the November 1944 transport of 120 women – mostly from Block 10 – was probably the largest. The Ravensbrück staff would also have known that this transport was the last to the castle gas chamber, which was about to be dismantled for good.

For the most part, the deaths at Castle Hartheim remained anonymous, as nearly all German records about the castle were destroyed, as well as the camp records about the transports. The only women victims from Ravensbrück whose identities are known for sure are those few whose names were known to Loulou Le Porz and the other 'staff' in Block 10.

In 2012, I tried to find out more about some of the women Loulou remembered. One was Marie Léger, and in order to help my research, Loulou's son, Jean-Marie Liard, tracked down a copy of the book that had led to Henriette and Marie Léger's arrest. He found it in the Bibliothèque Nationale in Paris. Entitled *Les voix du drapeau* (Voices of the flag), the book is a collection of patriotic ballads, written in praise of French military heroes of days past, and is dedicated 'to all those whose voice of agony and glory speaks to us down the years'. The introduction, written by the twins, speaks of 'those who fertilised our soil with the holiness of their blood – the heroes of the trenches of Ypres and Furnes', and implores readers to remember 'all the cruelties and betrayals of the Great War and the terrible use of gases in that war'. Marie and Henriette dedicated their book 'to those whose feet passed down the "road of blood"'.

Aerial view of Fürstenberg and Ravensbrück in the late 1930s, showing the Schwedtsee and the site where the camp was built on the far side of the lake

The camp wall, photographed from outside shortly after liberation in 1945 by Hanka Housková, a Czech prisoner

View from the roof of the headquarters building across the camp. This picture, taken in 1940–1, was displayed in the 'official' SS photograph album of the camp, which was used for propaganda purposes

Himmler entering through the camp gates with his entourage on a visit to Ravensbrück in January 1940. Visible behind him is the camp headquarters building

Himmler inspects the women guards, accompanied by Max Koegel. Behind Koegel is SS General Karl Wolff, Himmler's chief of staff. On the far right of the picture is Johanna Langefeld. To Himmler's right is the wall of the bathhouse and kitchen block

Johanna Langefeld, chief woman guard May 1939–March 1943

Fritz Suhren, camp commandant July 1942–April 1945

Max Koegel, camp commandant May 1939–July 1942

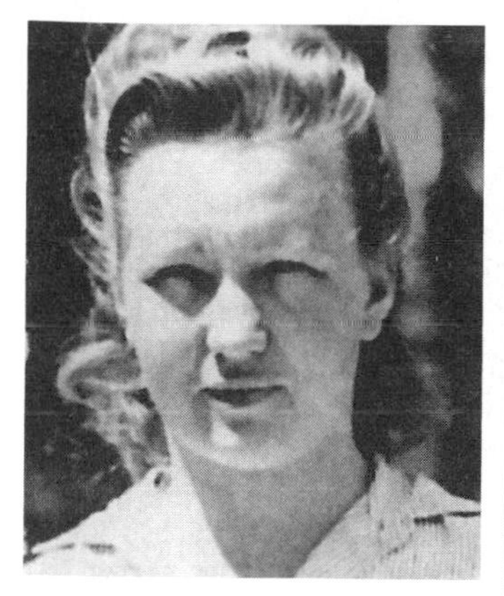

Dorothea Binz, Ravensbrück guard and later chief woman guard. This photograph was taken in the 1930s, its origins unknown

A guard, Herta, with her dog Greif at the Grüneberg subcamp. On the back of the photograph, she wrote 'In memory of my wonderful time working at Grüneberg, to my dear parents, your Herta, 24/03/1944. This is my faithful little Greif'

Studio portrait of Franziska Buchinger, a woman guard, taken in May 1940 by the Fürstenberg photographer A. Rudolph

Camp identity card of the guard Hildegard Schatz

Fr.-Konzentrationslager Ravensbrück

Ausweis Nr 656

Frl.

Hildegard Schatz

ist Angehörige des Fr.-Konzentrationslagers Ravensbrück. Alle öffentlichen Organe werden ersucht, ihr Schutz und Hilfe zu gewähren.

Der Lagerkommandant

SS-Hauptsturmführer.

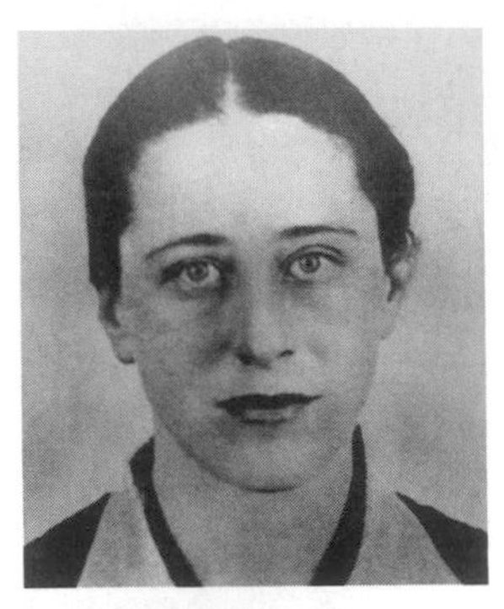

A pre-war portrait of the German Jewish communist Olga Benario

Doris Maase, the German doctor and communist released in 1942, photographed in 1944

Ilse Gostynski, the German Jewish communist prisoner, photographed in Berlin in the 1920s

Jozka Jaburkova, the Czech communist and women's rights campaigner

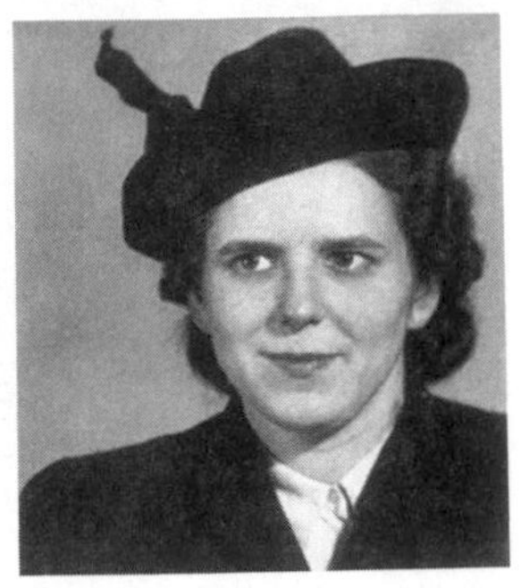

Anna Sölzer, arrested in Cologne for prostitution and sent to Ravensbrück as an 'asocial'

Käthe Leichter, the Austrian Jewish sociologist, by the Danube canal near Klosterneuburg, where before the war she and her husband Otto spent holidays

Grete Buber-Neumann, prisoner of Stalin and Hitler, speaking at a rally organised by the European Youth Organisation in Berlin, June 1952

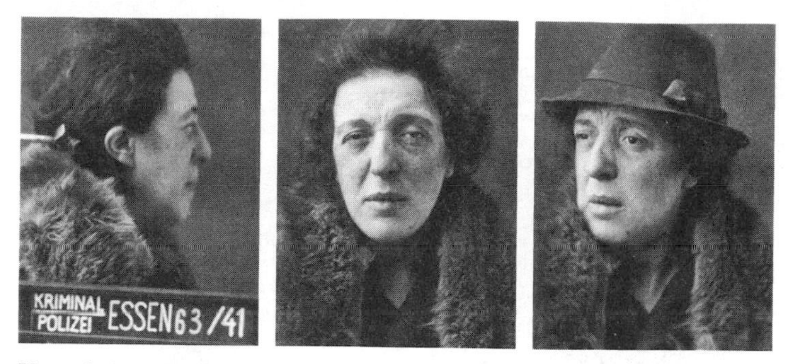


Herta Cohen, the German Jewish woman imprisoned for having sexual intercourse with a man with German blood

Wanda Wojtasik (later Półtawska), one of the Lublin 'rabbits'

Milena Jesenska, the campaigning Czech journalist and former lover of Franz Kafka

Krysia Czyż, the Polish 'rabbit' and secret letter-writer. The portrait was drawn by fellow Ravensbrück prisoner Grażyna Chrostowska when the two women were first imprisoned in Lublin Castle

The sisters Grażyna (seated) and Pola Chrostowska in the countryside near their home town of Lublin, 1930s

Digging in the sand: a photograph from the SS album

Marching to work at the Siemens factory. The post-war painting, probably by the German artist Rudolf Lipus, was displayed in the first camp exhibition in 1959, when the memorial site was inaugurated

*Le Rouleau* 'The roller' by Felicie Mertens, a Belgian communist prisoner

The guard Maria Enserer with other guards and SS friends. Enserer wrote 'A holiday at Hohenlychen' on the back of the photograph, referring to the nearby lakeside town where the SS medical clinic was based

The guard Hilde Hulan

The guards (*left to right*) sister Maria and Anna Enserer, and Ottilie Kaiser, with their guard dogs Gundo and Castor. The photograph was taken in 1940, and handwritten on the reverse are the words 'One Sunday morning out in the flowering heather'

Guards Helene Massar, Marga Löwenberg and one other out rowing on the Schwedtsee

The Polish 'rabbit' Maria Kuśmierczuk showing her deformed leg, which was injected with gas gangrene. The photograph was taken secretly behind a block by fellow Pole Joanna Szydlowska

Jadzinko - króliczku
kochany życzę Ci żeby ta
gwiazdka i ten Jezusik
nowo-narodzony przyniósł
Ci zdrowie i rychlejszy
powrót do domu —

Ravensbrück - 194?r.

A Christmas card given to Jadwiga Dzido, a 'rabbit', by another inmate. The card reads: 'Jadzienko Bunny, for Christmas I wish that baby Jesus will grant you health and hope that you will get back home'

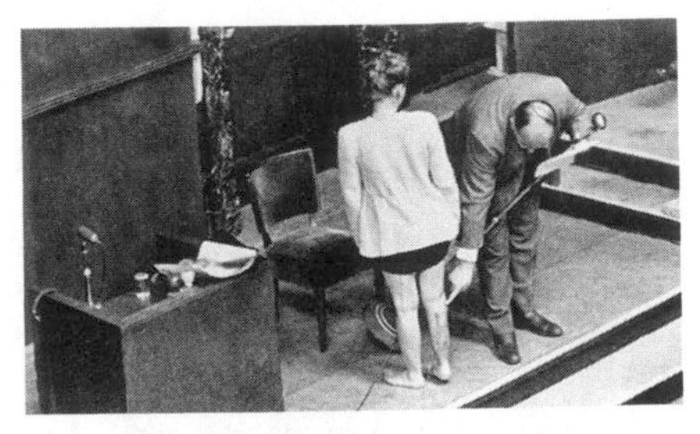

Jadwiga Dzido's leg is examined by Dr Leo Alexander at the Nuremberg doctors' trial in December 1946

*Koperta* (envelope) no. 5 is one of the secret letters written in urine by the Polish 'rabbit' Krysia Czyż. Here she tells her family in Poland that surviving rabbits are able to rest in the block and knit socks

Dr Karl Gebhardt, mastermind of the Ravensbrück medical experiments, with injured First World War veterans and sportsmen at the Hohenlychen SS clinic in the 1930s

*The Children's Christmas Party,* 1944. Painting by Ceija Stojka, the Austrian-Romani artist who was a child prisoner at the camp, having arrived from Auschwitz in 1944. The painting shows children with crosses on their backs, clearly identifying them should they escape

*Zimni Apel* ('winter *Appell*') by the Czech prisoner Nina Jirsíková

*Nourritures terrestres* by Violette Lecoq

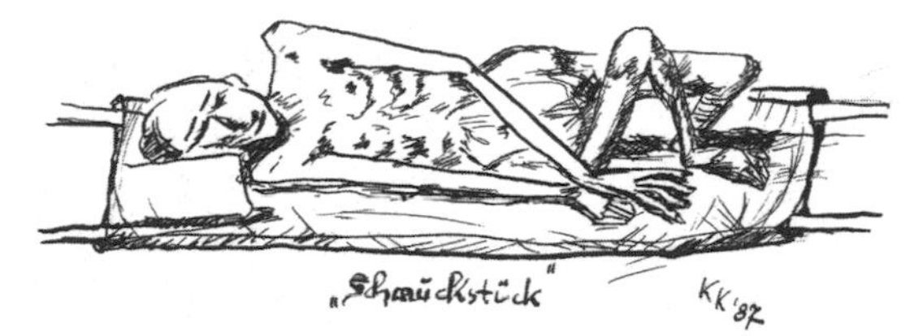


*Schmuckstück* by Katharina Katzenmaier, a Catholic nun who saw this woman dying in Block 10

Antonina Nikiforova as a young doctor in her Red Army uniform

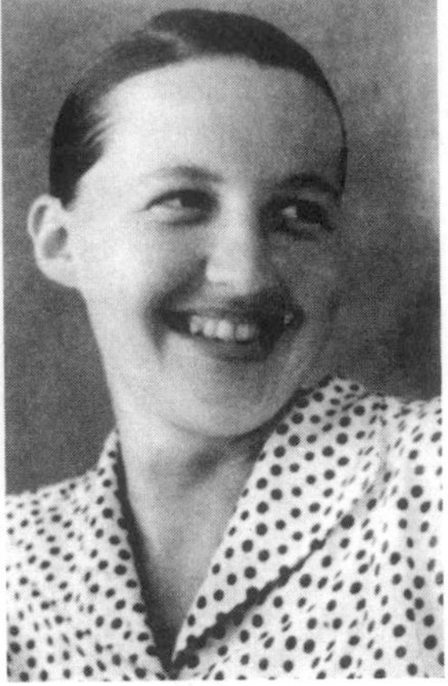

Zdenka Nedvedova, the Czech doctor. Probably taken in the mid-1930s

Stella Kugelman was four years old when she was taken to Ravensbrück with her Belgian mother

Yevgenia Klemm, the Red Army leader in the camp. This picture was probably taken in 1912, when Yevgenia was in her teens

Yevgenia Klemm's number and red triangle

Loulou Le Porz, the French Block 10 doctor. This photograph was taken in 1940, shortly before her arrest

Yvonne Baseden, the British SOE agent, on joining the WAAF in the early 1940s

The British agent Violette Szabo, on joining SOE, early 1940s

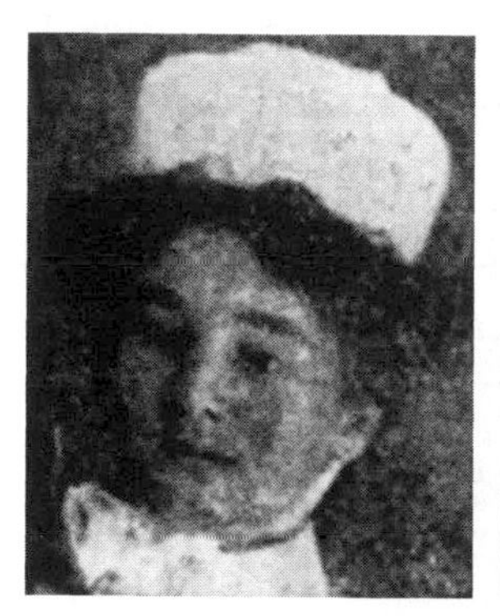

Mary Young, the Scottish nurse arrested in Paris for helping the resistance. This picture, believed to have been taken when she was a trainee nurse in the early 1900s, appeared in the *Aberdeen Journal* on 27 September 1945, and is the only known photograph of her

The Norwegian prisoner Sylvia Salvesen in 1957

Marie-Louise Zimberlin, the French resister, as a young teacher in Cluny, France

Countess Karolina Lanckorońska in 1938 at Rozdół Palace, her family's main country estate in Poland

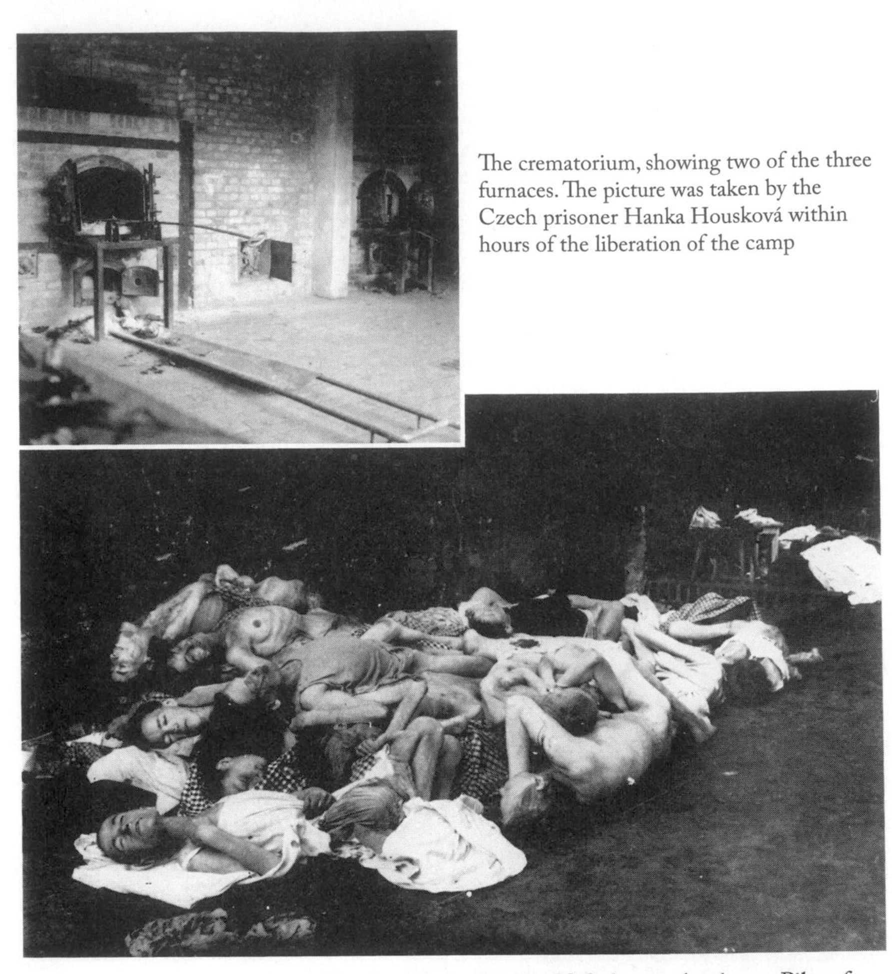

The crematorium, showing two of the three furnaces. The picture was taken by the Czech prisoner Hanka Housková within hours of the liberation of the camp

Bodies photographed by Hanka Housková soon after the SS fled on 29 April 1945. Piles of corpses lay all over the camp. Later, local people were sent to the camp to help bury them

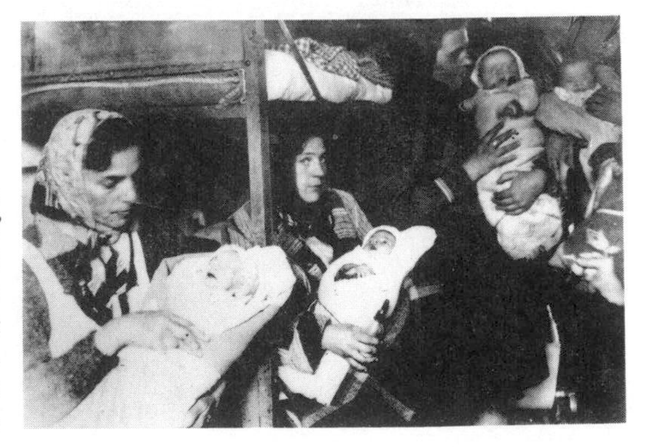

Ukrainian and Russian mothers and babies in the 'maternity block' photographed by Hanka Housková immediately after liberation. Words on the back of the picture say that one of the women was among those raped by the Red Army soldiers who liberated the camp

Women rescued by Bernadotte's White Buses on the boat to Malmö, Sweden

Folke Bernadotte (centre) discussing the rescue with an SS doctor and a Norwegian pastor in Hamburg, March 1945

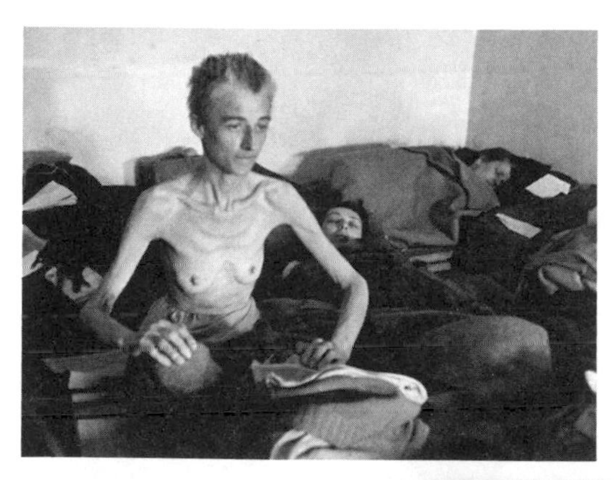

An unidentified French woman, rescued from Ravensbrück by the Swedish Red Cross, photographed in a Danish hospital in May 1945 by Tage Christensen

French women brought out of the camp by the International Committee of the Red Cross are welcomed with soup and blankets in a gymnastics hall in Kreuzlingen, Switzerland, 6 April 1945

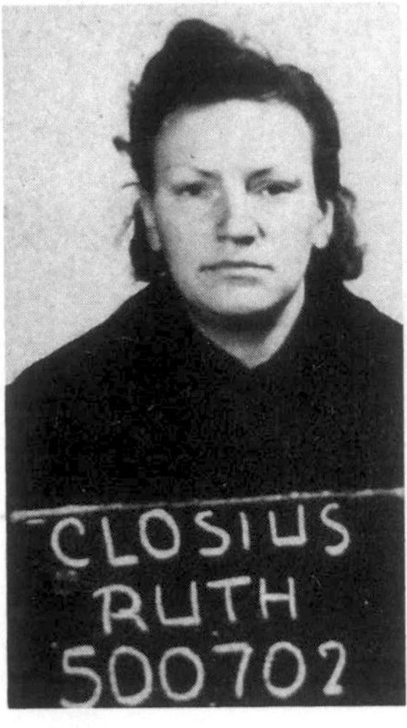


Ruth Closius (formerly Neudeck), chief guard at the Uckermark Youth Camp. This photograph was taken at the British internment camp at Paderborn in 1947, before her trial in Hamburg

Johann Schwarzhuber, Ludwig Ramdohr, Gustav Binder and Heinrich Peters (SS officer at the men's camp) in the dock at the Hamburg trial, which began in December 1946

Fritz Suhren, camp commandant 1942–5. Suhren probably wore these civilian clothes when he drove to American lines with Odette Sansom to give himself up

Dr Herta Oberheuser being sentenced at the Nuremberg doctors' trial, 20 August 1947

Dorothea Binz, Margarete Mewes, Grete Bösel, Vera Salvequart (in row behind) and Eugenia von Skene in the dock at the Hamburg trial

*Oberschwester* Elisabeth Marschall, Vera Salvequart, the prisoner-nurse at the Uckermark Youth Camp, and Dr Percival Treite being sentenced at the Hamburg trial

Carmen Mory, the Swiss prisoner and Blockova of Block 10, with her lawyer Dr Zippel

*Tragende* by Will Lammert

This sign – 'You are not forgotten' – was put up by a German survivors' group near the overgrown site of the Uckermark Youth Camp

A view of *Tragende* from outside the camp walls, looking across the lake towards Fürstenberg

# PART SIX

*Chapter 30*

# Hungarians

Eva Fejer was at school in Budapest in October 1944 when an announcement was made that all Jewish girls in her class should go to dig trenches because the Russians were coming. 'We were taken out to a field and we had to start digging. We slept on an open football ground. A few days later we were marched out towards the west.'

The October order came from the office of Adolf Eichmann, the man sent to Hungary, after the German invasion six months earlier, to implement this last stage of the Final Solution by rounding up the country's 750,000 Jews and sending them to Auschwitz. Time was pressing: the Red Army was closing in.

When the Hungarian roundups began in late March 1944 most Jews were unprepared. They knew about the slaughter of Europe's other Jews, but until now Hungary, a German ally, had been protected. Eva Fejer's father, a prominent lawyer, told his family: 'It won't happen here. Hungarian law won't allow it.' Franz Fejer was a Hungarian patriot and a German patriot too. The family all spoke German; Eva had a German nanny, and spoke fluent German by the time she was ten. The family took no precautions. 'I think my parents just didn't want to accept it. And my father didn't want to frighten his family, so he didn't warn us. He wanted us to have as much of our childhood as there was left.'

This time, however, the world outside recognised the signs. The moment that Hitler invaded, the warning went out to Western capitals that Hungarian Jews were about to be exterminated too. Berlin barely attempted to hide it. The Swedes sent envoys to issue Jews with protective passports and papers, and the International Red Cross tried to offer clothes and food to those forced into holding camps, but even as this went on, tens of thousands of Jews were being herded onto trains for Auschwitz, and one of the first to go was Eva's father. 'He was sixty-one but he was very fit,' said Eva, 'so we hoped he might have survived. He was a fine skater and brilliant pianist. Sometimes one hoped that someone might make it out in an air pocket or something, but not one of his transport came back.'

By July 1944, 430,000 of Hungary's 750,000 Jews had already been rounded up and sent to Auschwitz, where all but 100,000 were gassed. The only Hungarian Jews who avoided transport to Auschwitz were those deemed fit for munitions work, and they were sent on to the concentration camps in Germany. Hungarian arrivals at Auschwitz were also sifted for any who might make useful slave labourers.

In July 1944, four months after Eichmann's roundups in Hungary began, the deportations were put on hold. Miklos Horthy, the Nazis' puppet leader in Budapest, had shifted his allegiance to the Allies, refusing to cooperate with further Jewish expulsions. The 200,000 Jews who remained – mostly in Budapest – appeared to have been spared, including Eva Fejer and her mother. In early October, however, the Horthy government fell, and Eichmann was set to resume. By now Allied bombs had destroyed train lines and rolling stock across Hungary and Poland: trains could no longer be used. Furthermore, the Soviet front was driving forward so fast that even Auschwitz in southern Poland was preparing for evacuation; the gas chambers were about to be closed down, and the camp had stopped taking in more Jews.

Abandoning the roundups, however, was not an option; Hitler had ordered that every last Jew be removed from Hungary before the Red Army arrived. The only way Eichmann could achieve this was to force-march the remaining 200,000 men, women and children from Budapest to the Austrian border, a distance of 200 miles.

It was 16 October and frost was already on the ground when women and girls between the ages of sixteen and forty received the orders to leave. Eva had managed to pack her girl guide's rucksack – '1939 Jamboree' emblazoned on it – with food and spare clothes, smuggled to her by her German nanny. But she was unable to see her mother again before she left.

Eva didn't suffer on the march as much as most, she says. She'd learned first aid, and was sporty and strong. 'My father used to make me learn to do everything myself. He'd mend my bike the first time, but I'd have to watch and do it myself the next time.' She also knew the road the marchers set out upon, as the family used it before the war to visit relatives over the border. She marched all day and slept in football fields at night. It was cold, but Eva was wearing her culottes and had spare ski pants in her bag.

Most prisoners marched in families, or small groups. Margit Nagy insisted on coming with her daughters, Rosza and Marianne. 'I think she knew we might die and she wanted us all to be together. We held hands all the way,' said Rosza. Girls who were alone were 'adopted' by other families, but Eva preferred to march alone. Guards from the fascist Arrow Cross beat the stragglers. Passers-by stared, and sometimes offered food. In the Swabian mountains a man walked next to Eva and started asking questions about her father.

> He told me he'd been my father's valet in the First World War and that my father was good to him. He said: 'So you come with me and I'll see you're all right.' I could have gone, as nobody was really watching. But I thought we were only going to a labour camp and I'd be strong enough for that. I believed in my own strength. It was a hard decision, but I was worried about my mother; I didn't want anything to happen to her if I did something wrong.

After her father's valet had loaded her bag with quinces, Eva walked on.

Several days later the marchers reached the Danube and walked down planks to ferry boats. 'People lost their footing and fell off the plank. We saw the drowned corpses in the water but I kept on going and didn't fall.' Somewhere near Vienna the marchers were put in trains, locked in closed wagons, and the trains continued west. 'A guard asked if anyone spoke German and I quickly said yes, so I was made his interpreter and sat on a ledge where I could see out. I knew how to navigate by the sun, so I told the others the direction we were going.'

When the train pulled up at Jena, southwest of Leipzig, the men were taken out and sent to Buchenwald, but the women stayed on. 'We passed a medieval castle and I thought I must bring my parents here after the war.' About two days later the train pulled up at a tiny station called Ravensbrück. 'I'd heard of Auschwitz, Dachau and Mauthausen, but not Ravensbrück.'

After the departure of Eva's convoy from Budapest the final phase of the forced marches out of Hungary accelerated. The weather worsened, and of the many thousands of women marched towards Ravensbrück at least a third are thought to have perished. An envoy of the International Red Cross, sent to observe the exodus, was overwhelmed: 'The idea of standing by helplessly, powerless to do anything, is almost impossible to bear,' he wrote in his report to Geneva.

Deportations from other eastern countries that bordered the Reich accelerated too. Hitler was taking his last opportunity to clean out camps and ghettos ahead of the Russian advance. These Jews were still being deported in trains that criss-crossed what remained of Nazi-occupied lands, often stopping for days in sidings, as lines were bombed or communications broke down. On one of the trains was nineteen-year-old Basia Zajączkowska, who had survived the Kielce ghetto, in central Poland, because she worked in a gunpowder factory. As the Soviets approached, the workers were sent to Auschwitz. Basia escaped into the woods but was caught and sent to Ravensbrück instead, because by that time Auschwitz was beginning to shut down.

On 2 November 1944 Himmler halted the gassing at Auschwitz, but in the chaos some trains continued to turn up, including one from Slovakia whose passengers arrived in abject terror having received a graphic account of what to expect – two Slovakian men who had just escaped from Auschwitz and made their way back home told them about the gas chambers just before their transport left. On arrival at Auschwitz, one of the Slovakian women even asked an SS man where the gas chambers were. He replied: 'They aren't working any more. You are not to be gassed.'

The Slovakians were put on another train, which arrived on 10 November at Ravensbrück, where they once again expected to be gassed. The women were herded towards the Ravensbrück tent but they refused to go inside. 'Entering the tent the women were convinced they were entering a gas chamber,' said Halina Wasilewska, the tent Stubova. 'Many of them asked the tent personnel to tell them the truth – when could they expect to be gassed? – and they didn't really believe it when they were assured that there were no gas chambers at Ravensbrück at all. Although at that time there really were no gas chambers at Ravensbrück.'

With the arrival of thousands of Jewish women in the late autumn of 1944, Ravensbrück was once again swamped; squalor and disease spread on an unimaginable scale. First all new arrivals were herded into the tent, where neither straw nor blankets were any longer provided, so women who had marched in the snow now slept on cold wet cement blocks. Most of those who marched from Budapest had contracted pneumonia, gangrene and frostbite on the road. Many had the symptoms of typhus too, and were suffering from high fever, vomiting and diarrhoea.

The buckets overflowed. The canvas structure stank. Mothers tried to feed children, as well as feeding themselves. Amid this horror typhus broke out on a scale not seen here before. The SS sought desperately to control the killer disease by vaccinating not only SS staff but key prisoners – nurses and office staff, some of whom were too weak to endure vaccination, and caught typhus instead and died. A new rule was instituted that thirty patients from the tent could visit the *Revier* each day, but it was too few, and the rest were just sent back to die. Dead bodies mingled with the living and could not be easily extracted. Then when the corpse gang came to the tent they refused to take bodies because they didn't have numbers. Many in the tent were admitted without them, and died before the numbers were given out.

According to Halina, a new phenomenon specific to the tent broke out – 'feverish conversations of agitated people, complaining, fights over sleeping space, moans and screams of the sick, shouting back and forth in the crowd creating a constant deafening din, non-stop day and night'. Yet the tent 'block' nevertheless still had to stand for *Appell* like all the others. Those who couldn't stand were laid out to be counted on their backs in rows of ten.

After they had been in the tent a few days the first Hungarians to arrive were moved out to blocks; the healthier among them went to munition factories at subcamps. Straight away a new group of 1000 Poles (Aryans this time, noted Halina) came in from Auschwitz and refilled the tent. What made matters worse was that more and more sick women were returning from satellite camps. And not only were Ravensbrück subcamps sending their sick women back; more distant ones that had long ago been placed under the administration of men's camps such as Buchenwald were returning their sick (and pregnant) too. These camps had for many months been sending their exhausted women workers to Auschwitz, but this was no longer an option.

Closer at hand, Siemens too was sending more and more unsuitable women back to the main camp. Its few surviving monthly reports detailing prisoner turnover show a remarkable upturn in 1944. In October the company sent fifty unsuitables back to the main camp from the finishing shop alone. This compared with an average of three returned from the same small section eighteen months earlier.

Women rejected by Siemens went straight to the *Revier* blocks or joined others working outside in the labour gangs. Betsie ten Boom, sent back in October, worked levelling ground for a few more weeks before being admitted to the *Revier*, where she died in early December. Corrie saw her sister's naked body on a mattress: 'a carving in old ivory, I could see the outline of the teeth through the skin'. Then she caught sight of Betsie's body again, stacked up with other corpses against the *Revier* washroom wall, 'her eyes closed as if in sleep, the deep hollows of hunger and disease, simply gone. Even her hair was graciously in place, as if an angel had ministered to it.'

For the Siemens managers, replacing exhausted women was harder than ever, but young Jewish women were now pouring into the camp, some still agile and strong enough to work. Siemens had employed Jewish women at its Berlin factories at the start of the war, before the mass deportations, and valued their skills, so when Basia Zajączkowska, the Kielce ghetto survivor, appeared on the 'cattle market' they were swiftly put to work making electrical parts.

Throughout November and December more Jewish women continued to arrive from the East; most had to fight for their lives in the tent. A teenager called Sarah Mittelmann entered it to find 'women all around me having fits and beating each other. There was no room for anyone even to stretch out.' A new transport of Polish Jews arrived talking Yiddish, which the Hungarian Jews didn't understand. Selma Okrent, another young Hungarian, remembered the smell in the tent. As she stood in line for soup someone said: 'If you don't behave, you'll smell like that as well.'

> They took away my clothes and broke my earrings to get them out. I was given a red triangle and the number 79706 and told to watch out for green triangles, as they were thieves. I was made to work pulling stones and sometimes we had to schlepp out the dead. I had a skirt and was playing with the hem when I felt something in it and it was somebody's wedding ring.

Selma and Sarah got out onto good labour gangs by making sure the *Meister* chose them first. This was what Eva Fejer did almost as soon as she arrived. The man from Daimler-Benz snapped her up. 'He asked who spoke German and I said I did, so he said, "Yes, you'll do," and I became his translator at the factory in Berlin.' Before Eva left Ravensbrück she spotted her best friend arriving on the next transport from Budapest and shouted to her: '"Martha, whatever you do, get out of here as soon as you can," but she didn't believe me and died.'

Rosza and Marianne Nagy also managed to 'get out' to a munitions plant near Chemnitz, but at the last minute their mother Margit, who had been with them ever since Budapest, was made to stay behind. 'We were put in the back of a truck and driven away, and that was when we saw her for the last time.'

It used to be the new arrivals who stared in disbelief at the ravaged women in the camp. Now it was the other way around. Loulou Le Porz saw a group of new Hungarians. 'One ran up to me pleading: "*Bitte Schwester, bitte Schwester.*" I could see from her face she was going to die and I ran away because I couldn't tell her.'

Describing this period, survivors talk of seeing groups of newcomers, usually Jews, just wandering – perhaps detached from their transport – lost, around the camp. One day Nelly Langholm saw such a group on her way back from the kitchen, where she had gone to get water for women in the fabric shop. Since the typhus outbreak the kitchen had been the only source of safe water.

> I'd filled the jug and was walking back when I saw this group of women – they were Hungarian perhaps or Polish. They were in a dreadful state and had obviously just been brought in from somewhere, and probably hadn't drunk or eaten for days. They saw my water jug and swarmed all over me, so that most of it spilt and they fell on the ground to let some drops just touch their lips. I stood back and watched them.
>
> As I turned to go I saw a woman on the ground and stared at her. She was giving birth to a child, right there, and I watched. I was only twenty, and had never seen a woman giving birth, and she was giving birth there in the filth of the camp street.

Nelly didn't see the group again and doesn't know where they went. 'But the baby didn't go anywhere. The baby died right there. Of that I'm sure.'

It was about this time that Violette Lecoq came across a group of Jewish women as she went to the *Revier* to collect index cards.

> I saw in the yard five wheelbarrows that were normally used to cart manure; each one contained one woman. They were Jews who had dropped from exhaustion in the road on their way from work at Siemens and who'd been beaten to the brink of death by the *Aufseherinnen* in charge of them. Their comrades had been forced to pick them up and take them back to the camp. The *Oberschwester* forbade anyone to touch them. Two of them were dead when I saw them, the others were on the point of death.

In December the snows began to fall, and a group of women arrived clad only in straw. The prisoners in the camp stared at the straw women; they were frightened by them, and tried to keep away. Even Percival Treite was struck by the vision of women dressed in straw, saying later that the condition of these 1300 new arrivals was the worst he'd ever seen. These were mostly Hungarian Jews who had been deported earlier in the year, and taken first to Auschwitz and from there to a subcamp called Frankfurt Walldorf, in west Germany, to work in atrocious conditions building an airport. As fears grew in November 1944 that American forces would soon be approaching, the camp was shut down and the exhausted women brought to Ravensbrück.

One of those who observed the 'straw women' closely was Julia Barry, who described what she saw in evidence given at the Hamburg war crimes trial. She was on patrol near the gate when she first saw them. 'The women arrived dressed only in straw which was tied about their bodies.' Julia observed the women many times. 'They were constantly dying about the camp. These women I have seen drop down in the camp and die.' She also noticed that the women were regularly set upon by two German prisoners – not guards – and she took the trouble to investigate. One, it turned out, was a Pole called Anita.

> She was aged about twenty-six, tall, a lesbian dressed like a man, and had her hair cut accordingly. The other prisoner was a German girl called Gerda. She was fat, aged about twenty-two, about five feet three inches tall, and looked very common. Both women were savagely brutal to the Jewish arrivals and beat them without mercy with sticks and anything else that came handy on numerous occasions.

Unlike other prisoners, Julia Barry – herself a Hungarian Jew – rather than fearing these new arrivals, reached out to them. 'I met a Hungarian lady named Mrs Sebestyn. On her arrival her legs were in a terrible condition owing to her experiences in the wintry conditions on leaving Hungary.' Mrs Sebestyn was ordered out to work, 'and protested that she was unable to go'. Nevertheless she had to go, 'and later lost both her feet and died in the hospital'.

Julia Barry's evidence was always unusually detailed and frank, partly because as a policewoman she was able to observe a great deal that went on, and also because, unlike other camp policewomen, she was more than willing to describe what she saw, which in the last months of 1944 was death. Julia felt sure that the events she witnessed at that time were 'definitely designed to bring about death'. For example, in the hospital blocks the SS doctors 'put in one bed a patient with a foot injury and another with TB or typhus or other contagious disease, with the inevitable result that two deaths from the contagious disease would occur'.

Julia saw bodies everywhere, and seems to have looked for them too. In the death cellar, she saw bodies awaiting transport to the furnace. Near the crematorium she saw gold being extracted from the teeth of the dead. A little later she noticed an aunt of her husband's among the arrivals from Hungary. Hearing that the relative had been taken to one of the death blocks where prisoners with dysentery were left with no food until they died, she went to investigate. 'I tried to see her but the Blockova would not allow me in. I never saw my husband's aunt again.'

Julia listened too, and she reported what she'd heard people say. 'I remember a woman telling me that her newborn baby was dead having been eaten by rats in Block Eleven.' On another occasion she was patrolling near the crematorium and overheard a senior SS officer whom she didn't recognise. She noticed him again and again, sometimes with another officer, who was also new to the camp.

> I remember two senior officers. One of them was a man by the name of Höss, and I once heard him say that it was a waste of coal to burn the bodies of the dead prisoners, or words to that effect. The same Höss was a tall thin man aged about forty-five to fifty who always wore a fur-lined coat. He was not as bad as the other officer whose name I don't remember. This one was tall, stout, aged between forty-five and fifty – very good-looking and well dressed. He was one of the most brutal and cruel men I have seen in the camp.

A short time later Julia saw two more strangers to Ravensbrück – this time both were doctors, who she learned had come 'from Auschwitz'.

*Chapter 31*

# A Children's Party

Rudolf Höss, commandant of Auschwitz, moved to Ravensbrück just a few weeks after the Auschwitz gas chambers had shut down. Bank records prove it: on 30 November 1944, 'Höss, Rudolf' deposited 50 Reichsmarks in a Fürstenberg bank.

Höss was not the only Auschwitz boss to be seen around Ravensbrück in late 1944. The other man spotted by Julia Barry, 'one of the most brutal and cruel men I have ever seen', may have been the gassing expert Otto Moll, also present at this time, though it could also have been Albert Sauer, another former death-camp commandant.

One of the SS doctors seen by Julia Barry was probably Franz Lucas, who had previously worked on the ramp at Auschwitz; the other could have been Carl Clauberg, who masterminded Himmler's sterilisation experiments at Auschwitz. Both came to Ravensbrück in the winter of 1944–5. The sudden appearance at Ravensbrück of a pack of experienced exterminators was sinister, though the explanation was to some extent banal: they were out of a job. Their camps were all to the east, and had either been overrun by Russians or were about to be. The Auschwitz extermination programme had halted on 2 November; the Red Army was expected to reach the camp in early January.

Dr Franz Lucas had been moved from Auschwitz to Stutthof camp, near Danzig (Gdansk), early in 1944, but Stutthof too was about to be overrun. The camp of Riga-Kaiserwald, where Albert Sauer had been commandant, was overrun when the Red Army took Latvia in October.

There may also have been a simple reason to send quite so many unemployed SS men to Ravensbrück: there were few other KZs to go to. The remainder were commanded by high-ranking officers who would not want idle colleagues on their patches. Fritz Suhren, the women's camp's middle-ranking commandant, was not in so strong a position to complain, though even Suhren appears to have been irked by their arrival.

The most important reason for posting such men to Ravensbrück was, however, sinister in the extreme: as experts in mass murder they were needed to launch a new extermination programme. It is no coincidence that just before these men arrived, Himmler had issued a new directive requiring an immediate, massive increase in the rate of killing and construction of a gas chamber to carry it out.

Like so many other SS orders, Himmler's latest edict for Ravensbrück did not survive the destruction of Nazi documents and it took some time for details to emerge. When the first and most important Ravensbrück war crimes trials were held in Hamburg in 1946 and 1947, facts of extermination were certainly revealed but no evidence was presented showing that the killing order came direct from Himmler.

In fact the contents of the directive would have been entirely lost to history had it not been for Anni Rudroff, an Austrian doctor, who read the order when working as secretary to Edmund Bräuning in the camp HQ. In 1948, when the last Ravensbrück trial was being prepared, Anni was tracked down to the Soviet sector of Berlin by a British war crimes investigator looking for evidence against Artur Conrad, the executioner, whom she had known in the HQ. In a brief but damning statement Anni described Conrad's role in the shooting of Polish women. Almost as an afterthought she then mentioned Himmler's order.

> From 5 Jan until 16 Dec 1944 I worked in the camp office. In October there came an order from Himmler, which Schutzhaftlagerführer Bräuning left on the table and which I personally read. The order was directed to the Commandant and stated: 'In your camp, with retrospective effect for six months, 2000 people monthly have to die; Reichsführer SS.' The Schutzhaftlagerführer Bräuning got the order to construct the gas chambers.

Anni Rudroff's evidence is arguably the most important piece of testimony about Ravensbrück, showing that in these last months of the war Himmler had personally ordered a mass-extermination programme to begin at the women's camp. Perhaps because Anni's evidence came to light late in investigations, because it was presented with no fanfare, or because she herself then disappeared – as did Edmund Bräuning – the revelation received little attention. There is certainly no reason to doubt its veracity. The British investigator who took Anni's evidence was clearly impressed by her. 'She signed it – or rather, solemnly affirmed it as she did not belong to any religion,' stated Major Józef Liniewski.

In any case the prisoners all knew such an order must have been issued because well before gassing even started they saw a massive increase in killing.

Moreover, just as he had micro-managed every stage of the camp's evolution, it was entirely natural that Himmler should personally order extermination to begin. No prisoner could have invented the phrasing. Himmler wanted far more than 2000 a month killed but to disguise the extent of the required slaughter he camouflaged the facts with characteristic bureaucratic pedantry, ordering the killing to be 'retrospective for six months'.

Himmler's reason for ordering the extermination is also abundantly clear. Ravensbrück was out of control; disease was spreading and threatening the SS and the wider community. Order had to be restored before another vast influx of women arrived from Auschwitz, which was due to be evacuated within weeks. How else could control be reasserted without mass killing? No longer could the useless mouths be sent off to outside gas chambers: Majdanek and Castle Hartheim were already closed and the Auschwitz gas chambers shut down.

At other camps, already liquidated ahead of the Russian advance – Stutthof for example – mass killing had been done largely by shooting or by drowning in the Baltic. At Ravensbrück, however, with men like Höss on hand, extermination was to be done by gas. A number of concentration camps situated on German soil – Sachsenhausen, for example – had operated their own gas chambers or gas vans in the past, but Ravensbrück now became the only such camp to be fitted with a gas chamber for the first time, in order to carry out mass extermination on site in the final months of the war.

Everything that now happened quite clearly stemmed from the order seen by Anni Rudroff. The capacity of the crematorium was increased. A site was cleared where victims could be held while the gassing was done; the site chosen was the Uckermark Youth Camp, just half a mile away and hidden in the woods. By early December the Youth Camp had been evacuated, the teenagers and young women either freed or sent to Ravensbrück.

At the same time construction of new living barracks for the Siemens workers began; they were in future to sleep out at the plant itself. This was necessary so that the Siemens women wouldn't walk past the gas chamber which was to be sited near the crematorium by the south wall – in other words, right alongside the route they had hitherto taken to work.

Exactly who took charge of installing the gas chamber, and precisely when, the testimony does not reveal. There is evidence to suggest that as early as

October 1944 – about the same time Himmler's killing order came in – a plan for a sophisticated concrete gas chamber was drawn up. An electrician called Walter Jahn, a prisoner at the men's camp, said that he had been commissioned to design it. This chamber was to stand against the camp's north wall disguised as the *Neue Wäscherei* – new washroom. A German communist arrested in 1941, Jahn was an unlikely gas-chamber architect, but he was a talented electrician whose abilities had already been enlisted by the SS for projects including servicing the radios in Oswald Pohl's cars. It was while giving evidence at Pohl's trial that he described his plan for the gas chamber, but its construction was delayed, he said, apparently for want of materials, hard to come by at this stage of the war.

There had also been some dispute about who amongst the SS should oversee the construction. Another interesting fact revealed by Anni Rudroff was that Edmund Bräuning had refused to implement Himmler's order to organise the gassing, and we know he left the camp in disgrace in January, when Anni herself was locked in the bunker, presumably because she knew too much. It was therefore almost certainly Rudolf Höss, Albert Sauer and Otto Moll between them who selected the new site by the crematorium and agreed – at least as a stopgap while the *Neue Wäscherei* chamber was built – to construct a simple structure which would not demand materials. This temporary gas chamber was to be fashioned out of an old tool shed. It was Hanna Sturm who made the partitions and banged in the nails. As she did so she saw canisters of the gas Zyklon B (prussic acid) lying alongside the shed.

After Hanna had completed her work, the painting gang followed, as the French woman Suzanne Hugounencq explained. 'We passed in front of the crematorium in front of which lay bodies waiting for burning,' she recalled. 'That morning there were some very important SS men around, with loud voices and fat bellies, and they had the arrogance of people with great power.' The civilian boss of the painting gang received instructions from the fat men – 'very submissively but with apprehension' – and the job of painting the shed fell to Suzanne and two Germans.

Inside were large barrels containing chemicals used for mixing the paint. 'When the SS left there was an ominous silence. We had to get to work. We had to empty the building of all these materials. The building must have been four metres wide and six long. It had a large door and a window on the left side that let in the light. On the outside it had two shutters. It was like a garage for a car, perhaps.'

The women returned the next day, by which time the shutters of the window had been nailed down with a plank and something had been fixed to the wall. The three big chiefs came to inspect. 'One suggested that two holes were drilled about five centimetres wide and two holes were also pierced in the wall of the block. A special airtight cover was erected over the top to make sure everything was sealed tight. It was our job to plug all the gaps and holes with mastic, which was not easy to see in the total darkness we had to work in.'

After the painting gang finished their work, this 'temporary' gas chamber too was put on hold for a while. Perhaps Höss and his team were still expecting Jahn's concrete design to be built. More likely they just wanted to try another method of mass killing first – a method they were also familiar with.

Although shooting prisoners had been common at Ravensbrück for the past four years, the numbers shot in a month rarely exceeded forty, and to date these had mostly been termed executions, as the victims had been given 'death sentences' for a 'crime'. The shooting that now began was on an entirely different scale – fifty a night. It was called killing, not execution, and was done in such secrecy that today many questions about it remain unanswered. It is partly through Percival Treite, who as camp doctor had to be present, that we have any reliable detail at all.

Before his trial, in 1946, Treite talked openly of the shooting, but only through self-interest: after observing the shooting once he said he refused to be present again and hoped this would count in his favour with the judges.

Treite's testimony on the shooting came in three stages. In a statement given to British forces on 4 May 1945 – five days after giving himself up – he said that the extermination at Ravensbrück began with mass shooting in the winter of 1944–5.

'First of all fifty prisoners were killed daily in front of the crematorium by a shot through the neck,' he said. A doctor had to be there because 'one bullet doesn't always kill the prisoner immediately'. In a second statement, on 14 August 1946, he described how the victims were not only the old and sick but also 'young women capable of work', who were brought to a place near the crematorium and shot in the back of the neck with a small-calibre gun from a short distance – the *Genickschuss*.

It was always done at first light, said Treite. 'The dawn was enough for the executioners to see what they were doing.' Afterwards two prisoners from the men's camp brought the victims to the crematorium, where Treite waited to 'perform my task of certifying death'. Hellinger prised out the gold fillings and crowns 'and the bodies were burned'. In a further statement on 2 October 1946, Treite talked of an occasion when fifty prisoners were brought from the Youth Camp to be shot by rifle two at a time.

Treite claimed that he didn't remember who gave the orders, but it was almost certainly the Auschwitz man Otto Moll. Ravensbrück's own executioners said Moll was in charge and even brought his own team of assassins, which angered the local crew. Walter Schenk, the Ravensbrück crematorium chief, complained that while the killing was going on, the Auschwitz gang 'slept in my crematorium'.

Moll and his SS comrades would certainly have chosen the *Genickschuss* as their preferred method of shooting. They had practised it before – most notably to kill hundreds of thousands of Soviet POWs. It was fast and efficient – a prisoner could be shot in the neck every thirty seconds or so, then the body taken to be burned. The system was cleaner than mass shooting by rifle, and cheaper on ammunition.

Treite was quite clear that the shooting took place 'near the crematorium'. When the shot to the back of the neck was used it probably took place just inside the so-called shooting alley. The alley, about twenty metres long and two wide, lay between two high walls – one formed the back of the camp bunker and the other abutted garages. One end of the alley opened near the crematorium. The alley had been used for smaller-scale executions before, and obviously had advantages; the high flanking walls removed any risk of hitting bystanders and ruled out any chance of escape. They would also have ruled out witnesses, as well as muffling the sound, which goes to explain in part why not a single prisoner in the main camp seems to have heard any shots.

There is evidence to suggest that when overcrowding intensified, some arrivals – those from Hungary, for example, or from other subcamps – were never registered at Ravensbrück at all, but taken straight to be shot, or else held temporarily at the newly vacated Youth Camp, and then shot.

Such a system would also explain why the office prisoner secretaries, mostly reliable sources, say little of the early mass shootings, though they all heard Conrad, the Ravensbrück executioner, boasting about how he 'knocked off women with the butt of his gun'. In any case, as Christmas approached, the secretaries in the offices and other influential prisoners had other things to occupy their minds.

In early December 1944 prominent prisoners were planning a children's Christmas party. The idea began among the Germans and Czechs but quickly spread. In previous years Christians, as well as secular and even Jewish prisoners, had marked Christmas in small ways, by singing in their blocks, making decorations. Only the Soviets ignored the celebrations, and many seemed entirely ignorant of this 'festival that happened towards the end of the year'.

In 1944 the planned celebrations were far more extensive than ever before, largely because there were so many more children in the camp than before. A year ago the only children here had been the sixty-four under-twelves who arrived, mostly from Belgium and Holland, with the 'protected' Jewish families and a few other strays. Since then more Gypsy children had come from

Auschwitz, Polish children came during the influx after the Warsaw Uprising, and in the autumn children arrived with the Hungarian and Slovakian Jews. There were small numbers of Russian, Romanian, Yugoslav, French and Greek children too, making 4–500 in all. Many were Jews, but there were non-Jewish children as well, swept up and brought here from all corners of the war.

In the winter of 1944 children were seen all over the camp, playing quietly in the corners of blocks, running terrified from guard dogs or crouching in the mud, and all of them – like recent adult arrivals – had a black cross daubed on the back of their clothes to identify them as prisoners. Gypsy children delighted everyone, and were given free rein to roam the Lagerstrasse selling things – cigarettes stolen from SS officers' pockets, silk scarves from the 'Galeries Lafayette', scraps from the kitchen. One day a French prisoner was offered a copy of Molière's *Le Misanthrope*; the Gypsy seller said she came from Lille. Polish teachers organised classes in the blocks for more than seventy school-age Poles, while Blockovas smuggled in extra food.

By December 1944 the Blockova of Block 27, Ann Sheridan, counted forty children under her one roof, as well as seventy pregnant women. This was the mysterious 'British' woman whom survivors criticised after the war for being too close to the Germans. What they meant was never explained, but from her own testimony Ann made good use of her influence. Each day she persuaded the camp kitchen staff to give the children in her block an extra milk ration, 'though the mothers sometimes drank it themselves'.

Children lived in the blocks with their mothers if they had them or with adopted camp mothers if they didn't. The women's instincts towards the older boys were not always so maternal. Menachem Kallus, a ten-year-old Jewish boy who came from Holland with the 'protected' Jews in January 1944, recalls how Red Army women in his block took an interest in boys of his age: 'We were the only men. They came and played around with us. It was our first sexual experience. It was harmless. They taught us. But the Germans saw what was happening and moved us out to the men's camp.'

The arrival of more and more children encouraged more women to become 'camp mothers', and there was competition to adopt the prettiest orphans. The Russian Ekatarina Speranskaya recalled being adopted by Aunt Nastasya. 'She told me not to talk to anyone else and just to breathe the air. We slept together on the bottom bunk.' Ekatarina thinks Aunt Nastasya probably had her own children at home, 'or had lost them somehow'.

Camp mothers never lasted long; by December 1944 Stella Kugelman was on her fifth. Often they would fall sick or be posted to a subcamp, as happened to the Dutch nurse Claire van den Boom, probably Stella's favourite camp mother of all. Claire was sent to the underground munitions plant at Berndorf in September, after Carmen Mory reported her for smuggling food to patients in Block 10. Since then an Austrian called Frau Strassner, wife of a former president of the Viennese Supreme Court, had cared for Stella, and Karolina Lanckorońska helped out. She helped Stella write letters to her father, who, as they had found out, was in Buchenwald.

The sight of the children was the inspiration for the party, though as Sylvia Salvesen remarked, they were 'not as we think of children – starvation, suffering, shock and terror marked them all'. The grown-ups found it impossible to tell their ages. 'Children who looked four were eight, and twelve looked like eight-year-olds,' said Sylvia. Many didn't know their dates of birth, or their names. One Russian child, Nadia Bolanov, captured at first with her grandmother, was quite alone in the world by the time she was swept up at Auschwitz and sent on to Ravensbrück. 'I was like a little animal, very frightened,' she recalls.

By the second week of December planning for the Christmas party was well under way, with prisoners in the camp offices, the blocks and the *Revier* all involved. The German communist Hildegard Boy-Brandt ran the puppet show, while the Belgian nurse Emmi Gorlich organised parcels, and the Czechs created a children's choir. A 'Christmas man' was planned as a secular Father Christmas, in order not to alienate the communists.

As arrangements advanced, new bonds grew up between the different national groups, and a planning committee was formed with representatives from eleven nations. Such was the excitement that other groups joined too, including the Poles and the French. Everyone seemed to want to help prepare, making little toys and sewing decorations. The organisers hoped that the children's party would be a symbol of cooperation and reconciliation – 'a symbol for the future'.

In the winter of 1944, talk of the need for reconciliation after the war was heard more and more around the camp, especially among the German communists, who knew that among new prisoners coming from abroad, they were often hated just for being German. Grete Buber-Neumann recalls that as far as the many foreign women were concerned, 'all Germans were the same as the SS, and as they hated the SS, so they hated the Germans'. Grete observed that in later years even the foreign communists in the camp often shared this view. 'They regarded the German communists as beyond the pale and the German communists made no attempt to defend themselves.'

Such fractures may in part have caused the discord that erupted within the Christmas party committee. The Poles disliked being told what to do by the German communists and quite quickly decided to break away and hold their own party on a separate day. Other groups broke away as well and held their own separate events.

Despite the disagreements, however, a date around New Year was eventually agreed for the main party, and Dorothea Binz – to everyone's astonishment – agreed to allow the organisers to take over an entire block – Block 22 – for the event. Her stipulation was that only children would be admitted, along with twenty organisers. No mothers or camp mothers must attend.

In the final days the preparations were frantic. A Czech artist made the puppets and the forestry gang organised a tree that was decorated with tin-foil secured by a Siemens worker. French prisoners made toys out of rags, and each child was to have a small parcel and a large plateful of bread and butter, organised from the kitchen. The children's parcels were to contain five lumps of sugar donated by the Norwegians and Belgians – the only prisoners to be receiving food parcels at this time – and they were wrapped in envelopes from the stores. Sylvia Salvesen spent every evening for three weeks drawing on each parcel a picture of a Norwegian child on skis, wearing a red-tasselled cap, standing outside a small Norwegian cottage with a pine wood all around. Somehow she got hold of red, yellow and blue pencils.

As soon as the party began, however, things started to go wrong. Sylvia was posted at the door and led the children in. 'Most were like starved skeletons and some were so weak they had to be carried to their chairs.' The children were arranged in front of the stage. Bräuning said a few words, and he and Binz stayed for the singing of 'O Tannenbaum', during which the children began to cry. As the crying continued Binz and Bräuning stormed out.

When the puppet show started the children had no idea what to do. 'They hadn't the strength to laugh. They had forgotten how to laugh,' said Sylvia, and many were frightened of the puppets, particularly the dogs. 'One or two whimpered weakly from terror when Punch, with bells on his cap, appeared on the puppet stage. One or two cried hysterically and had to be carried out. The older ones clapped after each scene, but the little ones looked up terrified at the sound, which no doubt reminded them of blows they had received.'

Afterwards, when the food was given out the children fell on it 'like wolves', but couldn't eat it, as their stomachs couldn't tolerate it. 'Most could only manage a couple of mouthfuls. Tears began to roll down their thin cheeks, leaving little white strips on their dirty skin.'

Although the organisers gave accounts of the children's party after the war, the children's view has always been obscure. Most of the children who attended did not live for more than another two months. Of the handful who emerged from the camp alive, few have ever spoken of the party. Those who did have quite different memories from the organisers'. Naomi Moscovitch was seven at the time. There was a party, she recalls. And she was there because she was in the children's choir.

Naomi Moscovitch was one of the sixty-four Jewish children who arrived at Ravensbrück from Holland in the winter of 1943–4. She lives today in Netanya, north of Tel Aviv – a striking figure, with long dark curls, a flowing oriental style of dress, and an open, welcoming smile. Her younger sister, Chaya, smaller and fair, had come to talk too, but she doesn't remember a thing, she says, as she was only one when she reached the camp.

The girls' mother was originally Slovakian, and their father Hungarian. Before the war he was cantor in a synagogue in Bratislava – 'he had a wonderful voice' – and in 1938 was chosen as cantor of a large new synagogue in Amsterdam, so the whole family moved to Amsterdam, and hence their arrest in Holland. 'As my father got his Hungarian papers, and Hungary was with the Germans, we were OK,' says Naomi, meaning by that that they were not put on trains to the death camps. In fact her father was sent to Buchenwald and Naomi, Chaya and their brother Yair, aged eleven, came with their mother at the same time as Stella Kugelman to Ravensbrück.

Though they were the first significant group of children in the camp, they were treated just like other prisoners, says Naomi.

> Only difference was we got a bowl and two spoons – one extra as we were four people. I remember coming into the block for the first time and asking my mother who all these men were, as I'd never seen people without hair.
>
> My mother must have been so brave and strong. She was thirty-seven. Her name was Frieda Moscovitch and she kept all three of us going. She stood with the baby in her arms for hours and hours at the *Appell*, and at that age children got teeth and cried and cried. The food was terrible, one piece of bread for the whole day and a bowl of soup, but she smuggled in extra porridge somehow, and when I had typhus she got me an apple. I never knew how she got that apple. My brother got so thin he said one day: 'Look, I can see through my hands.'

When Naomi caught typhus she was kept in a hospital block and remembers a Jewish woman lying in the bed shouting in German: 'I'm going to kill anyone who comes near me.' Naomi, who spoke a little German, tried to calm her. 'The woman in the bed on my other side died. I woke up one morning and she was still. Dead. But we got used to that. No it didn't bother me at all, or haunt me. It's just like someone was there and then they were dead.'

The children played inside the block mostly, 'just jumping out of the window, things like that. There were no toys. We played in a kind of field, I remember, near the fence, and they told us not to go too close. And someone threw themselves against the fence and died and we weren't allowed to play there again.'

Naomi remembers a few big events: the Gypsies arriving in the summer, for example, and being told they were thieves. 'They came into our block and I remember thinking they were very dark. We were dark but they were darker. I don't know if they were really thieves, but I know my mother made a little bag to keep our bowl and spoons in and hid it under the pillow.'

In the autumn of 1944 the Hungarians arrived, and everyone was amazed by the state they were in. 'It was a terrible sight – they'd had no preparation, unlike us. We'd been in a camp before we got here – in Holland – but they had come straight from home or from the ghetto. They were in total shock and filthy.' Chaya interrupts to ask something about the camp and explains that she is always learning new things, 'because I never knew anything at the time – just that I was there, but where was it that I was? All I remember is sitting on a floor. When I came out I didn't know about most normal things. People always made fun of me and said – oh, you know, she's like that because of the camp.'

When the big groups began to arrive from Hungary and Slovakia, their mother, being Slovakian and her husband a Hungarian, would go and see if she knew anyone, 'and of course she spoke Hungarian'. One day she found her husband's sister, Aunt Chaya (Chaya was named after her), in the tent.

> And so my mother told our aunt that we couldn't get her out but we'd bring her things when we could. One day my brother comes and says: 'I think they are killing Aunt Chaya.' So my mother went to look, and because my aunt had tried to get out of that tent they hit her badly, and so we got her out somehow. Don't ask me how. I don't know how my mother managed that either, but Aunt Chaya came to the block and lived with us, so we stayed together as a family from then on.

After Naomi had talked a while longer she paused and looked at me, as if there was something specific she wanted to say. Then she asked if I knew about the children's choir. I said I didn't.

> So I was in this choir. It was the end of forty-four and they made a barracks for the children to go to. They said at Christmas we'd go there and we learned Christmas songs in German. Both my brother and I were in this choir. We both sang well, like our father. And we went to this barracks and there was a big Christmas tree and they said after the singing they would make a party and give us something. So we sang opposite the Germans and the women with the dogs.
>
> After the singing stopped my mother came and stood outside the window, and I don't remember exactly how this happened, but she must

have shouted to my brother and said we had to come out straight away, because this was not our religion and we couldn't stay to celebrate and we had to go with her back to the block.

And my brother took me by the hand and we climbed out of the window. I didn't know, but it was after that they said everything exploded and there were no barracks any more. So my mother saved us. And in the place where the barracks was, the next day was just water all frozen over. I didn't think about it, just that where the barracks was there was nothing any more. When I met some of the other kids years later I said I was in that choir and they said but how is it possible – how did you stay alive? These others told me that the Germans threw hand grenades in the window and that was how they wanted to finish off all the children.

I asked Naomi if she thinks it really happened, that they blew up the children in the barracks at the Christmas party. 'That is what I remember about what happened and what people say. I can't explain it all but that's what I know. And in Belsen it was terrible too.' She was talking now about what happened to the Ravensbrück children who were taken to Belsen a few weeks after the party. 'It was cold and we were in bags on the floor, no beds, no nothing. People were dying everywhere. And I remember my mother got typhus and my aunt saying look, we have three little children and everyone who schlepps out a dead body from the block should get an extra bit of bread.'

I wondered if Naomi had talked much about the bombing of the barracks when she went back to Holland after the war. Most people in Holland had not been in the camps, she said, and 'you didn't talk about it with children of your own age. A lot of people don't want to talk about what happened at the camps. My brother has never talked about it even to me, and won't talk now.'

Naomi Moscovitch's account of the bombing of the Ravensbrück Christmas party is not supported in any written testimony, and yet several other surviving children remember something similar. Stella also believes the story to be true.

Stella says she wasn't at the party herself because she was sick and unable to go. Her information came from her last camp mother, a Russian called Aunt Olympiada, who helped Stella in the final days. Aunt Olympiada told her that she'd once had a son, and that 'she'd lost him in the bomb'. She knew no more than that, but she is sure that Aunt Olympiada meant the bomb at the children's party.

After the war Stella met some of the grown-up party organisers, including the German communist Erika Buchmann. 'Erika would say to me: "But

Stella, you must remember how we gave you bread and everything at the party," but I didn't remember that at all.'

As no written evidence survives of the bombing, and the adults didn't talk of it, it is hard to believe the story, and yet, as this is the way the children remember things, for them it is clearly true. The horrors the same children went through in the weeks that followed were arguably far worse, and better-documented. The first of those horrors began a few days after the Christmas party.

In the last days of December prisoners in the *Revier* began to talk about another of the new Auschwitz men, one of the two doctors. He was 'a little man called the professor,' said Sylvia Salvesen, and not long after he arrived Gypsy children were called up for sterilisation. Their parents were told that if they agreed to the operation they would be freed. The man was Carl Clauberg, the doctor ordered by Himmler early in the war to find a means of mass sterilisation, as part of the drive to create a master race. For three years Clauberg had been experimenting at Auschwitz, maiming and killing hundreds of women, but all his experiments had failed. Now, in what he must have known were the last months of the war, he wanted to experiment again on new 'material' at Ravensbrück.

In the *Revier*, the message got out that Treite was to carry out the surgery under Clauberg's supervision. According to Sylvia Salvesen, Treite's secretary, the Belgian Emmi Gorlich, suddenly turned 'pale as death, with dark rings under her eyes – she knew what was going to happen'. The prisoner staff in the *Revier* all told Emmi to plead with Treite not to cooperate with Clauberg. 'And through the thin partition we heard her begging him. Voices rose, the door flew open. But Dr Treite stormed out saying: "Orders from Berlin."'

Emmi Gorlich said later that the sterilisation started with children aged eight to ten.

> All the Gypsies came into the hall. They were small children. They called out to me as I passed. I went to try and find them some sugar; they didn't understand what was going to happen. My friend, an Austrian doctor, often helped on operations. She was forced to do this. I told her you must not do this, they can kill you. She came back green in the face, saying Dr Treite had sent her away.

According to Zdenka Nedvedova, Clauberg carried out the sterilisation by spraying a substance into the womb under pressure and watching the effect on the fallopian tube through an X-ray screen.

Sylvia remembered two Gypsy girls coming into the *Revier* aged eight and ten – both called Elisabeth. 'They were asking: "We are already sterilised, why are we called in?" They put them in the room behind me and I asked to see Dr Treite to ask him to do nothing more to the children. Dr Treite said again: "It's no use. It's orders from Berlin." A child came out crying in a hysterical way.' Zdenka said the eight-year-old's screams went on for two hours after she was operated on.

As more and more children were sterilised, prisoners in nearby blocks also heard the children screaming and weeping. The prisoner medical staff became more and more desperate to find a way to stop it, and a German nurse called Gerda Schröder, who had recently joined the staff, offered to help. 'We pleaded with her to give them at least a painkiller, and she did this,' said Zdenka.

> Afterwards we took the children from the X-ray room and we put them in bed in a small treatment room where they lay bleeding from the uterus. Their poor little female bodies made a distressing sight, and at least two of the little martyrs died. In these cases both children suffered further from inflammation of their abdomens, which meant they died in desperate pain.

According to figures obtained by British war crimes investigators, between Christmas 1944 and February 1945 500 Gypsies were sterilised at Ravensbrück, including 200 young girls.

*Chapter 32*

# Death March

Grete Buber-Neumann said that you could always tell women who had arrived at Ravensbrück from Auschwitz, as they had a special hardness about them – especially those who survived the death march of January 1945. The Jews among the 20,000 women left at Auschwitz at the end were still there because they were 'lucky' enough to be young and fit when they arrived and so to be selected for work. Allegra Benvenisti was eighteen when she came from Thessaloniki in Greece to Auschwitz with her parents, sisters, brothers and cousins. At the first selection, the SS officer pointed her one way while almost all the rest of her family went the other way, to the gas chamber.

As Allegra noticed, many of these healthy girls then died of sickness after two or three weeks. She too fell sick and nearly died, but a Ukrainian nurse saved her by smuggling her out of her hospital block just before a truck took all the sick away – 'dead or alive'. Susi Bachar, another Greek, was also selected for work, along with her two sisters. One quickly died of typhus and the other of dysentery.

Throughout the summer of 1944, Susi, Allegra and other 'working' prisoners watched as Auschwitz reached the zenith of its power, exterminating 400,000 Hungarians in just two months. But during the autumn the churning of the trains back and forth, bringing victims for slaughter, was slowing as the Soviet advance continued and the camp prepared for evacuation. By October those still alive at Auschwitz dared to hope that they might survive, especially when on 2 November the furnaces stopped smoking. Lydia Vago remembered a civilian boss in the factory where she worked whispering to her: 'See to it that you get home now – there are no more chimneys.' For Lydia, home was in the Transylvanian mountain town of Gheorgheni, in Romania, where her father was a doctor and her mother a dentist. The whole family – Hungarian Jews by origin – had been rounded up in 1944 and Lydia, aged twenty, with her younger sister, Aniko, ended up in Auschwitz.

Late that year Auschwitz's blocks and streets began to thin out as prisoners were transferred to camps in Germany. Some of the most hated guards left too, among them Irma Grese, the farmer's daughter who had trained at Ravensbrück and risen to the post of chief woman guard at Birkenau. Now Grese and several of her Ravensbrück cohort were reassigned to Belsen.

With fewer guards, Maria Rundo, a Polish student, recalled an 'idyllic period' in Auschwitz in late autumn when the prisoners had more freedom of movement and were left to some extent to their own devices. The weak, old and sick went to the former Gypsy camp, where Maria found work as a nurse. 'We were saving the sick with our own hands; we cooked soup for them, bathed and combed them, deloused them.' Here babies were even born and could be looked after.

The divisions between Jews and non-Jews began to relax. A Polish-Jewish doctor, Alina Brewda, recalled being sent to live in a mixed block of Jews and 'Aryans'. 'It had been a strict rule that we be kept separate, but now we were living together.' The brothels closed down and one of the prostitutes asked Alina to treat her, as she was dying. In return she gave Alina a knitted black dress, felt shoes and a warm jacket, which served her well on the coming march.

In January 1945, with the Russians just a few days from Auschwitz, the SS began to prepare frantically for the evacuation. It soon became clear that anyone fit enough to walk was to be forced on the march, but anyone too weak was to be killed. As the moment came the guards began to cull the sick and dying by shooting. They also prepared to blow up the camp. Lydia Vago, who had fallen ill, was in the sickbay and she remembered a nurse shouting at her to get out now. Lydia left the *Revier*, and as she walked away she saw a truck arrive to take those too feeble to move, to be shot.

On 18 January work continued normally, including construction of a new block. As night fell, the call came to clear out. Maria Rundo remembered a total blackout in the hospital where she worked, and then the lights came back on and an SS man ordered the nurses to collect all the cards of the sick, which he took away. On the Lagerstrasse people shouted that all those able to march should return to their blocks, as the evacuation was to start. It was snowing, and as prisoners ran back to the blocks those too sick to march panicked. 'There was no doubt about their fate, as the SS would not let the sick be liberated,' said Lydia Vago.

Some didn't want to leave, hoping to greet their Soviet liberators. Alina Brewda, the Jewish doctor, hid with the sick, but an SS officer found her and threw her out. Some made for the clothes stores and collected whatever they could for warmth – blankets, coats, sweaters. Allegra, the girl from Thessaloniki, was on the night shift at the factory when the call came. She had no time to eat or get warm clothes and went straight to the line now gathering at the gate. Lydia Vago found time to get into the pharmacy of the small factory *Revier* and put aspirins and bandages into her small bag made of blue-grey uniform cloth. She and her sister Aniko carried extra clothes and blankets strung in bundles on their backs, the string clasped tight in their hands.

On the evening of the evacuation, those selected to leave gathered at the gates: men, women, Jews and non-Jews, Kapos and non-Kapos. Children were told they couldn't leave, but some came. Just before the gates opened the guards handed every prisoner a loaf of bread and told them to get in line, women at the back.

This was not the first death march. In the early years of the war the Nazis force-marched Jews into the ghettos and Red Army soldiers into the camps. In the summer and autumn of 1944 they marched many thousands of Hungarians to Germany. But this forced march of some 60,000 enfeebled, terrified Auschwitz survivors, including 20,000 women, out of the camp gates into the snowy night, with Russian artillery sounding just three miles away, surpassed all others in horror.

Lydia held on tight to Aniko. It was vital not to lose each other as the crowd now began to move. The guards shouted: '*Alles antreten*' – Fall in, line up. Get out. The dogs barked. An air-raid alert sounded and for some minutes all the lights went out, plunging the camp into darkness. People thought of hiding, but what was the point if the camp was going to blow up? As the prisoners moved away they knew the Red Army was close, as they could see 'Stalin's candles' – the Soviet Katyusha rockets – lighting up the skies.

The line shuffled out down the snowy road, the men in the front, the women at the back, with SS on all sides, carrying rifles. The temperature was plummeting. Alina Brewda remembered the guards ordering them to run, prodding with bayonets. While some ran, others stumbled. Before long they saw the first dead men lying in the snow, shot for falling over. Soon they saw women shot as well. Allegra kept slipping as snow got stuck on her wooden shoes. When Alina couldn't keep up, stronger runners on either side picked her up under the arms and carried her, so she 'ran' between them barely touching the ground.

Now they slowed a little. The SS had calmed down as they put more distance between themselves and the Russians. Guards started to overtake them on motorbikes or in cars. The factory workers' group tried to stay together, but soon they got mixed up with the massed ranks from Birkenau. Sisters, cousins, friends, all feared losing each other. They knew it meant death to be left alone amid the trudging crowd.

On the first day, the guards allowed them to rest a few times and relieve themselves on the side of the road. But they were afraid they'd fall asleep, squatting there, and freeze to death. They'd eaten their loaf of bread and anything grabbed before leaving. 'So we ate the snow,' said Maria Rundo, who noticed groups of male corpses, in prison stripes, near where she stopped. 'They'd had their skulls cut open right across the top of their heads with a knife, and their brains scooped out. We supposed the SS did it with long sticks, with some kind of wooden ball attached to the end. There were SS on the march who were armed with such sticks.' After this Maria tried not to look at the ground at all. 'I pretended it was all a fairy tale and watched the sunset and sunrise instead.'

Shots rang out repeatedly behind them, as the SS executed any stragglers. The marchers now trampled over corpses strewn along the road, shot where they slipped and fell. Lydia saw a blue-eyed boy under her feet and stepped over him. One girl and her mother carried an exhausted younger sister until they couldn't carry her any more. 'So we sacrificed her and she died.' They knew the guards had killed her, because they heard the shot seconds later.

After three days they lost track of time. In Lydia and Aniko's factory group the marchers reckoned they were already down from 500 to 300. Sometimes they seemed to be trudging with thousands, sometimes just with a small group, separated temporarily from the billowing crowd.

Mostly they tried to sleep at night in barns, but often there was no room, and many lay down in the road to freeze to death. Some even managed to flee, reaching nearby farms where Poles hid them. Others were found and shot. Once the guards sent Lydia and Aniko to a small barn with soft dry hay where they slept for a few hours. They thought of hiding in the hay and asking the Polish farmers for asylum, but next morning the Germans came and stabbed the hay with bayonets, shooting anyone they found. On another occasion they rested in a cowshed where peasants were milking the cows. The peasants gave the marchers bowls full of warm fresh milk.

Allegra remembered another night when the SS marched them to a barn with one guard carrying a can of gasoline. Everyone thought the SS were going to burn them all to death, 'but I was too tired to worry'. So she lay down in the barn and to her astonishment found her cousin Berry next to her, whom she hadn't seen since their arrival at Auschwitz. Berry had worked at 'Canada', the warehouse where the clothes and personal belongings of the gassed were sorted. She gave Allegra some spare warm clothes she had brought with her from 'Canada'.

'We vowed we wouldn't let anyone separate us again, and for the next days we marched in line holding each other.' More and more stragglers were being shot. At one point Allegra told Berry she couldn't go on – 'Let them shoot me.' Berry urged her on. Further ahead, they reversed roles, Allegra encouraging Berry. At one point a friend called Diamante joined the girls and carried Berry some of the way.

After two or three days the SS broke up the endless column, as they marched the men down different roads towards Mauthausen, Buchenwald or Gross-Rosen. The women kept on towards Ravensbrück, 420 miles northwest of Auschwitz. Yet often, straying in the Polish wasteland, the SS lost the way. Word of the chaos on the Polish roads got back to SS headquarters in Berlin, so Rudolf Höss, the former Auschwitz commander, was sent out to assess the evacuation.

In his memoir Höss said he was surprised to find that already the Russian armoured spearheads were fanning out on the east side of the Oder, while on every road and track west of the river he found prisoners stumbling through deep snow without food. He first ran into men bound for the concentration camp of Gross-Rosen, 'but most of the non-commissioned officers in charge of these stumbling columns of corpses had no idea how to get there.' On his first night out there he came across countless bodies of prisoners who had just been shot and were still bleeding.

Allegra and Berry's group marched for another 250 miles west and then north, passing through Prague and on into Germany, where shelling was intense. They spent one night in a field with dead bodies and dead horses and the next day the guards herded them onto train wagons. Just before the train left:

> I spotted loaves of bread on the ground. I don't know how I gathered the strength to run and steal two loaves and run back to Berry to give them to her. I picked up a blanket from a dead person and we climbed into the open train car, keeping the bread hidden. We covered ourselves with the blanket and during the night, while the train was moving through the snowfall, we ate the bread and also ate the snow from on top of the blanket. We travelled this way through the night and the following afternoon we reached Ravensbrück.

Alina Brewda, the Jewish doctor, was put in a covered train that went northwest through Hamburg and then doubled back to Berlin, where they saw mile after mile of ruins 'and rejoiced'. Guards loaded Lydia and Aniko's group onto open cattle wagons in Loslau in Silesia, with only standing room. Aniko had developed a septic sore, caused by the string of her makeshift bag, which had cut into her flesh.

'We were snowed in,' Lydia recalled. 'We were standing sardines. Falling was impossible, although we couldn't feel our frozen numbed feet, which had no strength to support us. Have you ever heard of human beings dying upright? That's what happened on the death trains.'

Lydia and Aniko stood near the front of the wagon where the SS guard sat on a bench with his German shepherd dog at his feet. The dog got up, and Lydia crawled under its belly and lay there for warmth. She was sure the guard would tell the dog to bite her, or he'd shoot her. But he just complained 'My dog has no space' and told her to get out of the way. 'We travelled this way through the night and the following afternoon we arrived at Ravensbrück.'

The Auschwitz women arrived at Ravensbrück in different groups over several days towards the end of January 1945. Walter Schenk, the crematorium chief, recalled there were so many dead amongst them that the furnaces couldn't cope so the Fürstenberg crematorium was used to burn the corpses as well. More transports kept coming.

'Half-frozen dead-on-their-feet women' fell out of the trucks, said Lydia of her trainload. There were untold numbers of dead, taken straight off for burning. At the gates the guards made what Lydia and Aniko thought at first was going to be a selection. Instead, 'a small ugly woman at a control table, whose cheeks and lips were red with lipstick, just directed them on through'. Lydia said: 'We kept guessing, would they gas us or shoot us?' The sisters feared Aniko's wound was now so septic that she would certainly be taken away for killing. 'I want to go to Mother,' she whimpered.

The guards sent almost all the women to the tent at first, to crouch in the mud. Allegra was soon allocated a barracks and grabbed a plank 'bed' of four narrow boards, sensing 'if I had to sit in the mud one moment more I'd die'. The bread came round, she looked away for a split second and a girl snatched one of the boards. 'I began to hit this girl, pulling the board and screaming at her: "I'm not going to die." Berry ... screamed at me, "You're killing her," and I said again: "I'm not going to die."'

Alina Brewda was among those new arrivals forced to sleep out in the snow. Zdenka Nedvedova, the camp's Czech doctor, who had arrived from Auschwitz herself six months earlier, came to look at the death-marchers:

> Everything was white with snow when they poured in – thousands of them; so many that the guards couldn't sort them out or separate them from other prisoners who went in among them and asked what had

> happened and looked for missing friends. They told of their terrible journey and how they'd left Auschwitz burning behind them. When we went to bed they were still out there and when we woke up they were still there too – halos of frost around their faces.

Lydia and Aniko were 'shovelled' into the tent, where Lydia tried to protect Aniko's septic hand as the soup was distributed to the surging crowd. A ladle splashed soup into the bowl tied on a string around Lydia's waist, and the two girls shared it.

Aniko now seemed close to death from her abscess, and the guards and Kapos shunned her because of the stink from the wound. Someone sent her to the *Revier*, where she was operated on and came back with a clean bandage, but the tent was so filthy that they soon grew lice-infested, 'like at Birkenau'.

After several days, when they thought they'd been abandoned to die, Lydia and Aniko were suddenly called to be registered. They weren't worried that this meant selection, as in that case surely the SS would have selected them at the gates. Lydia was made to stand on a measuring device. 'Why were they curious suddenly to know my height?' Then the girls received their new camp numbers on a slip of white cloth: 99626 for Lydia and 99627 for Aniko.

Soon after, the SS sent Aniko and Lydia to 'a place in the woods called the *Jugendlager*, Youth Camp' and set them to work filling straw mattresses. 'There was something odd about this Youth Camp that we couldn't grasp,' said Lydia.

> Some little women in grey were hurrying about in silence. Who were they and what was their business? And as we were not severely guarded, I opened a door, out of curiosity. A large room was crammed with old women sitting on the floor. I asked where they came from and one of them said Budapest. I looked around, horrified, thinking of my grandmother, whom I'd left in Budapest. I hurried out and opened the nearby door. It was a very small room containing several naked corpses.

Lydia and Aniko stayed only a few days at the Youth Camp, where they received an extra bowl of soup each day. Years later Lydia learned that they had filled straw mattresses for Ravensbrück's new extermination camp.

*Chapter 33*

# Youth Camp

As Lydia Vago watched women die at the Uckermark Youth Camp, Cicely Lefort and Mary Young were hearing rumours that the new camp was a far better place to go, with a well-equipped sickbay and good treatment. Some even called it a sanatorium. Sylvia Salvesen, the Norwegian *Revier* worker, and others said they'd heard such talk before; any change at Ravensbrück had always been for the worse. Then a new rumour started; the slum blocks heard that at the new camp they wouldn't even have to work or to stand for morning *Appell*. In the middle of January, with temperatures dropping to minus 30, women were now volunteering to go.

Cicely Lefort and Mary Young appeared outside Sylvia's window at the *Revier*. They needed to talk. They had put their names on a list for a new camp, they said. As Sylvia knew, the two were living in one of the most overcrowded blocks. The Norwegian woman had recently befriended them, particularly Mary, who was very frail. Aged sixty-two, her slight frame was bent with exhaustion, her legs were swollen and she was running a high fever.

Cicely, the SOE woman, once athletic, tall and sinewy, was also now bent and skeletal. Treite had operated on her in the autumn for stomach ulcers and swollen legs, but now she had acute diarrhoea. They'd heard 'excellent' reports about the new place; if only they could avoid roll call they might be able to hold out. It would only be weeks now, wouldn't it? Didn't Sylvia agree it was a good idea to go? asked Cicely. 'She blurted all this out in a rush, nervous and excited. Her eyes were terror-stricken and she was nervous of my answer.'

Sylvia tried to warn them, but they didn't want to listen, and nor did hundreds of others who also saw the Youth Camp as their only chance to hold on until the liberation. By mid-January General Konstantin Rokossovsky's second Belorussian Front, advancing through East Prussia, along the Baltic coast, was just 400 miles from Ravensbrück. In the west the Allies had smashed the Wehrmacht's counterattack in the battle of the Bulge and were driving on towards the Rhine. Nothing scared the women more than the prospect of dying in these last few weeks, before their liberators arrived.

Inside Ravensbrück signs multiplied that the end was imminent. Someone had set up a secret radio, and news of the Allied advance was shouted out at night between the blocks. Air raids were frequent, the guards on edge, and the Red Army women were walking tall, preparing for the Soviet arrival.

Rations had been cut again. Some days the soup seemed to be made of nettles or marjoram with hardly a potato. Then yet another rumour started. At the Youth Camp there would be potatoes 'twice a day'.

It was no coincidence that just as the Youth Camp myths began to spread, the tall slender figure of Johann Schwarzhuber appeared on the Lagerstrasse. Another redundant Auschwitz man, Schwarzhuber arrived at Ravensbrück early in January to carry out the orders Bräuning had refused to implement.

In his evidence later Schwarzhuber was confused about names and dates, and sanitised many of the events. Yet his testimony was informative for an SS man: he seemed more ready than his comrades to give a real sense of how things might have happened. For example, a conversation he recounts with Fritz Suhren, in which he received instructions to start gassing, has a strong ring of truth.

Soon after arriving at the camp, Obersturmführer Schwarzhuber said he and the chief doctor, Richard Trommer, were called to the commandant's office. 'Suhren told us that he had received an order from Reichsführer Himmler which stated that all women who were ill or incapable of marching were to be killed.' Until then the killing was still being done by shooting under the orders of Moll. 'This method did not seem to be going fast enough for the commandant. He said in my presence: "It isn't going fast enough, we shall have to use other methods."'

Artur Conrad, head of the camp shooting squad, had been saying the same thing to colleagues in the HQ building. 'He said: "Women are not dying fast enough. Something must be done about it,"' recalled Karla Kampf, an Austrian secretary.

Treite said later he too had heard that the reason gassing began was that 'shooting wasn't going fast enough'. Nobody suggested, however, that the shooting should stop – rather, both killing methods were now used. One of the crematorium workers, a male prisoner called Horst Schmidt, recalled that when he first began work at the crematorium at the end of January every evening about fifty women were shot and brought for burning – the same daily rate given by Treite. 'Occasionally some of the victims were still alive and were shot again before the cremation. Two doctors were present and one removed the gold teeth.'

Schmidt estimated that at least 600 women were shot from the end of January to the end of February 1945. He didn't know if the shootings went on past February – he only stayed in the job for two weeks – but recalled another worker coming to him soon after he left the crematorium and saying: 'Now we have gas.'

Meanwhile, Walter Schenk, the head of the crematorium gang, had received specific instructions from Schwarzhuber. 'He said to me: "We are going to start operations." I said: "What sort?" He said: "You'll hear about it when we start to gas." I said I had too much work to do already. He said, don't be stupid. It won't affect you. "There will be a team from Auschwitz to gas and burn."'

When he had first realised what 'other methods' meant, Schwarzhuber says in his trial statement that he tried to resist. 'I told the camp commandant that I was glad I had left Auschwitz and that I did not wish to take part in this a second time.'

The son of a printer from Bavaria, Johann Schwarzhuber had joined the SS at twenty-one. He was schooled in hardness at Dachau, before his graduation to Theresienstadt and Auschwitz. From 1942 he supervised the entire gassing programme at the Birkenau extermination plant.

High-cheekboned, with hooded eyes, Schwarzhuber was known among the women as 'a smirking SS lecher', although he was apparently happily married, with two boys who were often seen running about at Auschwitz. When one of them vanished one day, Schwarzhuber feared that he'd been taken to the gas chamber. From then on his boys wore signs around their necks, saying 'SS Schwarzhuber's son'.

Colleagues said Schwarzhuber was not as hard as other SS officers. He helped run the men's prisoner orchestra and also got Russian prisoners of war to perform folk dances while his family watched outside the fence. He liked the Gypsies and used to spend time talking to them.

One SS officer said he'd heard Schwarzhuber tell Rudolf Höss to his face that he had 'not joined the SS to kill Jews'. Höss doesn't mention this incident in his 1947 prison memoir, but he does recall that Schwarzhuber was very affected once by the gassing of Auschwitz Gypsies. 'Schwarzhuber told me that no extermination of the Jews had been so difficult, and he had a particularly hard time of it because he knew a lot of those inmates well and had a good relationship with them.' Another Auschwitz guard said it was quite common to see Schwarzhuber 'drunk and weeping' as inmates were led to the gas chamber.

However reluctant Schwarzhuber may have been to do the job a second time at Ravensbrück, he must have recognised there were enormous differences between the Auschwitz operation and what was to happen here. The target of 2000 deaths a month at Ravensbrück demanded by Himmler in October 1944 ('retrospectively') was tiny compared with the number gassed at Auschwitz, thought today to have been over a million. The setup here was primitive compared with the sophistication of the Birkenau extermination complex.

At Auschwitz the vast majority of those gassed were Jews. Ravensbrück mostly murdered non-Jews, chosen according to whether a woman was sick or incapable of marching, as Suhren had said. Jews clearly fell into this category, especially as the recent arrival of Auschwitz evacuees and Hungarians had raised their number from an average of one in ten to about one in five of the total population, which in mid-January was about 45,000 strong. But being Jewish was not by this time a reason for selection, as it had been at Auschwitz and the other death camps.

Indeed the entire context of the gassing at Ravensbrück was new. For the first time Nazi extermination had no stated ideological objective; it was impossible for the SS to persuade themselves or others that what was being done here was to cleanse the gene pool or to further the welfare of the master race. At Ravensbrück killing by gas in the closing months of the war was done to make space and save food, while also reducing the number of prisoners who might fall into enemy hands. Anyone who could march could be evacuated in time; those who could not were to be gassed. Furthermore, the gassing was to be done inside a concentration camp on German soil.

And because the Ravensbrück extermination programme had different goals, it posed different problems for its overseer. Perhaps the most important problem for Johann Schwarzhuber was how to keep the women calm as the gassing got under way. Himmler and his SS officers had understood that large-scale gassing could only succeed if the victims remained unaware and therefore calm.

At Auschwitz, calm had been easy to preserve. Most of the Jewish victims, even at the end, knew next to nothing about what was to happen to them. They arrived from the ghettos or from other camps, to be parted at once from those deemed fit to work and marched to the gas chamber with no time to question what was happening.

At Ravensbrück, however, it would not be easy to isolate those selected for gassing from the rest of the camp. They would not be in convoys delivered by train, as at Auschwitz, but women picked from an existing throng. Furthermore, the Ravensbrück victims could only be gassed in small groups, taking time, because the temporary gas chamber had a limited capacity, so that while those selected awaited their fate, fear could spread.

Previous selections at Ravensbrück for the black transports that took prisoners for killing elsewhere had been carried out in relative calm; but these earlier selections were smaller, and targeted to some extent at defined groups – the so-called 'lunatics', the acutely sick, Jews – groups that could be split in advance from the rest. Other, 'ordinary', prisoners could tell themselves that they were exempt from the black transport selections, and so had nothing to fear. Even at Ravensbrück such selections had been camouflaged, and when preparation was poorly disguised – as in the case of the Majdanek death transport – panic had erupted.

For all these reasons, Schwarzhuber grasped the need now for very careful camouflage. Hence, before selection had even begun, he had the camp flooded with rumours and lies to make the most vulnerable believe that they were going somewhere better. So easy to fool were these desperate women that Schwarzhuber had soon persuaded hundreds to queue up and volunteer to die.

Before it all started, however, he needed the staff – men and women he could trust. He could certainly trust the *Sonderkommando*, the special work gang who would operate the gas chamber itself, because he brought this group of eleven male prisoners with him from Auschwitz. Prisoners said later he brought with him some components of the Auschwitz gas chamber as well.

To work with his gassing team, he also needed Ravensbrück support, both men and women. At Auschwitz-Birkenau he had tended to employ people who had not long been in the camp, so they were not 'fixed in their ideas', and not at all close to the prisoners. This was a tactic he deployed at Ravensbrück too.

Within days of arriving Schwarzhuber recruited Ruth Neudeck, a woman recommended by Albert Sauer, who according to Schwarzhuber was now deputy commandant. A tall thirty-two-year-old blonde, who had arrived at Ravensbrück just three months previously, Neudeck first worked in the camp's bookkeeping office, but after a brief illness was posted to Block 27, where she caught Sauer's eye. He noticed she liked to thrash, and gave her a gift of a silver-handled whip. Loulou Le Porz later described her: 'Big. Ordinary looking. Vulgar. She held herself straight. I heard she was a widow. No children. Lived with her mother.'

Neudeck was swiftly promoted to the *Strafblock*, and after observing her at work, Schwarzhuber conscripted her to his team. To work alongside her he recruited a handful of other women guards, as well as two male SS hospital orderlies – probably also from Auschwitz – called Koehler and Rapp. This group were to be deployed at the new annex, the Youth Camp. Neudeck was to be the Youth Camp's chief woman guard.

When Lydia Vago, the Auschwitz death-marcher, was sent to work at the Youth Camp in mid-January 1945 she found that it was already a place of death. The Hungarians she saw there had obviously been left to die. At this stage the new camp's purpose had not been worked out; for now it was probably being used as an ad hoc dumping ground for surplus prisoners, brought there and left to die, or else shot. By late January, however, Johann Schwarzhuber had drawn up his extermination plan more thoroughly, and worked out the roles the Youth Camp and its staff would play.

Given the priority assigned to avoiding panic, not only were rumours and lies circulated about going to a sanatorium, but a plan was devised, most likely by Schwarzhuber, whereby the women to be gassed would not be selected direct from the main camp. Instead, selection would work in stages.

First, those women who had chosen to go to the 'sanatorium' or 'better camp', as well as others chosen by the SS, would be put together, perhaps 200 at a time, and assembled in and around blocks at the rear of the compound. This area – where the slum blocks were – was already fenced off, but the cordon was now reinforced and the area would soon be known as the 'death zone'. Whatever fears the women held here might develop, it would not be possible to communicate with others elsewhere in the camp.

At a given moment the selected women would be marched out of the death zone via a gate at the bottom right-hand side, and taken the half-mile or so through the woods to the Youth Camp. Here they would be kept for a while. Further such groups would gradually be marched out to join them. Another round of selections would then be carried out at the Youth Camp, and it would be those chosen in this second round who would be taken away for gassing. That would involve a further journey, this time by truck, to the gas chamber near the crematorium, beside the south wall. In a sense, the plan would take the victims full circle, but it would have the benefit of confusing them, while also keeping the selections for gassing out of sight.

Keeping selections out of sight would also ease the concerns of the wider camp staff, who would not need to be briefed, at least at first, in case discontent broke out in their ranks too. Prisoner doctors and nurses in the hospital blocks were the most likely source of protest, because they were already terrified of more black transports. Two SS doctors had even shown signs of rebellion: Percival Treite had refused to be present at the mass shootings that Otto Moll was still carrying out, and the other new doctor, Franz Lucas, who arrived in December, then refused too.

In order to hoodwink the medical staff – prisoners and SS alike – Schwarzhuber devised a charade with real actors and props. He sent a French prisoner doctor called Dora Revier to the Youth Camp before the first group of prisoners arrived, giving her medicines and a set of sham instructions to start a sickbay. Two nurses came with her. Now rumours spread that the new camp really was a sanatorium. Indeed, so effective was this latest deception that at first it fooled some of the *Revier*'s most experienced staff, including Loulou Le Porz, the Block 10 doctor, and Erika Buchmann, the German communist who had by now taken over from Carmen Mory as Blockova.

According to Buchmann, Treite also appeared to believe in the charade. He walked into Block 10 one morning and asked for a list of prisoners who were most acutely ill, explaining that they were to be 'transferred elsewhere for better treatment'. The transfers he referred to were almost certainly the first dispatch of prisoners for the Youth Camp. Testimony varies about when this was. Erika Buchmann said Treite's request came on 20 January, so the first women probably left very soon after that.

Erika had compiled the list straight away, 'without the slightest fear about what it might mean, in view of the terrible conditions in Block Ten'. At the same time the guards began calling out prisoners with pink cards and selecting among them for the new camp.

In the offices the 'old rat' secretaries – 'death secretaries' they called them at Auschwitz – collated the lists without a qualm. They surely should have known better, having assembled so many black transport lists since 1941. The Austrian communist Hermine Salvini remembered being told when the first group left to note beside their names: 'transferred to the new camp'. She said the secretaries had no idea of the conditions prevailing at this camp. 'We were even glad that the old women were going to a place where conditions were good and where they would only do a little knitting and no hard work.'

The Belgian nurse Renée Govers, however, had fears from the start. When the sick from the main *Revier* were taken off to join the group and she tried to give one woman a warmer coat, one of Schwarzhuber's guards shouted at Renée: 'You idiot. She won't need that now.'

It took several more days after the first departure before suspicion began to spread. Sylvia Salvesen got word of conditions at the Youth Camp from a Jehovah's Witness who ran an errand there and returned with news of prisoners starved, stripped of their clothes and left out in sub-zero temperatures. Dora Revier, the French doctor, and one of the nurses who went with her returned in a state of shock after a week, bringing back their unused medicines. The so-called *Revier* was an empty barracks with no mattresses or even running water. Dora complained at once to Treite, who replied that the Youth Camp was not his responsibility: Schwarzhuber was in charge.

Sylvia went to find Cicely and Mary to stop them going, but it was too late, they were already behind the barbed wire in the death zone at the end of the camp, waiting to leave. A third British woman, Mary O'Shaughnessy, was with them.

Mary O'Shaughnessy knew she was destined for the Youth Camp as soon as the guards started calling out pink cardholders; she held a pink card because she had an artificial arm. Of Irish immigrant stock, raised in Leigh, near Wigan, Mary had learned to cope with her disability from a young age. As a teenager she had set off to France to work as a governess and to seek adventure and independence. Following the French surrender in June 1940, Mary offered to help a local resistance cell, hiding stranded British servicemen on their way down escape lines to the Pyrenees. In Ravensbrück her artificial arm had often provoked beatings from women guards, but she had been spared the most gruelling labour, and after nine months in the camp she was still in a better state of health than her two British friends.

Mary Young, the Scottish nurse, was continuing to weaken. A tiny, slight figure, Mary was the daughter of a grocer's clerk from Aberdeen, who in 1909 had gone to France as a private nurse and then served in the field hospitals behind the trenches. She settled in Paris, where she was arrested in 1942 on suspicion of helping British airmen, and arrived at Ravensbrück in February 1944.

Mary's closest friend in the camp was Cicely Lefort, the forty-six-year-old SOE woman who had arrived on the same transport from Paris. In the 1930s Cicely, an accomplished yachtswoman, had travelled to France seeking adventure and fallen in love with a French doctor called Alex Lefort. He owned a yacht, which he sailed off the Brittany coast. The couple married, and when war broke out Alex encouraged Cicely to go back to England and volunteer for SOE, given her knowledge of France and the French coast. It was Alex Lefort who had first notified SOE in London that Cicely was in Ravensbrück, after receiving a letter from her with the camp address. During her first months in the camp Cicely had stayed in touch with her husband through the official camp mail, but during the summer of 1944, she received a letter from Alex asking for a divorce. Devastated, Cicely found the means to re-write her will in the camp, cutting him off; she even found a camp doctor to witness the document.

*

The group waiting to leave for the Youth Camp with the British women – probably the second group to leave so far – was a mixed crowd with almost every nationality represented, and all ages. Romana Szweda, a Polish teacher, was one of the first Polish prisoners to arrive in Ravensbrück and had helped build the first roads. In early 1945 she fell ill and was in the *Revier* when SS officers came to select for the Youth Camp.

Several long-standing German prisoners were also waiting to leave. A Frau Rissel from Wiesbaden was due to be released in January, but the guards forced her to stand outside the office in the freezing cold for several hours while she waited for her discharge documents. She caught frostbite on her face, and instead of going home now stood behind the wire. Frau Thüringer, who had lost three sons at the front, had only recently been arrested on spurious allegations of speaking out against Hitler; her selection may have been due to her grey hair, which she wore in pigtails. Another German, Gisela Krüger, had arthritis in one leg, which Dr Treite decided – quite unnecessarily – to amputate. She too was bound for the Youth Camp.

Recent arrivals from Hungary were also listed, including Klara Hasse, who lost her right foot on the forced march out of Budapest. Some seventy Dutch women included several who had worked at the Siemens plant before they fell too ill. Scores of Poles from the Warsaw Uprising were here, as well as survivors of the Auschwitz death march, plucked out of the Ravensbrück tent.

Members of the same family volunteered for the Youth Camp group so as not to be parted. They included the French Tambour sisters, who had worked on the SOE's ill-fated *Prosper* circuit near Paris. Madeleine Tambour was desperately sick, and when she was selected her sister Germaine volunteered to join her, having heard the rumours about better food and conditions.

Even now, new rumours of extra blankets and individual mattresses were circulating among the prisoners heading for the Youth Camp, and they couldn't help but feel some hope. The simple prospect of leaving the main camp and walking out into the trees gave the women some sort of cheer. Neeltje Epker, a Dutch midwife and Ravensbrück veteran, put it like this: 'Though we had experience not to believe all those things, we never could imagine that they were telling us such flagrant lies or that they could be quite so cruel. We never imagined that they were going to murder us.'

Irma Trksak, an Austrian-Czech prisoner in the group, recalled the same mood of tentative hope: 'You see, we wanted to believe so much. And our only chance by now was to believe in a miracle.' In any case, most knew they didn't stand a chance of getting off the list; the women selected had no influence in the camp.

Ilse Gohrig, another Dutch woman, simply accepted her fate, as did many others: 'I was sent to the Youth Camp because I was a knitter. I was not a Kapo. I would not be a Kapo as I knew the Kapos were the worst types. I was detailed to go there. I did not try to stay behind as I decided to do what God had decided to be my fate.'

The orders came to line up in ranks of five and the gates at the back of the compound opened. Ahead ran a track leading deep into the woods. 'Later we'd call them "the little woods of death" [*Todeswäldchen*],' remembered Janina Habich, one of the Poles. Those able to walk crunched through the snow, some of them pushing or pulling carts that carried amputees and other disabled women. It took more than an hour to cover the half-mile to the Youth Camp. When at last it came in sight, this huddle of five squat grey barracks ringed by wire seemed disconcertingly small, but the pines shimmering with snow made a pleasant impression on some.

When they got there, Cicely and the two Marys were crammed into one of the smaller blocks with about seventy other women, and no room to sit or lie down. The guards made out that this was just a temporary arrangement while their permanent quarters were made ready. Instead, they were left in the room for three days. No food or water was provided on the first two days, and no one could go out to relieve themselves; urine and excrement soon covered the floor.

Alina Brewda, the Jewish doctor who came on the Auschwitz death march, recalled reaching out of the window and grabbing snow to quench her thirst and to wash. Mary O'Shaughnessy said that during those first forty-eight hours, at least three women in her block died and their bodies remained where they lay. Another seventy women were locked up in an adjoining room, where Mary heard several screaming madly until they passed out, 'presumably through exhaustion'.

On the third day, the guards handed out a splash of watery soup and a scrap of bread before they moved the women into a larger block, along with several hundred other prisoners. There were beds of a sort – planks fixed to walls. The guards gave each woman a single blanket and a straw mattress, sopping wet from lying out in the snow. With the heat of their bodies the mattresses dried, but then seethed with lice. There was still nowhere to wash, and the latrines turned out to be an open ditch forty feet long on the far side of the camp.

Neeltje Epker, the Dutch midwife, remembered that women slept four or five to each plank, as the Youth Camp swelled to about 800 women. So small a gap was there between one plank and the one above that prisoners could barely squeeze onto them. 'Everyone had a fifteen-inch space.' Food was half of the rations issued at the main camp: half a litre of watery cabbage or swede soup at lunchtime, and 100 grams of bread.

One incentive for moving to the Youth Camp was the promised absence of an *Appell*, but on about the fourth day the women were woken at 3.30 a.m. and forced to stand outside in the freezing air for six hours. Some collapsed and died. The next night, the guards took the women's remaining blankets, and then their coats and jackets at the 3 a.m. *Appell*. They were standing in a snowstorm when the coats were taken, Neeltje Epker remembered. Leonarda Frelich, another Auschwitz death-marcher, recalled standing for seven hours. 'Many were passing out, but the group was still not allowed back into the blocks.'

When eventually the women were let back inside, the guards opened the windows wide. The prisoners sickened fast, with severe diarrhoea and swelling caused by starvation and exhaustion. Few had the strength to reach the filthy latrine, but Stijntje Tol, from Amsterdam, struggled over and saw a pile of confiscated clothing outside the back of the hut. 'When we stood for the next *Appell* we were dressed in nothing but thin dresses, in temperatures now dropping as low as −25 degrees centigrade.' All this time more women were being marched up from the main camp. The five wooden barracks were filling up fast, while the last barracks, used as a morgue, was piling up with corpses.

On about 5 February the chief guard, Ruth Neudeck, held a special roll call. Instead of lining up the prisoners as usual she called numbers from a list in her hand, ordering the women to step aside. Neudeck used her silver-handled whip on any woman who didn't respond fast enough, or else the sanitary workers Koehler and Rapp dragged the women forward. Neudeck herself said later she didn't at this stage know where the selected victims were going. Schwarzhuber had given her the list and written at the top: '*Schonungslager* Mittwerda' – 'Rest Camp Mittwerda'.

These Mittwerda lists, as they became known, named the prisoners marked for the gas chamber. Schwarzhuber's charade meant that prisoners, and possibly Neudeck herself, could share the brief delusion that a rest camp existed called Mittwerda.

At the main camp offices, the new lists caused the greatest surprise among the prisoner secretaries. Unlike previous black transport lists, these had to be signed by Suhren. Secretaries used to euphemisms like 'transferred to another camp' found Schwarzhuber's reference to a place called Mittwerda perplexing. So specific was the order that some thought it really meant somewhere better. Then someone thought to check on a map. Mittwerda was well east of Ravensbrück, in Silesia, and had already fallen to the Russians. Schwarzhuber – nicknamed the 'loving God of

Ravensbrück' – must have known his latest lie would be discovered by the prisoner secretaries, and that Ruth Neudeck and everyone else would find out soon enough what it meant.

The silver-topped riding crop – some called it a cane or stick – was the first thing people noticed about Neudeck though Leonarda Frelich also recalled that the woman wielding it was elegant and pretty. Appearing with this stick, she stalked up and down the ranks, using the curved handle as a crook round the necks of the selected prisoners, pulling them out. Any resistance was met by punching; the woman was thrown to the ground and kicked. Frelich also remembered that two men were usually at Neudeck's side and one was always drunk.

Usually Neudeck carried a list, but as Mary O'Shaughnessy observed, on some occasions she and the SS men simply chose women who seemed in poorer health, 'looking at the legs to see if they were swollen and the eyes to see if they had any life in them. If they didn't move quickly enough she hit them with the riding crop that she always carried in her hand.'

Janina Habich remembered Neudeck parading up and down the ranks 'with her thin black staff with a silver handle that she hooked around a prisoner's neck as she called "*Links*" [left]'. Several others testified after the war to the same effect, often adding: 'I saw this with my own eyes.' But there was never any danger that the survivors' evidence would be doubted, because, unlike most other women guards, Ruth Neudeck admitted everything they accused her of and more.

'I had to beat prisoners now and again because of a lack of discipline,' she said. 'I always gave them one or two strokes with the whip. I couldn't strike them with my hand because they were always infested with lice. In the punishment block I also beat three or four prisoners a day because they didn't want to go to work.'

Neudeck's lawyers attempted at one point to claim mistaken identity, suggesting that it was someone else, not she, who carried the silver-handled whip. Neudeck would have none of it. She told the court: 'During the second half of January I received from Sturmbannführer Sauer a cane that had a silver handle. I never lent it to anyone else and as far as I can remember nobody else in the camp had a similar one, or one with a silver handle.'

After the selected group were called they were made to stand to one side and then marched off to a large block known as the gymnasium; it had served as a gym when the camp housed teenage girls, but now it served as a holding zone for the gas chamber. Few details have ever emerged about what happened inside it, but Kapos and prisoner secretaries spoke of the 'dreadful tragedies played out there'. These prisoner Kapos handled most of the day-to-day running of the Youth Camp, in return for privileges, just as they did at the main camp.

One of the Kapos, Józefa Majkowska-Kruszyńska, an arrival from Auschwitz-Birkenau the previous summer, got work with the Youth Camp corpse commando, which was 'something like the *Sonderkommando* at Birkenau'. Sometimes she went to the gymnasium to remove the bodies of women who died before they were even sent for gassing. Once she was asked to extract gold teeth from the dead, but she refused, so someone called Dr Vera did it instead. The SS man Rapp was always drunk, said Jozefa, and Lotte Sonntag, the prisoner messenger, was always beating, but Neudeck was the worst.

It was usually just before dark when Neudeck ordered the detainees out of the gymnasium and into a lineup. Despite the snow, they were then made to strip off all their clothing. Mary O'Shaughnessy sometimes witnessed the scene through a slat in her hut wall. Once the prisoners were naked, a dark-haired young woman wearing a white coat would approach the group. This 'Dr Vera' wrote the women's camp number in indelible ink across their left forearm, or across the chest instead.

Next, the guards allowed the prisoners to put back on one article of clothing – usually a thin shirt or cotton dress. They stood outside for two or three more hours until it was nearly dark. At this point a motor lorry arrived, driven by Josef Bertl, the head of transport. Koehler and Rapp would appear, and Neudeck too. The women were told to get in. If they struggled, the guards threw them into the truck, as their screams rang through the Youth Camp. Eyes peered through windows and cracks, watching as Koehler and Rapp kicked any woman who resisted; or Neudeck screamed and lashed, or kicked out with her jackboots.

These scenes recurred on most nights. Neeltje Epker watched when the first Dutch group was taken, their numbers shouted at random.

> They were women we all knew from The Hague, Brabant, Friesland. They couldn't even take their bit of bread with them. We saw them appear naked on the square where they had handed over their shirts, dresses, knickers and shoes. In the afternoon with loud shouting and beating with straps the SS people forced them onto open trucks for their last journey. I still remember the faces of some of them – Mrs Dessauvagie, Mrs Zandstra, the two Gorter sisters, Mrs Storm and Mrs Grinsveen. And one was able to shout out to us and ask their families to be told what had happened and she said to tell the world that they had 'no regrets for having committed what the Germans called a crime'.

On another night the German woman Gisela Krüger watched as a young Russian, Halina Tschernitschenko, was taken. 'She limped from a fracture and refused to go. So the SS-man beat her with his strap until finally she was thrown into the truck and taken away.' Romana Szweda saw a Polish girl with an amputated arm and leg taken away. 'Neudeck seized the girl by the head and threw her into the truck. Rapp and Koehler were always there to make sure the victims were packed in and to make sure that Dr Vera had correctly scribbled the right numbers on all the arms.'

Dr Vera's real name was Vera Salvequart, twenty-six years old, the daughter of a Czech mother and a German father. She was another of Schwarzhuber's choices. Having reached Ravensbrück in December 1944, Salvequart spent her first three weeks in the freezing squalor of the tent. Treite, on the lookout for prisoner doctors and nurses, found she had some medical training from Prague University and sent her as a nurse to the typhus block, where about 1500 women were dying. Then Schwarzhuber spotted her and sent her to the Youth Camp with Dora Revier and one other nurse. He left her there alone when the others returned to the main camp.

Salvequart's personal history bore some similarity to Carmen Mory's. Before coming to Ravensbrück, she had several aliases and may have been a spy as well as a prostitute; at various times she was wanted by police in France, Denmark, Poland and Austria. For Schwarzhuber's ends, her greatest assets were probably her ready smile and apparently gentle manner: with these she could win the victims' trust.

According to Salvequart, she didn't want the Youth Camp job, but fellow prisoners said she was happy to do it, especially as Schwarzhuber sent her a Red Cross parcel every week and let her wander into the nearby men's camp. Salvequart also claimed that from the start Koehler and Rapp watched her, and told her not to talk about what she saw 'or I'd be shot'.

As the only medic left in the Youth Camp, 'Dr Vera' at first lived alone on one side of the *Revier*, until a few other helpers joined her. The Youth Camp *Revier* was just another plain wooden block, divided into two. There was a washroom of sorts, and a shed called an ambulance room. The other side, known as the day room, was empty. Her duties in the early days of the killing programme were straight forward: she had to fill out the death cards for all those who died and count the bodies. On one occasion the numbers didn't add up and she had to count them all over again.

Dr Vera also handled the formality of contacting, where possible, next of kin, and informing them that they could receive the ashes of the dead in return for a fee. She took all gold crowns and fillings from the corpses, using special pliers, and handed them to Koehler and Rapp. These jobs took much of her time, as from the start about thirty to forty women were dying a day at the Youth Camp, just from starvation, cold and disease. Then the gassing began, and she went to the gymnasium in the evenings to write the prisoners' numbers in indelible ink on their arms and check them off on the lists before the lorry took them away.

Back at the main camp, Suhren – still striving to meet Himmler's target – said the killing was still not going fast enough. Mass shootings by Moll and his men were proceeding, but they couldn't speed up. With only limited capacity inside the gas chamber, new ways were now found to boost the killing.

The sequence over the next weeks is not always clear, but at some point in late January or early February 1945 Schwarzhuber issued a starvation order: all prisoners at the Youth Camp, already on a starvation diet, were to be put on half-rations. This led to a new outbreak of diarrhoea and dysentery, forcing up the death rate from about forty to sixty a day. At about this time, the day room in the *Revier* became a starvation room where prisoners close to dying were locked up and denied all food and water. The guards crammed some seventy to eighty women into it, with a single latrine bucket. They had to lie on the floor, and at intervals Koehler and Rapp made notes, to monitor how long it took to die. Salvequart brought *Oberschwester* Marschall to visit one day with 'her friend', the prisoner Ragna Fischer. Vera said she took the chance to ask if she could leave, but Marschall told her she'd be shot if she asked again. 'She said this is a concentration camp, not a sanatorium.'

Treite also visited, but according to Vera he ran away when she showed him the starvation room. At his trial, Treite confirmed that at the Youth Camp, 'women were put on half-rations and made to stand for five to six hours a day in the open air. This was clearly meant to kill large numbers of the prisoners.' He estimated that fifty a day died in this fashion.

As the starvation order was applied at the Youth Camp, so Dr Trommer introduced mass poisoning as another means to kill, but according to Salvequart's testimony it was Koehler and Rapp who administered the poison and not her. She said the first time the poisoning happened was just after a group of new prisoners had arrived from the main camp. At 3 p.m., 'when the annihilation transport arrived as usual', Rapp abruptly ordered Vera not to cross off the names but to wait. She recalled: 'They made the women line up along the *Revier* corridor and then Koehler walked along, saying, "This woman is too weak, this woman is useless," as if they were looking for someone who still had some strength.'

The two men picked out a tall Polish woman called Irena Szyjkowska, who was suffering from 'dropsy', swollen legs, a fairly mild condition. Koehler and Rapp sent Irena, the wife of a Polish general, into the *Revier* washroom and gave the admissions list back to Vera to continue her checking. Koehler next went to the ambulance room to fetch a mug and a spoon. 'I saw him take a spoon of white powder and return to the washroom.' After a few minutes, they called Vera into the washroom. Irena lay on her back as Koehler knelt on her knees and held her hands. The men ordered Vera to squeeze Irena's nose, while they tried to force her mouth open. Vera said she refused and ran away, as Irena shouted: 'Why are you trying to murder me?' The prisoners standing outside the block heard Irena cry out.

Vera claimed she went to Neudeck to report the event and to ask again to be transferred, but Neudeck said there was nothing to be done. Salvequart returned to the washroom, where Rapp ordered her to watch Irena and report what she observed. 'It was about ten at night and I went to look after her. She spoke to me and told me that her husband was in a camp in Germany and asked me to tell her son, the editor of a Swiss newspaper, about the way she died.'

All night long Irena suffered convulsions and couldn't breathe. 'Foam came out of her mouth and ears. She died after about three hours. I was alone with her all this time. The only help I could give her was a camomile tea.' Vera said Rapp came in the morning and took the body away. Koehler put most of the rest of the poison in his private drug store, amounting to about 35 grams. 'I kept part of it to commit suicide, as I'd been told I would not leave the camp alive.'

Salvequart argued at her trial that whenever she complained about what happened she was punished, for example 'by being made to take out gold teeth without gloves'. She also denied getting parcels from Schwarzhuber, saying she only spoke to him three times, 'the first time to complain about a rat plague in the mortuary, but he didn't help'.

She protested that she was suspected of poisoning prisoners because she was the only individual seen entering and leaving the *Revier* and because she wore a doctor's white coat. She said she understood why nobody trusted her 'because I lived where people were killed ... But I never told anyone I was a doctor. I said I only studied medicine for one year. There are no eyewitnesses that I killed people.'

Gisela Krüger, the German prisoner whose leg Treite amputated, was one of many eyewitnesses who did see Vera kill people. Gisela kept a diary in which she described events at the *Revier* quite differently from Salvequart. According to her, she and twenty-five to forty other invalids were taken straight to the Youth Camp *Revier* on arrival early in February. Soon afterwards, Suhren appeared and commented: 'Good burning material for the crematorium. We can save on wood.'

On 7 February Gisela noted: 'There is little to eat and no medicine, but Vera has a powder, possibly for diarrhoea – but those who take "the powder" sleep and never wake up. I am very worried. I have pain down my right side but don't say anything because of "the powder".' On 8 February, Gisela wrote: 'All amputees have to go on a transport. My God where to? I had an argument with the SS man Rapp. I am on the list of amputees.' Gisela says the SS man then took her off the list of amputees, perhaps because he was a bit 'simple' or because Vera asked him to. 'Vera stood by me,' says Gisela.

Vera appears to have stood by Gisela because Gisela offered help with the paperwork. Salvequart had other helpers and 'favourites' who assisted in various ways, such as making clothes for her. Gisela said that Vera was obviously overloaded with work, 'so I wrote the death lists out for her. Just in the *Revier* we had about 150 to 180 patients, with 50 dead each day. Vera went from block to block to find new victims. I have seen myself that gold rings from fingers and gold crowns from mouths were taken.'

Over the days Gisela described how the *Revier* filled up with prisoners. Now, while the lorries removed the prisoners from ordinary blocks, the *Revier* patients died by injection, or the powder administered by Vera and the two SS men. Mrs Rissel, the frostbitten German from Wiesbaden, received two doses of the powder from Vera. Another recipient was the Hungarian who lost a foot on the march from Budapest. She had suffered badly from the pain in her unbandaged foot. 'Now blood comes from her mouth and nose but she has left all this behind her,' wrote Gisela.

Women who refused Vera's powder were often beaten until their mouths opened and 'she shoved it in'. At other times she 'took care of them with lethal injections'. Koehler and Rapp shot two who refused the powder three times.

Gisela also described how Frau Thüringer, the German mother who had lost three sons at the front, cried out to some Siemens plant civilians whom she saw passing the Youth Camp as she went to the latrine ditch. 'Help us, help us, we will be killed here,' she pleaded. The Siemens men went on their way and the next day Frau Thüringer was dead, murdered in a corridor near the latrine. 'She was recognised by her long pigtailed hair.' Next day brought a letter for Frau Thüringer from her husband, who wrote 'the war will end soon and all will be well again'.

Sometimes mothers and daughters were murdered together. Gisela recalled one invalid mother in the *Revier* with her seventeen-year-old daughter, who was deaf and could not communicate. Vera gave both of them the powder. The mother died quite fast. The daughter lasted forty-eight hours and was given another dose. Still she lived on. Salvequart then gave her a lethal jab direct into the heart, saying, within Gisela's earshot: 'This one gets on my nerves.'

Another of Vera's 'favourites' was a French prisoner called Irène Ottelard. Irène was so disabled that when selected for the Youth Camp in early February she was pulled through the muddy wood track on a cart with sixteen other sick prisoners. 'It took a long time to get there,' she told the Hamburg court, 'because the road was very bad and it was raining and very cold.' On arrival, Irène was put in an ordinary block where 'most inmates had dysentery so could not move at all and were just going to die. They were left there without being attended to in the slightest way.'

Irène was transferred to the *Revier* with some thirty other prisoners. She slept in a bed with her friend Madame Gabianuit and recalled the *Revier* had a washroom 'with a nice china basin'. But when she entered the washroom she saw three or four women lying there on the floor. 'They were quite naked and were moaning and groaning. I think they were Polish. I could only hear "water" but that was all.' Later Irène heard that Salvequart had injected the women. 'I saw her walk to the washroom with a syringe. I saw her give out some sort of white powder.'

Irène testified at Hamburg that Salvequart would tell women they needed the white powder to regain their strength, as they were going 'on a convoy'. 'The great majority who took it slept and snored, and by about three or four o'clock in the morning they were dead. Even my friend Madame Gabianuit took the white powder and I saw her dead at my side.' Irène's friend Madame Ridondelli suffered very badly from dysentery and was told if she dirtied her bed once more she would be given an injection. She could not help soiling the bed another time. 'Later I heard her calling out, "Irène, they've killed me," and I never saw this lady again.'

Many other prisoners, particularly those working as Kapos, runners or clerks, saw Dr Vera killing. Lotte Sonntag, the Austrian camp runner, said Salvequart told her that fifty lethal injections were given each day. She then showed Lotte the powder. When word spread that the white powder meant death, Salvequart found new ways to entice prisoners to take the poison. A former Auschwitz prisoner, Gerda Backasch, described an unknown woman staff member giving her a slice of bread with butter and honey one morning. Amazed, Gerda offered half to a friend. At that moment Salvequart, who was outside the block, knocked on the window and warned Gerda not to eat it, as it was poisonous.

The corpse commando woman, Jozefa Majkowska-Kruszynska, went to take away bodies from the *Revier* one day and found the corpse of her sister-in-law, Stanisława Pozlotko. Jozefa discovered that Stanisława had been fed the bread and honey that contained the white powder.

> After that I paid attention and ate no bread prepared by others. I also warned my suffering fellow prisoners. Not all of them wanted to believe me. One day we were offered bread and honey, and twelve of the 120 block inmates with me refused to eat it, and only the twelve survived. The others were all poisoned and died.
>
> When Vera established that we had survived she brought us bread, honey and margarine in their original packaging. She said this was extra rations for the heavy work that we did. I was extremely hungry, especially looking at the food that lay before me. Finally I cut myself a sliver of bread and spread margarine and honey over it. My comrades did the same. Soon afterwards I was sick. I had a fever and my body started shaking. Two of my female comrades who had also eaten the bread had red foam coming from their mouths. The watching prisoners suggested that I drink my own urine. I overcame my aversion and did. After that I repeated this therapy and my stomach was soon quite empty. Someone gave me three cups of milk to drink. My friends who ate the bread died that night.

As the poisoning continued, selections for gassing mounted and Mary O'Shaughnessy started to live in constant fear of Neudeck's cane. Given her artificial arm and her pink card, she was convinced she'd soon be selected. After about two weeks, however, it was Cicely Lefort's number that came up. Clearly her name had appeared on the day's 'Mittwerda list'.

'We were standing that day at *Appell* when two SS men guards came up with a list. Neudeck was present. She spoke to the SS man and he called Cicely out. In Cicely's case there was no reason for the selection. She had no pink card and no particular disability. Her physical appearance was better than many.'

Like many other prisoners at the Youth Camp, Mary O'Shaughnessy had understood by now that the lists were drafted largely at random. Neudeck would pick people herself, because she felt like it.

When the selections began the prisoners didn't know where the lorries went, but they did hear talk. Guards and Kapos told each other: 'She won't feel it soon,' or 'She won't need a blanket where she's going.' The Dutch woman Stijntje Tol was walking to the latrine ditch one night when she met a Yugoslav prisoner who worked in the gymnasium. 'She told me: "Tonight, about 500 were taken." We spoke in German and I asked where these 500 had gone and she said: "*Zur Himmelfahrt* [On the heaven trip]."' It wasn't long, however – and certainly well before Cicely Lefort was selected – before everyone knew that heaven was the gas chamber, because the whole camp was talking about it, including the guards.

During German investigations held in the 1960s and 1970s, these same guards either denied all knowledge, or stuck to the Mittwerda cover to explain their ignorance, or resorted to other lies. At his Hamburg trial, Josef Bertl, the truck driver, said he 'wasn't interested' in what happened to the Youth Camp prisoners and 'didn't ask'.

Ruth Neudeck, however, identified Bertl as the driver, saying he was ordered by Schwarzhuber to have a daily lorry ready for Uckermark, 'and every day he drove into the camp at 6 p.m.'. Bertl must have known that the transports were going to the gas chamber, said Neudeck, because of what Schwarzhuber told him. 'I heard Schwarzhuber speaking to him one day, saying: "Bertl, you do know about this gassing, this evening again."'

Neudeck described what happened from her point of view when the truck arrived at the Youth Camp. 'At first I stood down below to count the prisoners, so that there were not too few or too many. It did actually happen that a daughter wanted to travel with her mother or vice versa.' Neudeck said that she, Rapp and Koehler usually had to beat the women to get them onto the truck. 'Rapp and his friend also often stayed at the back of the truck, so that no prisoners would jump off.'

The truck then drove off towards the main camp, carrying the prisoners, Neudeck and other women guards, and Rapp and Koehler. It turned left towards the crematorium and gas chamber, always halting fifty metres short of the destination. Rapp was friendly with Alfred Cott, the man who ran the crematorium, and he and Cott usually fetched two women each from the truck and led them into the building. Neudeck and her fellow female guards stayed with the truck until the last prisoners had been unloaded. On one of the early trips, she said, Rapp told her what happened next.

'I had been at Uckermark three or four days before Rapp told me that the women we were selecting were gassed in the Ravensbrück crematorium. Rapp told me that when on account of the small number of victims [selected on a particular day] it did not pay to gas them, the women were simply shot in the crematorium.' On those occasions, said Neudeck, 'I myself and the other guards could hear the shooting. On the whole, however, most of the prisoners were killed by gassing.'

In her usual candid manner, Neudeck told the court that Mittwerda was 'an invention of Schwarzhuber, so that the prisoners would not know that they were to be gassed'. She could not tell the court what happened inside the gas chamber because she wasn't allowed to get close, which seems to have angered her. But Schwarzhuber himself gave an unusually detailed description in a statement at the trial. Although he minimised numbers his testimony was broadly correct. He said:

The gas chamber itself was about 9 metres by 4.5 and could contain about 150 people. It was about five metres from the crematorium. The prisoners had to get undressed in a shelter situated three metres from the gas chamber, from where they were led into the chamber via a small room. I was present at a gassing. They pushed 150 women at one time into the gas chamber. Hauptscharführer Moll ordered them to get undressed and told them that we were going to treat them for lice. One prisoner carried a gas mask and went on top of the roof and threw a box of gas down through the opening, which he closed very quickly. I heard the moaning and the crying. After about two to three minutes there was silence in the room. I didn't know if the women were dead or stunned. I wasn't there when they opened the doors.

*Chapter 34*

# Hiding

Once things at the Uckermark Youth Camp were running smoothly, the SS made little effort to prevent news of the horror reaching the main camp. Runners came and went between Ravensbrück and the Youth Camp, passing messages and carrying lists of the dead or of those selected for extermination. Bloodied clothes from the mass shootings piled up all the time at the *Effektenkammer*. The Jehovah's Witnesses, always willing to run errands, acquired a stash of cod liver oil and delivered it to the *Revier* at Uckermark. They returned with stories of white powder and poisoning.

The SS required Blockovas at the Youth Camp to pass on the numbers counted at each *Appell* to the main camp secretaries, who then matched the figures with their own records. By the middle of February, with selections increasing, as many as 1500 women had already been gassed. 'When we checked up on the death figures we realised with disgust what was going on there,' said Hermine Salvini, the Austrian prisoner now in charge of collating camp numbers. Prisoners in the slum blocks, which backed up against the interior wall on the south side of the main camp, could hear the trucks pull up outside the crematorium, which was just the other side. At first the prisoners wondered why the engines were left running for so long, then someone said it was to cover the screams from the gas chamber.

The bunker, just over the wall from the crematorium, was by now often engulfed in stinking smoke that billowed into the cells. A prisoner cleaning the bunker told Geneviève de Gaulle one day that the bodies had been packed too tightly in one of the ovens and the chimney had caught fire. Walter Schenk, the crematorium boss – a fire brigade man before the war – gave a further explanation for the blaze. In order to burn the ever-increasing pile of bodies the temperature had been turned up, and as a result, on the night of 25 February the crematorium roof was set alight.

Schenk said it was impossible to say how many were burned at this time because he was responsible solely for burning the bodies during the day and these were not those who were gassed. 'The bodies of the gassed were burnt at night. They were burnt by the Auschwitz gang. I had to requisition the coke for burning. In February 1945 the consumption went up.'

The plan to hide what was going on from the Siemens women by moving their barracks out to the plant had failed as well. The women enjoyed their clean new accommodation: food at the Siemens kitchen was better, the plant had its own doctor and sickbay, and everyone was delighted that they didn't have to march to and fro each day. However, as the plant was perched on a hill, it was bound to give prisoners a view of what happened below. Without even leaving the plant, everyone could hear the noise of trucks moving back and forth along muddy tracks. And those who cared to peer through the trees – leafless in winter – could see the little wooden watchtowers of the Youth Camp in the distance, and watch the trucks, loaded with half-naked women, heading towards the gas chamber.

Just before reaching the base of the Siemens hill the trucks swung round towards the main camp walls to stop outside the gas chamber and the crematorium, which were only about 300 yards away. 'I often stood and counted the vehicles loaded with bodies; they went one after the other, always following the same route,' recalled the Austrian-Czech Anni Vavak. 'We told the guards in the Siemens camp, who were concealing these facts from the civilian workers, and their hair stood on end with fear.'

Yvonne Useldinger, a Luxembourger, who started work at Siemens in January 1945, kept a diary. On 29 February she noted: 'Extermination transport to Uckermark went by our camp. The sun shone warmly.' Siemens women were also picking up news of selections from their contacts in the main camp, where prisoners were better informed by the day. The Polish woman Irena Dragan even volunteered to run an errand to the Youth Camp in order to see for herself.

Irena was a Polish student from Warsaw. After four years at Ravensbrück, including sessions in the bunker, she was 'campwise' and hard to shock. The wearer of a 7000 number, she had what she called 'honorary *Verfüg*' status, which meant she could play truant from the casual work roll-call almost without anyone caring, particularly during the chaotic final months of the war.

'Sometimes I pretended to be a night-shift worker,' she recalled. 'I didn't care about anything because I thought I was bound to die.'

One day in early March 1945 as Irena was sitting in her block, a Kapo came and asked for volunteers to go with a cart to fetch blankets from the Youth Camp. Irena stuck up her hand. A walk through the woods brought her to the gates, and the first thing she saw was a group of women standing in front of the blocks. 'They were shivering with cold and there were mounds of blankets lying next to them on the ground that had been taken away three weeks earlier. They were not allowed to touch them, and slept without any blankets.'

Irena started talking to the women, who asked her how much prisoners at the main camp were getting to eat. 'They yelled that they were hungry. They started giving me scraps of paper with the names of people they knew in the main camp, to help them. On one piece of paper someone had written that she wanted bread because she was hungry, but there was no name.'

Irena went to find a Polish Blockova who she knew was working at the Youth Camp. The Blockova told her that most of the women who had arrived in the first transports were already dead. Those still in her charge were almost naked and she had no clothes to give them. 'So she clothed them in paper and straw taken from the mattresses. I saw a woman dressed like that who reminded me of a fish caught in a net.'

As Irena chatted with her friend, Neudeck appeared, and a hush came down. 'She was smiling and holding a cane in her hand with a bent nickel tip, and she came up to the women standing in front of the block and started pointing at them.' The Blockova asked why she was selecting women now, as it wasn't the usual time.

> Neudeck said they were going to knit, and had them stand under the tree where one dead woman was lying already, looking more like a lump than a woman ... in the distance, other corpses, almost naked, were visible.
>
> While Neudeck was choosing, some women tried to smile at her and Neudeck said to them 'Why are you smiling at me?' and made them stand under the tree with the others.

As Irena loaded the blankets onto carts she saw another Polish woman she knew who was working here at the Youth Camp, and spoke to her. 'She told me that during the night there'd been an air raid and she had gone out behind the kitchen to try to find some potato peelings to eat. She saw lorries there and crouched down to watch as SS men got out and entered the *Revier* block. She saw young girls with bandaged feet and heads being brought out.'

This acquaintance explained that the girls were prisoners from subcamps who had been badly injured in bombing raids and were now useless for work. Their factory managers had sent the girls back to Ravensbrück to be killed. They had almost certainly not been registered in the main camp, and were being killed right here in a specially adapted truck, made for gassing. The Poles knew about these gassing trucks, which the Nazis used widely across Poland during the first years of the occupation. Irena's acquaintance described how they worked here at the Youth Camp.

> Young girls in bandages were pushed out of the *Revier* and into the truck by the SS. When the truck was full it was locked. The truck was completely covered. The SS man threw a tin can through the little window by the engine inside and only the clatter of the can hitting something could be heard. It lasted about a minute. There was a deathly silence. There were several trucks like that.

Irena had to leave the Youth Camp in a rush, as her friend had collected the clothes from the crematorium and was waiting to go. 'There were so many lice on the clothes that it looked as if someone had shovelled them on.' Back at Ravensbrück, Irena returned to her block and told everyone what she had seen. Soon the news was all over the camp.

It was now four months since Himmler's order to shut down the Auschwitz gas chambers – or, as Höss put it, to 'discontinue the Jew-exterminations'. With the end of the eastern death camps, however, the use of gas was not entirely 'discontinued': by mid-February 1945, at least 1500 women, Jews and non-Jews, had been gassed at Himmler's newest death camp, right here on German soil.

That mass murder should continue even now came as no surprise to those who had direct experience of the Nazi machine. In her evidence at Nuremberg, Marie-Claude Vaillant-Couturier, a prisoner at both Auschwitz and Ravensbrück, described the extermination programme at Ravensbrück as 'the systematic and implacable urge to use human beings as slaves and to kill them when they could work no more'. Rudolf Höss, the former Auschwitz commandant, also described the Nazis' inexorable urge to kill. His memoir, written as he awaited execution, leaves us with a powerful sense of how this urge to kill had been nurtured so long in the Nazi psyche that eventually it ran of its own volition, impossible to extinguish.

As far as the women themselves were concerned, the main aim of the killing was to destroy evidence of what had happened here well before the Allies arrived. Some feared they'd all be gassed by then. Others said this was impossible. Having heard rumours of what happened at Stutthof concentration camp, where a few weeks earlier 5000 male and female prisoners had been marched into the Baltic and machine-gunned, some said they'd all be shot out at sea.

And yet, although this rush to exterminate had plunged the camp into new depths of despair, at the same time, among some prisoners, it brought a surge of courage and of hope. This annihilation left no doubt that the Germans knew the end was very near, so all the more reason to try and hold on. Those with some remnant of strength knew they still had a chance of getting out alive, as long as they could withstand starvation, disease and random brutality.

It was plain that the SS and the guards knew the war was lost. Grete Buber-Neumann would sometimes prowl into the SS offices before *Appell* and look at the large-scale map of Europe pinned to the wall. On it were little flags marking the situation at the fronts – no longer according to official German reports, but placed according to news received by listening to enemy broadcasts. 'During the day we could read on their faces what the news was, and as it grew worse they were correspondingly depressed,' Grete recalled.

Discipline continued to crumble. It was even possible to miss *Appell* if you knew how, and those attending would often stand chatting or reading a newspaper. When an air-raid siren sounded the guards ran straight for cover. 'Order throughout the camp had completely broken down,' said Maria Moldenhawer, the Polish military instructor, who almost seemed to miss the old days of strict discipline. Germaine Tillion even found it possible to stage an operetta, which she'd secretly been writing for several months. A spoof of *Orpheus in the Underworld*, which she said was an attempt to help prisoners 'resist by laughing', the operetta was called *Le Verfügbar aux enfers* [The Verfügbar in the underworld] and was staged secretly at the back of a block. A chorus of *Verfügs* sang of 'a model camp with all comforts, water, gas, electricity – above all gas'.

At Siemens relations with the plant's civilians began to improve. 'They sympathised with us more as they were being forced to work as well. They too had no food,' said the Kielce ghetto survivor Basia Zajączkowska. In general, the guards seemed less present around the main camp and more inclined to let the prisoner Blockovas, the Kapos and the camp police take over. Elisabeth Thury, the Austrian head camp policewoman, became more prominent; Dorothea Binz faded from view.

It was the new SS doctor, Franz Lucas, whose behaviour changed most dramatically in these final months. Like many of the other new SS arrivals, one of his previous postings had been at Auschwitz, and like the others he had been closely involved in the atrocities, including selecting prisoners for the gas chamber. Loulou Le Porz saw no reason to trust Lucas when he first appeared: 'He wore the same SS uniform, the same cap.' But Loulou soon noticed that Lucas quickly began to behave differently from the other doctors. 'He brought us medicines, and he sometimes examined a patient. Treite used to touch them with his boot.'

One day Lucas examined a young Dutch woman suffering from TB, who was also pregnant. 'He showed real attention for the little Dutch girl, and when the baby was born he brought milk for the baby too. The poor woman gave birth but died very quickly afterwards and we never even learned her name. And soon afterwards the baby died too.'

At about the same time that Vera Salvequart was distributing white powder at the Youth Camp, a poisoning experiment was conducted at the main camp in Block 10. Schwester Martha Haake told Loulou and the new Blockova Erika Buchmann to follow her to a part of the block where the critically sick women were lying. Haake told the prisoners she had a special powder that would help them sleep, and asked for volunteers. Loulou knew instinctively that Haake meant to poison the women. She tried to signal not to volunteer, with no success; some women even took a double dose of the powder. Haake then left, asking Loulou to observe their reaction. Half an hour after falling asleep the women began to vomit red mucus. Next morning Loulou and Erika found five women dead. The others were groaning and near to death, with blood pouring out of their mouths, noses and ears.

Lucas was called, and was angry. Prisoners in the main part of the *Revier* heard him protesting to Marschall, Trommer and Treite. Later, he told Loulou and Erika that the experiments had been 'ordered by Berlin' and he knew nothing about them.

Sylvia Salvesen had also grown aware of Franz Lucas's readiness to help. In January Lucas informed Sylvia that her young Norwegian 'relative' Wanda Hjort and her father had visited the camp again. They were not permitted to see Sylvia, but left packages of medicines. Lucas passed the medicines to Sylvia, and offered to act as a go between with the Hjorts.

More channels of communication were opening between prisoners and the outside world. The Poles received a letter from Aka Kołodziejczak, the friend who had been released in early 1944 and was now in America, and they learned something of what Aka had done to publicise their story in the United States.*

At last, significant numbers of prisoners were receiving parcels. Denise Dufournier received a parcel from her brother Bernard – the one arranged by his Spanish diplomat friend in Berlin. The same Spaniard used his connections with the German Red Cross to gain access to the camp. One day in January, to her astonishment, Denise was called *nach vorn* and told she had a visitor. Here was her brother's friend, who was able to report back to

* When Aka eventually reached the United States in late 1944 she gave interviews to several newspapers and broadcasters, in which she described the conditions in Ravensbrück and the medical experiments in detail.

Bernard that she was, at least, alive. The rabbits suddenly started receiving small parcels too, containing sardines and religious 'blessings' – small emblems – which some believed had come from the Pope in response to their secret letters. In fact, the parcels seem to have come from Catholic missions in neutral Portugal, which had probably learned of the women's plight from Polish missions who picked up the news on SWIT.

In early 1945 rumours floated around Ravensbrück that prominent prisoners might be exchanged for German prisoners held in Allied camps. The *Schreibstube* secretaries saw papers pass across the commandant's desk. There were whispers that Geneviève de Gaulle and Gemma La Guardia Gluck might soon be freed.

The signals remained very mixed. Elisabeth Thury, the camp police chief, told Sylvia Salvesen one day that she'd been instructed to compile a list of intelligentsia in the camp who it was supposed would be used as hostages. Nothing seemed to come of the plan. Several days later a group of prominent hostages who had been held in the bunker for some time were taken away to be shot. Among them was Helmuth von Moltke, the German pacifist and leader of the resistance Kreisau Circle.

Meanwhile, Suhren summoned the Polish countess Karolina Lanckorońska to his office. The commandant inquired after her health, and asked whether she had enough food and clothes. 'He behaved like a shopkeeper offering his wares,' she said. 'I said there was nothing that I needed. At that, he grew impatient and repeated the question. At last I was taken back to my block.'

The sense that the wider world was throwing lifelines into Ravensbrück, even as selections for the Youth Camp redoubled, shored up some prisoners' morale and encouraged them to take on greater risks. The Red Army women protested to Suhren when they heard that a group of Russian children had arrived at the camp to be killed. Suhren allowed the children to live, as long as they stayed in the Soviet block.

When a further round of selections happened in Block 10, Loulou Le Porz and her friends Marie-Claude Vaillant-Couturier and Jacqueline d'Alincourt discussed whether they too should approach Suhren to protest. The three women met during the Sunday walking period on the Lagerstrasse and talked of what should be done. Loulou recalled:

> We were all in shock. We began to understand that they were out to annihilate all our sick and probably us too. Jacqueline wanted to go straight to the commandant and protest, and she would have gone to Suhren flying the French flag if she could. But I thought, what if I'm sent to the *Strafblock*, and I can't care for my sick at all? Marie-Claude was cautious too. So we decided not to protest but to help our prisoners in our own way.

In the NN block some of the rabbits were even daring to hope that they might go home after all, simply because they hadn't yet been shot. More than any other group, the rabbits had always had reason to believe they were to be killed, because they were living proofs. Just in case, one of them had recently secured a camera on the camp black market and persuaded Germaine Tillion to take photographs of their legs as insurance should the final execution happen.

Wanda Wojtasik, however, believed that if the SS had wanted to shoot them they'd have done it by now. 'We had started allowing ourselves to think of the prospect of freedom,' said Wanda. And Krysia Czyż, who could no longer write secret letters home, had instead been passing her time drawing intricate maps showing the roads along which she intended to walk home, all the way to Lublin.

When on 4 February, therefore, a messenger came with the news that all rabbits were to stay inside the block until further notice – this was a sentence of death, and all of them knew it – the shock was far worse than it might have been had they never begun to hope.

'Total and unimaginable silence followed the messenger's departure,' said Wanda Wojtasik. She looked at Krysia's face, which was grey – 'not pale but ashen-grey'. In seconds the news had spread around the whole block, and others who had not been operated on broke down, wailing about injustice. A peasant girl called Lodzia began sobbing, which set everyone off, and the whole block wept.

'Now we knew the war was drawing to an end and that we were to be exterminated completely. The experiments done on us and others were a crime against mankind, and as witnesses we had to be destroyed,' said Wanda. That evening rumours spread that they were to be evacuated to Gross-Rosen, not executed, but everybody knew this was a lie, as Gross-Rosen was already liberated.

All night the block held feverish meetings as prisoners discussed what to do and messages of support poured in from around the camp. Some passed the time 'waiting for death' by writing letters to their loved ones, which they handed to fellow prisoners to pass on. Other rabbits sang patriotic Polish songs.

One group made plans to resist by all means possible. It included stalwarts of earlier protests – Wanda, Krysia and Dziuba Sokulska – and many others. The leaders were Jadwiga Kamińska and Zofia Baj, who proposed a two-point plan. First, a delegation would make a statement to Fritz Suhren, challenging him to admit that the suggestion that they were bound for Gross-Rosen was a lie. They would then demand that their alleged crime be read out to them before their executions. 'We agreed that we would tell him that we had a duty to return to our motherland, or, if we were going to die, we wanted to die like soldiers on the battlefield,' Wanda said.

While the statement was made, the other rabbits would do whatever it took not to be taken and shot, which would mean hiding around the camp. One scheme involved smuggling themselves into work gangs of the *Zugänge* – newcomers – who did not yet have camp registration numbers.

They knew from experience that the first attempt to round them up would probably take place at morning *Appell*, so they had only hours to prepare. For the plan to succeed, the rabbits needed volunteers to take their places in line while the Poles hid. The word went out at once to friendly Blockovas, and by the time the siren sounded at 4 a.m. the volunteers were primed. Support came from the Red Army women, also in Block 24, some of whom gave the rabbits their ration of soup, saying: 'You'll need all your strength now, girls.' Szura, a Soviet electrician, promised to turn the lights out during *Appell* to cover the rabbits' disappearance. Two other Red Army girls sought out Karolina Lanckorońska and told her: 'Miss Karla, we won't surrender the rabbits.'

'An incredible, unheard-of thing happened – the whole camp decided that we were to be saved,' said Dziuba Sokulska. One rabbit was to be replaced by a Red Army doctor, another by a Yugoslav. A Norwegian prisoner told her rabbit friend that she would insist on being executed in her place. 'You should be the one to live to tell the world about the crimes committed against you. I am older. I can perish,' the Norwegian wept. Many Poles also came forward. An old Polish woman called Władka begged to replace Wanda, claiming she had cancer and was going to die soon anyway. If not Wanda, then Krysia, she insisted, so she should survive to tell the tale. Neither Wanda nor Krysia would agree.

Twelve rabbits offered to hide first, and by 4 a.m. they and their stand-ins were ready. As the parade got under way, the twelve slipped away and their replacements filled the gap before the guards began to count. Roll call started, and then prisoners heard a murmur from the far end, followed by voices shouting: 'They're coming for them! They're coming for them!' Wacława Andrzejak saw Suhren in the distance, surrounded by guards with dogs, walking down the Lagerstrasse. One of the guards held a sheet of paper with a list of names. The siren had not yet sounded for it, but the shout *Arbeitsappell!* – 'Work roll call!' – rang out from within the lines of prisoners, and they all broke ranks. Some shouted: 'We won't let you take them.' The guards tried to retake control, but at this moment the Red Army electrician threw a switch and the camp was plunged into pitch darkness.

Columns of prisoners collided blindly with each other, while more rabbits were collected and hidden by prisoners from other blocks. The guards held back, waiting for order to settle. Suhren had clearly ordered them not to shoot. By the time the grey light of dawn broke, the confusion was total. Work groups began to form up for the day with the wrong prisoners, while several rabbits succeeded in joining the unnumbered *Zugänge* groups of new arrivals. Others swapped numbers, preventing the guards from keeping track of prisoner movements.

When the Lagerstrasse finally cleared, only the two guinea-pig leaders, Jadwiga Kamińska and Zofia Baj, returned to their original block to coordinate the resistance. During the next hours they carried messages between prisoners in hiding and acted as public spokeswomen for the group while putting the second part of their plan into action. Zofia and Jadwiga confronted Suhren, challenging him to admit that the claim to be sending them to another camp was a lie. Sticking to their script, the women said if the rabbits were to be executed, it should be 'with honour'. Suhren refused to yield, and issued a fresh order for all prisoners to assemble. Out went the order from Zofia and Jadwiga: Stay in hiding.

Each day at roll call, the same stand-ins took the places of the missing rabbits; each day, Szura managed to switch off the lights just as the counting began. Suhren demanded extra roll calls, more searches and closer surveillance of the camp exits, but to no avail. Some rabbits left with the *Zugänge* for munitions plants many miles away; the rest were scattered across the whole camp. One of the rabbits, Maria Cabaj, was hiding on a hospital ward amid the sick and dying. Still in terrible pain from her own 'operation', she feared that she'd quickly be found because she couldn't move, and was terrified that she might then be thrown alive into the furnace. She found new energy – 'from where, in all my pain, I don't know,' she said later. 'I only know that in spite of everything I didn't want to die.'

Antonina Nikiforova, the Red Army doctor, hid Wacława Andrzejak on a typhus ward, registered as a Hungarian patient who had just died. Wacława lay for two days in terror, feigning unconsciousness. When she dared to see, she witnessed worse horrors than any in the guinea-pig block. 'Forty to fifty women died around me every day. There were women here who were no more than skeletons. They were starving and ate what was given to them but could digest nothing as they excreted it all immediately. The smell in the ward was almost unbearable.'

At first Wacława didn't dare go to the bathroom. At last she plucked up the courage, and found the bathroom heaped with corpses. 'After a few days I became indifferent to the sight of these naked corpses who had died of dysentery or typhus, and I got used to washing without glancing at them.'

All the time more women were entering the ward, where selections for the gas chamber were now regularly taking place. 'I couldn't hide there any longer in case I was selected myself – or else I lost my mind.' So Wacława returned to her own block, where other rabbits were hiding in the gap between the floorboards and the earth foundations. Maria Cabaj was equally appalled by conditions in the *Revier*. 'One day I felt I couldn't stand it any longer, so I jumped out of the window and went back to my old block. I'll stay here even if it's the end of me, I told myself.'

Wanda Wojtasik likened the rabbits' manoeuvring to 'a fearful game of hide-and-seek. The watchword "They're after the rabbits" was understood by everyone and warnings went out in a flash.' Leokadia Kwiecińska, another rabbit, looked back on those last months as a 'strange incomprehensible dream – a tragic dream, but one that had its comic aspects'.

Normally the rabbits took pride in their 'upstanding behaviour' and neat appearance. Now, 'as if a magic wand had been waved', they disguised themselves to 'look like the masses', while striving to conceal disfigured legs. Joanna Szydłowska cut off her magnificent long hair. Wanda and Krysia dressed up as *Goldstücke*, tying scarves under their chins 'Ukrainian fashion', plaiting hair over their foreheads and scrapping for food.

Krysia looked suddenly quite different. 'Without her glasses she had a pleasant little face and a look of uncertainty and excessive seriousness,' said Leokadia. As Leokadia couldn't manage without her spectacles, she covered half her face with a black kerchief.

Over the next two weeks, while the rabbits continued to live 'like hunted animals', not one of them was betrayed or captured. Some prisoners noticed that the guards didn't seem to rush to find them either, backing off 'perhaps because they were beginning to think about themselves and how to get out alive'.

Then came a new initiative from Suhren. Clearly exasperated, he summoned one of the rabbits, Maria Plater-Skassa, and offered her the chance to sign a declaration stating that her scars were caused by an ordinary accident in a workshop, not by experiments. Sign, and he would free her. She refused. Flanked by the 'delegation' women, Jadwiga Kamińska and Zofia Baj, Maria told Suhren that he should understand the whole world now knew their names, and killing them would simply exacerbate his crime. Suhren then indicated that he was aware the news had got out. It would not in principle be difficult for him to execute sixty women, he said, except in the rabbits' case, because 'the details are known in America, Britain and, more important, in Germany'.

Suhren explained that he could not take the initiative himself, but would ask Berlin what to do and 'try to resolve the issue in a humane way'. He added that he couldn't do so immediately as he 'had other things to think about'.

According to another account by Janina Iwańska, it was as a result of this meeting with Suhren that the girls now learned that the list of those to be executed had in fact been sent direct to Suhren by Karl Gebhardt, with instructions they be gassed. Suhren's annoyance at Gebhardt's interference was obvious to the rabbits at the time, and it was also obvious in his testimony after the war. Suhren evidently resented the fact that Gebhardt had used 'his' prisoners for these experiments in the first place, thereby implicating him and tarnishing his own record. Now, due to his friendship with the Reichsführer SS, Gebhardt was pulling rank on Suhren and ordering him to gas the women, which in the circumstances he was loath to do.

As Karolina Lanckorońska put it: 'The girls succeeded extremely well in frightening the authorities, especially Binz, whose name, as well as Gebhardt's and Suhren's, had by now been broadcast.'

Meanwhile, the other rabbits stayed in hiding, desperately hoping that the Russians would get here before the SS found them.

*Chapter 35*

# Königsberg

At the little camp of Königsberg, on the River Oder, Violette Szabo, the British SOE woman, was also clinging onto hope. She spoke of her baby, Tania, to friends in her block. 'In a few months I'll be able to hold her in my arms again.'

It was now nearly three months that these women, who had arrived together from Paris in September 1944, had been slaving at the Königsberg punishment camp – the result of refusing to make munitions at Torgau. After working on a frozen airfield, now they were digging a trench for a narrow-gauge railway and laying the track. Grasping the heavy steel rods with frostbitten hands, and stumbling on frozen feet, was more than most could do. The guards put the stronger Poles and Russians at the head of the line, but the French and the small group of British and Americans couldn't keep up with them.

At least on Sundays they could rest in the block and talk, which was when Violette befriended Christiane Le Scornet, a seventeen-year-old French girl. 'Violette treated me like a little sister,' Christiane remembered. 'She had a rare loyalty and a rare courage.'

All the SOE women were in Christiane's block. She recalled that Lilian Rolfe was extremely thin and shockingly pale, while Denise Bloch suffered terrible sores from malnutrition. The three Americans – Charlotte Jackson, Lucienne Dixon and Virginia Lake – were there too, and another Englishwoman called Jenny who kept aloof and didn't like to say she was British. Of the group, Violette was in the best state of health and cheered them all. 'She often spoke of Tania. She would say: "She's in London with my parents, loved and protected." She was certain that she would find her little girl again soon in good health.'

That Christmas, as the women decorated their block with pine branches, Violette had sung 'God Save the King' and Christiane joined in. Christiane described how she then turned to another French woman, Mathilde, and said: 'Now it's your turn to sing, come on, Mathilde, sing!' But Mathilde said: 'I'll sing when I've found my children and my husband.' When Christiane pressed her further, Violette, her eyes full of tears, said: 'Leave it, Crissi. I understand her, she can't.'

'Violette was like that,' said Christiane. 'She always had time for those suffering more than her, and tried to give them courage with her gentleness and her smile.' Christiane also remembered Violette's 'absolute conviction' that Germany had lost. 'She spoke all the time about how the Allies were advancing every day. "We must all hold on, we must be strong," she would say.'

Violette and all her fellow prisoners knew they were bound to be the first women of Ravensbrück liberated because of the subcamp's location. Königsberg was just six kilometres to the east of the River Oder and lay right in the path of the Red Army. In January 1945 the First Belorussian Front army had begun the major assault that would lead it on to Berlin. The roads around Königsberg were already filling with refugees fleeing west, while civilians working at the airfield began to pack up and leave.

January was the coldest month at Königsberg. Each morning at *Appell* women passed out on the snow. If a friend failed to carry them to the infirmary they stayed there. Those still on their feet were now only interested in saving themselves. 'One's first reaction was "I won't move, I can't help anyone, I'm so weak I must save the little strength I have, or I shall fall myself,"' said Virginia Lake. Jacqueline Bernard said many simply grew weaker and weaker, never realising they were dying. 'Most who died this way were never admitted to the hospital hut and were compelled to stand up every morning at roll call in the bitter cold. Many died before the roll call ended.'

Lilian Rolfe collapsed at *Appell* one morning in a fit of coughing. Denise Bloch could not help because she was suffering terribly from a septic foot. Violette and Virginia Lake, the strongest of the small group, helped lift Lilian to the sickbay, which was already full.

Suzanne Guyotat, a young French woman who huddled on the floor near Lilian, remembered the sickbay as more like a pigsty than a hospital. There were no medical supplies, no heat and no blankets, yet prisoners outside still longed for the *Revier* to escape the sub-zero temperatures outside. Virginia's friend Janette was among them, and with a temperature of 100 degrees was finally admitted, only to be kicked out when her temperature fell again.

Sick women who could not stay in the *Revier* were crammed into the ordinary blocks; festering sores covered their legs, their hearts and lungs were failing, and they clearly could not work. The Königsberg commandant despatched many of these useless mouths in trucks back to Ravensbrück, and the news would come back that they were dead. Furious at the number of sick still on his hands, the commandant made all those remaining stand for five hours in the snow at *Appell*, just as they did at the Youth Camp. Death by *Appell* was now a favoured weapon at several other subcamps too.

Those left on their feet went off to work. The weakest collapsed in the snow: Suzanne Guyotat noticed one of her friends was missing and found her dead body frozen fast to the ground. On another day Virginia discovered her friend Janette crouching behind stacks of sod and sobbing: 'I want to die. I can't stand it any longer. I want to die.'

Virginia recalled that one of the Anglo-Americans suggested their group should volunteer for the forest work gangs, said to be slightly less cold because the trees broke the wind. The long trek out took them through snow-drifts that clung so that they walked on snow platforms and kept wrenching their feet. Denise's foot had turned gangrenous, making the walk impossible, so she stayed in the block.

The forest work meant delving down to the base of tree stumps felled earlier and digging out the roots. As many as six would combine on a single great tree, disappearing as they dug down and piled earth up around them. It was gruelling labour, but it was also sheltered, and they could talk as they attacked the frozen soil. Several of the French remembered Violette working down among the roots, chatting away. Jeannie Rousseau, the Torgau protest leader, said Violette still had ideas of escaping, but couldn't figure out how. 'She never complained, that girl. She seemed unchanged by the work, unlike her two friends, who were in a terrible state.'

By midday the women were listening out for the distant motor of the soup truck. Its arrival meant a fight for a place in line against a 'herd of thundering Poles and Russians'. A female guard they nicknamed 'La Vachère' often kicked the pot so that the soup spilt. Back at work they talked about food: 'How thick was your soup? Shall we save our potatoes to make a sandwich tonight? Is it better to eat slowly? I wonder what tomorrow's soup will be like.' Then they wondered if they could snatch some sugar beets on the way back to the camp.

One day the women met French POWs on the road home; soon presents were being smuggled to them again – biscuits and chocolate – as at Torgau.

Then in mid-January Violette, Lilian and Denise were called out and told they were going back to Ravensbrück. Lilian, who was still in the *Revier*, was told to be ready to leave next morning at five. 'She was very thin by now, and very weak,' recalled her friend Jacqueline Bernard. Christiane Le Scornet says

Violette was warned the previous evening too. Violette said: '"It is King George who has asked for us. I will go and see him when I get back and demand a plane. I'll come and rescue you myself." Violette believed sincerely that she was going back to be liberated. She left with Lilian and Denise. I was so happy for them.'

According to Jeannie Rousseau, 'La Vachère' called the British names out at the morning *Appell* and Violette, Lilian and Denise marched off to a waiting truck. Jeannie also remembered that the trio thought they were going to be liberated. Violette may really have believed that the message she gave to their POW friends at Torgau had reached London, which had then negotiated a prisoner exchange with the Germans. She knew that her SOE comrade Odette Sansom was being held in the bunker as a hostage, along with Geneviève de Gaulle. And since the start of the New Year, there had certainly been talk of prisoner exchanges involving a group of French parachutists held in the main camp. Some of this talk may well have reached Königsberg with newly arriving prisoners.

Jeannie Rousseau remembers that they spoke of an exchange having been organised. 'They thought they were going to Switzerland first, but I wasn't so sure. There were some not very nice men who had come all the way from Ravensbrück to take charge of them. I didn't like the look of it much. And I thought, they're going to be shot.'

Julia Barry, the Guernsey woman, saw Violette, Lilian and Denise as soon as they arrived back at Ravensbrück, because the guards took them straight to the *Strafblock*, where she was on duty. 'They were all black and in rags,' Julia said. 'Lilian could hardly move and was terribly ill. So was Denise; only Violette was any better. They hadn't eaten food for weeks, or washed.'

The women were now held in the atrociously overcrowded *Strafblock*, where seven prisoners shared two lice-infested mattresses. Julia Barry did what she could for the British women. She fetched clothes, soap and towels from her own block and asked Mary Lindell in the *Revier* to get medicines. Mary in turn alerted Yvonne Baseden, the other SOE woman, who was suffering from TB and was now in the Ravensbrück *Revier*. Yvonne heard that while away at the subcamp, Lilian in particular had 'changed a lot and had been very ill'. She also gathered that the women were hopeful of an exchange, or at least of a transfer to another camp.

But Yvonne, more than most, had reason to fear the worst for her friends. As well as the mass shootings that were part of the extermination programme, regular executions of 'dangerous' prisoners were continuing, ordered by the Gestapo in Berlin. Just a few days before the British girls' return, four French women were executed at Ravensbrück, probably by hanging. These too were secret agents; they worked for De Gaulle's underground organisation BCRA

(Bureau Central des Renseignements et d'Action), and had parachuted into occupied France from French bases in North Africa. Their cases had always been closely linked to those of the British SOE women, and they had even been chained together for part of the original train journey to Ravensbrück.

On arrival the British had been taken to subcamps, while the French four had stayed here at Ravensbrück, where Yvonne had befriended one of them, Jenny Silvani. Like the British girls, the French had expected to be shot as spies, but nothing happened. Then, in early January, perhaps in view of the growing optimism about the end of the war, the French women decided to complain about their treatment. Jenny visited Yvonne in the *Revier* and told her that a comrade, Suzanne Mertzisen, had been to see Suhren to request the right to receive Red Cross parcels. Suhren took a courteous tone. 'I understand she was very well received by the SS officer and they said they would see what could be done,' Yvonne recalled.

Two days later Suzanne was recalled to see Suhren, this time with Jenny Silvani, who returned to Yvonne full of optimism. They were once again 'very well received and Jenny told me that the SS seemed to have received orders from Berlin about them on a blue telegram that was lying on the officer's desk, but she had no idea what the orders were. They were told that their demands had been considered and they would hear more about them but they should be available for call.'

A week later Jenny went to see Yvonne again, saying they had been recalled a third time. 'This was the last time I saw her. I heard a day later that the four girls had been seen standing in their striped dresses in front of the SS office, guarded by an armed SS guard, which was most unusual. They were taken away by lorry and I heard later that they had been hanged.'

Although no one had witnessed the hanging, it was 'more or less confirmed', said Yvonne, when their clothes came back. Amid the mountain of dead women's clothes at the *Effektenkammer*, someone found Suzanne Mertzisen's grey jumper. It had no trace of bullets or blood. A German who worked there took one look at it and held her hand against her neck to signal 'hanged'.

Lying in the hospital, Yvonne obviously took a very personal interest in all this, as she knew she'd suffer their fate if anyone found out that she too was SOE. She believes that it may have been the French women's decision to ask for better treatment that brought about their execution, and that of the British women. Going to Suhren drew attention to all of their cases. Execution orders lying gathering dust in Berlin, or perhaps destroyed in some Gestapo office hit by British bombs, were then checked and reactivated. As Yvonne saw it: 'I can only believe I escaped their fate because I had arrived at the camp with a different transport from Dijon, and under different circumstances, and because during my whole stay I remained as unobtrusive as possible.'

Julia Barry said the British women stayed in the *Strafblock* for three days and then a camp policewoman summoned them to the office. They were too sick to be moved. Violette could go, said Julia, but not the other two. A few minutes later the same policewoman came back with an assistant and Lilian and Denise were carried on stretchers, not to the office but to the bunker. Violette walked. They were taken not to the hostage cells where Odette and Geneviève de Gaulle were held, but to the punishment cells below. In her testimony, Barry said she didn't see the three of them again, 'but a woman came to me from the bunker the next day to say that the following day they were shot'. Two of the women, Lilian and Denise, had to be carried on stretchers to the place of execution.

Despite Barry's claim that they were shot, French evidence after the war suggested that, like their French comrades, the British women may have been hanged. Curiously, there was no indication that their clothes came back at all, blood-stained or not. But the French asked, if the French 'spies' were hanged, why not the British who were executed just a few days later? Further, on Himmler's order, hanging had by now become the preferred method for executing saboteurs and spies, supposedly to act as a new deterrent.

A year after the war Johann Schwarzhuber was arrested by the British and was interrogated about the fate of the SOE women by Vera Atkins, their staff officer, who had been searching for them ever since they went missing in France. Schwarzhuber told Vera that the three women's names had figured on a list drawn up by the Gestapo in Berlin of women to be executed. He was told to recall them from Königsberg. One evening in late January 1945 they were taken out to the small courtyard near the crematorium and shot. 'Suhren read out the execution order, they were shot by Corporal Schultz, using a small-calibre gun in the back of the neck. Present were Dr Trommer and Dr Hellinger, the dentist.' Prisoners in the *Schreibstube* heard that Dorothea Binz was present as well.

In his statement Schwarzhuber said the women's clothes were burned with their bodies. He was not pressed to explain why the clothes were not returned to the *Effektenkammer* for recycling, as always happened. 'All three were very brave,' he observed, 'and I was deeply moved. Suhren was also impressed by the bearing of these women. He was annoyed that the Gestapo themselves did not carry out these shootings.'

Schwarzhuber's comments were obviously an attempt to present a picture of the killings as properly carried out, according to some sort of military procedure – 'Suhren read out the execution order.' The tragic facts of these women's final days, however, were all too clear. At least three high-ranking SS officers looked on while these stricken women were dragged from their stretchers and either shot or hanged, we don't know which. Alongside Lilian and Denise stood Violette, who just three days earlier had said she was hoping to be freed 'by King George'.

At Königsberg in the last week of January 'we were watching ourselves die', said Virginia Lake. Women came back from the airfield with wild and haunted expressions on their faces. 'They were fighting not to lose their minds. It was as if they were struggling to hold on ... just a little longer until relief would come.'

By 30 January the Red Army was so close to Königsberg that the guns could be heard in the camp. All the civilian staff packed up overnight and left, as refugees poured westwards on the roads around the forest. The German guards were more and more jumpy, while the prisoners – particularly the Russians – rejoiced. The Russian prisoners talked of welcoming the Soviet soldiers with garlands; the French planned sumptuous dinners to celebrate their liberation. News came that the French POWs nearby had been evacuated and marched west ahead of the Russian advance. Perhaps the guards intended to evacuate the Ravensbrück subcamp women too, some said.

On 31 January the head woman guard drove off in a car with large bags and a young officer from the aviation camp. The commandant also left, as did all the other guards. Late that night the Russian prisoners broke loose and set the aviation camp on fire. Poles, Ukrainians and Russians now streamed through the camp, plundering. The French looked on, wondering what to do, and then joined in. Prisoners of all nationalities ransacked the SS quarters, grabbing everything in a mad race for spoils. Virginia and her group found wood and coal to burn in their block. Women swarmed through the kitchens, finding rooms piled to the ceiling with crates, cans and sacks of food. Sporadic German military patrols came into the camp and made half-hearted attempts to take control, but the looting continued. The French and Americans sat down to a meal of bread, spread with margarine and jam.

On 1 February French POWs turned up and reported that the Russians were only ten miles away. According to the French, the Germans now planned to evacuate all the prisoners at the last minute. In the sickbay, Suzanne Guyotat heard that all those in the hospital would be left behind and the building blown up. Others scoffed at the idea that the Germans would bother evacuating them now. That evening the French held a 'liberation banquet' and invited two of the French POWs. 'I woke up two or three times that night. I was too happy to sleep and every time I woke I ate a little lunch of jam and crackers,' recalled Virginia. Next morning the women learned that a German patrol had come upon the banquet and shot dead the two French POWs as they sat at a table.

That day the prisoners roamed wider, and found the guards' living quarters, which were in total disarray – empty liquor bottles, makeup, maps and clothes strewn everywhere. On 2 February news came that the Russians were only four kilometres away. Virginia tried to make crêpes with the food she had stolen, as it was the '*Jour des Rois*', a French holiday, but Janette had terrible dysentery and was unable to eat. Outside, women were digging graves for the shot Frenchmen, when a new commotion erupted. The girls ran inside to warn the others: 'It's the Germans. The SS from Ravensbrück. They've come to get us. They've ordered us to line up outside.'

Outside the prisoners saw the Ravensbrück men rampaging around like madmen. Having come to round up prisoners, but scared now of capture by the Russians, they were venting their terror on the women. One guard shot a young girl called Monique as she walked back to the block to retrieve something she'd forgotten. Others were shot simply for not moving fast enough towards the gates. The women who came into line were now marched off away from the Russian advance and back towards Ravensbrück, 200 miles to the west, but some stayed behind.

Suzanne Guyotat and about twenty others in the *Revier* couldn't join the exit march. As Suzanne had feared, the SS tried to blow up the *Revier*, but in their panic to escape they botched it; most of the women survived. For two more days 'we lay there, poor women freezing, moaning, shivering and dying,' said Suzanne. 'One beautiful morning – it was February 3rd – three Russians appeared outside our block. Where had they come from, these victors, dressed in their marvellous fur hats? They moved forward cautiously, bicycles in their hands.' Over the next days the Russians cared for the women, fed them, warmed them, and reassured them. One even made a wooden cross for Suzanne to put on the grave of a dead friend.

The Königsberg death-marchers reached Ravensbrück a week later, and the sight of these starved, dying women, packed in a mass of tangled bodies, some swollen and disfigured, others emaciated and shrunken, would never be forgotten by those who witnessed it. Many died on the journey, and the guards shot stragglers. Trucks brought the survivors on the final lap, arriving at intervals over the course of two days.

Mary Lindell was walking up the Lagerstrasse when two trucks pulled up and guards dumped bodies on the ground. At first she wondered why they didn't take the dead straight off to the crematorium, then she saw some were still alive. The guards started whipping them to make them move. Next day another truck came and some eighty women fell out. Their yellow skin stretched over bone and their eyes stared bright, they shivered in the cold. None of them could walk without help. Virginia Lake – a bag of bones herself – looked at her friend Janette and saw 'a shapeless heap lying in her own filth, unable to talk and no longer reacting to hunger or cold'.

The French heard that compatriots had returned from Königsberg and came to find old friends, only to recoil at the sight of 'the remains of that charming convoy of French women', as Denise Dufournier put it. These were the same women who had breezed into Ravensbrück six months earlier, all optimism and elegance, with their Hermès scarves. Now 'we were shocked at their haggard eyes'.

Many died as they lay on the Lagerstrasse, but it was the sight of the living that caused most distress. Loulou Le Porz hardly recognised her friend Nicole de Witasse, the young French Red Cross ambulance driver who had so nearly escaped during the train journey to Ravensbrück: 'That youthful, spirited girl I had known was now a wizened old woman who could barely move and had very little time to live. I have never forgotten the sight. The only consolation was that her parents would never see her like that.'

The onlookers learned that the Russians had almost liberated these Königsberg women. The stronger among them told the camp women here how they had heard the Russian guns, and as they marched away they had turned back to see the camp on fire. Now the Ravensbrück women understood that the same fate – forced evacuation – awaited them.

The memory of those Königsberg faces would haunt the camp women for another reason too. Everyone knew by now that the French convoy had been sent to the punishment camp because of the protest they had staged against making arms at Torgau. Loulou Le Porz was one of those who felt Jeannie Rousseau had made a tragic error of judgement by starting the protest that brought such terrible results. 'She was unusual – impulsive,' said Loulou. 'Of course – it is all very well to have courage but you must know how to use it.'

The guards herded the Königsberg death-march survivors into the tent and left them to die. Virginia Lake had first peered inside the tent on arrival in September, and seen its horrors from afar again on return to Ravensbrück in October. Now, on her third arrival, she was herself shoved into the stinking structure and left to seek inches of space for herself and for Janette.

Over the months the tent had changed. A partition now ran down the middle and there were bunks along one end, and lavatories of a sort, but the filth and overcrowding was worse than ever. Virginia and Janette tried to occupy a cranny in one corner where a Polish Blockova had marked out an area for herself and her entourage of hangers-on. The Blockova kicked Virginia and Janette away.

Corpses lay everywhere, covered with whatever came to hand. Everyone had dysentery and few had the strength to reach the lavatories. At night the situation grew 'frightful, unimaginable'. Women needing to reach the buckets crawled in the dark and groped over bodies. They were usually too late and the filth around the exit was atrocious. 'The Germans ordered holes to be dug about three feet in diameter outside the tent, and women would be found squatting around the same hole.'

Virginia watched her friends grow weaker every day. 'I knew I was like them. Janette was obviously dying. Her once bloated body was now a limp rag.' Virginia appealed to the Polish Blockova to let her take Janette to the *Revier*. This 'husky brute of a woman' refused, so Virginia and a French friend managed to drag Janette there anyway. Virginia said goodbye as Janette lay on a stretcher in a corridor, surrounded by corpses.

> The sadness, the tragedy and the horror of it all shocked me. Janette's eyes, which shortly before were expressionless, now seemed to glow with adoration as she gazed up into my face. I knew she loved me. I wondered whether she realised that she was dying. She was not suffering now. She was no longer cold, nor did she feel her hunger.

Virginia told her she was in the infirmary now, would be cared for and would soon be home with her mother. 'Good night. Sleep well,' she said, and left to go back to the tent.

The days dragged on. 'We were weak and listless and drugged by the horrors that surrounded us.' The Polish Blockova and her crew barred others from using a washroom of sorts at one end of the tent which also had a stove; she looked at her fellow tent dwellers as if they were 'untouchables, lice-ridden, filth'. One of the German hangers-on stole from the prisoners and struck them with a heavy rod if they came too close, as she didn't want their lice.

One day this German spotted Virginia's wedding ring and demanded it. Virginia's knuckles were so swollen that she couldn't pull it off. The woman goaded her until, in tears, she blurted out to another Austrian woman: 'I'm American. Does she steal the wedding rings of Americans too?' The Austrian said something in German to the thief, who looked at Virginia 'as though she had seen me for the first time'. She told Virginia she could keep her ring.

Several days later, the guards moved Virginia and a group of her Königsberg comrades into a regular block where the dire conditions seemed blissful compared with the tent. They were even sent to the bathhouse for a shower, although in a final humiliation, Virginia's head was shaved.

There was no call to leave the block now, and no *Appell*. The women lay listless on bunks, growing weaker every day. 'We were losing our friends one by one and were on the borderline of life and death,' said Virginia. They tried to hold on, forcing themselves to get up at least once a day to wash and forage for food. A friend from early days smuggled some extra soup to Virginia.

On 26 February, about a week after Virginia's arrival in the new block, the Blockova bawled: 'Will the American who was at Königsberg come immediately.' Virginia climbed down and a woman gave her new clothes. Two days later – on 28 February – the Blockova announced that Virginia d'Albert Lake was 'wanted at once'.

Terrified, Virginia was led across the camp to the office inside the bunker. Prisoner secretaries sat at desks and smiled at her with interest. One offered a seat. A woman guard entered, smiled, and explained something in German. Virginia didn't understand a word. A male SS officer then led her out of the gate to another office building where two women in Nazi uniform were sitting. To Virginia's astonishment, the higher-ranking of the two inquired in perfect English for her name and date of birth. The younger woman said: 'Tonight you will be happy. You are going away.'

Virginia was led to the *Revier*, where she was briefly examined, and on to the *Effektenkammer*, where staff were throwing clean clothes at German women busily undressing and dressing. The staff told Virginia to discard her dirty clothes in a bin and put on clean clothes that were handed to her; they didn't have the big black crosses that marked prisoners' clothes. Outside, the guards called the German women prisoners away, and Virginia understood they were being freed. She then found herself back in the bunker office, along with the English-speaking Nazi woman. The woman asked courteously: 'Sit down, won't you, there, beside the stove. You will have a short time to wait. Your train leaves at four-thirty.'

'But where am I going?'

'I'm not sure, but I think you're going to a Red Cross camp near Lake Constance.'

The Nazi woman spoke of how she'd been at Auschwitz until recently, and of her fear of the advancing Russians. She told Virginia it would have been better if the Americans were heading this way, and she turned and shook her fist at a portrait of Hitler on the wall. 'To think that that man is responsible for all of this.' Virginia asked the officer where she learned her English. 'In New York,' she said. 'I spent several months there with relatives of mine. America is a wonderful place.'

A door opened and a girl entered with two guards. It was Geneviève de Gaulle. Virginia had seen Geneviève before, and recognised her straight brown hair, dark eyes and easy smile. She learned that they were travelling companions; their release was part of an exchange for German prisoners of war.

Geneviève had been summoned earlier that day from her privileged bunker cell and told she was being set free. Like Virginia, she was given new clothes, including her own woollen coat from Paris, taken from her on the day she arrived at Ravensbrück, almost exactly a year before. Geneviève described later how during the earlier formalities in the camp office she also met a mysterious female Nazi officer who told her she loved Paris and asked her to sign her photograph album.

Now in the bunker office Geneviève saw two SS officers, as well as 'a terribly emaciated woman who looked very, very old'. On the woman's shaven skull, tufts of hair protruded here and there. 'She looked like Gandhi at the end of his life.' The two prisoners exchanged glances but didn't dare exchange words. Geneviève then took Virginia's hand and together they descended the three steps outside the bunker. Dawn was breaking. Flanked by SS officers and a female guard, they walked out of the gate and into the wind and snow.

*Chapter 36*

# Bernadotte

Within an hour of leaving Ravensbrück, Geneviève and Virginia, along with three SS guards, boarded a train at Fürstenberg, and by evening they were in Berlin, struggling across the smouldering city, sheltering in subways blocked with fallen timbers before catching a train on south. Two days later they reached Munich. It was midnight and the small group were once again stumbling across craters and rubble and staring up at carcasses of buildings, silhouetted against the night sky. Soon they were on a train bound for Ulm, but bombing raids halted the train and the group were forced to walk several miles, bypassing ruined tracks.

They stayed overnight at an inn where Germans huddled around a radio. Virginia recalled the radio announcer saying, 'A formation is over Ulm. Ulm is being bombed. A formation is leaving Ulm. The formation is over ...' and suddenly the building shook violently, chairs overturned and people ran terrified for the door. Virginia 'felt no fear' and didn't move. Getting up, she caught sight of herself in a mirror and thought: 'What ugly creature is this? A woman, yes, but neither hips nor breasts; great lustreless eyes staring out of a grey countenance.' Over the days, the SS guards grew friendlier, and one night one of the women guards shared a room with Virginia and Geneviève and showed them family photographs. At night 'she locked the door and put the key under her pillow'.

After a week on the move, the two women were delivered to an internment centre at Liebenau, near Lake Constance, where aliens – mostly Americans and British women and children – were held for the duration of the war, living in pleasant buildings set in rolling hills, with good food and care. Writing to her husband, Philippe, Virginia said: 'My own darling, how strange to be able to write to you. Last June seems so far away that you and my past life seem like a dream.' Geneviève was visited by delegates from the Geneva Red Cross, of whom she requested a few small 'luxuries' including 'underwear (not wool); a tailored suit (not too warm); a dozen handkerchiefs; six pairs of stockings; soap, vitamins and cigarettes'.

It isn't known whether the women learned why they had been released at this time. Virginia's transfer was arranged by General Eisenhower's office as part of an exchange for captured Germans. Her American mother's pleas had finally reached Eisenhower's desk, and when a deal was being struck to exchange a small number of Allied prisoners for Germans held in Allied hands, Virginia's name was put on the list.

Geneviève's release was requested by her uncle, General de Gaulle, now provisional president of France. She would always insist later on that her uncle had nothing to do with her release, and would never have 'favoured a member of his family', but correspondence held by the International Committee of the Red Cross tells a different story. Geneviève's father, Xavier de Gaulle, brother of Charles, first raised the alarm about his daughter, but the general let it be known that he too was seeking her release. In a letter on 15 September 1944 an official of the ICRC in Geneva wrote to the German Red Cross: 'The committee has been informed by one of its delegates of the anxiety of Monsieur le Général de Gaulle about his niece, Mademoiselle Geneviève de Gaulle, imprisoned in Ravensbrück, Block 122 [*sic*], no. 27372.' The letter inquired about her health and stated that the General 'particularly requested that she should be sent to Switzerland and treated in a sanatorium'.

Himmler's other two prize Ravensbrück hostages, Odette Churchill and Gemma La Guardia Gluck, remained unclaimed. There is no evidence that Himmler ever attempted to inform the British that a 'relative' of the prime minister was held in Ravensbrück, but even if Winston Churchill had learned of it, nothing would have been done: Odette had lied all along about her Churchill family connection. Nor is there evidence that Fiorello La Guardia knew at this stage that Gemma was in the camp. Had he known it seems unlikely that he would have tried to secure her release. Even after the war, when Gemma had to wait many months to return to the US, living in hardship in Berlin, her brother declined to help.

By this time La Guardia was running the UN's refugee programme, UNRRA. He knew by now the suffering that his sister had undergone, and that her husband had been murdered in Mauthausen. Nevertheless, La Guardia wrote to Gemma telling her he could not speed her passage home as he could not make exceptions for a family member. 'If any different treatment were applied to you it would cause hundreds of thousands of demands for the same treatment.'

The transfer of Geneviève and Virginia to the Liebenau internment centre was another sign of Himmler's growing eagerness to make concessions over certain prisoners in the hope that it would help him get a hearing in London and Washington for his fantastical ideas of a separate peace. As the two Ravensbrück women were being handed over, Himmler's aides were finalising the details of a far more ambitious prisoner release, through contacts in Switzerland.

On Himmler's instruction, Walter Schellenberg, his intelligence chief, agreed a deal in January with a Swiss politician and Nazi sympathiser, Jean-Marie Musy, by which every other month 1200 Jews of an estimated 600,000 still alive in Nazi camps would be transferred to Switzerland in return for 5 million Swiss francs for each transport. Because Hitler vehemently opposed all prisoner releases, Himmler stipulated that the deal stay secret. His purpose, once again, was public relations. 'The object of this action was to bring about a favourable reaction in the international Press, which, at a later date, would present Germany in a better light,' said Franz Göring, one of Schellenberg's aides, and the man charged to carry out the plan.

In a detailed report to British security service officials after the war, Göring gave an extraordinary insight into the fantasies many Nazi leaders and their friends had, even now, that they could keep their crimes a secret or at least present them to the world in a favourable light. According to Göring (no relation to Hermann Göring), Musy also proposed to Himmler that women from Ravensbrück be set free – Jews and non-Jews alike. The Swiss man said: 'the release of these women would create a terrific impression which in the course of time could redound to Germany's credit'.

Attempts to secure the Jewish releases began in the first weeks of 1945, when Göring set about requisitioning a rescue train and locating the 1200 names on Musy's list. Although an SS man, Göring was a foreign intelligence specialist, unfamiliar with the world of the camps, and seems to have been astonished by what he found there. To his surprise, many of the Jews he was looking for were dead or lost in the system, or else camp commandants refused to hand them over.

Göring was undeterred, and found two of the Jewish women on the list in Ravensbrück. Charlotte Wreschner and her sister Margarete, arrivals from Holland in 1944, were told in January 1945 that they were to be freed. Along with a Jewish mother and daughter from Turkey, and another Jewish woman, they were sent to the concentration camp of Theresienstadt, near Prague, where those on the release list were being assembled and where the rescue train to Switzerland would leave from.

A new problem then arose: according to Göring, instructions had been given to commandants that nobody should be released who knew about the gas chambers, as their stories would not yield 'favourable publicity'. Theresienstadt had been chosen as the gathering point for the prisoners, and the camp from which most on Musy's list were selected, precisely because there were no gas chambers at this 'show camp'. Although Jewish prisoners here had been regularly taken off to Auschwitz to be gassed, those who remained were supposedly ignorant of the true horror.

The Ravensbrück women, however, knew very well about the gas chambers, both at Ravensbrück itself and, from other prisoners, about Auschwitz. On arrival at Theresienstadt Adolf Eichmann, mastermind of the Jewish extermination programme, interrogated the Wreschner sisters in person to find out exactly what they knew. 'It became clear that we were isolated and that they did not want to allow us to enter the camp, out of fear we might know too much and that we might talk about it to the inmates of Theresienstadt,' said Charlotte Wreschner in evidence later. When the sisters promised not to talk of what they knew, Eichmann did allow them to mix with other prisoners, warning them that if they did talk they'd 'go up the chimney' themselves.

In the ongoing confusion Göring realised that many other prisoners on his list knew about the gas chambers too, and therefore could not leave on his train, which was by now waiting to go. Given a shortfall in numbers, Göring then invited other prisoners at Theresienstadt to volunteer to come to Switzerland, but no one wished to do so, which astonished him, until someone explained that the prisoners were terrified that the train was really a death train going to Auschwitz. It was only when Göring's train neared the Swiss border that the prisoners he had persuaded to come along relaxed, 'as though released from some frightful nightmare'.

A few days after the first group arrived safely, headlines in the Swiss press declared that 200 leading Nazis had secured asylum as a result. The stories may have been planted by Ernst Kaltenbrunner, head of Hitler's security police, and an opponent of Himmler, on purpose to scupper Himmler's plans. If so, Kaltenbrunner succeeded. Hitler was furious to hear that Himmler was releasing prisoners – albeit for money, which was how Himmler sought to justify his action to the Führer. Hitler ordered that from now on releases must stop, which ruled out the further Ravensbrück releases that had also been discussed with the Swiss.

*

Although in January 1945 the Swiss plan was scotched, Swedish plans to help prisoners had gathered pace. The previous autumn Himmler had signalled to the Swedes, via Felix Kersten, that he might be willing to release Norwegian policemen. In December that release was agreed, and fifty Norwegian policemen, as well as fifty Danish students, were delivered into Swedish hands.

The releases gave the Swedes reason to believe that Kersten exercised real influence over Himmler, who might now be persuaded to consider a far wider prisoner-release plan than any proposed to date. At the very least it was worth exploring, especially as, after the Swiss debacle in January, it became clear that no other government or international organisation was willing or able to act.

As the Allies prepared for their final assault on Germany, attitudes in Washington and London towards the fate of prisoners had, if anything, hardened. This was displayed in a bald statement issued in December 1944 by the western Allies' joint military leadership, the Supreme Headquarters Allied Expeditionary Force (SHAEF). The statement urged prisoners of all nations to 'stay put, await the arrival of allied forces and be prepared for an orderly repatriation after the end of the war'.

To anyone aware of the reality inside Hitler's concentration camps, the idea of 'staying put', let alone of 'orderly repatriations', appeared at best unrealistic and at worst absurd. Even as the SHAEF statement was being issued, in Ravensbrück death rates were edging up towards 200 a day as the gassing was stepped up. At Belsen, near Hanover, prisoners were dying of sickness and starvation at the rate of 300 a day. Yet the judgement at Allied headquarters meant that until Germany had surrendered, prisoners in the camps were on their own.

As the military fronts moved forward, however, there was nothing to stop the neutral Swedes from devising their own schemes; by January 1945 ideas first tabled in Paris and in Stockholm developed into a full-blown rescue plan, which envisaged a task force of buses and military vehicles, manned by volunteers, driving across the Danish border into Germany under the flag of the Swedish Red Cross.*

The objective, in the first instance, was to gather up all Scandinavian prisoners – mostly Danes and Norwegians, believed to number about 13,000 – and take them to a single camp near the Danish border, under Swedish care, before transferring them to Sweden for the rest of the war. Rescue of other nationals later was not ruled out.

* Bernard Dufournier got wind of this plan. On 11 January he received a letter from the Swedish mission in Paris, which he had contacted about Denise, saying that the Vice President of the Swedish Red Cross 'is at this moment very interested in doing something for the women's camp at Ravensbrück. He wishes to send parcels and send a delegate. I can't promise anything,' wrote a Swedish official.

Certain top officials in Stockholm scoffed at the idea of sending 'a pretty caravan of Swedes' into war-torn Germany, and on paper the ideas were so ambitious they must have seemed fanciful. However, new soundings from Kersten about Himmler's state of mind, and intelligence about the situation on the ground, gave Stockholm reason to believe the plan might work.

The key to rescuing the prisoners would be knowing precisely who and where they were; this called for detailed knowledge about the location of camps and the names and nationalities of people in them – information that only the Swedes possessed, due in large part to the work of Wanda Hjort and the Gross Kreutz group.

In recent months Wanda, with Bjørn Heger, the young Norwegian doctor, and other cell members, had risked their lives criss-crossing bombed-out Germany and securing all details they could about prisoners. Using information from Wanda's Norwegian contacts inside Sachsenhausen, linking up with a network of Danish and Norwegian pastors, and building links with the German communist resistance cells, the group had by January 1945 assembled an impressive database on the camps. They had also secured medicines from the Danish Red Cross, which they had managed to deliver to certain camps, using trusted intermediaries. The Swedish legation in Berlin was providing backup: Wanda and Bjørn Heger used a delegation car and the Gross Kreutz intelligence reached Stockholm via the Swedish diplomatic bag.

All this time the group had been appealing to Stockholm to implement their rescue plans, because there was no time to lose. In one report back to Sweden they passed on specific intelligence about the imminent annihilation of the camps. This new intelligence was based in part on a visit to a concentration camp by Wanda and her father, Johan Hjort, when they heard directly from an SS informer that the commandant planned to liquidate the camp 'to the very last detail' as soon as the Allies were close. The report didn't name the camp, but we know that Wanda Hjort and her father had visited Ravensbrück in December, and had been in touch with the SS doctor there, Franz Lucas, and with Sylvia Salvesen.

However invaluable the Gross Kreutz cell's intelligence, the Swedes could do nothing without Himmler's say-so. By January Kersten was assuring Stockholm that the Reichsführer was receptive, particularly if an intermediary was appointed whom Himmler could trust.

Count Folke Bernadotte was one obvious choice. Though some in Stockholm considered him too lightweight, he had strong German ties and an innate diplomatic charm. Furthermore, Himmler would be impressed by Bernadotte's royal blood and would know of his close connections with the Allies – the count had an American wife and had recently met Eisenhower in Paris. Bernadotte was certainly ready and eager to take on the role.

On 16 February Bernadotte flew into Berlin, where barricades were being erected, people lined up at food queues, and death and destruction increased every day. With the help of the Swedish ambassador he sought a meeting with Himmler. He waited three days, seeing other top Nazis first, before he was told that Himmler would see him. The venue chosen was Karl Gebhardt's SS clinic at Hohenlychen, sixty miles north of Berlin and five miles north of Ravensbrück.

Hohenlychen had long been one of Himmler's favoured locations for secret meetings and talks. His old friend Karl Gebhardt was entirely trustworthy and the clinic was both convenient for Berlin and secluded.

Bernadotte was driven out to the clinic on 20 February. Under the ornate portico of the main sanatorium building, Gebhardt was waiting to greet him. As they awaited Himmler, Gebhardt told Bernadotte that the clinic was packed with German children waiting to have amputations after being wounded by Allied bombs.

Suddenly Himmler was before him: 'in green Waffen-SS uniform without any decorations and wearing horn-rimmed spectacles' he looked 'the typically unimportant official', except for his 'well-shaped, delicate hands, which were carefully manicured'.

Bernadotte listened to Himmler for two and a half hours as he spoke of his loyalty to the Führer and of the 'chivalry' of British and French forces. The military situation was 'grave, very grave, but not hopeless'. Himmler told Bernadotte that he could never go against the Führer, and the Führer was against releasing prisoners. Himmler complained about his 'bad press' in Sweden. The two shared jokes. Bernadotte presented Himmler with a seventeenth-century Swedish work on Scandinavian runic inscriptions, which 'touched' Himmler greatly.

Eventually Bernadotte saw an opening and put his proposals for the prisoner rescue. Himmler at first 'reacted violently', but Bernadotte was patient and won him round, so that by the end of the meeting the plan for the Swedish task force to collect up Scandinavian prisoners from the camps was agreed. Before Bernadotte left Hohenlychen, Himmler checked that he had a good driver, warning that the roads back to Berlin were dangerous due to tank traps and barricades. Assured about the driver, Himmler replied: 'Good, otherwise it might happen that the Swedish papers come out with big headlines saying: "War criminal Himmler murders Count Bernadotte".'

*

The December visit to Ravensbrück by Wanda Hjort and her father, alluded to in their report to Stockholm, was made primarily in order to deliver medicines received from Denmark for Sylvia Salvesen to distribute. Their contact at Ravensbrück was Franz Lucas, the SS doctor, who had learned of their links with Sylvia and signalled his willingness to help.

Lucas's 'interest in' helping prisoners had by now become known throughout the *Revier*. He had refused to take part in selections for the Youth Camp, and protested over the poisoning by white powder in Block 10. One evening late in January he took Sylvia Salvesen aside in the *Revier* and offered his hand. 'Give me the address of your Hjort family. Perhaps I can manage to visit them,' he said. Astonished, Sylvia sat down and wrote out the address. The next day Lucas came to see her again and told her to write a letter to the Hjorts and he would deliver it. She had ten minutes to do so, he said, as he was leaving for good. Acutely anxious and excited, Sylvia wrote what she could, then hid the note in a box, and as Lucas coughed in the corridor outside she went out and smuggled it into his pocket. Schwester Gerda Schröder was standing there too.

Pretending he had not seen Sylvia, Lucas turned to Gerda, saying: 'Goodbye, Sister. I'm off. I'm a soldier and I'm going to fight the enemy, but I don't fight prisoners.' With this he left the camp for the last time, giving Sylvia a last look, which seemed to say: 'Depend on me.'

Despite his promise, Lucas failed to deliver the letter in time to help Sylvia or anyone else. He did, however, appear at Gross Kreutz nearly four weeks later – letter in hand – pleading with the Hjorts for refuge as the Red Army approached. Nevertheless, Sylvia very soon had a chance to write a second letter to the Hjorts, and this time Gerda Schröder offered to deliver it.

The prisoners had known Schwester Gerda longer than they had known Franz Lucas, and many not only trusted her, some spoke of her as a friend. She had helped on several occasions, particularly during the recent sterilisation of children, when against SS orders she administered pain relief to the stricken girls. Born in Bad Oeynhausen, where she trained as a nurse, Gerda Schröder worked in a Berlin hospital before being transferred to Ravensbrück in early 1944. When Lucas arrived the couple became lovers, and Gerda might well have encouraged him to help the prisoners. The evidence certainly suggests that they discussed how to help Sylvia by delivering a letter to Gross Kreutz.

It was a few days after Lucas left the camp with the first letter that Gerda proposed to Sylvia that she write another, which she, Gerda, would personally deliver. This time Sylvia had all night to write, but found it hard to know what to say to outsiders who couldn't possibly understand, especially as the letter might be intercepted. She tried to start at the beginning, describing how the camp had grown and how slave labour had begun, but soon the story of the latest horrors came spilling from her pen. In the hospital:

> there are 40 to 60 deaths a day … The camp has typhus, colitis and diphtheria … Prisoners are starving and living skeletons wander everywhere … 1000 prisoners stand daily naked to be selected for work, but they are bound to die in a short time, and if they don't they are disposed of in a camp whose horror no words can describe.

Sylvia evidently realised, as she wrote, that Wanda needed to know the whereabouts of Norwegian prisoners. Several had been sent to Majdanek and on to Auschwitz, 'an extermination camp where a million Jews have been driven into the gas chambers … If you can help us, I trust it will be soon.'

Some were still safe at Ravensbrück, she said. 'I helped Kirsten Brunvold get a job in the hospital and Solveig Smedsrud is knitting.' But now more were being sent away on transports. 'At this very moment I have received information that six Norwegians – Kate Johanssen, Maja Holst, Solveig Smedsrud, Live Carlmark, Singe Enger and Tora Jespersen – have been marked down to be moved.' Sylvia wrote that she had, just that evening, managed to have four taken off the convoy. 'I have been round to the two blocks where they are asleep and have spoken to them all. I will try to speak to Dr Treite and beg him to rescind the order.'

But Kate Johanssen and Maja Holst were down to go to Bergen-Belsen:

> unless we can stop them at the last moment. There are rumours today that the whole camp is to be evacuated in three weeks' time and it certainly looks as if anything might happen. Possibly this is the last and only sign of life that I shall be able to give, and if so please give Harald and the children a message from me. Say that I am not at all despairing or depressed. Tell him that the longing for him and the children has been the worst of all to bear. Second has been my longing for freedom, the longing to lead my own life without being a slave to others, and my longing for the forests and streams of Norway. And please deliver my message – which may be my last to my beloved husband, my dear old mother and my beloved children. Thank you for everything. Farewell.

Taking the letter from Sylvia, Gerda said she was leaving the camp the next day and would not return. Dr Trommer had told her she was being posted to the male concentration camp of Mauthausen, but Gerda had refused to go.

At four in the morning Gerda left with the letter and headed for Potsdam and Gross Kreutz. She got as far as the Oranienburg station on the outskirts of Berlin, but was delayed by air-raid warnings. At Potsdam more diversions were announced, and Gerda didn't reach Gross Kreutz until it was dark. The stationmaster knew nothing of a Norwegian family living in the area, but when Gerda mentioned five fair-haired children he pointed towards their house. In pitch darkness due to air raids, she found the house and knocked at the door. Nobody answered. In her bag was the incriminating letter.

More air-raid sirens sounded and a small girl appeared. Gerda asked if her family was at home. The girl led Gerda down to the cellar, where Mrs Hjort, Wanda's mother, and Joanna Seip, Arup Seip's wife, were sitting in the light of a tallow candle. Wanda, her father and the others were all away. Both women were afraid of the German stranger, but Gerda took out Sylvia's letter and showed them the long list of Norwegian names, and now they grasped the situation.

There was little time to talk, but the women scribbled some words for Gerda to take back with her, and told her to tell Sylvia that help was on its way. They explained that Count Bernadotte of the Swedish Red Cross was coming to Germany to rescue the Scandinavian prisoners.

With the air-raid sirens screaming again, Gerda suggested that Mrs Hjort and Joanna Seip might wish to send a parcel back to Sylvia with her, and they gathered up boots, socks and a bar of soap. Gerda left with the package and headed for Berlin. The two Norwegian women pored over Sylvia's letter. 'If you can help us, I trust it will be soon.'

*Chapter 37*

# Emilie

No rescue would come soon enough to stop the Belsen transport. The day after Sylvia wrote her second letter, a train left Ravensbrück carrying 3205 prisoners. Just before the train set out, the Belsen commandant, Josef Kramer, contacted the main camp administration office, saying: 'By telex of 28.2.45 you've told me I must receive a first delivery of 2500 prisoners from Ravensbrück. The reception is impossible. Prisoners are sleeping on the ground and we have an epidemic of typhus which is spreading fast.' Still the train left.

The purpose of the Belsen transport was to empty Ravensbrück of all young children and babies, mothers and pregnant women. All but a handful of the 400 or 500 children at the Christmas party were sent. Before the transport left, the *Kinderzimmer* in Block 11 had been extended, with new cots holding row after row of dying babies, so that Zdenka Nedvedova, the Czech child doctor, observing the sight one day, suddenly screamed out in anguish: 'Poles, where is your God now?' The block was now cleared.

Mothers were prepared to believe that any change must be better for their infants, and many volunteered for the Belsen transport. Others did too, including the Polish rabbit Maria Cabaj, who smuggled herself on board, thinking she had a better chance of surviving if she got out of Ravensbrück.

The journey to Belsen, 250 miles due west, took seven days. The prisoners were locked into closed cattle wagons, with no food or water and no space to lie. 'It was clear what was going to happen,' said Maria. 'The mothers had no milk to feed their babies and as the days passed they all began to die.'

By the time the train reached Belsen, every baby was dead. The women were unloaded about three kilometres from the camp and made to walk across fields. During the march those who could not walk were shot. As they came to the perimeter fence, the mothers laid the little bodies in a row along the barbed wire; white snow covered them. By morning they were gone. Maria Cabaj remembered:

> The despair of their mothers was terrible to see. I was already numb and indifferent. My children were already a part of the past. I couldn't even remember their faces. Sometimes I used to wonder if I had ever had any children, a home, a family. At Belsen there were gallows with men hanging from them, corpses burning in ditches, and against the wire.

With the Belsen transport the evacuation of Ravensbrück had begun, and with it the cleanup. The *Kinderzimmer* in Block 11 was scrubbed and painted. 'The Dutch prisoners said they weren't in the least surprised,' said Karolina Lanckorońska. 'They'd come from a camp in Holland that was evacuated just before the Allies arrived. A few days before they were cleared out, a children's block had been created, and the walls were hastily decorated with scenes from fairy tales.'

At the beginning of March the tent disappeared, and the occupants too. According to Halina Wasilewska, it contained at least 4000 women just before it came down, though in the end nobody knew how many were in there or how many died, as those consigned there often had no numbers and no recorded identity. When at last the tent Blockovas protested to the SS that there was no way to admit one woman more, another 500 were pushed inside – 'literally – one of the office workers pushed them through the flap with her knee', said Halina.

Specific images noted by Halina on her record of the tent's final days included:

> The body of an unknown deceased woman lying for 4 days in front of the door to the tent awaiting identification.
>
> A woman with scarlet fever, whose skin was in the final stages of coming off.
>
> Suzi Perekline-Rudolphino, a beautiful healthy eighteen-year-old, who went mad after two days in the tent and was taken to the *Revier*, where she died.

Once the canvas came down there was just a patch of wasteland and a pile of rubbish. A British aerial reconnaissance plane flew over soon after and photographed the camp. The picture showed an empty space where once the tent had been. Within a few days saplings were planted.

After the Belsen transport and the dismantling of the tent, the SS turned their attention back to the killing. Now that Dr Lucas was gone, Dr Treite was asked to take over the selections, but he too refused, so a former naval surgeon, Dr Adolf Winkelmann, was enlisted, who had worked at the Gross-Rosen camp overrun not long before by the Russians.

'Very tall and very fat, carrying a vast stomach, with enormous thick, very large shoulders, a bloated face, light eyes, and a neck that sank into his shoulders in thick flab' was how Loulou Le Porz described Winkelmann. Most prisoners couldn't look him in the face, but Loulou studied him and offered a diagnosis: she believed he suffered from a cell disorder known as mastocytosis, producing boils and growths on the skin. 'I know you should not judge people by their face,' she said, '*mais quand même!* [all the same!] He had the face of a professional killer. He came to the camp with a gun on his shoulder.'

Winkelmann didn't even pretend to behave like a doctor. He heaved his bulk through the door of Block 10, accompanied by an SS sister, then sat at a table and demanded to see a temperature chart. 'But he never looked at it,' said Loulou.

> There was no logic in his choices for death. He selected French women who would easily have lasted out until the liberation. He just decided if he didn't like the look of someone – no more than that. He was a very stupid man and even put Germans on his first list, a long time after they'd stopped gassing Germans. If any of us protested he would turn and give us a look as if to say we'd be next. He had very small light-coloured eyes. I heard he had two children and lived with his family near the camp.

Before long, however, the prisoners did see a pattern in Winkelmann's selections. Julia Barry noticed that he always looked down, at women's legs. Denise Dufournier said he often appeared with Hans Pflaum, the 'cattle merchant', but unlike Pflaum, 'also a hefty beast of a man', Winkelmann didn't beat the women. 'He just stood and looked at their legs.' Loulou said that in Block 10 he sometimes asked a nurse to yank off a blanket. 'Then standing well back, he slowly turned his thick neck, raised his eyes and allowed them to hover for a second or two over a terrified prostrate figure, particularly the legs.'

Winkelmann inspected only legs because the selection criteria had whittled down to just that: was a woman capable of walking, and therefore of joining the coming evacuation march? The Führer had insisted that no prisoner should be left alive in the camp when the Russians arrived, but it was clear by now that there wouldn't be time to gas everyone, so the rest must be force-marched out. Those who could not walk were to be gassed.

Within a week of Winkelmann's arrival the *Schreibstube* secretaries noticed that he had doubled the numbers going to the Youth Camp from about 50–60 a day to 150 or even 180. Most of those sent had swollen ankles and calves.

He also took over selections at the Youth Camp, where Ruth Neudeck was losing control. Prisoners were fighting back and some had escaped. A Hungarian managed to find her way to the main camp after being offered the white powder by Salvequart. She was hidden in a block and never found. According to Hedwig Kuna, a German assigned as Neudeck's interpreter, Adolf Winkelmann blamed Neudeck for these incidents. As soon as he arrived at the Youth Camp he accused Neudeck of choosing women for gassing 'who still had the strength to resist'.

A young woman from Warsaw was so strong when selected for gassing that she managed to escape from the gas chamber itself, ran back to the Youth Camp and described what she saw. As Irma Trksak, the Austrian-Czech Stubova, recalled:

> She told us that they were taken into a hut which had an opening in the roof. They were all told to lie down and go to sleep, as it was night, but the next thing they knew this gas was coming down through the opening in the roof. But not all the women died at first, and as this Polish woman wasn't completely dead, she managed to get away before the others were all taken to the crematorium.

The terrified woman had no idea where to flee, which was why she ended up back at the Youth Camp, and tried to hide there. The guards didn't see her at first, so knowing that the dogs would be on her any minute she hid in a ditch where prisoners' excrement was dumped, together with wet straw. 'She thought if she hid there, under the straw, the dogs wouldn't be able to smell her and she'd be safe,' said Irma.

At first the dogs didn't find her, but one stood there beside the ditch where the woman was and another prisoner – another Czech Stubova – saw this:

> The Stubova shouted: 'She's in the ditch, let's burn the straw.' So Neudeck set light to the straw, which smoked the Polish woman out. Straight away she was locked up again and put on a truck to the gas chamber the following day. As the truck took her off she shouted out from the back: 'It's all a lie. We're not going to Mittwerda, we're going to the gas chamber and to be burned.'

After this episode, not even the most crazed of Youth Camp prisoners believed in the Mittwerda lies.

In early March rumours spread around the Youth Camp that Winkelmann would pick anyone out with a pale face, so they would pinch their cheeks or rub them with something red. More and more women resisted, screaming, kicking and scratching, usually as they were loaded onto the lorries, often with women already dead. 'There were terrible scenes,' said Hedwig Kuna. One afternoon a young guard returned after going with a transport to the gas chamber, and her whole body trembled. 'She told me it was gruesome and she couldn't do it again.'

All this time Mary O'Shaughnessy still lived in terror of being selected because of her artificial arm. Then in early March the Scottish nurse Mary Young heard her number called out. Mary Young was very weak by now and unable to protest, said Mary O'Shaughnessy. 'That morning we were all going mad. We were led out to stand before our huts. SS men came and made us walk along for about twenty yards in ranks of ten. As we walked the SS picked out women to stand out. Before me was Mary Ellen Young with a French woman, Tambour. Mary and the Tambour woman were picked out by the SS men.'

The Tambour woman was Madeleine Tambour, who had worked with the British *Prosper* circuit near Paris. Her sister Germaine was with her in the Youth Camp but was not selected. Mary O'Shaughnessy said she had no idea why Madeleine Tambour and Mary Young were chosen this time. 'There was no logic in it. Mary seemed no weaker than anybody else.'

After selecting at the Youth Camp, Winkelmann returned to the main camp, which in March became the focus of his interest. During the first phase of gassing, women from Block 10 and some of the other death blocks were selected, but from late February onwards he selected from ordinary 'workers' sick blocks too.

Germaine Tillion was now writing a daily diary – 'the most essential facts; the ones that horrified most; that were too important to commit only to memory' – while still collating figures handed to her by the 'old rats'. Soon after Winkelmann arrived, after the first evacuation transports, Germaine noticed that the numbers in Ravensbrück started to go down for the first time. At the start of February there were 46,473 women counted there, which was probably the peak. At the start of March there were 37,699.

On 2 March women were called for a further mass evacuation transport, this time to Mauthausen camp, near Linz, in Austria. The transport was to take all Gypsies, a large number of old and sick, as well as all the NN prisoners. Germaine's diary records: 'This evening 1000 women – of which, all the NN (except those in hiding) and Gypsies with their children – were locked up in the *Strafblock*.' Germaine doesn't mention the 'essential fact – the one that horrified most' that she too was sent to the *Strafblock*, because, as 'NN', both she and her friend Anise Girard were listed for Mauthausen. Later she explained that thanks to an influential Czech friend, the artist Anicha Kapilova, both she and Anise were taken off the list at the last minute. Their places were taken by others who left next morning locked inside closed cattle wagons.

Reports of what happened to those who left for Mauthausen emerged only after the liberation. At least 120 women died on the journey of thirst and suffocation. On disembarking, those 'still dying', as one of the prisoners put it, were quickly 'finished off'. Walking towards the gates of Mauthausen, a Dutch woman called Sabine Zuur noticed a young woman in front of her holding a baby in one arm and holding the hand of a small child in the other.

> She marched two ranks ahead of me. She was at the end of her strength and kept tripping. When the SS hit her, those who marched beside her lifted her up, but she only fell again. So the SS pulled her out of the crowd and beat her up, leaving her at the end of the line. The other women had to look after her children. We were terrified of tripping and being beaten like her.

Once Anise and Germaine had been taken off the Mauthausen list, they were hidden – Anise in the block where Germaine's mother, Emilie Tillion, had been all along and Germaine, who was sick, in an ordinary *Revier* block. Word then spread that a *Generalappell* was due next day. *Generalappell* was a mass selection in which anyone might be chosen for gassing, but particularly the old, or women with bad legs. At sixty-nine years of age, Emilie Tillion was obviously at risk, but so was Germaine, who was not only sick but still limping heavily owing to her bout of diphtheria. While Emilie stayed in the block, tended by Anise, Germaine's friend Anicha smuggled her out to a safer *Revier* block. Anicha knew that Grete Buber-Neumann lay ill in the *Revier* at that time in a 'safe ward', meant for privileged prisoners.

'I was in the sickbay when the window was opened from outside by Anicha, who said excitedly that a general *Appell* was on the way and some hiding place must be found for Germaine,' Grete recalled. The only other woman in the safe ward was lying, very sick, on the mattress below Grete, so Grete was able to take Germaine into her bed and hide her under the blankets.

Outside the siren sounded the *Appell*, and more than 30,000 women lined up beside their blocks as Winkelmann, Suhren and a posse of guards and prisoner policewomen drew near. Among them, Zdenka Nedvedova noticed a woman guard with a cane forty centimetres long, with a silver crook. Each prisoner had to undress and quickly walk by them. Anyone with swollen legs, grey hair, wrinkled bodies and the like had to stand to one side.

> We stood in an extraordinary roll call on the Lagerstrasse while before our eyes half-naked women were taken from the hospital blocks and taken away on trucks. Among those taken I remember the writer Milena Blacarova Fischerova, who was suffering from TB, a mother of two children. She was taken to the gas chambers. We stood powerless and very shocked. Women who were led away cried out and fought. Lorries stood by waiting to take the victims.
>
> At the end the chosen prisoners were taken to another block and to the Youth Camp by truck. Those suffering from TB and the 'insane' were taken straight to the gas chamber. I saw them clad in nothing but a shirt piled up in heaps on lorries, and within an hour I observed flames spurting high from the chimneys and a thick suffocating smoke spread over the camp.

Zdenka and many other prisoners said the camp police helped the SS to round the women up and hunt down those who were hiding. Certain Blockovas helped too. The French later accused Karolina Lanckorońska, Blockova of their block, Block 27, of helping the SS to round up women.

As the mass selection continued Grete and Germaine heard the bawling of guards outside the blocks, 'and we knew the search parties would be going through the whole camp,' said Grete. 'We heard the sound of lorries starting up and driving off and various other sounds. After an hour, steps sounded in the corridor outside our room and Germaine hid further under the bedclothes. Three men came in – Treite, Trommer and Winkelmann.'

'How many sick are in this room? asked Treite. Grete answered, two. Treite looked at her, and at the dying woman below, then turned with the others and went out. Soon after the siren sounded the end of the *Appell*. 'Anise's face appeared at the window frozen with horror,' said Grete. 'She said, "Germaine, your mother has been taken to the gas chamber," at which Germaine sprang out of bed sobbing: "My mother, my mother."'

The selection was over and the women were returning to their blocks. Anise told Germaine that she and Emilie had tried to hide but had been forced to line up. Emilie had then been picked out and put on one of Winkelmann's lorries. The prisoners believed she was taken to the Youth Camp, and not direct to the gas chamber, so Germaine hoped there was still a chance of saving her.

Germaine wrote a message to her mother and asked Micky Poirier, a friend who worked in Hans Pflaum's office, to make sure the letter reached

Emilie in the Youth Camp. If anyone could get a letter to the Youth Camp it was Micheline 'Micky' Poirier, aged nineteen, who had arrived in Ravensbrück in July 1944 and quickly become the camp's most influential French prisoner. Largely because she was a fluent German-speaker, born in the border region of Alsace, but also because she was a clever administrator, Micky was made assistant to Pflaum, which meant she knew the whereabouts of almost every prisoner in the camp.

Germaine's message to her mother read: 'Watch your health and try to seem happy.' She asked her mother if she had seen two French women also sent to the Youth Camp – 'Have you news of Evelyne or Madame Bailly?' She sent a package too, containing painkillers, a piece of sugar and a biscuit. Germaine sent a second and a third letter to her mother over the next days, as well as packets containing pieces of charcoal for diarrhoea. 'For the charcoal you must scrape it very fine so as not to irritate the intestine,' she instructed.

Germaine waited days for an answer, but none came. A week later Micky gave Germaine the packets back, as well as the letters, telling her that her mother had gone to the gas chamber. The gassing of Emilie Tillion devastated the French, and sympathy poured out for Germaine, though some asked, and ask to this day, why it was that Germaine hadn't stayed with her mother. 'I think I would have made sure I went with my mother to the gas chamber, wouldn't you?' said Loulou Le Porz, when I asked her what she remembered of that day.

Others blamed Karolina Lanckorońska for not saving Emilie. Lanckorońska was Blockova of her block and had influence with Binz and Suhren. She could have intervened. Anise Girard blamed herself. She had promised her friend Germaine she would look after Emilie, to whom she was also very close.

Jeannie Rousseau, instigator of the Torgau protest in September 1944, was by this time back in the main camp, and says there was nothing anyone could have done to save Emilie Tillion:

> Germaine was in the *Revier* and could do nothing. Anise was with Emilie and said to her, look, you don't have to go. I can hide you. But Madame Tillion said to Anise: 'I have always looked my life in the face. I want to look my death in the face.' She didn't try to escape it. She didn't want to try. 'My moment has come and I must face it.' She had to go and see what it was.
>
> And Anise has always borne the guilt. She has not forgotten it for one second. Whenever she speaks about those moments. She weeps. Weeps. Weeps. That is why she won't leave Germaine's side even now.

I met Anise Girard twice. The second time was at Germaine's Paris house in 2009. Germaine was 100 years old and lying, very weak, upstairs. Anise sat in constant vigil over her dying friend. A picture of Emilie hung on the wall. I asked if it was true that Karolina Lanckorońska had refused to help prevent Emilie's selection.

> Yes, I thought Karolina would save Emilie. She was in the same circle in the camp. She was a professor of art like Madame Tillion and they both gave lectures on art in the block. They were in a group of intellectuals and ambassadors' wives – the *milieu culturel*. But Lanckorońska found most of the French detestable in the camp. The French were always refusing her orders and she had a big wooden stick and she hit us with this and she said: 'Mesdames, you have no civilisation.'
>
> Yes, she could have helped. She was near us when the selections happened, but she did nothing.

Anise started to cry. She had never talked about the camp at all 'until Faurisson', she said. Robert Faurisson, a British-born academic who lectured at the University of Lyon, wrote articles in the 1970s questioning the existence of Nazi gas chambers and saying there was no proof of a gas chamber at Ravensbrück. In support he cited the records of the International Committee of the Red Cross, which didn't mention a gas chamber at Ravensbrück. Faurisson's claims caused uproar around the world, and pain amongst Ravensbrück survivors, in particular those who had seen family and friends taken off to be gassed.

By the 1970s Germaine Tillion was busy studying African tribes again, so Anise Girard took on the task of refuting Faurisson. 'We were terribly tired as old deportees; we had wanted to forget and drive all that out of our lives, but when we read what Faurisson said we had to do something.'

If the International Red Cross files that he saw did not mention a gas chamber, it came as no surprise: Himmler fooled the ICRC over the gas chamber at Ravensbrück and much else besides. The facts were confirmed before the post-war Hamburg trials. Johann Schwarzhuber, the SS officer who conducted the gassing, described the gas chamber and outlined how the killing happened.

Later more SS evidence emerged. Fritz Suhren, who in early statements confirmed the existence of the gas chamber but denied any personal involvement, escaped just before the Hamburg trial. Recaptured, he appeared before a French court at Rastatt in 1949, where his role was proven. Suhren was even shown a 'Mittwerda list' with his signature at the bottom. The list, dated 6 April 1945, with 450 names of women selected for gassing, had been obtained by prisoners and secretly brought out to be used in evidence.

Other witness testimony later came to light, some of it given by survivors of the men's camp who had worked in or around the gas chamber. Because these survivors lived behind the Iron Curtain after the war, their evidence was at first almost unknown in the West, but it added important new details. Anise discovered the evidence of Emanuel Kolarik, a Czech prisoner who did odd jobs around the gas chamber – cleaning and moving bodies. He said that during his work he often spoke to the men who performed the gassing. These were the Jewish prisoners from Auschwitz imported by Schwarzhuber to form the Ravensbrück *Sonderkommando*.

> In the yard beside the building the women were given a small towel and a piece of soap and taken into the left side of the building, where they had to undress. They were told that they had to wash well, as this was important in the camp where they were going. In the gas chamber the SS shouted to them: 'Wash well, there's no hurry.'

According to Kolarik the men of the *Sonderkommando* took the dead bodies out of the gas chamber by dragging them with hooks. 'Many of the dead had obviously tried to escape or fight their way out at the last minute, because the dead women's fists were clasped tight, holding clumps of hair, and bodies were clinging to each other so that the workers couldn't disentangle them.'

On his way to do repairs near the gas chamber, Kolarik saw a Jewish worker picking up dead bodies and piling them up outside the crematorium like logs ready for burning. The worker wore an apron made of sacking as protection, and in the apron pocket he had some bread. 'This prisoner was so desensitised that he ate the bread he had in his apron while he went off to collect a new body. This spectacle made me vomit.' Kolarik called his boss over to show him the scene – an SS man – and he vomited too.

Anise also unearthed evidence suggesting that there may have been a second gas chamber at Ravensbrück. Both she and Germaine had always wondered how it was that the primitive wooden gas chamber described at Hamburg by Schwarzhuber and others had managed to kill so many, given its small capacity. Furthermore, the wooden structure was reportedly destroyed in the very first days of April, and yet there is overwhelming evidence to suggest that gassing went on longer than that. Other testimony shows that it went on until late April, so where?

It was Anise Girard who first drew attention to the little-known testimony of Walter Jahn, the electrician from Dresden and prisoner in Ravensbrück men's camp, who testified at the trial of Oswald Pohl that he had designed a concrete gas chamber for Ravensbrück, but the construction was delayed. Jahn's design was quite different from the makeshift wooden gas chamber that we know was used. His chamber, he said, commissioned by Schwarzhuber and Höss, was sited near the north wall, disguised as the *Neue Wäscherei* – the new washroom. Jahn said it was even inspected by Höss, Suhren and Pohl at the end of February, and again in March, and he implied that it did function.

'I did the electrical equipment myself, including the signalling side,' said Jahn. The entrance looked quite harmless, 'like a waiting room', but inside were two 'bathing rooms' with about thirty spray heads. In the middle was an exhaust with fan-extraction. The extractors cleared the poisoned air. Victims were taken out and thrown into a grave and their belongings removed by truck.

Since it came to light, Jahn's testimony has always caused controversy, as no sign of such a gas chamber has ever been discovered and survivors didn't mention such a building, leading to speculation that either Jahn was lying or his gas chamber was never used. It remains possible though that the camouflage was so effective that the building was not identified as a gas chamber. The site has never been excavated for signs of such a structure, nor has digging been done to find the mass graves that Jahn spoke of. Thus Jahn's testimony cannot be ruled out. And even if his gas chamber was never used, it could have been part of a plan to gas far more extensively at Ravensbrück than has hitherto been supposed.

The truth about Jahn's gas chamber will probably never be known. But we do have overwhelming evidence about other gassings at the camp. Particularly in the final weeks, scores of prisoners saw a mobile gas chamber – described as a gas van, a gassing truck and even a gassing railway carriage – partly concealed in the woods. Some prisoners said there was more than one gassing vehicle.

Karolina Lanckorońska spoke of a motor bus. It arrived in late March and was stationed in the woods close to the camp. 'The motor bus was painted green; the windows were painted and the wheels were quite close to one another.'

In a report to London, based on interviews with the survivors straight after the liberation, a British diplomat said the women he interrogated spoke of 'two gas chambers' – one of them 'a converted train wagon, brought in from Auschwitz'. Countless Polish survivors spoke of 'gas vans' and 'gas lorries'. Irena Dragan's account of bandaged women gassed in a lorry at the Youth Camp was one of the most vivid. Other prisoners at the Youth Camp talked of hearing 'the continual drone of the vehicle engines at night ... and a desperate crying'. The prisoner secretary Erna Cassens, a German communist, said she heard that a gas van was used when the gas chamber wasn't working well. 'It became known that women were loaded onto railway wagons on a spur in the woods. In the sealed wagons gas was introduced. After a certain time the wagons were opened and the bodies of prisoners unloaded and taken to the crematorium.'

Mary O'Shaughnessy believed the gas van was 'a railway wagon parked on a siding somewhere in the woods'. Immediately after the liberation, the Polish radiologist Mlada Tauforova described finding such a railway wagon in the woods, and she made a report on it to the Soviet authorities. Maria Apfelkammer described seeing inside 'a gas wagon, in the shape of a long bus'. Hanna Sturm, the Austrian carpenter, was ordered to dismantle one of the gas trucks. She said later that she didn't have time and it fell into Russian hands. Zdenka Nedvedova also saw the gassing trucks after the SS had gone: 'We found abandoned vehicles near the Youth Camp – something like removal vans – that had a mechanism allowing exhaust gases to be pumped inside.'

There are other reasons to believe that gassing trucks were used; for one thing, the expertise was here. The transport chief, Josef Bertl, had learned how to gas Jews in trucks while based in Lublin in the first days of the war. Among the new SS chiefs who arrived at Ravensbrück in the winter of 1944–5 was Albert Sauer, who had also used gassing trucks in Poland. Suhren was commandant of Sachsenhausen when experiments in the use of mobile gassing trucks were carried out there. All these men knew each other from previous postings and would almost certainly have pooled ideas on how to kill, especially as in March and April the numbers dying were still not high enough. Fritz Suhren told a colleague that he'd received direct orders from the Führer 'to liquidate the entire camp'.

For the best advice on mobile gassing, Suhren could go to Sturmbannführer Herbert Lange, who pioneered the technique. Ordered to oversee the murder of Poland's mentally ill at the start of the war, Lange operated a fleet of three-ton trucks, converted so that up to 100 people could be poisoned at a time as the truck's carbon monoxide exhaust fumes were fed into a cabin at the back. Lange was later posted to Drögen, the security police headquarters near Ravensbrück. In March 1945 he and Suhren may well have discussed how best to gas women in trucks. Perhaps Lange still had some of his trucks with him at Drögen. The fleet were said to have been returned to Berlin, but this wasn't far away.

In her diary for every day of March, Germaine Tillion noted '*la chasse, la chasse*' (the hunt), and Loulou Le Porz remembers that this was what it was like. 'It became dangerous to be out on the Lagerstrasse. It was "*la chasse à l'homme*" [manhunt]. Winkelmann or Pflaum would just appear with a lorry and say *Allez hop*, and you'd be taken. We certainly went out as little as possible during "*la chasse*".'

After the mass selection of 2 March the rules of *la chasse* kept on changing. In the first week of March it wasn't only the women herded into the wired-off death zone who had reason to fear selection. Now lorries drove down the Lagerstrasse, pulled up outside a block where Winkelmann had been selecting, and Neudeck, Koehler and Rapp jumped out to pile his victims straight into their truck. Blockovas and Stubovas were told to help, as was anybody passing by.

In early March, three of the painting gang, Denise Dufournier, Christiane de Cuverville and Claire Davinroy, passed by Block 11 where a truck was loading women. Seeing the French trio, the guards ordered them to help carry the victims, and they dared not refuse. The terrified women pleaded with the French girls to tell them where the truck was going and all three denied knowing.

As they stood back and stared in horror at the loaded lorry, the trio became aware of SS eyes lingering on them too. 'We sensed something unusual,' Denise said, 'as if the guards could not resist the idea of grabbing us too.' Glancing at each other, the three walked rapidly away.

By the middle of March selections were no longer confined to the sick blocks; they happened in ordinary blocks too, and at any time. A guard might simply turn up outside a block, shout '*Appell!*', and the women had to line up before Winkelmann, sometimes with Schwarzhuber or Pflaum at his side. Selections were even made in the privileged blocks. Sixty-four-year-old Gemma La Guardia Gluck, now grey and frail, was picked out from Block 2, at which she 'screamed like a child', crying out: 'I don't want to go up the crematorium chimney!' Hearing her, Gemma's Blockova reminded Fritz Suhren who Gemma's brother was, and she was taken off the list.

Selections took place at the Siemens plant too. Margareta van der Kuit remembers an SS officer coming to the new living barracks:

> Everyone had to stand outside and the officer called out numbers. Those chosen were often older women, whose daughters were also working at the Siemens camp. The daughters were very worried about where their mothers were going, so the officer said they would be taken to somewhere where they would be better off and where they wouldn't have to work so hard.

Basia Zajączkowska, the Jewish woman who survived the Kielce ghetto, said: 'We had a selection once – they sorted out older people who had injured legs and those who were generally well. Those sorted out were sent back [from Siemens] to Ravensbrück to the crematorium.' A Yugoslav prisoner called Vida Zavrl said Siemens prisoners had to line up and lift skirts in front of a commission who noted the numbers of those selected. Anyone judged incapable of working was now in danger of gassing, said Yvonne Useldinger, the Luxembourger at Siemens: 'Grey-haired prisoners began to colour their hair, but when it rained at roll call the colour ran down their faces.'

As part of the drive to empty the camp, selections for subcamps – those further west, away from the Russian front – were also stepped up. Large numbers were taken to subcamps attached to male concentration camps as well. Between January and March, 2000 Ravensbrück women were transported to Buchenwald subcamps alone, and more went to subcamps of Dachau and Flossenbürg. Pflaum entered the painting gang's block one day calling everyone out for a transport to Berlin to dig ditches. The painters climbed up into the attic of their block, while others flattened themselves under bunks as the 'cattle merchant' raged around the block beating prisoners out of the door. Survivors of the ditch-digging transport returned two weeks later, telling how many had died of exhaustion or had been killed by bombs.

Given the danger of *la chasse* many prisoners started trying to get out to a subcamp, expecting to be safer, only to find that the chances of survival at these camps were in some ways worse. Wanda Wojtasik and Krysia Czyż, the Polish rabbits, assumed the numbers of dead prisoners and managed to slip in amongst a column of women heading to the tiny subcamp of Neustadt-Glewe, where they found prisoners starving to death instead of being gassed. Cut off from all sources of supplies, the camp received no rations and the prisoners were fed on soup made of potato peelings. 'There were no beds, and a floor with a vast number of dead bodies jamming it solid,' said Wanda.

At Neubrandenburg Micheline Maurel had been slowly starving for many months. In March she was sick again and back in the *Revier*. 'All morning we waited for soup. Near the bunks of the dying those who could still eat lay in ambush.' SS selections were still made at the subcamps too. At night the trucks arrived, the numbers were read out, women were hoisted onto trucks and taken back to Ravensbrück to be gassed.

By the end of March the food at Ravensbrück too was running out. Meals were given out at random times and prisoners provided their own security squads to protect the soup gang from attack. Sanitation had largely broken down, walkways were littered with excreta, the washrooms in the sick blocks could hold no more dead bodies, the mortuary was overflowing and the crematorium working to capacity. A new death block was established to hold the excess corpses. Patrolling near by, Julia Barry saw inside the 'death block' where bodies were stacked high 'with eyes out of their sockets'.

Pflaum, Winkelmann and the posse roamed the camp, selecting people almost at random, but at least in the chaos it became easier to hide. The painting gang hid in the infectious diseases block; lying in a bed with a sick person was the safest of all places to hide.

By late March everyone seemed to know someone chosen for the Youth Camp or for another transport; mothers, daughters, friends were all trying to get names off lists, or onto a better list, or to find a way to hide. Some time in mid-March Mary Lindell heard that Yvonne Baseden was on a list. She rushed out onto the Lagerstrasse to find that Yvonne was already lining up to be taken away, probably to the Youth Camp. Yvonne stood 'skinny, hollow-eyes, morose and without hope', so Mary went to Micky, in Pflaum's labour office, for help. Mary had smuggled painkillers to Micky in the past; now she called in the favour. 'What's her name and number?' asked Micky, and struck off Yvonne's name.

As soon as Yvonne heard she'd been spared she pleaded that her friend, whom today she remembers only as Marguerite, be taken off too. Mary again asked Micky, who 'with a flick of a pen' erased Marguerite's name as well, and told Mary: 'Quick, get them away. Now it's your risk.' Mary hid the two women on a safe ward in the *Revier*, under Treite's protection.

Mary's relations with Treite were closer every day. She wrote affectionately of him in her memoir, saying how on one occasion, as he treated her for pneumonia, Treite injected her with a serum. 'I flinched, for everyone knew that injections in Ravensbrück were usually lethal,' wrote Mary. 'But Treite bent down and whispered in English: "It's all right, Queen Mary. The seals are intact."'

Towards the end of the month Violette Lecoq, the Block 10 nurse, noticed that the rules of *la chasse* had changed again. A truck that came to Block 10 to load up the sick returned empty just minutes later for another load. Next time the truck appeared Violette used a stopwatch, organised from the store, to time the round trip. It took just seven minutes, the time it would take to go to the gas chamber and back, which proved what Violette had suspected: that those chosen for gassing no longer went via the Youth Camp but went straight from their beds to the gas chamber.

It was 'bedlam' in Block 10 towards the end, said Loulou Le Porz, who was spending much of her time trying to move her sick out of Block 10 to avoid being selected. 'Most of our patients had no mattresses at all, no running water, nothing worked at all. We thought we were in hell. But our strategy was to concern ourselves with our block and our patients. And there were things we could suddenly do as well – things happened that didn't happen before. I remember getting a whole loaf of bread one day. It was incredible. A lorry came and someone said – do you want bread, just like that.'

I asked Loulou if she was sure she would survive until the end.

> I didn't know. For me it had always been obvious we would win the war, but when? We could see they were clearing us all out. We were isolated out there and forgotten by the entire world. People knew nothing about us. They didn't know where we were.

'Did you think they might never find you?'

> We thought we might die there, yes. My patients were dying in my arms. Madame de Lavalette-Montbrun told me she knew she wouldn't be going back, but she was still smiling. She was a fatalist. We all were by then. Claude Virlogeux was a physics teacher. I saw her pass me by on the back of a cart one day, quite dead. But we tried to help people hold on. On one mattress we had Madame Tedesco, she was well connected in the world of theatre and she got on very well with our *camarade* Zim. Then Madame Tedesco died of exhaustion in my arms, saying she would do it all again. I told Zim that she could still last out, it wouldn't be long. And she agreed to let us smuggle her to a safer block. Zim wanted to live so I persuaded her to take the risk.

By the end of March the camp was 'like a mysterious planet', said Denise Dufournier, 'where the macabre, the ridiculous and the grotesque rubbed shoulders in a fantastic irrational chaos'. Karolina Lanckorońska, watching the crematorium flames shooting higher every night, was reminded of the beginning of the *Iliad*. She was still giving lectures on Charlemagne and Gothic art as children in Block 27 played a game of selecting for the gas chamber. In the Red Army block the women were making red flags to hang out to welcome their liberators, while the painting gang had been sent to redecorate the maternity block, where, according to Zdenka's lists, 135 more babies were born in March, of which 130 died.

Hitherto servile Blockovas turned courageous, and might suddenly decide to save an entire column of prisoners by leading them out of line for the gas chamber, pretending they were a unit needed for work. Meanwhile, all around the camp groups of haunted women – faces never seen before in Ravensbrück, brought in perhaps from subcamps – were seen waiting for something and then being marched off. 'We sometimes saw passing by our workplace a small group of women we didn't know,' recalled Grete Buber-Neumann. 'Quite terrified, they passed about thirty metres away from us. We supposed they were taken straight to the gas chamber.'

Anna Stekolnikova, the Muscovite, remembers seeing 'women standing in a queue waiting to be burned, holding bundles of clothes'. Such was the chaos that by March no attempt was even made to issue these new arrivals with numbers, and any numberless woman was liable to be simply rounded up and sent for gassing. So when the German communist Änne Saefkow arrived – transferred from a Berlin prison at the end of the month – a communist friend in the *Schreibstube* gave her the number of a dead woman, 108273. Änne's was the last number issued in the camp.

As the Easter weekend approached the weather was warming up. Gypsies sat outside their blocks in the evenings singing, and the painting gang was sent to drag rowing boats out from a shed onto the lake. The guards wanted to go boating over Easter.

News reaching the prisoners was of a slowdown in the Russian advance, but the Western front was closing fast. 'We knew that victory was close at hand. We thought perhaps we only had to stand fast for a few days,' recalled Denise, whose strength was suddenly fading; her civilian boss remarked upon it as he fed her with cooked potatoes.

Rumours came and went. The camp secretaries had heard that the French were to be exchanged, but at the Youth Camp the only rumour was of a mass selection. The Easter weekend was coming up and the SS wanted a final clear-out. Several prisoners recorded the sequence of events.

On 28 March – a Wednesday – the Youth Camp prisoners were ordered to line up barefoot. Neudeck and an SS man carried out a selection, examining faces and legs. Those selected were sent to one side. Amongst them was Elise Rivet – otherwise known as Mère Elisabeth de l'Eucharistie, a Mother Superior from Lyon, brought to Ravensbrück for hiding resisters in her convent. The victims were stripped of everything except shirts and loaded on the trucks, their shoes and underwear left lying on the road. At least six women died in the lineup, and were hauled onto the lorries by their legs.

Two days later, on 30 March, Good Friday, the guards announced another mass selection, this time at the main camp. The women were told to line up with bare legs and torso and then they had to 'keep jackets on' but 'take shoes off'. As they stood for the selection, Russian guns were just audible for the first time in the distance. Winkelmann appeared. When he signalled, the women had to walk rapidly past him as he bent double and peered at their legs. When he raised a hand a prisoner was taken away to a waiting lorry. When a lorry was full it drove off to the Youth Camp. At Block 10 Violette Lecoq was ordered to help load women direct onto a truck, then she was chased onto the truck herself and driven off. At the Youth Camp her name was not on the guards' list so she was sent back.

After the new influx of prisoners from the main camp, seven empty lorries arrived at the Youth Camp that same afternoon. Each lorry was then filled with women, ready to go to the gas chamber. Then two more lorries arrived from the main camp, each loaded with about 250 women. When evening came all nine lorries prepared to leave, one after the other, for the gas chamber, but an air raid delayed departure. When the all clear came, some of the lorries left in the dark while the rest stayed at the Youth Camp, and left for the gas chamber next day, Saturday 31 March. More gassing happened on Easter Sunday, and by the end of the Easter weekend all the prisoners on these lorries – as many as 2500 – had been gassed and burned and the air was thick with choking smoke.

At the main camp on Easter Sunday another order went out: all the French were to line up next morning at the camp gates. Groups met to discuss what it might mean. Some believed it meant liberation. Others feared wholesale extermination, while another group believed there was to be an exchange of prisoners. There was talk of buses in the woods, not green ones but White Buses – belonging to the Red Cross.

That evening, Easter Sunday, French prisoners from the Youth Camp were marched down to the main camp and told to join the other French on the Lagerstrasse the next day. The French workers at the Siemens factory were also ordered to join the lineup on Easter Monday.

The painting gang returned to their block on Sunday evening and found a strange atmosphere. 'In the large room by candlelight couples danced languorously to the accompaniment of an accordion,' recalled Denise. 'The *Jules* dandled their girls, who were all dressed up, on their knees. There was a vague smell of greasy humanity in the air and in the darkest corners lovers were kissing. It was our last vision of Block Seventeen.'

*Chapter 38*

# Nelly

As trucks queued outside the Ravensbrück gas chamber over the Easter weekend, a small Swedish plane flew over the German coast, and then seemed to stall in the air as the pilot throttled back and began to circle over Stralsund. The Allies had mounted a daylight raid over Berlin and a huge black cloud of smoke was unfurling on the horizon.

Count Bernadotte was flying in for a second meeting with Heinrich Himmler, hoping to persuade him to grant permission for the Swedish rescue mission to be extended to include not only the Scandinavians but other nationalities as well. Amongst those high on Bernadotte's list were French women from Ravensbrück. Bernadotte had a particular concern for the French women's plight ever since learning first hand of the mass deportations when in Paris in the autumn. De Gaulle's government-in-waiting was also putting enormous pressure on Bernadotte to help the French prisoners.* As soon as the smoke lifted, Bernadotte's plane flew on, landing at Berlin's Tempelhof Airport just half an hour after the all-clear was sounded.

Since 10 February, when Himmler had given Bernadotte permission to rescue Scandinavians and hold them in a Swedish-run holding centre at Neuengamme, much had been achieved. By the second week of March more than 100 vehicles, mostly belonging to the Swedish army – trucks, buses, ambulances and motorcycles, manned by 250 Swedish soldiers, doctors and

* Bernadotte also had a personal interest in France; as a direct descendant of the Napoleonic marshal Jean-Baptiste Bernadotte he had a great deal of French blood.

nurses – had left southern Sweden, driven across Denmark and crossed into Germany.

Before the convoy left, the British, American and Russian delegations in Stockholm were all informed of the expedition. No objections were raised, but no guarantees of safe passage were offered either, although, just as the convoy was about to start boarding the Malmö ferry, the British sent out a last-minute request: all the vehicles were to be painted white with red crosses on the roofs and sides, so as to be easily identifiable by Allied aircraft. The job was done in haste on the ferry.

On 12 March the convoy set up its headquarters at Friedrichsruh, twenty-two kilometres east of Hamburg, near the Baltic coast, and instantly set about collecting up prisoners. By the end of the month nearly 5000 Norwegian and Danish men imprisoned at Sachsenhausen, Dachau and camps near Dresden had been brought to the Swedish holding centre at Neuengamme camp, close to the Friedrichsruh HQ.

The mission had run into many problems, including shortages of men, vehicles and fuel. The fronts were closing in so rapidly that the buses – all carrying at least one Gestapo man as minder – could only move through a sliver of land. Buses had been strafed by Allied planes, though as yet nobody was hurt.

Acute moral conflicts had arisen too. Each time the Swedes reached a camp and filled their buses with Scandinavians they left prisoners of other nationalities behind. At Neuengamme, they found themselves in a particularly invidious position when the commandant told them that only by helping clear out his sick and unwanted prisoners could room be made at his camp for the holding centre for the rescued Norwegians and Danes. After much debate, the Swedes did the SS commandant's bidding and took away his 'unwanted' prisoners, driving them in their Red Cross buses to another far worse camp, where many almost certainly died.

Another dilemma faced the mission. Throughout March it had not been possible for Bernadotte's buses to rescue the women of Ravensbrück. Sylvia Salvesen had smuggled out letters in early March that told of hundreds of corpses burned each day at the camp. Sylvia also warned that liquidation might occur 'within three weeks'. The way from Hamburg was still passable by road; Bernadotte's buses could at least have collected Ravensbrück's Scandinavian women. And yet, while they rescued the men, the women were having to wait till last. Why?

Bernadotte's memoir is silent on the subject, and so are the Swedish foreign ministry papers. But the answer lies, almost certainly, in the fact that to carry out his mission at all, Bernadotte was bound by Himmler's terms, and Himmler had not yet given permission for the White Buses to go to Ravensbrück.

Even as Himmler and Bernadotte first met on 10 February at Hohenlychen to discuss the first stage of the rescue, the gassing at Ravensbrück, eight miles down the road, was under way. By the end of March the extermination hit its peak. Anyone coming to the camp in that time would have smelt the choking brown smoke, and seen trucks packed with bodies. Local villagers were even complaining about the ash in the lake. At the other camps visited by the White Buses, gassing was not being carried out, so the rescues could start. But Himmler had decided that Bernadotte could not come to Ravensbrück until most of the gassing was done.

Whether Bernadotte was aware of the reasons for his exclusion remains unclear; there is certainly no evidence to suggest that he pressed for permission to go to Ravensbrück in the first weeks. What is clear, however, is that by the time he drove out to Hohenlychen for his second meeting with Himmler on 4 April, the gassing at the women's camp had begun to slow down. Probably the gassing vans alone were still in use, and they could move around and be easily hidden in the woods.

At first the chances of new concessions from Himmler did not look good. When he appeared this time the Reichsführer was 'not only grave, but nervy', Bernadotte recalled. Himmler spoke again of his duty to the Führer. At one point he got up to take a call and left the room, at which Walter Schellenberg, who was always present at these meetings, turned to Bernadotte and told him what was on the Reichsführer's mind.

Himmler wished the count to act as an intermediary with the Allies and go directly to Eisenhower to say that Himmler wished to negotiate an armistice on the Western front. Schellenberg said that Himmler had found himself unable to make this request directly to Bernadotte, and had left him to do it. Bernadotte replied by making clear to Schellenberg that the Western powers would not negotiate with Himmler and he could not offer himself as an intermediary.

When Himmler returned to the room, Bernadotte saw his chance to ask for the concessions he was seeking on the prisoner rescues. First, he asked for permission to take all the Scandinavians now held at Neuengamme straight to Denmark. Himmler said this was not possible, because Hitler would get to know, and would veto it. Himmler made his own counter-offer: 'Moving smaller numbers might be possible.' Bernadotte now proposed the release of all Norwegian and Swedish women – as well as Norwegian students and some Danes – direct to Sweden. Himmler agreed.

Perhaps because he judged that Himmler had conceded as much as he was willing for now, Bernadotte did not push his luck by asking for the French as well, as he had intended. But significant gains had been made: in particular, the White Buses could now head to Ravensbrück.

Bernadotte passed the news to his mission leaders and the Ravensbrück rescue date was set for 7 April. Before the Swedish buses set out, however, they learned that the Swiss had reached the women's camp first. In a further letter from Sylvia Salvesen, smuggled out on 4 April, Sylvia spoke of 400 French women 'fetched today by the Swiss International Red Cross'.

Given that for six years the International Committee of the Red Cross had refused to take a stand on the concentration camps, the appearance of their rescue buses outside Ravensbrück in early April was, as the prisoners themselves would say, 'a miracle'. It was, in part, a matter of mere rivalry. Learning that their rival neutrals, the Swedes, were launching a dramatic rescue mission, the Swiss didn't want to be outshone. Carl Burckhardt, the acting ICRC president, had his legacy in mind and had requested his own meeting with Himmler to discuss the camps.

The intervention signalled just how fast Geneva's attitudes had changed in the final weeks of war. Reports about what Hitler had planned for his prisoners in the last days exerted overwhelming pressure on the ICRC to act. Throughout January and February national Red Cross societies – Czech, Polish, Yugoslav, Greek, Romanian, French, British and American – had been urging the International Red Cross to take a lead. The World Jewish Congress was pressing hardest of all, horrified by what fate awaited those Jews left alive in German camps. De Gaulle's provisional government in France also pressed the ICRC to get off the fence, and the US State Department was calling for it to 'use every means at its disposal'.

Most communications were cut and roads impassable, but if the Swedes could do it, why not the Swiss? An opening appeared when Himmler – keeping the Swiss in play as well as the Swedes – accepted a suggestion from Burckhardt for a prisoner swap: 300 French women held at Ravensbrück to be exchanged for German civilian prisoners held in France. The deal was done in early March, but amid the chaos it proved hard to implement. It was largely thanks to the influence and contacts of a Swiss doctor that the exchange got off the ground at all.

Thirty-two-year-old Dr Hans Meyer, born in Zurich, had been appointed an ICRC delegate in Germany in January 1945. On the face of things he was an appropriate person to oversee the prisoner exchange, but his prior employment made him a breathtaking choice. Before joining the ICRC he had worked for two years as a doctor for the SS, based at the Hohenlychen clinic, where his chief was Karl Gebhardt, the man who – as the ICRC knew – had carried out medical atrocities at Ravensbrück.

Why, as the war drew to an end, Meyer suddenly left the SS clinic to take up a job as an ICRC delegate is easier to understand than how a man who had worked as an SS doctor came to be appointed as an ICRC delegate. Meyer must have known about – if not taken part in – Gebhardt's crimes. Now, however, Meyer turned his zeal to helping the other side as he tried to secure the 300 Ravensbrück prisoners' release, and his SS contacts soon proved indispensable.

When Meyer turned up at Ravensbrück to make arrangements he found that Suhren was away and no one knew a thing about the exchange. By this time the pace of the Red Army advance was about to make routes to the Swiss border impassable. In view of this Meyer drove the five miles up to Hohenlychen to see if his old SS friends could help speed things up. Only by direct appeal to Himmler – presumably arranged by Meyer's old boss, Gebhardt – was Meyer able to instruct the Swiss drivers to approach the camp and was Suhren finally instructed to release the women.

On arrival at Ravensbrück on 1 April, however, the Swiss drivers were still made to wait. The reason given was that the women had not yet been selected and properly prepared. The reason not given was that there was still some gassing and burning to be done. So the Swiss Red Cross buses parked a little way back in the trees, and waited for three more days.

The day that the buses turned up, word spread among the French in the camp that everyone was to gather next morning at the gates, but no confirmation came. All that night excitement and fear ran in conflicting waves through the French blocks. Someone in the offices had seen the Red Cross buses. The French Siemens workers had been brought to the main camp and the few surviving French from the Youth Camp had been brought back too.

Binz was going round the camp trying to tidy things up 'as if she was expecting visitors'. She told staff in the *Revier* to shut the broken windows so that missing panes didn't show. 'And lock the *Schmuckstücke* in washrooms,' shouted the *Oberaufseherin*.

Marie-Claude Vaillant-Couturier noted in her diary for that day: 'The sick were sent to the gas chamber yesterday and today we get on their behalf their share of Ovaltine as an Easter treat!' In another French block prisoners spent the day chatting around the stove, warming their Easter drinks, as truckloads of bodies continued to trundle past. 'Is that one French?' asked someone, perhaps recognising a face. 'No, Polish,' came the answer. 'You can only die once,' said a girl called Lily. 'But we mustn't die in Ravensbrück' – on that they were all agreed.

When the women went to their bunks, the Blockova shouted out: 'Tomorrow morning all the French at *Appell* at nine.'

As the French lined up, it was a horribly familiar sight. A selection took place, conducted by the cattle merchant. First, Pflaum picked out 400 French and moved them to one side. Then the same group were told they were to be selected again. Now 200 were picked out – but again no one knew why some were chosen and some not. Then others, not chosen the first two times, were told they had been selected after all, and the numbers rose again. Among those not selected at all were the most acutely sick and feeble – clearly the sight of these dying women would not redound to Germany's credit. The NN (Night and Fog) group were also not to be released.

Many of those not selected were relieved, as they knew that 'selection' was likely to lead to something worse. When they saw the chosen women led off to Block 31, inside the enclosure, where prisoners once waited to go to the Youth Camp, such fears intensified. Here the women were kept for forty-eight hours and made to pass twice through the showers, then left naked and shivering in the cold, 'filled with anxiety, fear and hope', until they were given new sets of ill-fitting clothes. Denise Dufournier inherited an evening dress, which she thought must have been used in a Polish cabaret. The women were then kept waiting in a wet block for three days.

On the third day, 3 April, came new torment: the women were called out and Suhren took a roll call, at the end of which he selected all those with aristocratic names and told them to return to their blocks. The aristocrats were to stay behind, but the rest, he said, would be freed the next day.

The aristocrats, guessing, rightly, that they were to be held as hostages, gathered in anger and a three-woman protest 'committee' – Christiane de Cuverville, Colette de Dumast and Jacqueline d'Alincourt – went to see Suhren to ask for an explanation. Colette did all the talking, as she spoke the best German. 'She asked Binz why we were not allowed to leave, and Binz looked astonished at being spoken to like that,' Christiane recalled. The chief guard then placed a piece of paper on the desk. If the titled ladies of France agreed to sign the paper saying they had been 'well treated', they would not be executed, she announced. 'We were horrified. Colette said there was no question of that,' said Christiane. As they returned to their block the three debated whether to tell the other 'aristocrats' of the offer. 'Colette said let's not tell them. So we decided not to in case there might be one or two who would sign,' said Jacqueline d'Alincourt.

Next morning – Wednesday 4 April – those still on the list were told to prepare to leave, and new names were added to fill the spaces of those removed, including a handful from Block 10. With the help of Violette Lecoq, Loulou sought out Zim in the block where she'd been hidden and managed to help her to her feet and out to the *Appell*. At the last minute, Winkelmann appeared and picked out any woman with swollen legs, or with her head recently shaved. Zim, however, was overlooked and found the strength to walk with the others to the gates. As the women filed out – 299 in total, still in ranks of five – Suhren closed the gates behind them and wished the group '*bon voyage*'. He hoped they wouldn't have a 'disagreeable recollection' of their stay at the camp.

The women looked ahead down the road. Half hidden in the pine trees about 1500 yards away, they saw a line of White Buses, each painted with a huge red cross. It seemed they had better walk on, and so they did, haltingly, staring ahead. Closer they saw soldiers in khaki standing beside the buses. A little closer still they saw the word Canada on the soldiers' sleeves. These were Canadian prisoners of war, freed by the Germans to drive the buses as part of the deal.

The French women stared at the buses and at the men in khaki, 'motionless and dazed', recalled Denise. 'I thought it was a dream,' said Loulou. 'Really, I did not believe it. It was surreal. We went forward and we saw soldiers – I think they were Canadians, and they cried when they saw us. When I saw them crying I began to think it was real.'

The women climbed inside the buses and the Canadians helped. Inside they were each given a piece of cake and a large piece of cold sausage. The vehicles started up and drove away. The women were told they were heading to Lake Constance and the Swiss border.

After the 299 French had gone, those left behind talked of who might go next. They knew that time for rescue was running out. The secretaries were holding daily bonfires burning documents and files. The front was closing fast, and with about 30,000 prisoners still held in Ravensbrück, orders to evacuate – or blow the camp up – were certain to come soon.

Sylvia Salvesen had given up hope. It was four weeks since the nurse Gerda Schröder had left, taking with her the second of Sylvia's smuggled letters and promising to pass it on to Wanda Hjort and the Norwegian cell at Gross Kreutz. 'She had been gone over a month and dreadful things had happened during those weeks,' Sylvia recalled.

Then on the day the French left for Switzerland – 5 April – Gerda reappeared. She came to Sylvia's bed that night, carrying a parcel and bringing news. Sylvia was astonished and overjoyed. Gerda was upset at the sight of her friend, who in four weeks had grown ravaged, white-haired and thin. She gave Sylvia the note sent back from Mrs Hjort and Mrs Seip, but Gerda had more recent news than this. She explained that after she left Ravensbrück in early March she'd been unable to get back to the camp due to the bombing of the train lines. Gerda had tried to get back to Gross Kreutz, but the lines to Potsdam were also bombed. On Easter Monday, however, Gerda managed to telephone Gross Kreutz and arranged to meet Wanda Hjort in Berlin.

Miraculously, given the turmoil in the city, Gerda and Wanda had found each other. Wanda brought with her the Norwegian Professor Arup Seip, a key member of the Gross Kreutz cell. They met in a small café near the central station, where trains were still arriving, though the front was so close now that they could see the wounded soldiers being brought in on the S-Bahn. All over the city the streets were plastered with notices saying: 'Berlin will never surrender.' It was rumoured that Hitler was in an underground bunker, said Gerda. Everyone knew the end was near.

Arup Seip had told Gerda that the previous day Bernadotte had met Himmler at Hohenlychen for a second time. He also told her that at the meeting 'Himmler had given the Red Cross permission to fetch the Norwegian and Danish women from Ravensbrück'. Sylvia was ecstatic. 'I shall never forget that evening,' she wrote later. 'I was told to write another letter with an up-to-date list of names, as Professor Seip was afraid that some of our prisoners had been moved.'

Gerda told Sylvia to write the list at once, as Wanda aimed to come to the camp next day to collect it, and take it to the Swedish task force. How Wanda would make the perilous journey to the camp Gerda had no idea: the lines had been bombed again, even since Gerda had made it through. Nor did Gerda know how Wanda would gain access to the camp. But she told Sylvia that she had given Wanda directions about where to find her in the nurses' quarters if she did get through the gates.

Sylvia now wrote her third letter to her Norwegian friends. In clearer terms that nobody this time could misunderstand, she told them that the women of Ravensbrück were being gassed.

> Thousands have been picked out and sent to the gas chamber. A number of them were ill but some of them were quite well, though older. It was almost enough just to have grey hair. The saddest scenes have been enacted here. Many had dyed their hair with shoeblack or soot. By a miracle I have escaped.

She gave names of ninety-six Norwegians and twenty Danes still in the camp. Fearing that, as with the French, the weakest might not be allowed to leave, Sylvia begged the Swedes to make sure that those too ill to walk should not be left behind. A group of French had been released that same day, she wrote, apparently to be exchanged for Germans. But many French 'intelligentsia and women of good families' had been kept back, which Sylvia clearly feared might happen to her. 'It will be terrible to be left alone without any other Norwegians,' she wrote.

Sylvia also gave as many names as possible of the Norwegians who were NN and had therefore been sent to Mauthausen, but she wasn't sure she had them all. 'We believe that they arrived [at Mauthausen] but have heard rumours that half of them were selected on arrival and sent on to another camp.' Others on the NN list were still at Ravensbrück, she said, and employed in the workshops, 'so they are in less danger of being chosen for the gas chamber'.

Sylvia gave her letter to Gerda. The next day Gerda told Sylvia that Wanda had made it to the camp, and she had handed the letter to her. Wanda had come with a message that the Swedish Red Cross buses would be here within a few days. 'You must pack your rucksack immediately. You must believe it,' Gerda told Sylvia, at which Sylvia took Gerda in her arms to hug her – 'A prisoner, daring to hug a German sister.'

Wanda Hjort had arrived at Ravensbrück just a few hours earlier. It was her most daring expedition yet. Bombing had disabled the railway line, so Wanda had come in the car loaned by the Swedish legation and driven by Bjørn Heger, the Norwegian doctor, who had joined the Gross Kreutz cell. The couple had worked on several dangerous missions together in recent months – they had also become lovers.

Wanda and Bjørn were receiving help now from the ICRC delegation in Berlin, who had given them Swiss Red Cross identity papers to get them past the camp gate. On arrival, the SS sentry let them in, at least as far as the camp offices, where Bjørn went to drop the parcels they brought. When no one was looking Wanda managed to slip away down an alley to look for Gerda, as arranged, in the SS nurses' block. It was hard to find. She felt conspicuous in her thick warm coat and good boots. 'All round me were women in rags, pulling carts with bare feet in wooden clogs.'

Wanda kept on walking, and found Gerda's room almost by chance. There was a bed, a chair, some artificial flowers in a vase. Nobody came and she feared she would be caught, thinking: 'If I'm tortured I'll give everything away – Gerda and Sylvia's names too.' But Gerda appeared, the letter was delivered, and Wanda made her way back to the camp gates. Bjørn was waiting, trying to look at ease. Wanda tried not to run. As they were leaving, the guard eyed the couple with a look that suggested to Wanda he had understood something – 'perhaps that we were all in peril now' – and he let them go.

Back in the car, Wanda broke down and sobbed. 'This time it was too much,' she said later. 'All these women – starving, humiliated and defenceless – and many my age.' They sped off to deliver Sylvia's list of names to the Swedes.

*

'Sylvia's to be freed,' said Zdenka to those in the *Revier* the following day. She was wearing an organised English tweed coat, and hugged her friend. The *Oberschwester*, Elisabeth Marschall, gripped Sylvia's hand and cried. Norwegians in the ordinary blocks had had no idea that rescue was close. Nelly Langholm and her Stavanger friends only learned when they were ordered into the showers the night before. 'But we didn't believe it,' said Nelly.

> The next day we came out in our new clothes and had to walk to the gate. We saw the buses and there were these Swedish men in grey uniforms with red crosses on their arms. They were just standing outside the gate. I think they told us: 'Now you will go to Sweden – now you will be free.' Before we left, the German big boss came and said: '*Meine Damen, Sie sind frei* – Ladies, you are free.' Can you imagine? Here was a German calling us *Meine Damen*. Were they really talking to us? We hadn't been called 'ladies' for such a long time. *Meine Damen*.

And Nelly laughed. 'Margrethe said to me: "I would rather he'd said *Meine Schweine*."'

Nelly recalled that other prisoners were standing in the camp and watching as they left. 'We were given bread to take with us and we took it; we didn't know when would be the next time we'd get something.'

'How did it feel, leaving the other prisoners behind?'

'I think we felt sorry. It is not easy to understand, but if something so good happens you feel sad at the same time. Very sad.'

'Could you say goodbye?'

'No, we couldn't, because we came out of this building straight to the buses.'

'Did you think they would be collected too?'

'I can't remember. But we heard that the camp was – that it was going to be blown up.'

Leaving on the bus was 'like a miracle', said Nelly.

> I was with Margrethe, and there were two Germans on the bus with us. So we thought, what are they doing here? What is going on? There was a Swedish driver and two on a motorbike in front. It was terrible to go through Germany. It was one month before the end and it was shocking to see a big town like Hamburg. I don't think I saw a house – not a whole house. We heard the shooting from the west – the Americans – and the Russians from the other side. But we found a way through all these ruins. These terrible ruins. Because the Germans, they repaired the roads very quickly you see. They needed a way through too.

From Hamburg the buses drove on to the Danish border. Nelly smiled as she remembered.

> And we saw the grass, the green grass – and we hadn't seen green grass for two years. So Margarethe and I asked if we could get down from the bus and go into the grass. We wanted to pee. And we wanted to pee in the grass. So they let us down and we ran across the field and took our knickers down. I will never forget the feeling of the green grass. It was a feeling so beautiful, cool and soft. Freedom – you know.

As the Swedes crossed the Danish border, 200 miles northwest of Ravensbrück, the 299 French who left with the Swiss were arriving at Kreuzlingen, 550 miles to the south on the German-Swiss frontier. They left three days earlier, but their journey the length of Germany was longer and harder. Loulou and Jacqueline Héreil, two of the Block 10 team, were on the bus, tending the sick and working with Hans Meyer, the Red Cross doctor. Violette Lecoq, their comrade from Block 10, classified 'NN', was left behind. All the way women cried out 'Are we at the frontier?' only to find they had stopped for another air raid. Zim told Loulou that all she cared about now was to cross the border so that she could die in France. Many were saying the same.

On 8 April at the town of Hof, on the road to Nuremberg, a bombardment held the convoy up all day. At dawn the buses moved off, as figures pushing carts and trolleys poured out of the city's burning ruins. 'Now it's their turn,' said the French, looking down at the wretched German faces. 'They're the prisoners now. See how they like it. And we are free.'

At nine that night the buses slowed to a halt in front of barred gates and sentry posts at the Kreuzlingen border post. Floodlights shone through a cold drizzle as the women were unloaded for a last *Appell* while German guards checked papers. The checking took over an hour. On the other side of the barriers figures gathered in the gloom – nurses, doctors, Samaritans, reporters, priests, and ordinary people come to welcome and to help. Their shouts and cheers died out at the sight of so many silent ghosts. As the gates opened a German shouted a command. That made a Swiss policeman step across the road, raise his arm and growl: '*Non, monsieur.* That is enough. Withdraw!' He turned to the women and smiled. 'You are free now.'

They boarded the buses again. Figures came forward to lift, embrace, and to offer gifts and food. 'You'll have soup and a hot bath.'

Just across the border they stopped for the night and were led into a warm gymnasium where soup was waiting and much more. Men cried as crumpled figures swathed in bandages were stretchered from the buses. Six women were taken straight to hospital, while others lay on mattresses of fresh straw covered with wool and piled with blankets.

Next morning officials of the ICRC in Geneva arrived. They advised the women not to speak about the camp, as it might be dangerous. Then they made assessments of needs. Doctors had already diagnosed dysentery, TB, typhus, gangrene and acute malnutrition, as one of the Red Cross men noted. 'A Doctoresse Le Porz and four other medically qualified prisoners are helping treat the sick,' he wrote. The women had arrived with nothing but the clothes they stood in – 'which obviously don't fit'. Those few with any small possessions were carrying them in Red Cross boxes. 'We've some here who are completely shaved.' One woman had lifted a sleeve to show a number tattooed on her arm; others had pieces of cloth with their numbers sewn on.

Swiss dignitaries came from Geneva, among them a woman who spoke to Loulou. 'She was very elegant. She said she was part of a delegation that had been to the camp and she talked about the charming commandant' – this was Suhren. A Swiss colonel told Loulou not to speak to the woman. 'You have friends still there. All you say to her will be transmitted to the Germans.' He told Loulou that the woman was the wife of 'some high-up person in Geneva'.

At midday the women were put on a train for France. According to the notes of the Red Cross escort, it was the same one used the previous day to take the exchanged Germans back to Germany, but no record survives of who those Germans were. We only know that they numbered 450. As only 299 French were released in return, there was plenty of room on the train, but not enough water to clean the WCs, 'which were in a lamentable state, in view of the cases of dysentery,' noted the Red Cross man.

At Berne a dying woman was taken off the train. At Annemasse, just across the border, more women were taken off the train to hospital. One of them was Zim. 'At the hospital she regained consciousness. She knew she was in France,' said Loulou, who had kept Zim's death notice and read it out: "'Mademoiselle Marie-Louise Zimberlin. Died 13.4.45." She lived two days after crossing into France. I was surprised she lived as long as she did. She was exhausted and very, very thin. But she still had her intelligence,' said Loulou. After the two days, Loulou and the others left on a train for Paris. Zim stayed in hospital in Annemasse. She wasn't married, but her sister Sophie had been alerted and was coming down from Cluny to be with her. Later Sophie wrote to Loulou, recounting Zim's last hours.

'On the morning of April 13th, I received a telegram from Annemasse saying come urgently. Marie-Louise is repatriated. We were mad with joy and made arrangements to bring her home. We received another call in the afternoon. She was not to be moved. We should go to Annemasse as it was urgent.' The trains were delayed so Sophie took a taxi. 'We drove like madmen. When I got there, I entered the room and only recognised her by the colour of her eyes. She smiled at me gently and said, "My sister is coming." I said, "Here I am. Here. It is me. Mimi." She said, "It is an angel." So I took out what I had bought for her. I had made a lemon drink with beautiful lemons. I gave her two spoons. Suddenly her eyes opened and she recognised me. "Oh my *chérie*, now I see it is you," and she took me in her thin, thin arms.'

'I told her, "I have never eaten anything or put on any clothes without thinking of you." She took my hand and looked at me. I understood that the last minute had arrived and I took my courage in two hands and pronounced the verses that came to my mind; God is love, there is no greater love than to give your life for your friends. I said the Credo. She looked at me in serenity. This lasted about ten minutes until a nurse told us that the heart was no longer beating.'

Crossing into France, the Red Cross officials told the women once again not to talk about the camp, but nothing now would stop the story from spilling out. The day the women reached the French border – 11 April 1945 – the US Third Army, commanded by General George Patton, liberated Buchenwald. It was the first camp liberated by Western Allies and Patton decided there should be no more secrets about concentration camps, calling for reporters and photographers 'to get the horrid details'.

A young American diplomat sent to report on the French Ravensbrück arrivals related those details – his shock evident in every word. He described 'a convoy of martyrs, frightfully mutilated, skeleton like – a terrifying spectacle ... The looks of pity and horror on the faces of the doctors responsible for the medical examination spoke more than all the speeches professional secrecy forbade them to make.'

The most significant account of Ravensbrück to emerge from this French convoy came from the only non-French prisoner in the group: Karolina Lanckorońska. During the negotiations on the prisoner swap, Carl Burckhardt, the ICRC chief, had again appealed to Himmler to release her, and on 2 April 1945 SS General Ernst Kaltenbrunner wrote to Burckhardt saying that Himmler had agreed on condition that the countess stay silent on the camp. Or, as Kaltenbrunner put it, 'conduct herself loyally' in respect of the Reich. Lanckorońska, however, had no intention of keeping quiet. In a twenty-two-page report written largely in the present tense, she described for Burckhardt and his Red Cross Committee exactly what she had seen, and, more important, what was still going on at Ravensbrück. In particular, she wrote of the danger still facing the Polish rabbits. 'They are under threat of death' and 'are in hiding as I write'. The rabbits 'are therefore in extreme danger and an intervention of the ICRC on their behalf is of the greatest importance'.

Karolina said that even as she was writing, the SS was clearing away the evidence of its crimes. Just before she was evacuated, she says, 'the gas chamber was dismantled and all evidence of what happened there destroyed'. She also tells the ICRC that 'A little before April 5th – the day our transport left – a machine appeared which resembled a bus and was in the forest near the camp. It was a mobile gas chamber and was painted green.'

*Chapter 39*

# Masur

In the days after the Swiss and Swedish convoys left, prisoners working outside the walls peered into the trees wondering if more White Buses would appear. None came. Instead the women saw more gassing vehicles, like the green-painted bus that Karolina Lanckorońska had described when she arrived in Switzerland.

Many women later confirmed what Karolina said on the timing of the destruction of the main gas chamber. According to Zdenka Nedvedova a group of women from Lidice were the last prisoners to be gassed there. They went to their deaths singing the Czech national anthem. 'After the gas chamber was destroyed and the place flattened, came the visit of the International Red Cross,' said Zdenka. Hanna Sturm, the Austrian carpenter, who had helped convert the shed into a gas chamber in the first place, helped dismantle it.

Suhren now knew the killing could not be finished in time. By the second week of April the Americans had reached the Elbe, seventy-seven miles west of Berlin, while the Red Army under Marshal Zhukov were massing at the Oder, ready to attack the capital from the east. On Zhukov's right flank General Rokossovsky's forces had taken Danzig and were marching west, so Suhren had perhaps a week or two to remove the evidence of extermination before Rokossovsky reached his camp.

The gassing, however – though reduced – hadn't stopped. From now on it was done in these green or black vehicles, which could be taken away when the order for evacuation came. Meanwhile, the process of clearing up accelerated. More trees were planted, more blocks painted, and pits were dug where bodies were burned because the three furnaces (and the two in Fürstenberg) could not burn them fast enough.

At the end of March and into April the clearance was done most urgently at the Youth Camp. Since the Uckermark Youth Camp first started operating as a death camp, at least 6000 women had been sent there, most of whom had been exterminated by the start of April. Arrivals had already slowed down. According to Vera Salvequart, the Youth Camp nurse, the last annihilation transport was brought here in early April. She remembers it because a Russian girl escaped, and everyone had to wait until Koehler found her. He brought her before the others and beat her to death with a piece of timber.

Selections for gassing at the Youth Camp continued, as did starvation and poisoning, but as killing was taking too long, more and more remaining prisoners were sent off to subcamps or marched back to the Ravensbrück main camp. As Neeltje Epker saw it: 'The enemy was fast approaching and they could not complete their plan.'

Many of the French at the Youth Camp had been returned to Ravensbrück over the Easter weekend. A few days later the Youth Camp guards had a bonfire of documents and logbooks. Polish prisoners in one block were told to destroy their bunks, 'which we did with enthusiasm,' said Natalia Chodkiewicz. A selection was then held and Natalia, with 200 others, was marched back to Ravensbruck. 'I stood with my eyes closed and hoped today that the black staff of the chief guard would choose me,' said the Polish woman Janina Habich. 'But at the end of the selection I was returned to Ravensbrück.'

Mary O'Shaughnessy still expected daily to be chosen. 'By this time we thought we were all going mad. All we did was wait on parade – or rather wait for orders to die.' Another mass selection was held, and the women chosen taken to be gassed, or possibly shot. But Mary O'Shaughnessy was selected to return to the main camp. In the end her false arm had proved irrelevant to her selection for life or death, as all that the selectors were interested in was the state of the women's legs.

As Mary lined up to walk back, Ruth Neudeck passed by and struck her across the mouth with her silver-handled riding crop. 'There was no reason. Two of my teeth had already been knocked out.' With a group of about 200 she headed back through the woods towards Ravensbrück, still bleeding from her mouth.

Numbers at the Youth Camp now rapidly thinned out and prisoners from the male camp were sent in to clear up more of the evidence. They burned rotting bodies and turned the starvation room in the *Revier* back into a normal day room.

Before Auschwitz was evacuated in January 1945, the SS had gone round shooting any Kapos who might have evidence of what had happened. All of the *Sonderkommando* – those prisoners who had worked in the Auschwitz gas chambers and the crematorium – were to be executed. Just before their execution, the

Auschwitz *Sonderkommando* had revolted. Though the revolt was put down, several men had escaped. Presumably to forestall any similar rebellion here, the eleven men who had worked in the Ravensbrück crematorium and gas chamber were taken to the camp bunker in early April and locked up. Also in early April, Vera Salvequart, the Youth Camp nurse, learned that she was to be shot.

Salvequart said later that it was Rapp who told her first that she would 'never get out alive'. It was probably after this that her behaviour changed. She was almost certainly under instructions to poison all those who remained in the *Revier*. Instead she was kind to them and tried to save some of them.

'When the first warm rays of the sun appeared Vera told sick people that they could go outside into the sun, and she arranged for the TB patients to be carried out,' said Irène Ottelard. 'She even went for walks with the patients, without the SS guards.' Many prisoners appreciated Vera's 'kindness', and on her birthday – 12 April – they gave her presents. By now Salvequart had a number of prisoners helping her in various ways; a Frau Schaper was her dressmaker.

'She invited people into her room and gave them bread and honey from her parcels,' said Irène – but this time there was no white powder in the sandwiches. In desperation, Gisela Krüger told Salvequart one day, 'If this fear and hunger doesn't stop soon, it's best to take the powder,' but Salvequart refused to kill her, saying: 'You can still have it, but you love life.' According to Gisela, Frau Schaper was to have been given the powder before the end, but she hadn't finished making Vera's clothes, so she was spared.

Salvequart also saved prisoners from death by swapping names on the death list. 'I must say that the behaviour of Vera Salvequart was a paradox,' said Irène. 'She did save some women, but she killed a large number too.' To save someone, she would replace the intended victim's name with the name of someone who had already died. Later she would claim she saved scores of women in this way, but Gisela Krüger said it was more like four or five.

Salvequart's own descriptions of her last days in the Youth Camp came in three rambling depositions made in 1946 before an assiduous British war crimes hunter called Charles Kaiser. An Austrian Jew who had parachuted behind the lines for SOE, Kaiser was renowned for getting his subjects to talk. Salvequart told him that towards the end, pregnant women were brought to the Youth Camp *Revier* to give birth. The women were mostly Jewish prisoners and their babies were killed by Rapp. Vera tried to save them, she said, by hiding them in the washroom. Some she adopted for herself and tried to raise, including 'the child of a Jewess called Weinert – a boy – which I brought up secretly'.

She received food for the baby from a prisoner in the male camp called Franz Eigenbrodt. Salvequart had struck up a friendship with Eigenbrodt when he came with one of the work gangs to carry out repairs. The existence of the baby became known in the male camp, and other male prisoners smuggled milk for the child. 'But Neudeck took the child away from me and threw it on the food wagon like a parcel of cloth. The wagon was dirty with spilt food. She also said to me: "A little Jew will be a very big Jew one day."' Salvequart told Kaiser that after this, she tried to poison Neudeck. The chief guard came to her complaining of a headache, and so she gave her the white powder, but Neudeck took too little to kill her.

After the killing of the Weinert baby all the babies born in Vera's *Revier* were taken away by Koehler, Rapp's colleague. Salvequart said she knew her days were numbered by then, as Rapp was following her around, saying that the *Oberschwester* suspected her of tampering with the death lists.

On one occasion, she said, a list of 180 women had been selected to go on a work transport to Belsen, but as the train lines were destroyed they were to be shot in the head instead. She took the chance to switch several names on the list with prisoners who were already dead, and as a result was called before *Oberschwester* Marschall and Dr Trommer to explain herself. They suspected Salvequart of keeping the original lists, which had their signatures on and would therefore incriminate them, so they ordered her to hand over the originals. It was at this point that she overheard Trommer saying, 'This woman mustn't fall into enemy hands,' and decided to escape.

A further horror strengthened her resolve. According to Salvequart a group of fourteen Polish nuns arrived at the Youth Camp in the final days. One of them was a Mother Superior called Isabella Mozynska. Salvequart told Kaiser that she remembered the name because the Mother Superior had asked for some tablets for her nuns, who were suffering from diarrhoea. Vera gave them the tablets and told them not to come to the *Revier* again, it was too dangerous. The Mother Superior thanked her and gave her a medallion, saying: 'May God protect you.' Vera told Kaiser that she had put the medallion on a necklace, which he could look at, if he liked, as it was in the personal effects safe of the Hamburg prison.

Next day when she was in one of the *Revier* rooms, sorting out gold teeth, Rapp and Koehler came in drunk.

> Rapp left the room and Koehler, who was very drunk, came over and tried to kiss me. I resisted, he ... threw me on an examination bed and tried to rape me. I resisted with all my force, and bit and scratched and kicked him with my feet. I kicked him in the abdomen, which must have hurt a lot as he fled into a corner of the room.

Salvequart escaped from the room and told one of the women guards, Erna Kube, what had happened. Kube was about to take a pile of lice-infested clothes to Ravensbrück for washing, so Salvequart asked her if she would take her too. While this conversation was going on, Rapp had fetched the fourteen nuns and brought them into a disused kitchen near the *Revier*.

> Suddenly we heard shots. When I was walking away with Kube I was called back by Rapp. He ordered me to bring the teeth pliers into the kitchen. When I entered the kitchen I saw a horrible picture. Some of the nuns were dead and some were severely injured by the shots and in great pain. I still remember the horrible picture of a nun whose eyes were shot out.

Vera ran out to join the guard, Kube, and the two of them went back to Ravensbrück, where Salvequart hid in a hospital block for two days until someone gave her away to Koehler. 'I was just lifting a corpse when Koehler came in, so I jumped out a window.' Prisoners helped her to hide, first in the rabbit hutches and then in Block 19, where the Swiss-American Blockova Ann Seymour Sheridan kept her in the roofspace. Salvequart gave Ann a sample of the white powder to smuggle out and asked her to give it as evidence to the Allies. An analysis of the sample – a cyanide poison – was presented to the Hamburg court.

Both Koehler and Rapp were now pursuing Salvequart. Koehler found her first and took her back to the Youth Camp. He was worried about the attempted rape. 'Koehler was terribly afraid that I had reported the matter to Schwarzhuber, as he asked me immediately whether I had seen Schwarzhuber and tried to apologise to me, saying he was drunk.' Again she escaped Koehler's clutches, this time by fleeing to the men's camp. Her friend Eigenbrodt had managed to smuggle some men's clothes to her through a group of male prisoners who were cleaning drains at the Youth Camp, so Salvequart got out disguised as a drainage worker.

Asked by Kaiser if she knew what happened to Koehler and Rapp, Salvequart said she'd heard Koehler was hanged by prisoners before the liberation, but she didn't know about Rapp. Asked what happened over the murdered Polish nuns, Salvequart said she'd heard that Ruth Neudeck 'dealt with it'.

Dealing with the murdered nuns must have been one of Neudeck's final tasks at the Youth Camp, because when the last of the prisoners had been killed, or had returned to the main Ravensbrück camp, the extermination annex was closed. Neudeck was promoted and sent to run the subcamp at Barth. Salvequart continued to hide out in the male camp, disguised as a male prisoner, awaiting the liberation.

The Uckermark Youth Camp prisoners who started arriving back at Ravensbrück, probably in late March, were greeted as if they'd returned from the hereafter. Some were shepherded into the *Revier* and cared for by friends. Irène Ottelard, who weighed just 29 kilos on return, wrote later: 'I would never have believed that I could experience such joy at seeing Ravensbrück again. And when I found myself in the hands of a French woman doctor it was like heaven.'

Others were not as lucky. Mary O'Shaughnessy was marched straight to the mayhem of the death-zone blocks behind the wire. Conditions were little better than at the Youth Camp, though she was glad to have a blanket. Youth Camp killing methods were being used here too. In early April hundreds of women suffering from dysentery were taken to Block 22, to be locked in for three days and three nights without food or water and with no means of relieving themselves, obviously in the expectation that they'd die. Julia Barry, the British camp policewoman, tried to get inside the death block, as one of the women taken there was her husband's aunt, who had come from Hungary in December. Mary was not allowed inside, 'but I did see through a door, bodies piled up on top of another, perhaps as many as thirty. I particularly noticed one corpse of which the eyes were hanging out of the sockets, which I believe was due to rats with which the block was infested.'

Mary O'Shaughnessy soon found herself facing Winkelmann again. The 1500 sick and dying women in her block were ordered to strip to the waist and run past him. As her false arm was exposed, she thought she was now bound to be selected, but at the last minute she was rescued by her Blockova, Ann Sheridan. Seeing the threat, Ann managed to bring Mary indoors after the count, along with several others, and hide them under a bed at the back of the block. 'This selection happened three times, and on each occasion I was able to avoid it with the help of Ann Seymour Sheridan,' said Mary O'Shaughnessy in her post-war testimony.

Once back in the main camp, Youth Camp survivors were also hunted by the 'cattle merchant', Pflaum, who was determined to send them off to the subcamps, no matter how near death they were. The Dutch midwife Neeltje Epker recorded that twenty-five of the seventy-nine Dutch survivors of the Youth Camp were put on a transport to a subcamp; seventeen were so weak that they died on the journey.

The roundups had by now assumed 'a tragicomic' form, observed Maria Moldenhawer. 'Pflaum would personally enter blocks and look under beds or climb up onto the highest bunks, while everyone who could would hide, and Winkelmann would come and look at women's legs.' Anna Hand, the Austrian camp secretary, saw Pflaum in the labour office at this time and observed that he was now 'permanently drunk'. She watched him ride through the camp on his bicycle with women scattering as they saw him coming.

The ordinary SS were seen about far less by now. 'They weren't idiots,' said Violette Lecoq. 'They knew the end was coming.' But Pflaum's 'special posse', SS men with revolvers and riding crops, were always present and would surround blocks day or night and take away entire columns of women to a subcamp as they were heading off for work. Whether they got there alive no longer mattered as long as they were sent somewhere to get them out of the camp. Hitler's orders had been reiterated to Suhren: not one prisoner must fall into Russian hands.

As the fronts advanced, Suhren's choice of subcamps to send his women to was dwindling by the day. They fell into an ever-shrinking band as the Red Army moved forward to the east, the British to the northwest and the Americans to the southwest.

On 15 April Belsen ceased to be an option for Ravensbrück's evacuees as British forces reached the camp, uncovering unimaginable horror. By this time the Americans were forming bridgeheads across the Elbe and air attacks intensified, so that any prisoners packed off in trucks or trains were almost certain to be hit. Even if women reached a subcamp alive they would starve as food supplies were cut off. The Polish woman Janina Habich, and 150 others, arrived back from the Youth Camp to spend three days digging a trench around Ravensbrück before being loaded onto trucks for a two-day journey, dodging Allied bombs on their way to the salt mines at Berndorf. Here they were set to work 200 metres underground making V2 rocket parts. 'In those first April days 140 of us women were held here for ten days and given only rotting carrots and turnips to eat.'

Eva Fejer, the Hungarian teenager, was sent to work in a factory on the southern edge of Berlin. When it was bombed the prisoners were sent to clear up, 'but we hid in the latrines instead'. Here they overheard the SS discussing whether to blow the whole place up, prisoners and all, but instead they marched them back into Berlin. 'They put us on the underground and we saw all the names of the stations that we knew from children's books, and the guards said: "Stay with us or you'll be spotted." Some escaped, but I didn't dare. I thought, if I've got this far I'll not jeopardise it now.' They were put on a train to Oranienburg, on the northern edge of Berlin, and taken to Sachsenhausen concentration camp.

> We were taken to the baths and led inside stark-naked. I don't know how long we were left there. I remember a child started screaming and I never saw her again. I sat with my head in my hands, thinking – whatever happens let it happen quickly – and the SS man came and opened the door. He shouted '*Raus, raus*' and we were loaded into a truck and taken to a proper bath and given a wash. We were loaded into another truck and taken back to Ravensbrück and we saw lots of commotion and bits of furniture being packed and were given Canadian five-kilogram parcels.

Women were moved out to Malchow, Barth and Torgau, three subcamps that lay furthest from the advancing fronts, but even as the trucks were leaving, prisoners from other camps, newly overrun, were brought back to

Ravensbrück. Many recalled the return by truck from Rechlin, the punishment camp 50 kilometres northwest of Ravensbrück. Hermine Salvine, the office secretary, said:

> On the lorry were lying dead bodies, dying and living prisoners all mixed up together. They were unloaded, reloaded and taken out through the gates. This happened late in the evening. All night the crematorium chimney smoked. In the morning when I had to write the daily strength return [prisoner count] I learned that they were all dead.

Evacuation transports were the new way to kill. Trains were crisscrossing, circling and doubling back between the ever-fewer camps and subcamps as yet out of reach of the Allies. Isabelle Donner had reached Ravensbrück by cattle truck from Budapest in December 1944 and was sent west by open rail wagon to a work camp at Dachau in February 1945. 'The train was bombed and two wagons had their tops blown off – there were many dead.' The group was taken off the train and marched north, and came under attack from the air, but they marched on west, away from the Soviet front. Helen Gaweda, a Pole, had marched from Auschwitz to Ravensbrück in December 1944, and was trucked out to the Malchow subcamp north of Ravensbrück in February 1945. In April 1945 she was evacuated south by train to Leipzig, and then again on foot, ahead of the advancing US and Russian troops.

Krystyna Dąbrówska, the seventeen-year-old from Warsaw, was evacuated from a subcamp near Hamburg as the British advanced and put on a train south to Leipzig. She sat on an open cattle truck, next to a wagon crammed with ammunition.

> As the Allied planes were flying over we looked up and we thought our friends will see us in these open wagons – the American pilots won't drop their bombs on us, but they did and our train was bombed as well as the ammunition train. There were so many dead nobody could count them. I remember seeing women still conscious with no legs. There was nothing anyone could do. We tried to run away but were brought back and marched back to another train.

Rosza Nagy, her younger sister Marianne and their mother Margit had marched almost all the way from Budapest to Ravensbrück in October 1944 and stayed together at the camp until January 1945, when the two girls were sent to a subcamp at Chemnitz, near the Czech border, leaving their mother behind.

'When Mother saw us go she didn't cry,' said Rosza. 'She just said: "Stay together, girls, and you'll be all right."' In mid-April, as the Russians approached from the east and the Americans from the west, they were put in closed cattle wagons bound for Mauthausen, a journey that took them directly between the Russian and American fronts.

'It was quite dark in the wagon and we had no food. We sat packed together, sixty to a wagon, like this' – Rosza folded her knees up to her chest.

> It was completely dark all the time but I held my sister's hand. Mother had told us never to let go of each other's hands. Then people gave up, and they started to die. So we tried to pile them up in one corner of the wagon. We could hear the cannons while we went along. We thought this was probably Dresden they were bombing, as we must have been close. We didn't know if it was the Russians or not.

After a few days many more people started to give up, and Rosza tried to urge her fellow passengers to hold on.

> I said we are going to stay alive. We are soon going to be free. I tried to talk to them to give them strength. But they didn't want to live any more. My sister gave up. She was only twenty and she was not as strong as me. I was sporty and went cycling and played tennis. My sister was a cellist and had a beautiful voice, but on the train she lost her strength.

After a week in the darkness of the wagon, the train started to pass through Czechoslovakia. Then it slowed and pulled to a stop. The doors were thrown open.

> There were people outside wanting to help. It was the Czech Red Cross but we couldn't get out. Eventually we crawled out on hands and knees, as we couldn't stand, and we crawled onto a field of grass so we ate the grass. In the wagon behind us were the dead people and they took them out.
>
> It was wonderful for a moment because we could breathe. And the sunlight was so bright it dazzled us. It was wonderful to see the light. When they opened the door it was like a miracle.

The women were ordered back in and the train moved on for another week. On arrival at Mauthausen more than half the passengers were dead. The living were herded into a tent. Rosza's sister Marianne died at Mauthausen two days later.

At Ravensbrück they all knew the final act was coming. On 12 April the Siemens women had been confined to their barracks. Two days later the Ravensbrück plant was emptied, the last prisoners marched to the main camp ready for evacuation, and all Siemens equipment loaded on barges and sent away out of the line of fire.

Some in the camp still hoped the Americans would reach Berlin – and therefore perhaps Ravensbrück – first. They weren't to know that on 15 April Eisenhower had told his stunned commanders at the Elbe bridgeheads to stand fast. Contrary to all expectations, the Supreme Allied Commander had decided to allow Stalin's forces alone to take Berlin.

At 3 a.m. on 16 April the Soviets' final thrust towards the capital began with a massive attack on the so-called Gates of Berlin – the Seelow Heights, fifty miles to the east – and such was the extraordinary firepower that the rumbling was heard even at Ravensbrück. That morning, the camp's selections for the gassing vans continued, and 'old rats' still filled in prisoners' names on transport lists as usual, but two days later, as news came that German resistance at Seelow had collapsed, the *Schreibstube* staff were told to burn the lists instead.

New orders had come through to destroy the most incriminating evidence of all – the prisoners' files, and with them all trace of every order that had ever been issued at Ravensbrück. At first the prisoners were ordered to form a human chain stretching from the camp offices to the crematorium, boxes of documents passed from hand to hand and into the furnace.

The guard in charge of the camp library, Irmgard Schröers, burned all the Nazi texts as well. She explained to her assistant, a Polish prisoner: 'Times have changed and the Germans will have to adjust to other people. You are going to be free and I am going to be locked up. Apparently that is how it must be.'

The *Effektenkammer* staff had been ordered to clear out evidence too. Prisoners' valuables – wedding rings, photographs, letters, carefully labelled and stored under lock and key since the earliest days of the camp – were now removed, loaded onto trucks and sent away. Suhren revealed later that the valuables were shipped first to Fortress Doemitz on the River Elbe, but as the Americans advanced they were moved again and 'stored in the vicinity of a youth hostel' – though whether the valuables ever arrived there, and what became of them, nobody ever knew.

In their blocks, the Red Army women were making preparations for the Soviets to arrive – preparing reports on the camp, drawing maps of the area, anything that might be of use to their Soviet liberators. Irma Dola had a brother fighting with Rokossovsky's army, who said he'd be there in days and he'd sort the SS out. Antonina Nikiforova was talking about making a film of it all after the war.

Recriminations broke out. The head camp policewoman, Elisabeth Thury, was accused by some of sucking up to the Red Army women now that their victory was assured. Blockovas who had been too close to the SS were carefully watched by other prisoners, and if necessary cut down to size. A new woman guard arrived, called Zetterman. She'd been transferred back to Ravensbrück from Belsen just before the British arrived. Zetterman roamed around Ravensbrück with a revolver, kicking and hitting, and threatening the women that she'd use her Belsen methods on them. The prisoners asked, 'But what will you do when you lose the war?', at which she scoffed and said she'd 'know to shoot herself' and roamed around and kicked and hit out some more.

Most guards talked not of revenge but of how they were going to get home. Rucksacks were the most wanted items in the camp, and the guards were willing to pay prisoners – who'd been making their own – in bread or potatoes to get their hands on one. They were also keen to bargain for a share of the prisoners' Red Cross parcels. The food in the staff canteen had been thin pickings of late, and now in the second and third weeks of April thousands of bulging five-kilo food parcels started arriving at the camp from the Canadian Red Cross, full of chocolate and jams, sausage and tinned meat. The parcels were designated for the French, the Jews and the Poles.

But whereas the SS had always felt at liberty to rifle prisoners' parcels, this seemed no longer to apply. Suhren was suddenly checking receipts, and a negotiation began between prisoners and SS about how the parcel contents should be divided up. The Poles, for example, were told that as long as they signed a receipt saying they had received their parcel, they could each receive one fifth – or else they'd get nothing at all. They debated the offer, and after several hours turned it down. Meanwhile the rabbits were offered an entire five-kilo parcel each, but only because Suhren was trying to buy them off. When they heard their compatriots were being cheated, the rabbits refused the parcels entirely. 'So that's what thanks I get for making sure the rabbits get their parcels,' Suhren was heard to say. Nevertheless the contents of the parcels found their way to some prisoners. 'We even stole back the cigarettes the SS had stolen from the parcels, so everyone was walking down the Lagerstrasse busily puffing away,' said Zofia Sokulska.

On 14 April Marie-Claude Vaillant-Couturier noted in her diary a conversation in which the *Oberschwester* reprimanded a nurse for stealing butter and chocolate from a prisoner parcel. The next day she noted that Dorothea Binz had shown concern for a Jewish prisoner. The chief guard had asked a Stubova why it was that the Jewish woman looked so pale and sick. 'The Stubova replied that the women had recently come back from the Youth Camp and now worked every day in the sand, to which Binz replied: "But that's a scandal, to make a woman work in a state like that; she must rest in her block." ' 'What a difference the advancing front can make,' observed Marie-Claude.

Trucks were still returning from subcamps with exhausted prisoners and bodies to be burned. Now rumours spread that charges had been placed all around the camp. Explosions could already be heard nearby as the SS blew up its installations in the area. Numbers on the Lagerstrasse were fast thinning out. On 15 April Gemma La Guardia Gluck was called to see Fritz Suhren and told she was being freed. On 19 April a group of fifty prisoners – mostly Germans – were rounded up to be shot. Hermine Salvini, the prisoner secretary, filled in the forms and remembers that they were mostly German criminals and asocials, as well as Russians. 'One was a woman with typhus who was brought from the *Revier* and carried on a stretcher. Most of those prisoners had been in the camp for many years.'

A few days later, Hermine herself and 500 privileged German prisoners were marched to the gates and set free. Grete Buber-Neumann was amongst them. Before she left, Grete gave a note to her friend Germaine Tillion, containing a list of dead prisoners, and she asked Germaine to give the list to the Allies if she got out. As Germaine and her friend Anise were both NN, they had not been allowed to go with the 299 French women who left for Switzerland. Nevertheless Grete had hopes that they would get out; she had heard from contacts in the offices that more Red Cross buses were on their way. There was also talk in the offices that a young German officer had entered the camp and an argument had broken out with the commandant in front of the other guards.

The officer seen arguing with Suhren was Franz Göring, Walter Schellenberg's man. Göring was one of only four people in Himmler's circle who on the night of 21 April had learned of a third secret meeting between Count Bernadotte and Himmler, during which Himmler agreed to release thousands more Ravensbrück women to the Swedish Red Cross. Straight after the meeting Göring was told to tell Suhren to start organising the releases, but when Göring arrived at the camp, Suhren refused.

The latest meeting between Himmler and Bernadotte had come about after renewed diplomatic contacts between Swedish officials and Himmler's aides. Outwardly Himmler had continued to display absolute loyalty to Hitler, but those around him were hoping that in these last days he would finally break his bond. With this in mind, Schellenberg had been desperately trying to keep channels open to the West, telling the Swedes once again that the Reichsführer SS would soon be ready to negotiate a separate peace. Schellenberg also kept the Swedes interested by hints of further concessions on prisoners.

Felix Kersten, meanwhile, was telling contacts in Stockholm a similar story, and was even boasting that he had won a written assurance from Himmler that he would stop all future evacuations and put a halt to the death marches. Himmler had given Kersten an assurance – so the masseur claimed – that from now on prisoners in the camps would be kept in place ready for an 'orderly evacuation' by the Allies. And he went further: Himmler was even ready to help the Jews. Kersten now made an astonishing proposal. He suggested to the Swedes that a meeting be set up between the Reichsführer and a senior Jewish representative to discuss Jewish releases.

Although Kersten claimed later that the idea of a meeting between Himmler and a Jewish representative was his own, the Swedes understood perfectly well that Kersten would not have seriously suggested it without a strong indication from Himmler that he should. It was therefore taken seriously in Stockholm from the start.

Himmler's motive in all this was, as always, clear: even now, as the Third Reich crumbled, he still clung to the extraordinary hope that the Allies might see him as a man they could deal with, once the Führer had gone. At this eleventh hour Himmler had a great deal to lose, but by making even more concessions, he still fantasised that he had something to gain. He was therefore manoeuvring more desperately than ever to present a reasonable face, even to the extent of offering to negotiate with a representative of the race he had tried to annihilate.

Talk of such overtures had spread fast from Stockholm to Jewish leaders abroad, who were piling ever greater pressure on Sweden to grab what chance it could to get more people out. The route to the south from Switzerland to Ravensbrück was now cut off, which meant the Swiss could not return, so the French were also pressing the Swedes even harder to take action, particularly after the appalling scenes uncovered at Belsen. The descriptions of dead women at Belsen – many of whom had been taken there from Ravensbrück – were some of the most disturbing. A British medical officer had seen 'The unclothed bodies of women in a pile 60 to 80 yards long, 30 yards wide and four feet high, within sight of children. Gutters were filled with dead. Men had gone to the gutters to die. Thousands were dying of typhus, TB and dysentery.' Cannibalism was reported too. 'There was no flesh on the bodies but the liver, kidneys and heart were cut out.'

For the Allied leadership, these latest horrors had caused great shock. At least a million prisoners were thought to be still alive in Hitler's concentration camps in April 1945, all threatened with massacre in the last days, and most dying the same horrible deaths already exposed at Belsen and Buchenwald. Nevertheless, apart from limited commando missions, no serious attempt to rescue or protect remaining prisoners was considered. The risk to Allied soldiers' lives was too high and, militarily, a rescue was deemed impossible. Eisenhower's decision not to move his men beyond the Elbe – taken largely to keep US soldiers out of the final battle – meant the camps were out of reach even for airborne operations.

Nor did the Allies, even after Belsen, consider giving assistance to Bernadotte, and were continuing to refuse safe passage to the white buses. The hands-off approach to Stockholm was due in part to fears that Stalin would suspect a backroom stitch-up if he heard of Allied dealings with the Swedes, but more important was the need to stay focused on winning the war. On his last visit, Bernadotte himself was fired on by Allied planes and had to dive out of his vehicle into a ditch. For the White Buses on the ground the situation was now doubly dangerous, as the Germans had started to camouflage their vehicles with white paint and red crosses. One White Bus had been strafed by a British fighter, killing a Swede and a Dane. When the Swedes protested to the Allies, the response in London was that the deaths were 'unfortunate', but planes flying at 400 miles per hour couldn't see the Red Cross markings. 'It is clear the Swedes don't understand what modern war is like.'

The Swedish government, however, was not deterred. If offers of more prisoners were to materialise out of the mounting chaos, somebody must be in place to take them, and nobody was better equipped than Bernadotte. A two-pronged strategy was therefore agreed in Stockholm: first, to pursue Kersten's plan for a meeting between Himmler and a Jewish leader, and second, to send Bernadotte back to Germany to track down Himmler in the burning wreckage of Berlin.

According to Bernadotte's memoir, he left Stockholm on this occasion intending, for the first time since his mission began, to push Himmler for the release of non-Scandinavians, including non-Scandinavian Jews. How exactly the Swedes decided their priorities for Bernadotte's mission is not clear from their records, or from Bernadotte's memoir. However, we do know that Jewish organisations, as well as the French and others, had been piling ever greater pressure on the Swedes to widen their remit.

Bernadotte was heading into a country in total turmoil, where communications were largely severed and the situation on the ground was changing by the hour. Amid these chaotic events it was clear to him that, whatever his brief, his only realistic objective was to find Himmler in the rubble, then roll the dice as best he could and get as many prisoners out as possible. The Russians were days away from Berlin, and this would surely be his last meeting with the Reichsführer SS.

Flying into the German capital was already almost impossible, so Bernadotte took a night train to Malmö, then the ferry to Copenhagen, and made his way down to the Swedish Red Cross base on the Danish-German border. Here he stopped off for a briefing by leaders of his White Bus mission, and heard that all links with the south of Germany were already cut off. On their last trip south to Theresienstadt, on 15 April, the Swedish buses had rescued 450 Danish Jews, but it was touch and go if they would get back, so fast were the fronts closing in. Now all of the 4200 Scandinavians rescued over the past six weeks were to be transported over the Danish border by an armada of vehicles sent by Denmark 'Dunkirk-style', including ninety-four buses, ambulances, motor cycles and trucks, as well as ten ten-ton fish vans.

Once this evacuation was complete the Swedes were planning to pack up and go home, as the possibility of further rescue seemed slim. Even the road east to Ravensbrück would not be open for long.

Bernadotte left at once for Berlin, arriving early on 20 April. There was a lull in the bombing, and as the count was driven to the Swedish legation he found a silent smouldering city. Sheltering in the legation cellars, he made contact with Schellenberg and requested an urgent meeting with Himmler, but Himmler was not to be found. He was in fact at a reception in the Führer's bunker congratulating Hitler on his birthday, along with Göring and Goebbels and others of the inner circle. Bernadotte waited. There were more air raids. The birthday reception was over, but now Himmler and the others were deep in conference with the Führer, discussing what was to be done when all land routes south were severed, which would happen any hour. Hitler should get out while he still could, said those with him, but still he refused.

Bernadotte, still waiting, received another message from Schellenberg: Himmler would see him that night at Hohenlychen. He took the legation car and headed north. The journey was slow, as refugees fled west and filled the road.

After some two hours Bernadotte passed once again close to Ravensbrück. With the Russian guns now clearly audible, and Katyushas lighting up the sky to the east, it must have occurred to him that the women's concentration camp was now the most vulnerable of all. He knew that any new concessions to be won from Himmler were likely to centre on Ravensbrück, not least because it was now almost the only camp his White Buses could still reach. Any rescues feasible at Mauthausen or Theresienstadt, both also yet to be overrun, would have to be made by the Swiss, to the south.

But what Bernadotte felt he could achieve, now that he was on his way to see Himmler for the third time, is hard to say: the evidence from Bernadotte himself is contradictory. The fact that during his stopover at the Danish border he had allowed several of his White Bus convoys to start heading home suggests that he did not expect a lot. He said later that he had sensed something significant was coming, but 'nothing as momentous as what happened'.

At Hohenlychen there was still no Himmler. Instead, Karl Gebhardt again welcomed Bernadotte. The two had dinner, which Bernadotte later described as perfectly convivial, suggesting that even as he wrote (a month after the war) he had no inkling of Gebhardt's own crimes. After dinner Himmler had still not appeared, so Gebhardt showed Bernadotte around the clinic, which was now packed with wounded soldiers from the eastern front. 'Professor Gebhardt even invited me to be present as some German soldiers were operated on,' wrote Bernadotte.

A message then came through that Himmler was even further delayed and would not be there until six in the morning. So with air raids sounding, Bernadotte turned in for the night.

After leaving the Führer's birthday party, and before seeing Bernadotte at Hohenlychen, Himmler had decided to stop off for another meeting at an estate close to Hohenlychen called Gut Hartzwalde. This was the estate that Himmler had given to Felix Kersten, his masseur. Here Kersten was also waiting to see the Reichsführer and to introduce him to another possible bridge to the Western Allies, a German Jew called Norbert Masur, who was a representative in Sweden of the World Jewish Congress.

In the past few days the parallel negotiations involving Kersten as intermediary had come to fruition. Himmler had given Kersten the go-ahead to set up a meeting at Gut Hartzwalde between him and a Jewish interlocutor whose personal safety while in Germany the Reichsführer SS had guaranteed. Himmler had even convinced Kersten that he was 'prepared to bury the hatchet with the Jews'.

While waiting for Himmler, Masur talked to Schellenberg and others in Himmler's entourage, finding 'these gentlemen', as he called them, 'courteous and ready to help'; he was particularly impressed by Franz Göring, Schellenberg's assistant, who was 'very efficient'. Masur formed the view that the men working for Himmler would try to help implement any agreement. 'We are definitely of the opinion that they will not carry out possible orders from Himmler regarding more acts of violence,' wrote Masur. 'They declare that they quite understand that every outrage – even against Jews – is a crime against the future Germany.' They were also, he noted, 'young men who wanted to live', and would therefore behave accordingly.

Masur's comments are contained in a report of his meeting with Himmler that he wrote for the Swedish government the very next day, and which is therefore remarkably fresh and almost contemporaneous.

At two in the morning Himmler appeared, 'impeccably dressed in a spotless uniform, and with decorations prominently displayed'. His manner was 'calm and self-controlled'. Masur was relieved to be greeted with a '*Guten Tag*' instead of '*Heil Hitler!*', and the small group sat down to tea and cakes, brought from Sweden.

Himmler then launched into a long monologue, reviewing Germany's history and rationalising the policy of 'driving out the Jews', though not, it seems, touching on their extermination. At one point he attacked the 'lies' told about Belsen. The foreign press had been 'mud-slinging', he complained; the crematoria at Belsen were built to help wipe out epidemics, not to commit mass murder.

Masur chose his moment to give Himmler a list of names of specific prisoners whose release was demanded by prominent Jewish families, but who, he must have known, were almost certainly dead by now, or would not be found in the mayhem of the camps. Masur called for a halt to more Jewish evacuations from the camps and good treatment for those remaining. In response, as Masur reported it, Himmler said that 'no more Jews were to be shot' and 'all evacuations to halt'.

Himmler then made another more specific offer – one that nobody had expected: he proposed the release of 1000 Jewish women from Ravensbrück 'as long as they were immediately fetched by the Red Cross'. The offer took Masur aback. Himmler's word was of course 'absolutely unreliable', he commented in his report the next day, and he was well aware that 'at the last moment there could be an order for the mass murder of all Jews'. Masur added: 'The danger for non-Jews is considerably less, and it is hardly probable that any Nazi leader would dare to give an order to mass murder non-Jews belonging to any of the enemy countries of Germany.'

Masur thought it was possible that Himmler 'really did want to do something at the last moment, and therefore I think he will give the promised orders'. On the offer to spare 1000 Ravensbrück Jews, Masur had particular reason to think it would happen, because the 'efficient' Franz Göring had already told him it would. Göring was already 'working on arrangements', Masur reported, and the women could be in Sweden within three days.

Himmler left Gut Hartzwalde just before dawn, telling his driver to take him on to Hohenlychen, where at 6 a.m. he sat down to breakfast with Bernadotte. According to Bernadotte, Himmler now seemed 'very tired and weary'. He couldn't sit still and kept 'tapping his teeth' – a sure sign, or so Bernadotte had been told by Schellenberg, that he was nervous.

Once more the discussions centred on the release of prisoners. After Bernadotte sought more concessions on the Scandinavians, Ravensbrück was back on the table. Bernadotte presented his proposal for the release of French women, and Himmler not only instantly agreed, but said that Bernadotte could 'take all nationalities'.

Himmler had just massively increased the offer he had made a few hours earlier to Masur. Bernadotte could send his White Buses to collect all the remaining prisoners of Ravensbrück – Jews and non-Jews – he declared. All of this was possible, said Himmler, simply 'because the camp was about to be evacuated'.

Himmler then left and Bernadotte headed off to his mission's HQ at Friedrichsruhe to try to stop the White Buses from leaving for home. The Swedish mission was about to become the biggest prisoner rescue of the Second World War.

*Chapter 40*

# White Buses

Franz Göring, not Bernadotte, delivered the message to the Swedish drivers first. He had signalled to the Gestapo men on board the buses, just as they were about to cross the Danish border, ordering them to turn round and head to Ravensbrück because there was more work to be done. Göring, still in Berlin, then set out to reach the camp himself. According to his account, given to British intelligence after the war, he left Berlin 'at the last minute' on the evening of 21 April as the Russians were fighting their way in. On his drive north further instructions reached him from Schellenberg that on arrival at Ravensbrück he was to 'inform the camp commandant of Himmler's decision and to make preparations for the removal of the women'. Schellenberg told Göring 'the transfers were to be continued on the largest possible scale, even if there were orders to the contrary'. He found instead that it was Hitler's orders Suhren was following.

At about midday on 22 April, Göring drove up to the Ravensbrück gates. There followed an immediate and 'fairly long' discussion during which Suhren showed a 'negative attitude towards the release of the detainees' and refused even to tell him how many women were in the camp, claiming he had 'destroyed documents and registries on orders of the Führer'.

It was clearly understood that the German prisoners, along with the Italians, Russians and other East European prisoners, were not included in the Swedish rescue deal, so Göring was less concerned about those. But to plan the transports he needed to know precisely how many Western prisoners there were, and Suhren would not tell him. The commandant was 'vague' about numbers, and 'avoided the question', eventually saying there were about 9000 Poles, 1500 French, Belgian and Dutch and about 3000 'Jewesses', though Suhren knew there were many more.

Suhren was particularly evasive when asked about two French women, a Madame Buteau and a Madame del Marmol, both Jews from Masur's special list. 'When I explained that Himmler was particularly interested in these persons, and had already ordered their release, Suhren became very nervous and after another half an hour told me that both had died in the camp a few weeks ago.' Göring tried to make his own arrangements for the rescue, but the commandant refused to cooperate. When Göring asked why not, Suhren replied that he was following orders from the Führer, not to let the women leave the camp.

Exasperated, Göring managed to get through to Karl Brandt, Himmler's personal secretary, asking for Himmler to intervene. A short time later Brandt called back, telling Suhren that Himmler's orders were to set the prisoners free. Suhren now turned to Göring. 'Suhren told me, between ourselves, that he no longer knew where he stood, for he had received the express order from the Führer, via Kaltenbrunner, to keep the prisoners in the camp and on the approach of enemy troops to liquidate them all.'

Suhren 'became very uncertain' and confided to Göring 'amongst other things' that he had another dilemma. Also in the camp, he said, was a special group of prisoners whom he was under express orders to kill. The women – fifty-four Polish and seventeen French – had had 'experiments made on them'. Suhren was referring to the rabbits, though who the French were is not known. Karl Gebhardt had ordered the rabbits' murder some weeks ago, but Suhren had not yet obeyed. Göring asked what sort of experiments they were, and Suhren told him the women had been subject to bone and muscle experiments and had been injected with bacteria.

Göring said later he could hardly believe it. 'I thereupon had two women brought before me to get proof of this affair.' Having seen the scarred legs of the two women – Jadwiga Kamińska and Zofia Baj – he told Suhren he was under no circumstances to kill them 'until a decision from Himmler was to hand'. Göring claimed later not to have known that it was Himmler who had ordered the experiments in the first place.

In any case, after seeing the women he called through to Himmler's office again, seeking a decision that 'on no account should these women be liquidated, because others who had been released already had knowledge of the experiments', by which he meant the world already knew about them. Göring had learned this because Jadwiga had told him so to his face.

Jadwiga and Zofia later gave their own version of this curious encounter to the other rabbits, as Wanda Wojtasik recalled:

> On entering Suhren's office, they saw a stranger in civilian clothes with a briefcase full of documents. Suhren whispered something to the stranger and pointed at their legs, saying these two 'weren't so bad but the others are in far worse shape'. The strange man didn't say a word and just stared at their legs.
>
> Then, always the reckless one, Jadwiga spoke out, telling the two SS officers that 'the whole world knew about the experiments', and she reminded Suhren about the parcels that had come for them from the outside world – the 'blessings of the Pope'. And she dared to say that the war was as good as over now and that if they were to shoot us now the consequences for them would be catastrophic …

At this Suhren looked uncomfortable and muttered something about 'orders from Berlin' and 'reaching an understanding' and dismissed them.

Shortly after this Suhren, seeing Jadwiga on the Lagerstrasse, gave his 'word of honour' that nothing would happen to them, and 'for once we believed him and began to crawl out of our holes'. In fact, Göring's request for them to be spared had been granted and Himmler had rescinded the order to shoot them. The Polish rabbits, once fodder for Himmler's butcher-doctors, were suddenly valuable bait to be offered to the West.

All over the camp, women were now crawling out of holes, as they'd heard the rumours that more White Buses were on their way. Even as Göring was talking to Suhren, a convoy of rescue vehicles, made up of fifteen Danish ambulances – the Danes had offered to supplement the mission – turned up outside the Ravensbrück gates. The ambulances had the capacity to take 115 women at the most, and Hans Arnoldssen, the Swedish doctor leading the convoy, had been instructed to take the sick first and come back for more. To everyone's astonishment, however, Suhren now strode out of his office and told Arnoldssen he could take every Western prisoner in the camp – about 15,000 women were left – and take them 'straight away'.

In the course of his conversation with Göring, Suhren had obviously changed his mind about the releases, influenced no doubt by the news that the Red Army was already ringing Berlin. Now the Swedes didn't know what to do, as even with every vehicle they had, they couldn't possibly remove that many women straight away. Göring said he'd try to requisition a train, but nobody believed he could do that, and anyway, warned Suhren, the Russians had now cut off the route to Berlin and could reach the camp 'within hours'.

All Arnoldssen could do for now was load up the first fifteen ambulances, requesting that the sick be released to him first. As soon as he directed the vehicles to roll into the camp, chaos erupted as women literally stormed the vehicles. 'They were grey, thin and tired,' he noticed, 'but most could at least walk.'

Rumours that the sick might be taken first this time were viewed with fear in Block 10, as this normally meant a gassing transport. The morning the ambulances arrived, Erika Buchmann, the Blockova, was given a list of twenty-four names, all of them acutely sick, and told to bring them outside. Instead Erika hid as many as she could around the block, or said they had died, which brought the list down to seventeen.

The seventeen were led to the offices and told to wait, which was unusual, so Erika dared to hope they were to be rescued after all, especially as she'd now seen the sick from ordinary *Revier* blocks taken to the ambulances. However, when the last of the ambulances pulled away, the seventeen Block 10 women were left behind. Soon after that, recalled Erika, they were returned to the block.

> They came back frozen and wet with rain – but at least they came back. Now the whole block hoped this was a sign that they were really going to let them go home next time, and the women themselves were convinced of it. That night our sick veered between the greatest hope and the greatest fear, and we with them. We all understood now that the whole camp had to be evacuated before the Red Army arrived. Some of the Germans had already left on foot. The Swedish Red Cross had already taken away some of the sick. Would they take ours?

At dawn the following day, 23 April, more prisoners were prepared for the next Swedish transport, and the same seventeen women were taken to stand by the offices again. After standing in the cold the night before, most were by now at death's door, said Erika, but not all. Edith Glodschey, a German from Königsberg, was one of the strongest – 'After each cough of blood, she stood up straight again.' The German Gypsy called Pfaus had a pneumothorax but she was well in general. Marta Meseberg, a German, was in a good state, 'and had only been with us two days'. Silvie Cernetic, a Yugoslav partisan, was also 'quite strong and well'.

When the group left the block for the second time the prisoner nurse Nadja Bunjac accompanied them, which was taken as another sign of hope. It was dawn when they left, but after three hours, Nadja came back, alone. She was weeping in despair.

> She told us that she had to wait with the patients all this time in the terrible cold in front of the office. The sick were lying on their thin coats on the ground. It was raining. They were in the worst state you could imagine. When the truck arrived eventually the SS who were with it made no attempt to hide the fact that they were going to murder them all. Nadja

> was ordered to carry each of the sick in her arms to the truck. She was ordered by the guards to drag them on the ground to make it easier. And when, beside herself, she cried, 'These are human beings and sick human beings,' the guards just laughed.

Erika now felt stupid for even thinking that anyone would be rescued from Block 10, or from the other sick blocks. That day Marie-Claude Vaillant-Couturier made another note in her diary: 'This day, in the *Revier*, they selected sick French women for a Red Cross Transport, and women with tuberculosis were selected for gassing. Sixteen were taken from Block 10.' The fact that Marie-Claude counted sixteen and not seventeen, as counted by Erika, meant that one had died before the gassing truck came.

As expected, the fifteen ambulances were swiftly followed by a second, larger convoy. Having led the ambulances safely back to Lübeck – now the Swedish base – Hans Arnoldssen had reached Bernadotte by telephone, calling urgently for more vehicles and warning that time was fast running out. A line of trucks and buses had been hurriedly assembled and set off at dawn. The urgency had redoubled with the news that the evacuation of Sachsenhausen, on Berlin's northern periphery, had just started. Himmler's promise to halt evacuations had been a lie.*

Just as he had done in January, when the Auschwitz death march began, Rudolf Höss went to take a look at the 'starving hordes' who trudged out of the Sachsenhausen gates in another 'mad evacuation', as he put it in his prison memoir. The 40,000 men were to trek 100 miles west, facing nothing but mass starvation and death. 'At least now it was warmer and drier,' he observed, 'but these prisoners faced the constant menace of low-flying Allied planes which "shot up the road".' Among the Sachsenhausen death marchers were at least 2–3000 women, sent to the camp in recent weeks, many from Ravensbrück.

To pre-empt a similar Ravensbrück death march, an ICRC delegate was told to make his way to the camp and to formally request that Ravensbrück be handed over at once to International Red Cross control. He could not get close. Just north of Berlin his car was swamped by a torrent of refugees, trucks, bicycles, animals and field guns fleeing the Russians. They forced him to turn around and try to find another way, but he knew it was probably too late.

At the camp the women waited for more Swedish White Buses. Jeanne Bommezjin de Rochement, a Dutch woman, had been living for weeks in a

* Anton Kaindl, commandant of Sachsenhausen, revealed later that his first orders, received on 19 April, had been to liquidate the camp by embarking all prisoners into barges lying in the western harbour of Berlin and taking them up the canals into the North Sea to be sunk. He refused, and was told to march the prisoners out instead.

small attic hideout to avoid selection for the gas chamber. She now felt confident enough to come out. In her diary she wrote:

> The Red Cross is coming to take us away. The few Dutch and French that remain are mad with excitement. But I am past believing rumours. I'm much more likely to believe another rumour, namely that they are about to shoot the lot of us now, and that the camp is surrounded by the advancing allies so the food supply is about to be cut off. If this is true we can do nothing.

All over the camp the SS staff were busier than ever, cleaning, tidying, brushing, painting and burning, ready for the arrival of the Red Army. Everything had to seem normal before the Russians came. Bodies were taken from the washrooms, from the mortuary and from the stacks around the camp, to be burned in ditches, as the crematorium was too slow. In Block 10, as the sick were selected for gassing, the guards replaced the holes in the glass that all winter long had let in the wind, rain and snow, helping to kill the sick.

In the bunker the beating *Bock* was dismantled and burned. Prisoners held in the privileged cells as useful hostages were now deemed useless encumbrances and shot. Odette Sansom (alias Churchill) was still in a privileged cell, and watched as the others were led away, knowing her turn must come soon. Certainly there appeared to be no question of the British being rescued by the Swedes – not a single British name had featured on any rescue list – so Mary Lindell took it upon herself to find out why. After drawing up her own list of British women, she walked over to Suhren's office, to ask him if they were to be included in the rescue transports.

Suhren turned to Binz and said wearily: '*Die Engländerin!* Despite her stay here she is still as arrogant as when she first arrived.'

'On what authority do you still keep us here?' demanded Mary.

'Do you realise that I can still have you shot?' said Suhren, but before Mary left the room he changed his tune, and asked her to give him the British list. He told her that the women should all line up outside Pflaum's office the next morning, and he would make sure they received passes for release. Mary reported the conversation back to Yvonne Baseden. Yvonne was still in the *Revier*, ravaged by TB, and far too weak to consider what Suhren's offer might mean. 'By that time I was reconciled to the idea that I would probably die,' she said.

A few hours after her conversation with Suhren, the chief of the camp police, Elisabeth Thury, came to the *Revier* to warn Mary that Suhren's real intention was to kill the British women. If she brought them tomorrow to Pflaum's office, as Suhren had suggested, they would be shot. The source of the tip-off was Micky Poirier, the French-Alsatian woman working in Pflaum's office. Instead,

Thury advised, Mary should confront Suhren again. She had nothing to lose, and Suhren, like everyone now, was interested in saving his own skin.

So Mary entered the commandant's office again. '*Ach so, die Engländerin!*' said Suhren as she came in. Mary retorted: 'Well? In England our word is our bond. Obviously you have a different code in Germany.' Suhren, seeing she had learned what he intended, apologised. 'I'm sorry,' he said, 'but orders came from Berlin that you were not to be released after all.'

'I see,' said Mary. 'But what do you intend to do with us?' Suhren replied that the English were to remain in the camp, though he said nothing of shooting them, implying instead that they were now all to be held as hostages, like Odette. He walked to a large cupboard in his office, opened it, and showed Mary stacks of tinned food, obviously rifled from Canadian Red Cross parcels. 'To show you my good faith I give you permission to take this food for the British and Americans.'

'But how do you expect me to carry so many tins?' asked Mary. Suhren signalled to Binz, who left the room and returned with several camp policewomen carrying large washing baskets, as well as police to act as guards, to keep away the starving women who by now were roaming the camp 'like wild beasts'. Before the women left with the food, Mary took out several tins and left them on Suhren's desk, saying: 'You may need food yourself before too long.' He took her hand and kissed it. 'That is not for you. It is for England.'

By the time the next Red Cross convoy arrived on 23 April the *Oberschwester*, Elisabeth Marschall, was sporting a Red Cross emblem on her uniform. The prisoners could see there were so many trucks and buses this time that they would surely be able to take hundreds – some said thousands. The Dutch woman Jean Bommezijn de Rochement was told to line up with the rest of her block in the passage beside the *Revier*. The Blockova whispered to them that they were going – leaving the camp – and would probably be set free. Jean noted in her diary:

> This sounds too good to be true, and we do not believe it, we know better. When we have waited a while, the SS man Hans Pflaum and a woman guard appear. They sit behind a table and call our numbers from the lists before them. When the person whose number has been called steps forward, the guard tears the number and the triangle off her sleeve. For the first time since we arrived we stand, though still in prison rags, as individuals not numbers.

Whip in hand, Pflaum herded the women forward. 'A shabby procession of creatures that barely look human,' noted Jean. 'But where are we going?'

Terrified, they were marched not to the gates but out into the woods. After about fifteen minutes the women realised they were heading towards the men's camp, which was nearly deserted, and the block they were taken to was filthy, stinking and dilapidated. Simone Gournay, a French woman, was also with this group and saw 'ghostlike men' appear who tried to talk to the women but were beaten back by the SS.

Jeanne Bommezjin de Rochement saw 'A long row of men, or what must have been men at one time, for now they are living skeletons, a macabre collection. They greet us with their eyes. For a moment something like joy illuminates their features, joy at the sight of fellow martyrs, their sisters in sorrow.'

The same afternoon, one group of these women was led back again to the women's camp. Jeanne was not among them but the French woman Simone Gournay was. 'At 4 a.m. we were marched in lines of five to the exit, beaten and kicked as we went,' said Simone.

> The SS now seemed hysterical. They were shouting and kicking us. Just before the gate [of the men's camp] they tore from us anything we were still holding – little bags that we had made with souvenirs of our friends who had died. We passed by a pile of corpses. We were a miserable line of women. We weren't thinking of liberation. We weren't thinking of anything. We were in a trance.

They re-entered the women's camp and were lined up just inside the gates to wait.

Now they caught sight of tall blonde men wearing grey and green. The women were marched out and the men tried to help, 'but we didn't understand and we pushed them away'. It took Simone a while to realise who these men were, and that the blue and yellow emblem on their shoulders was the Swedish colours. Dazed, she climbed into one of the buses. 'We drove off. With the daylight we could see the countryside. We saw lines of carts and people carrying boxes and bags. It was the German exodus. Once we had to stop because of the bombing, but nobody was hurt. Then we reached Lübeck and stopped for a picnic on the grass. It was my first feeling of liberty.'

The Swedish drivers remembered the women's picnic too. One recalled: 'When we stopped the women ran around looking for green herbs, which they picked and ate. Particular favourites were dandelion leaves, which had just begun to sprout in the spring weather. Using twigs they dug up the plants by the roots, dusted off the soil, and ate them.' Drivers also remember that during the 'picnic' the women told them about the camp, and for the first time the rescuers heard about the gas chamber, and learned that gassing was still going on, reinforcing the rescuers' determination to get back to the camp as soon as they could.

At the same time word had reached the Lübeck HQ that Franz Göring had opened discussions with the Reichsbahn about requisitioning a train.

When the next White Buses appeared at the camp gates confusion broke out about who was to leave this time. One large convoy of vehicles with several Canadian and Swedish drivers, led by a Dane called Gösta Hallqvist, arrived on 24 April and left early the next day. Among those aboard was Jeanne Bommezjin de Rochement, the Dutch woman.

Jeanne and her friend Toto had not slept the previous night and had passed the time standing outside their stinking hut, talking in the night air. 'We are nervous, very nervous, even if we pretend we are not,' she wrote. 'Like two children we play our fantastic little game of make-believe, what it will be like to be home again, who will be there to receive us, where shall we go. We go back in the hut, which is dreadful, the smell overpowering.'

At lunchtime the women were still in the camp and a couple of pots of watery turnip soup and some bread were handed out. 'And we wait, wondering what is going to happen to us.' At about 5 p.m. they hear a whistle and they are told to move.

> We leave the camp, and find ourselves moving in the direction of the gas chambers, and for many of us this is too much. A few are seized by a kind of nervous fit, and we have to calm them, and drag them with us in the column. It is only a few minutes, but the tension lasts hours, and we are safely past the gas ovens. On we go, not daring to think of liberty ... for if it doesn't happen after we have counted on it, we are lost. We move and see the back of the camp – here are the stores, there is Siemens. Some of the inmates appear behind the windows and the barbed wire, looking at us. By their faces I can see that they wonder what is going to happen to us and where we are being taken. They know that 'transport' usually mean death.

The group found themselves on the main road in front of the camp, standing in front of the SS living quarters. Faces stared from the windows. 'And suddenly pandemonium breaks loose; we scream, weep and cheer as a white truck, flying the Red Cross flag, with red crosses on the doors and bonnet, appears round a bend in the road. And the people inside smile at us and wave their hands.' As the prisoners made for the vehicles, the men beside the buses smiled.

> At last we see men who do not beat us, shout and swear at us. These men are deeply moved when they see us, and there are tears in their eyes as they speak to us. We must have looked dreadfully wretched indeed, if these men, who are certainly used to seeing terrible things, weep when they meet us. More and more cars appear on the road, all marked with the Red Cross. The officials ask us if we will mind the long journey, if we will be nervous or afraid. They do not know that for years we have faced death every moment of the day.
>
> Suddenly as we are about to mount the buses there is a scramble as people fight for places, as nobody wants to be left behind. But quite a number have to remain behind and the Red Cross men promise they will come back with more. And we are off, stared at by the SS and the guards, whom we mock to their faces. We can laugh at them now.

As the buses left the women turned and were horrified to see what Jeanne described as: 'a high earthen embankment fitted with gun emplacements and guns trained on the camp'. Like others who had left before them they now understood that the SS really had planned to destroy the camp and everyone in it.

Jeanne's convoy moved off into the night. The drivers told the women that there was a risk of attack from Allied fighters: many German military vehicles were using the roads and many were being hit. As night fell the rescue trucks drove with no lights, but luckily there was a full moon. For safety's sake, they split up: one group of vehicles headed north on the Wismar road, the other went south via Schwerin.

Jeanne was on the Schwerin road, and as the convoy moved close to the front line, word came that there could be an attack at any minute. The buses pulled off the road into the thick of a wood, and the women watched tanks and cannon go past on the main road ahead. 'The sky is as bright as day and we hear the explosions of bombs and rumble of the guns, but nothing matters to us as we are alive and approaching freedom,' wrote Jeanne. As they waited in the darkness, the women talked to their Danish protectors, who told them it was touch and go whether the Red Cross buses would be able to come for them.

When dawn broke the convoy moved off again. All was well. The fighter planes had moved away for now, but a few hours later they had to stop again, and this time the drivers told all the women to get out fast and take cover in the bushes alongside the road.

> There are planes on the way and we are going to be attacked. We are too slow to take cover, as we don't really believe it. They urge us on, telling us we are in real danger, but we are sceptical because we have noticed that it

> is usually factories that are bombed and not the concentration camps. So why fear that a Red Cross column will be attacked? Nobody had told us that the Germans use red crosses as cover for their own transports.

Crawling and helping each other, the women reached the bushes. Jeanne lay under a bush with two other women, and a little further on she saw two more take cover under another bush. Planes appeared and dived lower and lower,

> and suddenly we are machine-gunned. Through the roar of the planes we can hear the whistling bullets raining down on us. The shots pass so close to me that one singes my hair. For a moment I taste the bitter irony of being killed by our own Allies on the road to freedom, and they are gone and I live. Looking around I see a terrible scene. Behind me a woman is bleeding to death. A bright red stream of blood is pouring out of her in gushes. Her lips are bluish white and her eyes break as I look at her.
>
> Another woman has a small hole-like burn in her dress where she has been shot through the breast. There are many victims. Blood and pieces of flesh are everywhere but we are quiet and calm. There's no screaming or moaning. We have to act, and quickly, for the drivers tell us they will be back to attack us again. And so it happens, there is another attack, but it's not so bad this time. When it's all over we put the corpses together on one truck, along with the wounded.

Further on down the road the convoy reached a French POW camp, where the White Buses were able to stop safely. The drivers and SS staff were traumatised and new vehicles and new drivers were sent for. The women waited, talking to the French POWs, who were astonished by their appearance and asked who they were and where they were going. They said they were going to Sweden with the Swedish Red Cross, and the Frenchmen laughed. 'You'll never make it. You're surrounded on all sides and you'll end up in the firing line of our own side.'

Hours later the relief buses arrived. Early next morning Jeanne's convoy crossed the Danish border and the women saw the Red Cross camp. 'People are smiling and waving at us. We are indescribably happy. They feed us porridge and hot milk.' The Danish flag, however, flew at half-mast. The second convoy that took the Wismar road to the north had also been attacked, and at least ten women killed.

How many died on the Schwerin road convoy nobody knew, or ever would. Some reports say nine women died, some say seventeen. Jeanne Bommezjin de Rochement said at the time that there might have been far more. The Danish convoy leader, Gösta Hallqvist, was also seriously injured, and one driver killed, a Canadian called Eric Ringman. Ringman was buried at the Red Cross camp in Denmark, and a Norwegian seamen's pastor said prayers over his grave. Then the women and their drivers and helpers headed on to Sweden. After a further Swedish protest, Sir Victor Mallet, British ambassador in Stockholm, telegraphed London reporting a number of deaths in three attacks that day 'by low-flying British aircraft' on Red Cross convoys from Ravensbrück. 'Nobody knows the nationalities but it is possible that among them were British and American women.'

News of the slaughter on the Schwerin road reached the camp, but it meant little to those still hoping to leave on the next Swedish convoy: they would far rather run the risk of being hit in an air attack than face the prospect of a death march.

All around the camp were the signals that evacuation threatened. Suhren had put a map on his office wall, marking out the route. The last of the documents from the offices were being burned and in the bunker all newly vacated cells were scrubbed, chairs installed and mirrors hung on the walls. In the punishment cells the most important cleaning up was now carried out.

Since the beginning of April, as their work diminished, the *Sonderkommando* – the eleven men who worked on the gassing and burning gang – had been gradually brought into the bunker cells, where they remained locked up until the last of the gassings was carried out. The precise date of the final gassing at Ravensbrück is not known, but Adolf Winkelmann told the Hamburg court that he had gone on selecting for gassing until 24 or 25 April.

Winkelmann's evidence on the dates ties in with the testimony of several prisoners, and is consistent also with what Mina Lepadies, a Jehovah's Witness, revealed about the murder of the *Sonderkommando* men in her statement for the 1946 Hamburg trial. Their killing, she said, took place on 25 April, and she described what happened.

Mina worked in the bunker under Margarete Mewes, the chief bunker guard, whom she helped by cleaning and serving the prisoners' coffee and food. The first Mina knew of anything amiss was when the men were put two to a cell. Then the coffee pot disappeared. 'I looked all over for it, and when I couldn't find it I got another. Mewes came with the missing pot and told me to give them their coffee.'

At first, Mina suspected nothing, but some of the men would not drink, so she grew suspicious and stopped taking the coffee round. Mewes took it instead, and those who drank it died. At ten in the morning their bodies were removed. At midday an SS man came with the soup and told Mina to serve it to the men still left alive. She refused, so he served it himself. Two men, those in cell 47, refused to drink the soup, but two in another cell drank it and by evening they too were dead. That evening Mina was told to serve the soup to the remaining two in cell 47.

> So I looked at the two men in cell 47 and asked if they wanted to eat. They both said: 'Yes, if it's you who's serving it.' They were very nervous and said that they were going to be executed anyhow. Next morning their cell was empty. Everything had been taken away. There was a hammer on the table and a bloodstain, which someone had tried to cover over with soil, but the bench was covered with bloodstains too, and so were the walls.

Mina was ordered to scrub the cells.

It was also on 25 April that the biggest convoy yet, with twenty Swedish White Buses, finally made it to Ravensbrück to collect more prisoners. Its Swedish mission leader, Åke Svensson, predicted that this would be the last time the buses got through, as conditions on the road were already almost impassable. The buses were fired on again as they approached. At Torgau, 200 miles to the south, Russian and American forces linked up that day, cutting Germany in two.

For the prisoners the day began with an *Appell* for all remaining French and Belgians, and the Poles were brought out in groups, mothers and babies first. 'We were suddenly told to bring our dressed babies onto the camp square,' said Stefania Wodzynska, who carried her baby girl Wanda, two months old. The women were told they were going to Sweden and they saw the Swedish Red Cross vehicles already waiting beyond the gates.

Stasia Tkaczyk was here too, carrying Waldmar, who was just twelve days old. Stasia, aged eighteen, like many of the mothers, had arrived at the camp the previous September after the Warsaw Uprising. Back then, knowing that she was already two months pregnant, she decided to save herself and her baby by concealing her pregnancy. She was sent to the Königsberg subcamp, where she worked on the frozen airstrip. In February, six months pregnant but still undetected, she joined the death march back to Ravensbrück. She was selected to work in a munitions factory near Berlin, twelve hours a day on a diet of cabbage soup, and sleeping in a cellar as the bombs dropped. In March she passed out at work and was sent to Ravensbrück again, where Czech nurses cared for her in the *Revier*. On 13 April, Waldmar was born. He was very sick, and now Stasia stood with him in her arms, wrapped in rags, waiting for the buses.

Svensson, the transport leader, recalled that as the day wore on the selections for the buses got more and more confused, and negotiations for places out of hand, so that in the end 'we took everybody we could without asking'. The biggest argument was over the rabbits. Suhren had not obeyed his orders to shoot them, but when the Swede asked him to hand them over he refused. At least three managed to smuggle themselves on board, including the Lublin lawyer Zofia Sokulska.

It was on this convoy of 25 April that the first large group of Ravensbrück's Jews were taken. In his meeting with Norbert Masur four days earlier Himmler had made his dramatic offer to release 1000 Ravensbrück Jews, and had then increased the offer over breakfast with Bernadotte a few hours later, when he said that 'all the women of Ravensbrück' could leave, which meant Jews and non-Jews.

The first the Polish Jewish women knew of this was the previous day, when according to the Siemens worker Basia Zajączkowska, an order was issued that all Polish Jews in the camp should come forward. 'We were placed in the *Strafblock*. No food was available and no access to toilets. We were viciously beaten at the lineup. We suspected they were going to send us to the crematorium, despite rumours of liberation.' Erna Solewicz, another Polish Jew, remembered a sudden order given in her block that 'all Jewish women had to leave the camp'. The Blockova took them *nach vorn*, where they received a piece of bread and a Red Cross parcel.

Next day the first of these Jewish groups were taken towards the gates. Guards 'tore off our marks and numbers,' said Basia. Exactly how many Jewish women left with Bernadotte's evacuation transports is impossible to say, but it must have far exceeded the 1000 offered by Himmler. Suhren had told Göring there were '3000 Jewesses' in the camp, which meant there were certainly many more. Statements from other prisoners suggest that as many as half of the women taken on the buses were probably Jews, and far more would follow three days later when Franz Göring – miraculously – would announce that he had managed to requisition a train.

Meanwhile, during the scramble for bus places the non-Jewish Poles complained of Jewish women taking places assigned for them. 'The Jewish women stormed the buses, which meant we couldn't get in,' complained one. For their part the Jewish women themselves later complained of being 'bumped off buses' and having to fight for places. Frieda Zetler, a Polish nurse who had come from the Łódź ghetto and Auschwitz, had been due to travel on one of the earlier buses, but learned later that the bus she had failed to get onto was the one that was bombed. But she made it onto the buses of 25 April instead.

Even the Jewish women themselves often didn't know if others were Jews or not. In order to conceal the Jewish releases from Hitler, Himmler had ordered they all be disguised as Poles. And as Basia Zającskowska said, they had to tear off their 'marks and numbers' before leaving the camp, so as the women embarked on the buses none of them wore triangles that marked them as Jews or as any other group.

Nor was any count attempted on arrival in Sweden: nobody wished to proclaim their Jewish origins after what they had been through. As always in the camp, there were countless women who had never avowed their Jewishness for the same reasons. For example, Maria Rundo, the young Pole who survived the Auschwitz death march, got out on the White Buses, as did the Dutch-Jewish woman Margareta van der Kuit, who had disguised her Jewishness since her arrest in 1943.

When Basia and her Jewish group were finally led out of the camp, each was given a Red Cross parcel. 'Outside were the White Buses of the Swedish Red Cross. We were free. We could not believe it and tried to make sure by asking the drivers, and even at the last minute the guards shouted at us and called us names.'

When the last of the twenty buses began to pull away, the names of the British women had still not been called, raising fears that the threat to hold them as hostages was real. Then, at the very last minute, Fritz Suhren had yet another change of mind. The British were suddenly called up, raising hopes that they too might be released.

Accounts vary of how this came about, but there is little doubt that it was the French prisoner Maisie Renault who first drew the Swedes' attention to the cases of the British and American women. Maisie had got away on a convoy the previous day, but before leaving she promised her French-American friend Lucienne Dixon, who was left behind, that she would pass on her name to the Swedish drivers, as well as those of other Americans and English, so that they could be collected next time.

When Maisie handed over her list it was the first the Swedes knew of the presence in Ravensbrück of any British or American women. Maisie had only been able to remember eight names, out of about twenty altogether. When the Swedes returned next day and asked Suhren to produce these eight names, he at first denied they existed. One of the Gestapo liaison officers, a man called Danziger, then pressed Suhren to come clean and hand the women over. It was not Danziger who persuaded Suhren to change his mind, however, but Percival Treite.

In these last weeks of the war several prisoners had observed Treite as he sought to ingratiate himself with the British prisoners, in the hope, presumably, that they might testify in his favour when the time came.

His hypocrisy sickened most of the British. He had done nothing to prevent Mary O'Shaughnessy being sent to the Youth Camp, nor to prevent the gassings of Cicely Lefort or Mary Young. But while most viewed Treite with disgust, Mary Lindell – his 'Queen Mary' – was not among them. Mary's obsequiousness towards Treite, and the salacious rumours about the favours she was granting him, had alienated her from almost all her compatriots by the last days of the war. On the other hand, as Mary would point out, she had won some favours too, in particular where Yvonne Baseden was concerned. Without Treite's protection, granted at Mary's request, there can be little doubt that Yvonne, who was dying of TB, would have been gassed.

When the question of the British releases was put before Suhren, and Treite heard the argument it caused, he saw his chance to intervene, and to do the biggest favour yet for Mary and the British women. He entered Suhren's office and persuaded the commandant that releasing the British women would serve more purpose than keeping them hostage. Perhaps, he suggested, Mary Lindell might even put a word in for the commandant too. After hearing Treite out, Suhren sent for Mary Lindell. A voice outside the *Revier* shouted: '*Die Engländerin Marie, die Engländerin Marie.*' Mary was sitting with Yvonne, who could barely move without coughing blood and weighed just 35 kilos. Hearing her name called, Mary got up to leave. Yvonne tried to stop her, fearing the worst, but Mary wanted to see why she was being called.

When she reached the Appellplatz, Mary saw Suhren waiting outside to talk to her. The commandant was leaning on a bicycle. His first words to her were 'Do you trust me?' to which Mary retorted: 'As a matter of fact I don't.' Suhren told Mary to gather up all the English women and bring them to his office. He told her that 'Dr Treite had suggested all the English and Americans should be freed.' Mary put the word out to the British group, and very soon they were assembled beside the *Revier*, with the understanding that they too were to go on the White Buses.

According to the accounts of several British survivors, given later, it was only thanks to one of the Swedish leaders, Sven Frykman, that they weren't all left behind. Frykman spotted their group and asked who they were. On being told they were British and Americans, he collected them himself and put them on the bus.

Mary Lindell had a slightly different version. She described how as she was marched towards the buses Suhren picked her out. He had apparently changed his mind yet again, and told Mary that she must stay behind after all. Yvonne saw what happened, and said that she would not go if Mary could not go too. 'Don't be such a fool, Yvonne,' said Mary. 'Go on, for God's sake, before it's too late.' At this point, said Mary, Yvonne walked towards the buses, tears pouring down her cheeks. Treite saw that Mary had been sent back to the camp. He erupted in fury, marched Mary in person to the White Buses, and put her on board himself.

Yvonne's memory differs again. She recalls being told by Mary Lindell that she had to leave her bed in the *Revier* and get herself to the Red Cross bus. 'She said it was our last chance, we had to try and get out.' Yvonne walked towards the camp gate and lined up with some others. Too sick to be aware of anything much, she doesn't remember if the other women were English or not.

> I just remember Mary told me to keep walking towards the buses. That is what I did. So I just attached myself to these people and kept walking and avoided any contact with the guards or anything like that. I remember being very worried that I might be stopped at any minute. I was very afraid of not getting on the bus, but I got on it. And we drove off at great speed. The drivers were very worried about not getting through because the front was now so close. I learned later that I was on the last bus.

As the twenty White Buses sped away, carrying 934 women, the drivers once again split up as a precaution. Some came under Russian artillery fire, but this time no one was hurt. Red Cross parcels were handed out and nurses tried to tend the sick. They passed two White Buses lying in a ditch, the ones shot up two days before. Somewhere along the route a German 'spy' was unveiled on board one of the buses, and on another a baby was born. The baby was nicknamed 'Per Albin', after the Swedish prime minister.

For the drivers this convoy was 'one long nightmare' as they threaded through swelling crowds of refugees. But inside the buses the Poles began to sing, as they saw the misery of the Germans, 'and we cheered and hung little Polish flags up at the windows,' said Maria Rundo. 'When the buses slowed down young German boys tried to rip down the flags and shook their fists.' The buses came up close to German hospital trains – so close that they could talk to the injured soldiers. 'They asked us for cigarettes and chocolates, which we gave them from our Red Cross parcels. And when we drove through Kiel and saw the terrible destruction it filled us with joy.'

Yvonne remembers little of the journey through Germany, but she remembers arriving at the Danish border and being greeted by members of the Danish royal family. And it was only when she was safely across the border that she discovered that Mary had managed to get onto one of the buses after all.

As Treite had hoped, Mary Lindell later spoke up for him at his trial, and submitted a plea for clemency when in February 1947 he was sentenced to hang. Mary was not the only prisoner to plead for Treite's life. Among the others was Yvonne Baseden herself. Her plea, submitted to the Hamburg judges read:

> I believe that Dr P Treite was mainly responsible for the safe evacuation of the British and American prisoners on the last convoy of the Swedish

> Red Cross in April 1945. Orders had been given that we were to be kept as hostages and it is only through Dr P Treite and the Lagerführer's help that we were evacuated with this last convoy. Furthermore, during my stay in the camp from September 1944 to April 1945 I came before Dr P Treite as a patient twice and on both occasions he treated me quite decently. I therefore plead clemency on his behalf.

When I asked Yvonne how the plea for clemency had come about, she explained that she had still been too weak to attend Treite's trial in Hamburg in 1946, but while Treite was awaiting execution she had received a letter from Mary asking her to say something to spare him the hangman's rope.

'Mary certainly believed Treite had saved her own life,' said Yvonne.

'Do you think he saved your life?'

'I think he made sure I was put on the bus. Otherwise I might not have got out. I was very weak by then.'

I asked if she believed that Treite should have been granted clemency, as she had requested.

'You see, I didn't know very much at that time. I had been so ill in the camp. I was grateful to Mary and did as she asked.'

I wondered how Yvonne felt when she learned that Treite had killed himself. Two weeks after the appeals for clemency were rejected, he cut his wrists and was found dead in his cell.

Yvonne was silent for a while. 'I can see now he helped us to save his own skin. But without him I would probably not be here now.'

*Chapter 41*

# Liberation

'Everything is on fire. Looting is in full swing. Women's screams are heard from open windows,' wrote the Soviet journalist Vasily Grossman as he observed the Red Army cross the German border and push towards Berlin in the first months of 1945.

Grossman had travelled with the Red Army forces all the way from Stalingrad. The Soviet columns were an extraordinary sight: a mixture of the modern and the medieval, their tanks with black-helmeted drivers churned forward alongside Cossacks on horseback, Chevrolets carrying mortars, and horses and carts carrying loot and supplies, and even accordion players. Grossman had watched Stalin's armies roll back Hitler's forces, liberate destroyed cities and overrun the death camps, exposing their gruesome secrets.

When the Red Army crossed into Germany, however, the soldiers' discipline went to pieces. Incited by cries for vengeance, a million drunken *frontiviki* (frontline troops) began to loot, murder and rape. 'Horrible things are happening to German women,' wrote Grossman, who was clearly disgusted by the rape, condoned by many senior officers.

The troops raped and then raped again. 'An educated German is explaining in broken Russian that his wife has already been raped by ten men today,' wrote Grossman. A breast-feeding mother spoke of being raped in a barn. 'Her relatives came and asked her attackers to let her have a break, because the hungry baby was crying the whole time.' The Soviet troops did not only rape German women. They raped Poles, French and even Soviet women who fell in the *frontiviki*'s path. These victims were usually young slave labourers, brought here to work in German farms and factories.

By the middle of April, as Soviet columns rolled on west, terrified refugees passed through Fürstenberg, recounting what they'd seen, so by the end of the month, most of the town's people had fled too.

In Ravensbrück all SS wives and families had been evacuated. Many SS men were permanently drunk and talking openly of the need to head towards the relative safety of American lines, or better still, to vanish. Most had already packed civilian clothes and decided on a civilian identity. Suhren, however, was vacillating about when to give the evacuation order. With several thousand prisoners still in the camp, the commandant was left at a loss.

The Führer's clear instructions had been to evacuate them all, and kill any who couldn't walk. No prisoners were to fall into enemy hands. But with links to Berlin severed and Hitler holed up in his bunker, Suhren had no new orders. His own superiors – Höss, Glücks, Himmler himself – were fleeing the advancing fronts and could no longer be contacted. As commandant of one of the few camps still not overrun, he was on his own. The fate of the last remaining Ravensbrück women lay in his hands.

The Swedish White Buses had already taken most of the west European prisoners and many Poles and Jewish women. That left the Russians, Germans, Austrians and East Europeans, amongst them still a large number of Jews. Many of these prisoners predicted that Suhren would order a massacre. Others believed the camp was mined, or that they really would be marched to the Baltic coast – the only escape route – put on boats and drowned. As for those too weak to walk, Suhren had threatened many times to shoot anyone unable to join the evacuation.

On 27 April came news that forces of Rokossovsky's Second Belorussian Front had taken Prenzlau, fifty miles to the east. The German army now blew up fuel depots and military bases around Fürstenberg, ready for the final retreat. Suhren's men started setting fire to workshops at the back of the compound while Suhren and Binz were seen 'black with soot and sweat' frantically burning more papers. Hans Pflaum cycled around the camp, selecting more women to exterminate. 'Pflaum hunted down the weak and sick prisoners from their blocks and then shot them on the Lagerstrasse,' said Zdenka Nedvedova.

Other last-minute killings went on. A German prisoner, Anni Sinderman, recalled a group of evacuees brought in just before the end. 'They were lying on the floor in the bathhouse whimpering and whining.' These women were not seen again, says Anni. Possibly they were killed in the gas van, or simply shot. Odette Sansom, still held as a hostage in her bunker cell, saw live prisoners driven into the crematorium. 'I could hear them screaming and struggling and I heard the oven doors being opened and shut. Then I didn't see the women any more.'

On the question of the final massacre, Suhren could not decide how far to go. Marie-Claude Vaillant-Couturier noted in her diary that orders were 'changing every two hours'. One minute the SS announced that all those incapable of marching would be killed and the camp swept clean before the Russians arrived. The next minute Suhren was issuing instructions that the sick could stay and the rest would march.

As Pflaum was shooting women outside, Dr Treite called the prisoner doctors to his office. He asked who would stay behind after the evacuation to care for the sick until the Russians arrived. Several women told Treite they would remain, including the prominent communists Zdenka Nedvedova, Antonina Nikiforova and Marie-Claude Vaillant-Couturier.

And even if Suhren had intended to kill all the old and sick, how would he have destroyed the bodies in time? The Führer had also ordered that all evidence be eradicated before the enemy arrived, but the crematorium couldn't burn bodies fast enough, as the Austrian prisoner secretary Friederike Kierdorf discovered when she saw inside.

Friederike was still working in the *Schreibstube*, filling in details on prisoners' cards, until the very last minute.

> But then suddenly we were told to put the cards down and burn the lot. We were told the office was to be destroyed and we had to take all the last dossiers in trunks to the crematorium for burning. Inside the crematorium there were three ovens, which we now saw for the first time. But as we stood there with the trunks the men working the ovens told us: 'We can't burn paper because we're burning people.' One of them told us: 'We burn sixteen thin ones or four fat ones in one oven.' So we had to carry the documents away again and burn them in sandpits.

Friederike says she didn't see the burning of the *Schreibstube*, but the office building wasn't there when she went back again after the war.

Before the workshops were torched too, the SS were determined to lay hands on any loot. They snatched rolls of cloth just before the flames reached them. Friederike was astonished when a senior SS man thrust a roll of luxury red cloth into her arms. 'He said it was better I had it than it fell into Russian hands. I think he felt protective towards me. He said he had a daughter like me – I was very young.' The 'protective' SS officer then handed her civilian clothes and told her to join the first convoy of SS and guards who on the evening of 27 April prepared to leave the camp. Suhren had made up his mind.

'The SS had horses and carts that they stole from the farmers, and one of the officers put me in a cart,' said Friederike. 'There were about eight to ten carts and the SS luggage went in the first one.' She felt scared to be with the SS. 'Everyone was loaded up with stolen goods – much of it jewellery. They asked me why I didn't have jewellery on me. They couldn't understand why I hadn't taken any.'

As the convoy left, Suhren drove past them, shouting: 'Get to Malchow as quick as you can.' Suhren had chosen the subcamp of Malchow, about seventy kilometres northwest, because it would not be overrun for a few days and probably lay in the path of the Americans – or so he thought.

In the small hours of Saturday 28 April the main exodus from Ravensbrück began. The day before, at half-past midnight, Suhren had visited Odette in her bunker cell. 'He stood at the door and made a gesture with his finger indicating a throat being cut.' Odette thought her turn for liquidation had come. 'He told me to get my things ready and be prepared to leave the camp early the next morning.' At eight in the morning an SS man came and ordered her onto the Lagerstrasse. Suhren appeared and put her into a prison van whose *Prominente* passengers included an Italian naval commandant, the Lithuanian minister of war, a Polish baron and two French women aristocrats. The group were sent on to Malchow, to wait until Suhren arrived.

All next day the guards massed large groups of prisoners at the gates. The kitchen and office staff marched out before daylight and ordinary prisoners followed. Any who refused were chased down by Pflaum, now using dogs. A French woman found hiding in the attic of a block was beaten to death with a hammer.

When the Austrian teenager Fritzi Jaroslavsky joined one of the columns, she saw Suhren drive past in his car, urging the women on to Malchow. 'But we hadn't got very far when Russian planes flew very low over us and we scattered in all directions.' Fritzi and her group reached a small town where they took cover in an empty house. 'Then quickly we realised we were free, so we turned and made our way back to Fürstenberg, where we thought we'd be safer.'

Johanna Sultan from Kiel had set off with an earlier group that was also attacked by Russian fighter planes. Everyone dived for cover – guards, dogs and prisoners alike. Now they took cross-country routes, trying to hide from the planes under trees, but the leaves were not out, and the planes attacked again as the women trudged on across vast ploughed fields, hard with frost. Everyone scattered, and apart from a single female guard, all the SS ran off. Then the woman guard fled too and the prisoners were alone. 'We met up with a Ukrainian peasant in the field who showed us the way to a nearby farm, where a group of French prisoners arrived who had also escaped. We all hid there and waited for the Russians or Americans to arrive.'

Many other SS guards escaped from the Malchow march by hastily changing into civilian clothes and fleeing north. The men hoped to disappear in the refugee flows, or find a way to the Danish border. Women guards often just made for home. After abandoning the march, Margarete Rabe and a fellow woman guard headed for Margarete's uncle's house in the nearby town of Schwerin.

At Ravensbrück, women prisoners were now streaming out of the gates. Maria Apfelkammer left with 300 or 400 prisoners, lined up five abreast. SS numbers were dwindling fast. Most of the guards in the escort were 'old men with guns out of a museum', as one prisoner put it. They were members of the Volkssturm, a conscript militia created the previous October. Artur Conrad, the SS executioner, brought up the rear of Apfelkammer's Malchow column, saying he would drive the women to American lines. 'After about three hours we had a short rest by the road. Two women sitting on stones said they could no longer go on, so Conrad shot them. Conrad then shot several other stragglers.'

They marched all day, slept in a barn, then marched again. A Czech woman, Stefanie Jokesch, spent the second night in a wood. She didn't remember shootings but did recall many women who 'lay down and died'. The third day she fled. 'But there was nowhere to go. I was in the middle of no-man's-land so I hid in some trees.'

In these last days of April, it was not only the main camp that was disgorging its prisoners; so were all remaining Ravensbrück subcamps, many of which were dotted along this as yet unconquered strip of Germany. Two hundred miles south, Eileen Nearne, the British SOE woman, imprisoned in a subcamp near Leipzig, had fled an evacuation column and was also lurking under trees, wondering how far away the Americans were. Even further south, across the Czech border, Maria Bielicka, evacuated from the Neurolau subcamp, was marching with a column of prisoners over the Sudeten Mountains. They hoped to reach American lines, though she feared it was more likely she would be shot.

> The Russians were a few miles away to the east and the Americans a few miles to the west but nobody knew quite where. Many women had already died on the road as they couldn't go on, and others had been shot. Then they put us in a giant beer warehouse for the night. The SS didn't know where to go or what to do with us.

At the subcamps the final evacuations were often more chaotic than at Ravensbrück. At Neubrandenburg on 26 April the guards told everyone to stop work as both Allied fronts edged closer. The French sat for two days on their bunks, wagering whether the Americans or Russians would reach them first, while the Russian prisoners pillaged the kitchens. 'All around our block nibbling could be heard,' remembered Micheline Maurel. 'On a nearby bunk a Russian was eating raw spaghetti. She smiled broadly and offered me a handful.'

Then the chief guard fired at women looting flour bags and suddenly it was '*Raus, raus, schnell!*' and shots came through the window. As the women were rounded up outside, Micheline trod on something soft, a tiny pack of margarine, and picked it up. 'Night was falling. It was raining and the guns rumbled as the outer gate swung open.' She clutched her friend Michelle's arm and told her she couldn't possibly march. 'You can. You are going to march,' said Michelle, and she did, telling herself: 'Keep walking, don't stop, don't look round, don't speak, don't think.'

At dawn Micheline took out the margarine and ate it with Michelle. Then they set out again and marched all day. It was raining, the horizon was ablaze and the guard Edith Fraede brought up the rear, riding a truck with a machine gun. That night they slept in a wet barn where several exhausted women died, among them Marthe Mourbel, a professor of philosophy from Angers. She might have lived had she stayed behind: the day after the evacuation a lone Swedish Red Cross ambulance turned up at Neubrandenburg and rescued women left in the sickbay.

Columns of marchers crisscrossed no-man's-land, exhausted and maddened by thirst and hunger. 'A mother stopped and began to pull up grass to eat,' recalled Lise Lesèvre. 'The daughter sprang from the rows of marchers to help her mother and the guards shot both of them.' Further back a Red Cross truck had pulled up with food parcels for the same column, and was handing them out even as the shots rang out.

The marchers came across many other gruesome murder scenes. Near Rostock on the Baltic coast, a group of women escaping from a column found a mass of dead men in striped clothing hanging from trees. Along the road to Malchow lay dozens of women's bodies shot by Conrad and his crew. Women who ran into fields to dig for potatoes were shot, as were a group who raided bread from an SS car. Fritz Suhren shot a prisoner who stooped to pick up a cigarette butt in the road.

Women evacuated from a subcamp near Leipzig were marched into a field where lines of dead men in striped camp clothes lay face down. These were prisoners from a Buchenwald subcamp who had apparently been marched here and then shot en masse. 'We were forced to walk over the corpses to get to our resting place at the other end of the field,' one woman recalled. 'We couldn't help treading on the bodies.'

A flight of planes flew overhead. Everyone scattered, but the planes tipped their wings and began to circle before gaining height again, 'and above our heads was a blaze of colour as flags floated down to let us know that our friends had recognised us. Then we were marched off again.'

Despite the terrors of no-man's-land, with the Allies so close, the chance of escape had never seemed greater. Packed into the beer warehouse in the Sudeten Mountains, Maria Bielicka and her friends decided to take the risk.

> We climbed inside the empty beer crates to hide and then we waited. In the morning we could hear the SS shouting '*Raus raus, schnell schnell*', and dogs were barking. Then they left, but one man came back with his dog and my ear was squashed against my friend's chest and I could hear her heart going 'boom boom' and I thought, my God, the whole world can hear this, but then he left, leaving us and all the sick behind. We waited several hours and we could hear the sick women calling out for water in every language, water, *Wasser*, *Wasser*. There were many and they were dying. Then the SS came back and shot them.

The SS didn't find Maria and her friends, who waited a few more hours, hiding inside their crates, then crept back out.

At some subcamps the guards fled before the evacuation began. In Genthin, the prisoners, left alone, took revenge by murdering the civilian factory bosses. 'I remember seeing two of our civilian factory managers lying dead, still with their white coats on,' said the Russian prisoner Evdokia Domina.

> They were not bad people. Then someone just opened the gates and we walked out. We found a house to stay in and someone gave us a horse, but we didn't know how to ride this horse so we went on foot and saw places burned and torched. We just thought to head east. We walked into deserted houses and found the bedrooms with beds to sleep in. And it was so nice with these sheets and quilts. We ate the food and never washed the plates, just took another one.

Before long the guards were escaping across no-man's-land faster than the prisoners. Piles of uniforms lay discarded at the roadside by women guards and the SS as they changed into civilian clothes and fled. Columns of marching prisoners would suddenly look around and find that they were free. Ekatarina Speranskaya was with a group of Russians heading north when one of them shouted: '"Girls! Are you animals? Are you just cattle? There aren't even any guards left any longer and still you all march." And we looked around and others shouted: "Hurrah, comrades, we've been liberated."'

Yet this first 'freedom' didn't yet mean liberation, as many women were to learn. At least one group of prisoners were killed in error by American sniper fire as they moved close to US lines. The Poles feared running into Russian lines. Krystyna Zając was one of the first to encounter Russian soldiers.

> Immediately they saw us they chased us. A Russian said he wanted to dance with me. Then they tried to rape us. I fell down. They even tried to get my mother and to rape her. We said we were Poles, not Germans, and we were prisoners, but they didn't care. Then in the night they killed a mother who was protecting her daughter. Eventually we found a safer place in a German house.

By 29 April the few remaining prisoners at Ravensbrück were increasingly giving the orders as the Soviet army approached. Treite came once more to the *Revier* to press Zdenka to leave, but she refused. He then told Zdenka that she was now in charge of all the sick left in the camp, a decision that riled Antonina Nikiforova, who believed that the role should pass to her as the senior Red Army doctor.

Antonina and the other doctors and nurses had counted at least 1500 women in the camp who were too sick to move, many of whom were close to death. Twenty-two women found at the back of Block 32 were 'barely more than human remains', wrote Marie-Claude in her diary. 'We moved them to the *Revier* but I doubt they'll live.' Kamila Janovic, a Polish nurse, said that in the days before the Russians arrived unknown numbers of women died and piles of bodies lay everywhere and were gnawed by rats, but there was no time to bury them.

Electric power had been turned off, so prisoners organised a chain gang to haul pails of water to the *Revier* blocks. In the kitchen Marta Baranowska, the Polish Red Cross leader, took charge. 'This morning Binz appeared at the kitchen and asked Marta if there was any food for the guards who had been left behind and had nothing to eat,' wrote Marie-Claude. 'Marta told Binz that everything we had was for the sick and Binz would have to go and ask at the SS canteen – how things are changing.'

The guards had enough authority left to order the last of the prisoners to march out of the camp gates, but such was the confusion that several hid at the last minute, including Rosa Thälmann, wife of the former German Communist Party president. German comrades smuggled her out and hid her in a house in Fürstenberg.

This latter group of marchers were mostly Russians, and included all the Red Army women, as well as the children who had been living in their block. Olga Golovina seized the cart used for pulling the soup kettles and used it as a pram to carry small children, dragging it out of the camp gate.

Stella Kugelman, who was five years old when she was evacuated, says today she can't remember exactly how she and the other children got out. She recalls that the children quickly became separated from the adults, possibly after an air attack. Then a woman she calls 'Aunt Olympiada' took care of them. 'I remember suddenly being outside on a road, and I think Aunt Olympiada just found us there and decided to look after us. I didn't know her in the camp. She put us back on this cart and pushed us along and later she found some food to feed us.'

Instead of heading for Malchow, northwest of Ravensbrück, the Volkssturm, backed by a few SS guards, drove the Red Army prisoners northward to the sea, directly in the line of the Soviet advance. 'The roads were full of people and carts,' said Yekaterina Boyko. 'And when we saw we were going towards the Baltic we thought we were going to be taken to Africa as slaves.'

Georgia Tanewa, the Bulgarian, was marching close to Yevgenia Lazarevna Klemm. In 1943 Klemm had passed orders down the lines when the Red Army women were marched west to Germany; now she resumed the same commanding role as they marched towards their liberators. 'Our guards were just old men who looked like they'd been dressed in uniforms for the day,' said Georgia, who lives today in east Berlin. 'But Yevgenia Lazarevna was really the one in charge. She'd say: "Stay together, girls, do as I say, just keep marching." So we marched along the road in our wooden clogs. Clack, clack, clack' – and Georgia bangs the table to make the sound.

> In Fürstenberg we walked past beautiful empty houses – we'd forgotten what civilisation was. And then we thought, what are these old [Volkssturm] men going to do with us? They aren't going to kill us in this little town. They knew the war was lost and were probably thinking, what are we going to do with this stinking bunch of starving women? Then we thought they might bring us to some big prison or other. And when we realised we were heading north we thought: 'Aha! They're marching us towards the sea to drown us.'

Did Georgia believe this might happen?

> That is what I personally thought, yes. The sea was actually very far away, but we didn't know that. Then suddenly we had been marching some hours and looked around, and there were no soldiers, but our clogs were still banging on the road, clack, clack, clack. There was nobody on the road at all except for us. We kept looking around and nothing happened. We didn't know where we were, and there were only these ploughed fields for miles.

The front half of the column carried on up the road, hoping to find the Russian front. Those near Yevgenia Lazarevna asked her what to do. 'She said we must find a wood and hide,' says Georgia.

> We ran like mad over this ploughed field and then there was a wall on the edge of a wood and we were running on pine needles. There were pine needles everywhere and we were in the forest and we looked around and there were eyes all around us and then the eyes popped up and we found they belonged to prisoners from Sachsenhausen who were hiding. So we lay down in the pine needles and had a rest, and it was wonderful.

When Georgia woke up she saw a boy on the road.

> I spoke a little German so I asked the boy for water. He took me to a village and we found a pump and some pots. We walked around the village and people hiding in their houses thought we were going to kill them, but of course it didn't cross our minds. Everything was empty. Kaputt. We asked the boy where the road went and he said to Neustrelitz. He said the Soviet army are in Neustrelitz, so we headed to Neustrelitz.

On the way some of the women were caught in crossfire. 'I was lying on the ground and got hit by a piece of shrapnel,' said Ekaterina Speranskaya.

> Then I remember the tanks and lots of bodies, and it was then I heard Russian spoken and saw our soldiers. When they came close the Russian captain said: 'My God, where are you from? Have you come from the grave?' And when we stepped forward in our striped uniform, all dirty and tired, they started laughing and crying and said 'sisters' and they welcomed us and gave us food and so we carried on to Neustrelitz.

By midday on 29 April the last evacuees were marching out of the main camp. Fritz Suhren darted up and down the evacuation columns and then returned to Ravensbrück, where he was seen pacing nervously beside the gates. 'Then suddenly he ordered the guards: "Close the gates. Those still inside, shoot them" – I heard this diabolical statement myself,' recalled Elfriede Meier.

If Suhren did issue this order, it wasn't carried out. Zdenka recalled a different parting gesture: 'He sent me two large sacks of salt, a few sacks of musty flour and a rack of loaves of bread with which we were supposed to feed the sick.' Marie-Claude said that Suhren's last instructions were that the remaining prisoners should dig a ditch to bury unburned corpses, 'then we should fill it in properly and make a cross to place on top. To think that a few days before women were still being gassed.'

By the middle of the afternoon, Fritz Suhren and the entire SS contingent – Binz among them – had driven off in trucks and cars, or on horses and carts, to Malchow.

As soon as the SS had gone the women began to explore their camp. They found piles of Red Cross parcels in the cellars of the headquarters buildings and in the SS houses; some had been rifled, some left unopened. One cellar was full of sugar, dried milk, porridge, Swedish bread, conserves, soap, toothpaste, all with Swedish labels except for the American cigarettes. Next, the women inspected the crematorium, piled with partly burned corpses, and peered into the half-destroyed gas chamber, where they saw empty tins of chemicals bearing the name Zyklon. They also found eight cases of documents, which they put aside to give to the Russians.

It was now, walking out into the woods, that the women found the remains of gassing vans, which Zdenka compared to removal vans with 'a mechanism allowing exhaust gases to be pumped inside'. She said they were found near the Youth Camp.

Venturing over to the men's camp, also evacuated, they found some 400 sick men who had been left behind. 'They'd been without water for a week and were dying of hunger and thirst,' wrote Marie-Claude. 'They didn't look like men but like ghosts, and the suffering had driven them mad. Nobody, but nobody, could have described it – nobody would have believed it. We did what we could to help them, but we had so little ourselves.'

On 30 April, the women awoke to the roar of Russian artillery, which grew louder by the hour, the gunfire so close that the sky above the perimeter wall lit up. 'Women ran in a panic onto the Lagerstrasse and one of them lifted her arms to the sky, her hair all wild, and knelt in the middle of the road, praying at the top of her voice,' said Zdenka. A small group went out of the gates to find out just how near the Red Army were. Others prepared beds for wounded Soviet soldiers and made a red banner to hang across the camp gates when they knew liberation was assured. Some still expected the Germans to blow up the camp. 'We came out one day and there was no siren, so we said let's get ready to be blown up, let's say goodbye,' said Maria Vlasenko, one of the Odessa nurses who had stayed behind.

The first Red Army soldier to enter the gates of Ravensbrück was a young man on a white horse, wearing a golden fur hat – or so Zdenka Nedvedova remembered. Marie-Claude said he rode on a bike: 'At 11.30 the advance guard of the Red Army arrived, and seeing the first cyclist ride through the camp gates my eyes filled with tears of joy and I remembered my tears of rage when I saw the first German motorcyclist ride through the Place de l'Opéra five years earlier.'

Antonina Nikiforova saw the cyclist too. 'Everyone who could run ran out to greet him.' Then the Russians came through the gates in tanks and cars. 'We ran up and kissed them and showered them with cigarettes until they told us to stop. "Are you mad?" they shouted. "It's enough to kiss us!" And we surrounded them and stared at them and cried. There they were all covered in dust, but to us they were the most precious things in the world.'

Maria Gorobotsova, from Tbilisi in Georgia, said the soldiers 'looked terrified when they saw the state we were in. Then they said: "Girls, let's kill a pig and eat."' Maria Vlasenko saw a tank commander jump down from his vehicle and walk towards them. 'He asked us, Is there anyone here from Maykop, which was his home town. He had lost his sister, he said. And his sister then came forward. He could barely recognise her and he cried.'

According to Red Army testimony, the first soldiers arrived on motorbikes. Alexander Mednikov, a captain with the Second Belorussian Front, reported that a reconnaissance patrol was riding near Fürstenberg when it came across a high wall topped with rows of barbed wire. 'Our submachine gunners got down from their motorbikes and one accidentally touched the wire with his hand, and received a strong electric shock [suggesting the electricity had not been turned off after all] which knocked him to the ground.'

A few armed men, probably elderly Volkssturm militia, were still defending the camp. 'As our men rode along the wall, they found the gate, which also had a thick tangle of barbed wire over it. And suddenly from the other side a machine gun started chattering. Our men had already understood what sort of place this was and decided to enter, at which Hitler's men fled and tried to hide behind some barracks.'

Minutes later, Colonel Mikhail Stakhanov arrived in a tank:

> After fighting all the way across Russia and Poland, I happened to take part in the liberation of the women's camp of Ravensbrück. We drove over the barbed wire in our tanks and broke the camp gates. And then we stopped. It was impossible to move further as the human mass surrounded the tanks; women got under our tanks and on top of them, they shouted and they cried. There was no end to them. They looked awful, wearing overalls, skinny; they didn't look like human beings. There were 3000 sick, so sick it was impossible to take them away, they were too weak.

It was probably the day after the advance guard arrived that Yaacov Drabkin turned up at Ravensbrück. Driving a jeep with loudhailers attached,

Drabkin entered the camp gates, looked around briefly, then swung his vehicle around and headed out again; he was looking for someone.

Drabkin was a young Jewish political officer attached to the 49th Army of the Second Belorussian Front. His job was to pick up intelligence and put out propaganda to undermine enemy morale. By the end of April Drabkin was based in the small town of Gransee, ten miles south of Fürstenberg. 'I remember celebrating my birthday the day we crossed the Oder, so it must have been a few days after that that I heard about Ravensbrück. I don't think we'd known of the women's camp before, though we'd passed by Auschwitz, Majdanek and all the other camps. For a Jew it was of course particularly hard to see these things.'

Once in Germany Drabkin gathered intelligence from Russian and Ukrainian teenagers brought as slave labour for farms, and now fluent in German. 'They passed us notes saying this German is a good guy, don't kill him, or this one treated us badly, kill him.' The boys told Drabkin a great deal about Ravensbrück, which he passed on to his headquarters. His superiors ordered him to get to the camp straight away and try to find Rosa Thälmann.

The Soviets knew by now that Ernst Thälmann, once the head of the German Communist Party, had been executed at Buchenwald. 'They still hoped to find his wife alive, they wanted to know what she knew,' said Drabkin, seated in his book-lined Moscow study. He failed to find Rosa at Ravensbrück, so he drove around Fürstenberg, calling her name on the empty streets through a loudhailer.

> The Germans had all fled. It took a few hours but eventually I found her. She'd been hidden away in a small house in a back street. She was in a very bad state – emaciated, barely alive, the way everybody was. She was still wearing her prison clothes. She already knew her husband was dead, and all she wanted to know was what had happened to her daughter.

Twenty-six-year-old Irma Thälmann had been taken to Neubrandenburg subcamp some weeks earlier. Rosa had no idea if her daughter was dead or alive.

> My instructions were to tell her that our commanders were pleased she had survived and would do everything to help her. We wanted to know what she could tell us, about the camp, the party, certain people we were interested in. But she wasn't able to tell me anything, she was too distressed. She was terrified in case anything she said might put her daughter in more danger somehow. She was a tiny shrunken figure.

What was Yaacov's response when he saw Rosa?

'It's hard to say,' he said, moved by the memory. 'A mixture of compassion and pity.'

Drabkin and the rest of the Soviet advance guard soon moved on west, promising the prisoners that Red Army units in the rear would bring supplies and medics to help them. While they waited, for two or three days more, the women hung their red banner over the entrance 'to announce to the world that we were free,' said Antonina. The Czechs asked Antonina for 'permission' to hang their national flag on their block, and soon every nation was flying its flag. Antonina described how everyone redoubled their efforts to help the sick, drawing up calorie charts, scavenging for food and mattresses, trying to start a cleanup. She did not mention that both in the camp and outside, Russian soldiers were now systematically raping prisoners and German civilians.

The Red Army's sexual rampage at Ravensbrück was witnessed by Ilse Heinrich, a German asocial who was too weak to leave her bed when the Soviet advance guard arrived. A few hours later, Ilse and other bed-ridden prisoners saw Soviet soldiers, drunk, and bent on raping even the women who were sick and dying. 'And then it began,' she said. 'I had only one thought at that time – to die, because I was little more than a corpse. Later, when the senior officers arrived and they set up their quarters in the camp, we had some peace and order. But first, we had to undergo that! It was the worst thing. And half dead as I was.'

How many rapes occurred inside the walls of the main camp of Ravensbrück is hard to put a figure to: so many of the victims – already, as Ilse Heinrich said, half dead – did not survive long enough after the war to talk about it. Antonina, the senior Red Army woman left in the camp, apparently never mentioned it and nor did the other prominent communist prisoners. Only Zdenka chose to speak out later, revealing that not only were the sick and dying raped but so were women in the camp's maternity block. Left behind after the evacuation were scores of women too pregnant to march, and many women with newborn babies, all housed in the same block. Soon after the Red Army liberators arrived one of these women ran to Zdenka screaming. 'She cried that the soldiers had come and locked themselves in the block and tried to rape the women.' Zdenka immediately went to the senior Soviet officer, Major Sergej Bulanov – a doctor, who was much respected – pleading for help. Bulanov must have quickly established that the men had done far more than threaten the women, because after a short time the prisoners heard shots. 'And the next morning we learned that the soldiers had been executed,' recalled Zdenka. 'At the time we thought this punishment may have been too hard.'

While many older Soviet women were reluctant to talk of the rape, younger survivors feel less restraint today. Nadia Vasilyeva was one of the Red Army nurses who were cornered by the Germans on the cliffs of the Crimea. Three years later in Neustrelitz, northwest of Ravensbrück, she and scores of other Red Army women were cornered again, this time by their own Soviet liberators intent on mass rape.

Nadia was one of those who accompanied Yevgenia Lazarevna Klemm on the road to Neustrelitz, where they ran into more Russian soldiers. 'At first they greeted us as sisters,' said Nadia. 'I remember a soldier came up to us and said: "It's OK now; you can come with us." We saw our own tanks on the road and we were overjoyed.'

Soon the soldiers' behaviour changed. It was dark when the column got to Neustrelitz, and 'they started walking beside us, chasing us and goading us, and wouldn't leave us alone. Then they turned into animals. They were drunk.'

It became obvious that there was nowhere for the women to sleep in the town.

> There were many other women here too, not just the Red Army girls, so we were taken to a big building like a warehouse. We were led into a big room and all the time they were harassing us but we were tired and needed to sleep so we went into the room. It was on the first floor. The soldiers followed us. We shut the door, trying to keep them out. Yevgenia Lazarevna tried to barricade us in. They shouted to us to come out. They asked for the youngest women. It was terrifying. I was one of the youngest in the group. Then they said: 'Anyone who's a virgin come out to us.' They started banging at the door and on the window and I saw one man swing in at the window and fall into the room drunk. They were starting to break down the doors and Yevgenia Lazarevna tried to do everything she could to protect us, telling them we were Red Army women who had been at the front at Stalingrad, Leningrad and the Crimea. We had been in the concentration camp for two years. 'You can kill me but don't touch the girls,' she said.

Another of the Odessa nurses, Ilena Barsukova, remembers the women screaming and crying and Yevgenia Lazarevna calling for calm and trying to reason with the soldiers. But she couldn't hold all of them back, and several got in.

> Then a major came and threw out the drunk ones and Yevgenia Lazarevna pleaded with him to stay and protect us from our own soldiers. And he agreed. Then in the morning the commanding officer came and restored

order. All the girls there would have been raped that night in Neustrelitz if it hadn't been for Yevgenia Lazarevna. Yevgenia Lazarevna defended us in every way she could. But I know lots of girls who were raped by our soldiers; even girls who stayed in the camp were raped, and not only in our group.

Olga Golovina, the Red Army radio operator, now living in Moscow, described how her group, which had split off from Yevgenia Lazarevna's column, found themselves in a deserted village already taken by Soviet soldiers.

They allocated a house for us and gave us food, but then the soldiers started making advances. They hadn't had a woman for ages. My friend Masha was so strong, like a man she defended us and beat them off. We went to the commandant to complain and he gave us two soldiers, who guarded us. They sat outside at first then we took pity on them and asked them to come inside and have some tea. In the morning they told us that only now did they realise what we have been through. 'One of you was singing in her sleep and another crying out loud and another one sobbed. What we heard made our hair stand on end,' they said.

Other women make no excuses for the Soviet rapists. 'They were demanding payment for liberation,' said Ilena Barsukova. 'The Germans never raped the prisoners because we were Russian swine, but our own soldiers raped us. We were disgusted that they behaved like this. Stalin had said that no soldiers should be taken prisoner, so they felt they could treat us like dirt.'

Like the Russians, Polish survivors were also reluctant for many years to talk of Red Army rape. 'We were terrified by our Russian liberators,' said Krystyna Zając. 'But we could not talk about it later because of the communists who had by then taken over in Poland.' Nevertheless, Poles, Yugoslavs, Czechs and French survivors all left accounts of being raped as soon as they reached the Soviet lines. They talked of being 'hunted down', 'captured' or 'cornered' and then raped.

In her memoirs Wanda Wojtasik, one of the rabbits, says it was impossible to encounter a single Russian without being raped. As she, Krysia and their Lublin friends tried to head east towards their home, they were attacked at every turn. Sometimes the approach would begin with romantic overtures from 'handsome men', but these approaches soon degenerated into harassment and then rape. Wanda did not say she was raped herself, but describes episodes where soldiers pounced on friends, or attacked them in houses where they sheltered, or dragged women off behind trees, who then reappeared sobbing and screaming. 'After a while we never accepted lifts and didn't dare go near any villages, and when we slept someone always stood watch.'

Izabela Rek, one of the rabbits whose legs had been badly mutilated, had no hope of getting away from the Soviet soldiers. With the help of friends, Izabela tried to escape into the woods.

> Suddenly we were walking towards a river and the Russian soldiers arrived. One soldier told me not to worry but the others were dragged off and I could hear them screaming very badly nearby; crying and shouting. Then they attacked us all and raped us, even though they knew we were prisoners. When we reported what happened to another group of soldiers they said come with us and we'll look after you. Two girls went with them but we never saw them again.

The French teacher Micheline Maurel, who by the end of the war weighed only 35 kilos and was ravaged by dysentery and scabies, described the systematic rapes in detail. On 1 May Micheline saw her first Red Army soldier. 'A big burly fellow, gay and debonair', he walked into the courtyard of the barn where she and her friends Michelle and Renée were hiding after escaping from the Neubrandenburg evacuation march. 'He immediately raped Michelle and then left, running across country as bullets flew past him.' Later that day, while looking for food in the burning town of Waren, Michelle and Renée were both raped again several times by Russians who were staying in looted houses.

On the second day of 'liberation' the three friends were still hiding in the same barn when a company of Cossacks arrived. 'They looked just like their pictures – superb men, wearing high astrakhan caps, long, fitted coats and spurred boots and riding magnificent horses that pranced around the farmyard. They brought us a gramophone and played dance music. They offered us vodka in big cups and this helped our pains.'

Micheline says the only reason she wasn't raped was that she persuaded the soldiers that her sores were deadly and infectious. But her friend Michelle had no sores. 'I tried to protect her but it did no good,' said Micheline. 'Nor was it really a question of protection, for the Russians had no evil intent, no animus whatever against us. Quite the contrary, they were filled with extreme cordiality, brimming over with affection, which they had to demonstrate immediately. "French? You French, me Russian, it's all the same! You are my sister. Come lie down here."'

Each day the French trio's health deteriorated; each day more Russians assaulted the women as they went on their way. The story was always the same. 'Whether they were big blondes with drooping moustaches, little yellow Mongols with bowed legs, superb dark Cossacks, to each we had to explain: "Two years in the camp, we are exhausted, leave us alone." But they wanted to make love to their French sisters.'

One of the Russians, on hearing the women were French concentration-camp survivors, rose to his feet indignantly and declared: 'You are one of the conquerors like ourselves and you sleep in straw, while a German family next door sleeps in beds.' At which he picked up his rifle saying: 'I'm going to kill them. You shall have their bed.' The Russian then marched the French women to the house where a family of Germans, including several children, were eating. As the Russian pointed his rifle at the Germans screaming '*Kaputt, kaputt*', Micheline interpreted for the family. The German farmer rose and led the women to a room that contained beds. The Russian then left, embracing the French women and taking one of the German girls with him. 'Later that night she returned to the farmhouse sobbing.'

There is little doubt that the worst violence was meted out to German women. 'I remember my mother held my little sister tight to her bosom as a kind of protection. She said the Russians have respect for little children,' recalled Wolfgang Stegemann, then a twelve-year-old Fürstenberg schoolboy. The German soldiers had left Fürstenberg about one hour before. 'It was very silent, then came a great noise, and the Russians came into the village on foot. Most were drunk and they came into the houses and destroyed everything. There were a lot of atrocities. A lot of rapes.'

Rudolf Rehländer, who grew up in the same village as Dorothea Binz, three miles away, remembered what happened when the Red Army arrived at Altglobsow. 'The first ones rampaged through our houses. Everything was looted – boots, clothes. They left the village with five or six watches on their arms. Then they started to rape. The first troops were the worst. They were the ones who carried out most of the rape. Almost every woman in the village was raped unless she had managed to hide.'

I wondered if Dorothea's mother was still in the village. Rudolf thought she was, because his family ran the village bar where Rose Binz drank. 'I had the job of filling glasses and I couldn't fill Rose Binz's glass quick enough.'

It was the same everywhere, says Rudolf, and there were hardly any men in the village at the time; either they were at the front or they had fled or killed themselves. Rudolf, just seventeen, was one of the oldest left behind, so he and the other boys had to bury the bodies. The mayor and three other top Nazis in the village killed themselves.

> I remember we were burying the mayor when someone shouted, 'Come quick,' because they'd found the Ortsbauernführer [the peasant leader]. We

ran there and it was a horrible sight. Both he and his wife had been hanged, but their bodies had been taken down and were lying on the ground. The woman was naked from the waist down and had a stick up her vagina. She was just lying there in the forest and I had to bury them.

I asked the Red Army intelligence officer Yaacov Drabkin what he thought of the atrocities.

Yes, everything happened. After what our soldiers had seen and been through it was difficult to tell them not to kill every German they saw. When the war was over I had to talk to the German population, explaining that the Red Army was not so bad. I had to respond to the German nation for all our crimes and I always heard in reply about the rapes.

I asked him about the rape of the Ravensbrück prisoners. At first he expressed surprise that it had happened, 'as they were in such a terrible state'. He said:

One should understand that it was a terrible, terrible monstrous war and everyone had gone completely inhuman. The soldiers had just fought their way through the fires of Danzig. The whole city was in flames. After that they just wanted to stay alive until the end. And remember that at Fürstenberg it was not yet over. Berlin had not been taken yet. There were still several days to go.

By early May, the fighting troops had largely moved on past Ravensbrück but Major Bulanov stayed behind to impose order, moving into Dorothea Binz's villa. He 'behaved decently' and tried to help the women, but the camp was now in chaos, with male and female prisoners roaming around looting and destroying. He and his staff could not determine how many prisoners were here, or who they were. They could not keep track of the death toll. 'Women started dying faster than ever after the Russians arrived,' said Kamila Janovic, a Pole who stayed behind to help. 'I think they had tried so hard to hold on until the liberation that when they relaxed they died.' There was no means to burn or bury them, so the corpses continued to pile up. Many prisoners died miles away from the camp, possibly because they ate and drank too much for their emaciated bodies to digest.

Prisoners began wandering around Fürstenberg. 'I remember them sitting in the street and under trees,' said Wolfgang Stegemann. 'They seemed very quiet. Very shy.' Major Bulanov ordered local people – now mostly women – to go to the camp to help clear up and bury the dead. 'When my mother came back she was very sad and depressed, but she never told me what she saw,' Stegemann recalled.

The Soviets brought in better food, as well as blood and medicines, and restored the electricity. Camilla Sovotna remembers a French priest arriving, and a British woman called Pat turned up to help.

One day Marie-Claude went looking for mattresses in the SS houses, and found a male prisoner asleep in a big bed, 'his head on a feather pillow under a pink satin quilt'. Another day she entered Suhren's house. She found a piano and played on it for hours. 'I felt welling up in me hopes and desires that had so long been buried.'

Fifty miles northwest, Fritz Suhren was fleeing for his life.

Suhren's gamble that the subcamp of Malchow would be a last safe haven for the SS had backfired. By 2 May it was clear that the Red Army, not the Americans, were closing in on Malchow, which would be overrun within hours. According to Odette, held hostage there for the past four days, the camp was littered with bodies as the SS periodically opened fire on the prisoners.

When more prisoners poured in and the carnage mounted, Odette asked Suhren to open the gates and let everyone go. She described the scene outside Suhren's office to her biographer. A radio was blaring out the news that Berlin had fallen, the Germans had surrendered in Italy, and the British had taken Lübeck. Inside, she found Suhren in tears. 'Adolf Hitler, the Führer of Germany, is dead. He died as a hero in the forefront of battle,' Suhren told her, 'his mouth twitching in ungovernable grief'.

Suhren told Odette to get into his black Mercedes-Benz car, along with two Polish women who had worked for him at Ravensbrück, and his white dog Lotti. They drove off, escorted by armed SS packed into cars in front and behind. After about two hours the cars stopped by a wood. 'He [Suhren] opened the back of the car, took out an armful of official papers, walked to the edge of the trees, and made a fire. They were Ravensbrück records. When the papers were consumed he stirred the ashes with his foot, making sure that there was nothing left.'

Suhren then turned to Odette and said: 'So that's that. Are you hungry?' He produced sandwiches 'wrapped in a white napkin', a pot of crystallised cherries and a bottle of wine. He showed her the label – Nuits-Saint-Georges – and said: 'There you are. A real French Burgundy.'

The convoy drove on, and after a while Suhren told Odette he was taking her to the Americans. She didn't believe him, telling Suhren that when the Americans saw the SS escort they would open fire 'and we will all be killed'. Suhren replied, 'You are quite right,' and he stopped to tell the other cars to keep a good distance behind him.

After nightfall they reached the small village of Rostoff. Odette saw a group of soldiers in unfamiliar uniforms at a point where the road narrowed. 'One of them cradled a gun in the crook of his arm, stood in the middle of the road and shouted for the car to stop.' In broken English, Suhren told the American soldier: 'This is Frau Churchill. She is related to Winston Churchill, the Prime Minister of England.' Odette said she then stepped out of the car and added: 'And this is Fritz Suhren, commandant of Ravensbrück concentration camp. Please take him as your prisoner.'

As the Allies moved on forward, seizing the last slice of territory, prisoners wandering around in no-man's-land suddenly ran into advancing American, Russian, French and British troops. By 5 May every remaining subcamp had been liberated except for Neurolau in the Sudeten Mountains. Here, that day, Maria Bielicka and her Polish comrades were still waiting for the end of the war.

After the SS guards had left them hiding in the beer warehouse, Maria and her group had retraced their steps back to Neurolau. They knew that the German manager of the porcelain factory was probably still there, but they also reckoned that all the SS guards must have fled. Neurolau seemed the safest place to wait for liberation.

Across the Sudeten Mountains, just a few miles from Neurolau, one of the final battles of the war in Europe was under way. US forces had surrounded more than 100,000 German soldiers, including two panzer divisions, whose commanders were refusing to surrender.

'We had no idea what was going on,' said Maria.

> We began to wonder if the war would ever be over. Then one day we discovered somehow that it was finished, and crying like mad, we decided we were not going to sit there any longer. We discovered the Russians were only fourteen kilometres away and we didn't want to fall into their hands. But we had to act fast if we were to get to the Americans in time.
>
> So I went to the factory director and said: 'For tomorrow I need a lorry and a driver, thirty loaves of bread and three sacks of potatoes.' He said OK, but can you send the lorry back with the driver when you've finished with it. He said the Russians would be there soon and would want to check his inventory and he'd be in trouble if the lorry was missing. Stupid man, he should have escaped in it instead of worrying about that.

I asked her what happened to the man.

> I don't know and I don't care. He was probably shot. But we got the lorry. And you know, before we left he invited us to see his display of fine porcelain. I remember he showed us a beautiful dinner service made before the

war for our president, with the Polish Eagle on it. He wanted to show that he was on our side. Then he wished us well and tried to shake my hand. I said: 'No, I won't do that.' It was too late for that.

The lorry driver took about thirty women five kilometres up the road and dropped them at a crossroads to return for a second load. 'As we stood there we suddenly saw an American soldier. He was sitting all alone on the side of the road, smoking, just like that,' said Maria, imitating someone drawing slowly on a cigarette.

We walked up to him and he said: 'Who on earth are you?' We said: 'We are from a concentration camp.' He said: 'What's that?' We were speaking English, but we soon discovered he was a Pole from Chicago.

He said: 'Oh my God, what do I do with you? Are you hungry?'

Then he looked at us some more and said: 'Look, we can't do anything for you today, we are rather busy. We've just taken about a million Germans as prisoners.' Then the American stood up and said: 'Come over here a minute.' We thought this is strange and he led us up to the top of the hill and pointed down, and we were looking over this sea of Germans. He told us it was the whole of Hitler's Seventh Army. They had just surrendered. There were heaps of them as far as you could see. They were lying, sitting, standing. There were tanks and mountains of ammunition. And there we were, in our prisoner clothes, standing looking over them. You can imagine our joy.

# Epilogue

On 28 April, under a blustery sky, the midday ferry from Copenhagen pulled up to the docks at Malmö and the first prisoners rescued from Ravensbrück by Bernadotte's White Buses came down the gangplank.

'All in thin rags, shoes made of paper and wood and odds and ends,' wrote a journalist. Some were carried on stretchers. Some clutched Red Cross boxes, and small parcels containing lists of the dead. Ann Sheridan carried a pot of poison smuggled out of the Youth Camp. A Dutch woman, Anne Hendrix, carried her two-month-old baby lying sleeping in a box.

Once on land the women looked ahead to see a series of tents, from which men in white coats appeared and asked them to strip; the women screamed in horror. Inside the tents they were sprayed with disinfectant and asked to stand under showers. 'We thought, what is this nightmare all over again?' remembers Yvonne Baseden.

For their part, the doctors who examined the women on arrival were horrified by what they saw. One recalled how a woman screamed out when she saw him – a man in a white coat. She kept crying: 'I don't want to burn, I don't want to burn.' Some of the nurses fainted.

The first night the women were put up in the towering Malmö citadel, part of which housed a museum; Yvonne found herself sleeping beneath a dinosaur.

By the time George Clutton, second secretary at the British legation in Stockholm, arrived to report on the British contingent's arrival, the women were recovering strength, and greeted him wearing Union Jack badges that Lady Mallet, wife of the British ambassador to Sweden, had sent them. Some had curled their hair and acquired handbags and jewellery, offered by the people of Malmö. To the young diplomat, the British women presented an astonishing picture. Julia Barry, the Hungarian camp policewoman, was 'a very cheerful lady and pathetically patriotic about the Channel Islands. Her main anxiety is to get back to her island and find the three bottles of sherry she hid in her piano just before her arrest,' noted Clutton. Barbara Chatenay had 'obviously suffered much' but was 'cheerful and serene'. She had twice been chosen to be gassed, she told Clutton, but after protesting that they couldn't gas an Englishwoman, was spared both times.

Most remarkable was Countess Françoise de Laverney, who had 'suffered with six weeks' solitary confinement, during which she was fed only once a week. She was very emaciated but absolutely on top of the world. She had in her possession a valuable diamond ring, a diamond bracelet and a diamond brooch which she claimed to have kept from the Germans by swallowing constantly.'

Clutton said that the women showed 'a joy in life that I have never encountered in a human being', adding this may have been due to their feeling of 'triumph over death and evil'. It was certainly down to a knowledge they had survived by pure luck.

He noted that other British women had not been lucky. A Miss Jackson was murdered at the Youth Camp and a Mrs Gould from Jersey had been 'gassed and burned'. Clutton heard of an Irish woman 'who starved to death in Block 22', while the British golf champion Pat Cheramy was 'Sent to Mauthausen. Fate unknown.' Mary Young, the Scottish nurse, was 'killed at the Youth Camp, too ill to resist'. News of the murder of the SOE women was reported back to Baker Street. One of the SOE group, Yvonne Rudellat, was thought to have been on the last transport to Belsen.

Clutton was also instructed to file a report on the camp itself, which was difficult as the women's accounts 'telescoped backwards', but he found ' a very intelligent French woman called Germaine Tillion' on whose information he was able to rely. Germaine, who began passing on her analysis of the camp as soon as she reached safety, briefed Clutton on slave labour, saying it meant 'giving prisoners only enough food to keep them alive for the time they might be useful, then killing them and replacing them with someone else'.

When it landed on Foreign Office desks back in London, Clutton's report elicited little comment on the remarkable stories of these British women snatched from Ravensbrück.

There was far more to be said as to whether it might be appropriate to ask the Treasury to stump up for a token of Britain's appreciation for Sven Frykman, the Swedish driver who had been responsible for getting the British women out. A series of official notes on the question reached a view that it would be best to give Frykman a gold watch.

Back in Germany, the camp was emptying fast. By mid-May the last survivors were heading home – some walked all the way to Prague, Warsaw and even Vienna, joining the millions of refugees, ex-prisoners and captured German soldiers on Europe's roads. Micheline Maurel and her friend Michelle stopped a passing cart, which was flying a French flag, and hitched a lift.

Reaching a US camp, they joined a long line of men queuing for soup. An American soldier spotted them, took their hands and ushered them to the front, saying: 'Ladies first.' Micheline tried to thank him but cried instead.

Mothers all over Europe wept on seeing daughters suddenly turn up at their doors, but many survivors had no homes to go to. Gypsies reaching home in Austria found entire villages destroyed. Many waited at home and nobody returned. The Spanish Jew Louis Kugelman, freed from Buchenwald, learned that his wife had died at Ravensbrück and that his five-year-old daughter Stella had disappeared without trace; he began to search.

The Russians had to wait the longest to go back. All were held for several months in so-called 'filtration camps' where they were forced to undergo checks carried out by SMERSh, which had already started looking for 'traitors'. Antonina Nikiforova was one of their first victims. As she awaited repatriation Antonina passed the time gathering more material for her book, but the SMERSh got to hear of this, seized her notes and manuscript, and used it to concoct evidence showing she was a Nazi collaborator. They then persuaded Antonina's comrade Valentina Chechko to accuse her. Chechko made a statement to SMERSh on 15 June 1945, stating that Antonina Nikiforova 'took part in the selection of people for extermination' at Ravensbrück and that she 'twice gave ill people poison'. Valentina also confessed to selecting people for extermination herself. This was the same Valentina Chechko who would later face trial at Simferopol and accuse other comrades.

In another filtration camp Yevgenia Klemm bided her time working as a translator for a Russian general. Others worked at a Soviet military court where Ravensbrück camp guards were put on trial, though several German guards were lynched instead.

By the end of the year most of the Russian women were piling into trains east, taking with them trunks, bags, sacks, all packed with items looted from abandoned German homes. Ilena Barsukova recalled that Yevgenia Klemm took more than anyone; her carriage was piled with pots and pans, books, blankets, old clothes. 'She knew she had nothing to go back to,' remembered Ilena. 'My mother had a cow and a chicken, so at least there would be food, but Yevgenia had no family left.'

Against the tide of Europe's refugees, a victors' army – different from the fighting forces – was moving into Germany. These were men and women, civilians as well as soldiers, assigned to set up the military government, carve Germany into zones of occupation and hunt down war criminals.

Fritz Suhren, arrested at a US checkpoint with Odette Sansom, was one of the first Ravensbrück criminals to fall into Allied hands. Hearing that the commandant of Ravensbrück had been captured, the British SOE officer

Vera Atkins flew out to Germany to interrogate him about her missing women agents. Accompanied by a Scottish major, Angus Fyffe, Vera – in WAAF uniform – entered the interrogation room at a Paderborn internment camp to find the once-dapper Suhren standing in socks, breeches and shirt. Suhren saluted, but Atkins got nothing out of him; he even denied there were any British women in Ravensbrück, apart from Odette.

In the last chaotic days at the camp Suhren had floundered, cut off from orders, but now he was quite clearly following orders again; these commands, spread among captured SS men held in internment camps, were that none of them should admit to anything at all, in order not to implicate comrades.

Vera then interrogated two women guards held at the same camp. According to Angus Fyffe, one was 'a middle aged woman of very low mentality' and the other 'looked half silly'. These guards confirmed there were English women in the camp, so Atkins and Fyffe confronted Suhren again; he still admitted nothing but 'started slightly' at mention of the crematorium. 'By this time it was dark and the cell was lit by a fluorescent strip, which gave Suhren a sickly colour,' recalled Fyffe.

Not long after, Percival Treite gave himself up at a British checkpoint, saying he had deserted his position at Ravensbrück on 30 April 'in order to avoid fighting as his father was a British subject'.

Dorothea Binz – last seen fleeing Malchow subcamp on a bicycle – was soon picked up, and after some months was taken to a small British prison in the woods near Minden. Approaching the jail, Binz collapsed in fear and had to be carried in. Perhaps she had heard about the fate of her Ravensbrück colleague Irma Grese, a graduate of Auschwitz and Belsen as well as Ravensbrück, who had recently been hanged. Grese uttered one last word to the British hangman, Albert Pierrepoint: '*Schnell.*' Inside the British prison Binz was given some knitting to settle her down.

By the autumn of 1945 the world's attention was focused on Nuremberg, where the Allies were trying the major Nazi war criminals: Göring, von Ribbentrop, Hess, Speer and the like. These were 'the grand conspirators', said Robert H. Jackson, the United States chief prosecutor, 'men of station and rank who did not soil their own hands with blood, but who knew how to use lesser folk as their tools'. The purpose of the military tribunals at Nuremberg was to expose how the Nazi conspiracy evolved. The 'grand plan' was carried out, in Jackson's words, by 'achieving one goal then setting out to achieve a more ambitious one'.

As the twenty-four men 'of station and rank' were led from the Nuremberg dock, sixteen 'lesser folk', seven women and nine men, filed in to the dock of No.

1 War Crimes Court in Hamburg. It was 5 December 1946 and the women's camp of Ravensbrück was about to come under its own spotlight in the first of six cases prepared by British investigators. Located as it was in the Russian sector of occupied Germany, Ravensbrück should have been tried by the Russians, but Moscow showed no interest. As the British had special knowledge, largely due to Vera Atkins's search for SOE women, Britain took on the trial.

The backdrop – rubble-strewn streets and bomb craters – was reminiscent of Nuremberg, but the atmosphere at Hamburg was entirely different: less grandiose, more intimate, more feminine.

The female defendants, including three Kapos, were the first to enter the dock; then the men shuffled in and began animated conversations with their lawyers. Each prisoner wore a black number on a white card around his or her neck. Absent were both commandants: Max Koegel had hanged himself with a strip of blanket. Fritz Suhren had escaped from his cell just days before the trial. Others too had disappeared. Nevertheless, those in the dock were representative of the crimes, especially as Johann Schwarzhuber, the gassing specialist trained at Auschwitz, had latterly fallen into British hands. The accused certainly all had a great deal of blood on their hands, though these 'lesser folk' did not look like mass murderers.

It would be another fifteen years before the American writer Hannah Arendt coined the phrase 'the banality of evil' in her account of the 1961 trial in Jerusalem of Adolf Eichmann, but a writer called Jerrard Tickell, sitting on the Hamburg press bench, identified the same phenomenon here. The women guards in the dock 'might have stepped out of a bread queue in any German city,' he wrote.

Binz had even taken the trouble to perm her hair for the occasion. Elisabeth Marschall 'sat bolt upright as if upholstered in granite stays', said Tickell. More noticeable were the Kapos: Carmen Mory, the Block 10 Blockova, wore a grimace and a red fox fur; Vera Salvequart – 'Dr Vera', the Youth Camp 'nurse' – had a look of 'lazy carnality' and also wore a fur coat, acquired – it was said – by selling gold teeth, which she kept in the back of a car given to her by American servicemen while on the run.

The men looked ordinary too. Only Percival Treite stood out; he would have looked 'more at home in a Harley Street consulting room', said Tickell, probably a studied pose to underline his English roots.

But it was precisely the ordinariness of the Hamburg defendants that made this drama so shocking. At Nuremberg the court heard about the motivations of the 'grand conspirators' but here they learned about local girls called Binz and Bösel who came to work at Ravensbrück, then did as they were told.

Asked why she had committed her crimes, Grete Bösel replied: 'I behaved decently but then after two weeks I changed and accepted the methods that were generally used.' When Dorothea Binz was asked why she didn't tell anyone about the atrocities she witnessed, she responded by saying: 'There was no point as everyone knew.' Aged nineteen when she started work at the camp, Dorothea was a blank slate. She learned about life during her six years as a guard at Ravensbrück; the world of the camp seemed – to her – normal.

Nuremberg had heard about 'crimes against humanity', whereas here the judges heard about crimes against women, and these would have a particular power to shock – and to revolt. The prosecution lawyers knew this. The junior counsel John da Cunha, aged twenty-three, who had barely begun his legal training, was physically sick when he first read through the Ravensbrück testimony in preparation for the case. 'I became hardened after a while – coarsened,' he told me. 'One does.'

The male judges, though stiff in their military uniforms, were not yet 'hardened', so Stephen Stewart, the chief prosecutor, paced his opening speech. 'In Mecklenburg, about fifty miles north of Berlin, there is a group of lakes to which the gentry of that once great capital used to go for weekends,' he said, before moving on to speak of 'nameless things done to women's bodies', as if trying to tone down the special horrors that were to come.

It wasn't long before the 'nameless things' were laid bare, but they were hard to describe to those who hadn't been there. At Nuremberg the court was assisted by films 'which turned the stomachs of the world' and by tons of captured Nazi documents. There were almost no photographs at Hamburg, and few documents other than those the women themselves had smuggled out. So the prosecution produced drawings by the prisoner Violette Lecoq 'to bring home how Ravensbrück must have appeared'; among them was her pen-and-ink sketch 'Agonies Juives', showing five women's bodies slumped in five barrows as Violette had seen them after they collapsed on their way to the Siemens plant. 'The intelligence of the judges accepts the evidence but their imagination reels from it,' commented Tony Somerhough, head of the British war crimes unit.

Germaine Tillion would later criticise the trials on the grounds that it was impossible to try the crimes of the 'abnormal world' of concentration camps within the confines of a 'normal' court. The two worlds were bound to collide because neither judges nor lawyers could possibly comprehend the unprecedented horror of the camps. Only the accused and witnesses understood the 'abnormal world', said Germaine, which made them partners in the sharing of this awful knowledge; the rest of the court was in the dark. For example, nobody in the court could possibly imagine what had happened in the *Idiotenstübchen* (idiots' room), but Loulou Le Porz, Violette Lecoq and Jacqueline Héreil shared this piece of awful knowledge with Carmen Mory, whom they accused from the witness stand as the former Blockova glared back with venom and fired off notes to her lawyers accusing the 'French bitches' of lying. Treite also knew about the *Idiotstübchen*; he had carried out experiments on the brains of the 'idiots' to see what made them 'mad', apparently unaware of where the real insanity lay.

Johann Schwarzhuber may have had an inkling. On advice from lawyers, he never took the stand, but he often looked up from the dock and tried to catch the eye of John da Cunha. 'It was as if he wanted me to know he understood somehow.'

It has often been said that the SS and their underlings found it easy to kill in the death camps in Poland because they didn't get to know their victims, such was the speed and the industrial scale of the murder. But at Ravensbrück, so much smaller, and in existence for such a long time, they often knew the prisoners well.

So personal was Irène Ottelard's hatred of Dr Treite that on the witness stand Irène – nearly blind – asked for a guiding hand so she could step down and approach the dock in order to look him in the eye. Treite's refusal to treat her infected leg had meant she was selected for the Youth Camp, 'where people laid about and died'. Asked how she survived the Youth Camp, she said: 'I should think it was my destiny, because it was necessary for some witnesses at least of what happened to return to tell the truth. That is why I am alive.'

As there were at Nuremberg, there were accusations at Hamburg of 'victors' justice': only crimes committed against Allied nationals were examined, which left lasting bitterness among German survivors. Nevertheless, the prosecution here achieved a great deal. Within a short time the court collated the single most important body of evidence about Ravensbrück, and established in the clearest terms the simple fact that everything about the camp was designed to kill. Of the total number who passed through the camp – estimated at that time to have been 123,000 – about 90,000 died, the court heard, though this figure would later be disputed. In the end, said Stewart, the camp became 'an enormous extermination machine', the 'most terrible women's prison in history'.

The hearings also shone light on the courage of the prisoners, not least because much of the evidence the prosecution relied on had been smuggled out of the camp at great risk. At the related Nuremberg medical trials, where Karl Gebhardt and his Hohenlychen team were tried for carrying out medical experiments, the case rested in large part on documents secured in the camp by Zofia Mączka, the Polish radiologist.

But Zofia did more than help convict the guilty. Her most memorable contribution was her impassioned statement about the Polish prisoners.

Speaking as if they had emerged victorious from a front-line battle, Zofia said it was 'their heroism, super-human tenacity and exceptional willpower to survive that were decisive'. The experiments had proved nothing for science, but they had proved something for humanity. 'The soldiers who have received the Order Virtuti Militari can proudly stand at attention before Maria Kusmierczuk,' said Zofia. Maria very nearly died when Gebhardt's doctors infected her with tetanus but fought her way back to life. Gebhardt insisted to the end that the experiments on the Polish rabbits had been dreamt up by Himmler and he was only following orders, but the defence of 'following orders' had already been rejected at the main Nuremberg trial. In any case it was clear by now that everyone was following Himmler's orders – the Reichsführer SS decided on everything that happened in the camps. In case of doubt on this point, the astonishing 'Order on Flogging' discovered by the Allies, showing each beating was to be reported direct to the Reichsführer 'for approval', gave the proof. Himmler himself, however, never had to answer for his crimes because he swallowed a cyanide capsule shortly after capture.

The Allied Ravensbrück trials continued for two years. In that time Binz, Schwarzhuber, Binder, Ramdohr, Salvequart, Neudeck and Gebhardt were among those executed. When Binz was led to the gallows she gave her pendant to an officer and was reported to have said: 'I hope you won't think that we were all evil people.'

Carmen Mory was sentenced to death, at which she fired off more angry letters, this time to the judge – 'you sly hypocritical British fox' – then slit her wrist rather than hang. Treite was also sentenced to death. He secured several pleas for clemency, including one from his 'Queen Mary' (Mary Lindell) and one from Yvonne Baseden, but all were rejected, at which he too slit his wrists.

By 1948 the Allies had lost their appetite for punishing the Nazis and both the war crimes trials and the process of 'de-Nazification' – whereby Nazi supporters were brought to book and denied top jobs – were shut down. There were exceptions. Fritz Suhren was recaptured in 1949 and executed, along with Hans Pflaum, the labour chief, after a further Ravensbrück trial held at Rastatt in France. However, from 1949 the main responsibility for investigating Nazi war crimes was handed to the new German courts.

The reason the Allies cut short their trials was clear: the Cold War was under way, Germany was about to split in two and the new priority was to help West Germany rebuild so it could join in the fight against the communists. Most notable amongst the perpetrators let off the hook were German industrialists. Whatever their complicity with the Nazi horror, or their profits from slave labour, these companies were needed to help the West fight the Cold War. Not a single member of the Siemens board, or the Ravensbrück Siemens staff, was ever charged with war crimes at Ravensbrück or anywhere else where they used slave labour.* The only known legal action against a Siemens employee was a de-Nazification case launched in 1946 by the British in Berlin against Wolf-Dietrich von Witzleben, the head of personnel, when he was cleared of past crimes and continuing Nazi links. The case was reopened in 1948 after communist witnesses brought new accusations against Siemens and von Witzleben. In 1949, as the Soviet blockade of Berlin intensified, the accusations were again thrown out – obviously in part because the communists' motives were not trusted – and the case shut down.

As the trials ended, and the transcripts were locked away in London for thirty years, Allied prosecutors exhorted historians to pick up where they had left off, to make sense of the Nazi crimes. But history soon forgot Ravensbruck.

Survivors found that nobody back home wanted to hear about the camp; there were many reasons. In London, the Special Operations Executive was wound up amid evidence of bungling and betrayal, which had contributed to the capture of the SOE women taken to Ravensbrück. To close the scandal down, SOE veterans were told never to speak of their wartime work again, which meant no talk of the camps.

Those British women who had volunteered for resistance work while in France found no interest in their stories either. The governess Mary O'Shaughnessy, who had survived the Youth Camp, hoped to write a book about what she'd witnessed, but was told by a friend in Fleet Street that the British public would not want to read it.

Returning to her home in Stavanger, on Norway's west coast, Nelly Langholm tried to tell her family and friends about her experiences, 'but my sister took me aside and told me not to talk like that again as people thought I'd gone mad'.

For the French, there was a particular taboo about the atrocities committed on the women. Many were asked if they had been raped. Most had not, but they were treated as if they had been collectively violated nonetheless, and felt ashamed. 'I was a young girl before the war, I wasn't married and I was supposed to be pure. I couldn't explain what it had been like so I said nothing. It was easier that way. We weren't proud of what we'd been through,' said Christiane de Cuverville.

Denise Dufournier went to Switzerland to convalesce and wrote her memoir while events were fresh in her mind, and Germaine Tillion began work on her first Ravensbrück history, but most of their compatriots stayed

* Two Siemens directors, both SS members, committed suicide in 1945, no doubt because they anticipated war crimes trials. Otto Grade, the Siemens manager at Ravensbrück, disappeared without trace.

silent. Some French women found it easier to make up stories about what happened, knowing that people simply wouldn't believe the truth. Loulou Le Porz, however, had to tell the truth in her first few weeks back in Paris because she was given the task of providing information to families looking for missing loved ones.

A French doctor came to Loulou one day, looking for his sister. 'She died in Block 10 – a woman of about sixty. She had told me how she hid British airmen in her house but her brother didn't even know why she had been arrested. So I told him the full story. He was a typical old-fashioned type, standing there in a stiff suit with a melon [bowler] hat. As I talked I saw that straight away there were tears in his eyes.'

In post-war France trying to come to terms with its own collaboration with the Nazis, the stories of the real resisters – and those who returned from the camps could prove it better than most – were often unwelcome. Moreover, the French resistance was considered an entirely male affair. 'These men who had done nothing strutted on the streets with their medals,' scoffed Loulou. On her return to Paris Michèle Agniel could barely stand, and as a result was given a permit to jump the ration queues. 'But when I did a man complained, so I said I had just come back from a concentration camp. He said, "*Mais quand même*, they know how to queue in concentration camps, don't they?" I hit him.'

Back in Bordeaux, Loulou Le Porz returned to her work as a doctor, and decided to respect 'her dead' in the camp by keeping her memories to herself. 'I'd watched my friends die so courageously amidst the vermin and the filth that I couldn't talk about them now with those who wouldn't understand.'

One person Loulou did talk about, however, was Anne Spoerry ('Claude'), the Swiss-French doctor who had been 'bewitched' by Carmen Mory and helped beat and kill the 'lunatics' in Block 10. Spoerry had refused to attend the Hamburg trial, and a deal was done for her to be tried in Switzerland instead, where she was cleared. After the Swiss trial, Loulou, Violette Lecoq and other French women were determined she shouldn't practise medicine in France and secured a ban. Spoerry left for Kenya, where she lived and worked as a flying doctor, devoting the rest of her life to the poor and needy, seeking redemption and trying to forget her past.

Yevgenia Klemm could never forget her past. As soon as she arrived back in Odessa she tried to rebuild her life. Her flat had been taken from her, but a fellow teacher gave her lodgings and she secured her old job, teaching how to teach history at the Odessa College.

Harassment by SMERSh soon began again. In March 1946 six Ravensbrück women were found guilty by a court in Leningrad of collaborating with 'the fascists' and were sent into exile in Siberia. After this all survivors lived in terror. Stella Kugelman, aged five at the end of the war, was taken by her last camp mother, Aunt Olympiada, to an orphanage outside Moscow. Aunt Olympiada never came back. 'Nobody came to see me because they didn't want to advertise they'd been in the camp, and nobody wanted to adopt me as I was too thin and yellow,' says Stella. 'In the orphanage we were taught not to laugh or cry and to be as quiet as possible and nothing would happen, so that's what I did.'

The terror reached its zenith in 1949, when the Simferopol doctors' trial took place, as a result of which the three Ravensbrück doctors, Lyusya Malygina, Maria Klyugman and Anna Fedchenko were found guilty of collaborating with the SS and sent to Siberian camps.

Klemm was often interrogated during this investigation but not accused. Then in the early 1950s Stalin's campaign against 'cosmopolitans' – foreigners and Jews – began and rumours spread around the Odessa College that Klemm must be a spy as she had been in the West during the war. As a result, her teaching work was cut back. Friends spoke later of 'wicked and unfair accusations made against Klemm' by comrades who 'worked for the organs' – for 'SMERSh'.

In March 1953 Stalin died and the atmosphere began to ease, but inside the Odessa College harassment of Klemm intensified, and in early September, on the eve of a new term, she received news that she would no longer be able to teach at all. The following morning – 3 September 1953 – Yevgenia was found dead. She had hanged herself in the small kitchen of her friend's flat. In a suicide note she said that she had taken her life because she was not allowed to teach any more and nobody had bothered to tell her why.

'All my life I have worked honestly, with all my soul and energy. And to this day I do not know what I have done wrong ... Was it because I was taken prisoner by the fascists in Sevastopol and spent nearly three years in a death camp? Am I really such a criminal that I am not worth talking to? I cannot live any longer.' For many years Klemm's suicide could not be spoken of; most of her comrades never learned that she had died. Her body was buried in an unmarked grave.

Although their case was the most extreme, the Russians were not the only survivors to be terrorised into silence after the war. Amongst many others, now living behind the Iron Curtain, the Czechs were constrained in what they could say about Ravensbrück; they certainly couldn't talk of their dear friend Milena Jesenska. Reviled as a traitor to communism, Milena's courage in opposing the Nazis before her capture and spirited resilience in the camp were obliterated from her country's history.

Three years after the war the site of the camp itself, now in the German

Democratic Republic (DDR), lay abandoned; piles of human ashes lay beside a mass grave outside the crematorium. A Soviet tank regiment then moved into the main compound, destroying the remaining barracks and flattening the site.

A group of former German prisoners – 'mothers for peace' – led moves to create a memorial to honour the memory of the dead, but the political reality of the Cold War meant that only the communist resisters were remembered: like the other camps in the DDR – Buchenwald and Sachsenhausen – Ravensbrück soon became an official communist shrine. The centrepiece of the memorial was the statue called *Tragende*, inspired by Olga Benario and said to represent 'a strong woman, with knowledge, who helped her weaker comrades'. It was a monument to 'our heroines who fought'; in other words, the communist ideal of womanhood. The fact that Olga was also a Jew, and was murdered because she was Jewish, was not mentioned. Non-communist prisoners – as well as Gypsies, asocials and other Jews – were also largely ignored by the East German camp history.

One of the leading camp communists, Maria Wiedmaier, became head of the officially backed Victims of Fascism (VVN), with power to rule on who should qualify as a true 'fighter against fascism' and who should receive help and money.

Mina Rupp, another veteran camp communist, was not one of them. On arrival in the camp Rupp had been sentenced to a thrashing for stealing half a carrot, and when appointed a Blockova turned to thrashing prisoners herself. In 1948 Maria Wiedmaier reported Rupp to the Soviet police for crimes in the camp. She confessed at her trial to selecting prisoners for gassing, and was sentenced to twenty-five years' forced labour at a prison in Dresden.

By the mid-1950s Wiedmaier and several other 'mothers for peace' were working for the East German secret police, the Stasi. In 1956, under the cover name Olga, Wiedmaier was given forty West German marks and sent through the Iron Curtain to 'observe the mood of the population' in areas of NATO training.*

In the 1960s the Stasi rounded up Ravensbrück guards found living in the East and launched their own war crimes trials, during which the accused were often persuaded to invent new horrors, as the Eastern courts sought to show that they had done a better job at trying Nazi crimes than the West. Their position was perhaps understandable; not only had the Allies let the majority of war criminals walk free, but by the early 1950s most of those they had sentenced were out of prison. Herta Oberheuser, the Ravensbrück camp

* The Stasi also kept a file on Grete Buber-Neumann. Her groundbreaking book *Under Two Dictators* (1948) revealed in greater detail than anyone to date the horrors of Stalin's Gulag camps and was naturally banned in the East. Even today, the work has not been translated into Russian.

doctor, was even practising medicine again as a children's doctor in Stocksee, in Schleswig-Holstein.

Siemens's role at Ravensbrück and other camps remained hidden until the 1960s, when investigators seeking compensation for Jewish claimants unearthed the facts. The company reluctantly paid out small sums into a fund, but accepted no liability, saying it was coerced.

Later trials held by the West German courts had produced few convictions, and pitiful sentences. In 1963 a much-vaunted Auschwitz trial was held at Frankfurt where Franz Lucas, a doctor at Auschwitz as well as at Ravensbrück, faced war crimes charges. Lucas had helped prisoners in Ravensbrück and Loulou Le Porz felt duty bound to testify on his behalf; she remembered in particular how Dr Lucas had brought milk for a pregnant Dutch woman who then died in childbirth in Block 10. However, as the trial exposed details of Lucas's previous crimes, including his selection of Jews for gassing at Auschwitz, his humanity at Ravensbrück looked more like an attempt to save his skin. Nevertheless, Loulou said she didn't regret speaking up for Lucas; the help he gave to patients in Block 10 was not in dispute. After Lucas was freed, just four years later he pushed his luck by asking Loulou for a character reference so he could recoup his confiscated possessions. She refused: 'I said no. That's enough. This matter of his possessions had nothing to do with me.'

All this time survivors East and West battled to keep memories alive. In 1955 Antonina Nikiforova returned from exile in Siberia, where she had adopted an orphaned boy, and immediately started her research on Ravensbrück all over again by writing to survivors, asking for their memories of the camp and trying to find ways of speaking out.

In 1957 a toothless woman also expressed a need to speak out. Johanna Langefeld knocked on Grete Buber-Neumann's door in Frankfurt, determined to unburden herself of her story. Before Langefeld reminisced about her earlier life and the camp, however, the former chief guard told Grete about her post-war 'odyssey', including her many years hiding in Poland with the help of former prisoners and the Catholic Church.

After being fired from Ravensbrück in 1943 for helping the Polish rabbits, Langefeld was cleared of disciplinary offences by an SS court and sat out the war living with her sister in Munich. In 1946 she was picked up and interrogated by both the British and American war crimes investigators, who then extradited her to Poland to face charges at the Auschwitz trial in Kraków in 1947. Held in a Polish jail, she learned from the prison director that Polish women, former inmates from the camp, knew of her presence in custody and were determined to get her out 'because of what she had done for Poles in the camp', she told Grete.

However, when Langefeld did eventually escape, she did so of her own volition, or so she claimed. It was Christmas Eve 1947 and she had been assigned a task cleaning the prison stairs. Seeing an opportunity, she fled out of the front door into the dark, snowy Kraków streets before being invited to take shelter in a convent. From there, she was taken to safety in another convent in another Polish city.

Much is known today about the role of the Catholic Church in helping Nazi war criminals evade capture, but the story of Johanna Langefeld's escape has a curious twist: it was former Ravensbrück prisoners who persuaded the Church to help her. Polish survivors today refuse to divulge details, but it was almost certainly they who snatched her from jail and then hid her for the next ten years. In 1957 Langefeld became 'homesick', she told Grete, and wished to see her son again, so Langefeld's Polish protectors smuggled her back through the Iron Curtain. She reached West Germany in 1957, which was when she sought out Grete Buber-Neumann to 'explain her behaviour'.

After hearing her out, Grete concluded that Langefeld was 'a broken human being, who is repressed by heavy feelings of guilt'. The two women kept in touch, and Grete once visited Langefeld in Munich, where she lived. 'She had lost the strength to start her life anew. She told me that she'd like to be in prison, at least for two years, to pay for her crimes.' Langefeld died in Augsburg in 1975.

In the post-war years mainstream historians did little to investigate the detailed stories of the camps, preferring to theorise about the Nazi leadership and its coming to power rather than tell what happened on the ground. The camp for women – always low down the SS pecking order – was of no interest to historians at all, particularly as there were no official documents; oral history was distrusted. In the wake of the 1961 Eichmann trial, however, new interest was sparked in the Jewish death camps and writing on the Holocaust began to burgeon. But this in turn seemed to push the Germany-based concentration camps into the background. In the late 1960s certain historians searching for new narratives began to question the existence of gas chambers at Ravensbrück. The Ravensbrück survivors were in despair.

Michèle Agniel was sitting at home in Paris when her mother, who had lost her husband in the war, and had always spoken out about war crimes, walked in and slammed a newspaper down on the desk in front of her. The paper contained an article by one such historian. 'She said, "Now look. They are saying it never happened. You have no right to be silent any more." She was right. Many of us felt guilty we hadn't spoken out earlier. We should have had more courage.'

*

By this time, the children of survivors were beginning to ask questions, but most found answers hard to come by. As I talked to survivors, their children and grandchildren often came to listen; few had ever heard their mothers talk in detail about the war. Many in this second generation had been damaged, perhaps by years of separation when mothers were in the camp, or disturbed in later years by what their mothers had suffered and could not discuss. Maria Wilgat, daughter of Krysia, the secret letter writer, saw her mother erupt in fury when she heard the German language or if she saw red salvia flowers, but Krysia never told her daughter why. I heard of several in the second generation who had taken their own lives. Mina Rupp, the German communist, who confessed before a Soviet court to selecting fellow prisoners for gassing, was pardoned in 1954. Her daughter committed suicide by gassing herself two months before Rupp was freed from prison in Dresden.

Naomi Moscovitch, one of the Jewish children who arrived in the camp in 1943, spoke of a very different family tragedy. She had gone to live in Israel after the war, and when I met her there she talked for many hours about Ravensbrück, describing, most memorably, her recollections of a bomb at the children's Christmas party in 1944. As I got up to leave we talked about her new life in Israel, and she said it had been hard. She asked me if I knew about the Sbarro Pizzeria suicide bombing. On 9 August 2001 a Palestinian suicide bomber and his female accomplice walked into the Jerusalem pizzeria where Naomi's daughter, her daughter's husband and their three children were eating. The entire family were among the dead.

In the early 1980s a young West German schoolgirl was having difficulty finding out about Ravensbrück; it was a place she had heard her parents mention when they were talking about her grandfather Walter Sonntag, one of the first doctors at Ravensbrück and the most sadistic.

At the camp Sonntag married his fellow camp doctor Gerda Weyand and they had a child, Heidi. Clara,* Heidi's daughter, was born in 1966. She was five when she first sensed the taboo about her grandfather; her parents talked of how he had worked at the camp and afterwards was put in prison, but it had been a case of mistaken identity. 'I couldn't find out any more. At school we learned about Belsen, Dachau and the death camps, but not much about Ravensbrück. And the teaching didn't relate to real life. Teachers had to be careful what they said. They knew that parents or grandparents might have been involved.' The mystery about her grandfather made Clara unhappy. She developed a face rash, which she says worsened as the sense of taboo intensified. Clara's grandmother, Gerda, was still alive, but kept a distance from her

* Not her real name: she wishes to remain anonymous.

own daughter, telling her nothing. 'So my mother was brought up with all these losses and tried to make a nice world for herself saying her father wasn't such a bad guy.'

As a teenager Clara started her own research but did not know where to turn. 'I went to the Bundesarchiv but they told me I had to get permission to read anything. It isn't easy to find things out if you don't know how. I looked in books but Ravensbrück wasn't in the index.'

The end of the Cold War brought change for Ravensbrück. A West German director moved in to run the memorial site and plans were made to abolish the communist exhibits. Debate began about how the site should be preserved: as a cemetery, a crime scene or as a place of education and academic study? Changes came slowly; the Russians did not move out until 1994, and until then nobody could visit. But in 1995, the fiftieth anniversary of the liberation, survivors were invited back and many were able to come from the West for the first time. For those who had buried memories of the camp for so long, the return brought the deepest pain.

As Loulou Le Porz walked around the compound, she saw in her mind bodies piled up in the Block 10 washroom and spilling out of the mortuary. The speeches and the chattering crowd that had gathered for the memorial event presented a ridiculous backdrop to these visions of the dead and Loulou was pleased to get away. Michèle Agniel looked around and could not imagine this person – her younger self – who once had been here. 'It was as if it was someone else.'

After German reunification in 1990 small sums of compensation were at last paid to survivors in the East, which encouraged women who had never done so before to talk about the camp, and archives in Russia and Eastern Bloc countries were opened for the first time, revealing new evidence. A flurry of new material came to light in the West too – letters of a former SS man hidden in a chimney stack; diaries of mothers, never read before. Scholarly research on all the camps multiplied.

In America a new immigration computer helped US war crimes hunters trace Elfriede Huth, the former dog-handler at the camp who had entered the US illegally in 1959. Huth had lived in California, where she married a Jewish man called Fred Rinkel, whose parents had died at Auschwitz. Elfriede was extradited back to Germany, but there was little chance of a trial. Of the estimated 3500 women guards who passed through Ravensbrück only a fraction have ever come under investigation in the German courts, which don't even keep a record of the numbers they have charged. It is probably less than twenty-five, with even fewer convicted. I tracked Elfriede down to a well-appointed old people's home in Willich, near Düsseldorf, hoping to talk to her about the camp.

Her name was on a buzzer. 'Forget it. There is nothing to say. Forget it,' she barked down the intercom.

The end of the Cold War made it possible for Dr Sonntag's granddaughter Clara to visit the camp. 'I worried the staff would point a finger at me accusingly saying, Why didn't you come earlier or something, but in fact they were very nice.' Clara found out a lot about her grandfather and the camp, and noticed her face rash clear. But she needed to know more and made her way to London to read the trial testimony at the National Archives. She stayed in a bed and breakfast a long way from the archives. 'It sounds crazy but I was frightened someone might put two and two together and realise who I was.'

I asked Clara what it was she was trying to find out. She had always been puzzled by the stories of her grandfather's drunkenness. 'They said he rode his bicycle around the surgery table. Sometimes you think it can't be true. Blood is thicker than water – you know – and I had always had this feeling that there was something of him in me. So I was looking for excuses for him, I suppose. I mean, did his drinking mean he had a conscience? Was he an arsehole or a drunk? Then, reading all that stuff, I knew it was true.'

* * *

In December 2013 I went back to Ravensbrück. Fürstenberg seemed just the same, sullen, with its back turned to the camp across the lake. The town had paid dearly for its ties to the women's concentration camp. The Red Army ransacked homes and raped women as it passed through in 1945, then when the DDR came into being locals were forced to become communists and worship at the camp's new communist shrine. When the Russians left the town the locals sought permission to build a supermarket on the site. The request was turned down.

In the woods by the lake the sun was burning the frost off the trees. There had been changes at the site: a new exhibition had been set up, and beside the lake a visitor centre. Ravensbrück now receives 150,000 visitors a year, though its brother camp of Sachsenhausen, closer to Berlin, gets far more – and more money as a result. 'We were always on the margins of the story,' says Insa Eschebach, director of the memorial site.

There have been many excuses for marginalising this camp: it was smaller scale than many others; it didn't fit easily into the central narrative; camp documents had been destroyed; it was hidden behind the Iron Curtain; the prisoners were only women. And yet it is precisely because this was a camp for women that Ravensbrück should have shaken the conscience of the world. Other camps showed what mankind was capable of doing to man. The Jewish death camps showed what mankind was capable of doing to an entire race. Ravensbrück showed what mankind was capable of doing to women. The nature and scale of atrocity done here to women had never been seen before. Ravensbrück should never have had to fight 'on the margins' for a voice: it was – and is – a story in its own right.

The Nazis committed atrocities against women in many other places too: more than half the Jews killed in the death camps were women, and towards the end of the war women were held at several other camps. But just as Auschwitz was the capital of the crime against Jews, so Ravensbrück was the capital of the crime against women. Deep in our collective memory, throughout literature of every period and every country, atrocities against women have always horrified. By treating the crime that happened here as marginal, history commits a further crime against the Ravensbrück women, and against the female sex.

At the memorial site today the story is told more fully than before. In the new exhibition, chapters largely left out when communists had control of the story – the asocials, the prostitutes, the Gypsies, the Jews – are now included, while the chapter extolling the communist heroines has been toned down – perhaps too far. Cold War rhetoric is certainly out of place in the twenty-first century, but the German women who stood up to Hitler – many of them communists – were indeed 'fighters against fascism' and should be recognised as such. I was glad to see *Tragende* was still standing. Her foot raised as she seems to step out over the lake, Olga Benario deserves her place as a 'strong woman who helped her weaker comrades'.

I wandered towards the crematorium. More ashes have recently been found in a mass grave nearby. Plans to plant a thousand roses on top of the grave are held up by a dispute about whether this will desecrate the remains.

A new academic study of surviving lists and figures has revised the estimate of numbers killed at Ravensbrück, slashing the figure of 90,000 set at the Hamburg trials, and agreed by most camp historians since, to a precise 28,000. The British calculations were too crude and took no account of releases over the years, or of women released from subcamps, says the study. But these new calculations should be treated with caution too. Digging rather than academic analysis might produce more truth – it would certainly produce more ashes, more mass graves.

The whole site is a cemetery, the lake itself a grave. The real number killed here can never be known. Many of the victims – particularly in the last months – were not even registered on camp lists. No attempt has been made to find out the truth of gassings in lorries and buses in the final weeks, or to excavate around the site of the second gas chamber, camouflaged as the *Neue Wäscherei*.

In fact, re-examining the figures exposes just how little of the horror is known, even today. Are those sent away on 'black transports' for gassing to be counted? If so, how many were there? Nobody knows. Counting deaths at subcamps complicates the story further. Are all the murdered babies included in the revised figure of 28,000? How many were killed in the final evacuations, when prisoners were piled on trains in the sure knowledge they'd be bombed by the Allies? The women killed on the death marches are not included – neither those marched out of Ravensbrück itself nor those marched from the multiple subcamps. Those killed in the White Buses, hit by Allied fire, remain uncounted – nobody knows how many there were.

The original estimate of 90,000 dead was almost certainly too high. A figure of between 40,000 and 50,000 – depending on which deaths are included – is probably as close as it is possible to get to the truth. But does the precise number of dead really matter? Survivors think names are more important than numbers. 'The Germans were always counting us,' scoffed Loulou Le Porz. 'Now the academics count us again. Some study us like ants.' The author of the 'Memory Book', Bärbel Schindler-Saefkow, also believes that names matter more than numbers. Her *Gedenkbuch* now contains 13,161 names, but a lack of funding has stopped her research.

I walked over to the Siemens camp to see what had changed there, but the path was blocked by barbed wire. Access to information from the company's Munich headquarters is also still largely blocked.

When I first approached Siemens for information about its involvement with Ravensbrück I received a glossy brochure about the company's successes. Later the company's official history, published in 1998, came through the post. 'Siemens felt forced to cooperate, however reluctantly, with the regime,' said the introduction. In 2013 the company announced its archives were open, but the few documents made available on Ravensbrück contained not a single prisoner's name. When I asked to speak to a Siemens director about how the company today viewed its involvement with the Third Reich, I was told that only the company archivist could speak about the past, so I sent him my questions.

And yet from the top of the Siemens hill, which I reached via a back route, the company's past at Ravensbrück is clear for all to see. The skeleton of an old workshop still stands, and in the dip below are the old rail tracks which took parts back and forth. Also clear to see are the wooden trails along which trucks carried women to the gas chamber once they were 'taken off the lists' as too weak to work.

During the British post-war de-Nazification case against the Siemens head of personnel Wolf-Dietrich von Witzleben, claims were made of the ill-treatment of prisoners and that Siemens 'made gas ovens for the concentration camps'. A British adjudicator noted that the defence statement in the case was 'rather woolly', but no evidence was found to support the claims, which were rejected.

That Siemens staff didn't know about the existence of the 'gas ovens', or that in the latter period their exhausted workers at Ravensbrück were gassed, is impossible to believe, however, especially from the top of the Siemens hill. The crematorium chimney is less than 300 yards away; its stinking smoke blew right over the Siemens plant. By January 1945 the gas chamber stood alongside the crematorium. Anni Vavak, the Austrian-Czech prisoner, described how in the last months of the war she stood there watching trucks loaded with half-naked women driving from the Youth Camp, past the Siemens plant and then heading to the gas chamber. When Anni told the Siemens civilian staff what she saw they 'winced'. Selma van de Perre and other survivors recall selections for gassing taking place at the Siemens plant itself during the last months.

When I eventually received a response from the Siemens archivist Dr Frank Wittendorfer, it came in the form of a brief statement which began: 'During World War Two, German industrial companies were incorporated by the NS dictatorship into the "war economy" system.' In other words, Siemens was reiterating its long-held argument that it was 'forced to cooperate' with Hitler from the start, and therefore, even today, accepts no legal responsibility for its actions. The statement gave details of its compensation payments made over the years, while stressing it had 'no legal obligation' to make any such payments. It mentioned the company's 'profound regret', but omitted to give any details about what was regretted.

These mealy-mouthed words were distasteful and contrasted with responses of other German institutions which, increasingly in recent years, have had the courage to face their past. During the Nazi era a doctorate awarded by Heidelberg University to Käthe Leichter, the Jewish-Austrian sociologist imprisoned in Ravensbrück and gassed at Bernburg, was revoked. When her son Franz Leichter asked for it to be reinstated, the university rector, Dr Stefan Maul, replied describing Käthe's case as 'a harrowing testament to our country's and our university's shameful past and the many unjustified and unspeakable crimes committed'. The removal of the doctorate by his predecessors was a 'blatant violation of human rights', and he added: 'Today in 2013 we are whether we like it or not the successor of those who committed this injustice, those who let it happen and hushed it up.' The employment of slave labourers by Siemens was surely a far more shocking violation of human rights, but it was also more costly to rectify, and when in 1993 a Ravensbrück prisoner, Waltraud Blass, sought to use new laws brought in since German reunification in order to secure payment of her lost wages in a Munich court, Siemens refused to accept liability and the case was thrown out. There is evidence, however, that some within Siemens – apart from the archivist – may be ready to look back. At the instigation of the camp's educational staff and of Siemens's trade unions, workshops are held at Ravensbrück for Siemens trainees, where they can study the camp 'in an environment that makes them feel safe about confronting their past', as the head of the camp education section put it. In December 2013 a Siemens director asked to meet two survivors, including Selma van de Perre, and reportedly spoke of his company's 'guilt'. The meeting, however, was held behind closed doors; the expression of guilt, 'hushed up'. And while groups of employees are helped to 'feel safe' as they learn about the past, up at the Siemens plant there is not even a 'safe' place for survivors to stand nor a shelter to keep off the rain. There is no rose bed here, no memorial to the Siemens victims. The name Siemens is nowhere to be seen. Before long the remains of the Siemenslager will be entirely overgrown.

I left the Siemens plant and headed across a strip of waste ground towards the Youth Camp. Fog was closing in. Once again it was hard to find the way. A rusty railway track disappeared into the trees. Just beyond it was a clearing with a little shrine made of shells, put up by the Berlin feminist group Gedenkort in memory of the teenage girls imprisoned here before the Youth Camp became a death camp, as well as those who died later.

Piles of ugly concrete and sheets of zinc stick up out of the ground nearby. Perhaps this was one of the blocks.

Then, suddenly, six wire-mesh figures appeared out of the trees.* Like ghosts they seemed to be tilting forward as if to welcome me. Between February and April 1945 an estimated 6000 women were marched out into these woods from the Ravensbrück main camp. They were told they were coming somewhere where they would be treated better, but instead they were brought here and most were murdered, or taken by truck to the gas chamber and gassed or shot.

What happened on this forsaken patch of land was Ravensbrück's most abominable crime. Yet nobody passing by would ever know. There is no reason even to pass by; the land, owned by the state of Brandenburg (as is the Siemens site) and not even incorporated into the main Ravensbrück memorial site, is far off the beaten track. Nobody seems to want to lay claim to it, except the feminists of Gedenkort. A shortage of money is given as one reason why the Youth Camp seems to have been forgotten. More important is a dispute over terminology. The camp director proposed that the former Youth Camp be called an extermination camp, but members of the Jewish council of Germany objected, saying only the Jewish death camps, set up

* Gedenkort also made the wire-mesh figures, called Maschas, and placed them at the site.

under the terms of the Final Solution, can be defined as such.* Yet again, nobody can quite think how to tell the Ravensbrück story. There is a reluctance to take what happened here as seriously as other Nazi crimes, so the site lies abandoned 'on the margins'.

The SS men who devised the final killing at Ravensbrück would certainly have called it extermination – they were the same exterminators who had murdered the Jews at Auschwitz. They'd be pleased to see how well their secret has been kept: seventy years ago they deliberately tucked this women's extermination camp away in the woods so nobody would know about it. The exterminators also invented a name for the place, calling it Mittwerda and pretending it was a sanatorium.

There were certainly differences from earlier exterminations: the scale was smaller, and to save money the killers first tried to kill as many women as possible by starving them, or leaving them to stand almost naked in the snow for hours on end 'without hair, without name, with no more strength to remember, her eyes empty, her womb cold like a frog in winter', as Primo Levi wrote when he asked us to 'Consider If This Is a Woman'. He urged his readers: 'Meditate that this came about. I commend these words to you. Tell your children.' Levi wrote about Auschwitz but his message was universal.

We should certainly 'meditate' upon what happened here, and also give this extermination camp for women its rightful name and place in history. At Nuremberg Robert H. Jackson said the Nazi conspiracy 'set one goal then, having achieved it, moved on to a more ambitious one'. Ravensbrück, which spanned the war years, is a useful prism through which to watch those goals evolve. The camp helped Hitler achieve some early aims: elimination of 'asocials', criminals, Gypsies and other useless mouths, including those unable to work; the first such group of women were gassed at Bernburg, an atrocity which the world today knows almost nothing of. The camp played a small part too in the more 'ambitious goal' – the annihilation of the Jews, not least by providing women guards and Kapos for Auschwitz's women's camp. Then, in the final weeks of the war, Ravensbrück moved centre stage, becoming the scene of the last major extermination by gas carried out in the Nazi camps before the end of the war.

Unlike the earlier phases of extermination, however, this final killing had no 'goal' because the creation of a master race had been abandoned. The

* Germany's central office for the investigation of Nazi war crimes at Ludwigsberg has also recently ruled that Ravensbrück was 'not a death camp'. For this reason, the office is no longer investigating crimes committed by guards or SS officers at Ravensbrück; it is only investigating crimes at death camps. Absurdly, this ruling means that none of the crimes connected with the Ravensbrück extermination will be investigated. When Ravensbrück women guards moved on to work at a 'death camp', however, their crimes there can be investigated, and the central office is currently investigating alleged crimes committed by a small number of Ravensbrück guards while they were working at Majdanek.

prisoners of Ravensbrück therefore – old, young, of many different nationalities, non-Jew and Jew, with nothing to unite them except that they were women – were killed just to make more room. Then they were killed because their legs weren't good enough to join the death march. In reality these final gassings happened because the exterminators couldn't stop. This was no marginal atrocity; it was where the Nazi horror ended – with the mass murder of women in the most bestial fashion with no cover of ideology, however obscene, for no reason at all.

As I left the clearing the rain was coming down heavily. I passed the wire-mesh figures again. Had Ravensbrück stayed so stubbornly 'in the margins' of the story because of some kind of collective guilt about the victims – sisters, mothers, daughters, wives – abandoned here, the world unable to offer any help? Or perhaps the facts are just too horrible to contemplate – too painful. There is certainly testimony from Uckermark that I had found too troubling to report.

Is it best to leave these ghosts alone? It is certainly difficult to know how to remember such a place, but a clearer sign through the woods would at least help those who wish to come here to find the way.

Walking back to the main camp I entered the compound through the rear gate – the same gate through which the Youth Camp women left, and through which some, in the very last weeks, returned. By March 1945 the last extermination was extended to the whole of Ravensbrück. Across what is today just a vast empty space dotted by linden trees, the Nazis gave vent to their inexorable desire to kill, as Rudolf Höss described it, for several more weeks.

Parked in the trees while the murders reached a climax were Red Cross buses. What better image can there be of the world's impotence in the face of the slaughter carried out in Hitler's camps than these buses patiently waiting until the gassing was over before the rescue began? And yet Bernadotte's mission was the only major prisoner rescue of the war.

By mid-April 1945 the Allies were closing in fast on Berlin; the Americans had uncovered Buchenwald and the British had found Belsen. There could now be no doubt about the horror in the camps, and that horror was still unfolding in several places not yet liberated, including Ravensbrück, where women were being lined up for gassing. Political and military realities, however, meant no change of strategy was considered that might protect the remaining camps in the last weeks of the war.

Negotiating with Himmler over the camps had never been an option either. Churchill's edict of 'no truck with Himmler' ensured that the Allies never compromised their objective, which was to win the military war, crushing the Nazis and all they represented. Even offering safe passage to Bernadotte's White Buses was a compromise too far for the Allies and was refused.

And yet it is impossible not to follow the story of the White Bus rescue without cheering them on, in the knowledge that with Bernadotte's mission under way at last someone was putting prisoners' lives first. Bernadotte certainly had to compromise in order to carry out his rescue, which was done on Himmler's terms. Not only was he obliged by Himmler to wait for the killing to subside at Ravensbrück, he was unable to rescue Jews until the last days. Had he not compromised, however, Bernadotte would not have got 17,000 prisoners out. He received little thanks. After the war he was still accused of failing to rescue enough Jews, though he eventually saved at least 7000. In 1947 Bernadotte was chosen to be the United Nations mediator in the Arab-Israeli war. On 17 September 1948 he was assassinated in Jerusalem by the Zionist militant group the Stern Gang.

In later years survivors wanted more than anything for their accounts of Ravensbrück to be heard and believed. They knew that if the next generations did not know the facts, they would never learn the lessons.

Antonina Nikiforova spent the proceeds of her first book on buying a small dacha near Leningrad and retreated there in order to write more. 'My impressions of the camp were so strong, I could only quieten them by writing books,' she wrote in a letter to another survivor.

Others decided to talk after decades of silence. Some spoke to me of things never mentioned before – sometimes they were surprising.

Nelly Langholm, the Norwegian from Stavanger, revealed the secret of her arrest. When the Germans occupied Norway in 1940 Nelly, a schoolgirl, came home one wet evening to find a German officer playing the piano in her house. 'He said, "Now begins the Grimm's fairy tale." He said his name was Wolfgang Grimm and he had come to see me. I didn't know why and he wouldn't say. But he talked to me and he was so lovely and sweet and played the piano. And he came back the next day. And the next day. And I fell in love with him.'

Soon afterwards Nelly's uncle was blown up by a German bomb and a cousin was captured. 'Eventually I realised that it could not be and I wrote to him and said don't come to my house any more because you are the enemy and I can't see you any more. And then the next day the Gestapo came to my house and arrested me. They told me they had read the letter in which I said I was an enemy of Germany. I didn't know if he had handed the letter into the Gestapo or if it was just the censor.'

Nelly said it 'felt right in a way' that she was sent to Ravensbrück. 'I had done this terrible thing and fallen in love with a German and the Germans had killed our family. I thought I should be punished.'

When Nelly was first arrested one of her friends asked her mother why she had let the German into the house in the first place. Nelly's mother told the friend that he had looked so miserable and cold and wet she couldn't leave him out there. 'She was so beautiful, my mother. That was just like her to do that,' said Nelly.

In the 1960s, on a visit to Berlin, Nelly saw Wolfgang Grimm again. 'I was walking in the street with a friend and I suddenly saw him. He was standing up stock still like a statue staring at me. I just walked past and said nothing. There was nothing I could say.'

Listening to the voices of the Ravensbrück women I looked for clues about why this group survived. I could almost hear Maria Bielicka banging her fists on the table as she tried to explain why survival was in the blood of every Polish woman, 'passed on from mother to daughter'.

Jeannie Rousseau, the French woman who passed on intelligence about the V2 bombs to Churchill, survived because she refused not to. At Torgau she refused to make German arms. At the punishment camp of Königsberg she refused to die on the freezing airfield and escaped back to the main camp, hiding in a typhus truck. When Bernadotte arrived, Jeannie was locked in the *Strafblock* but refused to be left behind, and persuaded the Blockova to let her out.

'You can refuse what is happening. Or go along with it. I was in the refusal camp,' she said.

I asked her how she had the courage.

'I don't know. I was young. I thought if I do it, it will work. You simply cannot accept some things. Certain things.'

Many refused in other ways; they refused to accept the annihilation of what they knew, praying, talking, writing, reading, teaching whenever they could – the Polish teachers taught their young students in the camp so well that when they got home they were even awarded their exam certificates. Some 'refused' by remaining detached from events, which may have protected them. Natalia Chodkiewicz said: 'The entire time I was in the camp it was as if I had a double personality. My real self seemed to be observing what was happening to my physical self.'

None would have survived without luck, particularly with their health. None would have survived without friends, ad hoc families, which helped them keep their heads. Such families appear to have formed more readily in the women's camp than in the men's camps. Loulou's 'family' was Block 10; sitting in her conservatory, I came to know many of them. Loulou could be very sombre: 'I find it abominable that we still talk of war. I often think we have learned nothing at all.' But then suddenly she would brighten as she remembered the courage of 'her sick' and 'her dead'.

It helped, said Loulou, that she had a role. 'As a doctor I was able to help people a little – to live and to die.' She once gave a young Polish woman a little morphine so she would not be taken away by Winkelmann. 'I said she is going to die any minute, so he left her. She did die, but not until a few days later. And she died on her mattress with someone at her side. That was important. She wasn't gassed.'

When she returned from the camp Loulou very nearly entered a convent. 'One didn't believe in the goodness of human nature any more. I had to learn it again. And I did.' She paused. 'But it took a long time.'

Many women broke down in tears as we talked. There was often laughter. Nobody was bitter. But nor – I think – did many forgive; certainly nobody would forget. At one memorial weekend I met Wanda Wojtasik again. I had first interviewed Wanda, one of the youngest Polish *Kaninchen*, at her apartment in Kraków. Now she was throwing roses onto the Ravensbrück lake. She told me that one of the SS doctors, Fritz Fischer, had recently contacted her asking for her forgiveness. 'I told him there was nothing I could forgive him for. He would have to seek forgiveness from God.'

# Acknowledgements

My intention in this book was to tell the story of Ravensbrück primarily through the voices of the women themselves, but time was already running out. My initial task was to search for the last survivors. For this, I needed guides, and my first thanks go to them.

Survivors in Russia and the East were bound to be the hardest to find, not least because so few names were known.

I first met Dr Bärbel Schindler-Saefkow in her sunny allotment in East Berlin, a stone's throw from the Karlshorst mansion where Nazi forces surrendered to the Red Army on 9 May 1945. The daughter of a communist survivor, Bärbel had grown up in East Germany living and breathing the story of Ravensbrück, and the East European survivors had become her 'family'. Their stories first came alive for me sitting at a table in Bärbel's allotment and from there I set off on trails which led to Moscow, St Petersburg, Kiev and Donetsk. Bärbel helped in countless ways to the very last days of my research.

My introduction to the Polish women came from Wanda Półtawska, who invited me to talk to her in Kraków and put me in touch with other survivors, including other Polish 'rabbits' whom I found in Gdansk, Lublin and Warsaw. I was assisted in this by Anna Pomianowska, translator, companion and guide. The Polish historian Eugenia Maresch passed on names of Polish survivors in the UK and, later, Eugenia unearthed priceless testimony about the camp in the National Archives.

My first introduction to the French survivors came through Dr Annette Chalut, President of the Ravensbrück International Committee, and Denise Vernay, general secretary of the French survivors' body, L'Association nationale des anciennes déportées et internées de la Résistance (ADIR), which led me to dozens of French survivors. I was particularly grateful in the early days to Anise Postel-Vinay, Christiane Rème, Michèle Agniel, Françoise Robin and Marie-Jo Chombart de Lauwe, for their hospitality and advice and for pointing me to others, and to Richard de Courson.

In Israel I met Irith Dublon-Knebel, who advised not only on the Jewish survivors but on Ravensbrück's place in Holocaust history. In the Netherlands I was assisted by Joke van Dijk-Bording. Selma van de Perre, a Ravensbrück survivor and my neighbour in West London, helped with countless questions, particularly on Siemens. For contacts and background on Austrian prisoners I am indebted to Brigitte Halbmayr and Helga Amesberger, whose research on the Burgenland Sinti and Roma was of particular value, not least since they were the hardest group to reach. Gerhard Baumgartner gave valuable advice on the Austrian story as did Gerhard Unger at the Dokumentationsarchiv des österreichischen Widerstandes in Vienna.

From the start, and at every later stage, the help of staff at the Ravensbrück Memorial site was invaluable. I am particularly grateful to Insa Eschebach, Director of the Memorial, for her support, to Alyn Bessman for her excellent research and tireless answers to questions, and to Matthias Heyl for his suggestions about themes to pursue. I would also like to thank Sabine Arend, Monika Herzog, Cordula Hundertmark, Janna Lölke, Britta Pawelke and Monika Schnell for advising on the Memorial's archives and collections, and Sigrid Jacobeit, the former Memorial director, for her advice.

Searching for survivors and testimony, I relied on many local guides as well as translators who often proved as committed to the story as me. Lyuba Vinogradova, the Russian journalist and author, climbed to the top of Moscow apartment blocks and plunged into St Petersburg's labyrinthine subways time and again as we sought out survivors and looked for testimony. Marina Sapritsky (now Nahum) translated and advised as we trekked through dusty Black Sea villages to find old ladies who hadn't known we were coming but who welcomed us, filled their tables with food and talked of Ravensbrück, often for the first time. Ilena Izugrafova took overnight bus trips with me across the Ukraine and then waited outside closed doors for hours, certain they would eventually open – which often they did. Many stepped in to help along the way, including Vyacheslav Gorlinsky, an eighty-five-year-old Buchenwald survivor who had taken on the task of delivering small payments to survivors around Odessa, so knew every woman's name and address. And I would like to thank Vova Chaplin of Odessa's Jewish Museum, who explored the city's archives and graveyards for me and even found the tomb of Yevgenia Klemm. I owe an enormous debt to Georg Loonkin, a former Soviet journalist, who had researched Klemm's life and gave me his dossier, containing the story of one of the most remarkable women in the camp. William Bland did a terrific job translating Russian archival material.

In Germany I relied heavily on several translators and researchers, none more so than Henning Fischer, who helped me from beginning to end with every aspect of the story, not only translating but researching, advising, proofreading and answering countless queries. Beate Smandek's assiduous research and insights in the early stages were invaluable. Helmut Ettinger offered to translate on numerous occasions and always did more, filling in background and context and opening doors. For help with the Polish material I am enormously grateful to Barbara Janic, who gave her time to reading and translating books and testimony. I could not have covered the Polish story without Barbara, who also read the final proofs. Many others kindly provided assistance at various stages, including Andrew Smith, Tanja Röckemann, Sophia Schniederat, Tomasz Małkuszewski, Agnes Fedorowicz, Zakhar Ishov, Daniel Knebel and Esther Hecht, who all translated and helped follow trails. I would also like to thank Nikita Petrov and his staff at the Memorial human rights body in Moscow as well as Len Blavatnik and Eugeniusz Smolar for making introductions in the Ukraine and Poland respectively.

Nobody followed the Ravensbrück trails more widely or more assiduously on my behalf than the Second World War historian Stephen Tyas. With instincts second to none, Steve searched archives in Germany and the UK, finding testimony, often previously unknown. He not only dug in the archives but in the undergrowth of Mecklenburg forest, as we trekked through fields searching for Himmler's Brückenthin house, or wandered in the desolate woods at Uckermark before driving the 600 miles back to Calais, to catch the midnight ferry home.

Many of my helpers were the children or relatives of survivors. Anita Leocadia Prestes, daughter of Olga Benario, gave me advice and showed me her mother's letters. Judith Buber Agassi talked about her mother Grete Buber-Neumann and provided insights into the Jewish story, while Tania Szabo shared her memories of her mother Violette and her own research material. I am also grateful to Marlene Rolf, daughter of Ilse Gostynski; Caroline McAdam Clark, daughter of Denise Dufournier; Franz Leichter and Kathy Leichter, son and granddaughter of Käthe Leichter; and to Irena Lisiecki, sister of Aka Kołodziejczak. Maria Wilgat, daughter of Krysia Czyż, and Krysia's brother Wiesław, talked about Krysia's secret letter-writing, and Maria passed me copies of all her mother's letters.

I am indebted to the granddaughter of the SS doctor Walter Sonntag, who agreed to talk about him and her own life, and passed on his letters.

Jean-Marie Liard, son of Dr Louise Liard-Le Porz, not only passed on advice and translated, but gave up time to carry out research and read my first draft, correcting errors and giving suggestions for which I am enormously grateful.

Dozens of helpers stepped in at different stages: Wolfgang Stegemann and Wolfgang Jacobeit talked about Fürstenberg; Keith Janes helped find Comet Line women; Anna-Jutta Pietsch talked about Olga Benario; Michael Pinto Duschinsky talked about Siemens. Nikolay Borodatin attempted, with great skill and in no time, to explain life under Stalin's purges. I should also like to thank David Coulson, Hella Pick, Father Edward Corbould, Martyn Cox, Michael Hegglin, John Heminway and Krzysiak Lukasz. Ian Sayers and Peter Hore helped with details of British survivors, and Fiona Watson at NHS Grampian Archives and Richard Hunter at Edinburgh City Archives helped trace Mary Young, who was gassed at Ravensbrück. The details on Mary, as well as other lesser-known British women, were particularly hard to come by. This failure to recognise their courage and suffering should bring a shame on their country.

For the stories of the SOE victims and the general context, I was again grateful to Professor Michael Foot, Duncan Stuart, Gillian Bennett, Francis Suttill and Tim Mant, who had helped with my first book on Vera Atkins. I made use of material, photographs and memories of John da Cunha, who was part of the prosecution team at Hamburg. My early talks with John were in many ways the inspiration for this book.

It was an enormous pleasure to meet Wanda Hjort, who had brought help to the Ravensbrück prisoners and played a key role in the Swedish White Bus rescue led by Count Bernadotte. For background on the story of the White Buses, I am also grateful to the Swedish historian Sune Persson, to Ricki Neumann and to Bertil Bernadotte.

Several German historians advised on specific aspects of the camp's history. Bernhard Strebel's exhaustive study of Ravensbrück was an essential resource. I am particularly grateful to Stefan Hördler, whose work on the SS at Ravensbrück, Lichtenburg and other concentration camps has been groundbreaking, and who readily sent material, corresponded and met to talk. Johannes Schwarz, Simone Erpel, Christa Schikorra, Linde Apel, Loretta Walz, Irmtraud Heike, Susanne Willems and Grit Philipp were among other historians who helped.

For the wider historical background I am grateful to Sir Martin Gilbert, who generously gave time to talk, and made suggestions. I would also like to thank Anne Applebaum, Antony Beevor, David Cesarani, Richard Evans, Peter Longerich and Nikolaus Wachsmann, who all gave advice.

Lord Weidenfeld passed on his unique memories of the period and Anita Lasker-Wallfisch, a survivor of Auschwitz, kindly talked of her time in the camp.

Others whose assistance I have valued include the journalist Andrew Gimson, the columnist Joan Smith, the professor of English Philip Davis, the biographer Nancy Wood and the politician and author Denis MacShane.

There are countless others who lent books, looked up references, and passed on names and testimony found while researching their own book or simply encouraged me at difficult moments. There are too many names to mention here; I am grateful to them all.

Material was drawn from archives and libraries in a dozen countries and I am indebted to the archivists for their advice and help. In the UK I was particularly reliant on staff at the National Archives, the London Library, the Weiner Library, the Imperial War Museum, the Polish Study Trust, the Polish Institute and Library and the BBC Written Archives at Caversham. In France I was assisted by staff at the Musée de la Résistance in Besançon, the Bibliothèque de Documentation Internationale Contemporaine (BDIC) in Paris and in Germany at the Bundesarchiv in Ludwigsberg, the Stasi Archives in Berlin and the Landesarchiv Nordrhein-Westfalen Staatsarchiv. I would like to thank Frank Wittendorfer at the Siemens Archives, Munich, and Barbara Oratowska at the Muzeum Martyrologii 'Pod Zegarem' in Lublin.

At the ITS (International Tracing Service) in Bad Arolsen I received help from Reto Meister and his staff, and at the ICRC (International Committee of the Red Cross) in Geneva by the chief archivist Fabrizio Bensi. In Jerusalem, Alexander Avram at Yad Vashem gave valuable advice. I am also grateful to Brigitta Lindholm at Lund University Library, to staff at Oslo's Hjemmefrontmuseet and to Gro Kvanvig at Stiftelsen Arkivet, Kristiansand.

My gratitude to the Ravensbrück survivors themselves is, of course, immeasurable. I am grateful not only for their memories, their patience and their inspiration, but for their hospitality and friendship as I asked them – sometimes time and again – to recall a painful past.

Amongst those women I met were women who fought at Stalingrad, defended the Crimea, dropped by parachute into Nazi-occupied France, stared Himmler in the eye, permed Dorothea Binz's hair and marched in protest to the commandant of a concentration camp. I was honoured to meet every one of them; each story enriched my own life.

I would like to express particular gratitude to Yvonne Baseden, whom I met many times, and whose modesty about her own remarkable courage left a profound impression. Anise Postel-Vinay (née Girard) provided the most incisive analysis of the SS regime and of the French group. The Red Army parachutist Olga Golovina talked with humour but gripped my hand with steel. Loulou Liard-Le Porz was not only an oracle on Ravensbrück but also a friend, and provided confirmation that humanity can surmount the greatest degradation. Jeannie de Clarens (née Rousseau) I will remember for her pure courage. I will not forget the tears in the eyes of Zofia Cisek (née

Kawińska) as she recalled the deaths of fellow rabbits, the inability of Stella Nikoforova (née Kugelman) to smile, nor Nelly Langholm's sheer delight at having come out alive. They all gave me many, many hours of their time.

While grateful for help with my research, support during the writing has been invaluable too. I would like to thank those who advised on early drafts, including Katrina Barnicoat, Tony Rennell and Bernardo Futscher Pereira. I am particularly grateful for the suggestions and support of Richard Tomlinson, who advised on the first draft, made countless excellent suggestions and has always been on hand to help.

I have strived for accuracy, but there are bound to be errors in the text, and I hope where this occurs readers will alert me so corrections can be made.

I would like to thank my agent Natasha Fairweather for her unfailing support, and my editors at Little, Brown, Ursula Mackenzie and Tim Whiting, who have waited patiently, offering guidance along the way. I am also grateful to Ronit Wagman, my editor at Doubleday, and to Zoe Gullen at Little, Brown for suggestions and encouragement. In the last months Zoe Gullen took on the task of editing the final text, which she has done with remarkable skill, judgement and patience.

I owe a very great deal to my own family. I will always be grateful to my father, a doctor on the Normandy battlefields, whose curiosity about the world and love of literature first drew me to writing, and to my mother, who served as a Wren in the Royal Navy. My daughters Jessica and Rosamund have helped in every way they can.

The writing was not easy and the words would not have emerged onto the page at all without the help of my husband Jonathan, who has talked the story through, read every chapter more than once, edited and given advice and encouragement every step of the way. I sincerely doubt that any other author has ever had such support from a partner. I owe him my deepest thanks.

# Notes

*Abbreviations*

| | |
|---|---|
| AICRC | Archives of the International Committee of the Red Cross, Geneva |
| ARa | Archiv Mahn- und Gedenkstätte Ravensbrück |
| Atkins | Vera Atkins papers, held at the Imperial War Museum, London |
| *Beyond* | *Beyond Human Endurance: The Ravensbrück Women Tell Their Stories*, edited by Wanda Symonowicz, a compilation of survivors' testimonies. |
| Buchmann coll. | Erika Buchmann collection, Archiv Mahn- und Gedenkstätte Ravensbrück |
| BA | Bundesarchiv Berlin |
| BAL | Bundesarchiv Ludwigsberg |
| BStU | Stasi Archives, Berlin |
| Czyż letters | Letters and papers of Krystyna Czyż-Wilgat (Krysia Czyż) |
| *Dictators* | *Under Two Dictators: Prisoner of Stalin and Hitler* by Margarete Buber-Neumann |
| DÖW | Dokumentationsarchiv des österrichischen Widerstandes, Vienna |
| *Dreams* | *And I Am Afraid of My Dreams* by Wanda Półtawska |
| FO | Foreign Office records held at The National Archives |
| GZJ | Geschichtsarchiv Zeugen Jehovas, Selters/Taunus |
| HS | Special Operations Executive files held at The National Archives |
| IISH | International Institute for Social History, Amsterdam |
| ITS | International Tracing Service, Bad Arolsen |
| IWM | Imperial War Museum, London |
| KV | Security Service records held at The National Archives |

| | |
|---|---|
| Lund | Records of the Polish Research Institute, Lund University. These are detailed reports of Polish survivors who arrived in Sweden in 1945. |
| Nikif papers | Antonina Nikiforova papers, Archiv Mahn- und Gedenkstätte Ravensbrück |
| NARA | National Archives and Records Administration, Washington, DC |
| LAV NRW | Landesarchiv Nordrhein-Westfalen |
| SA | Siemens Archives, Munich |
| TNA | The National Archives, Kew |
| WL | Wiener Library, London |
| WO | War Office records held at The National Archives |
| YV | Yad Vashem, Jerusalem |

## PART ONE
### Chapter 1: Langefeld

3 *'The year is . . .'*: Buber-Neumann, *Die erloschene Flamme.*

4 *'Trespassers Keep Out'*: What Langefeld saw on her early visit is reconstructed from testimony of the first arrivals, for example: Hanna Sturm (who came with the advance party), *Die Lebensgeschichte einer Arbeiterin*; Maase, WO 309/416 and BAL B162-9896/9828; Gostynski, eyewitness account, WL P.III.h. No. 159; Maria Hauswirth, WL P.III.h. No. 948; Clara Rupp memoir, ARa. Early maps and the SS photo album also show the layout, ARa.

5 *fewer guards*: By the end of 1939 there were about fifty-five women guards and by the end of the war about 3300 had worked in the camp. See Heike, *Johanna Langefeld.*

6 *'feminine matters'*: On Langefeld's role and attitude, see her only known interrogation, dated 26 and 31 December 1945, in the US National Archives (NARA, NAW RG 338-000-50-11). See also: Johannes Schwarz 'Geschlechtsspezifischer Eigensinn' and his 'Das Selbstverständnis Johanna Langefeld als SS-Oberaufseherin' in Fritz, Kavčič and Warmbold (eds), *Tatort KZ*; Heike, *Johanna Langefeld*; and Müller, *Die Oberaufseherinnen.* Several survivors described Langefeld to me, including Edith Sparmann, Wojciecha Zeiske (née Buraczyńska), Maria Bielicka, Fritzi Fruh (née Jaroslavsky), Irma Trksak and Barbara Reimann. Rudolf Höss gives a view in *Commandant.*

7 *ran away from home*: See Anna-Jutta Pietsch, 'Jakob-Klar-Straße 1:

das Elternhaus von Olga Benario', in Ilse Macek (ed.), *Ausgegrenzt – Entrechtet – Deportiert: Schwabing und Schwabinger Schicksale 1933 bis 1945* (Munich: Volk, 2008). In the 1920s Olga's father Leo, a social democrat lawyer, fought for striking workers' rights in Munich courtrooms, encouraging his daughter's radical streak. The man she snatched to freedom was Otto Braun, a senior figure in the secret service of the German Communist Party.

8 *'re-educating prostitutes'*: Langefeld first worked as a teacher of home economics in Neuss, near Düsseldorf. Her Brauweiler ID card (in Archiv des Landschaftsverbands Rheinland) shows she started at the workhouse in 1935. Detail courtesy of Hermann Daners.

8 *new saviour in Adolf Hitler*: For Langefeld, God's teaching would have seemed compatible with the teaching of Hitler. By the early 1930s the Lutheran church in her home town of Kupferdreh was a stronghold of *Deutsche Christen*, the fanatical Nazi Christians. See Busch, *Kupferdreh und seine Geschichte*.

8 *'Hitler rode into . . .'*: Shirer, *Berlin Diary*.

9 *'What's up?'*: Haag, *How Long the Night*.

11 *'I'm a wretched prattler'*: Himmler's diaries, quoted in Padfield, *Himmler*.

11 *'show their teeth . . .'*: Höss, *Commandant*.

12 *wrote to her sister*: Cited in Herz, *The Women's Camp in Moringen*.

13 *'I always know . . .'*: Cited in Koonz, *Mothers in the Fatherland*.

14 *'as a gift'*: Details in a British Security Service file on Arthur Ernest Ewert, another of the Comintern cell. He was married to Elise Saborowski Ewert (alias Sabo), who came back on the steamer with Olga; KV 2/2336.

14 *defuse the row*: Protests against Olga's capture did nevertheless continue, including a march in London's Hyde Park attended by communists and sympathisers, including the Labour peer Lord Listowel.

14 *'So you have to excuse . . .'*: Prestes and Prestes (eds), *Anos Tormentosos*. The extracts from Olga's letters are from this book, and also the collection in the papers of Ruth Werner, Olga's friend and biographer (BA NY 4502).

16 'Asoziale': Kriminalpolizei and Gestapo personal files, NRW. See also Schikorra, '" . . . ist als Asoziale anzusehen"'.

17 *site was too small*: In *Commandant*, Höss decribes a site meeting at Ravensbrück in 1938, which he attended with Pohl and Eicke to discuss construction. Many survivors were convinced that the land on which the camp was built was the personal property of Heinrich

Himmler. No proof of this has emerged, but during a recent legal dispute over plans to build a supermarket on the site, papers were found showing the land was owned by the Munich branch of the SS, where Himmler cut his teeth well before the coming of the camp. Site plans, ARa.

18 *Doris Maase*: Police file, LAV NRW. She was arrested in Düsseldorf when trying to get in touch with the illegal communist resistance.

18 *fulfil her vocation*: Langefeld interrogation, 26 and 31 December 1945, NARA, NAW RG 338-000-50-11. Several other guards claimed they came believing their job would be to 're-educate' women: see Pietsch, BAL B162/981, and Zimmer, WO 309/1153.

18 *'incapable of improvement'*: Police file, LAV NRW 2034/177.

19 *'no sense'*: Haag, *How Long the Night* and author interview.

19 *'like dripping mice'*: See reports in GZJ. The spraying of the Jehovah's Witnesses was recalled with horror by most Lichtenburg survivors; see also Haag, *How Long the Night*, and Maase, WO 309/416.

19 *Himmler visited*: Gostynski, eyewitness account, WL P.III.h. No. 159, says he visited every year. She once saw him close up and remembered his 'terrifying eyes … evil, cold and grey'.

21 *On 15 May*: Some say 15 May was the date when the camp officially opened, but that the first big transfer – of 867 from Lichtenburg – happened on 18 May. Others say that the transfers happened gradually over the course of the first week or so. There is no certainty on the point. See Heike, *Johanna Langefeld*.

22 *'a sparsely populated …'*: Ullrich, 'Für Dich', ARa.

23 *This first group:* For descriptions of arrivals, first days in the camp and rules and procedures see multiple testimonies, including: Gostynski, eyewitness account, WL P.III.h. No. 159; Wachstein, Vienna report, ARa; Ullrich, 'Für Dich', ARa; Sturm *Die Lebensgeschichte einer Arbeiterin*, and Schwarz and Szepansky (eds), … *und dennoch blühten Blumen*.

23 *colza rape seed*: Maria Zeh, interview in Walz, *'Und dann kommst Du dahin an einem schönen Sommertag'*.

## Chapter 2: Sandgrube

25 *men were not allowed*: See Wicklein, BAL B162/9808, and Maase, BAL B162-9896/9828.

25–6 *'The blanket …'*: Author interview.

27 *'… fancy stuff later,'*: Author interview.

27 *syphilis*: Agnes Petry's camp health card, ITS Bad Arolsen. A batch

of Ravensbrück prisoner health cards came into the possession of the ITS after the war. These cards, complete with prisoner numbers, names and dates of birth as well as health details, have been a means of confirming some identities.

27 *974 prisoners*: Figures cited in Strebel, *Ravensbrück*.

28 *'It will be impossible . . .'*: Koegel to Eicke, ARa.

29 *'Next I remember . . .'*: Wachstein, Vienna report, ARa.

31 *'Iron Gustav'*: von Luenink, WO 309/416.

31 *'Be hard . . .'*: Insa Eschebach, 'Das Fotoalbum von Gertrud Rabestein', in Erpel (ed.), *Im Gefolge der SS*.

32 *often on heat*: Schiedlausky trial testimony (WO 235/309). Testimony in general contains multiple accounts of serious injury caused by dog bites.

32 *'. . . give up their God'*: Berta Hartmann and Klara Schwedler, 'Bei der Sandarbeit', in Hesse and Harder (eds), *'. . . und wenn ich . . .'*. Testimony of Anna Kanne and others in reports provided by GZJ.

33 'Abdecken': von Luenink, WO 309/416.

33 *I looked out*: Wachstein, Vienna report, ARa.

34 *'I wish I could be . . .'*: Maase letters, Studienkreis Deutscher Widerstand 1933–1945.

34 *finding Tolstoy*: Sturm, *Die Lebensgeschichte einer Arbeiterin*.

36 *'a young woman . . .'*: Gostynski, eyewitness account, WL P.III.h. No. 159.

37 *On arrival at the camp Jozka*: Werner, *Olga Benario*.

38 *lived in Burgenland*: I have drawn from accounts, published under pseudonyms, in Amesberger and Halbmayr, *Vom Leben und Überleben*. I also spoke to Rudolf Sarkozi about his mother Paula, and with the Burgenland Gypsy Ceija Stojka, who was sent first to Auschwitz then Ravensbrück. See also Friedlander, *The Origins of Nazi Genocide* and Thurner, *National Socialism and Gypsies in Austria*.

39 *'A multicoloured dress . . .'*: Gestapo transport order, 20 July 1939, in VVN, *Olga Benario*. The story of the attempt to secure Olga's release is told in the family correspondence and was also explained to me by Anita Leocadia Prestes. See also Apel, 'Olga Benario – Kommunistin, Jüdin, Heldin?', in Eschebach, Jacobeit and Lanwerd (eds), *Die Sprache des Gedenkens*.

42 *'She's lying here dead . . .'*: Doris Maase also saw the killing of the unnamed Gypsy. WO 309/416.

42 *'suicide by stab wounds . . .'*: Copy of death notice, ITS/ANF/KL Ravensbrück Indiv-Unterlagen.

42 '*... lunatic asylum must be like*': Sturm, *Die Lebensgeschichte einer Arbeiterin*.

43 *Zimmer screamed*: The prisoner Berta Maurer (and many others) said Zimmer was usually 'ill-tempered and drunk', BAL B162/9809.

44 *The work that we have*: Wachstein, Vienna report, ARa.

## Chapter 3: Blockovas

47 '*I saw Binz...*': Maase, BAL B162/9828.

47 *The daughter of*: See Duesterberg, 'Von der "Umkehr aller Weiblichkeit"' and Johannes Schwartz, 'Handlungsräume einer KZ-Aufseherin. Also Dorothea Binz – Leiterin des Zellenbaus und Oberaufseherin', in Erpel (ed.), *Im Gefolge der SS*. Early signs of sadism were noted by many survivors: Erika Buchmann said Binz beat 'until she saw blood coming from the nose and the mouth'. She also used 'the heels of her boots' to kick women on the ground. WO 235/318.

48 '*treat orders as...*': Höss, *Commandant*. For regime change on the outbreak of war in other camps see Sofsky, *The Order of Terror* and Kogon, *The Theory and Practice of Hell*.

49 '*September prisoners*': Luise Maurer left two important statements; one is in Ludwigsberg (BAL B162/9809) and the other is in Elling, *Frauen im deutschen Widerstand*.

49 '*until hands were...*': Moldenhawer, Lund 420. On early Polish arrivals see also Kiedrzyńksa, *Ravensbrück*.

51 *Kapos*: For a study of the Ravensbrück Kapo system, see Annette Neumann, 'Funktionshäftlinge im Frauenkonzentrationslager Ravensbrück', in Röhr and Bergkamp (eds), *Tod oder Überleben?*

52–3 '*Zimmer surrounded herself...*': Wiedmaier statement, ARa

54 '*A Jewish woman...*': Wachstein, Vienna report, ARa.

55 *It was 5 p.m.*: LAV NRW R RW-58/54910.

55–6 '*Not married. 138 cm...*': LAV NRW R RW 58/63779.

56 *Dear Mutti*: Eckler, *Die Vormundschaftsakte*.

57 '*bourgeois Jews...*': Werner, *Olga Benario*. Olga's comarade Ruth Werner (née Ursula Ruth Kuczynski) became one of the Soviet Union's most famous secret agents. Codenamed Sonya, she worked after the war with the German atomic spy Klaus Fuchs, sending British and American nuclear secrets to Moscow.

61 *Brother, have you*: Leichter family papers.

61 '*My release must have been*': Hirschkron, WO 309/694.

63 '*The child was ill...*': Samulon (née Bernstein), BAL B162 9818.

## Chapter 4: Himmler Visits

64 *On 4 January 1940*: Phillip and Schnell, *Kalendarium*.

65 *'the cold-blooded murder . . .'*: Kersten, *Memoirs*.

65 *'with such a narrow pedantry . . .'*: Trevor-Roper, *The Last Days of Hitler*.

67 *'He let the guards . . .'*: Erna Ludolph, '"Das war der Weg, den ich gehen wollte" – Hafterfahrungen in den Frauen-KZ Moringen, Lichtenburg, Ravensbrück und andere Erinnerungen von Erna Ludolph' in Hesse and Harder (eds), *'. . . und wenn ich . . .'* and many accounts of the Jehovah's Witnesses' protest in trial testimony and memoirs.

67 *cover of war*: Hitler said in 1935 that he would deal with the problem of the mentally ill once war broke out. He 'took the view that in wartime measures for a solution to the problem would be put through more easily and with least friction, since the open opposition which must be expected from the Church could not then, in all the circumstances of war, exert so much influence as it would in the time of peace,' said Karl Brandt, his personal physician, at the Nuremberg doctors' trial. The trigger to start was, according to Brandt, a petition in 1939 direct to Hitler from the father of a deformed child requesting a 'mercy killing'. Brandt went to see the child in Leipzig. 'It was a child who was born blind, an idiot – at least it seemed to me an idiot – and it lacked one leg and part of an arm'. Cited in Mitscherlich and Mielke, *Death Doctors*.

68 *In one of the rooms*: Buber-Neumann, *Die erloschene Flamme*.

69 *Mariechen Öl and Hilde Schulleit*: Phillip and Schnell, *Kalendarium*.

69 *Himmler had personally approved*: Binz, along with several other accused, testified that each beating – including the number of lashes – had to be approved by Himmler in person. This was proved to be true by Himmler's 'flogging order', uncovered after the war (WO 309/217). In the early days the staff followed Himmler's 'verbal orders' on procedures, which were later written down (see p. 303).

## Chapter 5: Stalin's Gift

73 *In February 1940*: *Dictators*.

77 The *communist coup:* See *Sturm, Die Lebensgeschichte einer Arbeiterin and statement* (DÖW 4676 1-6). Also Rentmeister testimony, 30 April 1947, at the trial by Landgericht Dresden against Knoll, BstU

Ast 32/48. Also see Annette Neumann, 'Funktionshäftlinge im Frauenkonzentrationslager Ravensbrück', in Röhr and Bergkamp (eds), *Tod oder Überleben?*, and see Strebel, *Ravensbrück*.

79 *At that time*: von Luenink, WO 309/416. Susi's daughter, Tanja, first learned of her mother's death when a card she sent for her birthday was returned with a notification of her death. The cause of death was given as heart failure. Benesch correspondence, DÖW 02110 and 08815.

79 *exhumed his corpse*: Haag, *How Long the Night*.

80 *her later Stasi file*: After the war, Maria Wiedmaier and several others of those meeting on Käthe Rentmeister's bunk were recruited by the Stasi to spy on the West. See p. 644.

80 *Barbara Reimann*: Author interview.

81 *'We were't allowed . . .'*: Rosa Jochmann, 'Wenn der Elferblock voll gewesen ist, dann . . .', <http://www.doew.at/erinnern/biographien/erzaehlte-geschichte/haft-1938-1945/rosa-jochmann-wenn-der-elferblock-voll-gewesen-ist-dann>.

82–3 *Don't forget*: Ibid.

83–4 *Prisoners liked*: Clara Rupp memoir, ARa.

85 *'She could have got out . . .'*: Author interview.

## Chapter 6: Else Krug

89 *A number of them*: Herbermann, *The Blessed Abyss*.

89 *'we set right what we could'*: Teege statement, 'Hinter Gitter und Stacheldraht', ARa 647.

90–1 *They said I was a traitor*: In Schikorra, '. . . ist als Asoziale anzusehen'.

91 *'but we know . . .'*: LAV NRW R BR 2034/83.

92 *Ottilie Gorres's life story*: This is told in a file at the Landesarchiv NRW, along with that of Elisabeth Fassbender and many other 'asocials'. Also see Schikorra, *Kontinuitäten*.

97 *The letter states*: Correspondence in VVN files, BA.

99 *'There she is . . .'*: Maase, WO 309/416, and echoed in many prisoner testimonies.

## Chapter 7: Doctor Sonntag

Much of the Hamburg trial testimony on Sonntag is in WO 309/416, but is also scattered in other files at TNA.

101 *'Himmler left Berlin . . .'*: Witte et al. (eds), *Dienstkalender*.

101 *'Häschen'*: Himmler, *The Himmler Brothers*. Local historians believe that the house at Brückenthin was built by prisoner labour. Exactly when the land was bought and when Häschen moved in is unclear. Before Brückenthin was available Himmler may have stayed with her at a new experimental farm he had set up, which was also close to Ravensbrück and where he reared livestock. Today Brückenthin is a children's holiday camp; details of Himmler and Häschen's sojourns there were exposed in the *Schweriner Volkszeitung*, 30 June 2003.

103 *'For several weeks . . .'*: Cited in Friedlander, *The Origins of Nazi Genocide*.

103 *'The power over . . .'*: Ibid.

104 *'whether and how . . .'*: Ibid.

104 *instructed his chief surgeon*: Himmler to Grawitz, 3 February 1940, cited in Witte et al. (eds), *Dienstkalender*.

105 *'Reproduction by . . .'*: See Stoll, 'Walter Sonntag'.

107 *'extreme pleasure'*: Buchman deposition, 23 January 1948, WO 309/416.

108 *'I remember a woman . . .'*: Apfelkammer, BAL B162/9818.

108 *'You old pig . . .'*: Vera Mahnke, WO 309/416.

109 *'Sonntag, the greatest scoundrel . . .'*: Wiedmaier statement, 6 July 1958, ARa.

109 *what was left of his breakfast*: *Dictators*.

110 *try it out at Ravensbrück*: As was revealed at Nuremberg, Rudolf Brandt, Himmler's personal physician, wrote to Clauberg on 10 July 1942, requesting he go to Ravensbrück to perform mass sterilisation experiments on Jewesses 'according to your method'. Brandt said that by 1941 'it was an open secret' that Hitler planned to exterminate all Jews. The purpose of the sterilisation experiments was to come up with an alternative to total extermination. In view of the labour shortage the idea was to preserve about two to three million Jews who were fit to work, but to sterilise them. Cited in Mitscherlich and Mielke, *Death Doctors*.

110 *I remember one day*: Buchmann deposition, 23 January 1948, WO 309/416.

111 *'I have never been happier . . .'*: Sonntag family papers.

112 *'We heard him enter . . .'*: WO 309/416.

112 *I was asked one day*: Teege statement, 'Hinter Gitter und Stacheldraht', ARa 647.

## Chapter 8: Doctor Mennecke

115 *'The women seemed . . .'*: Teege statement, 'Hinter Gitter und Stacheldraht', ARa 647.

116 *'In the camp . . .'*: *Dictators.*

116 *'Have you ever seen . . .'*: Hayes (ed.), *The Journalism of Milena Jesenska.*

118 *'The woman stopped . . .'*: Anička Kvapilová, cited in Buber-Neumann, *Milena.*

120 *first execution*: See Kiedrzyńska, *Ravensbrück.*

122 *'big and pleasant room'*: Chroust (ed.), *Friedrich Mennecke.*

122 *Several times a week*: Friedlander, *The Origins of Nazi Genocide.*

123 *'accustomed to their own atrocities'*: Longerich, *Heinrich Himmler.*

125 *'medical commissioners will shortly . . .'*: Cited in Mitscherlich and Mielke, *Death Doctors.*

125 'My dearest Mummy! . . .': Chroust (ed.), *Friedrich Mennecke.*

127 *'We had to get out . . .'*: Cited in Strebel, *Ravensbrück.*

132 *'an* Appell *for Blockovas'*: My account of how prisoners viewed events in the camp that followed Mennecke's arrival are compiled from interviews, as well as a series of testimonies in WO 235/416 and WO 235/318, and Rosa Jochmann, 'Wenn der Elferblock voll gewesen ist, dann . . .', <http://www.doew.at/erinnern/biographien/erzaehlte-geschichte/haft-1938-1945/rosa-jochmann-wenn-der-elferblock-voll-gewesen-ist-dann>. Also: *Dictators*; Herbermann, *The Blessed Abyss*; Clara Rupp memoir, ARa; Teege statement, 'Hinter Gitter und Stacheldraht', ARa 647.; and Luise Mauer, BAL 162/9809 and in Elling, *Frauen im deutschen Widerstand.*

135 *'Take my hand . . .'*: *Dreams.*

## Chapter 9: Bernburg

136 *'very ordinary – nothing'*: Author interview.

138–9 *'Tuesday 13 Jan . . .'*: Witte et al. (eds), *Dienstkalender.*

140 *'dearest baby'*: Chroust (ed.), *Friedrich Mennecke.*

142 *'The guard Zimmer . . .'*: Falkowska, 'Report to the History Commission', Institute for National Memory, Poland.

143 *'. . . extermination transport'*: In addition to the testimony and memoirs cited above, events immediately after are based on statements of Wiedmaier statements, ARa, witnesses and guards in further Hamburg trial evidence (e.g. Quernheim, Zimmer and Bernigau in BAL B162/9811) and Apfelkammer, BAL B162/9818.

146 *'Visit of RFSS . . .'*: Witte et al. (eds), *Dienstkalender*.
148 *'so we knew . . .'*: von Skene, WO 235/316.
151 *All our hopes*: Leichter family papers.
152 *Herta 'Sara' Cohen*: LAV NRW R RW-58/54910.
155 *'exemplary'*: Lina Krug letters in VVN files, BA.

## PART TWO

This section draws in particular on interviews with Polish survivors, most notably Maria Bielicka, Wanda Półtawska (née Wojtasik), Wojciecha Zeiske (née Buraczyńska) and Zofia Cisek (née Kawińska).

I have also used the statements of scores of Polish survivors at the Polish Institute at Lund and now held in the Lund University Library. These long, invaluable accounts were taken down within months of liberation, on the initiative of Zygmunt Lakocinski, a Polish art historian living in Lund. They were made public only in 1996.

### Chapter 10: Lublin

160 *'They couldn't get . . .'*: Michalik, Lund 117.
161 *'He took off his clothes'*: Jezierska, Lund 402. On the torture of Poles before reaching the camp, see also Wanda Kiedrzyńska, introduction to *Beyond*.
161 *St Adalbert's bookshop*: Details of Krysia and Wanda's meeting, resistance and imprisonment in Lublin from author interviews and *Dreams*.
161 *Michał Chrostowski*: Chrostowska, *Jakby Minęło Już Wszystko* and documents at Museum of Martyrology 'Pod Zegarem' (Under the clock), a branch of the Lublin Museum (Muzeum Lubelskie w Lublinie).
162 *'Write if you know something . . .'*: Chrostowska papers, Museum of Martyrology 'Pod Zegarem' (Under the clock), a branch of the Lublin Museum (Muzeum Lubelskie w Lublinie).
162 *hidden in a palm:* Author interview with Maria Wilgat.
162 *a train left Lublin*: Author interviews, also *Dreams* and Lund, various.
162 *'We were all pleased . . .'*: Stefaniak, *Beyond.*
166 Schmuckstücke: See also Tillion, *Ravensbrück*: 'the human debris that at Ravensbrück they threw outside'. In Auschwitz, the jargon for poorest of the poor was *Muselmann* (Muslim). The supposed

fatalism of Muslims is a possible reason for the word, says Sofsky in *The Order of Terror*. In Majdanek they were called 'donkeys', in Dachau 'cretins', in Mauthausen 'swimmers'. Sofsky says in Ravensbrück the term 'Muselweiber' (female Muslims) was used, but I did not find the term in the course of my research.

167 *telling stories*: Wińska, *Zwyciężyły Wartości.*

167 *Helena Korewina*: See Kiedrzyńska, *Ravensbrück*, and *Dictators.*

168 *Verfügbare*: *Dreams.* Also Młodkowska, *Beyond.*

168 *brought new rules*: Moldenhawer, Lund 420.

170 *'But don't sing out loud'*: Author interview with Maria Bielicka; also Kiedrzyńska, *Ravensbrück.*

170 *Polish farm girl*: Michalik, Lund 117.

171 *Gerda Quernheim*: Testimony and memories of Quernheim and Rosenthal is plentiful. See, for example, WO 309/416.

172 *'She asked me . . .'*: Tanke, BAL B162/472.

172 *We often caught sight*: Housková, BAL B162/455.

173 *'I didn't return the smile'*: LAV NRW 3997. The interrogation of Leni Bitterhoff (née Reinders), who was categorised as an asocial, is in her criminal police file. The fifth of eleven children, she was the daughter of a farmer and worked as a maid near Kleve. Her husband died at the front on 25 October 1941. She had no previous convictions and no interest in politics.

173 *'Can't you see . . .'*: *Dreams.*

174 *tiny little gifts*: Author interview.

174 *Grażyna composed*: Author interview.

174 *ugly and inhuman acts*: *Dreams.* On the spread of lesbianism see also: Moldenhawer, Lund 420; Młodkowska, *Beyond*; Morrison, *Ravensbrück.*

175 *beginning to starve*: *Dreams*; Dragan, Lund 239; Michalik, Lund 117.

177 *'Langefeld was full of affection . . .'*: Kiedrzyńska, *Ravensbrück.*

## Chapter 11: Auschwitz

179 *'. . . disastrous confusion'*: Buber-Neumann, *Die erloschene Flamme.*

180 *At first I didn't*: Author interview.

181 *3 March 1942*: Himmler's desk diary for 3 March 1942 states that he visited FKL Ravensbrück between 1100 and 1400 hours. Witte et al. (eds), *Dienstkalender.*

182 *entire corps of guards*: See Langefeld interrogation, 26 December 1945, NARA, NAW RG 338-000-50-11; also *Dictators* and Strebel, *Ravensbrück*.

182 *26 March*: According to Danuta Czech, the chronicler of Auschwitz, they arrived on a Thursday. See Czech, *Kalendarium*.

182 *We have little information*: The political prisoner Klara Pförtsch went as a Kapo and amongst the guards sent to Auschwitz remembers Hasse and Drechsel, terming the latter a 'bloody bitch' (BAL B162/9809).

183 *Philomena Müssgueller*: WO 309/412. See report in this file dated 19 April 1947 from US investigators, saying that a Philomena Muesgueller [*sic*], alias Mimi Heller, had been caught and according to her statement – was an 'oberkapo' in several camps since 1939. At Ravensbrück she confessed to having been in charge of the punishment company and at Auschwitz she ran the 'infamous Kommando Sauna' (the clothing stores at the gas chambers). The notes say Jewish prisoners who had been at Auschwitz accused Müssgueller of torture and 'causing death'. There are also notes about a possible extradition to the British sector to stand trial, but she was not apparently charged or tried. Inteviewed by German investigators in April 1965, she described herself as 'a housewife' living in Oberpfalz. She admitted to having been in Ravensbrück as a Stubova, saying she was 'released' in 1942, which was in fact when she was posted to Auschwitz. She says nothing about Auschwitz in this later interview and, not apparently pressed on the issue, was allowed to go home (BAL B162/9818).

183 *vivid accounts*: Luise Mauer report in Elling, *Frauen im deutschen Widerstand*. Teege statement, 'Hinter Gitter und Stacheldraht', ARa 647.

183 *arrived from Poprad*: Czech, *Kalendarium*.

185 *'piled high to the ceiling'*: Höss, *Commandant*.

187 *'I took the first . . .'*: Langefeld interrogation, December 1945, NARA, NAW RG 338-000-50-11. Also see Buber-Neumann, *Die erloschene Flamme*.

188 *Nora Hodys*: See Langbein, *People in Auschwitz*.

189 *17 July 1942*: See Hoss, *Commandant*, and Rees, *Auschwitz*.

191 *Gorlitz*: See Buber-Neumann, *Die erloschene Flamme*, Langefeld interrogation, December 1945, NARA, NAW RG 338-000-50-11, and Höss, *Commandant*.

## Chapter 12: Sewing

The story of the sewing shop has been pieced together from scores of prisoner accounts, including: Wiedmaier, untitled statement on the sewing shop, 29 December 1946, ARa; Alfredine Nenninger, 'Erlebnisse in Frauenkonzentrationslager Ravensbrück und bei den Wirtschaftsbetrieben der Waffen-SS', DÖW; Müller, *Klempnerkolonne*; *Dictators*; Wińska, *Zwyciężyły Wartości*; and testimonies at Lund as well as French and Russian statements.

194 *sold toys*: Dąbrówska, BAL B162/9813.

194 *local links*: Strebel, *Ravensbrück*.

195 *Herr Wendland's work*: *Dictators*.

196 *'reduced the impetus . . .'*: Moldenhawer, Lund 420.

197 *circle of friends*: See Feldenkirchen, *Siemens*, the company's official history.

197 *To make up the shortfall*: By the end of 1940, Siemens was heavily reliant on Jewish labour in Berlin. The Jewish workers were kept separate and had less favourable working conditions from others. Ibid.

198 *adapted for precision work*: Ibid.

198 *shipment of Germany's Jews*: When the deportations began Carl Friedrich von Siemens told a Jewish Siemens manager he found it 'upsetting' to have to dismiss him. However, von Siemens added that if he had objected to Hitler's policies he 'would be risking the existence of the entire house of Siemens'. Cited in ibid.

198 *'encourage the men . . .'*: Himmler to Pohl, 23 March 1942, BA NS 19/2065. See also Sommer, 'Warum das Schweigen?'.

198 *'The women chosen . . .'*: Schiedlausky, WO 235/309.

199 *Texled was professionally run:* See Strebel, *Ravensbrück*. Trial testimony is divided between the first, main case in which Binder was a defendant (WO 235/305–319), and the trial of Opitz and Graf a year later (WO 309/1150).

199 *'women's work'*: Cited in Iris Nachum and Dina Porat, 'The History of Ravensbrück Concentration Camp as Reflected in its Changing and Expanding Functions', in Dublon-Knebel (ed.), *A Holocaust Crossroads*.

200 *word comes that she has died*: Accounts of such deaths are plentiful. See, for example, Ilse Gohrig and Neeltje Epker, in WO 235/433 and WO 309/1150.

201 *Suddenly Schinderhannes*: See Alfredine Nenninger, 'Frauenkonzentrationslager Ravensbrück Abteilung Industriehof', DÖW, Ravensbrück f. 143.

202 *Kawurek*, *Ryczko* and *Zaremba*: Wińska, *Zwyciężyły Wartości*

203 *'It was a kind of history lesson . . .'*: Dragan, Lund 239.

203 *'took the money and gold . . .'*: Wiedmaier, WO 309/42. She also talks of army uniforms coming for repairs 'covered in blood and muck'.

203 *'laden with Jewish furs'*: Biega, BAL B162/9818.

203 *'lifting our chins . . .'*: Dragan, Lund 239.

204 *'Even today when . . .'*: Michalik, Lund 117.

204 *'beautiful sunny day'*: *Dreams.*

205 *'Fanatical patriot . . .'*: Bielicka. Kiedrzyńska, in her introduction to *Beyond*, said evidence emerged that the death sentences on these women had not been formally agreed by Odilo Globocnik, the Lublin police chief.

205 *sewing on buttons*: Młodkowska, *Beyond.*

206 *'scream of unbearable longing . . .'*: *Dreams.*

207 *'I knew they were . . .'*: Falkowska, 'Report to the History Commission', Institute for National Memory, Poland.

208 *'like medieval penitents'*: *Dictators.*

208 *'Pola pointed a finger . . .'*: *Dreams.*

208 *'a truck carrying prisoners . . .'*: Pietsch, BAL B162/981.

208 *'At 6 p.m. roll call . . .'*: Adamska, WO 235/318.

208 *'We stood there . . .'*: *Dictators.*

## Chapter 13: Rabbits

210 *'caused by bacteria . . .'*: Quoted in MacDonald, *The Assassination of Reinhard Heydrich.*

211 *They were holding*: Hozáková, *Und es war doch.* Also see Russell, *The Scourge of the Swastika*, and Uwe Naumann (ed.), *Lidice: Ein böhmisches Dorf* (Frankfurt: Röderberg, 1983).

212 *Karl Gebhardt had no interest*: Interrogated by the Americans in October 1945, Gebhardt poured scorn on other high-up Nazi doctors, saying, unlike him, they had joined the SS for personal advancement. Had he (Gebhardt) not carried out the sulphonamide tests they would have had no scientific basis at all and been assigned to some incompetent like Dr Rascher, whose experiments were 'ridiculous'. For Himmler, the experiments were simply a way of finding 'a new device' to impress the Führer. NARA M 1270.

213 *'visiting some relations . . .'*: Cited in Mitscherlich and Mielke, *Death Doctors.*

213 *born at Hohenlychen*: Himmler, *The Himmler Brothers*. It was a difficult forceps delivery.

214 *'you horse . . .'*: Ostermann, Buchmann coll.

214 *Wanda was picked out last*: The doctors said at Nuremberg that during what they called this 'second' phase of experiments from September to early October, thirty-six women were chosen, divided into three groups of twelve. In total seventy-four Polish women were operated on. See Mitscherlich and Mielke, *Death Doctors*.

218 *'How many deaths . . .'*: Ibid.

## Chapter 14: Special Experiments

223 *Kazia Kurowska*: Kurowska had tried to escape the camp a few weeks before the experiments, as if instinct had pre-warned her. She illegally joined an outside work group then ran from one work team to another 'like a frightened deer' before being caught. See Grabowska, *Beyond*.

224 *spies through keyholes*: Mączka, Lund 228.

226 *'Look here,'*: *Dreams*.

226 *Gebhardt left*: Zofia Mączka, the Polish doctor, later said that one day she overheard Oberheuser admit that 'there was at least one good thing about the operations: I got a bit of practice with surgery, and I have a chance of getting a position at Hohenlychen now'.

227 *'I can also imagine . . .'*: Cited in Mitscherlich and Mielke, *Death Doctors*. Himmler's mania for experimentation became clear to Keith Mant, the British war crimes pathologist, when preparing for the Nuremberg cases. 'I discovered when reading the SS documents in Nuremberg during preparation for the trial of the doctors that he [Himmler] had personally read and initialled virtually every document dealing with human experiments which were in the SS HQ files'. Note on a file, Atkins.

227 *'showed unobjectionably Nordic . . .'*: Mitscherlich and Miekle, *Death Doctors*.

227–8 *'very quickly grasped . . .'*: Ibid.

228 *opposed Stumpfegger's tests*: Nuremberg testimony, cited in ibid. Details of these experiments also in Mączka, Lund 228, and Mant report, WO 309/416.

231 *A little Gypsy girl*: Housková, BAL B162/455.

231 *'marks of hypodermic needles . . .'*: *Dictators*.

232 *mostly to Auschwitz*: In autumn 1942 the Ravensbrück women were still unclear what happened at Auschwitz, but news arrived with a

group of 'extreme' Jehovah's Witnesses, sent from Ravensbrück to Auschwitz for making trouble, then returned – nonsensically – a few weeks later to be executed. Grete Buber-Neumann managed to speak to one of them, who said: 'You won't believe it, I know, but living human beings are thrown into the fire there, including little children. Jews chiefly.' Grete didn't believe her. She looked delirious. She'd obviously gone mad. See *Dictators*. At the same time as the Jewish prisoners left for Auschwitz in October 1942, so Emma Zimmer, the senior guard, was transferred to work there; she said her job was supervising the SS accommodation (WO 309/1153).

232 *'They were often sick . . .'*: Hoffmann, Buchmann coll.

233 *a Ukrainian girl*: Winkowska, Lund 285, and Grabowska, *Beyond*. There were at least ten of these 'special experiments', says Zofia Mączka (Lund 228).

234 *Russian doctor in Kiev*: Mitscherlich and Miekle, *Death Doctors*.

234 *shoulder blade*: Ibid, and Mączka, Lund 228.

234 *One of these women*: Also see Grabowska, *Beyond*.

## Chapter 15: Healing

237 *Kazimiera Pobiedzińska*: See Grabowska, *Beyond*, and Falkowska, 'Report to the History Commission', Institute for National Memory, Poland.

237 *'these unscrupulous Kapos . . .'*: Höss, *Commandant*.

238 *On the ground*: Pery Broad affidavit, 14 December 1945, NI-11397, Staatsarchiv Nürnberg.

239 *backroom boy*: In training SS chiefs found Suhren 'a little hesitant and awkward' and lacking 'military sentiment' but his conduct was 'irreproachable', as were his National Socialist convictions. See Strebel, *Ravensbrück*. The German prisoner Isa Vermehren noted he had a 'cultivated demeanour' (TNA TS/895). Also see note for p. 354, below.

239 *SS corruption*: Ramdohr's so-called 'investigation' centred on SS looting in the fur workshop, but according to Ella Pietsch, a particularly observant guard, it was a cover-up. A key witness – a junior SS man called Verchy – was shot before he could spill the beans. Ramdohr told Pietsch that Verchy 'died a natural death' but she didn't believe him (BAL B162/981).

239 *lethal toll*: Death figures cited in Strebel, *Ravensbrück*.

241 *'Each prisoner's output . . .'*: *Dictators*. Also see samples of monthly reports in SA, showing the turnover of 'useless' workers and numbers

rejected due to 'death'. In *Siemens*, Feldenkirchen notes that management found output 'impressive' due to 'exemplary' fitting out of workshops and 'order that reigned in the workplace'.

242 *'wriggling between . . .'*: *Dictators*. Helena Strzelecka, Lund 192, described the couple's 'drunken orgies' in the *Revier*. Quernheim put on 'macabre shows' for those she was going to kill, bathing them first and decorating the bath tub with flowers, then combing their hair.

244 *sneaking little luxuries*: Grabowska and Maćkowska, *Beyond*.

244 *'I'll just try . . .'*: *Beyond*.

245 *'We were silent . . .'*: *Dreams*.

246 *'painful sight'*: Michalik, Lund 117.

246 *'telling the world'*: *Krysia* Czyż-Wilgat (née Cycż) essay, describing the genesis of the plan, in *Beyond*, and author interview with Wanda Półtawska (née Wojtasik) and Wojciecha Zeiske (née Buraczyńska). See also *Dreams*.

248 *'It seemed out of context,'*: Author interview.

249 *'This was the only story . . .'*: Author interview.

249 *The letter writing began*: Czyż-Wilgat, *Beyond*.

253 *protest march*: The march was described to me by Wojciecha Zeiske and is in testimony of several cited above, in particular Pelagia Maćkowska, and Eugenia Mikulska in *Beyond*.

254–5 *'knew nothing of the operations'*: Lanckorońska, 'Report of the Camp of Ravensbrück', AICRC.

256 *a near-mutiny*: Czyż letters. See also Kiedrzyńska, *Ravensbrück*.

257 *I sat at my typewriter*: *Dictators*.

## PART THREE
### Chapter 16: Red Army

For the story of the Red Army women I interviewed more than thirty survivors and have also drawn on others' interviews, notably those with the German historian Loretta Walz, who was the first Western writer to work on an oral history of the camp.

Trial testimony is limited. Crimes against Russians were not investigated in Western post-war trials, and nor did Russians give evidence, which is in part why the story has never been told. A few ad hoc trials were held at Neustrelitz, near Ravensbrück, by Soviet prosecutors after liberation but details are few.

Papers relating to a Soviet Investigative Commission into Ravensbrück have recently come to light in GARF, the State Archive of the Russian Federation, and were invaluable though incomplete.

261 '... *orders came to mobilise*': Author interviews. Also see Shneer, *Plen*, and Mednikov, *Dolya Bessmertiya*.

262 *800,000 Soviet women*: Cited in Strebel, *Ravensbrück*.

263 *'Malygina was ...'*: The account of the last battle on the Crimean cliffs, the swim, the march west and the shooting of Jews is based on my interviews, as well as the account of Leonida Boyko in Mednikov, *Dolya Bessmertiya* and Konnikova, GARF. Also Tschajalo, report to the Military Medicine Museum, St Petersburg.

264 *'depraved creatures'*: Cited in Strebel, *Ravensbrück*. Also see Shneer, *Plen*.

267–9 *used for slave labour*: Author interviews. Also see Tschajalo, report to the Military Medicine Museum, St Petersburg, and Shneer, *Plen*.

## Chapter 17: Yevgenia Klemm

270 *From the train*: Author interviews. Also: Konnikova, GARF; Tschajalo, report to the Military Medicine Museum, St Petersburg; Losowaja, ARa; and Nikif papers.

272 *'war status'*: Author interviews, and see discussion in Strebel, *Ravensbrück* and Favez, *The Red Cross and the Holocaust*.

273 *'official' Russians*: *Dictators*. Grete Buber-Neumann's memoir, first published in West Germany in 1949, was viewed in the East as the work of a fascist traitor and is still today not translated into Russian.

273 *'They came from ...'*: Hájková, 'Ravensbrück', Prague 1960, ARa.

273 *'contemptible'*: *Dictators*.

273 *post-war censorship*: On Nikiforova's fight with censors I drew on interviews with Stella Nikiforova (née Kugelman) and Bärbel Schindler-Saefkow.

274 *born in Odessa*: Klemm's background is based on survivors' accounts and Georg Loonkin's papers, including an article he wrote in 1968 for the *Communist Flag*. The article was groundbreaking as it extolled the heroism of the Soviet women at a time when Hitler's Red Army prisoners were still viewed by many in Russia as traitors.

276 *I found the camp*: Yekaterina Olovyannikova, Nikif papers.

276 *'I don't see Lyusya ...'*: Anna Fedchenko, Nikif papers.

278 *'extremely beautiful clothes'*: Letter in Nikif papers.

278 *'always held high'*: Hájková, 'Ravensbrück', Prague 1960, ARa.

278 *more were arriving every day*: Increasing overcrowding is described in most accounts of the period; see for example Moldenhawer, Lund 420. Also see the SS photo album showing building work

(ARa) and Plewe and Köhler, *Baugeschichte Frauen-Konzentrationslager Ravensbrück.*

278 *her favoured Blockovas*: Amongst other Blockovas sacked and sent to the bunker when Langefeld was dismissed were Rosa Jochmann, the Austrian trade unionist and Helena Korewina, the Polish countess.

279 *Spitzel*: Multiple accounts in Hamburg trial testimony and BAL. See Apfelkammer BAL B162/9818, and Ramdohr's own testimony, WO 309/416.

279 *'strolling up and down . . .': Dictators.*

279 *'beautiful beast'*: Exactly when Binz officially became chief guard is not clear. At first she shared the post with a newcomer to the camp, Anna Klein-Plaubel, but Klein-Plaubel made little impression on prisoners and claimed in post-war interrogations that she had no direct contact with inmates (WO 309/115). From 1943 onwards most prisoners believe Binz was only chief guard; she certainly had the most power.

279 *Binz paid a visit*: Author interview with Ilse Halter, childhood acquaintance of Binz.

280 '*It was 4 a.m. . . .*': Nikif papers.

280 *stand outside in the cold and rain*: Konnikova, GARF. New forms of water torture were always being invented. Anna Stekolnikova recalled digging sand from the lake floor, standing waist-deep in water to do it. Author interview.

280 *'Suddenly from machine to machine . . .'*: Nikif papers.

283 *sang an aria*: Tschajalo, report to the Military Medicine Museum, St Petersburg, says it was an aria from *Carmen*. Anise Girard recalled singing an aria with the Soviet women when she lived in the same block.

284 *'Only the proletarians . . .'*: Hájková, 'Ravensbrück', Prague 1960, ARa, on the march and also author interview with Galina Gorbotsova.

## Chapter 18: Doctor Treite

285 *he donated*: Strebel, *Ravensbrück.*

285 *Youth Camp*: Construction of the Uckermark camp was carried out at about the same time the Siemens plant was built, and was also done by prisoners from the men's camp. Once again the death toll was shocking. Witnesses said ten to fifteen men were shot each day, as they collapsed of hunger and exhaustion, or tried to escape.

286 *'I absolutely wanted . . .'*: Vavak, 'Siemens & Halske im Frauenkonzentrationslager Ravensbrück', DÖW, Ravensbrück f. 49.

286 *'It is incomprehensible . . .'*: SA uncatalogued file, cited in Feldenkirchen, *Siemens*.

286 *to work at the death camp*: Ehlert, BAL B162/452.

287 *'I wanted to go back . . .'*: Strebel, *Ravensbrück*.

287 *'As the housing . . .'*: Ibid.

287 *'Under our eyes . . .'*: Bontemps, 'Siemens-Arbeitslager-Ravensbrück', ARa.

287–8 *'After three months . . .'*: Author interview.

288 *'It was one of the . . .'*: Author interview.

288 *had never halted*: The sewing shop kept lists of the 'useless' too. WO 235/433.

288 *black transports*: Schiedlausky, WO 235/309. Also see Tillion, *Ravensbrück* and her evidence at Rastatt, Archives diplomatiques du ministère des Affaires étrangères, Colmar. Also Anise Postel-Vinay (née Girard), 'Les exterminations par gaz à Ravensbrück', in Tillion, *Ravensbrück*, 3rd edition.

289 *'They chose us . . .'*: Maurel, *Ravensbrück*.

290 *the contracts*: See Strebel, *Ravensbrück*; also Speer, *The Slave State*.

290 *'whether because of . . .'*: Czyż letters.

291 *clandestine radio station*: SWIT came under the Politcal Warfare Executive, a British wartime secret service, which oversaw all underground radio propaganda. A women's branch of SWIT was started too, at the instigation of a Polish woman lawyer called Krystyna Marek.

292 *The first time*: Author interview. Poles had also been sent to work as labourers at Hohenlychen clinic, from where they got letters out from in the ordinary mail.

292 *'produced a feast'*: Silbermann, 'SS-Kantine Ravensbrück', DÖW, Ravensbrück f. 140.

294 *'With such a high rate . . .'*: NI-10815, Staatsarchiv Nürnberg.

294 *'. . . only those suffering . . .'*: Himmler, NO-1007, Staatsarchiv Nürnberg.

294 *'I didn't want to do it'*: Konnikova, GARF.

294 *at least two abortions*: Rosenthal's officer file, copy in ARa.

295 *family background*: See Salvation Army yearbooks (various editions), 'Jubilee Memories of Lt-Col K. Treite' and other papers in the Salvation Army archives, London. Family tree in Percy Treite officer file, BA.

295 *reorganised the Revier*: See, for example, Maria Grabska, 'Bericht über das Revier Frauenkonzentrationslager Ravensbrück', ARa.
296 *'After her illness . . .'*: *Dictators.*
297 *'Even the SS guards . . .'*: Ibid.
298 *'Bolshevik cow'*: Konnikova, GARF.
298* *officially secret letter*: Cited in Mitscherlich and Mielke, *Death Doctors.*
299 *'The conditions . . .'*: *Dictators.*
300 *'And looking at me . . .'*: Tillion, *Ravensbrück.*
300–1 *This for me*: Salvesen, WO 235/305.
301 *'no other hospital on earth'*: Salvesen, *Forgive.*
301 *'Are you the daughter . . .'*: WO 309/149
301 *'Was he a Jew?'*: See Nikoforova report in Buchmann coll.
301–2 *'Treite often came . . .'*: Nedvedova, Prague statement.
302 *'I thought it might . . .'*: Salvesen, *Forgive.*
302 *'Except one day . . .'*: Author interview.
302 *'The conversation turned to . . .'*: Hanka Housková, handwritten memoir, ARa. Also see Jirásková, *Kurzer Bericht über drei Entscheidungen.*
303 *Two inmates*: Elisabeth Thury, the camp policewoman, said by 1943 the prisoner-beaters lived in a special room in the bunker, WO 235/318.
303 *urinating in terror*: Multiple testimonies, for example Epker, WO 309/1150, and Konnikova, GARF.
303 *'Flogging of Female Prisoners'*: WO 309/217.
304 *'perhaps because he was . . .'*: Nedvedova, Prague statement.
305 *'Armed with a broom . . .'*: Salvesen, *Forgive.*
306 *they were to be bribed*: Konnikova, GARF, and see French refusal in *Les Françaises à Ravensbrück*, also Poles refusing in Lund testimony.
306 *'Girls, we must show . . .'*: Quoted in Mednikov, *Dolya Bessmertiya.*
306 *Today we have learned*: Nikif papers.

## Chapter 19: Breaking the Circle

307 *own style of terror*: Ramdohr's own trial statement WO 309/416. Unusually for an SS man, he was condemned in court testimony by his own SS colleagues and he condemned them too. Treite spoke of Ramdohr's brutal methods and Suhren said he 'heard Ramdohr was very cruel'. Rastatt testimony, Archives diplomatiques du ministère des Affaires étrangères, Colmar.

307 *Binz looked shocked*: Falkowska, 'Report to the History Commission', Institute for National Memory, Poland. Also multiple reports of atrocity, for example: Anna Hand, WO 235/318, and Vermehren, *Reise durch den letzten Akt*.

308 *'When he buried . . .'*: WO 235/312. In Nazi war crimes trials several SS men produced evidence of kindness to animals to support pleas in mitigation of their cruelty to humans.

308 *network of camp spies*: WO 309/416.

309 *'It is not easy to control women . . .'*: Cited in Strebel, *Ravensbrück*.

309 *'They were very young . . .'*: *Dictators*.

309 *These recruits arrived*: Silbermann, 'SS-Kantine Ravensbrück'.

309 *'The original female supervisors . . .'*: Höss, *Commandant*.

310 *women's prisoner orchestra at Auschwitz*: When Mandl arrived at Auschwitz in 1943 a men's orchestra already existed, and she wanted a women's orchestra 'as a matter of prestige'. The two orchestras were kept entirely separate; the men's was of far higher quality. Author interview with Anita Lasker-Wallfisch, the only cellist in the Auschwitz women's orchestra.

311 *'Girls, look, it's an airport'*: The main narrative of Barth is drawn from my interview in Kiev with Valentina Samoilova from which her comments in the text are drawn, unless otherwise stated below.

314 *thick with maggots*: Sabrodskaja, ARa.

314 *more locals*: See Elga Kaletta in Radau, *Nichts ist vergessen und niemand*.

314 *'She was the first . . .'*: Maurel, *Ravensbrück*; see also *Les Françaises à Ravensbrück*.

315 *the Hangman, Baba Yaga, Squinty Eye*: Homeriki, BStU.

315 *glass eye*: Evdokia Domina, author interview on Genthin subcamp.

315 *Blondine*: For the story of Ilse Hermann (later Göritz; aka Blondine) and Ramdohr's methods see testimony of the 1965 trial in the DDR of three guards, Göritz (née Hermann), Frida Wötzel and Ulla Jürss, in BStU.

315 *'We were never out of touch . . .'*: Author interview. Also her testimony in Buchmann coll. and Tschjalo, report to the Military Medicine Museum, St Petersburg. Contact between Klemm and Red Army women in other subcamps was mentioned in several author interviews.

316 *Vera Vanchenko*: Nikif papers, particularly letters of Antonina Kholina, in prison with her and later in Ravensbrück. Also author interview with Stella Kugelman-Nikiforova.

317 *'Psychology, this is the secret'*: Cited in Strebel, *Ravensbrück*.

317 *Julie Wolk*: See anon, 'Report on Julie Wolk', Prague 1945, Buchmann coll.

318 *ran into the wire*: Nikif papers and Pikula, Buchmann coll.

319 *strung two nooses up*: What happened next is pieced together from several accounts which vary in detail but survivors are in broad agreement that as a result of the protests both Samoilova and Malygina were subjected to water torture and threatened with the gallows, at which one, or possibly both, gave up their resistance.

320 *Stasi inquisitors*: The responses of Ilse Göritz (née Hermann; aka Blondine) to Stasi questioning throws light not only on what happened at Barth but on the Stasi interrogators' determination to find out about Ramdohr's spy ring. Göritz was interrogated eighteen times between 6 March 1964 and 25 May 1965, in Rostock Prison, DDR, and each time a little more detail was eked out of her (see BStU, ZUV 1). Göritz's statements must be read against the backdrop of the Cold War and in the knowledge that her interrogators wanted her to embellish Nazi war crimes; see Angelika von Meyer, '"Ich wollte eine Uniform tragen": der "Rostocker Prozess" in den Unterlagen des Ministeriums für Staatssicherheit', in Erpel (ed.) *Im Gefolge der SS*. However, the details she gives of her banal daily routine, carrying out Ramdohr's orders to crush Soviet prisoners, combined with matching testimony from the prisoners, gives a compelling picture of extermination of subcamp slave labour, and of the Red Army's desperate resistance at Barth.

321 *Belsen fodder*: Göritz interrogation, 16 April 1964, BStU ZUV 1.

324 *'at the operating table . . .'*: 1956 letter, Nikif papers. Tatyana Pignatti herself was suspected by several comrades, including Antonina Nikiforova, of working after the war 'for the organs' (i.e. SMERSh). Antonina told Stella Kugelman-Nikoforova that Pignatti was one of those who denounced people. 'You had to be careful with Pignatti,' said Stella when we met in St Petersburg. 'She behaved all right in the camp but afterwards she was transformed. Maybe she had been persecuted and became sick. Who knows.' See note for p. 643, below, on Stella's post-war family ties to Antonina.

## Chapter 20: Black Transport

325 *'the potato-cake girl'*: Author interviews with Wanda Heger (née Hjort), Nelly Langholm and Norwegian survivors. Also see Heger, *Tous les vendredis*, and Persson, *Escape from the Third Reich*.

326 Sippenhaft: See Padfield, *Himmler*.

328 'Die Salvesen . . .': Salvesen, *Forgive*.

330 *I rang the bell*: Author interview.

330 *'magnificent hospitality'*: Cited in Moorehead, *Dunant's Dream*.

330 *ingratiating letters*: Favez, *The Red Cross and the Holocaust*.

331 *hitherto sceptical*: The Allied Joint Declaration, issued on 17 December 1942, was supported not only by Britain, the US and the Soviet Union, but eight governments in exile and General de Gaulle's French National Committee. For debate see Gilbert, *Auschwitz and the Allies*.

331 *crisis meeting*: For a vivid account of this meeting, see Moorehead, *Dunant's Dream*.

332 *the designation NN*: Wanda was one of the first, if not the first, to get news of the *Nacht und Nebel* order out to the West. Author interview.

333 *'In the concentration camp . . .'*: Polish Study Trust collection 3.16, note of 30 July 1943 relating to signal reveived on 29 July 1943.

333 *Regarding experiments*: Polish Study Trust collection 3.16, note of 8 May 1943. Also see the note of 22 May 1943 in the same collection, which shows that an appeal was also sent by the Polish Embassy in the Vatican to the Pope on 20 March, asking His Holiness to intervene on behalf of the several hundred Polish women imprisoned in Ravensbrück.

334 *'We could hear motorbikes . . .'*: Sokulska, Lund. Also see Wińska, *Zwyciężyły Wartości*, Kiedrzyńska, *Ravensbrück*, and Dąbrówska, BAL B162/9813.

334 *Judas soup*: Młodkowska, *Beyond*.

335 *shinbone snapped*: Sokulska, Lund.

335 *'crumpled up in the bed . . .'*: Salvesen, *Forgive*.

336 *death rates were rising*: Death rates were also high among women given late and botched abortions who were susceptible to TB. And new arrivals were in a far worse condition than before. A Polish woman arriving in 1943 was handcuffed en route but her hands were so thin 'my handcuffs fell off' and the clogs issued at the camp were 'so heavy I could not lift them off the ground'. Cieplak, Lund 143.

336 *five stretchers*: Sprengel, 'Wie Siemens an Häftlingen verdiente'.

336 *'pitiable'*: Cited in Strebel, *Ravensbrück*.

336 *'Many women had to be . . .'*: Sprengel, ARa; also in Strebel, *Ravensbrück*.

337 *'capitalist toes'*: Maurel, *Ravensbrück*.

337 *According to Carmen Mory*: WO 309/419.

337 *'I asked him if . . .'*: Some of Mory's most credible evidence, particularly her description of black transports, emerged during a detailed interrogation carried out by the Belgian War Crimes Commission in 1946; a copy is filed in WO 309/419.

338 *'showed affection . . .'*: Tillion, *Ravensbrück.*

338 *'Transports of the sick . . .'*: Czyż letters.

338 *I went to Triete*: Salvesen, *Forgive.* For details on selections, Treite's role and selections also see statements and trial transcripts in WO 235/317 and 318 and Mant report, WO 309/416.

339 *'Difficult decisions . . .'*: Boy-Brandt, 'Überlick über die Reviertätigeit vom März 1942–Ende 1945', Buchmann coll.

339 *'One day a woman . . .'*: Tillion, *Ravensbrück.*

339 *'Then we hid her . . .'*: Author interview.

340 *'They beat us . . .'*: Quoted in Mednikov, *Dolya Bessmertiya.*

340 *'I give you my word . . .'*: Mory, WO 309/419.

341 *Yvonne Le Tac*: Testimony in Fonds (collection) Tillion, Musée de la Résistance et de la Déportation, Besançon.

341 *'sent to Lublin . . .'*: Sprengel, ARa.

341 *On 3rd Feb 44*: Czyż letters.

342 *Later came more news*: Zofija Daniejel-Osojnik, report in ARa. Anna Hand, one of the Polish prisoner secretaries, said that such was the chaos of the Majdanek transport that nobody knew 'of the 800' who had finally gone, so a woman guard called Laurenzen went to Majdanek to find out. 'With gruesome cold-bloodedness she reports back that out of 800 prisoners, sixteen died during the transport in the cattle waggons. The waggons had been left unopened on a siding for several days. The women had no blankets, very little straw, and had not been given any food or water. They had had nowhere to relieve themselves.' WO 235/318.

343 *'Vivisection in Ravensbrück'*: FO 371/39396.

## PART FOUR
### Chapter 21: Vingt-sept Mille

351 *The inspection by Himmler*: Tanke, BAL B162/472.

351 *'depressed in mind . . .'*: Kersten, *Memoirs.*

354 *it was only when her brother*: Isa's account of her brother's defection and how it led to her arrest is given in a long statement to British investigators in Capri in May 1945. Isa found herself in Capri with a group of other Allied hostages (*Prominente*) who had been smuggled out of Germany and into Austria under SS escort in the last

days, and were then liberated by the British who took them to Capri for immediate debriefing. See Vermehren statements, TNA TS 26/895.

355 *so, in the strictest secrecy*: Himmler's letter to Burkhardt, dated 21 July 1942, in reply to Burkhardt's letter of 1 June 1942, is in the ITS archives (TID 800 176). For later correspondence see Favez, *The Red Cross and the Holocaust*, and below, p. 576.

357 *'protected' Jews*: On 'protected' Jews, see Buber Agassi, *Jewish Women Prisoners of Ravensbrück.*

## Chapter 22: Falling

362 *'Clap' Wanda*: Lundholm, *Das Höllentor.*

362* *'Holy Ghost–Kommando'*: Baumann, BAL 162/448.

365 *'It is for the Reich . . . '*: WO 309/416.

365 *Someone said: 'Come and see . . . '*: Author interview.

365 *'were very emotional . . . '*: Author interview.

365* *unprecedented visit*: Siemens monthly report, 23 February 1944, SA.

366 *'high culture'*: Lanckorońska, *Those Who Trespass Against Us.*

368 *I came onto*: Author interview.

369 *'From my window . . . '*: WO 309/149

370 *promptly destroyed:* Germain Tillion said in evidence at the Rastatt trial that she received information from camp secretaries and others to suggest that about sixty small 'black transports' left the camp in 1943 and 1944. Tillion, 'Procès Verbal', 11 June 1949, Tribunal Général de Rastatt; held at Archives diplomatiques du ministère des Affaires étrangères, Colmar.

## Chapter 23: Hanging On

375 *'Oh yes, Elfriede . . . '*: Author interview.

376 *'Sometimes they would . . . '*: Author interview.

376 *'and put it at the back . . . '*: Silbermann, 'SS-Kantine Ravensbrück', DÖW, Ravensbrück f. 140.

377 *'international association'*: Moldenhawer, Lund 420.

378 *'Every morning . . . '*: Lundholm, *Das Höllentor.*

378 *'She believed . . . '*: Author interview.

378 *'At first . . . '*: Author interview.

379 *I asked her*: Author interview.

380 *'. . . punched me violently . . . '*: Mary O'Shaughnessy statement, Atkins.

## Chapter 24: Reaching Out

383 *'We are in touch . . .'*: Dufournier family papers, courtesy of Caroline McAdam Clark.

384 *German officials evacuated*: Falkowska said 'the big Eichmann office' was re-located here, in other words the staff of part of Eichmann's notorious department for Jewish affairs, 1VB4 of the RSHA (Reich Security Head Office) were evacuated to the Ravensbrück woods. *Report*.

384 *Those lucky enough*: Maurel, *Ravensbrück*.

385 *'Look at the colour . . .'*: Buber-Neumann, *Dictators*.

387 *'But Germaine . . .'*: Author interview.

387 *'These other women's . . .'*: Czyż letters.

388 *'If the idea . . .'*: Private letter cited in ibid.

389 *conditions were 'tragic'*: Note in Favez, *The Red Cross and the Holocaust*.

390 *The daily routine*: FO 371/39395.

390–1 *'At first sight . . .'*: *Dreams*. See also Kiedrzyńska, *Ravensbrück*.

391 *Allied landings*: Falkowska, 'Report to the History Commission', Institute for National Memory, Poland.

391 *'in a loud voice'*: Lanckorońska, *Those Who Trespass Against Us*.

391 *'Now ladies . . .'*: Author interview.

392 *A Hungarian Jewish woman*: La Guardia Gluck, *Fiorello's Sister* and notes on her ITS file.

393 *Among the group was*: Vaillant-Couturier, Nuremberg testimony, proceedings of 28 January 1946, Staatsarchiv Nürnberg.

394 *'But I thought . . .'*: Author interview.

395 *In a little-noticed footnote*: Bundsarchiv Koblenz, N 1126/38.

395 *cars and all inmates*: Schinke, BAL B162/9817.

396 *'He sat on a chair . . .'*: Vermehren, *Reise durch den letzten Akt*.

397 *Outside women*: Author interview.

397 *'ridiculous dresses . . .'*: Dufournier, *La maison des mortes*.

# PART FIVE

## Chapter 25: Paris and Warsaw

401 train de la mort: *Livre mémorial.*

402 *'And the Allies? . . .'*: Litoff (ed.), *An American Heroine in the French Resistance*.

404 *A sixteen-year-old girl*: Krystyna Dąbrówska, author interview and her unpublished essay, 'Through the Concentration Camp to Freedom'.

405 *'What news of Warsaw?'*: Author interview with Półtawska and *Dreams.*
406 *'There were badges . . .'*: Lanckorońska, *Those Who Trespass Against Us.*
406 *The original tent*: Wasilewska's report on the tent, 'Block 25, Zelt', Lund 434.
407 *'The strong snatched . . .'*: Hand, BAL B192/9819.
407 *'They seemed to have . . .'*: *Dreams.*
409 *She had faced Mengele*: Wellsberg and Minsburg, author interviews; also testimony in YV.
409 *not be 'recorded on the lists'*: Stutthof Camp Archives, AMSt. I-IIB-7, cited in Hördler, *Ordnung und Inferno.*
410 *Her long hair*: Lundholm, *Das Höllentor.*

## Chapter 26: Kinderzimmer

411 *'on the grounds . . .'*: Lanckorońska, *Those Who Trespass Against Us.*
412 *Stasia Tkaczyk*: Author interview.
412 *felt contractions*: Kopczynska's account in *Die Frauen von Ravensbrück* (1980), a film directed by Loretta Walz. Also see *Ravensbrückerinnen* (Berlin: Hentrich, 1995).
412 *allow the birth of babies*: The details of births come from my interview with Marie-Jo Chombart de Lauwe (née Wilborts); Nedvedova, Prague statement and WO 235/317; Sylvia Salvesen, WO 235/305 and *Forgive*; Ilse Reibmayer, interview with Loretta Walz and in DÖW; Anna Weng Seidermann statements in WO 235/318 and Nikiforova, *Plus jamais.*
415 *'hanging pictures . . .'*: Himmler, *The Himmler Brothers.*
416 *deliberate starving of babies*: See Friedlander, *The Origins of Nazi Genocide.*
416 *Hermann Pfannmüller*: Ibid.
418 *'They would count them off'*: Cited in *Les Françaises à Ravensbrück.*
418 *'It was a dreadful sight . . .'*: Cited in Strebel, *Ravensbrück.*
418 *'They died without crying . . .'*: Author interview.

## Chapter 27: Protest

421 *'Do you know that feeling . . .'*: Author interview.
421 *Her friends could see*: Testimony of Anne-Marie de Bernard, in the archives of Loir et Cher, 55.j.4, and of Marguerite Flamencourt, HS 6/440. Both Bernard and Flamencourt were members of the ill-fated British Prosper circuit.

422 *'Ravensbrück was by this time . . .'*: Moldenhawer, Lund 420.
422 *satellite network*: See Tillion, *Ravensbrück*, on multiplying transports to satellite camps.
428 *'piled high . . .'*: Wynne, *No Drums, No Trumpets*.
428–9 *'She always thought . . .'*: Author interview.
429–30 *'I told him . . .'*: WO 235/318. Odette was given a cover name of 'Shurey' in the camp, probably 'so others wouldn't know there was an important person in the camp,' she thought.
430 *'too close to the Germans'*: FO 371/50982. See also Julia Barry in same, and her testimony in Atkins and WO 235/318. The stories of the 'British' women – including Sheridan – also came to light in letters they wrote to Aubrey Radnall Davis, an autograph collector, after the war.
431 *'already belonged here'*: Litoff (ed.) *An American Heroine in the French Resistance*.
431 *'She talked of . . .'*: Author interview.

## Chapter 28: Overtures

433 *Vera Atkins travelled*: See Sarah Helm, *A Life in Secrets: The Story of Vera Atkins and the Lost Agents of SOE* (London: Little, Brown, 2005).
433 *'delivered to this country by hand'*: From the files of the Liaison Committee of the Women's International Organisation, IISH.
434 *Born in the United States*: Details on Aka Kołodziejczak were kindly provided by her sister Irena Lisiecki in Michigan, and also came from Maria Bielicka.
434 *rules forbade*: Minutes in the files of the Liaison Committee of the Women's International Organisation, IISH.
434 *'The information is so terrible . . .'*: Minutes of the 133rd meeting of Polish station managers to discuss BBC/Polish broadcasts, E.1. 1,148, Poland, BBC Written Archives, Caversham.
434 *'probably the greatest . . .'*: Churchill to Anthony Eden, 11 July 1944, facsimile, Churchill Papers, Churchill Archives Centre, Cambridge.
436 *When they met in Paris*: Bernadotte, *The Fall of the Curtain*.
436 *There were other reasons*: On early overtures see also Persson, *Escape from the Third Reich*.
437 *'No truck with Himmler'*: Cited in ibid.
438 *'He seemed put out . . .'*: de Gaulle, WO 235/318.
439 *'I saw a Russian girl . . .'*: WO 235/318; see also Tickell, *Odette*.
439 *'Madame Baroness'*: ten Boom, *The Hiding Place*.

### Chapter 29: Doctor Loulou

For the story of Block 10 I drew on several long interviews with Dr Louise Liard (née Le Porz) at her house in Bordeaux, as well as her testimony and private archive. The Hamburg trial evidence on Block 10 is extensive, and is largely in WO 235/317, WO 235/318 and WO 309/416.

440 *'Instead we hoped . . .'*: Litoff (ed.), *An American Heroine in the French Resistance.*

440 *'Sunday: My bread . . .'*: Maurel, *Ravensbrück.*

442 *It was night*: Author interview. Loulou was by no means the only prisoner to talk of making a film. Many others, including Käthe Leichter, Antonina Nikiforova and Milena Jesenka, thought a film would be the only way to make people believe what happened at Ravensbrück.

443 *'neglect killing'*: Mant report, WO 309/416.

447 *an English teacher*: Like the Poles, a large number of the French prisoners had been teachers, probably because they were useful to the resistance as couriers – they could move around unobtrusively and had good contacts.

449 *She was called Joanna*: Author interview.

449 *'They were a little odd . . .'*: Maurel, *Ravensbrück.*

450 *In her own testimony*: Mory's trial statements (particularly to the Belgian commission, WO 309/419); also Spoerry, Lecoq and Héreil in WO 235/318 and Spoerry's May 1945 report to the ICRC.

452 *attacking each other*: See Le Porz, Héreil, Lecoq and Mory, WO 235/317 and 318.

453 *'because Mory detested her'*: WO 235/318.

453 *'When they passed . . .'*: Barry, WO 309/417, and letter, Atkins.

## PART SIX

### Chapter 30: Hungarians

459 *'We were taken . . .'*: Author interview.

461 *a tiny station*: In 1944 the railway was extended from Fürstenberg to Ravensbrück village, where a small station opened, to be closer to the camp.

462 *On one of the trains*: Zajączkowska, Lund 50.

462 *'Entering the tent . . .'*: Wasielewska, Lund.

462 *typhus*: See Nedvedova, Prague statement. Nedvedova also talks of a diphtheria epidemic when inoculations were carried out. In some

cases the diphtheria caused paralysis: 'It passed to me to obtain strychnine injections so that the diphtheria cases with paralysis were also healed.'

463 *'a carving . . .'*: Ten Boom, *The Hiding Place*.

464 *'women all around . . .'*: Mittelmann, YV.

464 *'If you don't behave . . .'*: Okrent, YV.

464 *'We were put . . .'*: Author interview.

465 *I'd filled the jug*: Author interview.

465 *I saw in the yard*: Lecoq, WO 235/318.

465–6 *'The women arrived . . .'*: Barry, WO 235/318.

## Chapter 31: A Children's Party

468 *Bank records*: Copies in ARa. Höss has also been made head of Bureau D of the WVHA (camp inspectorate), a job performed while lending a helping hand at Ravensbrück.

469 *appears to have been irked*: See Suhren's three statements in 1946, WO 235/318. Suhren claims he handed over command of Ravensbrück to Sauer for several weeks early in 1945 (when the mass killing began) as he had to go away to deal with the disbandment of subcamps. It was easy for him to claim this as Sauer was by now dead, killed in action during the battle for Berlin. Suhren's direct role in the extermination would be set out by Johann Schwarzhuber – see statements of 15 and 30 August 1946, WO 235/309 – and would emerge at the Rastatt trial.

469 *facts of extermination*: For example, Schwarzhuber, WO 235/309.

469 *From 5 Jan:* WO 309/693 and WO 235/526.

469–70 *'She signed it . . .'*: WO 235/526.

471 *This chamber was to stand*: Jahn had given a statement about the men's and women's camps, including the gassing, to US investigators as early as 9 May 1945. NARA, Memorandum, Walter Jahn, Atrocities Committed in the Ravensbrück Concentration Camp. For his later evidence on the stone gas chamber – including a plan – see Staatsarchiv Nürnberg NO-3109.

471 *for want of materials*: Charlotte Müller, a German prisoner, had even been sent to Berlin to bring back fire clay and firebricks.

471 *There had also been some dispute*: In his 1946 evidence Suhren again placed the blame on Sauer, saying Sauer had installed the gas chambers in his absence, on orders from August Heissmeyer, a senior SS administrator.

471 *It was Hanna Sturm*: Sturm, *Die Lebensgeschichte einer Arbeiterin*.

471 *Zyklon B*: There was a lot of talk in the *Schreibstube* about orders for Zyklon B at this time, though nobody was sure if it was for gassing people or killing lice. 'Conrad decided the amount and signed the orders,' said a prisoner secretary (WO 235/526).

471 *'We passed in front . . .'*: Cited in Anise Postel-Vinay (née Girard), 'Les exterminations par gaz à Ravensbrück', in Tillion, *Ravensbrück* (3rd edition).

472 *'First of all . . .'*: Treite statement, 5 May 1945, WO 235/309.

472 *'young women capable of work'*: WO 235/309.

472 *'The dawn was enough . . .'*: Ibid.

473 *'festival that happened . . .'*: Note in Nikif papers.

474 *Polish teachers organised classes*: Kiedrzyńska, *Ravensbrück*.

474 *seventy pregnant women*: From November there were about 100 births per month, according to Gerda Schröder, the German camp nurse. Most died of pneumonia. WO 235/318.

474 *'We were the only men . . .'*: Author interview.

475 *'not as we think of children . . .'*: Salvesen, *Forgive*. Also see Müller, *Die Klempnerkolonne*, on the party.

477 *'he had a wonderful voice'*: Author interview.

479 *'she'd lost him in the bomb'*: Author interview.

479 *German communist Erika Buchmann*: Erika had been released in 1941 but was brought back to the camp a year later, charged again with 'treason'. On return she was first made Blockova of the *Strafblock*, then Block 10.

480 *'a little man called the professor'*: Salvesen, *Forgive*.

480 *All the Gypsies*: WO 235/317. There is further extensive evidence about the sterilisation of children. See Mant report, WO 309/416, and Winkowska (Treite's secretary), Lund 285. Other forms of medical experimentation on prisoners took place until the last days. See evidence of Dr Trommer's butchery of Russian male prisoners in the cellar of the Kommandatur (WO 235/526). Several Warsaw women later claimed they were subject to gynaecological experiments and Treite spoke of cyanide experiments (WO 235/317), but the true extent of the experimentation will never be known.

## Chapter 32: Death March

Several women who witnessed the last days at Auschwitz and then set off on the death march to Ravensbrück left accounts at Yad Vashem, including Lydia Vago and Allegra Benvenisti. Maria Rundo's account is in Lund 189. Alina Brewda's story is recounted in *I Shall Fear No Evil* by R. J.

Minney. Rudolf Höss's account is drawn from his memoir, *Commandant of Auschwitz*. I also interviewed survivors including the Belorussian Valentina Makarova.

## Chapter 33: Youth Camp

The account of the Youth Camp and gassings makes use of almost all the Hamburg testimony, but the most important material is in the first trial (series beginning WO 235/305) where Schwarzhuber and Salvequart were accused, and in the trial of Ruth Neudeck (WO 235/516a). I also drew on testimony at Rastatt and that given to German investigators in the 1970s when a new investigation was carried out in the Youth Camp. See series BAL B162-9810. Most survivor testimony and memoirs of this period contain accounts of selections and gassings. Remarkably, several prisoners survived the Youth Camp and returned to tell the tale. I interviewed one of them, Irma Trksak.

489 *'excellent' reports*: Salvesen, *Forgive*.
490 *'Suhren told us . . .'*: WO 235/309.
491 *'Now we have gas'*: WO 309/421.
491 *'SS Schwarzhuber's son'*: Langbein, *People in Auschwitz*.
494 *two male SS hospital orderlies*: Very little known about these men. Franz Koehler was Slovakian, Rapp (who is never given a first name) a Yugoslav. Both disappeared after the war.
495 *'transferred elsewhere . . .'*: WO 235/318.
496 *asking for a divorce*: Atkins.
497 *'Though we had experience . . .'*: WO 235/318.
497 *'You see, we wanted . . .'*: Author interview. For further testimony of others in this group, see Lund, BAL and TNA.
498 *'presumably through exhaustion'*: Mary O'Shaughnessy's testimony about the Youth Camp is the most valuable. She began writing her account almost as soon as she was liberated, and then made a series of statements for the Hamburg trial. The most vivid details are in her six-page handwritten account (WO 235/516a). Also see WO 309/417 and Atkins.
499 *'Rest Camp Mittwerda'*: WO 235/516a.
502 *'or I'd be shot'*: WO 235/317.
503 *'women were put on half-rations . . .'*: 5 May 1945 statement, WO 235/309.
506 *'It took a long time . . .'*: WO 235/317.
507 *After that I paid*: BAL B162/9814.

## Chapter 34: Hiding

510 *'When we checked . . .'*: WO 235/318
511 *'The bodies of the gassed . . .'*: WO 235/526.
511 *'I often stood and counted . . .'*: Vavak, 'Siemens & Halske im Frauenkonzentrationslager Ravensbrück', DÖW, Ravensbrück file 49.
511 *'Extermination transport . . .'*: Useldinger diary, ARa.
512 *'She was smiling . . .'*: Dragan, Lund 239.
514 *It was the new SS doctor*: Several prisoners talked about Lucas's help, particularly Loulou Le Porz and Salvesen in *Forgive*.
515 *Aka Kołodziejczak*: Author interview with Mary Bielicka, and Lanckorońska, 'Report of the Camp of Ravensbrück', AICRC.
515 *Denise Dufournier received a parcel*: From her autobiographical essay, written before *La maison des mortes*. A copy of the essay was kindly passed to me by her daughter, Caroline McAdam Clark.
515* *she gave interviews*: Aka gave interviews to *Time* magazine and the Hearst Press, with headlines such as SHE SCREAMED THROUGH THE NIGHT. In a radio interview in New York in February 1945, Aka was asked, 'Is everything we hear about the cruelty of Germans to women and children actually true?'
516 *taken away to be shot*: Frank Chamier – 'Frank of Upwey 282' (see p. 354) – was probably tortured and executed at this time. Chamier was the only MI6 agent known to have parachuted into Germany during the war. He was captured on landing and questioned, probably at the security police HQ at Drogen, five miles from Ravensbrück, which was why he was kept in a cell at the camp. For the story of Chamier, his German torturer and the post-war British cover-up about his death, see Sarah Helm, 'The Wartime Hero Abandoned by MI6', *Observer*, 21 May 2005, and 'A Nazi in Her Majesty's Secret Service', *Sunday Times Magazine*, 7 August 2005.
517 *drawing intricate maps*: Krysia's drawings hang in the Museum of Martyrology 'Pod Zegarem' (Under the clock), a branch of the Lublin Museum (Muzeum Lubelskie w Lublinie).
518 *An incredible, unheard-of thing*: This account of the hiding is drawn from Sokulska (WO 235/318), *Dreams* and several other Polish testimonies.
518 *'They're coming for them! . . .'*: The uproar is best described in Kiedrzyńska, *Ravensbrück*. See also Lanckorońska, 'Report of the Camp of Ravensbrück', AICRC.
518 *plunged into pitch darkness*: Lanckorońska says that if it hadn't been

for the presence of mind and courage of the Red Army women who short-circuited the lighting at the crucial moment, the hiding might have failed. See ibid., and also the descriptions of the drama in *Beyond* and *Dreams*. The same sources contain the account of Suhren's 'new initiative' and his subsequent retreat.

520 *Suhren explained*: In a post-war statement Suhren said he had once refused a request from Gebhardt to hand over 'human material' for experiments, and as a result Gebhardt 'insulted' him and said he'd speak to the Reichsführer and have him sacked. 'Annoyed and a little frightened' Suhren then apologised to Gebhardt and was forced to 'obtain humans' for him after all. WO 235/318.

521 *'The girls succeeded . . .'*: In her 'Report of the Camp of Ravensbrück', written and delivered while the events were still going on, Lanckorońska also said that the SS's main motive in meeting with the rabbits at this time was to elicit information about Aka Kołodziejczak. They knew Aka had been talking about experiments in the US and that SS names were known. 'Furthermore new arrivals at the camp were well informed on the subject, which had been commented upon at length by the London wireless' – a reference to SWIT broadcasts.

## Chapter 35: Königsberg

For the last weeks of Königsberg I drew particularly on *An American Heroine in the French Resistance*, the memoir of Virginia Lake, on Jacqueline Bernard's 1946 letter about Lilian Rolfe and on a letter sent to me in 2008 by Christiane Cizaire, recalling her friendship with Violette Lecoq.

523 *more like a pigsty*: Guyotat, *Königsberg sur Oder*.

524 *'I want to die . . .'*: Litoff (ed.), *An American Heroine in the French Resistance*.

525 *'They were all black . . .'*: Barry, WO 309/417 and Atkins.

526 *'This was the last time . . .'*: Baseden testimony for the Hamburg trial: she was too sick to attend in person (HS 437) and author interviews. For details of the French parachutists, see Tillion, *Ravensbrück*, and testimony at the Musée de la Résistance et de la Déportation, Besançon.

527 *'Suhren read out . . .'*: Schwarzhuber statement in Atkins and WO 235/309.

530 *'the remains of . . .'*: Dufournier, *La maison des mortes.*

533 *'a terribly emaciated . . .'*: De Gaulle-Anthonioz, *Dawn of Hope.*

## Chapter 36: Bernadotte

534 *'What ugly creature . . .'*: Litoff (ed.), *An American Heroine in the French Resistance.*

535 *'The committee has been . . .'*: 'Note à l'intention de Monseiur Berber', 15 September 1944, AICRC, B G 44/CP-227 023.

535–6 *'If any different . . .'*: La Guardia Gluck, *Fiorello's Sister.*

534 *'The object of this action . . .'*: KV 2/98.

539 *'a pretty caravan . . .'*: Cited in Persson, *Escape from the Third Reich.*

539 *via the Swedish diplomatic bag, 'to the very last detail'*: See Persson, *Escape from the Third Reich*, and Heger, *Tous les vendredis.* Wanda Heger (née Hjort) describes how the neutral Swedes, through their legation in Berlin, had shown 'extraordinary zeal' in putting her Norwegian Gross Kreutz cell in touch with the Norwegian delegation in Stockholm. Norwegian officials had begun to view the cell as their own 'secret committee in Berlin'.

539 *had visited Ravensbrück in December*: Johan Hjort, BAL B162/27217.

540 *'in green Waffen-SS uniform . . .'*: Bernadotte, *The Fall of the Curtain.*

541 *Gerda Schröder*: The German camp nurse is an elusive figure. One of only a handful of German women employed by the SS who were universally liked and even admired by prisoners, she was not called to give evidence at Hamburg, but did give a statement to Vera Atkins, saying she had worked as theatre sister before the war and was 'forcibly' transferred to Ravensbrück. She assisted Treite with his experimental operations, including sterilisations and abortions 'on debilitated German women and gypsies': WO 235/318. Letters written by Gerda after the war to Sylvia Salvesen, who remained a close friend, show her anguish: 'I was not a prisoner, but I was locked up. My hands were tied but I tried to help.' Salvesen archives, Norges Hjemmefrontmuseet.

541 *'Goodbye, Sister . . .'*: Salvesen, *Forgive.*

541 *pleading with the Hjorts for refuge*: Johan Hjort said Lucas turned up at Gross Kreutz on about 23 April, pleading for refuge. On learning that the Americans had stopped at the Elbe he feared falling into Soviet hands. Hjort hid Lucas for a few days, then gave him an old bicycle and the SS doctor pedalled away. BAL B162/27217.

## Chapter 37: Emilie

544 *'Prisoners are sleeping . . .'*: Cited in Strebel, *Ravensbrück.*

544 *'It was clear . . .'*: Cabaj, *Beyond.* The testimony of the Belsen transport is some of the most horrifying. Stanislawa Michalik, in ibid., says the women were so weak on arrival that 'just one strong blow was enough for someone to fall down dead. The same thing happened to women and children.'

545 *'The Dutch prisoners . . .'*: Lanckorońska, 'Report of the Camp of Ravensbrück', AICRC.

545 *'. . . with her knee'*: Wasilewska, Lund 434.

546 *'Very tall . . .'*: Author interview.

547 *She told us*: Author interview.

548 *'That morning . . .'*: WO 235/516a and related testimony, TNA.

548 *now writing a daily diary*: Tillion, *Ravensbrück.*

549 *She marched*: Cited in Strebel, *Ravensbrück.*

549 *'I was in the sickbay . . .'*: *Dictators*, and Tillion, *Ravensbrück.*

550 *We stood*: Nedvedova, Prague statement.

553 *In the yard*: Emanuel Kolarik, 'Tábor u jezera', Roudnice 1945.

554 *'I did the electrical equipment . . .'*: Jahn statement, NO-3109-311, Staatsarchiv Nürnberg.

554 *'The motor bus . . .'*: Lanckorońska, 'Report of the Camp of Ravensbrück', AICRC.

554 *a British diplomat*: FO 371/50982.

554 *'two gas chambers'*: Barry, WO 235/318.

554 *'gas vans' and 'gas lorries'*: For samples of testimony about gassing trucks see: Erna Cassens, BAL B162/9816; Dragan, Lund 239; O'Shaughnessy, WO 309/690; Tauforova, GARF; Sturm, *Die Lebensgeschichte einer Arbeiterin* and WO 309/416; and Nedvedova, Prague statement.

555 *'to liquidate the entire camp'*: KV 2/98.

556 *'We sensed something unusual'*: Dufournier, autobiographical essay, Dufournier family papers.

556 *'screamed like a child'*: La Guardia Gluck, *Fiorello's Sister.*

556 *Everyone had to stand*: Author interview.

556 *'We had a selection . . .'*: Zajączkowska, Lund 50.

558 *'skinny, hollow-eyes . . .'*: Wynne, *No Drums, No Trumpets.*

560 *final clear-out*: See multiple testimony in the Hamburg trial papers, for example WO 235/516a for the trial of Youth Camp guards. Also: Tillion, *Ravensbrück*; Nedvedova, Prague statement; testimony in Lund; *Les Françaises à Ravensbrück*; and Dufournier, *La maison des mortes.*

## Chapter 38: Nelly

563 *smuggled out letters*: Wanda Hjort says today that Bernadotte was well aware of the content of Sylvia's letters by this time. Author interview.

564 *'not only grave, but nervy'*: Bernadotte, *The Fall of the Curtain.*

565 *Before joining the ICRC*: On Meyer's role, see his report and personal file, AICRC, BRH 1991 000.491/DP 4066; also author interview with Loulou Le Porz.

566 *'The sick were sent . . . '*: Cited in *Les Françaises à Ravensbrück.*

567 *'She asked Binz . . . '*: Author interview.

568 *'bon voyage'*: According to Denise Dufournier in *La maison des mortes*, before Suhren bade farewell the German camp staff handed each departing prisoner half a pound of butter, a packet of cake and a large piece of cold sausage.

570 *also become lovers*: Heger, *Tous les vendredis*. Wanda and Bjørn Heger were married in the summer of 1945.

571 *The next day we came out*: Author interview.

573 *'A Doctoresse Le Porz . . . '*: See reports of the ICRC escorts Dr Auguste Jost and Mademoiselle Jung, who met the arrivals at the Swiss border and accompanied the train to France, in AICRC, BRH 1991 000/390.

573 *'some high-up person . . . '*: Author interview.

574 *'a convoy of martyrs . . . '*: Special Agent Edward A. Chadwell was assigned to a US war crimes investigations unit in Lyon, France, when he was sent to report on the Ravensbrück arrivals. Chadwell noted that the women recounted the horrors with 'a complete absence of emotion and feminine sentiment'. He reported: 'It is impossible to feel their emotion when they speak of the death of their mothers or sisters who were there with them or of the death of their husbands.' They still seemed to be in a state of shock, he said, but the majority had 'splendid morale and were still determined to fight for their country; some of them have even asked how they can go about volunteering'. NARA war crimes file.

574 *'conduct herself loyally'*: Letter from SS General Ernst Kaltenbrunner to the President of the ICRC, 2 April 1945, reproduced in Lanckorońska *Those Who Trespass Against Us.*

575 *'They are under threat of death'*: Lanckorońska, 'Report of the Camp of Ravensbrück', AICRC.

## Chapter 39: Masur

576 *'After the gas chamber . . .'*: Nedvedova, Prague statement.
577 *'I stood with my eyes closed . . .'*: BAL B162/9814.
578 *'When the first warm rays . . .'*: Ottelard, WO 235/310.
578 *rambling depositions*: WO 235/317.
583 *As the Allied planes*: Author interview.
583 *'When mother saw us . . .'*: Author interview.
585 *Eisenhower had told*: On the Americans at the Elbe see Beevor, *Berlin*.
585 *Suhren revealed later*: WO 235/318.
586 *'So that's what thanks . . .'*: Sokulska, WO 235/318.
586 *'"But that's a scandal . . ."'*: *Les Françaises à Ravensbrück*.
587 *'One was a woman . . .'*: Salvini, WO 235/318.
588 *'orderly evacuation'*: Kersten, *Memoirs*.
588 *commando missions*: These were to be carried out by special forces of Operation Vicarage and the SAARF (Special Allied Airborne Reconnaissance Force) teams who would drop by air into camps to warn the SS that the Allies were approaching in the hope of preventing more atrocity. One or two such missions to POW camps had limited success. See Foot and Langley, *MI9*.
588 *refuse safe passage*: The Swedes provided the British with routes and timings of the convoys. On 5 March the British promised that their planes would be instructed to avoid attacks on the Swedish convoys, but no concrete guarantees came. On 8 March the British told the Swedes the government was 'in principle in agreement with the action but was unable to give a safe-conduct', saying Swedes entering Germany did so 'at their own risk'. Cited in Persson, *Escape from the Third Reich*. Also see correspondence in FO 371/48047.
589 *When the Swedes protested*: See FO telegrams, FO 371/48047.
591 *'prepared to bury the hatchet . . .'*: Kersten, *Memoirs*.
591 *'these gentlemen'*: Masur report, 23 April 1945, Central Zionist Archives, Jerusalem.
592 *'very tired and weary'*: Bernadotte, *The Fall of the Curtain*.

## Chapter 40: White Buses

593 *'at the last minute'*: KV 2/98.
592 *' . . . liquidate them all'*: Ibid.
595 *On entering Suhren's office*: *Dreams*. What happened next and when is not always clear; the sequence of events reported here is pieced

together from accounts of Swedish drivers cited in Persson, *Escape from the Third Reich*, Fritz Göring's report to MI5 (TNA KV 2/98) and testimony of prisoners including Buchmann, Vaillant-Couturier and Nedvedova, as well as ICRC delegates and those leaving on buses.

597 *He could not get close*: The delegate, Albert de Cocatrix, eventually reached the camp and gave a surreal description of its last days as he was shown around by Suhren, who pulled the wool over his eyes with consummate ease. 'Before I left the camp I thought of asking Suhren to show me the gas chamber and crematorium. I didn't do it . . .'. Report on visit to Ravensbrück between 20 and 23 April 1945 (precise date unclear), AICRC, G 44/13-0.02.

598 *The Red Cross is coming*: Diary of Jeanne Bommezjin de Rochement, IWM 06/25/1.

598 'Die Engländerin! . . .': Wynne, *No Drums, No Trumpets.*

599 *This sounds too good*: IWM 06/25/1.

600 *'ghostlike men'*: *Les Françaises à Ravensbrück.*

603 *and suddenly we are machine-gunned*: In his report on the attacks (and the second on the Wismar road) the Swedish mission leader Sven Frykman said they followed reconnaissance flights by the aircraft and both were 'entirely intentional, the planes probably British'. Frykman called for 'energetic protests' to be sent to the British, Americans and French. Cited in Persson, *Escape from the Third Reich.*

604 *After a further Swedish protest*: FO 371/48047. On 1 May Mallet wrote to the Swedes expressing 'regret' at the attacks 'claimed' to be British, and reminding the Swedes of warnings previously issued (i.e., that safe passage could not be guaranteed). Letter to C. Günther, 1 May 1945, SRA/UDA, HP 1619.

605 *So I looked*: Cited in Tillion, *Ravensbrück.*

605 *'We were suddenly told . . .'*: Lund.

605 *'we took everybody we could . . .'*: Persson, *Escape from the Third Reich.*

606 *'We were placed . . .'*: Lund.

606 *'all Jewish women . . .'*: Lund.

607 *Maisie handed over*: Renault, *La grande misère.*

608 *sent for Mary Lindell*: Wynne, *No Drums, No Trumpets.*

608 *Sven Frykman*: Sven Frykman's role in identifying and collecting up the British prisoners who would otherwise have been left behind is also set out by British diplomats' reports in FCO 371/50982.

609 *I just remember*: Author interview.

609–10 *I believe that*: WO 235/308.

## Chapter 41: Liberation

611 *'Everything is on fire . . .'*: Grossman, *A Writer at War*.
612 *'I could hear them . . .'*: WO 235/318.
615 *The Russians were a few miles*: Author interview.
616 *'All around . . .'*: Maurel, *Ravensbrück*.
617 *They were not bad people*: Author interview.
619 *In Fürstenberg we walked*: Author interview.
622 *'Girls, let's kill a pig and eat'*: Author interview.
622 *'Our submachine gunners . . .'*: Mednikov, *Dolya Bessmertiya*.
622 *After fighting all the way*: 'A la guerre comme à la guerre', interview with Michael Ivanovich Stakhanov, now a retired colonel, by journalist Natalia Eryomenkova in *Russkaya Gazeta* no. 17/2005.
623 *'I remember celebrating . . .'*: Author interview.
625 *There were many*: Author interview.
625–6 *Then a major*: Author interview.
626 *They allocated a house*: Author interview.
626 *'handsome men'*: *Dreams*.
627 *Suddenly we were walking*: Author interview.
627 *'A big burly fellow . . .'*: Maurel, *Ravensbrück*.
628–9 *I remember we were burying*: Author interview.
629 *Yes, everything happened*: Author interview. Odette's flight with Suhren is described in Tickell, *Odette*, and in her May 1946 statement (WO 235/318).
631 *We began to wonder*: Author interview.

## Epilogue

633 *'I don't want to burn . . .'*: Mant report, WO 309/416. Seeing the arrivals, an American diplomat sent a cable to Washington describing women 'in appalling condition . . . starved and beaten. Still 5000 left at Ravensbrück and refugees believe Germans will exterminate them en masse when the camp is threatened. Many lives would be saved if camp could be taken by surprise attack.' Cable 1621 from S. Johnson in Stockholm to Secretary of State Washington, DC, received 1 May 1945, NARA.
633 *'a very cheerful lady . . .'*: FO 372/50982.
634 *last transport to Belsen*: Yvonne Rudellat, the Prosper circuit woman, died at Belsen a few days after liberation. As many as 15,000 men, women and children died at Belsen in the two weeks after liberation, many of typhoid and starvation. Soon after arriving at Malmö

Yvonne Baseden was flown back to Scotland, then took a train to London where Vera Atkins met her at Euston Station. Eileen Nearne, the other SOE woman at Ravensbrück, who in the last days had escaped from an evacuation march near Leipzig, reached American lines and eventually returned home. She died in Torquay in 2010. For the story of the search for missing SOE women, see Sarah Helm, *A Life in Secrets: The Story of Vera Atkins and the Lost Agents of SOE* (London: Little, Brown, 2005).

635 *'took part in the selection . . .'*: Chechko, GARF.

636 *'By this time . . .'*: Author interview and Fyffe's diaries. I interviewed Angus Fyffe about Vera Atkins at his home in Scotland in 2003. He also read out extracts from his extensive diaries recounting with wry humour how as a young Scottish major he had hunted down war criminals in the rubble of post-war Germany. The diaries are now in the IWM.

637 *'might have stepped out . . .'*: Tickell, *Odette*. In a diary kept during the hearing Syliva Salvesen describes Winkelmann 'sitting with his head in his hands' and Marshall showing 'rage and despair', while Carmen Mory 'looks insolent and sometimes laughs hysterically'. Salvesen archives, Norges Hjemmefrontmuseet.

637 *acquired – it was said – by selling gold teeth*: The extraordinary story of Salvequart's shenanigans while on the run from war-crimes hunters in the chaos of Allied-occupied Germany (including getting a job with American counterintelligence and blackmailing Nazi suspects – see Atkins papers) is matched only by Carmen Mory's escapades. Mory was hired by British intelligence and posted as an informer in a UN refugee camp, until a young British investigator called Hugh Trevor-Roper uncovered her true story, describing her as 'a very undesirable person indeed'. TNA investigation files.

641 *Not a single member*: The head of Siemens, Hermann von Siemens, was arrested by the Americans in 1945 and remained in prison until 1948, though his arrest was not connected to his role at Siemens but to his position at Deutsche Bank. He was released without charge.

642 *Anne Spoerry*: According to a handwritten note on a page of the Hamburg trial transcript, Hélène Roussel, a French survivor, attended an 'honour court' in Paris in 1946, where Spoerry was summarily tried by former Free French. WO 235/317.

643 *'Nobody came to see me . . .'*: At the age of eighteen Stella left the orphanage and traced her father, who had remarried and was living in Brazil. By this time Antonina Nikiforova had befriended Stella,

and Stella married Antonina's adopted son Arkady. She lived with Arkady at Antonina's St Petersburg flat, where she still lives today

643 *'All my life . . . '*: Georg Loonkin papers.

644 *'fighter against fascism'*: Rupp and Wiedmaier, BStU files.

645 *The company reluctantly paid out*: Benjamin Ferencz, a former Nuremberg prosecutor, describes his battle to get Siemens to pay up in *Less Than Slaves*.

645 *pitiful sentences*: There were no West German trials between 1949 and 1989 concerning crimes commited by female SS guards in Ravensbrück. A handful of women guards were tried at the Majdanek trial in Dusseldorf between 1975 and 1981. One, Hermine Braunsteiner, who had been tracked down to New York by the Nazi hunter Simon Wiesenthal, was sentenced to life imprisonment but was freed in 1996 for health reasons. She died in 1999.

646 *question the existence of gas chambers*: In 1968, the French historian Olga Wormser-Migot produced a study on the Nazi camps in which she claimed there was no proof that gas chambers existed anywhere on German soil.

649 *'Forget it . . . '*: See Sarah Helm, 'The Nazi Guard's Untold Love Story', *Sunday Times Magazine*, 5 August 2007.

651 *almost certainly too high*: For details of how the British prosecutors arrived at their figure of 90,000 dead, see the interim report on the Ravensbrück investigation, WO 235/316.

# Bibliography

## Archives

*Germany*
Archiv Mahn- und Gedenkstätte Ravensbrück
Archiv Gedenkstätte Buchenwald
Bundesarchiv Berlin
Bundesarchiv Ludwigsberg
Geschichtsarchiv der Zeugen Jehovas
International Tracing Service, Bad Arolsen
Landesarchiv Nordrhein-Westfalen
Siemens Archives, Munich
Staatsarchiv Nürnberg
Stasi Archives
Studienkreis Deutscher Widerstand 1933–1945
Stutthoff Concentration Camp Memorial Archives

*Austria*
Dokumentationsarchiv des österreichischen Widerstandes

*Switzerland*
International Committee of the Red Cross

*United Kingdom*
BBC Written Archives, Caversham
Imperial War Museum
Polish Institute Library, London
Polish Underground Movement Study Trust
Sikorski Institute

The National Archives
Wiener Library

*France*
Archives diplomatiques du ministère des Affaires étrangères, Colmar
Archives of the Association of French Deportees of Ravensbrück, Bibliothèque de Documentation International Contemporaine
Bordeaux City Archives
Le Havre City Archives
Musée de la Résistance et de la Déportation, Besançon

*United States*
National Archives and Records Administration
United States Holocaust Memorial Museum

*Sweden*
The Polish Research Institute in Lund, Lund University Library

*Poland*
Museum of National History, Warsaw
Museum of Martyrology 'Pod Zegarem' (Under the clock), a branch of the Lublin Museum (Muzeum Lubelskie w Lublinie)

*Russia*
GARF Military Archives
History Library, Moscow
Memorial Library, Moscow

*Israel*
Central Zionist Archives
Yad Vashem

*Netherlands*
International Institute for Social History

*Norway*
Hjemmefrontmuseet

## Published sources

Amesberger, Helga, and Brigitte Halbmayr, *Vom Leben und Überleben – Wege nach Ravensbrück: das Frauenkonzentrationslager in der Erinnerung*, vol. 2 (Vienna: Spuren, 2001)

Applebaum, Anne, *Gulag: A History* (New York: Doubleday, 2003)

——, *Iron Curtain: The Crushing of Eastern Europe 1944–1956* (London: Allen Lane, 2012)

Arendt, Hannah, *Eichmann in Jerusalem: A Report on the Banality of Evil* (New York: Viking, 1963)

Arndt, Ino, 'Das Frauenkonzentrationslager Ravensbrück', *Studien zur Geschichte der Konzentrationslager: Schriftenreihe der Vierteljahrshefte für Zeitgeschichte*, 21 (Stuttgart, 1970)

Beckett, Francis, *Stalin's British Victims* (Stroud: Sutton, 2004)

Beevor, Antony, *Berlin: The Downfall, 1945* (London: Viking, 2002)

——, *D-Day: The Battle for Normandy* (London: Viking, 2009)

——, *The Second World War* (London: Weidenfeld & Nicolson, 2012)

Bernadac, Christian, *Le camp des femmes: Ravensbrück* (Paris: Michel Lafon, 1971)

Bernadotte, Count Folk (trans. Count Eric Lewenhaupt), *The Fall of the Curtain: Last Days of the Third Reich* (London: Cassell, 1945)

Beßmann, Alyn, and Insa Eschebach (eds), *The Ravensbrück Women's Concentration Camp: History and Memory. Exhibition Catalogue* (Berlin: Metropol, 2013)

Bock, Gisela, '"No Children at Any Cost": Perspectives on Compulsory Sterilization, Sexism and Racism in Nazi Germany', in Judith Friedlander, Alice Kessler-Harris, Carroll Smith-Rosenberg and Blanche Wiesen Cook (eds), *Women in Culture and Politics: A Century of Change* (Bloomington: Indiana University Press, 1986)

Borowski, Tadeusz (trans. Barbara Vedder), *This Way for the Gas, Ladies and Gentlemen* (London: Cape, 1967)

Bower, Tom, *Blind Eye to Murder: Britain, America and the Purging of Nazi Germany – A Pledge Betrayed* (London: André Deutsch, 1981)

Breitman, Richard, *The Architect of Genocide: Himmler and the Final Solution* (London: Bodley Head, 1991)

Broszat, Martin, 'The Concentration Camps, 1933–1945', in Hans Buchheim, Martin Broszat, Hans-Adolf Jacobsen and Helmut Krausnick (eds), *Anatomy of the SS State* (New York: Walker, 1965)

Brown, Daniel Patrick, *The Beautiful Beast: The Life and Crimes of SS-*

*Aufseherin Irma Grese* (Ventura, Calif.: Golden West Historical Publications, 1996)

Buber Agassi, Judith, *Jewish Women Prisoners of Ravensbrück* (Oxford: One World, 2007)

Buber-Neumann, Margarete (trans. Ralph Manheim), *Milena* (London: Collins, 1989)

——, *Die erloschene Flamme: Schicksale meiner Zeit* (Frankurt: Langen Mueller, 1991)

—— (trans. Edward Fitzgerald), *Under Two Dictators: Prisoner of Stalin and Hitler* (London: Pimlico, 2008)

Busch, Johann Rainer, *Kupferdreh und seine Geschichte (mit Byfang und Dilldorf)* (Essen: Bürgerschaft Kupferdreh, 2008)

Caplan, Jane, and Nikolaus Wachsmann (eds), *Concentration Camps in Nazi Germany: The New Histories* (Abingdon: Routledge, 2010)

Černa, Jana (trans. A. G. Brain), *Kafka's Milena* (London: Souvenir Press, 1987)

Chombart de Lauwe, Marie-Jo, *Toute une vie de résistance* (Paris: Pop'Com, 2002)

Chrostowska, Grażyna (ed. Alojzy Leszek Gzella), *Jakby minęło już wszystko* (Lublin: Gal, 2002)

Chroust, Peter (ed.), *Friedrich Mennecke. Innenansichten eines medizinischen Täters im Nationalsozialismus. Eine Edition seiner Briefe 1935–1947*, vols 1 and 2 (Hamburg: Hamburger Institut für Sozialforschung, 1987, 1988)

Czech, Danuta, *Kalendarium der Ereignisse im Konzentrationslager Auschwitz-Birkenau 1939–1945* (Hamburg: Rowholt, 1989)

Davies, Norman, *God's Playground: A History of Poland* (Oxford: Oxford University Press, 2005)

de Gaulle-Anthonioz, Geneviève (trans. Richard Seaver), *The Dawn of Hope: A Memoir of Ravensbrück* (New York: Arcade, 1999)

Delbo, Charlotte (trans. Rosette C. Lamont), *Auschwitz and After* (New Haven: Yale University Press, 1995)

*Documents relating to the work of the International Committee of the Red Cross for the benefit of civilian detainees in German concentration camps between 1939 and 1945* (Geneva: ICRC, 1975)

Dublon-Knebel, Irith (ed.), *A Holocaust Crossroads: Jewish Women and Children in Ravensbrück* (London: Vallentine Mitchell, 2010)

Duesterberg, Julia, 'Von der "Umkehr aller Weiblichkeit": Charakterbilder einer KZ-Aufseherin', in Insa Eschebach, Sigrid Jacobeit and Silke Wenk (eds), *Gedächtnis und Geschlecht: Deutungsmuster in Darstellungen des nationalsozialistischen Genozids* (Frankfurt: Campus, 2002)

Dufournier, Denise, *La maison des mortes: Ravensbrück* (Paris: Hachette, 1947)

Ebbinghaus, Angelika (ed.), *Opfer und Täterinnen: Frauenbiographien des Nationalsozialismus* (Nördlingen: Greno, 1987)

Eckler, Irene, *Die Vormundschaftsakte 1935–1958: Verfolgung einer Familie wegen "Rassenschande": Dokumente und Berichte aus Hamburg* (Schwetzingen: Horneburg, 1996)

Elling, Hanna, *Frauen im deutschen Widerstand, 1933–1945* (Frankfurt: Roderberg, 1981)

Ermoliuk, L. I., and N. V. Zinovkina, *Sedye deti voĭny: vospominaniia byvshikh uznikov fashistskikh kontslagerei* (Kaluga: Fridgel'm, 2003)

Erpel, Simone, *Zwischen Vernichtung und Befreiung: Das Frauen-Konzentrationslager Ravensbruck in der letzen Kriegsphase* (Berlin: Metropol, 2005)

—— (ed.), *Im Gefolge der SS: Aufseherinnen des Frauen-KZ Ravensbrück: Begleitband zur Ausstellung* (Berlin: Metropol, 2007)

Eschebach, Insa, Sigrid Jacobeit and Susanne Lanwerd (eds), *Die Sprache des Gedenkens: Zur Geschichte der Gedenkstätte Ravensbrück 1945–1995* (Berlin: Hentrich, 1999)

Evans, Richard J., *The Third Reich in Power, 1933–1939* (London: Allen Lane, 2005)

Fabius, Odette, *Un lever de soleil sur le Mecklembourg: mémoires* (Paris: A. Michel, 1986)

Favez, Jean-Claude (ed. and trans. John and Beryl Fletcher), *The Red Cross and the Holocaust* (Cambridge: Cambridge University Press, 1999)

Feldenkirchen, Wilfried, *Siemens 1918–1945* (Munich: Piper, 1995)

Ferencz, Benjamin, *Less Than Slaves: Jewish Forced Labor and the Quest for Compensation* (Bloomington and Indianapolis: Indiana University Press, 1984)

Foot, M. R. D., *SOE in France: An Account of the Work of the British Special Operations Executive in France, 1940–1944* (London: HMSO, 1966)

——, and J. M. Langley, *MI9: The British Secret Service That Fostered Escape and Evasion, 1939–1945, and Its American Counterpart* (London: Bodley Head, 1979)

Friedlander, Henry, *The Origins of Nazi Genocide: From Euthanasia to the Final Solution* (Chapel Hill: University of North Carolina Press, 1995)

Fritz, Ulrich, Silvija Kavčič and Nicole Warmbold (eds), *Tatort KZ: Neue Beiträge zur Geschichte der Konzentrationslager* (Ulm: Klemm & Oelschlager, 2003)

Füllberg-Stolberg, Claus, Martina Jung, Renata Reibe and Martina Scheitenberger (eds), *Frauen in Konzentrationslagern: Bergen-Belsen, Ravensbrück* (Bremen: Temmen, 1994)

Garnett, David, *The Secret History of PWE: The Political Warfare Executive, 1939–1945* (London: St Ermin's Press, 2002)
Gellately, Robert, and Nathan Stoltzfus (eds), *Social Outsiders in Nazi Germany* (Princeton: Princeton University Press, 2001)
Gilbert, Martin, *The Holocaust: A History of the Jews of Europe during the Second World War* (New York: Holt, Rinehart & Winston, 1985)
——, *The Second World War: A Complete History* (London: Weidenfeld & Nicolson, 1989)
——, *Auschwitz and the Allies* (London: Pimlico, 2001)
Goldhagen, Daniel Jonah, *Hitler's Willing Executioners: Ordinary Germans and the Holocaust* (London: Little, Brown, 1996)
Götz, Aly, Peter Chroust and Christian Pross (trans. Belinda Cooper), *Cleansing the Fatherland: Nazi Medicine and Racial Hygiene* (Baltimore: Johns Hopkins University Press, 1994)
Greayer, Agneta, and Sonja Sjöstrand (ed. Martin Wikberg, trans. Annika and Peter Hodgson), *The White Buses: The Swedish Red Cross Rescue Action in Germany during the Second World War* (Stockholm: Swedish Red Cross, 2000)
Grossman, Vasily (ed. Antony Beevor, trans. Luba Vinogradova), *A Writer at War: Vasily Grossman with the Red Army 1941–1945* (London: Pimlico, 2006)
Guyotat, S., *Königsberg sur Oder* (Paris: Éditions de la France, 1946)

Haag, Lina, *How Long the Night* (London: Victor Gollancz, 1948)
Hany-Lefèbvre, Noémi, *Six mois à Fresnes* (Paris: Flammarion, 1946)
Hautval, Adélaïde, *Médecine et crimes contre l'humanité* (Arles: Actes Sud, 1991)
Hayes, Kathleen (ed.), *The Journalism of Milena Jesenska: A Critical Voice in Interwar Central Europe* (New York: Berghahn, 2003)
Heger, Wanda (trans. Luce Hinsch), *Tous les vendredis devant le portail* (Montford-en-Chalosse: Gaïa, 2009)
Heike, Irmtraud, 'SS-Aufseherinnen und weibliche *Funktionshäftlinge* in den Konzentrationslagern Ravensbrück und Bergen-Belsen', unpublished thesis, Hanover University, 1991
——, *Johanna Langefeld: Die Biographie einer KZ-Oberaufseherin* (Hamburg: Ergebnisse, 1995)
Herbermann, Nanda (trans. Hester Baer; ed. Hester Baer and Elizabeth R.

Baer), *The Blessed Abyss: Inmate #6582 in Ravensbrück Concentration Camp for Women* (Detroit: Wayne State University Press, 2000)

Herz, Gabriele (trans. Hildegard Herz and Howard Hertig, ed. Jane Caplan), *The Women's Camp in Moringen: A Memoir of Imprisonment in Germany 1936–1937* (Oxford: Berghahn, 2006)

Hesse, Hans, and Jürgen Harder (eds), '*... und wenn ich lebenslang in einem KZ bleiben müßte ...*': *Die Zeuginnen Jehovas in den Frauenkonzentrationslagern Moringen, Lichtenburg und Ravensbrück* (Essen: Klartext, 2001)

Hilberg, Raul, *The Destruction of the European Jews* (New York: Holmes & Meier, 1985)

Himmler, Katrin, *The Himmler Brothers: A German Family History* (London: Macmillan, 2007)

Hördler, Stefan, 'Before the Holocaust: Concentration Camp Lichtenburg and the Evolution of the Nazi Camp System', *Holocaust and Genocide Studies*, 25 (2011)

——, *Ordnung und Inferno: Das KZ-System im letzten Kriegsjahr* (Göttingen: Wallstein, 2014)

——, and Sigrid Jacobeit (eds), *Lichtenburg: Ein deutsches Konzentrationslager* (Berlin: Metropol, 2009)

Höss, Rudolf (trans. Constantine Fitzgibbon), *Commandant of Auschwitz: The Autobiography of Rudolf Höss* (London: Wiedenfeld & Nicolson, 1959)

Housková, Hanka, *Monolog* (Berlin: Hentrich, 1993)

Hozáková, Vera, *Und es war doch ...: To přece bylo* (Berlin: Hentrich, 1995)

Jacobeit, Sigrid (ed. with Simone Erpel), '*Ich grüße Euch als freier Mensch*' (Berlin: Hentrich, 1995)

——, and Grit Philipp (eds), *Forschungsschwerpunkt: Ravensbrück. Beiträge zur Geschichte des Frauenkonzentrationslagers* (Berlin: Hentrich, 1997)

Jacobeit, Wolfgang, and Wolfgang Stegemann (eds), *Fürstenberg/Havel – Ravensbrück, vol. 2: Wechselnde Machtverhältnisse im 20. Jahrhundert* (Berlin: Hentrich & Hentrich, 2004)

Jirásková, Marie, *Kurzer Bericht über drei Entscheidungen. Die Gestapo-Akte Milena Jesenská* (Frankfurt: Neue Kritik, 1996)

Kershaw, Ian, *Hitler 1889–1936: Hubris* (London: Penguin, 2001)

——, *Hitler 1936–1945: Nemesis* (London: Penguin, 2001)

Kersten, Felix, *The Kersten Memoirs, 1940–1945* (London: Hutchinson, 1956)

Kiedrzyńska, Wanda, *Ravensbrück: Kobiecy obóz koncentracyjny* (Warsaw: Książka I Wiedza, 1961)

Klier, Freya, *Die Kaninchen von Ravensbrück: Medizinische Versuche an Frauen in der NS-Zeit* (Munich: Droemer-Knaur, 1994)

Klimek, Helena, *Książka: Ponad ludzką miarę: Wspomnienia operowanych w Ravensbrück* (Warsaw: Ksiazka i Wiedza, 1969)
Kogon, Eugen, *The Theory and Practice of Hell: The German Concentration Camps and the System Behind Them* (New York: Farrar, Straus and Giroux, 1950)
——, Herman Langbein and Adalbert Rückerl, *Les chambres à gaz, secret d'État* (Paris: Éditions de Minuit, 1984)
Koonz, Claudia, *Mothers in the Fatherland: Women, The Family, and Nazi Politics* (New York: St Martin's Press, 1987)

La Guardia Gluck, Gemma (ed. Rochelle G. Saidel), *Fiorello's Sister: Gemma La Guardia Gluck's Story* (Syracuse, N.Y.: Syracuse University Press, 2007)
Lanckorońska, Karolina (trans. Noel Clark), *Those Who Trespass Against Us: One Women's War against the Nazis* (London: Pimlico, 2005)
Langbein, Hermann (trans. Harry Zohn), *Against All Hope: Resistance in the Nazi Concentration Camps, 1938–1945* (London: Constable, 1994)
—— (trans. Harry Zohn), *People in Auschwitz* (Chapel Hill: University of North Carolina Press, 2004)
Le Tac, Monique, *Yvonne Le Tac: Une femme dans le siècle: de Montmartre à Ravensbrück* (Paris: Tirésias, 2000)
Leo, Annette Leo, '"Das ist so'n zweischneidiges Schwert hier unser KZ (...)". Das Frauenkonzentrationslager Ravensbrück in der lokalen Erinnerung', *Dachauer Hefte*, 17 (2001)
*Les Françaises à Ravensbrück* (Paris: Gallimard, 1965)
Levi, Primo, *If This Is a Man* (London: Abacus, 1979)
——, *The Drowned and the Saved* (London: Abacus, 1988)
Lifton, Robert Jay, *The Nazi Doctors: Medical Killing and the Psychology of Genocide* (New York: Basic Books, 1986)
Litoff, Judy Barrett (ed.), *An American Heroine in the French Resistance: The Diary and Memoir of Virginia d'Albert-Lake* (New York: Fordham University Press, 2006)
*Livre-Mémorial* (Paris: Fondation pour la Mémoire de la Déportation, Theresias, 2004 )
Longerich, Peter, *Heinrich Himmler* (Oxford: Oxford University Press, 2002)
Lundholm, Anja, *Das Höllentor: Bericht einer Überlebenden* (Hamburg: Reinbek, 1988)

MacDonald, Callum, *The Assassination of Reinhard Heydrich* (Edinburgh: Birlinn, 2007)

Mant, Keith, 'The Medical Services in the Concentration Camp of Ravensbrück', *Medico-Legal Journal*, 18 (1949)

Marzac, Jacques, and Denise Rey-Jouenne, *Irma Jouenne: Disparue à Ravensbrück* (Jaunay-Clan: Éditions NC, 1995)

Maurel, Micheline, *Ravensbrück* (London: Anthony Blond, 1959)

Mednikov, A. M. *Dolya Bessmertiya* (Moscow: Sov. Pisatel, 1973)

Minney, R. J., *I Shall Fear No Evil: The Story of Dr Alina Brewda* (London: Kimber, 1966)

Mitscherlich, A., and F. Mielke (trans. James Cleugh), *The Death Doctors* (London: Elek, 1962)

Moorehead, Caroline, *Dunant's Dream: War, Switzerland and the History of the Red Cross* (London: HarperCollins, 1998)

Morais, Fernando (trans. Ellen Watson), *Olga* (London: Halban, 1990)

Morrison, Jack G., *Ravensbrück: Everyday Life in a Woman's Concentration Camp* (Princeton: Markus Wiener, 1999)

Müller, Charlotte, *Die Klempnerkolonne in Ravensbrück: Erinnerungen des Häftlings Nr. 10787* (Berlin: Dietz, 1987)

Müller, Monika, 'Die Oberaufseherinnen des Frauenkonzentrationslagers Ravensbrück: Funktionsanalyse und biographische Studien', unpublished thesis, Freiburg University, 2001

Naumann, Uwe (ed.), *Lidice: Ein böhmisches Dorf* (Frankfurt: Röderberg, 1983)

Niethammer, Lutz (ed.), *Der 'gesäuberte' Antifaschismus: Die SED und die roten Kapos von Buchenwald. Dokumente* (Berlin: Akademie, 1994)

Nikiforova, Antonina, *Plus jamais: Ravensbrück* (Moscow: Éditions en Langues Etrangères, 1957)

Nordling, Raoul, *Sauver Paris: Mémoires du consul de Suède (1905–1944)* (Paris: Payot, 2002)

Padfield, Peter, *Himmler* (New York: MJF Books, 1990)

Paul, Christa, *Zwangsprostitution: Staatlich errichtete Bordelle im Nationalsozialismus* (Berlin: Hentrich, 1994)

Persson, Sune, *Escape from the Third Reich: Folke Bernadotte and the White Buses* (Barnsley: Frontline, 2009)

Philipp, Grit, and Monika Schnell, *Kalendarium der Ereignisse im Frauen-Kozentrationslager Ravensbrück 1939–1945* (Berlin: Metropol, 1999)

Phillips, Raymond (ed.), *Trial of Josef Kramer and Forty-four Others: The Belsen Trial* (London: William Hodge, 1949)

Plewe, Reinhard, and Jan Thomas Köhler, *Baugeschichte Frauen-Konzentrationslager Ravensbrück* (Berlin: Hentrich, 2001)

Półtawksa, Wanda, *And I Am Afraid of My Dreams* (London: Hodder and Stoughton, 1964)

Prestes, Anita Leocadia, and Lygia Prestes, *Anos tormentosos Luiz Carlos Prestes – Correspondência da prisão (1936–1945)*, vol. 3 (São Paulo: Paz e Terra, 2002)

Radau, Helga, *Nichts ist vergessen und niemand: Aus der Geschichte des Konzentrationslagers in Barth* (Kückenshagen: Scheunen, 1995)

Rees, Laurence, *Auschwitz: The Nazis & the 'Final Solution'* (London: BBC Books, 2005)

Renault, Maisie, *La grande misère* (Paris: Chavanne, 1948)

Röhr, Werner, and Brigitte Berlekamp (eds), *Tod oder Überleben? Neue Forschungen zur Geschichte des Konzentrationslagers Ravensbrück* (Berlin: Organon, 2001)

'Rosane' (Renée Lascroux), *Terre de cendres: Ravensbruck et Belsen, 1943–1945* (Paris: Oeuvres Françaises, 1946)

Russell of Liverpool, Lord (Edward Russell), *The Scourge of the Swastika: A Short History of Nazi War Crimes* (London: Cassell & Co., 1954)

Saidel, Rochelle G., *The Jewish Women of Ravensbrück Concentration Camp* (Madison: University of Wisconsin Press, 1999)

Saint-Clair, Simone, *Ravensbrück: l'enfer des femmes* (Paris: Tallandier, 1945)

Salvesen, Sylvia (trans. Evelyn Ramsden), *Forgive – but Do Not Forget* (London: Hutchinson, 1958)

Schikorra, Christa, '"... ist als Asoziale anzusehen" – Frauen im Zugriff der Kölner Kriminalpolizei', in Harald Buhlan and Werner Jung (eds), *Wessen Freund und wessen Helfer?: Die Kölner Polizei im Nationalsozialismus* (Cologne: Emons, 2000)

——, *Kontinuitäten der Ausgrenzung: 'Asoziale' Häftlinge im Frauen-Konzentrationslager Ravensbrück* (Berlin: Metropol, 2001)

——, 'Prostitution of Female Concentration Camp Prisoners as Slave Labor: On the Situation of "Asocial" Prisoners in the Ravensbrück Women's Concentration Camp', in Wolfgang Benz and Barbara Distel (eds), *Dachau and the Nazi Terror 1933–1945, vol. 2: Studies and Reports* (Dachau: Dachauer Hefte, 2002)

Schindler-Saefkow, Bärbel, '14 f 13 – Ravensbrück – Bernburg – Das Geheimnis um die Massenvernichtung in Bernburg', in Sigrid Jacobeit, Wolfgang Schade and Bärbel Schindler-Saefkow (eds), *Gedenkbuch für die Opfer des Konzentrationslagers Ravensbrück 1939–1945: Vorläufiger Zwischenbericht* (Berlin: Metropol, 2000)

——, and Monika Schnell, *Gedenkbuch für die Opfer des Konzentrationslagers Ravensbrück 1939–1945* (Berlin: Metropol, 2005)

Schoppmann, Claudia, *Days of Masquerade: Life Stories of Lesbians during the Third Reich* (New York: Columbia University Press, 1996)

Schwartz, Johannes, 'Geschlechtsspezifischer Eigensinn von NS-Täterinnen am Beispiel der KZ-Oberaufseherin Johanna Langefeld', in Viola Schubert-Lehnhardt (ed.), *Frauen als Täterinnen im Nationalsozialismus* (Gerbstedt: Mansfeld Druck, 2005)

——, 'Handlungsoptionen von KZ-Aufseherinnen. Drei alltags- und geschlechtergeschichte Fallstudien', in Helgard Kramer (ed), *NS-Täter aus interdisziplinärer Perspektive* (Munich: Martin Meidenbauer, 2006)

Schwarz, Helga, and Gerda Szepansky (eds), *... und dennoch blühten Blumen: Dokumente, Gedichte und Zeichnungen vom Lageralltag 1939–1945* (Potsdam: Brandenburgische Landeszentrale für politische Bildung, 2000)

Sebag Montefiore, Simon, *Stalin: The Court of the Red Tsar* (London: Weidenfeld & Nicolson, 2003)

Segev, Tom (trans. Haim Watzman), *The Seventh Million: The Israelis and the Holocaust* (New York: Hill and Wang, 1994)

Sereny, Gitta, *Into That Darkness: From Mercy Killing to Mass Murder* (London: Deutsch, 1974)

——, *Albert Speer: His Battle with Truth* (London: Macmillan, 1995)

Shirer, William L., *Berlin Diary: The Journal of a Foreign Correspondent, 1934–1941* (New York: Knopf, 1941)

Shneer, Aron, *Plen. Sovetskie voennoplennye v Germanii, 1941–1945* (Moscow: Mosty Kul'tury, 2005)

Sofsky, Wolfgang (trans. William Templer), *The Order of Terror: The Concentration Camp* (Princeton: Princeton University Press, 1999)

Sommer, Robert, 'Warum das Schweigen? Berichte von ehemaligen Häftlingen über Sex-Zwangsarbeit in nationalsozialistischen Konzentrationslagern', in Insa Eschebach and Regina Mühlhäuser (eds), *Krieg und Geschlecht: Sexuelle Gewalt im Krieg und Sex-Zwangsarbeit in NS-Konzentrationslargern* (Berlin: Metropol, 2008)

——, *Das KZ-Bordell: sexuelle Zwangsarbeit in nationalsozialistischen Konzentrationslagern* (Paderborn: Schöningh, 2009)

Speer, Albert (trans. Joachim Neugroschel), *The Slave State: Heinrich Himmler's Masterplan for SS Supremacy* (London: Weidenfeld & Nicolson, 1981)

Stratton Smith, T., *The Rebel Nun* (London: Pan, 1967)

Strebel, Bernhard, *Das KZ Ravensbrück: Geschichte eines Lagekomplexes* (Paderborn: Schöningh, 2003)

Sturm, Hanna, *Die Lebensgeschichte einer Arbeiterin: Vom Burgenland nach Ravensbrück* (Vienna: Verlag für Gesellschaftskritik, 1982)

Symonowicz, Wanda (ed.) (trans. Doris Ronowicz), *Beyond Human Endurance: The Ravensbrück Women Tell Their Stories* (Warsaw: Interpress, 1970)

Szabo, Tania, *Young, Brave and Beautiful* (St John: Channel Island Publishing, 2007)

ten Boom, Corrie, with John and Elizabeth Sherrill, *The Hiding Place* (London: Hodder and Stoughton, 1972)

Thurner, Erika (ed. and trans. Gilya Gerda Schmidt), *National Socialism and Gypsies in Austria* (Tuscaloosa: University of Alabama Press, 1998)

Tickell, Jerrard, *Odette: The Story of a British Agent* (London: Chapman and Hall, 1949)

Tillion, Germaine, *Ravensbrück* (Paris: Seuil, 1946)

——, *Le Verfügbar aux enfers. Une opérette à Ravensbrück* (Paris: La Martinière, 2005)

——, *Fragments de vie* (Paris: Seuil, 2013)

*Topography of Terror. Gestapo, SS and Reich Security Main Office on Wilhelm- and Prinz-Albrecht-Straße. A Documentation* (Berlin: Topographie des Terrors, 2008)

Toulouse-Lautrec, Béatrix de, *J'ai eu vingt ans à Ravensbrück: La victoire en pleurant* (Paris: Perrin, 1991)

Trevor-Roper, H. R., *The Last Days of Hitler* (London: Macmillan, 1947)

Tusa, Ann and John Tusa, *The Nuremberg Trial* (New York: Skyhorse, 2010)

Tuvel Bernstein, Sara, with Louise Loots Thornton and Marlene Bernstein Samuels, *The Seamstress: A Memoir of Survival* (New York: Berkley, 1999)

United Nations Information Organisation, *Women under Axis Rule* (London: HMSO, 1943)

Vermehren, Isa, *Reise durch den letzen Akt. Ravensbrück, Buchenwald, Dachau: eine Frau berichtet* (Hamburg: Christian Wegner, 1946)

*Voix et visages, Bulletin de l'Association nationale des anciennes déportées et internées de la Résistance, Paris*

VVN Westberlin, *Olga Benario: Das Leben einer Neuköllner Antifaschistin* (Berlin: VVN, 1984)

Wachsmann, Nikolaus, *Hitler's Prisons: Legal Terror in Nazi Germany* (New Haven: Yale University Press, 2004)

Wagnerová, Alena, *Milena Jesenská* (Frankfurt: Fischer, 1997)

Walz, Loretta, *'Und dann kommst Du dahin an einem schönen Sommertag': Die Frauen von Ravensbrück* (Munich: Kunstmann, 2005)

Weindling, Paul Julian, *Nazi Medicine and the Nuremberg Trials: From Medical War Crimes to Informed Consent* (Basingstoke: Palgrave Macmillan, 2004)

Werner, Ruth, *Olga Benario: Die Geschichte eines tapferen Lebens* (Berlin: Neues Leben, 1961)

—— (trans. Renate Simpson), *Sonya's Report* (London: Chatto & Windus, 1991)

Wiesen, S. Jonathan, *West German Industry and the Challenge of the Nazi Past, 1945–1955* (Chapel Hill: University of North Carolina Press, 2001)

Wińska, Urszula, *Zwyciężyły wartości: Wspomnienia z Ravensbrück* (Gdanks: Marpress, 1985)

Witte, Peter, Michael Wildt, Martina Volgt, Dieter Pohl, Peter Klein, Christian Gerlach, Christoph Dieckmann and Andrej Angrick (eds), *Der Dienstkalender Heinrich Himmlers 1941/42* (Hamburg: Hans Christians, 1999)

——, and Stephen Tyas, *Himmler's Diary 1945: A Calendar of Events Leading to Suicide* (Stroud: Fonthill Media, 2014)

Wood, Nancy, *Germaine Tillion, une femme-mémoire: D'une Algérie à l'autre* (Paris: Éditions Autrement, 2003)

Wynne, Barry, *No Drums, No Trumpets: The Story of Mary Lindell* (London: Arthur Barker, 1961)

# Picture Credits

**Plate Section One**

p. 1
*top:* Collection of Robert H. Wiese, Eppelheim
*middle*: Hanka Housková; copy in Mahn- und Gedenkstätte Ravensbrück/Stiftung Brandenburgische Gedenkstätte
*bottom*: Mahn- und Gedenkstätte Ravensbrück/Stiftung Brandenburgische Gedenkstätte

p. 2
*top:* Mahn- und Gedenkstätte Ravensbrück/Stiftung Brandenburgische Gedenkstätte
*middle:* Mahn- und Gedenkstätte Ravensbrück/Stiftung Brandenburgische Gedenkstätte
*Johanna Langefeld:* Mahn- und Gedenkstätte Ravensbrück/ Stiftung Brandenburgische Gedenkstätte
*Fritz Suhren:* Atkins papers, Imperial War Museum
*Max Koegel:* Copy in Mahn- und Gedenkstätte Ravensbrück/Stiftung Brandenburgische Gedenkstätte

p. 3
*All photographs*: Copies in Mahn- und Gedenkstätte Ravensbrück/Stiftung Brandenburgische Gedenkstätte

p. 4
*Olga Benario:* Copy in Mahn- und Gedenkstätte Ravensbrück/Stiftung Brandenburgische Gedenkstätte
*Doris Maase:* Courtesy of Kaspar Maase
*Ilse Gostynski:* Courtesy of Marlene Rolfe
*Jozka Jaburkova:* Copy in Mahn- und Gedenkstätte Ravensbrück/Stiftung Brandenburgische Gedenkstätte
*Anna Sölzer:* LAV NRW R BR 0234/83
*Käthe Leichter:* Courtesy of Franz and Kathy Leichter
*Grete Buber-Neumann:* The German National Library. German Exile Archive 1933–1945, Frankfurt am Main

p. 5
*Herta Cohen:* LAV NRW R RW-58/54910
*Wanda Wojtasik:* Museum of Martyrology 'Pod Zegarem' (Under the clock), a branch of the Lublin Museum (Muzeum Lubelskie w Lublinie)
*Milena Jesenska:* © INTERFOTO/Alamy
*Kryzia Czyż:* Museum of Martyrology 'Pod Zegarem' (Under the clock), a branch of the Lublin Museum (Muzeum Lubelskie w Lublinie)
*Grażna and Pola Chrostowska*: Museum of Martyrology 'Pod Zegarem' (Under the clock), a branch of the Lublin Museum (Muzeum Lubelskie w Lublinie)

p. 6
*top:* Mahn- und Gedenkstätte Ravensbrück/Stiftung Brandenburgische Gedenkstätte
*middle:* Mahn- und Gedenkstätte Ravensbrück/Stiftung Brandenburgische Gedenkstätte
*bottom:* Copy in Mahn- und Gedenkstätte Ravensbrück/Stiftung Brandenburgische Gedenkstätte

p. 7
*All photographs*: Mahn- und Gedenkstätte Ravensbrück/ Stiftung Brandenburgische Gedenkstätte

p. 8
*Maria Kuśmierczuk:* United States Holocaust Memorial Museum, courtesy of Anna Hassa Jarosky and Peter Hassa
*Christmas card:* United States Holocaust Memorial Museum, courtesy of Anna Hassa Jarosky and Peter Hassa
*Koperta:* Courtesy of Maria Wilgat
*Jadwiga Dzido:* © Ullstein Bild/Topfoto
*Karl Gebhardt:* From *Verhandlungen des Historischen Vereins für Niederbayern*. Courtesy of Stadtarchiv Landshut

## Plate Section Two

p. 9
*The Children's Christmas Party*: © DACS 2014
*Zimni Apel*: Terezín Memorial
*Nourritures terrestres*: Courtesy of Richard Lecoq
*Schmuckstück*: Copy in Mahn- und Gedenkstätte Ravensbrück/Stiftung Brandenburgische Gedenkstätte

p. 10
*Antonina Nikiforova:* Mahn- und Gedenkstätte Ravensbrück/Stiftung Brandenburgische Gedenkstätte
*Zdenka Nedvedova:* Mahn- und Gedenkstätte Ravensbrück/Stiftung Brandenburgische Gedenkstätte
*Stella Kugelman:* Courtesy of Stella Kugelman-Nikiforova
*Yevgenia Klemm:* Courtesy of Georg Loonkin
*Klemm's triangle and number:* Mahn- und Gedenkstätte Ravensbrück/Stiftung Brandenburgische Gedenkstätte

p. 11
*Loulou Le Porz:* Courtesy of Jean-Marie Liard
*Yvonne Baseden:* Atkins papers, Imperial War Museum
*Violette Szabo:* Atkins papers, Imperial War Museum
*Mary Young: Aberdeen Journal*
*Sylvia Salvesen:* Imperial War Museum
*Marie-Louise Zimberlin*: Lycée la Prat's de Cluny
*Karolina Lanckorońska:* Archiwum Nauki PAN i PAU, sygn. K III-150, fot. nr 337, 329

p. 12
*All photographs:* Hanka Housková; copies in Mahn- und Gedenkstätte Ravensbrück/Stiftung Brandenburgische Gedenkstätte

p. 13
*top left:* Nordiska museet
*top right:* Nordiska museet
*middle:* Polfoto
*bottom:* Photothèque CICR (DR)

p. 14
*top left:* Copy in Mahn- und Gedenkstätte Ravensbrück/Stiftung Brandenburgische Gedenkstätte
*top right:* John da Cunha, The National Archives
*bottom left:* The National Archives
*bottom right:* © Topfoto

p. 15
*All photographs:* John da Cunha, The National Archives

p. 16
*top left:* © Stephen Tyas
*top right:* © Sarah Helm
*bottom:* © Sarah Helm

# Index